Perl: The Complete Reference
Second Edition

Perl:
The Complete Reference
Second Edition

Martin C. Brown

Osborne/**McGraw-Hill**

New York   Chicago   San Francisco
Lisbon   London   Madrid   Mexico City
Milan   New Delhi   San Juan
Seoul   Singapore   Sydney   Toronto

Osborne/**McGraw-Hill**
2600 Tenth Street
Berkeley, California 94710
U.S.A.

For information on translations or book distributors outside the U.S.A., or to arrange
bulk purchase discounts for sales promotions, premiums, or fund-raisers, please
contact Osborne/**McGraw-Hill** at the above address.

Perl: The Complete Reference, Second Edition

1234567890 DOC DOC 01987654321

ISBN 0-07-212950-6

Publisher
  Brandon A. Nordin

Vice President & Associate Publisher
  Scott Rogers

Acquisitions Editor
  Rebekah Young

Project Editors
  Betsy Manini
  LeeAnn Pickrell
  Patty Mon
  Lisa Theobald

Acquisitions Coordinator
  Paulina Pobocha

Technical Editor
  Mark Strivens

Copy Editors
  Andy Carroll
  Robert Campbell

Proofreader
  Paul Medoff

Indexer
  David Heiret

Computer Designers
  Gary Corrigan
  Roberta Steele

Illustrator
  Michael Mueller

This book was composed with Corel VENTURA™ Publisher.

To Darcy and Leon, two little kittens
who do try to help daddy with the typing,
but usually just end up typing
"jjskdjjvoookko00000000000000000000000"

About the Author

Martin C. Brown is the author of six Perl books, including the first edition of *Perl: The Complete Reference*, *Perl Programmer's Reference*, *ActivePerl Developer's Guide*, and *Debugging Perl*. In addition to Perl, he has worked in Python, Java, Visual Basic, and other languages. A programmer for 15 years, he is the former IT director of a large advertising agency dealing with blue chip clients such as Hewlett Packard, Oracle, and Cable & Wireless.

Contents at a Glance

Contents

Part I
Fundamentals

Part II

Programming with Perl

Part III

Developing Applications

Part IV
Fine-Tuning Applications

Part V

Appendixes

Acknowledgments

First of all, I'd like to thank my wife. Two years ago, based on the offer for the first edition of *Perl: The Complete Reference*, she stood by me when I wanted to start writing full time. Without her continued support, I wouldn't have written the first edition or the various other books that I've written since then, or been able to do this second edition. Meanwhile, she still gives advice, listens to my rants when things aren't going well, and continues to be impressed when each book arrives.

Next, I'd like to thank all the people at Osborne who made this book possible. That includes Wendy Rinaldi for offering me the opportunity, Rebekah Young for keeping me in check, LeeAnn Pickrell and Betsy Manini for getting it through production, the desktop compositors for laying out each chapter, and Andy Carroll and Bob Campbell for doing the copy editing.

For technical input, thanks again to Mark Strivens, Ann-Marie Mallon, Huga van der Sanden, Jon Nangle, and a myriad of others, including those people on Cix who gave me ideas and input about topics and tricks that should be included in the book.

It's not possible to write a Perl book without thanking Perl's original author and the current maintainers—that includes Larry Wall, Tom Christiansen, Randal L. Schwartz, Sriram Srinivasan, Gurusamy Sarathay, and many many others. It continues to amaze me how much you can cram into one language, and these people are the ones who do it.

If there's anybody I've forgotten to acknowledge, I apologize unreservedly in advance. I have done my best to check and verify all sources and contact all parties involved, but it's perfectly possible I made a mistake.

Introduction

The idea of this book is to provide a reference guide to everything you could possibly want to know about Perl. I've done my best to try and cover all the different aspects, from the core of the language to the different functions, and on into the different tasks and areas of the Perl language. I even cover how to debug your software, write documentation, and then build and distribute your applications or modules to the world at large. Along the way, we also look at some nonstandard features and extensions, including better ways of networking, web programming, and designing interfaces.

Throughout the entire book, you'll find real-world examples and guides on how to approach real problems using Perl—not just how to use the features of Perl. If all you want is a quick reference guide to the different areas of Perl, then use the appendixes at the end of the book and on the Web at **www.osborne.com**, which cover basic components, functions, the Perl standard library, CPAN (Comprehensive Perl Archive Network) extension library, a complete guide to errors and warnings, and a list of resources for more information.

Perl: The Complete Reference

What's Changed Since the First Edition?

Beyond the obvious updates and fixes for the newer versions of Perl, we've also changed the overall layout of this edition. We got a lot of feedback on the first edition and its pitfalls and problems. The most requested feature was a better introductory guide to the language. As such, we've completely restructured the first section of the book to provide a well-rounded introduction to the language, for people new to programming and for those migrating from another language.

The second and third sections have been updated, with many of the chapters modified to provide a more solution-oriented approach, and that means the order and content of many of the chapters has been changed. We've expanded on the content in many areas, including more information on networking, database access (which now covers the **DBI** extension and **Win32::ODBC** module) and web programming.

The last section has also been modified into a guide for the final processes behind turning your Perl program into a distributable application. This includes debugging and retuning your script and using the Perl compiler to improve performance and find coding errors. The chapter on Perl documentation has also been updated to provide information on using the supplied documentation and information on how to write your own. Finally, we cover the topics of cross-platform development and the packaging and distribution of your application or module.

Overall, I've tried to make the book less Unix-centric and cover more of the issues surrounding cross-platform development throughout the book, instead of concentrating the information into a few chapters at the end.

Who Is the Book For?

I haven't targeted the book at any specific group of Perl users. To put it simply, if you program in Perl, you will find this book useful. As a reference, most people should find it useful to keep on the desk or the shelf just as a quick means of looking up a particular function or feature. For learners and expert users alike, the information in this book will be invaluable.

You should also find the book useful if you want to know how to do a particular task in Perl, since you'll also find working real-world examples of the different features of Perl within the book. If you are looking for more examples, you might want to look at *Perl Annotated Archives*, which contains over 100 scripts to solve a myriad of different problems. For more information on migrating Unix scripts to the Windows platform, especially when using the ActivePerl distribution, try *ActivePerl Developer's Guide*.

If debugging and tuning are more your thing, then look at *Debugging Perl*. You can get more information on all of these titles and many others, in Appendix C.

How to Use This Book

Pick it up, look up the feature you want to get more information on from the contents or the index, and read! The scripts and script fragments included in the book should all work without modification on your machine. Be aware though that not all platforms support all Perl features—Chapter 24 provides a guide to most of the issues surrounding cross-platform development.

If you want purely reference information—that is, you want to look up the arguments and return values to a function—then use the appendixes at the back of the book and on the Web at **www.osborne.com**. For discussion, examples, and detailed information on a particular feature, use one of the earlier chapters. You should find references between the chapters and appendixes in both directions to help you get more information.

Chapter Breakdown

Each chapter in the book attempts to cover a different aspect of the solutions that Perl is able to provide.

Chapter 1 looks at the background of Perl and the fundamental abilities that you will need to use and understand in order to make the best use of Perl.

Chapter 2 examines the basic processes behind programming in Perl, from installing Perl onto your machine (Unix, Windows, and Mac OS are covered), to writing and executing your first script. We also look at some of the key terms that you come across while reading the book and using Perl.

Chapter 3 covers all of the basic semantics and parsing rules behind the Perl language, including an outline of how the execution process works, and all of the different components that make up a Perl script.

Chapter 4 looks at the Perl variable types; Perl supports three basic types, the scalar, the array and the hash (or associative array).

Chapter 5 details the statement and control structures that will control the flow and execution of your program.

Chapter 6 starts off by covering the theories behind dissecting a program into different components, from simple subroutines, right up to the more complex issues of creating your own modules.

Chapter 7 covers the use of files, from the basics of printing information to the screen to reading information from multiple files.

Chapter 8 details the processing behind data processing—by far the most useful and popular use of Perl. We start by looking at basic ways of manipulating strings and arrays before covering the Perl regular expression mechanism.

Chapter 9 looks at the basic mechanisms available for identifying and trapping errors and bugs, and how to go about handling the situation without upsetting the user.

Chapter 10 looks at the more complex data structures available in Perl—arrays and hashes. We go beyond the normal uses of these structures and look at other ways they can be employed to aid in the programming process. We also take the opportunity to examine references, which provide a different way of accessing and using information stored in variables, and this leads us on to nested data structures and object-oriented programming. This final section also leads to tied data structures—a system whereby information from an external source can be attached to an internal data structure.

Chapter 11 covers the different ways of finding out system information, such as information about users and groups, time and how to manipulate time values, and finally the environment and how it can affect the execution of your script.

Chapter 12 describes the processing required within Perl to support communication over standard network sockets, such as those used for communication over the Internet.

Chapter 13 looks at the storage of information in external databases, both homegrown and using systems such as DBM, Oracle, and ODBC sources.

Chapter 14 discusses the processes involved in interprocess communication, using both standard filehandles and System V IPC functions. The chapter also describes the methods available for creating, controlling, and communicating with external processes.

Chapter 15 details the more advanced methods of executing Perl scripts, from supplying arguments to the command line, to executing scripts within scripts (using **eval**), to multi-threaded execution.

Chapter 16 covers the basic processes behind getting and communicating information back to your users through a structured interface on the command line and back through the Perl reporting mechanism.

Chapter 17 takes a detailed look at user interfaces, especially at Perl/Tk—the Perl interface to the Tk user interface development system.

Chapter 18 describes the environment available to you when you are writing web scripts. This covers the physical environment of a script and also the ways of communicating between the web server, the user's browser, and a Perl script, otherwise known as CGI. We then go on to look at smarter ways of handling the web-development process and the specifics of web programming with Perl, including a useful checklist of the security issues surrounding the web-programming process.

Chapter 19 looks at ways in which you can control the execution of your Perl script. Perl uses a series of pragmas to improve the monitoring of potential problems in your script, provide additional warnings and error messages, and change the way in which different aspects of your scrip are interpreted.

Chapter 20 details the methods behind extending Perl through external C functions and libraries or through embedding Perl into your existing applications.

Chapter 21 covers the essential process of debugging Perl scripts, both at a simple level and at deeper levels within the Perl interpreter. We also look at how to debug regular expressions and how to use the Perl profiler to determine which parts of your Perl script need optimization.

Chapter 22 looks in detail at the Perl compiler. This supports several different systems that take a Perl script and produce a number of different reports and output formats. At a simple level, this includes a parsing tree that describes the real execution profile of your script, and at the other end of the scale, the compiler that supports the creation of stand-alone Perl binaries.

Chapter 23 details the use and development of Perl documentation, both when reading supplied documentation and writing your own.

Chapter 24 concentrates on ways in which you can write Perl programs that are cross-platform compatible, even if you don't know what the destination platform is. We look at the basics of using Perl in different environments, the major differences and things to watch out for, and also ways in which you can make a script more aware of its surroundings.

Chapter 25 discusses the processes involved in releasing a Perl module to the Perl community. In particular, it describes the **MakeMaker** utility for creating Perl Makefiles that can compile and automatically install Perl extensions.

The appendixes at the back of the book provide a quick reference resource for Perl functions (**Appendix A**) and the standard Perl library (**Appendix B**). **Appendix C** gives a list of all of the different areas—books, websites, mailing lists, and newsgroups—that can provide more information on how to use and program with Perl.

The appendixes on the Web (**www.osborne.com**) provide a reference to the core Perl constructs (**Web Appendix A**), the extensions for Perl available from CPAN (**Web Appendix B**), and a complete list and description of all the warnings and error messages generated by the Perl interpreter (**Web Appendix C**).

Conventions Used in This Book

All Perl keywords are highlighted in **bold**, but functions are listed without parentheses. This is because the C functions on which the Perl versions may be based are shown like **this()**.

```
Examples and code are displayed using a fixed-width font.
```

Function descriptions are formatted using the same fixed-width font.

 Notes are formatted like this and include additional information about a particular topic. You'll also find similarly formatted "Cautions" and "Warnings," which highlight possible dangerous tools or tricks to watch out for when programming.

Contacting the Author

I always welcome comments and suggestions on my work. I particularly appreciate guides and recommendations on better ways of achieving different goals, especially with a language as varied and capable as Perl. The best way to contact me is via email. You can use either **books@mcwords.com**. Alternatively, visit my website, **http://www.mcwords.com**, which contains resources and updated information about the scripts and contents of this book. You can find the homepage for this book at **http://www.mcwords.com/projects/books/pcr2e/**.

The Complete Reference

Part I

Fundamentals

The
Complete
Reference

Perl

Chapter 1

Perl Backgrounder

Perl is many different things to many different people. The most fundamental aspect of Perl is that it's a high-level programming language written originally by Larry Wall and now supported and developed by a cast of thousands. The Perl language semantics are largely based on the C programming language, while also inheriting many of the best features of **sed**, **awk**, the Unix shell, and at least a dozen other tools and languages.

Although it is a bad idea to pigeonhole any language and assign it to a specific list of tasks, Perl is particularly strong at process, file, and text manipulation. This makes it especially useful for system utilities, software tools, systems management tasks, database access, graphical programming, networking, and web programming. These strengths make it particularly attractive to CGI script authors, systems administrators, mathematicians, journalists, and just about anybody who needs to write applications and utilities very quickly.

Perl has its roots firmly planted in the Unix environment, but it has since become a cross-platform development tool. Perl runs on IBM mainframes; AS/400s; Windows NT, 95, and 98; OS/2; Novell Netware; Cray supercomputers; Digital's VMS; Tandem Guardian; HP MPE/ix; Mac OS; and all flavors of Unix, including Linux. In addition, Perl has been ported to dozens of smaller operating systems, including BeOS, Acorn's RISCOS, and even machines such as the Amiga.

Larry Wall is a strong proponent of free software, and Perl is no exception. Perl, including the source code, the standard Perl library, the optional modules, and all of the documentation, is provided free and is supported entirely by its user community.

Before we get into the details of how to program in Perl, it's worth taking the time to familiarize yourself with where Perl has come from, what it can be used for, and how it stacks up against other languages. We'll also look at some popular "mythconceptions" about what Perl is and at some success stories of how Perl has helped a variety of organizations solve an equally varied range of problems.

What Does PERL Stand For?

There is a lot of controversy and rumor about exactly what PERL stands for and if, in fact, it stands for anything. According to Larry Wall, the original acronym stood for Practical Extraction and Reporting Language, and this relates to the original development purpose, which was to process a large amount of textual report information.

Over the years, other solutions have been proposed for the PERL acronym. The most popular recent version is Pathologically Eclectic Rubbish Lister. Luckily, a rough translation of that expansion equates to the original version!

Versions and Naming Conventions

The current version of Perl (at the time of writing—Nov 2000) was Perl 5.6, with a develop version, v5.7, already in production. Some sites are migrating to v5.6, others seem to be dragging their heels, although there are no major compatibility problems.

Up until March 2000, the situation concerning the available versions of Perl was quite complex, but we'll start with the "current" version first. From the release of Perl 5.6 there are two very simple strands. Even version numbers, such as 5.6 and 5.8 are considered to be "stable" releases of the language. Odd version numbers, such as 5.7 and 5.9, are development releases.

Perl 5.6 was a long time coming—over two years since the last major release— but it also set a landmark for Perl's development. It was the first version that really reunited the core and Win32 versions of Perl, as well as providing some compatibility enhancements. For example, the Windows ports now support **fork**, something not natively provided by the Windows operating system. Also updated were the Perl compiler and the threading system (which actually supports the Windows **fork** function), and the addition of a new keyword, **our**, which handles global variables in the same way as **my**.

Discussions have already started for Perl 6. Unlike Perl 5, which was a complete rewrite of Perl 4 and was developed and coded almost entirely by Larry, Perl 6 will have its feature set determined by the people that use it, through a series of RFCs (Requests for Comments). The language's core code will be developed by a team of programmers with input and assistance from Larry, and with features agreed upon by committees, rather than solely by Larry. This will make Perl 6 a language designed by the people that use it, rather than by the person who invented it.

Perl, perl or PeRl?

There is also a certain amount of confusion regarding the capitalization of Perl. Should it be written Perl or perl? Larry Wall now uses "Perl" to signify the language proper and "perl" to signify the implementation of the language. Therefore, perl can parse Perl. In essence, however, it really doesn't make a huge amount of difference. That said, you will find that the executable version of perl is installed with its name in lowercase!

Life Before Perl 5.6

Before Perl 5.6, version numbers were far more confusing. Before version 5 came version 4, the highest incarnation of which was 4.036, released in 1993. Version 5 is still in development, with version 5.005_03 being the last stable release before the current 5.6. However, many sites were using Perl 5.005_56—this was a developmental release, but stable enough that some sites used it in preference to 5.005_02. Although there were changes between these versions, they were bug fixes rather than the significant improvements in Perl 5.6.

As to naming, you will see references to perl4 and perl5, and more recently, perl5.6. Since most people will be using at least perl5, it's probably safe to refer to Perl simply as Perl!

Perl History

Perl is a relatively old language, with the first version having been released in 1988. The basic history is shown in Table 1-1.

If you want a more detailed history of Perl, check out the **perlhist** documentation installed with Perl, or visit CPAST, the Comprehensive Perl Arcana Society Tapestry at **history.perl.org**.

Version	Date	Version Details
Perl 0		Introduced Perl to Larry Wall's office associates
Perl 1	Jan 1988	Introduced Perl to the world
Perl 2	Jun 1988	Introduced Harry Spencer's regular expression package
Perl 3	Oct 1989	Introduced the ability to handle binary data
Perl 4	Mar 1991	Introduced the first "Camel" book (*Programming Perl*, by Larry Wall, Tom Christiansen, and Randal L Schwartz; O'Reilly & Associates). The book drove the name change, just so it could refer to Perl 4, instead of Perl 3.
Perl 4.036	Feb 1993	The last stable release of Perl 4
Perl 5	Oct 1994	The first stable release of Perl 5, which introduced a number of new features and a complete rewrite.
Perl 5.005_02	Aug 1998	The next major stable release
Perl 5.005_03	Mar 1999	The last stable release before 5.6
Perl 5.6	Mar 2000	Introduced unified **fork** support, better threading, an updated Perl compiler, and the **our** keyword

Table 1-1. *Perl Version History*

Main Perl Features

Perl contains many features that most Perl programmers do not even know about, let alone use. Some of the most basic features are described here.

Perl Is Free

It may not seem like a major feature, but, in fact, being free is very important. Some languages, such as C (which is free with compilers such as GNU's **gcc**), have been commercialized by Metrowerks, Microsoft, and other companies. Other languages, such as Visual Basic, are entirely commercial. Perl's source code is open and free—anybody can download the C source that constitutes a Perl interpreter. Furthermore, you can easily extend the core functionality of Perl both within the realms of the interpreted language and by modifying the Perl source code.

Perl Is Simple to Learn, Concise, and Easy to Read

Because of its history and roots, most people with any programming experience will be able to program with Perl. It has a syntax similar to C and shell script, among others, but with a less restrictive format. Most programs are quicker to write in Perl because of its use of built-in functions and a huge standard and contributed library. Most programs are also quicker to execute than other languages because of Perl's internal architecture (see the section, "Perl is Fast" that follows). Perl can be easy to read, because the code can be written in a clear and concise format that almost reads like an English sentence. Unfortunately, Perl also has a bad habit of looking a bit like line noise to uninitiated. Whether or not your Perl looks good and clean really depends on how you format it—good Perl is easy read. It is also worth reading the Perl style guidelines (in the Perl style manual page that comes with Perl) to see how Larry Wall, Perl's creator, likes things done.

Perl Is Fast

As we will see shortly, Perl is not an interpreter in the strictest sense—when you execute a Perl program it is actually compiled into a highly optimized language before it is executed. Compared to most scripting languages, this makes execution almost as fast as compiled C code. But, because the code is still interpreted, there is no compilation process, and applications can be written and edited much faster than with other languages, without any of the performance problems normally associated with an interpreted language.

Perl Is Extensible

You can write Perl-based packages and modules that extend the functionality of the language. You can also call external C code directly from Perl to extend the functionality further. The reverse is also true: the Perl interpreter can be incorporated directly into many languages, including C. This allows your C programs to use the functionality of the Perl interpreter without calling an external program.

Perl Has Flexible Data Types

You can create simple variables that contain text or numbers, and Perl will treat the variable data accordingly at the time it is used. This means that unlike C, you don't have to worry about converting text and numbers, and you can embed and merge strings without requiring external functions to concatenate or combine the results. You can also handle arrays of values as simple lists, as typical indexed arrays, and even as stacks of information. You can also create associative arrays (otherwise known as hashes) which allow you to refer to the items in the array by a unique string, rather than a simple number. Finally, Perl also supports references, and through references objects. References allow you to create complex data structures made up of a combination of hashes, lists and scalars.

Perl Is Object Oriented

Perl supports all of the object-oriented features—inheritance, polymorphism, and encapsulation. There are no restrictions on when or where you make use of object-oriented features. There is no boundary as there is with C and C++.

Perl Is Collaborative

There is a huge network of Perl programmers worldwide. Most programmers supply, and use, the modules and scripts available via CPAN, the Comprehensive Perl Archive Network (see Web Appendix B at **www.osborne.com**). This is a repository of the best modules and scripts available. Using an existing prewritten module can save you hundreds, perhaps even thousands, of hours of development time.

Compiler or Interpreter

Different languages work in different ways; they are either compiled or interpreted. A program in a compiled language is translated from the original source into a platform-specific machine code. This machine code is referred to as an *executable*. There is no direct relation between the machine code and the original source: it is not possible to reverse the compilation process and produce the source code. This means that the compiled executable is safe from intellectual property piracy.

With an interpreted language, on the other hand, the interpreter reads the original source code and interprets each of the statements in order to perform the different operations. The source code is therefore executed at run time. This has some advantages: Because there is no compilation process, the development of interpreted code should be significantly quicker. Interpreted code also tends to be smaller and easier to distribute. The disadvantages are that the original source must be supplied in order to execute the program, and an interpreted program is generally slower than a compiled executable because of the way the code is executed.

Perl fits neither of these descriptions in the real sense. The internals of Perl are such that at the time of executing a Perl script, the individual elements of the script are compiled into a tree of *opcodes*. Opcodes are similar in concept to machine code—the binary format required by the processor in your machine. However, whereas machine code is executed directly by hardware, opcodes are executed by a Perl virtual machine. The opcodes are highly optimized objects designed to perform a specific function. When the script is executed you are essentially executing compiled C code, translated from the Perl source. This enables Perl to provide all the advantages of a scripting language while offering the fast execution of a compiled program. This mode of operation—translation and then execution by a virtual machine is actually how most modern scripting languages work, including Java (using Just In Time technology) and Python.

Keeping all of that in mind, however, there have been some advances in the most recent versions of a Perl compiler that takes native Perl scripts and converts them into directly executable machine code. We'll cover the compiler and Perl internals later in this book.

Similar Programming Languages

We already know that Perl has its history in a number of different languages. It shares several features and abilities with many of the standard tools supplied with any Unix workstation. It also shares some features and abilities with many related languages, even if it doesn't necessarily share the same heritage.

With regard to specific features, abilities, and performance, Perl compares favorably against some languages and less favorably against others. A lot of the advantages and disadvantages are a matter of personal preference. For example, for text handling, there is very little to choose between **awk** and Perl. However, personally I prefer Perl for those tasks that involve file handling directly within the code, and **awk** when using it as a filter as part of a shell script.

Unix Shells

Any of the Unix shells—**sh**, **csh**, **ksh**, or even **bash**—share the same basic set of facilities. They are particularly good at running external programs and at most forms of file management where the shell's ability to work directly with many of the standard Unix utilities enables rapid development of systems management tools.

However, where most shells fail is in their variable- and data-handling routines. In nearly all cases you need to use the facilities provided by shell tools such as **cut**, **paste**, and **sort** to achieve the same level of functionality as that provided natively by Perl.

Tcl

Tcl (Tool Command Language) was developed as an embeddable scripting language. A lot of the original design centered around a macro-like language for helping with shell-based applications. Tcl was never really developed as a general-purpose scripting language, although many people use it as such. In fact, Tcl was designed with the philosophy that you should actually use two or more languages when developing large software systems.

Tcl's variables are very different from those in Perl. Because it was designed with the typical shell-based string handling in mind, strings are null terminated (as they are in C). This means that Tcl cannot be used for handling binary data. Compared to Perl, Tcl is also generally slower on iterative operations over strings. You cannot pass arrays by value or by reference; they can only be passed by name. This makes programming more complex, although not impossible.

Lists in Tcl are actually stored as a single string, and arrays are stored within what Perl would treat as a hash. Accessing a true Tcl array is therefore slightly slower, as it has to look up associative entries in order to decipher the true values. The data-handling problems also extend to numbers, which Tcl stores as strings and converts to numbers only when a calculation is required. This slows mathematical operations significantly.

Unlike Perl, which parses the script first before optimizing and then executing, Tcl is a true interpreter, and each line is interpreted and optimized individually at execution time. This reduces the optimization options available to Tcl. Perl, on the other hand, can optimize source lines, code blocks, and even entire functions if the compilation process allows. The same Tcl interpretation technique also means that the only way to debug Tcl code and search for syntactic errors is to actually execute the code. Because Perl goes through the precompilation stage, it can check for syntactic and other possible or probable errors without actually executing the code.

Finally, the code base of the standard Tcl package does not include many of the functions and abilities of the Perl language. This is especially important if you are trying to write a cross-platform POSIX-compliant application. Perl supports the entire POSIX function set, but Tcl supports a much smaller subset of the POSIX function set, even using external packages.

It should be clear from this description that Perl is a better alternative to Tcl in situations where you want easy access to the rest of the OS. Most significantly, Tcl will never be a general-purpose scripting language. Tcl will, on the other hand, be a good solution if you want to embed a scripting language inside another language.

Python

Python was developed as an object-oriented language and is well thought out. It is an interpreted, byte-compiled, extensible, and largely procedural programming language.

Like Perl, it's good at text processing and even general-purpose programming. Python also has a good history in the realm of GUI-based application development. Compared to Perl, Python has fewer users, but it is gaining acceptance as a practical rapid application development tool.

Unlike Perl, Python does not resemble C, and it doesn't resemble Unix-style tools like **awk** either. Python was designed from scratch to be object oriented and has clear module semantics. This can make it confusing to use, as the name spaces get complex to resolve. On the other hand, this makes it much more structured, which can ease development for those with structured minds.

I'm not aware of anything that is better in Python than in Perl. They both share object features, and the two are almost identical in execution speed. However, the reverse is not true: Perl has better regular expression features, and the level of integration between Perl and the Unix environment is hard to beat (although it can probably be solved within Python using a suitably written external module).

In general, there is not a lot to tip the scales in favor of one of the two languages. Perl will appeal to those people who already know C or Unix shell utilities. Perl is also older and more widespread, and there is a much larger library of contributed modules and scripts. Python, on the other hand, may appeal to those people who have experience with more object-oriented languages, such as Java or Modula-2.

Both languages provide easy control and access when it comes to the external environment in which they work. Perl arguably fills the role better, though, because many of the standard system functions you are used to are supported natively by the language, without requiring external modules. The technical support for the two languages is also very similar, with both using websites and newsgroups to help users program in the new language.

Finally, it's worth mentioning that of all the scripting languages available, Perl and Python are two of the most stable platforms for development. There are, however, some minor differences. First, Perl provides quite advanced functions and mechanisms for tracking errors and faults in the scripts. Making extensive use of these facilities can still cause problems, however. For example, calling the system **truncate()** function within Perl will cause the whole interpreter to crash. Python, on the other hand, uses a system of error trapping that will immediately identify a problem like this before it occurs, allowing you to account for it in your applications. This is largely due to the application-development nature of the language.

Java

At first viewing, Java seems to be a friendlier, interpreted version of C++. Depending on your point of view, this can either be an advantage or a disadvantage. Java probably inherits less than a third of the complexity of C++, but it retains much of the complexity of its brethren.

Java was designed primarily as an implementation-independent language, originally with web-based intentions, but now as a more general-purpose solution to a variety of problems. Like Perl, Java is byte compiled, but unlike Perl, programs are supplied in byte-compiled format and then executed via a Java virtual machine at execution time.

Because of its roots and its complexity, Java cannot really be considered as a direct competitor to Perl. It is difficult to use Java as a rapid application development tool and virtually impossible to use it for most of the simple text-processing and system-administration tasks that Perl is best known for.

C/C++

Perl itself is written in C. (You can download and view the Perl source code if you so wish, but it's not for the faint-hearted!) Many of the structures and semantics of Perl and C are very similar. For example, both use semicolons as end-of-line terminators. They also share the same code block and indentation features. However, Perl tends to be stricter when it comes to code block definitions—it always requires curly brackets, for example—but most C programmers will be comfortable with the Perl environment.

Perl can be object oriented like C++. Both share the same abilities of inheritance, polymorphism, and encapsulation. However, object orientation in Perl is easier to use, compared to the complexities of constructors and inheritance found in C++. In addition to all this, there is no distinction between the standard and object-oriented implementations of Perl as there is with C and C++. This means you can mix and match different variables, objects, and other data types within a single Perl application—something that would be difficult to achieve easily with C and C++.

Because Perl is basically an interpreted language (as mentioned earlier), development is generally quicker than is writing in native C. Perl also has many more built-in facilities and abilities that would otherwise need to be handwritten in C/C++. For example, regular expressions and many of the data-handling features would require a significant amount of programming to reproduce in C with the same ease of use available in Perl.

Because of Perl's roots in C, it is also possible to extend Perl with C source code and vice versa: you can embed Perl programs in C source code.

awk/gawk

Although a lot of syntax is different, **awk**, and **gawk** (the GNU projects version) are functionally subsets of Perl. It's also clear from the history of Perl that many of the features have been inherited directly from those of **awk**. Indeed, **awk** was designed as a reporting language with the emphasis on making the process of reporting via the shell significantly easier. Without **awk**, you would have to employ a number of external utilities, such as **cut**, **expr**, and **sort**, and the solution would be neither quick nor elegant.

There are some things that Perl has built-in support for that **awk** does not. For example, **awk** has no network socket class, and it is largely ignorant of external files, when compared to the file manipulation and management functions found in Perl. However, some advantages **awk** has over Perl are summarized here:

- **awk** is simpler, and the syntax is more structured and regular.
- Although it is gaining acceptance, Perl has yet to be included as standard with many operating systems. **Awk** has been supplied with Unix almost since it was first released.
- **awk** can be smaller and therefore much quicker to execute for small programs.
- **awk** supports more advanced regular expressions. You can use a regular expression for replacement, and you can search text in substitutions.

Popular "Mythconceptions"

Despite its history and wide use in many different areas, there are still a number of myths about what Perl is, where it should be used, and even why it was invented. Here's a quick list of the popular mythconceptions of the Perl language.

It's Only for the Web

Probably the most famous of the myths is that Perl is a language used, designed, and created exclusively for developing web-based applications. In fact, this could not be more wrong. Version 1.0 of Perl, the first released to the world, shipped in 1988— several years before the web and HTML as we know it today were in general use. In fact, Perl was inherited as a good design tool for web server applications based on its ease of use and flexibility. The text-handling features are especially useful when working within the web environment. There are libraries of database interfaces, client-server modules, networking features, and even GUI toolkits to enable you to write entire applications directly within Perl.

It's Not Maintenance Friendly

Any good (or bad) programmer will tell you that anybody can write unmaintainable code in any language. Many companies and individuals write maintainable programs using Perl. A lot of people would argue that Perl's structured style, easily readable source code, and modular format make it more maintainable than languages such as C, C++, and Java.

It's Only for Hackers

Perl is used by a variety of companies, organizations, and individuals. Everybody from programming beginners through "hackers" up to multinational corporations use Perl to solve their problems. It can hardly be classed as a hackers-only language. Moreover, it is maintained by the same range of people, which means you get the best of both worlds—real-world features, with top-class behind-the-scenes algorithms.

It's a Scripting Language

In Perl, there is no difference between a script and program. Many large programs and projects have been written entirely in Perl. A good example is Majordomo, the main mailing-list manager used on the Internet. It's written entirely in Perl. See the upcoming section "Perl Success Stories" for more examples of where Perl has made a difference, despite its scripting label.

There's No Support

The Perl community is one of the largest on the Internet, and you should be able to find someone, somewhere, who can answer your questions or help you with your problems. The Perl Clinic (see Appendix C) offers free advice and support to Perl programmers.

All Perl Programs Are Free

Although you generally write and use Perl programs in their native source form, this does not mean that everything you write is free. Perl programs are your own intellectual property and can be bought, sold, and licensed just like any other program. If you are worried about somebody stealing your code, source filters and bytecode compilers will render your code useful only for execution and unreadable by the casual software pirate.

There's No Development Environment

Development environments are only really required when you need to compile source code into object files. Because Perl scripts are written in normal text, you can use any editor to write and use Perl programs. Under Unix, the favorites are **emacs** and **vi**, and both have Perl modes to make syntax checking and formatting easier. Under Windows NT, you can also use **emacs**, or you can use Solutionsoft's Perl Builder, which is an interactive environment for Perl programs. Alternatively, you can use the ActiveState debugger, which will provide you with a direct environment for executing and editing Perl statements. There are also many improvements being made in the ActiveState distribution that will allow Perl to be used as part of Microsoft's Visual Studio product under a project called VisualPerl. On the Mac, the BBEdit and Pepper editors have a Perl mode that colors the syntax of the Perl source to make it easier to read.

Additionally, because Perl programs are text based, you can use any source-code revision-control system. The most popular solution is CVS, or Concurrent Versioning System, which is now supported under Unix, MacOS and Windows.

Perl Is a GNU Project

While the GNU project includes Perl in its distributions, there is no such thing as "GNU Perl." Perl is not produced or maintained by GNU and the Free Software Foundation. Perl is also made available on a much more open license than the GNU Public License.

Note   *GNU stands for the recursive "GNU's Not Unix," and is part of the Free Software Foundation, an organization devoted to providing a suite of useful user software for free.*

Perl Is Difficult to Learn

Because Perl is similar to a number of different languages, it is not only easy to learn but also easy to continue learning. Its structure and format is very similar to C, **awk**, shell script, and, to a greater or lesser extent, even BASIC. If you have ever done any form of programming, you're half way toward learning programming in Perl.

In many cases, you will only use a very small subset of Perl to complete most tasks. The guiding motto for Perl development is "there's more than one way to do it." This makes Perl's learning curve very shallow and very long. Perl is a large language with a great many features, and there is a lot you can learn if you want to.

Perl Success Stories

Perl has been used by thousands of different corporations to tackle and solve different problems. For most people, it has reduced the development time for their desired application by days, weeks, or even months. Below is a sample of the bigger companies that have used Perl. I've tried to include testimonials and deeper examples of how Perl was the better solution, where the information has been available.

- **Amazon.com**, one of the Internet's best known and most successful e-commerce sites, used Perl to develop an entire editorial production and control system. This integrates the authoring, maintenance (including version control and searching), and output of the editorial content of the entire Amazon.com website.

- Netscape engineers wrote a content management and delivery system, with logging, analysis, and feedback on use, in three months using Perl.

- In order to get around many cross-platform development problems, SPEC (the Standard Performance Evaluation Corporation) used Perl as a wrapper around the C code that is used to test performance. With Perl's ability to import and dynamically use external C code in combination with its object-oriented abilities, SPEC generated a test system that was easily portable from Unix to the Windows NT platform.

■ Using an old 60MHz Pentium and Perl, a New England hospital implemented a distributed printing system that connected 20,000 PC workstations to 3,000 printers spread over an entire city.

On a personal level, I have Perl scripts that create users, add new virtual WWW servers to Apache, monitor all the machines and storage on my network, keep track of all my archives and e-mail, and even scripts that download weather information from my weather center and get the TV listings every day!

Chapter 2

Perl Overview

erl is a relatively unstructured language. Although it does, of course, have rules, most of the restrictions and rules that you may be used to in other languages are not so heavily enforced. For example, you don't need to worry too much about telling Perl what you are expecting to do with your program (or script or application), or what variable's subroutines or other elements you are either going to use or introduce. This approach leads to what is called "There Is More Than One Way to Do It" (TIMTOWTDI, or tim toady for short) syndrome—which refers to the fact that there are different ways of achieving the same result, all of which are legally valid.

In fact, a Perl program is as easy as

```
print "Hello World\n";
```

Note that there's nothing before that statement to tell Perl what it needs in order to print out that message. Compare it to a similar C program:

```
#include <stdio.h>

int main()
{
    printf("Hello World\n");
}
```

In Perl there is no "main" (well, not in the same sense as there is in C)—execution of a Perl script starts with the first statement in the list and continues until the end of the file. We don't need to tell Perl to explicitly exit the program, or give a return value to the caller; Perl will handle all of that for us.

The rest of this chapter is given over to describing how to create Perl scripts and use Perl to execute scripts, and to describing the basic components that make up a Perl program. The rest of this section of the book is devoted to giving more detail on each of these elements (and more) so that you will have a complete understanding of how to write basic Perl programs. The rest of the book looks at more advanced topics, such as object orientation, networking, and interface and web development.

Installing and Using Perl

Perl is available for a huge array of platforms, but the chances are that you are using Perl on one of the main three—Unix, Windows, and Mac OS. The use of Perl under all these platforms varies slightly, so we'll look at the Perl implementation on each one in turn.

As a basic rule, however, Perl works the same way on every platform—you create a text file (using your favorite editor: vi, emacs, kedit, Notepad, WordPad, SimpleText, BBEdit, Pepper), and then use Perl to execute the statements within that file. You don't have to worry about compiling the file into another format first—Perl executes the statements directly from the raw text.

Writing a Perl Script

Ignoring the platform-specific issues for a moment, producing a Perl script is not as difficult as it sounds. Perl scripts are just text files, so in order to actually "write" the script, all you need to do is create a text file using your favorite text editor. Once you've written the script, you tell Perl to execute the text file you created.

Under Unix, you would use

```
$ perl myscript.pl
```

and the same works under Windows:

```
C:\> perl myscript.pl
```

Under Mac OS, you need to drag and drop the file onto the MacPerl application.

In each case, Perl reads the contents of your text file, interpreting the file as Perl statements and expressions.

The file-naming system is part convention and part rule. Generally, Perl scripts have a .pl extension, even under Mac OS and Unix. This helps to identify what the file is by name, although it's actually a requirement. Other extensions you may come across include .pm for a Perl module, .ph for a Perl header file, and .pod for a Perl documentation file (POD stands for Plain Old Documentation).

Perl Under Unix

Because much of Perl's early development originated on a Unix platform, it is not surprising that this is still one of the most strongly supported Perl environments. Perl under Unix is available in a number of formats and distributions. The main, or "core," distribution comes from the main Perl developers and is available in precompiled binary and source format. There is also a distribution of Perl that comes from ActiveState—the original developers of the Windows port of Perl—that comes as a binary bundled with some additional extensions and the Perl Package Manager (PPM), an alternative to the **CPAN** module distributed with the core release. Currently the ActiveState release is available only for Linux (x86), Solaris, and, of course, the original Windows.

Installation

Perl is available for Unix in both precompiled binary and source format. Precompiled binaries can be downloaded, extracted, and then installed without any need to compile the source code. They are available both as compressed tar archives, RPM (RedHat Package Manager) packages, and Solaris packages. The best place to get Perl is from the main Perl website, **www. perl.com**. You should find links to most binaries on that site.

If you want to compile from the sources (useful if you want to enable certain extensions and options), then you need to download the source and then configure and compile it.

You'll need a C compiler installed on your system—both commercial environments such as Sun Microsystem's Forte for C/C++ and free systems such as GNU CC should work fine. Once you've downloaded the source from **www.perl.com**, do the following:

1. Extract the source code from the archive using **tar** and **gunzip**, for example:

```
$ $ gunzip -c perl.tar.gz | tar xvf -
```

2. Change to the newly created directory. It's worth checking the README and INSTALL files, which contain general Perl information and specific details on the installation process, respectively.

3. Run the configuration script:

```
$ ./configure.gnu
```

This is, in fact, a GNU-style execution of the real **Configure** script. The standard Perl **Configure** script is interactive, requiring input from you on a number of questions. The GNU-compatible execution answers the questions automatically for you, making a number of assumptions about your system, though it still shows the process going on behind the scenes.

The former GNU style-configuration script will probably install Perl into /usr/local, with the interpreter and support scripts ending up in /usr/local/bin and the Perl library being placed into /usr/local/lib/perl5. This obviously requires suitable access privileges to install the files to this location. You can change the install directory by using the **--prefix** command line option:

```
$ ./configure.gnu --prefix=/home/mc/local
```

4. Run **make** to build the application:

```
$ make
```

The application and support files have now been compiled. It's a good idea at this point to run **make test,** which will run a standard selection of tests to ensure that Perl has compiled properly. If there are any problems, you want to check the build process to see if anything failed. On the mainstream systems, such as Linux and Solaris, it's unlikely that you will notice any test failures.

5. Once the build has completed, install the application, scripts, and modules using **make**:

```
$ make install
```

Remember that the installation prefix will by default be /usr/local/, although the exact setting will depend on your OS. Providing you didn't specify different directories, the usual directory specification will install Perl into the /usr/local/bin and /usr/local/lib/perl5 directories. You will need to add /usr/local/bin or the installation directory you chose (specified by the **$installation_prefix/bin** variable in the makefile) to your **$PATH** environment variable, if it is not already in it.

FUNDAMENTALS

Executing Scripts

There are two ways of executing a Perl script under Unix. You can run the Perl application, supplying the script's name on the command line, as in the first example, or you can place the second example on the first line of the file (called the shebang line),

```
$ perl myscript.pl #!/usr/local/bin/perl
```

where the path given is the path to the Perl application. You must then change the file mode of the script to be executable (usually 0755). You can change the mode using the **chmod** command:

```
$ chmod 755 myscript.pl
```

Note that it is common to have different versions of Perl on your system. In this case, the latest version will always have been installed as /user/local/bin/perl, which is linked to the version-specific file, for example, /user/local/bin/perl5.6.0.

The Perl libraries and support files are installed in $prefix/lib/perl5. Since version 5.004, each version of Perl has installed its own subdirectory such that the actual location becomes /user/local/lib/perl5/5.6.0/, or whatever the version number is. User-installed (site-specific) scripts should be placed into /user/local/lib/perl5/site-perl/5.6.0.

Whenever a script is run, unless it has been redirected, standard input, output, and errors are sent via the terminal or window, the same as in the shell environment, except in the case of CGI scripts, where standard input is taken from the web server, standard output is sent back to the browser, and standard error is sent to the web server's log file.

Installing Third-Party Modules

For most modules (particularly those from CPAN), the installation process is fairly straightforward:

1. Download the module, and extract it using **tar** and **gunzip**, for example:

   ```
   $ gunzip -c module.tar.gz | tar xf -
   ```

   This should create a new directory with the module contents.

2. Change to the module directory.

3. Type

   ```
   $ perl5 Makefile.PL
   ```

   This will check that the module contents are complete and that the necessary prerequisite modules are already installed. It will also create a makefile that will compile (if necessary) and install the module.

   As in the original installation process, a **make test** will verify that the compilation and configuration of the package works before you come to install it. You should report any problems to the package's author.

4. To install the module, type

```
$ make install
```

This will copy the modules and any required support files into the appropriate directories.

A better, and less interactive, solution is to use the **CPAN** module to do the downloading, building, and installation for you. See Web Appendix B at **www.osborne.com** for information on how to use the **CPAN** module.

Perl Under Windows

Perl has been supported under Windows for some time. Originally, development concentrated on providing a Windows-compatible version from the core libraries, and then the development split as it became apparent that providing a lot of the built-in support for certain functions (notably **fork**) was unattainable. This lead to a "core" port and a separate development handled by a company called ActiveWare. ActiveWare worked on providing not only Perl, but also a suite of extensions that allowed you to perform most operations normally handled by the built-in functions that were only supported under Unix.

ActiveWare later became ActiveState, and their changes were rolled back into the core release. Now there is only one version of the Perl interpreter that is valid on both platforms, but there are now two distributions. The "core" distribution is identical to that under Unix, so it comes with the standard Perl library but not the extension set originally developed under the original ActiveWare development.

ActiveState still provides a prepackaged version of Perl for Windows that includes the core Perl interpreter and an extended set of modules that include the Perl Package Manager, a number of Win32-specific modules (see Table 2-1), and some general extensions like Graham Barr's libnet bundle and Gisle Aas's LWP (libwww-perl) bundle. The main ActiveState Perl distribution is called ActivePerl (and is now also available under Solaris and Linux x86), but they also supply a number of extras, such as the Perl Development Kit, which provides a visual package installer and debugger, and PerlEx, which speeds up execution of Perl scripts when used under Microsoft's Internet Information Server.

Module	Description
Archive::Tar	A toolkit for opening and using Unix tar files.
Compress::Zlib	An interface for decompressing information entirely within Perl.

Table 2-1.   *Default Modules Installed by ActivePerl*

Module	Description
LWP	Gisle Aas's Lib WWW Perl (LWP) toolkit. This includes modules for processing HTML, URLs, and MIME-encoded information, and the necessary code for downloading files by HTTP and FTP.
Win32::ChangeNotify	Interface to the NT Change/Notify system for monitoring the status of files and directories transparently.
Win32::Clipboard	Access to the global system clipboard. You can add and remove objects from the clipboard directory.
Win32::Console	Terminal control of an MSDOS or Windows NT command console.
Win32::Event	Interface to the Win32 event system for IPC.
Win32::EventLog	Interface to reading from and writing to the Windows NT event log system.
Win32::File	Allows you to access and set the attributes of a file.
Win32::FileSecurity	Interface to the extended file security options under Windows NT.
Win32::Internet	Interface to Win32's built-in Internet access system for downloading files. For a cross-platform solution see **Net::FTP**, **Net:HTTP** or the LWP modules elsewhere in this appendix.
Win32::IPC	Base methods for the different IPC techniques supported under Win32.
Win32::Mutex	Interface to the Mutex (Mutual/Exclusive) locking and access mechanism.
Win32::NetAdmin	Network administration functions for individual machines and entire domains.
Win32::NetResource	Provides a suite of Perl functions for accessing and controlling the individual Net resources.
Win32::ODBC	ODBC interface for accessing databases. See also the DBI and DBD toolkits.
Win32::OLE	Interface to OLE automation.
Win32::PerfLib	Supports an interface to the Windows NT performance system.

Table 2-1.   *Default Modules Installed by ActivePerl* (continued)

Module	Description
Win32::Pipe	Named pipes and assorted functions.
Win32::Process	Allows you to create manageable Win32 processes within Perl.
Win32::Registry	Provides an interface to the Windows registry. See the **Win32API::Registry** module and the **Win32::TieRegistry** module for a tied interface.
Win32::Semaphore	Interface to the Win32 semaphores.
Win32::Service	Allows the control and access of Windows NT services.
Win32::Shortcut	Access (and modification) of Win32 shortcuts.
Win32::Sound	Allows you to play .WAV and other file formats within a Perl script.
Win32::TieRegistry	A tied interface to the Win32 registry system.
Win32::WinError	Access to the Win32 error system.
Win32API::Net	Provides a complete interface to the underlying C++ functions for managing accounts with the NT LanManager.
Win32API::Registry	Provides a low-level interface to the core API used for manipulating the registry.

Table 2-1.   *Default Modules Installed by ActivePerl* (continued)

Installation

There are two ways of installing Perl—the best and recommended way is to download the ActivePerl installer from **www.activestate.com**, run the installer, and then reboot your machine. This will do everything required to get Perl working on your system, including installing the Perl binary, its libraries and modules, and modifying your **PATH** so that you can find Perl in a DOS window or at the command prompt. If you are running Perl under Windows NT or Windows 2000, or are using Microsoft's Personal Web Server for Windows 95/98/Me, then the installer will also set up the web server to support Perl as a scripting host for web development. Finally, under Windows NT and Windows 2000, the ActivePerl installer will also modify the configuration of your machine to allow Perl scripts ending in .pl to be executed directly—that is, without the need to pass the script names to Perl beforehand.

The alternative method is to compile Perl from the core distribution. Although some people prefer this version, it's important to note that core distribution does not come with any of the Win32-specific modules. You will need to download and install those modules separately.

If you want to install a version of the Perl binary based on the latest source code, you will need to find a C compiler capable of compiling the application. It's then a case of following the instructions relevant to your C and development environment. The supported C compilers are described here. Other versions and C compilers may work, but it's not guaranteed.

- Borland C++, version 5.02 or later: With the Borland C++ compiler, you will need to use a different make command, since the one supplied does not work very well and certainly doesn't support **MakeMaker** extensions. The documentation recommends the **dmake** application, available from **http://www-personal.umich.edu/~gsar/dmake-4.1-win32.zip**.

- Microsoft Visual C++, version 4.2 or later: You can use the **nmake** that comes with Visual C++ to build the distribution correctly.

- Mingw32 with EGCS, versions 1.0.2 and 1.1, or Mingw32 with GCC, version 2.8.1: Both EGCS and GCC supply their own make command. You can download a copy of the EGCS version (preferred) from **ftp://ftp.xraylith. wisc.edu/pub/khan/gnu-win32/mingw32/**. The GCC version is available from **http://agnes.dida.physik.uni-essen.de/~janjaap/mingw32/**.

Also, be aware that Windows 95/98 as a compilation platform is not supported. This is because the command shell available under Windows 95/98 is not capable of working properly with the scripts and make commands required during the building process. The best platforms for building from the core source code are Windows NT or Windows 2000 using the standard **cmd** shell.

In all cases, ignore the **Configure** utility that you would normally use when compiling under Unix and Unix-like operating systems. Instead, change to the win32 directory and run the make command for your installation. For example:

```
c:\perl\win32> dmake
```

For Microsoft's Visual C++, you will need to execute the VCVARS32.BAT batch file, which sets up the environment for using Visual C++ on the command line; for example:

```
c:\perlsrc\win32>c:\progra~1\micros~1\vc98\bin\vcvars32.bat
```

You may need to increase the environment memory on your command.com for this batch file to work properly—you can do this by modifying the properties for the

MS-DOS Prompt shortcut. Select the shortcut within the Start menu, and then choose the Program tab. You should modify the "Cmd Line" field to read

```
C:\WINDOWS\COMMAND.COM /E:4096
```

This boosts the environment memory for the command prompt up to 4K—more than enough for all the variables you should need.

Remember that compiling and installing Perl from the source distribution does not give you the integration facilities or modules that are included as standard within the ActiveState version.

You will need to manually update your **PATH** variable so that you have access to the Perl interpreter on the command line. You can do this within Windows 95/98 by modifying the AUTOEXEC.BAT file. You will need to add a line like

```
SET PATH=C:\PERL\BIN\;%PATH%
```

This will update your search path without replacing the preexisting contents. The C:\PERL\BIN\ is the default install location; you should modify this to wherever you have installed the binary.

On Windows NT/2000, you will need to update the **PATH** variable by using the **System** control panel.

Executing Scripts

Once installed correctly, there are two basic ways of executing a Perl script. You can either type

```
C:\> perl hello.pl
```

in a command window, or you can double-click on a script in Windows Explorer. The former method allows you to specify command line arguments; the latter method will require that you ask the user for any required information.

Under Windows NT, if you want a more Unix-like method of executing scripts, you can modify the **PATHEXT** environment variable (in the System control panel) to include .pl as a recognized extension. This allows you to call a script just like any other command on the command line, but with limitations. The following will work:

```
C:\> hello readme.txt
```

However, redirection and pipes to the Perl script will not work. This means that the following examples, although perfectly valid under Unix, will not work under Windows:

```
C:\> hello <readme.txt
C:\> hello readme.txt|more
```

The other alternative, which works on all Windows platforms, is to use the **pl2bat** utility. This wraps the call to your Perl script within a Windows batch file. For example, we could use it to convert our **hello.pl** utility:

```
C:\> pl2bat hello.pl
C:\> hello
```

The big advantage here is that because we are using batch file, it works on any Windows platform, and we can even add command line options to the Perl interpreter within the batch file to alter the behavior. Furthermore, pipes and redirection work correctly with batch files, which therefore also means the options work with our Perl script.

If you want to specify any additional command line options, you can use the normal "shebang" line (#!) to specify these options. Although Windows will ignore this line, the Perl interpreter still has to read the file, and so it will extract any information from the line that it needs. So, for example, to turn warnings on within a script, you might use a line such as

```
#!perl -w
```

Note that you must still comment out the line using a leading hash character.

Installing Third-Party Modules

Although it's possible to use the **CPAN** module to do the installation for you, it requires access to the **make** command and often a C compiler in order for it to work properly. Instead, ActivePerl comes with the Perl Package Manager (PPM). This works along the same basic premise as the **CPAN** module, except that PPM modules are precompiled and ready to be installed—all the PPM tool actually does is copy the files downloaded in a given package into their required location.

Using PPM is very easy. You start PPM from the command line:

```
C:\> ppm
PPM interactive shell (1.1.1) - type 'help' for available commands.
PPM>
```

Once there, you use **search** to find a suitable package, and **install** to install it. For example, to install the **Tk** interface module,

```
C:\> ppm
PPM interactive shell (1.1.1) - type 'help' for available commands.
PPM> install Tk
```

And you then let PPM install the files for you. The number of PPM files is smaller than CPAN, largely because the modules on CPAN are uncompiled, and those for use under PPM need to be precompiled. To add to the headaches for developers many of the CPAN packages rely on libraries and functions only available under Unix.

PPM packages are stored in a number of repositories. The main repository is at ActiveState, but others are available. A list of repositories is given in Table 2-2.

Perl Under Mac OS

Compared to Unix and Windows, Mac OS has one significant missing feature: it has no command line interface. Mac OS is a 100 percent windowed GUI environment. This presents some potential problems when we consider the methods already suggested for running Perl programs.

The solution is a separate "development environment." The MacPerl application supports both the execution of Perl scripts and the creation of the scripts in the first place. In addition to direct access to the execution process (scripts can be started and stopped from menus and key combinations), MacPerl also permits you interactive use of the Perl debugger in a familiar environment, and complete control of the environment in which the scripts are executed.

Quite aside from the simple interface problem, there are also underlying differences between text file formats, the value of the epoch used for dates and times, and even the supported commands and functions. There are ways of getting around these problems, both using your own Perl scripts and modifications and using a number of modules that are supplied as standard with the MacPerl application.

The current version of MacPerl is based on v5.004 of Perl, which makes it a couple of years old. Although the developer, Matthias Neeracher, has promised to work on a new version, there is currently no set date for a Perl 5.6 release. In fact, it's possible that MacPerl may not be updated until Perl 6 is released toward the end of 2001.

Repository	URL
ActiveState	http://www.activestate.com/packages
Jan Krynicky	http://jenda.krynicky.cz/perl
Roth Consulting	http://www.roth.net/perl/packages/
Achim Bohnet	http://www.xray.mpe.mpg.de/~ach/prk/ppm
RTO	http://rto.dk/packages/

Table 2-2.   *PPM Repositories*

For those of you interested in developing with Perl under Mac OS X, you'll be pleased to hear that Mac OS X's Unix layer is used to provide the same basic functionality as any Unix distribution. In fact, Mac OS X actually comes with Perl installed as standard.

Installation

Perl is available in a number of different guises, depending on what you want to do with it and how extensible and expandable you want the support modules to be. The basic distribution, "appl", includes the MacPerl binary, all the Perl and MacPerl libraries and modules, and the documentation. The "tool" distribution works with MPW (the Macintosh Programmer's Workshop), allowing you to develop and release Perl programs that are part of a larger overall application while presenting you with the same interface and development environment you use for C/C++ and Pascal Mac applications. Because MacPerl provides an almost transparent interface to the underlying Mac toolbox, you can use Perl and C/C++/Pascal programs and code interchangeably. The source, in the "src" distribution, including all of the toolbox interfaces, is also available.

Installing the application is a case of downloading and decompressing the installer, and then double-clicking on the installer application. This will install all the modules, application, and documentation you need to start programming in Perl. Starting MacPerl is a simple case of double-clicking on the application.

Executing Scripts

Perl scripts are identified using the Mac OS Creator and Type codes. The MacPerl environment automatically sets this information when you save the script. In fact, MacPerl specifies three basic formats for running scripts and one additional format for use with Mac-based web servers. The different formats are outlined in Table 2-3.

File Type	Description
Droplet	A droplet is a mini-application that consists of the original Perl script and a small amount of glue code that uses Apple events to start MacPerl, if it is not already running, and then executes the script. Using droplets is the recommended method for distributing MacPerl scripts. To save a script as a droplet, go to Save As under the File menu, and choose Droplet in the file type pop-up at the bottom of the file dialog box. Files dragged and dropped onto a droplet's icon in the Finder have their names passed to the script as arguments (within **@ARGV**). If you plan on distributing your scripts to other people, droplets require that the destination users have MacPerl already installed. This might make initial distributions large (about 800K), although further updates should be smaller.

Table 2-3.   *MacPerl Script Types*

File Type	Description
Stand-alone applications	A stand-alone application creates a file composed of the Perl application and the script and related modules. This creates a single, "double-clickable" application that runs and executes your script. This can be a great solution if you want to provide a single-file solution for a client, or if you want to save clients the task of installing MacPerl on their machines. However, this is still an interpreted version. The script is not compiled into an executable, just bundled with the Perl interpreter into a single file.
Plain text file	A plain text file can be opened within the MacPerl environment and executed as a Perl script. Make sure that if the script has come from another platform, the script is in Mac OS text format. These files will not automatically execute when you double-click them. They open either the built-in editor within MacPerl or the editor you usually use for editing text files (for example, SimpleText, BBEdit, or emacs).
CGI Script	This creates a script suitable for execution under many Mac-specific web servers, including the one supported by Apple's AppleShare IP 6.0.

Table 2-3. *MacPerl Script Types* (continued)

When a script is executing, **STDIN**, **STDOUT**, and **STDERR** are supported directly within the MacPerl environment. If you want to introduce information on a "command line" (other than files, if you are using a droplet), you will need to use the Mac-specific toolbox modules and functions to request the information from the user.

Installing Third-Party Modules

Installation of third-party modules under MacPerl is complicated by the lack of either standard development tools or a command-line environment that would enable you to execute the normal Perl makefiles for **make** tools.

Scripts that rely on external modules, such as those from CPAN (especially those that require C source code to be compiled), may cause difficulties, not all of which can be easily overcome. The process for installing a third-party module is as follows:

1. Download and then extract the module. Most modules are supplied as a gzipped tar file. You can either use the individual tools, MacGzip and suntar, to extract the file, or use Aladdin System's Stuffit Expander with the Expander Extensions.

Whichever application set you use, remember to switch line-feed conversion on. This will convert the Unix-style Perl scripts into Macintosh text files, which will be correctly parsed by the MacPerl processor.

2. Read the documentation to determine whether the module or any modules on which it relies use XS or C source code. If they do, it's probably best to forget about using the module. If you have access to the MPW toolkit, you may be able to compile the extension, but success is not guaranteed. You can also ask another MacPerl user, via the MacPerl mailing list, to compile it for you.

3. Ignore the **Makefile.PL** file. Although it might run, it will probably report an error like this:

```
# On MacOS, we need to build under the Perl source directory or
have the MacPerl SDK installed in the MacPerl folder.
```

Ignore it, because you need to install the Perl modules manually. Even if the **Makefile.PL** runs successfully, it will generate a makefile that you can't use on the Mac without the addition of some special tools!

4. Create a new folder (if you don't already have one) to hold your site-specific and contributed modules. This is usually located in **$ENV{MACPERL}sitelib:**, although you can create it anywhere, as long as you add the directory to the **@INC** variable via the MacPerl application preferences or use the **use lib** pragma within a script.

   Remember to create a proper directory structure if you are installing a hierarchical module. For example, when installing **Net::FTP**, you need to install the **FTP.pm** module into a subdirectory called Net, right below the **site_perl** or alternative installation location.

5. Copy across the individual Perl modules to the new directory. If the modules follow a structure, copy across all the directories and subdirectories.

6. Once the modules are copied across, try using the following script, which will automatically split the installed module, suitable for autoloading:

```
use AutoSplit;
my $instdir = "$ENV{MACPERL}site_perl";
autosplit("$dir:Module.pm", "$dir:auto", 0, 1, 1);
```

   Change the **$instdir** and module names accordingly. See Appendix B for more details on the **AutoSplit** module.

7. Once the module is installed, try running one of the test programs, or write a small script to use one of the modules you have installed. Check the MacPerl error window. If you get an error like this,

```
# Illegal character \012 (carriage return).
File 'Midkemia:MacPerl ƒ:site_perl:Net:DNS:Header.pm'; Line 1
# (Maybe you didn't strip carriage returns after a network transfer?)
```

then the file still has Unix-style line feeds in it. You can use BBEdit or a similar application to convert these to Macintosh text. Alternatively, you could write a Perl script to do it!

Perl Components

Describing language—whether coded, written, or spoken, is fundamentally difficult because in order to understand the language components (nouns, verbs, adjectives) you also need to need to understand the semantics that convert those components in isolation into an understandable language that allows you to communicate. Unfortunately, it's impossible to describe those semantics without giving examples of their use!

As a rule, Perl lets you do what you want, when you want to, and, more or less, how you want to. Perl is far more concerned about letting you develop a solution that works than it is about slotting your chosen solution into a set of standards and a rigid structure.

The core of any program are the *variables* used to hold changeable information. You change the contents of those variables using *operators*, *regular expressions*, and *functions*. *Statements* help to control the flow of your program and enable you to declare certain facts about the programs you are running. If you can't find what you want using the base Perl function set, you can make use of a number of *modules*, which export a list of variables and functions that provide additional information and operations. If you want to work in a structured format, modules also support objects, methods, and object classes. You can, of course, also make your own modules that use your own functions.

We'll have a quick look at some of the elements and components within Perl that will help when we start to look at these individual items in more detail in future chapters.

Variables

Variables hold variable pieces of information—they are just storage containers for numbers, strings, and compound structures (lists of numbers and strings) that we might want to change at some future point.

Perl supports one basic variable type, the scalar. A scalar holds numbers and strings, so we could rewrite the simple "Hello World" example at the beginning of this chapter as

```
$message = "Hello World\n";
print $message;
```

In this example, we've *assigned* a *literal* to a variable called **$message**. When you *assign* a value to a variable, you are just populating that variable with some information. A *literal* is a piece of static information—in this case it's a string, but it could have been a number. By the way, when you assign information, you are assigning the value to the right of the *assignation operator* (the = sign) to the *lvalue* on the left. The *lvalue* is the name given to a variable or structure that can hold information. Normally this is a variable, but functions and objects are also types of lvalues.

You'll notice in the preceding example that the variable, **$message**, has a "funny" character at the beginning. In this case, it's a dollar sign, and it identifies the variable as being a scalar. You always use a dollar sign when accessing a scalar value. The way to remember a scalar is that the **$** sign looks like an "s", for scalar!

There are also some compound variable types—namely the array and the hash. The array is a list of scalar variables—thus we can store a list of days using

```
@days = ('Mon','Tue','Wed','Thu','Fri','Sat','Sun');
```

The leading character for an array is an **@** sign (think "a" for array), and you always access an array of one or more values using an **@** sign. You access the values in an array by the numerical index; the first value is at index 0, so to get the first day of the week from the preceding list, we'd use **$days[0]**. Note the leading **$** sign—this is required because we are accessing the scalar value at index 0 from the array.

Perl also supports a *hash*—this is a list that uses not numerical indices, but instead a string "key" to access each "value"—the so-called key/value pair. Hash variables start with a **%** sign—think of the two "o" characters in the **%** as the key and value. Thus we could create a hash that contains month names (as the keys) and the days in that month (as the values):

```
%months = ('January' => 31,
           ...
           'November' => 30,
           'December' => 31);
```

Now all we need to do when we want to know how many days are in November is access the value in the **%months** hash with a key of "November":

```
print "Days in November:",$months{'November'},"\n";
```

Perl also supports some other types of variables, such as filehandles (which allow us to read from and write to files) and typeglobs (which allow us to access a variable via the internal symbol tables). We also use references, which just point to other variables without actually containing a value themselves.

The special characters used to access variables are a vital part of the Perl language—they enable us to identify the variables easily and let the programmer *and* Perl know what sort of variable we are expecting to use. We'll see more information on variables in Chapter 4.

Operators

Operators perform some sort of operation on a value or variable. For example, the **+** operator adds two numbers together:

```
$sum = 4 + 5;
```

Other operators allow you to perform other basic math calculations, introduce lists of values (for use with functions and variables), and assign values to variables and subroutines.

There are also operators that enable us to use regular expressions that can "match" information contained within a string against an expression, or perform a substitution so that we can replace and translate information without having to explicitly define its contents.

We'll be looking at Perl operators, and the core mechanics of how Perl takes a raw script and interprets the contents, in Chapter 3.

Statements

Statements enable us to control the execution of our script—for example, we might use the **if** statement to test the value of a variable or operation so that the script can make an informed decision about what to do next. Other statements include the loops, which allow us to repeat a process on the same piece of data or on a sequence of data. Statements also include declarations, such as those that allow us to define variables and subroutines.

We'll be covering statements and control structures in Chapter 5.

Subroutines (Functions)

When you want to perform an operation on a variable a number of times, or the same operation on a number of variables, it makes sense to place that sequence of operations into a subroutine or function. Now when you want to perform that operation, you send the variable to the subroutine, and then use the value returned from that subroutine.

Perl includes a number of subroutines that perform different operations—including the **print** subroutine, which sends information to the screen (or to a file). Other subroutines built into Perl include those for opening and communicating with files, talking over a network, or accessing information about the system. Other built-ins provide simple ways for performing different operations on variables and values.

You can also produce your own subroutines—something we'll be looking at in Chapter 6.

Modules

Once you have a collection of subroutines that you find useful, then you'll probably want to use them in other scripts and applications that you build with Perl. You could copy them to the new scripts, but a much better solution is to make your own modules. These are the libraries that extend the functionality of Perl.

Perl comes with its own, quite extensive, set of modules that allow you to communicate over a network (see Chapter 12), develop user interfaces (see Chapter 17), access external databases (see Chapter 13), and provide an interface for communicating with a web server and a client browser when developing web solutions (see Chapter 18).

If you can't find what you want within the standard Perl distribution, then there is a central repository of modules built by other programmers called CPAN. This contains literally thousands of modules to handle everything from accessing data sources through to handling XML (Extensible Markup Language).

We'll be looking at how to build our own modules in Chapter 6.

Where Next?

The answer to that question is really up to you—Perl will let you do almost anything. If you need to understand the basics of how Perl works and how scripts are interpreted, their elements identified, and rules followed, then continue reading Chapters 3 through to 6. If you want a little more detail on the sort of things Perl can do and how you might approach them, read Chapters 7 through 9.

If you already know the basics and want to use Perl to solve a particular problem, use the Chapters in Part 2, which cover everything from Perl's object-orientation system to extending Perl with external libraries.

The Complete Reference

Chapter 3

Perl Parsing Rules

Perl, like all languages, has its own set of rules for parsing the Perl script, identifying the different components that make up the Perl language, and then actually executing the script that you've supplied.

As we've already seen in the last chapter, Perl is pretty casual about certain aspects of the script's layout. For example, in Perl the simplest, and classic, Hello World program is as straightforward and complete as

```
print "Hello World\n";
```

We don't have to worry about any preamble or tell Perl to include required files before we can do anything useful. We also don't have to tell the interpreter how to end the program—Perl is quite happy for the source to simply end.

In this chapter, we're going to take a detailed look at some of the core elements of the Perl language. We'll start with the method used by Perl to actually interpret a source script and the process behind identifying and interpreting some of the core elements of the language. We'll also take our first look at the core operators used by Perl for manipulating and working with variables and other information.

The Execution Process

The first step to understanding how Perl parses a script is to take a top-level look at how Perl takes the source text and executes it. Perl works in a similar fashion to many other script-based languages—it takes raw input, parses each statement and converts it into a series of opcodes, builds a suitable opcode tree, and then executes the opcodes within a Perl "virtual machine." This technique is used by Perl, Python, and Java, and it's one of the most significant reasons why Perl is as quick as it is—the code is optimized into very small executable chunks, just like a normal program compiled for a specific processor.

To summarize, the basic sequence works as follows:

1. Read the source code and parse the contents to verify the source against the "core" rules. This is also the stage at which external modules are imported—Perl imports modules in their source format, and they are interpreted and parsed in the next stage along with your original script.

2. Compile the source into a series of opcodes. This involves the use of a parser, which translates the Perl source into the opcode structures. It's actually here that the majority of source errors are identified and raised.

3. Execute the opcode tree.

We will look in more detail at the specific process and the internals of the system in Chapters 20 and 22.

Outwardly, Perl actually classifies only two stages—the parsing stage and the execution or run-time stage. Errors reported at the parsing stage relate to problems with the layout or rules of the Perl language—for example, forgetting a quote or parenthesis, or trying to import a module that cannot be found. Run-time errors relate to the execution of a statement—for example, trying to divide a value by zero, or supplying an unexpected value to a function or subroutine.

Syntax and Parsing Rules

The Perl parser has to consider a number of different items when it takes in a source script and attempts to execute the statements. The primary purpose is, of course, to identify the different elements within each line as operators, terms, and constants, and then evaluate each sequence to produce a particular result—this might include calling a function (which itself will need the same statement examination) or performing a calculation.

Even before Perl gets to these elements, however, the parser must examine the individual source lines for information—comments need to be identified and removed. The basic layout of the line has to be validated—does it have a trailing semicolon, does it run on to the next line, and so on.

In fact, the Perl parser thinks about all of the following when it looks at a source line:

- **Basic syntax**   The core layout, line termination, and so on
- **Comments**   If a comment is included, ignore it
- **Component identity**   Individual terms (variables, functions and numerical and textual constants) are identified
- **Bare words**   Character strings that are not identified as valid terms
- **Precedence**   Once the individual items are identified, the parser processes the statements according to the precedence rules, which apply to all operators and terms
- **Context**   What is the context of the statement, are we expecting a list or scalar, a number or a string, and so on. This actually happens during the evaluation of individual elements of a line, which is why we can nest functions such as **sort**, **reverse**, and **keys** into a single statement line
- **Logic Syntax**   For logic operations, the parser must treat different values, whether constant- or variable-based, as true or false values

All of these present some fairly basic and fundamental rules about how Perl looks at an entire script. From the basic Hello World script to entire database applications, each line is executed in the same manner using the same basic rules.

Basic Syntax

The basic rules govern such things as line termination and the treatment of white space. These basic rules are

- Lines must start with a token that does not expect a left operand—for example,

  ```
  = 99;
  ```

  is invalid, because the = operator expects to see a valid lvalue on the left side of the expression. As a general rule, functions and variables are the primary token in a line, with some exceptions.

- Lines must be terminated with a semicolon, except when it's the last line of a block, where the semicolon can be omitted. For example:

  ```
  print "Hello\n"
  ```

  is perfectly legal as a single-line script. Since it's the last line of a block, it doesn't require any semicolon, but

  ```
  print "Hello "
  print "World\n"
  ```

  will cause a fault.

- If you split a line within a quoted string, then the line termination becomes part of the string.

- White space is only required between tokens that would otherwise be confusing, so spaces, tabs, newlines, and comments (which Perl treats as white space) are ignored. The line

  ```
  sub menu{print"menu"}
  ```

  works as it would if it were more neatly spaced.

- Lines may be split at any point, providing the split is logically between two tokens. The following is perfectly legal:

```
print
"hello"


                "world";
```

All of the preceding are examples of the core rules for executing a script. Any errors picked up at this point are reported during the compilation stage—before any code is actually executed (there are some exceptions; see Chapter 5 for details on **BEGIN** and other special blocks).

It's also important to remember that while the examples above are perfectly legal Perl, they don't make your program easier to read, which will make it harder to maintain in the long run.

Comments

Comments are treated by Perl as white space—the moment Perl sees a hash on a line outside of a quoted block, the remainder of the line is ignored. This is the case even within multiline statements and regular expressions (when the /x modifier is used):

```
matched = /(\S+)      #Host
          \s+         #(space separator)
          (\S+)       #Identifier
          \s+         #(space separator)
          (\S+)       #Username
          \s+         #(space separator)
          \[(.*)\]    #Time
          \s+         #(space separator)
          "(.*)"      #Request
          \s+         #(space separator)
          (\S+)       #Result
          \s+         #(space separator)
          (\S+)       #Bytes sent
          /x;
```

Comments end when Perl sees a normal line termination. The following is completely invalid:

```
print("Hello world");   # Greet the user
                          and let them know we're here
```

There is also no way of indicating to Perl that you have a multiline comment to include, short of placing the hash symbol before each comment segment.

If the comment includes a "line directive"; in this instance the information is stored within the opcode tree and used to populate the __LINE__ and __FILE__ special tokens. These are available directly and are also used as the basis for error messages raised by **die** and **warn** when no trailing newline is supplied.

In order to introduce the directive, you must use the word **line**, followed by a line number and an optional string. The match is actually made by a regular expression:

```
/^#\s*line\s+(\d+)\s*(?:\s"([^"]+)?\s*$/
```

The first group, **$1** (the first matching parenthesized block, see *Regular Expressions* in Chapter 8 for more details), populates __LINE__, and **$2** populates __FILE__. For example:

```
# line 200 "Parsing engine"
die "Fatal";
```

produces

```
Fatal at Parsing engine line 200
```

Note that the line directive actually modifies the __LINE__ token, which is normally automatically parsed and populated by the Perl interpreter based on the current line within the script. So this script:

```
#line 200 "Parsing engine"
print "Busy\n";
print "Doing\n";
print "Nothing\n";
die 'Fatal';
```

actually reports this:

```
Busy
Doing
Nothing
Fatal at Parsing engine line 203.
```

It reported an error on line 203, not the real source line 4—the earlier line directive has permanently modified the line-numbering counters. You can update the line directive with any number, such that

```
#line 200 "Parsing engine"
print "Busy doing nothing\n";
warn "Warning";
#line 100 "Post-process engine"
print "Working the whole day through\n";
die "Fatal";
```

generates this:

```
Busy doing nothing
Warning at Parsing engine line 201.
Working the whole day through
Fatal at Post-process engine line 101.
```

Comments and line directives can be a useful way of debugging and documenting your scripts and programs. We'll return to the topic in Chapter 21.

Component Identity

When Perl fails to identify an item as one of the predefined operators, it treats the character sequence as a "term." Terms are core parts of the Perl language and include variables, functions, and quotes. The term-recognition system uses these rules:

- Variables can start with a letter, number, or underscore, providing they follow a suitable variable character, such as **$**, **@**, or **%**.

- Variables that start with a letter or underscore can contain any further combination of letters, numbers, and underscore characters.

- Variables that start with a number can only consist of further numbers—be wary of using variable names starting with digits. The variables such as **$0** through to **$9** are used for group matches in regular expressions.

- Subroutines can only start with an underscore or letter, but can then contain any combination of letters, numbers, and underscore characters.

- Case is significant—**$VAR**, **$Var**, and **$var** are all different variables.

- Each of the three main variable types have their own name space—**$var**, **@var**, and **%var** are all separate variables.

- Filehandles should use all uppercase characters—this is only a convention, not a rule, but it is useful for identification purposes.

Once the term has been extracted using these rules, it's compared against Perl's internal symbol table and the symbol table of the current package. Quotes and constants are also identified and either resolved or tagged at this stage as being bare values.

If after all this, the item has still not been identified, then the item is treated as a bare word—see the "Bare Words" section further on in this chapter for more information on how these items are parsed. Quotes are also a special case; because their values may be interpolated, they are actually resolved at this stage—see the "Quoting" section in Chapter 4 for information on constants and quoting and the interpolation of variables into quoted strings.

Operators and Precedence

Like most languages, Perl's parsing rules are based on precedence—the order in which individual elements of a line are evaluated and then processed. As a general rule, Perl parses statements from left to right, except in situations where the rightmost value may affect the evaluation of a term on the left. A good example is the += operator, which adds and assigns a value to a variable—if the right side of this operator wasn't evaluated first, Perl would be unable to determine what value should be added to the variable on the left side.

The information in this section is quite complex, and I don't expect all readers to understand all of the principles and techniques shown on their first read through. It's impossible to describe the mechanics of a language without giving some examples. My advice is to read this section through, follow up with the remainder of the chapters in this section, and then come back and re-read this section again. Hopefully, it should all make more sense the second time around!

The list of operators in Table 3-1 gives the individual operator precedence, and the overall precedence for all operators.

Name	Precedence	Examples
Terms and list operators	Left	
The arrow (dereference) operator	Left	->
Auto-increment and auto-decrement	Nonassoc	++ --
Exponential	Right	**

Table 3-1. *Operators in Order of Precedence*

Name	Precedence	Examples
Symbolic unary operators	Right	! ~ \ and unary + and −
Regular expression bindings	Left	=~ !~
Multiplication	Left	* / % x
Addition and subtraction	Left	+ − .
Shift operators	Left	<< >>
Named unary operators	Nonassoc	**-X** file test, some functions
Relational operators	Nonassoc	< > <= >= lt gt le ge
Equality operators	Nonassoc	== != <=> eq ne cmp
Bitwise AND	Left	&
Bitwise OR and Exclusive OR	Left	| ^
Symbolic logical AND	Left	&&
Symbolic logical OR	Left	||
Range operators	Nonassoc	.. ...
Conditional operator	Right	?:
Assignment operators	Right	= += −= *= etc.
List operators	Left	, =>
List operators	Nonassoc	
Logical NOT	Right	not
Logical AND	Left	and
Logical OR and Exclusive OR	Left	or xor

Table 3-1.   *Operators in Order of Precedence* (continued)

The operators in Table 3-1 are also listed in overall precedence, from top to bottom—the first item in the table, terms and list operators, have the highest precedence and will always be evaluated by Perl first when used within a compound statement.

You can see, for example, that * has a higher precedence than +. This means that the statement

```
$a = 5*6+4;
```

is evaluated as

```
$a = (5*6)+4;
```

and not

```
$a = 5*(6+4);
```

which produces a result of 34, and not 50.

Understanding the Precedence System

If you want to check the precedence rules, you can use the Perl compiler **Deparse** backend. This takes a Perl script and regurgitates it after the precedence rules have been applied and optimization has taken place. The output is then reformatted, according to the precedence rules, using parentheses to highlight the precedence rules.

For example:

```
$ perl -MO=Deparse,-p -e '$a + $b *$c / $d % $e'
-e syntax OK
($a + ((($b * $c) / $d) % $e));
```

You can see here that the statement has been grouped according to the precedence rules. Any statement or script can be run through the backend. However, because the output includes any optimization (see the "The Execution Process" section at the beginning of this chapter), passing in statements that include constant values will not yield what you want:

```
$ perl -MO=Deparse,-p -e '$a = 5*6+4;'
($a = 34);
-e syntax OK
```

The compiler and its backends, which can provide useful nuggets of information about your script, such as this one, will be discussed in more detail in Chapter 22.

Terms and List Operators

Terms have the highest precedence in Perl, and they include the following:

- Variables
- Quotes
- Any parenthesized expression
- Function calls with parentheses
- The **do** {} and **eval** {} constructs
- Subroutine and method calls
- Anonymous constructors for arrays, [], and hashes, {}

The basic effect can be seen with a simple calculation:

```
print 6*(5+4);
```

prints out 54, the **5+4** is evaluated first, because it's in parentheses, even though the precedence rules state that the * operator has a higher precedence.

However, if you embed a term within a list, then the terms are evaluated left to right before being returned as a list to the caller; for example, in the fragment,

```
sub add { print 'Result:' }
print(2,3,add);
```

the call to the **add** function is evaluated before the **print** statement. As a general rule, the terms are evaluated from left to right, such that

```
sub first { print 'First' }
sub second { print 'Second' }
print(2,3,first,second);
```

generates

```
FirstSecond2311
```

This also affects embedded terms that accept further list operators:

```
print 2,3,sort 2+2, 1+1;
```

Here, the arguments on the right of the **sort** term are immediately gobbled up and then evaluated left to right, before the elements before **sort** are evaluated. This results in the entire statement printing "2324".

In general, this left-to-right term evaluation produces the behavior you expect when you embed calls to other functions within a statement,

```
print "Warning:", sort ('A','B','C'), "\nContinuing";
```

But it also has the effect of ignoring further arguments, or earlier arguments if the script or function returns or forces the script to terminate. For example,

```
print "Warning:", die("Error"), "Exiting";
```

outputs this:

```
Error.
File 'Untitled'; Line 1
```

This script:

```
sub add
{
    print "Sum: ",return($_[0]+$_[1]);
}

print add(1,2);
```

outputs "3", the return value of the function, missing the prefix string, which would only have been printed if the evaluated list had been supplied to the **print** function.

Finally, the statement

```
print(4+5) + 1, "\n";
```

is unlikely to do what you expect. The call to **print** will be made and evaluated, but using only the evaluated **4+5** expression—the parentheses define the list of values that is returned to the **print** statement. Then Perl will attempt to add the return value from the **print** subroutine call, which is actually void, to 1, while the newline character is just discarded as a useless constant. If you switch on warnings, you'll get more information:

```
Useless use of integer addition (+) in void context at t.pl line 1.
Useless use of a constant in void context at t.pl line 1.
9
```

But the **Deparse** backend is more explicit:

```
((print(9) + 1), '???');
t.pl syntax OK
```

The first part shows the result of **print** and 1 being added together, but the newline argument is never properly evaluated or included in the statement. Note that Perl still treats the syntax as being okay—there is nothing invalid about the statement as far as the parser is concerned, it just doesn't make any sense.

The Arrow (Dereference) Operator

The arrow or infix dereference operator is used to access the properties and methods of an object or the data contained within hash or array references. Because we are accessing the contents of variables, the precedence has to be high enough for the values to be determined before they are included as part of other statements.

References, which support nested structures and Perl's object-oriented mechanism are the subject of another chapter. Please refer to Chapter 10 for further examples and explanation of the dereference operator.

Auto-Increment and Auto-Decrement

The auto-increment and auto-decrement operators allow you to immediately increment or decrement a value without having to perform the calculation within a separate expression. This operates in the same fashion as the C equivalent and can be placed before or after a variable for the increment or decrement to take place before or after the variable has been evaluated. For example:

```
$a = 1;
print ++$a; # incremented before, outputs 2
print $a++; # incremented after, outputs 2, $a now equals 3
print --$a; # decremented before, now outputs 2
print $a--; # decremented after, outputs 2, $a now equals 1
```

The increment operator also has special meaning when applied in a string context. If applied to a string that equates to a number, then it returns the number incremented as normal. For example:

```
print ++($foo = '99'); # Outputs 100
print ++($foo = '100'); # Outputs 101
```

However, when used on an alphanumeric string, the increment applies to the string, applying the increment within the character's range. For example:

```
print ++($foo = 'b1'); # Outputs c2
print ++($foo = 'Qz'); # Outputs Ra
print ++($foo = 'zz'); # Outputs aaa
```

Note the result of the last line—the "characters" are incremented, introducing a new character "a", just as if we were incrementing numbers. The rule applies to all "natural" rollovers: "z" increments to "aa", and "Z" increments to "AA" and so on. But, the application is against the entire string as if it was a number. Thus a rollover of the last character from "z" to "a" also increments the preceding character. This can be seen better with:

```
print ++($foo = 'Qx'); # Outputs Qy
print ++($foo = 'Qy'); # Outputs Qz
print ++($foo = 'Qz'); # Outputs Ra
```

The last letter worked in exactly the same fashion as the tens column in a decimal number, thus it would have changed "Zz" to "AAa".

You can only use increment in this fashion; the decrement operator does not work in the same way.

Note, as well, that the operators can only be applied to variables—the statement

```
print ++'aa';
```

will fail.

The increment and decrement operators have no significant precedence. They are listed in the table as non-associative—this is because there are no left or right arguments; the operators work directly on the variable or string supplied. If they are placed before a variable, the variable's value is incremented or decremented before the variable's value is used. If placed after, then the variable is incremented or decremented after the variable has been evaluated. This means that the statement:

```
$a = 3;
print $a++ * $a
```

Actually prints the result of the calculation 3*4—the increment is executed immediately after the value of the variable has been extracted.

Exponentiation

The exponential operator raises the value on the left of the operator to the power of the right. For example:

```
print 9**3;
```

Outputs 729, or 9*9*9. The operator evaluates the expression on the right before the one on the left, such that:

```
$a = 2;
print $a**++$a;
```

prints 27, that is, 3^3 and not as you might expect 2^3.

Caution *Care should be taken to ensure you aren't executing nested exponential statements that are parsed in this order. It's possible to create a large value, or even evaluate items in the wrong order if you are not careful—if you're unsure, either use **Deparse** to check the entire syntax and sense of the statement, or try to devolve the statement into a number of individual lines.*

Symbolic Unary Operators

The symbolic (or ideographic) unary operators modify an expression in some way:

■ Unary ! performs logical negation (not); for example !0 is equal to 1, and !1 is equal to 0.

■ Unary − negates the expression if it is numeric, as in **−10**. If the expression is a string, then it returns the string with the operator prefix. For example **−option** is equivalent to **"−option"** just as if the string had been quoted.

■ Unary ~ performs bitwise negation (1s complement) on a numerical value. If the argument is a string, then individual bits of the string are flipped.

■ Unary + does nothing on numerical or string values. However, if placed before an expression that would otherwise be interpreted as a list, it forces the expression to be returned as a single argument.

■ Unary \ creates a reference to the expression or term following it. See Chapter 10 for more information on references.

Regular Expression Bindings

The =~ and !~ operators are regular expression binders—they bind the expression on the left to the pattern match, substitution, or transliteration (translation) on the right. As such, they are a special case, and we'll be looking in more detail at their operation in Chapter 8.

Multiplication

The *, /, and % operators are fairly straightforward, doing the normal numerical multiplication, division, and modulus (remainder) on two numbers. For example:

```
print 2*10; # Outputs 20
print 20/2; # Outputs 10
print 20%7; # Outputs 6 - the remainder
```

The x repetition operator is useful when you want to repeat a string:

```
print 'Ma' x 8; # outputs MaMaMaMaMaMaMaMa
```

If you supply a numerical value on the left side, then the number is converted to a string:

```
print 123 x 2; # outputs 123123
```

You should be careful, however, when using it with lists and arrays. If the item on the left side of the operator is a list, then the entire list is repeated:

```
print (join(',',(1,2,3) x 2)); # outputs 1,2,3,1,2,3
```

With arrays, you must enclose them in parentheses so that they are treated as lists, not scalars. The fragment,

```
@abc = ('a','b','c');
@abc = @abc x 5;
print join(',',@abc);
```

generates "33333"—the **@abc** array has been populated with a list consisting of one element, the scalar value of **@abc** (its length) repeated five times.

To resolve this, place parentheses around the source array:

```
@abc = ('a','b','c');
@abc = (@abc) x 5;
print join(',',@abc);
```

Finally, if you supply an array on the right and a list on the left, the result is a repetition based on the scalar value of the array, effectively setting each item of a non-empty array to the list you supply. If the array on the right is empty, then an empty list is returned. For example, this:

```
@abc = ();
@abc = (5) x @abc;
print "First: ",join(',',@abc),"\n";
@abc = ('a','b','c');
@abc = (5) x @abc;
print "Second: ",join(',',@abc),"\n";
```

generates this:

```
First:
Second: 5,5,5
```

Addition and Subtraction

Addition and subtraction operators work on numerical values as you would expect:

```
print 10+2; # Outputs 12
print 10-2; # Outputs 8
```

You cannot use the same operators for concatenating strings; instead use the . operator:

```
print $hello . $world;
```

The . operator does not include a space in the concatenation, so this would output "HelloWorld". You'll either have to explicitly add the space or use double-quoted strings and interpolation:

```
print "$hello $world";
```

Shift Operators

The shift operators shift the bits of an expression right or left, according to the number of bits supplied. For example:

```
2 << 8;
```

is 512. Be aware that if a floating point value is supplied to a shift operator, it is converted to an integer without rounding, that is, it is always rounded down, such that:

```
2.9 << 7.9;
```

produces 256, 2 shifted to the left 7 times.

Named Unary Operators

Certain Perl functions are really named unary operators, that is, functions that take a single argument and return a value. The exact list of unary operators is difficult to determine manually, but as a guide, the Perl source defines the following functions and operations as unary operators:

alarm	gethostbyname	log	sin
caller	getnetbyname	lstat	sleep
chdir	getpgrp	my	sqrt
chr	getprotobyname	oct	srand
chroot	gmtime	ord	stat
cos	goto	quotemeta	uc
defined	hex	rand	ucfirst
delete	int	readlink	umask
do	lc	ref	undef
eval "string"	lcfirst	require	-X tests
exists	length	return	
exit	localtime	rmdir	
exp	lock	scalar	

If any of these are followed by an opening parenthesis, then they automatically have highest precedence; however, if you use them without parentheses, then their precedence is as listed within Table 3-1—lower than most calculations, but higher than most of the relational and logical operations.

For example, the **rand** function has a lower precedence than the multiplication operator, so

```
rand 10 * 20;  # rand (10*20)
rand(10) * 20; # (rand 10)*20;
```

Tip   *You can always check these functions with **Deparse** if necessary.*

Also, remember that a comma automatically terminates a named unary operator, such that

```
print rand 10, 2;
```

prints a random number up to 10, immediately followed by the number 2.

However, care needs to be taken with these operators in situations where Perl defaults to using the **$_** operator. For unary operators that do default to **$_**, failing to explicitly specify the variable may cause Perl to actually interpret any following operator as the start of a term. For example,

```
print if length < 1;
```

will trick Perl into interpreting the < operator as the start of a filehandle input operator. Other examples include *, which can be identified as a typeglob, and /, which can be misinterpreted as a regular expression pattern. See Table 3-2 for a complete list.

If a term was expected and it happens to be of the form **–X**, then Perl treats the operator as a file test operator—see Chapter 7 for a complete description of the **–X** operators.

Character	Operator	Misinterpreted as
+	Addition	Unary plus
–	Subtraction	Unary minus
*	Multiplication	Typeglob (*var)
/	Division	Regex (/pattern/)
<	Less than	Filehandle (<HANDLE>)
<<	Left shift	Here document (<<EOF)
.	Concatenation	Value (.1)
?	? Test	Regex (?pattern?)
%	Modulus	Hash (%hash)
&	Logical AND	Subroutine call (&sub)

Table 3-2. *Misinterpreted Unary Operators*

Relational and Equality Operators

The relational and equality operators enable you to test the equality of numbers and strings, respectively. The full list of relational and equality operators is given in Table 3-3.

Operator	Action
<	Returns true if the left statement is numerically less than the right statement
>	Returns true if the left statement is numerically greater than the right statement
<=	Returns true if the left statement is numerically less than or equal to the right statement
>=	Returns true if the left statement is numerically greater than or equal to the right statement
==	Returns true if the left statement is numerically equal to the right statement
!=	Returns true if the left statement is numerically not equal to the right statement
<=>	Returns −1, 0, or 1 depending on whether the left statement is numerically less than, equal to, or greater than the right statement, respectively
lt	Returns true if the left statement is stringwise less than the right statement
gt	Returns true if the left statement is stringwise greater than the right statement
le	Returns true if the left statement is stringwise less than or equal to the right statement
ge	Returns true if the left statement is stringwise greater than or equal to the right statement
eq	Returns true if the left statement is stringwise equal to the right statement
ne	Returns true if the left statement is stringwise not equal to the right statement
cmp	Returns −1, 0, or 1 depending on whether the left statement is stringwise less than, equal to, or greater than the right statement, respectively

Table 3-3. *Equality and Relational Operators*

To logically compare numerical values, you use the symbolic equality and relational operators, for example:

```
if ($a > 0)
```

For string comparisons, you must use the text operators:

```
if ($a gt 'a')
```

A common mistake is to use the wrong operator on the wrong type of value but fail to notice it, because for 99 percent of situations it would resolve true anyway. The statement

```
if ($a == $b)
```

will work fine if both values are numerical. If they are textual, then Perl compares the logical value of the two strings, which is always true. This may seem confusing, but even the undefined value resolves to true when comparing it numerically. For example, the following tests all return true:

```
undef == 'a'
undef == undef
'a' == 'a'
'a' == 'b'
```

The reverse is not true when using string comparisons on numerical values. The statement

```
0 eq 9
```

will return false, and

```
0 eq 0
```

will return true—this is because Perl automatically converts the numerical values to strings, because that's what the operator is expecting, and then compares those values.

There is a very simple rule to follow here: if you are comparing numbers, use symbolic operators, and if you are comparing strings, use text operators.

See the "Logical Values" section at the end of this chapter for details on the logical value of different constant expressions.

Bitwise AND, OR, and Exclusive OR

The bitwise AND, **&**, returns the value of two numbers ANDed together on a bit-by-bit basis. If you supply two strings, then each character of the string is ANDed together individually, and the new string is returned. If you supply only one integer and one string, then the string is converted to an integer and ANDed together as for integers.

For example:

```
print '123' & '456'; # Outputs 001
print 123 & 456;      # Outputs 72
print 123 & '456';    # Outputs 72
```

Bitwise OR, **|**, and Exclusive OR, **^**, work in the same fashion.

Symbolic Logical AND

The Perl logical AND, **&&**, works on a short-circuit basis. Consider the statement

```
a && b;
```

If **a** returns a false value, then **b** is never evaluated.

The return result will be the right operand in both scalar and list context, such that

```
@list = ('a','b');
@array = ('1','2');

print(@list && @array);

$a = 'a' && 'b';

print $a;
```

produces "12b".

See the following "Symbolic Logical OR" section for details on using the operator for comparisons and tests.

Symbolic Logical OR

The Perl logical OR, **||**, works on a short-circuit basis. Consider the statement

```
a || b;
```

If **a** returns a true value, then **b** is never evaluated. However, be wary of using it with functions that only return a true value. For example:

```
select DATA || die;
```

will never call **die**, even if **DATA** has not been defined.

Also, be careful when using it with functions and terms that accept list arguments. The statement:

```
print DATA "The answer is ", 0 || warn "Can't write: $!";
```

actually performs a logical OR between the argument 0 and the call to **warn**, and **warn** will be called before the 0 is evaluated and returned to **print**:

```
Can't write:  at t.pl line 1.
The answer is 1
```

The solution is to use the **or** operator, which has a much lower precedence:

```
print DATA "The answer is ", 0 or warn "Can't write: $!";
```

or to enclose your statements in parentheses to give them higher precedence:

```
print DATA ("The answer is ", 0) || warn "Can't write: $!";
```

Range Operators

The range operators, .. and ..., allow you to create ranges on the fly, and can also act as simple "flip-flop" operators. The value of each .. operator is unique, with each operator maintaining its own state. The value returned by the operator is false as long as the left operand is false. When the operand changes to true, the operator returns true until the right operand is also true, and then at the next execution the operator becomes false again.

If the operands are scalars or constant expressions, then the operand is compared against the **$.** operator—the current input line number.

In a list context, the operator returns a list of values between the supplied ranges:

```
@hundred = (0 .. 100);
```

It also operates in a similar fashion to the increment operator when supplied string values:

```
@characters = ('a' .. 'z');
```

Conditional Operator

The conditional operator is like an embedded **if...else** statement (see Chapter 5). The format is

```
EXPR ? IFTRUE : IFFALSE
```

If **EXPR** is true, then the **IFTRUE** expression is evaluated and returned, otherwise **IFFALSE** is evaluated and returned.

Scalar and list context is propagated according to the expression selected. At a basic level, it means that the following expressions do what we want,

```
$value = $expr ? $true : $false;
@list  = $expr ? @lista : @listb;
```

while

```
$count = $expr ? @lista : @listb;
```

populates **$count** with the number of elements in each array. On the flip side, you can also do

```
$result = $wantcount ? @list : join(',',@list);
```

returning the array size or merged array accordingly. The conditional operator is evaluated as a single element when used within a list, so don't confuse the interpreter by inserting additional list operators without qualifying them. This means that if you want to return more than one item based on a conditional operation, you'll need to parenthesize the expression you want to return. The script

```
$name = <STDIN>;
chomp $name;
print "Hello ",length($name) ? $name,', how are you today?'
                             : 'nobody',"\n";
```

should be written as

```
$name = <STDIN>;
chomp $name;
```

```
print "Hello ",length($name) ? ($name,', how are you today?')
                              : 'nobody',"\n";
```

You can also use the conditional operator for assignment, providing the two options are valid lvalues (see the following "Assignment Operators" section). You'll need to qualify the entire expression, however:

```
($group ? $a : $b) = 'users';
```

To use the conditional operator for choosing an assignment value, use the conditional operator as the assignment value, rather than embedding the assignment expression:

```
$a = $group ? 'is a group' : 'not a group';
```

Assignment Operators

The assignment operators assign a value to a valid lvalue expression—usually a variable, but it can be any valid lvalue. An lvalue, or left-hand value, is an expression to which you can assign a new value. Assignment happens with the = and associated operators. Valid lvalues include

- Any recognizable variable, including object properties
- **vec** function (for setting integer values)
- **substr** function (for replacement strings)
- **keys** function (for setting bucket sizes)
- **pos** function (for setting the offset within a search)
- Any lvalue-defined function (Perl 5.6 only)
- **? :** conditional operator
- Any assignment expression

As well as the basic = operator, there are also combined expression assignments that translate into embedded expressions. For example,

```
$a += 10;
```

is equivalent to

```
$a = $a + 10;
```

The full list of assignment operators includes the following:

=	**=	+=	*=	&=	<<=	&&=
		-=	/=	| =	>>=	| |=
		.=	%=	^=		
			x=			

Note that assigning a value to an assignment expression should be read from left to right, such that

```
($a += 10) *= 5;
```

reads as

```
$a += 10;
$a *= 5;
```

and

```
($match = $source) =~ tr/a-z/A-Z/;
```

resolves to

```
$match = $source;
$match =~ tr/a-z/A-Z/;
```

Finally, assignment works differently according to context when assigning lists. In a list context, a list assignment causes the lvalue to be resolved into a list of lvalues to be assigned to. That means this:

```
($a, $b) = (1,2);
```

is in effect

```
$a = 1;
$b = 2;
```

See Chapter 4, where we deal with Perl's variables, for more information on assignment.

Comma Operator

The comma is the list operator, and arguments are evaluated in order from left to right. In a scalar context, when used in an implied list, the left argument is evaluated, then thrown away, and the right-hand argument is returned. For example:

```
$a = (1,4);
```

This will assign a value of 4 to **$a**. In a list context, it evaluates all arguments from left to right and then returns them as a list:

```
@a = (1,2);
```

Be careful when using the list operators in a scalar context without parentheses. Here the first element of the list will bind tighter than the right-hand arguments, since the list operator has a lower precedence than most other statement forms. For example,

```
$a = 1,2;
```

will populate **$a** with a value of 1, because it's interpreted as

```
($a = 1),2;
```

Similarly, with a named unary operator,

```
chdir 'tmp','etc';
```

This will change the current directory to **tmp**, not **etc**.
    The same is true of arrays, so the line

```
@a = 1,2;
```

is interpreted as

```
(@a = 1),2;
```

The **=>** operator is just an alias to the **,** operator, best used when separating the key and value of a hash element:

```
%hash = ('key' => 'value');
```

Since Perl 5.001, the **=>** automatically implies that the left argument should be interpreted as a string, making

```
%hash = (key => 'value');
```

perfectly legal, even with warnings and the **strict** pragma in force.

List Operators (rightward)

The rightward list operators govern the interpretation of the list operator's arguments. The right side of a list operator has a very low precedence, with only the **and**, **or**, **xor**, and **not** having a lower precedence. This interpretation causes the problems when using implied lists and the symbolic logical operators:

```
tie %oldhash, NDBM_File, $old, O_RDONLY, 0444
                    || die "$0: Error opening source $old: $!\n";
```

This is actually interpreted as the last list argument being logically compared with the **die** statement. Use the named logical operators, which have lower precedence, to solve the problem.

Named Logical NOT

The logical **not** provides a logical negation for the item on the right of the operator. Any term on the left will immediately raise an error, so the statement

```
$a = $b not $c;
```

is completely nonsensical. Use | | if you want to choose between two values.

Named Logical AND

This **and** works identically to the symbolic logical AND (**&&**), including the short circuit execution. The only difference is that it has a lower precedence.

Named Logical OR and Exclusive OR

The named logical **or** works like the symbolic logical OR (| |), including the short circuit execution. Its main benefit is that it operates at very low precedence—in the lowest precedence of all statements—and is therefore useful in control statements

Care should be taken when using **or** in assignment statements. Because it has the lowest precedence, the assignment operator will bind tighter than the **or** operator, so

```
$a = $b or $c;
```

is interpreted as

```
($a = $b) or $c;
```

It's better to write it as

```
$a = $b || $c;
```

The same is true of any other statement where you want to make comparisons—the **or** operator is really only useful when you want to check the return value of a function without affecting the value returned.

The **xor** operator returns the exclusive OR of two expressions.

Bare Words

Bare words within a script are essentially a bad idea. First Perl tries to identify whether the bare word is a proper value—if it can be resolved to a function within the symbol table, then the function is called; otherwise it's treated as a string. The script below demonstrates this quite neatly:

```
sub hello
{
    return 'Hello user!';
}

$message = hello;
print "$message\n";

$message = goodbye;
print "$message\n";
```

This outputs

```
Hello user!
goodbye
```

If you have warnings switched on, then Perl will warn you if it sees an all-lowercase bare word that it can't otherwise identify as a term:

FUNDAMENTALS

```
Unquoted string "goodbye" may clash with future reserved word at t.pl line 10.
```

A mixed-case bare word is interpreted as a string in most instances, and it should raise a suitable error when warnings are switched on. However, there is one exception—where a bare word is used in a situation that requires a filehandle, the bare word is used as the filehandle name. For example, the code:

```
print Tester;
```

prints the value of **$_** to the filehandle **Tester**, assuming it's open and writable. If you try

```
print Tester, "Hello World\n";
```

you'll get an error when warnings are switched on because Perl assumes that **Tester** is the name of a filehandle.

If you have the **subs** portion of the **strict** pragma invoked, then execution will terminate because of the bare word:

```
Bareword "goodbye" not allowed while "strict subs" in use at t.pl line 10.
```

If you have both warnings and the **strict** pragma in effect, then the pragma takes precedence.

We'll be looking at pragmas and warnings in more detail in Chapter 8.

Contexts

Perl supports a number of different contexts, which are identified for each operator or term during the parsing process. The exact effects vary according to the operator or term concerned. Contexts affect the operation of different statements and functions, and they are worth covering, at least briefly—we'll look at the details of contexts in Chapter 6.

Scalar and List Context

There are two basic contexts that all programmers are aware of: scalar and list. These two contexts affect the operation of the function or operator concerned by implying the accepted value, or value returned. For example:

```
$size = @list;
```

Here, the **$size** variable is a scalar, and it therefore implies scalar context on the array, which causes it to return the array size, rather than the array values. Conversely, the statement

```
sort @list;
```

is evaluated in list context, since the **sort** function expects a list of values.

Within a function, you can identify the requested context using the **wantarray** function, which returns true if the caller is expecting a list (or array, or hash) to be returned instead of a scalar value.

Numerical and String Context

Some of the internal Perl functions also distinguish scalar context between numerical and string contexts. A classic example is the **$!** special variable, which holds the error status for the previous operation. In a numerical context, this variable returns the numerical error number of the last error that occurred, and in a string context, the associated message. The interpreter uses this context as the basis for the conversion of values into the internal integer, floating point, or string values that the scalar value is divided into.

Unfortunately, there's no way of determining from within a script what the expected numerical or string context is—you must leave it up to Perl to make the decision for you, converting the value accordingly.

Boolean Context

Boolean context is where an expression is used solely to identify a true or false value. See the "Logical Values" section, later in the chapter, to see how Perl treats individual values and constants in a logical context.

Void Context

Void context is a special case and is an extension of the scalar context. It identifies areas of the code where a constant has been introduced but never used. At its simplest point, the statement

```
99;
```

would be identified as a void context, since introducing a constant at this point does nothing. You'll only be notified of this instance if you have warnings switched on.

Other more common areas where void context applies include the instance where the precedence rules would cause a portion of the statement to be ignored. For example,

```
$a = 1,2;
```

causes the "2" to be identified in a void context. Look at the earlier precedence rules for details on why this and similar statements cause void-context warnings.

Interpolative Context

The Perl documentation identifies the interpolation of variables into interpolating quoted values as a separate context. This is good way of describing why some quoted blocks interpolate—that is, they are identified as interpolated context—but it doesn't really do the process justice. We'll look more closely at the interpolation process in Chapter 3.

Logical Values

Perl's Boolean logic relies on its ability to identify different variable and constant types as having a true or false value. As a general rule, anything that is undefined, empty, or 0 is taken as a false value, whilst any other value is taken as true. You can see a more explicit list in Table 3-4.

To check for the undefined value, you can use the **defined** function. This returns a positive integer (true) if the variable contains a valid value, or 0 (false) if the variable equals the **undef** value.

Value	Logical Value
Negative number	True
0	False
Positive number	True
Empty string	False
Non-empty string	True
Undefined value	False
Empty list	False
List with at least one element	True

Table 3-4. *Values and Their Logical Equivalents*

Perl Coding Styles

How you actually lay out and format your Perl scripts is entirely up to you—it's perfectly legal for you to place everything on a single line—but remember that at some future point in time, you'll probably want to look at the code again, and then things may not be so clear.

Using comments is obviously good practice, and writing some form of documentation will also help, but when it comes to the actual flow and style of the script, it's worth remembering that you may not be the only person looking at the code.

Larry Wall, the inventor of Perl, has some ideas for how to format code, although he doesn't necessarily enforce them. The only one he feels strongly about is that a closing brace (on a block) should be lined up with the statement that started it.

Personally, I have my own list of guidelines that I've been using for a number of years. My guidelines call for code that is specially designed to be readable on paper and is the style used throughout this book. If you want to use the guidelines that Larry prefers, see the **perlstyle** guide in the Perl documentation.

I use the following rules:

- Use four column indents for all types of blocks.

- On loops and other blocks, the statement goes on its own line, the opening brace on its own line, and the enclosing code is indented. The final brace is also on its own line. Thus, a **foreach** statement becomes

```
foreach (@list)
{
    # code goes here
}
```

and an **if...elsif...else** statement becomes

```
if ($expr)
{
}
elsif ($expr)
{
}
else
{
}
```

■ Short blocks can be on one line:

```
while ($expr) { $expr++ }
```

■ The final semicolon (which is optional) is included in all blocks, unless the block is on a single line.

■ There should not be a space between the statement and semicolon.

■ There should not be a space between the function name and its parenthesized arguments.

■ All non-standard functions calls should have parentheses.

■ Spaces after commas in lists are optional for numerical arguments, but required on all others.

■ Long lines are broken *after* an operator, but *before* logical operators such as **and** or **||**.

■ Line up corresponding items:

```
my $one   = 1;
my $two   = 2;
my $three = 3;
```

■ Always use a space to separate groups of code that do different things, for example *avoid*

```
sub funca
{
}
sub funcb
{
}
```

■ Avoid using the same delimiter or quotes in **q//**, **qq//** and **qx//** operators or regular expressions if you need to use them within the expression. For example, using the forward slash / in a regular expression that works on directories is messy.

■ Use here documents, rather than multiline double-quoted strings or repeated **print** statements.

■ Use arrays to hold lists of data, and then use **join** to output it instead of trying to build the string on the fly.

- Give your variables sensible names; for example, **$keyword** makes more sense than **$foo**.

- Avoid using the **$_** in situations where **$variable** would look clearer.

For a list of further hints, check out the remaining chapters of this book. Above all, remember to be consistent; don't change your style half way through the script, and remember that other people, including yourself in ten years' time, may need to revisit the code!

Chapter 4

Variables and Data

Variables, a core part of any language, allow you to store dynamic values into named locations. Perl supports one basic variable type—the scalar. Scalars are used to contain a single value, although the value itself can be either a numerical or string constant or a reference to another variable.

Two other variable types are basically variations on the scalar theme. The array, for example, is essentially a sequence (list) of scalar values accessible through a numerical index. The hash is a list of key/value pairs that allow you to access a value by name rather than the numerical index offered by arrays. Both the key and the value use scalars to hold their contents.

In this chapter, we're going to look at these base variable types, literals—the values you assign to these variables—and the variable types and values. We'll also take the opportunity to look at the different quoting mechanisms, which control how strings are determined and interpreted by Perl. The last part of the chapter looks at the standard Perl variables and some of their effects.

Basic Naming Rules

Before we look at the specifics of the different variables and how to use them, it's worth looking at the basic rules that apply to the naming of variables within Perl:

- Variable names can start with a letter, a number, or an underscore, although they normally begin with a letter and can then be composed of any combination of letters, numbers, and the underscore character.

- Variables can start with a number, but they must be entirely composed of that number; for example, **$123** is valid, but **$1var** is not.

- Variable names that start with anything other than a letter, digit, or underscore are generally reserved for special use by Perl (see "Special Variables" later in this chapter).

- Variable names are case sensitive; **$foo**, **$FOO**, and **$fOo** are all separate variables as far as Perl is concerned.

- As an unwritten (and therefore unenforced) rule, names all in uppercase are constants.

- All scalar values start with **$**, including those accessed from an array of hash, for example **$array[0]** or **$hash{key}**.

- All array values start with **@**, including arrays or hashes accessed in slices, for example **@array[3..5,7,9]** or **@hash{'bob', 'alice'}**.

- All hashes start with %.

- Namespaces are separate for each variable type—the variables **$var**, **@var**, and **%var** are all different variables in their own right.

■ In situations where a variable name might get confused with other data (such as when embedded within a string), you can use braces to quote the name. For example, **${name}**, or **%{hash}**.

Just remembering those simple rules should help to eliminate a number of common problems.

Variables are also subject to the lexical scope within which they have been declared—we'll cover that in more detail in Chapter 6.

Scalar Variables

As I've already mentioned, the *scalar* variable is the most basic variable type within Perl. A scalar always contains a single value, either a number, a string, or a reference to another variable. If the variable has no value, then it is said to be "undefined" or to contain the "undefined" value. See the section "The defined Function and the Undefined Value" later in this chapter for more information on the effects of this value on variables.

Although scalar values appear to contain a value of a specific type, the truth is they don't—Perl doesn't distinguish (as far as we're concerned) between numerical values and strings, nor does it care whether a numerical value is an integer or a floating point value.

In fact, internally, Perl stores numbers as signed integers, or as double precision floating point values if the value contains a decimal component. Also be aware that Perl doesn't have infinite precision for its floating point values; the calculations 10 / 3 and 1 / 3 * 10 will not always equal the same value.

Strings are held internally as a sequence of characters. There is no limit on the length of a string, and there are no terminators or other characters used to "delimit" the content of the string (unlike C, which uses the null value).

However you are using a scalar, it is converted to the most appropriate format when you use it. So when printing a numeric scalar, we don't have to use a special format; it's automatically converted to a string for us. Perl also automatically converts between integer and floating point values as required and will even convert strings into numbers if it deems them necessary. The caveat to this last feature is that a failure to convert a string results in a numerical value of zero.

To create a scalar variable, just select a name and assign it a value:

```
$int = 123;
$float = 123.45;
$string = 'Hello world!';
```

The last example assigns a string value to the scalar—note the quotes, which are a required component. We'll return to the topic of quotes later in this chapter (see "Quotes").

We can also assign a scalar an empty (undefined) value:

```
$nothing = undef;
```

The **undef** is actually the name of a built-in function that returns the undefined value. Don't worry about it too much for the moment, but be aware that assigning a variable the undefined value empties its contents.

Literals

Literals are the raw values that you insert into your source code; they can be made up of the normal numerical values and strings. Perl also supports a number of advanced literals that enable you to store specific types of data such as version strings.

Numeric Literals

Perl supports a number of a fairly basic methods for specifying a numeric literal in decimal:

```
$num = 123;           # integer
$num = 123.45;        # floating point
$num = 1.23e45;       # scientific notation
```

You can also specify literals in hexadecimal, octal, and binary by specifying a preceding character to highlight the number types:

```
$num = 0xff;          # Hexadecimal
$num = 0377;          # Octal
$num = 0b0010_0000;   # Binary
```

Note that the numbers are not stored internally using these bases—Perl converts the literal representation into a decimal internally. Also note that the system that handles the automatic conversion of strings to numbers does not support the base prefixes; use the **oct** function to convert strings (see Chapter 8).

When specifying large numbers, it's tempting to use commas to separate the thousands. Because Perl uses the comma as an operator, it's not practical. Instead, you can use the underscore character to separate the thousands:

```
$num = 1_234_456_789;   # underlines separate 000s for clarity
```

String Literals

Strings are generally surrounded by either single or double quotes. The effects of the quotes are different, however, and they follow the same rules as the Unix shell. When using single quotes, the value of the string is exactly as it appears—no form of interpretation or evaluation is performed on the contents of the string (except for \' and \\).

When double quotes are used, the effects are quite different. For a start, double-quoted strings are subject to backslash and variable interpolation, just as they are under Unix. For example, we can use double-quoted strings and the \n backslash sequence to add newline characters to a string. Other backslash (or escape) sequences supported by Perl are listed in Table 4-1.

Code	Meaning
\n	Newline
\r	Carriage return
\t	Horizontal tab
\f	Form feed
\b	Backspace
\a	Alert (bell)
\e	ESC (escape) character
\XXX	Character specified in octal, where XXX is the character's ASCII code.
\xXX	Character specified in hexadecimal, where XX is the character's ASCII code.
\x{XXXX}	Character specified in hexadecimal, where XXXX is the character's Unicode number.
\cX	Control character, where X is the character—\cC is Control-C.
\N{NAME}	Named Unicode character.

Table 4-1. *Backslash (Escaped) Character Sequences*

The backslash sequence is often called an escape sequence because you "escape" the normal interpretation.

For example:

```
$string = 'hello world';          # hello world
$string = 'hello world\n';        # hello world\n
$string = "hello world\n";        # hello world with trailing newline
$string = "\tHello World\a\a\n";  # hello world with preceding tab and
                                  # double bell, with trailing newline
```

Incidentally, the quotes work across line boundaries, so we could rewrite the second example as

```
$string = 'hello world
';
```

The newline from the source is included in the final string. Because of this, you need to be careful when using quotes and ensure that you terminate them properly. One of the most common errors is to embed a quote in your string. For example:

```
$message = 'Can't write to device';
```

This will fail because the second quote on the line will terminate the first. You can get around this in both single and double quotes by escaping the quote:

```
$message = 'Can\'t write to device';
$text = "She said \"I can't do that!\"";
```

Note that in the last example the single quote is not escaped; this is because a single quote has no meaning within double quotes other than as a quote character; thus we could rewrite the first example:

```
$message = "Can't write to device";
```

The same is true in reverse; we could have written the second example:

```
$text = 'She said "I can\'t do that!"';
```

You can also modify the case of a string specified within double quotes using a number of translation escapes, as listed in Table 4-2.

Code	Meaning
\u	Force next character to uppercase.
\l	Force next character to lowercase.
\U	Force all following characters to uppercase.
\L	Force all following characters to lowercase.
\Q	Backslash (escape) all following non-alphanumeric characters.
\E	End a \U, \L, or \Q escape.

Table 4-2.   *Translation Escapes*

The examples that follow demonstrate the use of translation escapes in your strings:

```
$string = "\uhello world";        # Hello world
$string = "\Uhello world\n";      # HELLO WORLD
$string = "\Uhello\E \LWorld\E\n"; # HELLO world with trailing newline
$string = "\Q'Hello World'\E";    # \'Hello\ World\'
```

Double-quoted strings are also subject to variable interpolation—this means that you can embed a variable directly into a double-quoted string and have the value of that variable inserted into the string. For example:

```
$name = 'Martin';
$greeting = "Hello $name!\n";     # Generates Hello Martin!
```

Note that this technique only works on double-quoted strings:

```
$greeting = 'Hello $name!\n';     # Generates Hello $name!\n
```

Note that you can only interpolate scalars and arrays—trying to interpolate an entire hash will only result in the string '%hash' being included in the literal value. See the later section "Interpolation of Array Values" for information on how arrays are interpolated into strings.

Also, because we sometimes want to include a variable name directly within the contents of a string that might otherwise upset Perl's evaluation of that variable name, we can use one of the rules we saw earlier:

```
$message = "This is ${name}s computer";
```

Any identifier within the braces is interpreted as a string, and because it has a leading **$** sign, the **${name}** becomes the full name for the variable we are accessing.

Quotes

The quotes we have already seen in Perl are actually operators—they operate on the embedded string. In the case of single quotes, this leads to the introduction of a string, and in the case of double quotes, it leads to the introduction of a string that has been evaluated according to the escapes and interpolation rules we have already seen.

Perl actually supports a number of quoting operators, most of which do more than simply introduce strings. Not all of the quoting operators interpolate, and each has a customary form. They do, however, share the same basic construction, allowing you to select the quote character that you want to use. The full list is given in Table 4-3.

Customary	Generic	Meaning	Interpolates
"	q//	Literal string	No
""	qq//	Literal string	Yes
``	qx//	Execute external command	Yes
()	qw//	Generate word list	No
//	m//	Regular expression pattern match	Yes
s///	s///	Regular expression substitution	Yes
y///	tr///	Character translation	No
""	qr//	Quote regular expression	Yes

Table 4-3.   *Quoting Mechanisms*

We have already seen examples of the first two mechanisms in Table 4-3 in their customary forms. One of the problems with the customary forms is that if you want to embed quotes of the same type (i.e. single in single), you must escape the quote. Using the quote operator, you can circumvent this:

```
$message = q/Can't send to device/;
$text = qq/She said "I can't do this!"/;
```

The character immediately following each operator is the delimiter—the delimiter specifies the limits of the construct you are creating. You can use any alphanumeric or non-whitespace character (that is, other than space, tab, newline) for a delimiter, but the delimiters must match or complement each other. That means that we could use an exclamation mark

```
$message = q!Can't send to device!;
```

or we can use a complementary pair of characters such as parentheses, braces, square brackets, or even angle brackets:

```
$text = qq{She said "I can't do this!"};
$text = qq<She said "I can't do this!">;
```

Which one you choose will depend entirely on what you are embedding within the construct, and you'll probably find that in most instances you end up using the same delimiting character.

Also note that the interpolation rules apply according to Table 4-3:

```
$message = q!Hello $name\n!;     # Still outputs Hello $name\n
$message = qq/Hello $name\n/;     # Outputs Hello Martin with a newline
```

Interpolation of Array Values

When you embed an array into a string, the elements of the array are included in order separated by the contents of the $" special variable, which by default is a space:

```
@list = ('hello', 'world');
print "@list\n";               # Outputs 'hello world'
```

Perl will determine whether the name you have supplied is correct, and it'll raise an error if you've tried to interpolate an array that doesn't exist. This can lead to problems:

```
print "mc@mcslp.com";
```

In this instance, Perl is expecting to find an array called **@mcslp**, and it will obviously fail because we haven't defined such an array. Generally, Perl will warn you of this error during compilation and tell you to escape the @ sign:

```
print "mc\@mcslp.com@;
```

Here Documents

If you want to introduce multiline strings into your programs, you can use standard quotes:

```
$string = 'This is
a multiline
string';
```

But this is messy and is subject to the same basic laws regarding interpolation and quote usage. We could get around it using the **q//** or **qq//** operator with different delimiters, but that won't change the underlying issue of delimiter choice and on-screen clarity.

To get around this, Perl supports "here" documents—these are multiline strings, which interpolate, that continue indefinitely until the multicharacter delimiter that you specify is reached. For example:

```
print <<EOF;
This is
a multiline
string
EOF
```

The resulting contents are interpolated as normal, and they contain any special characters such as tabs and newlines in the final string.

The delimiter should be placed immediately after the **<<**, a space is treated as a null identifier, and the delimiter should be specified on its own line with no leading or trailing spaces. You can also quote the delimiter during specification:

```
print <<'EOF';
This is
a multiline
string
EOF
```

or

```
print <<"EOF";
This is
a multiline
string
EOF
```

The null identifier (an empty string or space) matches the next empty line:

```
print <<'';
This is
a multiline
string

print "This is a new statement\n";
```

The here document just becomes a special type of literal, so we can combine it with other components

```
print <<'' x 5;
This message will repeat 5 times
```

and use them as arguments for function calls:

```
print(<<"EOFA", 99, <<"EOFB");
This is the first
argument...
EOFA
This is the second
EOFB
```

We can also use a here document to execute commands if we use backticks instead of normal single or double quotes:

```
print <<`BUILTIN`
ll
echo "Finished!"
BUILTIN
```

The important thing to remember is that everything contained between the initial specification and the delimiter that you have specified is taken verbatim. This means that any leading spaces in the text will need to be removed (if you want them to be!):

```
($string = <<'EOF') =~ s/^\s+//gb;
    These lines will have their leading
    spaces removed for clarity.
EOF
```

V-Strings

You probably think of v-strings as a method for the introduction of version numbers, although in reality they are slightly more complex. Any literal that begins with a v and is followed by one or more dot-separated elements is treated as a string literal composed of the characters with the specified values.

For example:

```
$name = v77.97.114.116.105.110;
```

Actually equates to 'Martin'. If there are more than two dots (i.e. more than three integers), then you can omit the leading 'v':

```
$name = 77.97.114.116.105.110;
```

V-strings can be a useful way of introducing version numbers and IP addresses into Perl. It means you are no longer restricted to using simple decimals (1.0003) for version numbers, and it also eliminates the need to build IP addresses manually with **pack** when you want to introduce a fixed IP address into some code.

Of course, it also means that these strings are illegible to the human eye. You'll need to use the **v** format with the **printf/sprintf** function to format these values nicely.

Arrays

An array is just a set of scalars. It's made up of a list of individual scalars that are stored within a single variable. You can refer to each scalar within that list using a numerical index. You can use arrays to store any kind of list data, from the days of the week to a list of all the lines in a file. Creating individual scalars for each of these is cumbersome, and in the case of the file contents, impossible to prepare for. What happens if the input file has 100 lines instead of 10? The answer is to use an array, which can be dynamically sized to hold any number of different values.

Creation

Array variables have are prefixed with the @ sign and are populated using either parentheses or the **qw** operator. For example:

```
@array = (1, 2, 'Hello');
@array = qw/This is an array/;
```

The second line uses the **qw//** operator, which returns a list of strings, separating the delimited string by white space. In this example, this leads to a four-element array; the first element is 'this' and last (fourth) is 'array'. This means that you can use newlines within the specification:

```
@days = qw/Monday
           Tuesday
           ...
           Sunday/;
```

We can also populate an array by assigning each value individually:

```
$array[0] = 'Monday';
...
$array[6] = 'Sunday';
```

However, you should avoid using square brackets to create a normal array. The line

```
@array = [1, 2, 'Hello'];
```

initializes **@array** with only one element, a reference to the array contained in the square brackets. We'll be looking at references in Chapter 10.

Extracting Individual Indices

When extracting individual elements from an array, you must prefix the variable with a dollar sign (to signify that you are extracting a scalar value) and then append the element index within square brackets after the name. For example:

```
@shortdays = qw/Mon Tue Wed Thu Fri Sat Sun/;
print $shortdays[1];
```

Array indices start at zero, so in the preceding example we've actually printed "Tue." You can also give a negative index—in which case you select the element from the end, rather than the beginning, of the array. This means that

```
print $shortdays[0];   # Outputs Mon
print $shortdays[6];   # Outputs Sun
print $shortdays[-1];  # Also outputs Sun
print $shortdays[-7];  # Outputs Mon
```

Remember:

- Array indices start at zero, not one, when working forward; for example:

```
@days = qw/Monday
           Tuesday
           ...
           Sunday/;
print "First day of week is $days[0]\n";
```

- Array indices start at –1 for the last element when working backward.

 The use of $[, which changes the lowest index of an array, is heavily deprecated, so the preceding rules should always apply.

Be careful when extracting elements from an array using a calculated index. If you are supplying an integer, then there shouldn't be any problems with resolving that to an array index (provided the index exists). If it's a floating point value, be aware that Perl always truncates (rounds down) values as if the index were interpreted within the **int** function. If you want to round up, use **sprintf**—this is easily demonstrated; the script

```
@array = qw/a b c/;

print("Array 8/5 (int)   is: ", $array[8/5], "\n");
print("Array 8/5 (float) is: ",
      $array[sprintf("%1.0f",(8/5))],"\n");
```

generates

```
Array index 8/5 (int)   is: b
Array index 8/5 (float) is: c
```

The bare 8 / 5, which equates to 1.6, is interpreted as 1 in the former statement, but 2 in the latter.

Slices

You can also extract a "slice" from an array—that is, you can select more than one item from an array in order to produce another array.

```
@weekdays = @shortdays[0,1,2,3,4];
```

The specification for a slice must a list of valid indices, either positive or negative, each separated by a comma. For speed, you can also use the .. range operator:

```
@weekdays = @shortdays[0..4];
```

Ranges also work in lists:

```
@weekdays = @shortdays[0..2,6,7];
```

Note that we're accessing the array using an @ prefix—this is because the return value that we want is another array, not a scalar. If you try accessing multiple values using **$array** you'll get nothing, but an error is only reported if you switch warnings on:

```
$ perl -ew "print $ARGV[2,3];" Fred Bob Alice
Multidimensional syntax $ARGV[2,3] not supported at -e line 1.
Useless use of a constant in void context at -e line 1.
Use of uninitialized value in print at -e line 1.
```

Single Element Slices

Be careful when using single element slices. The statement

```
print @array[1];
```

is no different than

```
print $array[1];
```

except that the former returns a single element list, while the latter returns a single scalar. This can be demonstrated more easily using the fragment

```
@array[1] = <DATA>;
```

which actually reads in all the remaining information from the **DATA** filehandle, but assigns only the first record read from the filehandle to the second argument of the array.

Size

The size of an array can be determined using scalar context on the array—the returned value will be the number of elements in the array:

```
@array = (1,2,3);
print "Size: ",scalar @array,"\n";
```

The value returned will always be the physical size of the array, not the number of valid elements. You can demonstrate this, and the difference between **scalar @array** and **$#array**, using this fragment:

```
@array = (1,2,3);
$array[50] = 4;

print "Size: ",scalar @array,"\n";
print "Max Index: ", $#array,"\n";
```

This should return

```
Size: 51
Max Index: 50
```

There are only four elements in the array that contain information, but the array is 51 elements long, with a highest index of 50.

Hashes

Hashes are an advanced form of array. One of the limitations of an array is that the information contained within it can be difficult to get to. For example, imagine that you have a list of people and their ages. We could store that information in two arrays, one containing the names and the other their ages:

```
@names = qw/Martin Sharon Rikke/;
@ages  = (28,35,29);
```

Now when we want to get Martin's age, we just access index 0 of the **@ages** array. Furthermore, we can print out all the people's ages by printing out the contents of each array in sequence:

```
for($i=0;$i<@names;$i)
{
    print "$names[$i] is $ages[$i] years old\n";
}
```

But how would you print out Rikke's age if you were only given her name, rather than her location within the **@names** array? The only way would be to step through **@names** until we found Rikke, and then look up the corresponding age in the **@ages** array. This is fine for the three-element array listed here, but what happens when that array becomes 30, 300, or even 3000 elements long? If the person we wanted was at the end of the list, we'd have to step through 3000 items before we got to the information we wanted.

The hash solves this, and numerous other problems, very neatly by allowing us to access that **@ages** array not by an index, but by a scalar key. Because it's a scalar, that value could be anything (including a reference to another hash, array, or even an object), but for this particular problem it would make sense to make it the person's name:

```
%ages = ('Martin' => 28,
         'Sharon' => 35,
         'Rikke'  => 29,);
```

Now when we want to print out Rikke's age, we just access the value within the hash using Rikke's name as the key:

```
print "Rikke is $ages{Rikke} years old\n";
```

The process works on 3000 element hashes just as easily as it does on 3:

```
print "Eileen is $ages{Eileen} years old\n";
```

We don't have to step through the list to find what we're looking for—we can just go straight to the information. Perl's hashes are also more efficient than those supported by most other languages. Although it is possible to end up with a super-large hash that takes a long time to locate its values, you are probably talking tens or hundreds of thousands of entries. If you are working with that level of information though, consider using a DBM file—see Chapter 13 for more information.

Creation

Hashes are created in one of two ways. In the first, you assign a value to a named key on a one-by-one basis:

```
$ages{Martin} = 28;
```

In the second, you use a list, which is converted by taking individual pairs from the list: the first element of the pair is used as the key, and the second, as the value. For example,

```
%hash = ('Fred' , 'Flintstone', 'Barney', 'Rubble');
```

For clarity, you can use **=>** as an alias for **,** to indicate the key/value pairs:

```
%hash = ('Fred' => 'Flintstone',
         'Barney' => 'Rubble');
```

When specifying the key for a hash element, you can avoid using quotes within the braces according to the normal brace expansion rules:

```
$ages{Martin} = 28;
```

However, if the contents are a more complex term, they will need to be quoted:

```
$ages{'Martin-surname'} = 'Brown';
```

You can also use the **-** operator in front of a word, although this makes the key include the leading **-** sign as part of the key:

```
%hash = (-Fred => 'Flintstone', -Barney => 'Rubble');
print $hash{-Fred};
```

For single-letter strings, however, this will raise a warning; use single quotes to explicitly define these arguments.

Extracting Individual Elements

You can extract individual elements from a hash by specifying the key for the value that you want within braces:

```
print $hash{Fred};
```

Care needs to be taken when embedding strings and/or variables that are made up of multiple components. The following statements are identical, albeit with a slight performance trade-off for the former method:

```
print $hash{$fred . $barney};
print $hash{"$fred$barney"};
```

When using more complex hash keys, use **sprintf**:

```
print $hash{sprintf("%s-%s:%s",$a,$b,$c)};
```

You can also use numerical values to build up your hash keys—the values just become strings. If you are going to use this method, then you should use **sprintf** to enforce a fixed format for the numbers to prevent minor differences from causing you problems. For example, when formatting time values, it's better to use

```
$hash{sprintf("%02d%02d",$hours,$min)};
```

than

```
$hash{$hours . $min};
```

With the former, all times will be displayed in the form '0505' instead of '55'.

Extracting Slices

You can extract slices out of a hash just as you can extract slices from an array. You do, however, need to use the @ prefix because the return value will be a list of corresponding values:

```
%hash = (-Fred => 'Flintstone', -Barney => 'Rubble');
print join("\n",@hash{-Fred,-Barney});
```

Using **$hash{-Fred, -Barney}** would return nothing.

Extracting Keys, Values, or Both

You can get a list of all of the keys from a hash by using **keys**:

```perl
%ages = ('Martin' => 28, 'Sharon' => 35, 'Rikke' => 29);
print "The following are in the DB: ",join(', ',keys %ages),"\n";
```

You can also get a list of the values using **values**:

```perl
%ages = ('Martin' => 28, 'Sharon' => 35, 'Rikke' => 29);
print "The following are in the DB: ",join(', ',values %ages),"\n";\
```

These can be useful in loops when you want to print all of the contents of a hash:

```perl
foreach $key (%ages)
{
    print "$key is $ages{$key} years old\n";
}
```

The problem with both these functions is that on large hashes (such as those attached to external databases), we can end up with very large memory-hungry temporary lists. You can get round this by using the **each** function, which returns key/value pairs. Unlike **keys** and **values**, the **each** function returns only one pair for each invocation, so we can use it within a loop without worrying about the size of the list returned in the process:

```perl
while (($key, $value) = each %ages)
{
    print "$key is $ages{$key} years old\n";
}
```

The order used by **keys**, **values**, and **each** is unique to each hash, and its order can't be guaranteed. Also note that with **each**, if you use it once outside of a loop, the next invocation will return the next item in the list. You can reset this "counter" by evaluating the entire hash, which is actually as simple as

```perl
sort keys %hash;
```

Checking for Existence

If you try to access a key/value pair from a hash that doesn't exist, you'll normally get the undefined value, and if you have warnings switched on, then you'll get a warning generated at run time. You can get around this by using the **exists** function, which returns true if the named key exists, irrespective of what its value might be:

```
if (exists($ages{$name}))
{
    print "$name if $ages{$name} years old\n";
}
else
{
    print "I don't know the age of $name\n";
}
```

Sorting/Ordering

There is no way to simply guarantee that the order in which a list of keys, values, or key/value pairs will always be the same. In fact, it's best not even to rely on the order between two sequential evaluations:

```
print(join(', ',keys %hash),"\n");
print(join(', ',keys %hash),"\n");
```

If you want to guarantee the order, use **sort**, as, for example:

```
print(join(', ',sort keys %hash),"\n");
```

If you're accessing a hash a number of times and want to use the same order, consider creating a single array to hold the sorted sequence, and then use the array (which will remain in sorted order) to iterate over the hash. For example:

```
my @sortorder = sort keys %hash;
foreach my $key (@sortorder)
```

Size

You get the size—that is, the number of elements—from a hash by using scalar context on either **keys** or **values**:

```
print "Hash size: ",scalar keys %hash,"\n";
```

Don't use **each**, as in a scalar context it returns the first key from the hash, not a count of the key/value pairs, as you might expect.

If you evaluate a hash in scalar context, then it returns a string that describes the current storage statistics for the hash. This is reported as "used/total" buckets. The buckets are the storage containers for your hash information, and the detail is only really useful if you want to know how Perl's hashing algorithm is performing on your data set. If you think this might concern you, then check my *Debugging Perl* title, which details how hashes are stored in Perl and how you can improve the algorithm for specific data sets (see Appendix C for more information).

Lists

Lists are really a special type of array—essentially, a list is a temporary construct that holds a series of values. The list can be "hand" generated using parentheses and the comma operator,

```
@array = (1,2,3);
```

or it can be the value returned by a function or variable when evaluated in list context:

```
print join(',' @array);
```

Here, the **@array** is being evaluated in list context because the **join** function is expecting a list (see Chapter 6 for more information on contexts).

Merging Lists (or Arrays)

Because a list is just a comma-separated sequence of values, you can combine lists together:

```
@numbers = (1,3,(4,5,6));
```

The embedded list just becomes part of the main list—this also means that we can combine arrays together:

```
@numbers = (@odd,@even);
```

Functions that return lists can also be embedded to produce a single, final list:

```
@numbers = (primes(),squares());
```

Selecting Elements from Lists

The list notation is identical to that for arrays—you can extract an element from an array by appending square brackets to the list and giving one or more indices:

```
$one = (5,4,3,2,1)[4];
```

Similarly, we can extract slices, although without the requirement for a leading @ character:

```
@newlist = (5,4,3,2,1)[1..3];
```

Selecting List Elements from Function Calls

We can even use list notation on the return value from a function call. For example, the **localtime** function returns a list of time values (hours, minutes, days, and so on), and we can extract just the elements we want:

```
($hours,$minutes) = (localtime())[2..3];
```

Note that the parentheses go around the expression that returns the list, to imply list context on the overall expression. The following are all examples of how *not* to extract individual elements from a function that returns a list:

```
$hours = localtime()[2];
$hours,$minutes = localtime()[2..3];
($hours,$minutes) = localtime()[2..3];
```

List Assignment

We've now seen an example of list assignment, but it's a useful feature that can be applied to any statement or sequence of statements. You can use list assignment to assign a series of values to a series of valid lvalues; for example, we can shorten

```
$one = 1;
$two = 2;
$three = 3;
```

to

```
($one, $two, $three) = (1,2,3);
```

Note that you need list context on both sides of the assignment operator. If you don't want one of the values, you can also assign to the undefined value:

```
($one, undef, $three) = (1,2,3);
```

Finally, you can assign a value to an empty list, which will force list context on to the function, although any value it returns will be lost:

```
() = function();
```

Arrays in List Context

When accessing an entire array or slice, arrays work as lists—that is

```
@array = (1,2);
($a, $b) = @array;
```

is equivalent to

```
($a, $b) = (1, 2);
```

Hashes in List Context

In the same way that hashes are essentially populated using a list, if you evaluate a hash in list context, then what you get is a list of key/value pairs. For example,

```
my %hash = (Fred => 'Flintstone', Barney => 'Rubble');
@list = %hash;
print join(', ',@list);
```

produces

```
Barney, Rubble, Fred, Flintstone
```

Typeglobs

The *typeglob* is a special type of variable that literally means "everything called...." In fact, a typeglob is a pointer to a symbol table entry. Typeglobs start with an asterisk; the typeglob ***foo** contains the values of **\$foo**, **@foo**, **%foo** and **&foo**. Typeglobs are useful when you want to refer to a variable but don't necessarily know what it is.

Although this isn't particularly useful for the three main data types, it can be useful for exchanging filehandles:

```
$myfh = *STDOUT;
```

This is useful when you want to use filehandles within a function call—although it's more natural to use references. See Chapter 6 for some more examples of this use.

The defined Function and the Undefined Value

The undefined value, **undef**, is an alternative to the null value used in C. In essence, **undef** means that the variable has had no value assigned. This is useful if you want to create an undefined variable—one that has no value. Compare the undefined value with an integer with a value of 0 or an empty string, both of which indicate valid values.

The undefined value will always evaluate to false if used in an expression, for example the test in this fragment:

```
$value = undef;
if ($value)
{
...
```

will always fail. It will also raise an error because you've tried to access the contents of an undefined value. In these situations, you can use the **defined** function to check the value of a scalar. The **defined** function returns true if the scalar contains a valid value, or false if the scalar contains **undef**:

```
if (defined($value))
{
...
```

Just to confuse you, **defined** will return false if a variable has never been named or created, and also false if the variable does exist but has the **undef** value.

Note that the same rules apply to the scalar components of arrays or hashes: they can contain the undefined value, even though the index or key is valid. This can cause problems if you only use **defined** on a hash element. For example:

```
$hash{one} = undef;
print "Defined!\n" if (defined($hash{one}));
print "Exists!\n" if (defined($hash{one}));
```

This will only print "Exists!," since the element's *value* remains undefined.

Default Values

It's not necessary within Perl to initialize variables with some default values. Perl automatically creates all scalars as empty (with the **undefined** value). Lists and hashes are automatically created empty. That said, there is nothing wrong with setting the initial value of a variable—it won't make any difference to Perl—it's good programming practice if only for its sheer clarity effect, especially if you are using **my** to declare the variables beforehand. See Chapter 6 for information on using **my**.

Other Tokens

Perl supports a few other tokens that are identified by Perl as containing a value or indicating a state, even though they are aren't truly variables. These are listed in Table 4-4.

Special Variables

Perl keeps an internal list of special variables that supply information and data about the current scripts environment. The subsections that follow include standard variables built into the interpreter, variables that have special meanings to core modules (such as pragmas and **Exporter**), and also the special filehandles used for communicating with the outside world.

Token	Value
_ _LINE_ _	The current line number within the current file.
_ _FILE_ _	The name of the current file.
_ _PACKAGE_ _	The name of the current package. If there is no current package, then it returns the undefined value.
_ _END_ _	Indicates the end of the script (or interpretable Perl) within a file before the physical end of file.
_ _DATA_ _	As for __END__, except that it also indicates the start of the **DATA** filehandle that can be opened with the **open**, therefore allowing you to embed script and data into the same script.

Table 4-4. *Literal Tokens in Perl*

Note that Perl uses a combination of special characters and names to refer to the individual variables. To use the long (named) variables, you must include the **English** module by placing

```
use English;
```

at the top of your program. By including this module, you arrange that the longer names will be aliased to the shortened versions. Although there is no standard for using either format, because the shortened versions are the default, you will see them used more widely. See Web Appendix A for a listing of the variables and their **English** module equivalents. The named examples are given here for reference.

Some of the variables also have equivalent methods that are supported by the **IO::*** range of modules. The format of these method calls is **method HANDLE EXPR** (you can also use **HANDLE->method(EXPR)**), where **HANDLE** is the filehandle you want the change to apply to, and **EXPR** is the value to be supplied to the method.

_ (underscore)   The underscore represents the special filehandle used to cache information from the last successful **stat**, **lstat**, or file test operator.

$0
$PROGRAM_NAME   The name of the file containing the script currently being executed.

$1..$xx   The numbered variables **$1**, **$2**, and so on are the variables used to hold the contents of group matches both inside and outside of regular expressions.

$_
$ARG   The $_ and $ARG variables represent the default input and pattern searching spaces. For many functions and operations, if no specific variable is specified, the default input space will be used. For example,

```
$_ = "Hello World\n";
print;
```

would print the "Hello World" message. The same variable is also used in regular expression substitution and pattern matches. We'll look at this more closely in Chapter 7.

Perl will automatically use the default space in the following situations even if you do not specify it:

- Unary functions, such as **ord** and **int**.
- All file tests except **-t**, which defaults to STDIN.
- Most of the functions that support lists as arguments (see Appendix A).
- The pattern matching operations, **m//**, **s///**, and **tr///**, when used without an =~ operator.
- The default iterator variable in a **for** or **foreach** loop, if no other variable is supplied.
- The implicit operator in **map** and **grep** functions.
- The default place to store an input record when reading from a filehandle.

$&
$MATCH   The string matched by the last successful pattern match.

$`
$PREMATCH   The string preceding the information matched by the last pattern match.

$'
$POSTMATCH   The string following the information matched by the last pattern match.

$+
$LAST_PARENT_MATCH   The last bracket match by the last regular expression search pattern.

$*   Set to 1 to do multiline pattern matching within a string. The default value is 0. The use of this variable has been superseded by the **/s** and **/m** modifiers to regular expressions.

Note   *Use of this variable should be avoided.*

@+
@LAST_MATCHED   Contains a list of all the offsets of the last successful submatches from the last regular expression. Note that this contains the offset to the first character *following* the match, not the location of the match itself. This is the equivalent of the value returned by the **pos** function. The first index, **$+[0]** is offset to the end of the entire match. Therefore, **$+[1]** is the location where **$1** ends, **$+[2]**, where **$2** ends.

@-

@LAST_MATCH_START   Contains a list of all the offsets to the beginning of the last successful submatches from the last regular expression. The first index, **$-[0]**, is offset to the start of the entire match. Therefore, **$-[1]** is equal to **$1**, **$-[2]** is equal to **$2**, and so on.

$.
$NR

$INPUT_LINE_NUMBER   The current input line number of the last file from which you read. This can be either the keyboard or an external file or other filehandle (such as a network socket). Note that it's based not on what the real lines are, but more what the number of the last *record* was according to the setting of the $/ variable.

$/
$RS

$INPUT_RECORD_SEPARATOR   The current input record separator. This is newline by default, but it can be set to any string to enable you to read in delimited text files that use one or more special characters to separate the records. You can also undefine the variable, which will allow you to read in an entire file, although this is best done using **local** within a block:

```
{
    local $/;
    $file = <FILE>;
}
```

@ISA   The array that contains a list of other packages to look through when a method call on an object cannot be found within the current package. The **@ISA** array is used as the list of base classes for the current package.

$|
$AUTOFLUSH
$OUTPUT_AUTOFLUSH

autoflush HANDLE EXPR   By default all output is buffered (providing the OS supports it). This means all information to be written is stored temporarily in memory and periodically flushed, and the value of $| is set to zero. If it is set to non-zero, the filehandle (current, or specified) will be automatically flushed after each write operation. It has no effect on input buffering.

$,
$OFS
$OUTPUT_FIELD_SEPARATOR   The default output separator for the print series of functions. By default, print outputs the comma-separated fields you specify without any delimiter. You can set this variable to commas, tabs, or any other value to insert a different delimiter.

$
$ORS
$OUTPUT_RECORD_SEPARATOR   The default output record separator. Ordinarily, **print** outputs individual records without a standard separator, and no trailing newline or other record separator is output. If you set this value, then the string will be appended to the end of every **print** statement.

%OVERLOAD   Set by the **overload** pragma to implement operator overloading.

$"
$LIST_SEPARATOR   This defines the separator inserted between elements of an array when interpolated within a double-quoted string. The default is a single space.

$;
$SUBSEP
$SUBSCRIPT_SEPARATOR   The separator used when emulating multidimensional arrays. If you refer to a hash element as

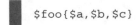
```
$foo{$a,$b,$c}
```

it really means

```
$foo{join($;,$a,$b,$c)}
```

The default value is "\034."

$#   The default number format to use when printing numbers. The value format matches the format of numbers printed via **printf** and is initially set to **%.ng**, where **n** is the number of digits to display for a floating point number as defined by your operating system (this is the value of **DBL_DIG** from float.h under Unix).

Note   *The use of this variable should be avoided.*

$%

$FORMAT_PAGE_NUMBER

format_page_number HANDLE EXPR   The page number of the current output channel.

$=

$FORMAT_LINES_PER_PAGE

format_lines_per_page HANDLE EXPR   The number of printable lines of the current page; the default is 60.

$-

$FORMAT_LINES_LEFT

format_lines_left HANDLE EXPR   The number of lines available to print to on the current page.

$~

$FORMAT_NAME

format_name HANDLE EXPR   The name of the current report format in use by the current output channel. This is set by default to the name of the filehandle.

$^

$FORMAT_TOP_NAME

format_top_name HANDLE EXPR   The name of the current top-of-page output format for the current output channel. The default name is the filehandle with **_TOP** appended.

$:

$FORMAT_LINE_BREAK_CHARACTERS

format_line_break_characters HANDLE EXPR   The set of characters after which a string may be broken to fill continuation fields. The default is "\n-," to allow strings to be broken on newlines or hyphens.

$^L

$FORMAT_FORMFEED

format_formfeed HANDLE EXPR   The character to be used to send a form feed to the output channel. This is set to "\f" by default.

$@

$EVAL_ERROR   The error message returned by the Perl interpreter when Perl has been executed via the **eval** function. If empty (false), then the last **eval** call executed successfully.

$$
$PID
$PROCESS_ID   The process number of the Perl interpreter executing the current script.

$<
$UID
$REAL_USER_ID   The real ID of the user currently executing the interpreter that is executing the script.

$>
$EUID
$EFFECTIVE_USER_ID   The effective user ID of the current process.

$(
$GID
$REAL_GROUP_ID   The real group ID of the current process. If the OS supports multiple simultaneous group membership, this returns a space-separated list of group IDs.

$)
$EGID
$EFFECTIVE_GROUP_ID   The effective group ID of the process. If the OS supports multiple simultaneous group membership, this returns a space-separated list of group IDs.

$!
$ERRNO
$OS_ERROR   Returns the error number or error string of the last system call operation. This is equivalent to the **errno** value and can be used to print the error number or error string when a particular system or function call has failed.

%!
%ERRNO
%OS_ERROR   Defined only when the **Errno** module has been imported. Allows you to compare the current error with an error string as determined by the C **#define** definitions in the system header files.

$[The index of the first element in an array or of the first character in a substring. The default is zero, but this can be set to any value. In general, this is useful only when emulating **awk**, since functions and other constructs can emulate the same functionality.

Note   *The use of this variable should be avoided.*

$]
$OLD_PERL_VERSION   The old version + patchlevel/1000 of the Perl interpreter. This can be used to determine the version number of Perl being used, and therefore what functions and capabilities the current interpreter supports. The **$^V** variable holds a UTF-8 representation of the current Perl version.

$a   The variable used by the **sort** function to hold the first of each pair of values being compared. The variable is actually a reference to the real variable so that you can modify it, but you shouldn't—see Chapter 8 for information on usage.

@_
@ARG   Within a subroutine (or function), the @_ array contains the list of parameters supplied to the function.

ARGV   The special filehandle that iterates over command line filenames in **@ARGV**. Most frequently called using the null filehandle in the angle operator <>.

$ARGV   The name of the current file when reading from the default filehandle <>.

@ARGV   The @ARGV array contains the list of the command line arguments supplied to the script. Note that the first value, at index zero, is the first argument, not the name of the script.

ARGVOUT   The special filehandle used to send output to a new file when processing the **ARGV** filehandle under the **-i** switch.

$b   The variable supplied as the second value to compare when using **sort**, along with the $a variable.

$^A
$ACCUMULATOR   When outputting formatted information via the reporting system, the **formline** functions put the formatted results into **$^A**, and the **write** function then outputs and empties the accumulator variable. This the current value of the **write** accumulator for **format** lines.

$?
$CHILD_ERROR   The status returned by the last external command (via backticks or **system**) or the last pipe close. This is the value returned by **wait**, so the true return value is **$? >> 8**, and **$? & 127** is the number of the signal received by the process, if appropriate.

$^C
$COMPILING   The value of the internal flag associated with the **-c** switch. This has a true value when code is being compiled using **perlcc** or when being parsed with the **-MO** option.

DATA   The filehandle that refers to any text following either the _ _END_ _ or _ _DATA_ _ token within the current file. The _ _DATA_ _ token automatically opens the **DATA** filehandle for you.

$^D
$DEBUGGING   The current value of the internal debugging flags, as set from the **-D** switch on the command line.

%ENV   The list of variables as supplied by the current environment. The key is the name of the environment variable, and the corresponding value is the variable's value. Setting a value in the hash changes the environment variable for child processes.

@EXPORT   The list of functions and variables to be exported as normal from a module when using the standard **Exporter** module.

%EXPORT_TAGS   A list of object groups (in the keys) and objects (in the values) to be exported when requesting groups of objects when importing a module.

$^E
$EXTENDED_OS_ERROR   Contains extended error information for operating systems other than Unix. Under Unix the value equals the value of **$!**. We'll look more closely at the use of this variable when we study the use of Perl as a cross-platform development solution.

@F   The array into which the input lines fields are placed after splitting when the **-a** command line argument has been given.

%FIELDS   The hash used by the **fields** pragma to determine the current legal fields in an object hash.

$^F
$SYSTEM_FD_MAX   The maximum system file descriptor number, after **STDIN** (0), **STDOUT** (1) and **STDERR** (2)—therefore it's usually two. System file descriptors are duplicated across **exec**'d processes, although higher descriptors are not. The value of this variable affects which filehandles are passed to new programs called through **exec** (including when called as part of a **fork**).

$^H   The status of syntax checks enabled by compiler hints, such as **use strict**.

@INC   The list of directories that Perl should examine when importing modules via the **do**, **require**, or **use** construct.

%INC   Contains a list of the files that have been included via **do**, **require**, or **use**. The key is the file you specified, and the value is the actual location of the imported file.

$^I   The value of the inplace-edit extension (enabled via the **-i** switch on the command line). True if inplace edits are currently enabled, false otherwise.

$^M   The size of the emergency pool reserved for use by Perl and the **die** function when Perl runs out of memory. This is the only standard method available for trapping Perl memory overuse during execution.

$^O
$OSNAME   The operating system name, as determined via the configuration system during compilation.

$^P
$PERLDB   The internal variable used for enabling the Perl debugger.

$^R
$LAST_REGEXP_CODE_RESULT   The value of the last evaluation in a **(?{ code })** block within a regular expression. Note that if there are multiple **(?{code})** blocks within a regular expression, then this contains the result of the last piece of code that led to a successful match within the expression.

%SIG   The keys of the %SIG hash correspond to the signals available on the current machine. The value corresponds to how the signal will be handled. You use this mechanism to support signal handlers within Perl. We'll look at this in more detail when we examine interprocess communication in Chapter 10.

$^S
$EXCEPTIONS_BEING_CAUGHT   The current interpreter state. The value is undefined if the parsing of the current module is not finished. It is true if inside an **eval** block, otherwise, false.

STDERR   The special filehandle for standard error.

STDIN   The special filehandle for standard input.

STDOUT   The special filehandle for standard output.

$^T

$BASETIME   The time at which the script started running, defined as the number of seconds since the epoch.

$^V

$PERL_VERSION   The current revision, version, and subversion of the currently executing Perl interpreter. Specified as a v-string literal.

$VERSION   The variable accessed to determine whether a given package matches the acceptable version when the module is imported. For example

```
use Module 2.5;
```

would check **$Module::VERSION** to see whether it was equal to or greater than 2.5.

$^W

$WARNING   The current value of the warning switch (specified via the **-w**, **-W**, and **-X** command line options).

$^X

$EXECUTABLE_NAME   The name of the Perl binary being executed, as determined via the value of C's **argv[0]**. This is not the same as the name of the script being executed, which can be found in **$0**.

${^WARNING_BITS}   The current set of warning checks enabled through the **warnings** pragma.

${^WIDE_SYSTEM_CALLS}   The global flag that enables all system calls made by Perl to use the wide-character APIs native to the system. This allows Perl to communicate with systems that are using multibyte characters sets, and therefore wide characters within their function names.

The Complete Reference

Perl

Chapter 5

Statements and Control Structures

A s in any other language, Perl scripts are made of a combination of statements, expressions, and declarations. We've already seen some examples of expressions that use operators and variables. We'll be looking at declarations—the specification of variables and other dynamic components, such as subroutines—in the next chapter.

Statements are the building blocks of a program. They control the execution of your script and, unlike an expression, which is evaluated for its result, a statement is evaluated for its effect. For example, the **if** statement is evaluated and executes a block based on the result of the expression.

Examples of other statements include the loop statements, such as **for**, **while**, and **do**. We'll look at all of these and the other basic components of a Perl script, but we'll start with a core component of any statement—the code block.

Code Blocks

A sequence of statements is called a code block, or simply just a block. The block could be an entire file (your script is actually a block of code), but more usually it refers to a sequence of statements enclosed by a pair of braces (curly brackets)—{}. Blocks also have a given scope, which controls the names and availability of variables within a given block—we'll cover scope separately in Chapter 6.

For example, consider the following simple script, which first assigns an expression to a variable and then prints the value:

```
$a = 5*2;
print "Result: $a\n";
```

As the only two lines within the script, they make up a single block. However, if we place those two statements into a braced block as part of an **if** statement, like this:

```
if ($expre)
{
    $a = 5*2;
    print "Result: $a\n";
}
```

then we have two blocks in the script—once block consists of the entire file, and the second block is made up simply of those two lines that perform and then print the result of a calculation.

Blocks are a vital part of Perl—they allow you to segregate sequences of code for use with loops and control structures, and they act as delimiters for subroutines and **eval** statements. They can even act as delimiters for accessing complex structures. Because of this, we'll actually be returning to blocks again and again throughout the book.

We'll be referring to a brace-enclosed block as **BLOCK**, and while we're at it, an expression will be identified as **EXPR**, and lists of values as **LIST**.

Conditional Statements

The conditional statements are **if** and **unless,** and they allow you to control the execution of your script. The **if** statement operates in an identical fashion, syntactically and logically, to the English equivalent. It is designed to ask a question (based on an expression) and execute the statement or code block if the result of the evaluated expression returns true. There are five different formats for the **if** statement:

```
if (EXPR)
if (EXPR) BLOCK
if (EXPR) BLOCK else BLOCK
if (EXPR) BLOCK elsif (EXPR) BLOCK ...
if (EXPR) BLOCK elsif (EXPR) BLOCK ... else BLOCK
STATEMENT if (EXPR)
```

In each case, the **BLOCK** immediately after an **if** or **elsif** or in the last form the **STATEMENT** immediately before the **if** is only executed if **EXPR** returns a true value (see the "Logical Values" section in Chapter 3).

The first format is classed as a simple statement, since it can be used at the end of another statement without requiring a block, as in

```
print "Happy Birthday!\n" if ($date == $today);
```

In this instance, the message will only be printed if the expression evaluates to a true value. Simple statements are a great way of executing a single line of code without resorting to the verbosity of a full **BLOCK**-based statement. The disadvantage is that they can only be used to execute a single line.

The second format is the more familiar conditional statement that you may have come across in other languages:

```
if ($date == $today)
{
    print "Happy Birthday!\n";
}
```

This produces the same result as the previous example (providing the expression returns true), but because we are using a **BLOCK**, we could execute multiple statements. Note, by the way, that unlike C/C++, the braces are required, even for single-line blocks.

The third format allows for exceptions. If the expression evaluates to true, then the first block is executed; otherwise (**else**), the second block is executed:

```
if ($date == $today)
{
    print "Happy Birthday!\n";
}
else
{
    print "Happy Unbirthday!\n";
}
```

The fourth form allows for additional tests if the first expression does not return true. The **elsif** can be repeated an infinite number of times to test as many different alternatives as are required:

```
if ($date == $today)
{
    print "Happy Birthday!\n";
}
elsif ($date == $christmas)
{
    print "Happy Christmas!\n";
}
```

The fifth form allows for both additional tests and a final exception if all the other tests fail:

```
if ($date == $today)
{
    print "Happy Birthday!\n";
}
elsif ($date == $christmas)
{
    print "Happy Christmas!\n";
}
else
{
    print "Happy Unbirthday!\n";
}
```

The sixth form is a short form used to evaluate a single line statements, providing the evaluation of the expression applied to **if** is true. For example:

```
print "Happy Birthday!\n" if ($date == $today);
```

would only print "Happy Birthday" if the value of **$date** equaled the value of **$today**.

The **unless** statement automatically implies the logical opposite of **if**, so **unless** the **EXPR** is true, execute the block. This means that the statement

```
print "Happy Unbirthday!\n" unless ($date == $today);
```

is equivalent to

```
print "Happy Unbirthday!\n" if ($date != $today);
```

However, if you want to make multiple tests, there is no **elsunless**, only **elsif**. It is more sensible to use **unless** only in situations where there is a single statement or code block; using **unless** and **else** or **elsif** only confuses the process. For example, the following is a less elegant solution to the preceding **if...else** example,

```
unless ($date != $today)
{
    print "Happy Unbirthday!\n";
}
else
{
    print "Happy Birthday!\n";
}
```

although it achieves the same result—TIMTOWTDI (There Is More Than One Way To Do It) syndrome!

The final conditional statement is actually an operator—the conditional operator. It is synonymous with the **if...else** conditional statement but is shorter and more compact. The format for the operator is

```
(expression) ? (statement if true) : (statement if false)
```

For example, we can emulate the previous example as follows:

```
($date == $today) ? print "Happy Birthday!\n" : print "Happy
Unbirthday!\n";
```

Furthermore, because it is an operator, it can be incorporated directly into expressions where you would otherwise require statements. This means you can compound the previous example to the following:

```
print "Happy ", ($date == $today) ? "Birthday!\n" :
"Unbirthday!\n";
```

Loops

Perl supports four main loop types, and all of them should be familiar to most programmers. Perl supports **while, until, for,** and **foreach.** In each case, the execution of the loop continues until the evaluation of the supplied expression changes. In the case of a **while** (and **for**) loop, for example, execution continues while the expression evaluates to true. The **until** loop executes while the loop expression is false and only stops when the expression evaluates to a true value. The list forms of the **for** and **foreach** loop are special cases—they continue until the end of the supplied list is reached.

while Loops

The **while** loop has three forms:

```
while EXPRLABEL
while (EXPR) BLOCKLABEL
while (EXPR) BLOCK continue BLOCK
```

The first format follows the same simple statement rule as the simple **if** statement and enables you to apply the loop control to a single line of code. The expression is evaluated first, and then the statement to which it applies is evaluated. For example, the following line increases the value of **$linecount** as long as we continue to read lines from a given file:

```
$linecount++ while (<FILE>);
```

To create a loop that executes statements first, and then tests an expression, you need to combine **while** with a preceding **do {}** statement. For example,

```
do
{
    $calc += ($fact*$ivalue);
} while $calc <100;
```

In this case, the code block is executed first, and the conditional expression is only evaluated at the end of each loop iteration.

The second two forms of the **while** loop repeatedly execute the code block as long as the result from the conditional expression is true. For example, you could rewrite the preceding example as:

```
while($calc < 100)
{
    $calc += ($fact*$ivalue);
}
```

The **continue** block is explained later in the chapter, in the "The continue Block" section.

until Loops

The inverse of the **while** loop is the **until** loop, which evaluates the conditional expression and reiterates over the loop only when the expression returns false. Once the expression returns true, the loop ends. In the case of a **do...until** loop, the conditional expression is only evaluated at the end of the code block. In an **until (EXPR) BLOCK** loop, the expression is evaluated before the block executes. Using an **until** loop, you could rewrite the previous example as

```
do
{
    $calc += ($fact*$ivalue);
} until $calc >= 100;
```

for Loops

A **for** loop is basically a **while** loop with an additional expression used to reevaluate the original conditional expression. The basic format is

```
LABEL for (EXPR; EXPR; EXPR) BLOCK
```

The first **EXPR** is the initialization—the value of the variables before the loop starts iterating. The second is the expression to be executed for each iteration of the loop as a test. The third expression is executed for each iteration and should be a modifier for the loop variables.

Thus, you can write a loop to iterate 100 times like this:

```
for ($i=0;$i<100;$i++)
{
...
}
```

You can place multiple variables into the expressions using the standard list operator (the comma):

```
for ($i=0, $j=0;$i<100;$i++,$j++)
```

This is more practical than C, where you would require two nested loops to achieve the same result. The expressions are optional, so you can create an infinite loop like this:

```
for(;;)
{
...
}
```

foreach Loops

The last loop type is the **foreach** loop, which has a format like this:

```
LABEL foreach VAR (LIST) BLOCK
LABEL foreach VAR (LIST) BLOCK continue BLOCK
```

This is identical to the **for** loop available within the shell. For those not familiar with the operator of the shell's **for** loop, let's look at a more practical example. Imagine that you want to iterate through a list of values stored in an array, printing each value (we'll use the month list from our earlier variables example). Using a **for** loop, you can iterate through the list using

```
for ($index=0;$index<=@months;$index++)
{
    print "$months[$index]\n";
}
```

This is messy, because you're manually selecting the individual elements from the array and using an additional variable, **$index**, to extract the information. Using a **foreach** loop, you can simplify the process:

```
foreach (@months)
{
    print "$_\n";
}
```

Perl has automatically separated the elements, placing each element of the array into the default input space. Each iteration of the loop will take the next element of the array. The list can be any expression, and you can supply an optional variable for the loop to place each value of the list into. To print out each word on an individual line from a file, you could use the example here:

```
while (<FILE>)
{
    chomp;
    foreach $word (split)
    {
        print "$word\n";
    }
}
```

The **foreach** loop can even be used to iterate through a hash, providing you return the list of values or keys from the hash as the list:

```
foreach $key (keys %monthstonum)
{
    print "Month $monthstonum{$key} is $key\n";
}
```

> **Note**   *As far as Perl is concerned, the **for** and **foreach** keywords are synonymous. You can use either keyword for either type of loop—Perl actually identifies the type of loop you want to use according to the format of the expressions following the keyword.*

The continue Block

We have up to now ignored the **continue** blocks on each of the examples. The **continue** block is executed immediately after the main block and is primarily used as a method for executing a given statement (or statements) for each iteration, irrespective of how the current iteration terminated.

Although in practice it sounds pointless, consider this **for** block:

```
for (my $i = 0; $i<100; $i++)
{ ... }
```

We could rewrite this as

```
{
    my $i = 0;
    while ($i<100)
    { ... }
    continue
    {
        $i++;
    }
}
```

You can see from this that a **for** loop is really just a **while** loop with a **continue** to increase the iteration variable **$i**. As a general rule, the **continue** block is not used much, but it can provide a handy method for complex multistatement iterations that can't be specified within the confines of a **for** loop.

Labels

Labels can be applied to any block, but they make the most sense on loops. By giving your loop a name, you allow the loop control keywords (explained in the following "Loop Control" section) to specify which loop their operation should be applied to. The format for a labeled loop is

```
LABEL: loop (EXPR) BLOCK ...
```

For example, to label a **for** loop:

```
ITERATE: for (my $i=1; $i<100; $i++)
        {
            print "Count: $i\n";
        }
```

Labels can also be a useful way of syntactically commenting the purpose of a piece of code—although you might find using actual comments an easier method.

Loop Control

There are three loop control keywords: **next**, **last**, and **redo**. The **next** keyword skips the remainder of the code block, forcing the loop to proceed to the next value in the loop. For example,

```
while (<DATA>)
{
    next if /^#/;
}
```

would skip lines from the file if they started with a hash symbol. This is the standard comment style under Unix. If there is a **continue** block, it is executed before execution proceeds to the next iteration of the loop.

The **last** keyword ends the loop entirely, skipping the remaining statements in the code block, as well as dropping out of the loop. This is best used to escape a loop when an alternative condition has been reached within a loop that cannot otherwise be trapped. The **last** keyword is therefore identical to the **break** keyword in C and Shellscript. For example,

```
while (<DATA>)
{
    last if ($found);
}
```

would exit the loop if the value of **$found** was true, whether the end of the file had actually been reached or not. The **continue** block is not executed.

The **redo** keyword reexecutes the code block without reevaluating the conditional statement for the loop. This skips the remainder of the code block and also the **continue** block before the main code block is reexecuted. This is especially useful if you want to reiterate over a code block based on a condition that is unrelated to the loop condition. For example, the following code would read the next line from a file if the current line terminates with a backslash:

```
while(<DATA>)
{
    if (s#\\$#)
    {
        $_ .= <DATA>;
        redo;
    }
}
```

In all cases, the loop control keyword affects the current (innermost) loop. If you label the nested loops, then you can supply each keyword with the optional label name so that the effects are felt on the specified block instead of the innermost block. This allows you to nest loops without limiting their control:

```
OUTER:
while(<DATA>)
{
    chomp;
    @linearray=split;
    foreach $word (@linearray)
    {
        next OUTER if ($word =~ /next/i)
    }
}
```

This would skip the current input line from the file if there was a word "next" in the input line, while still allowing the remainder of the words from the file to be processed.

Unqualified Blocks

You can introduce a block into a script without actually qualifying the block as being part of a subroutine or statement. In this instance, the unqualified (or bare) block is interpreted in an identical fashion to a loop, except that the statements are executed only once. Because an unqualified block acts as a loop, we can use the loop control statements (**next**, **last**, and **redo**) within the block, something that can't be done with **if** or **unless**, or the quasi-block statements of **eval**, **sub** (for subroutines), and **do**.

This operation can be useful for complex selections when you don't want to use multiple **if...else** statements or complex logical comparisons. For example, we could drop out of an **if** statement by enclosing the **if BLOCK** within an unqualified **BLOCK** so that the statements are identified as loop:

```
if (/valid/)
{
    {
        last if /false/;
        print "Really valid!\n";
    }
}
```

The **last** keyword would drop us out of the entire **if** statement.

A more obvious example is the emulation of the Shellscript **case** statement, or the C/C++ **switch** statement. The easiest solution is to use **if** statements embedded within a named block. For example:

```
SWITCH: {
    if ($date == $today) { print "Happy Birthday!\n";   last SWITCH; }
    if ($date != $today) { print "Happy Unbirthday!\n"; last SWITCH; }
    if ($date == $xmas)  { print "Happy Christmas!\n";  last SWITCH; }
}
```

This works because we can use the loop control operators **last**, **next**, and **redo**, which apply to the enclosing **SWITCH** block. This also means you could write the same script as

```
SWITCH: {
    print "Happy Birthday!\n",   last SWITCH if ($date == $today);
    print "Happy Unbirthday!\n", last SWITCH if ($date != $today);
    print "Happy Christmas!\n",  last SWITCH if ($date == $xmas);
}
```

or for a more formatted solution that will appeal to C and Shellscript programmers:

```
SWITCH: {
    ($date == $today)      && do {
                                print "Happy Birthday!\n";
                                last SWITCH;
                           };
    ($date != $today)      && do {
                                print "Happy Unbirthday!\n";
                                last SWITCH;
                           };
    ($date == $xmas)       && do {
                                print "Happy Christmas!\n";
                                last SWITCH;
                           };
}
```

Note that in this last example, you could exclude the label. The **do** {} blocks are not loops, and so the last command would ignore them and instead drop out of the parent **SWITCH** block. Also note that because **do** is not strictly a statement, the block must be terminated by a semicolon.

goto

BASIC programmers will be immediately happy when they realize that Perl has a **goto** statement. For purists, **goto** is a bad idea, and in many cases it is actually a dangerous option when subroutines and functions are available. There are three basic forms: **goto LABEL**, **goto EXPR**, and **goto &NAME**.

In each case, execution is moved from the current location to the destination. In the case of **goto LABEL**, execution stops at the current point and resumes at the point of the label specified. It cannot be used to jump to a point inside a block that needs initialization, such as a subroutine or loop. However, it can be used to jump to any other point within the current or parent block, including jumping out of subroutines. As has already been stated, the use of **goto** should be avoided, as there are generally much better ways to achieve what you want. It is always possible to use a control flow statement (**next**, **redo**, etc.), function, or subroutine to achieve the same result without any of the dangers.

The second form is essentially just an extended form of **goto LABEL**. Perl expects the expression to evaluate dynamically at execution time to a label by name. This allows for computed **goto**s similar to those available in FORTRAN, but like **goto LABEL**, its use is deprecated.

The **goto &NAME** statement is more complex. It allows you to replace the currently executing subroutine with a call to the specified subroutine instead. This allows you to automatically call a different subroutine based on the current environment and is used by the autoload mechanism (see the **Autoload** module in Appendix B) to dynamically select alternative routines. The statement works such that even the caller will be unable to tell whether the requested subroutine or the one specified by **goto** was executed first.

Chapter 6

Subroutines, Packages, and Modules

123

Everything covered so far makes up the basics of programming Perl. We've looked at how to communicate with the users, how to manipulate basic data types, and how to use the simple control statements that Perl provides to control and manage the flow of execution in a program.

One of the fundamentals of any programming language is that there are often repeated elements in your programs. You could cut and paste from one section to another, but this is messy. What happens when you need to update that sequence you just wrote? You would need to examine each duplicated entry and then make the modifications in each. In a small program this might not make much of a difference, but in a larger program with hundreds of lines, it could easily double or triple the amount of time you require.

Duplication also runs the risk of introducing additional syntactic, logical, and typographical errors. If you forget to make a modification to one section, or make the wrong modification, it could take hours to find and resolve the error. A better solution is to place the repeated piece of code into a new function, and then each time it needs to be executed, you can just make a call to the function. If the function needs modifying, you modify it once, and all instances of the function call use the same piece of code.

This method of taking repeated pieces of code and placing them into a function is called *abstraction*. In general, a certain level of abstraction is always useful—it speeds up the programming process, reduces the risk of introducing errors, and makes a complex program easier to manage. For the space conscious, the process also reduces the number of lines in your code. There is a small overhead in terms of calling the function and moving to a new section of the script, but this is insignificant and far outweighed by the benefit.

Once you have a suite of functions, you will want to be able to share information among the functions without affecting any variables the user may have created. By creating a new *package*, you can give the functions their own *name space*—a protected area that has its own list of global variables. Unless explicitly declared, the variables defined within the package name space will not affect any variables defined by the main script.

You can also take this abstraction a stage further. Imagine you have created a suite of functions that extend the standard mathematical abilities of Perl for use in a single script. What happens when you want to use those same functions in another script? You could cut and paste, but we already know that's a bad solution. Imagine what would happen if you updated the original script's function suite—you would need to do the same for each script that used the same set of functions.

The solution is yet another stage in abstraction: you move the function suite from the original file and place it into a new file with the same name as that of the package the functions belong to. In Perl, this process is called creating a new *module*. Each script that wants to use the functions defined in the module can import them and use them just like the functions that Perl has built in. You import the functions from a module with the **use** command. The examples of **use** you have seen up to now are all importing modules and promoting code reuse.

In this chapter, we'll be looking at how to create new functions for use within your Perl scripts and how to group functions and variables to create new packages. Then we'll examine how to convert a package into a module before moving on to the differences between the available methods for importing and using packages and modules within your scripts.

Functions

A function is a named code block that is generally intended to process specified input values into an output value, although this is not always the case. For example, the **print** function takes variables and static text and prints the values on the screen.

You can define functions anywhere within a program, including importing them from external files or having them generated on the fly using an **eval** statement. Furthermore, you can generate *anonymous subroutines*, which are functions that are attached, by reference, to a variable. This enables you to treat a subroutine as any other entity within Perl, even though you may consider it to be a fundamental part of the blocks that make up the Perl language.

Function or Subroutine?

The two terms *function* and *subroutine* are used interchangeably in Perl. If you want to be strict on the semantics, small pieces of named blocks of code that accept arguments and return values are called subroutines. The built-in subroutines in Perl are usually referred to as Perl's functions, because they provide additional functionality. A subroutine created as part of a class definition is called a method—see Chapter 10 for more information.

In truth, there's not a lot between subroutines and functions, although personally I prefer the latter.

Subroutines, like variables, can be declared (without defining what they do) or declared and defined. To simply declare a subroutine, you use one of the following forms:

```
sub NAME
sub NAME PROTO
sub NAME ATTRS
sub NAME PROTO ATTRS
```

where **NAME** is the name of the subroutine you are creating, **PROTO** is the prototype for the arguments the subroutine should expect when called, and **ATTRS** is a list of attributes that the subroutine exhibits. The **PROTO** and **ATTRS** arguments are optional—we'll be discussing these elements separately in the "Prototypes" and "Attributes" sections later in this chapter.

An undefined subroutine does nothing, but it does let the rest of the script know that such a subroutine exists. When used in combination with prototypes, it allows calls to subroutines to be checked. However, declaring subroutines without actually defining them is not required—we do not need to tell Perl the names of the subroutines we expect to create.

If you want to declare and define a function, then you need to include the **BLOCK** that defines its operation:

```
sub NAME BLOCK
sub NAME PROTO BLOCK
sub NAME ATTRS BLOCK
sub NAME PROTO ATTRS BLOCK
```

You can also create *anonymous* subroutines—subroutines without a name—by omitting the **NAME** component:

```
sub BLOCK
sub PROTO BLOCK
sub ATTRS BLOCK
sub PROTO ATTRS BLOCK
```

However, you can't create an anonymous subroutine without a definition (Perl has no way of later attaching the definition without knowing the subroutine's name). You will also need to assign the subroutine to a scalar variable so that you can call it later; for example:

```
$myfunc = sub BLOCK;
```

We'll be looking at anonymous subroutines (and other reference types) in Chapter 10. In all cases, the most important parts of a subroutine are its name and the block that defines what it does. To give a quick example of a simple subroutine:

```
sub message
{
    print "Hello!\n";
}
```

To call this function you would use one of the following forms:

```
NAME
NAME LIST
NAME (LIST)
&NAME
```

All the forms accept a LIST of arguments; unless you've declared through the prototyping mechanism that a subroutine should accept one argument, all subroutines accept a list of arguments, even if ultimately they use one (or even none) of them. In the first and second forms, the subroutine must have been declared and/or defined before the call was made; otherwise Perl will be unable to determine whether the bare word was a bare word or a subroutine call. The third option removes the need to predeclare the subroutine, because the parentheses automatically indicate the name's status.

The last form is the true name of the function—this is the name that should be used when referring to the function as a whole, such as when creating a reference to the subroutine (see Chapter 10). Think of the **&** as the notation character for a subroutine in the same way as **$** indicates a scalar and **@** indicates an array.

Arguments

Perl has a very simple attitude toward function arguments. In C, Pascal, and other languages the specification of a function is fixed, both in the form of the data types that can be supplied and the total number of arguments. Although C supports the "varargs" option, this is the exception, rather than the rule. Within Perl you can pass any type of argument and any number of arguments to a function (unless you've prototyped the function—see the "Prototypes" section later in this chapter). For most situations, this is an incredibly practical solution to the problem of argument passing.

What actually happens is that the arguments you supply to a subroutine are placed into the @_ array. This means that the first argument you pass to the subroutine is available within the function as **$_[0]**, the second argument is **$_[1]**, and so on. For example, this simple function adds two numbers and prints the result:

```
sub add
{
    $result = $_[0] + $_[1];
    print "The result was: $result\n";
}
```

To call the subroutine and get a result,

```
add(1,2);
```

The preceding subroutine is fairly simple, but what if you wanted to have named arguments? The simple answer is to assign the values of @_ to a list of variables:

```
sub add
{
    ($numbera, $numberb) = @_;
    $result = $numbera + $numberb;
    print "The result was: $result\n";
}
```

Note the syntax here—we're assigning a list of values (from @_) to a list of variables (**$numbera** and **$numberb**) so we must supply a list of variables, enclosed in parentheses so that each value in @_ is assigned to a corresponding variable.

Finally, because we probably don't want to create those variables in the global name space, we ought to use **my** to declare them all locally:

```
sub add
{
    my ($numbera, $numberb) = @_;
    my $result = $numbera + $numberb;
    print "The result was: $result\n";
}
```

See the "Scope" section later in this chapter for information on the effects of **my** and the other scoping mechanisms.

Using shift

The **shift** function is one of the "stack" operands supported by Perl. The **shift** function returns (and removes) the first element of an array. For example:

```
@list = qw/first second third/;
$a = shift @list;
```

The **$a** variable will now contain "first", while the **@list** array will contain the two elements "second" and "third". The **shift** function actually defaults to using the @_ array when used in a subroutine, so we could get our arguments using

```
sub add
{
    my $numbera = shift;
    my $numberb = shift;
    my $result = $numbera + $numberb;
    print "The result was: $result\n";
}
```

The effect is exactly the same; we've just obtained the arguments in a different way.

The only downside to this **shift** solution is that @_ is now empty. The advantage is that we can use the **shift** function to work through a list of supplied arguments without worrying about how many arguments there are:

```
sub add
{
    my $result;
    while(@_)
    {
        $result += shift;
    }
    print "Result: $result\n";
}
```

Now we can call the function with any number of arguments,

```
add(1);
add(1,2);
add(1,2,3,4,5,6,7,8,9,10,11);
```

Or a list:

```
add(@values);
```

See the "Passing Lists to Subroutines" section later in this chapter for information on passing multiple lists to a function.

Counting Arguments

If you want to count the number of arguments that you have received, just access the @_ in a scalar context:

```
my $count = @_;
```

If the subroutine expects a specific number of arguments, then your function should check for the correct number. The most obvious way of doing this is to check the scalar value of the @_ array:

```
carp "Not enough/too many arguments in mysub" unless(@_ == 2);
```

Note here the use of **carp** to report a problem, rather than using **warn** or **die**—this is to ensure that the error is reported back to the caller. (See Appendix B for information on the **Carp** module, which supports the **carp** function.)

We can use a count to allow a variable number of arguments to be supplied to a function:

```
sub greeting
{
    if (@_ == 2)
    {
        ($fname, $sname) = @_;
    }
    elsif (@_ == 3)
    {
        ($fname, $sname, $title) = @_;
    }
...
}
```

Alternatively, we could have used **shift** to progressively take arguments from the stack. However, if you're going to use the **shift** method, then it's a good idea to set default values for any arguments that you consider to be optional, for example:

```
sub greeting
{
    my ($fname, $sname, $title) = ('Nobody','','');
    my $fname = shift;
    $sname = shift if (@_);
    $title = shift if (@_)
...
}
```

Note that when using **shift** we don't have to explicitly check the number of arguments supplied or use a compound **if** statement to extract them.

Note

If you're going to support a function that accepts multiple arguments, remember to use ***my*** *to declare the variables before the tests and assignation. If you define the variables within the **BLOCK** of an **if** statement, they will have gone out of scope before the rest of the subroutine is executed.*

Passing Lists to Subroutines

Because the @_ variable is an array, it can be used to supply lists to a subroutine. However, because of the way in which Perl accepts and parses lists and arrays, it can be difficult to extract the individual elements from @_. To understand the reasons better, let's start by looking at the ways in which we can call a subroutine that accepts three arguments. All three of the following are valid:

```
mysub(1,2,3);

@args = (2,3);
mysub(1,@args);

@args = (1,2,3);
mysub(@args);
```

All of these calls will work and will supply exactly the same information to the subroutine. Because each of the preceding examples results in an @_ variable that contains three elements, we have no way of knowing which of the preceding arguments was supplied as an array and which was supplied as a scalar.

If we extend the subroutine to accept four arguments, the effects become even more apparent:

```
@args = (1,2);
@moreargs = (3,4);
mysub(@args,@moreargs);
```

Now @_ contains four elements: 1,2,3,4. Perl has compounded the two arrays into a single array.

This has some advantages over a normal, explicitly named argument list as supported in C or Python. For a start, it means that we can easily blend lists together and end up with a single new list, as in this call to a sorting function:

```
@sorted = simplesort(@lista, @listb, @listc);
```

We can call the same function using scalars, and still end up with a sorted list:

```
@sorted = simplesort($valuea, $valueb, $valuec);
```

The function itself is very simple—in fact we cheat and use the built-in sort function:

```
sub simplesort
{
    sort @_;
}
```

Because the argument list has been combined, we can just walk through the entire list of arguments and return them.

The downside is that if you want to actually supply a number of lists without them getting combined into a single list, the semantics get slightly more complicated. The format that you might expect to work:

```
(@listc, @listd) = simplesort(@lista, @listb);
```

simply won't work. Perl combines **@lista** and **@listb** into **@_**. All the subroutine does is sort **@_** and then return it. Perl assigns the entire returned list to **@listc**—it has no way of knowing which elements from **@lista** and **@listb** should be placed into **@listc** or **@listd**.

If you want to work with and identify the individual lists passed to Perl, then you need to use references:

```
(@listc, @listd) = simplesort(\@lista, \@listb);
```

The leading \ character tells Perl to supply a reference, or pointer, to the array. A reference is actually just a scalar, so we can identify each list by assigning the reference to each array within our subroutine. We'll cover references and how to access and use their values in Chapter 10.

The fundamental rule to remember in this example is that when passing arrays or lists to subroutines you can pass only one array or list, and it must be the last argument supplied. If you want to extract an array from a list of arguments, then specify the array list:

```
sub process
{
    my ($first, $second, @rest) = @_;
...
}
```

If you try to extract the array as the first element, then it will immediately gobble up all of **@_**, even if there are arguments after the array leaving any scalar entries empty. The following won't do what you want at all:

```
sub process
{
    my (@rest, $first, $second) = @_;
...
}
```

The **$first** and **$second** arguments will never be filled, no matter how hard you try!

The exception to this rule is when you use prototypes; see the "Prototypes" section later in this chapter.

Passing Hashes to Subroutines

When you supply a hash to a subroutine or operator that accepts a list, the hash is automatically translated into a list of key/value pairs. For example:

```
%hash = ('name' => 'Tom', 'age' => 19);
print %hash;
```

This will output "nameTomage19". However, the same process works in reverse, so we can extract a list and convert it to a hash:

```
sub display_hash
{
    my (%hash) = @_;
    foreach (%hash)
    {
        print "$_ => $hash{$_}\n";
    }
}
```

In this case, we output the key/value pairs of the hash properly, displaying each pair on its own line. As with arrays, care needs to be taken if you expect to pick out a single hash from a list of arguments. The following will work because we extract the hash last:

```
sub display_has_regexp
{
    my ($regex, %hash) = @_;
...
}
```

while this one won't because we try to extract the hash first (there will be an extra element, and Perl won't know how to assign this to the hash):

```
sub display_has_regexp
{
    my (%hash, $regex) = @_;
```

```
    . . .
}
```

If you want to work with multiple hashes, then use references. For example, the following subroutine returns the key intersection of two hashes:

```
sub intersection
{
    my ($hasha, $hashb) = @_;
    my %newhash;
    foreach my $key (keys %{$hasha})
    {
        $newhash{$key} = $$hasha{$key} if (exists $$hashb{$key});
    }
    return %newhash;
}
```

To use the subroutine:

```
%hasha = ('a' => 'b',
          'b' => 'b',
          'c' => 'b');

%hashb = ('b' => 'b',
          'c' => 'b',
          'd' => 'b');

%newhash = intersection(\%hasha, \%hashb);
```

Identifying Values and Types

If you need to verify the value or type of an individual argument, then you can use regular expressions or other methods to validate the information before you use it. For example, to verify that two arguments are numerical:

```
sub square
{
    die "Not a number" unless($_[0] =~ /^[0-9]+$/);
    return($_[0] * $_[0]);
}
```

Default Values

For functions that accept varying numbers and/or types of arguments, you should be setting the variable used within the subroutine to a default value. This will help to ensure that when an argument is not supplied, the variable still contains either valid data or a value that can be ignored or tested when it needs to be used. The default value of any declared but unassigned variable is the undefined value, or an empty list or hash. For example, the **power** function that follows raises the first argument to the power of the second argument, or to 2 if there is no second argument:

```perl
sub power
{
    my $base = shift;
    my $power = shift || 2;
    return $base**$power;
}
```

Here I've used **shift** to take off the arguments and then used the | | operator to set the power to a default value if **shift** fails. If called with a single argument, the function will return the square of the supplied value, and if supplied with two arguments, it'll return the first raised to the power of the second.

Dynamic Arguments

There are times when there is no set argument order for a function, but you still want to accept changes to the function's variables. The way to do this is to accept a hash, where each key of the hash is the variable that you want to accept, and the value is the data for that variable. This method has the advantage of allowing you to pass a variety of scalars, arrays, and hashes without directly worrying about the order of the references you supply.

For example, we could rewrite the **power** function from the previous section like this,

```perl
sub power
{
    my (%args) = @_;
    my $base = $args{base} || 2;
    my $power = $args{power} || 2;
    return $base**$power;
}
```

which means that we can now call the function in a number of different ways:

```
print power(base => 16, power => 3); # returns 16384
print power(base => 16);             # returns 256
print power(power => 8);             # returns 256
print power();                       # returns 4
```

The order of the arguments is no longer an issue, which makes supporting default values and/or multiple options within a single subroutine significantly easier.

Note *If you want to use this option, consider using **-argument** as the argument string. That way you won't need to quote the hash key each time—the preceding hyphen translates the bareword to a string.*

Return Values

The return value of any block, including those used in subroutines, is taken as the value of the last evaluated expression. For example:

```
sub myfunc
{
    $_[0]+$_[1];
}
```

The return value here is the result of the calculation.

You can also explicitly return a value using the **return** keyword:

```
sub myfunc
{
    if (@_)
    {
        return $_[0]+$_[1];
    }
    else
    {
        return 0;
    }
}
```

When called, **return** immediately terminates the current subroutine and returns the value to the caller—if you don't specify a value then the return value is **undef**.

Error Notification

The easiest way to report an error within a subroutine is to return the undefined value **undef**—this is universally accepted within Perl as notification of some form of failure and is also identified by any testing mechanism as a false (and therefore failure) value.

If you want to report the error directly within the function, then use **die** (see Chapters 7 and 9) or use the **carp** function from the **Carp** module (see Appendix B).

Context

The *context* of a subroutine or statement is defined as the type of return value that is expected. This allows you to use a single function that returns different values based on what the user is expecting to receive. For example, the following two calls to the **getpwent** function return a list or a scalar, according to what was used in the assignation:

```
$name = getpwent();

($name, $passwd, $uid, $gid, $quota,
 $comment, %gcos, $dir, $shell) = getpwent();
```

In the first case, the user expects a scalar value to be returned by the function, because that is what the return value is being assigned to. In the second case, the user expects an array as the return value, again because a list of scalars has been specified for the information to be inserted into.

This can be confusing, since most other languages support only one type of return value. In fact, it's very practical, because it reduces the amount of code required to achieve different results. Here's another example, again from the built-in Perl functions, that shows the flexibility:

```
my $timestr = localtime(time);
```

In this example, the value of **$timestr** is now a string made up of the current date and time, for example, Thu Nov 30 15:21:33 2000. Conversely,

```
($sec,$min,$hour,$mday,$mon,$year,$wday,$yday,$isdst) = localtime(time);
```

now the individual variables contain the corresponding values returned by **localtime**. We can now use these values to build our own string, instead of relying on the default value returned in a scalar context.

In order to discover the context in which a function has been called, you use the **wantarray** function. This returns true if the function has been called in a list context, and false otherwise. Consider the following script, which prints a scalar or list-based message, according to how the **hw** function was called:

```
sub hw
{
    if (wantarray)
    {
        return('Hello','World',"\n");
    }
    else
    {
        return "Hello World\n";
    }
}

$scalarmsg = hw();
$listmsg = join('--',hw());

print "Scalar is $scalarmsg";
print "List is $listmsg";
```

The list context is implied here because the **join** function expects a list as the second argument. If you run this program, you get this,

```
Scalar is Hello World
List is Hello--World--
```

which we know to be correct and is the result we expected.

If you supply a hash, then the hash is translated into a list of key/value pairs. Note that there is no equivalent **wanthash** function. If you want to exchange and work with hashes in your subroutines on a hash level, use references (see the "Passing Hashes to Subroutines" section earlier in this chapter).

You can force a function to return a scalar value with the **scalar** keyword. This forces the context of the function to be recognized as a scalar, not a list, value. To use it, just place the **scalar** function before the statement or expression that you want to be forced into scalar context:

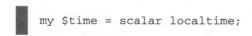
```
my $time = scalar localtime;
```

Attributes

Subroutine attributes are another new feature of Perl. Although an attributes feature has been available for some time, the definition has now been merged into the main subroutine-declaration process. To define an attribute, you specify a white space or colon separated list of keywords.

The attributes system is currently underused, although it's expected that attributes will form an important part of new versions of Perl, including Perl 6.0 when it becomes available.

Currently Perl supports only three attributes: **locked**, **method**, and **lvalue**.

The locked Attribute

The **locked** attribute allows you to define a subroutine so that a lock is obtained before the subroutine is executed when called in a script that supports multiple threads. For example:

```
sub func : lock { ... }
```

You can also use it in combination with the **method** attribute to ensure that only one thread is allowed to use the function on a given object at one time:

```
sub func : lock method { ... }
```

The exact semantics are identical to those for the **lock** function—see Chapter 15 for more information on threads.

The method Attribute

The **method** attribute currently only marks the subroutine so that you *don't* get a warning when a given method can't be resolved properly (normally highlighted as "Ambiguous call resolved as CORE::%s". See Web Appendix C for a full description of the likely cause of this error.

The lvalue Attribute

You can get a subroutine to act as a valid **lvalue** providing that you have declared the subroutine with the **lvalue** attribute. Using **lvalue**, a subroutine can be used as a modifiable scalar value. For example, you can do this:

```
mysub() = 5;
```

This is particularly useful in situations where you want to use a method on an object to accept a setting, instead of setting the value on the object directly. To create the subroutine, you must provide a scalar variable in the subroutine, which will be used both as the value that is assigned to the subroutine when it is used as an **lvalue**, and the return value when the subroutine is called as part of an expression. For example:

```
sub mysub : lvalue
{
    $val;
}
```

Look up the **attributes** pragma in Chapter 19 for more information on attributes, including creating your own customized values.

Prototypes

The dictionary defines *prototype* as "an original type, form, or instance that serves as a model on which later stages are based or judged." Within Perl, the act of prototyping a function tells Perl (or a programmer, if he's looking) what arguments the function expects or requires. As with other elements of the Perl process, the arguments passed can also imply the format of the information returned by the function. For example, the built-in **syswrite** function could be declared like this:

```
sub syswrite($$$;$)
```

The prototype is used by Perl to make decisions about the number and type of arguments that are supplied to the function. The prototypes only affect function calls in the "new" form, that is, without a leading ampersand. If it looks like a built-in function, Perl will treat it as such. If you call a function using the "old" ampersand style, prototypes are ignored. In all cases, Perl only checks at compile time, so the function and calls must be visible at the time the functions are compiled.

You specify the function arguments by using the special characters that precede normal variables as indicators of the variable type expected. In the preceding example, the dollar signs signify that scalar values are expected. The @ and % characters, as expected, specify arrays and hashes. However, except in the upcoming case (where a subroutine is treated as a named unary operator), unbackslashed entries gobble up all the remaining arguments, regardless of the rest of the prototype. In addition, the **$** implies a scalar context, and @ and % imply list context accordingly.

An ampersand requires an anonymous subroutine that can be specified without the **sub** keyword or the trailing comma, if it is specified as the first argument. A * character specifies a typeglob, typically used to supply filehandles.

Any backslash-quoted character signifies that the argument absolutely must start with that character—for example, \@ would require that the function call specify a list as the first argument. A semicolon separates the required arguments from optional arguments in the prototype. The semicolon is used to distinguish between the arguments that are required and those that are optional. Table 6-1 shows some examples taken from the perlsub man page.

In the last three examples in Table 6-1, Perl treats the declarations slightly differently. The **mygrep** function is passed as a true list operator, interpreting the following arguments as elements of a list and not as further arguments to the original **mygrep** function. The **myrand** function behaves like a true unary operator, and the **mytime** function is treated as a function with no arguments at all. This means you can get away with statements like

```
mytime +2
```

and you'll end up with the return value of **mytime** added to the static value, instead of Perl calling **mytime** with an argument of **+2**.

Declaration	Example Call
sub mylink ($$)	mylink $old, $new
sub myvec ($$$)	myvec $var, $offset, 1
sub myindex ($$;$)	myindex &getstring, "substr"
sub mysyswrite ($$$;$)	mysyswrite $buf, 0, length($buf) - $off,
sub myreverse (@)	myreverse $a, $b, $c
sub myjoin ($@)	myjoin ":", $a, $b, $c
sub mypop (\@)	mypop @array
sub mysplice (\@$$@)	mysplice @array, @array, 0, @pushme
sub mykeys (\%)	mykeys %{$hashref}
sub myopen (*;$)	myopen HANDLE, $name
sub mypipe (**)	mypipe READHANDLE, WRITEHANDLE
sub mygrep (&@)	mygrep { /foo/ } $a, $b, $c
sub myrand ($)	myrand 42
sub mytime ()	mytime

Table 6-1.   *Sample Prototype Declarations*

You should be careful when specifying prototypes, since many of the options imply the context in which the function should return and, therefore, affect some of the function-specific utilities such as **wantarray**. In general, therefore, you should use prototypes only on new functions, rather than retrofitting them to functions you have already written. This will prevent the effects of imposing a scalar context on a function that is expecting to return in a list context. For example, consider a function with a single argument:

```
sub printmsg($)
{
    print "Message: ", shift, "\n";
}
```

Calling this function with an argument that returns a single element list wouldn't produce the same results. The call

```
printmsg(@message);
```

would actually print a value of 1, since the scalar prototype has imposed that the list argument supplied be converted to a scalar.

In the case of a list, the scalar value of a list variable is the number of elements in the list. Worse, using a function such as **split**, which uses the context in which it is called to determine where it puts its results, would cause a more serious problem. If used as the argument to the prototype function, **split** would execute in the scalar context, messing up your @_ argument list.

Packages

The main principle behind packages in Perl is to protect the name space of one section of code from another, therefore helping to prevent functions and variables from overwriting each other's values. Despite what you may have seen up to now, there is no such thing as a global variable—all *user* variables are created within the realms of a package. If no package name is specified, then the default package name is **main**.

You can change the current package to another by using the **package** keyword. The current package determines what symbol table is consulted when a user makes a function call or accesses a variable. The current package name is determined at compile and run time because certain operations, such as dereferencing, require Perl to know what the "current" package is. Any **eval** blocks are also executed at run time, and the current package will directly affect the symbol table to which the **eval** block has access.

All identifiers (except those declared with **my** or with an absolute package name) are created within the symbol table of the current package. The package definition remains either until another package definition occurs or until the block in which the package was defined terminates. You can intersperse different package names in the same file and even specify the same package multiple times within multiple files. The **package** declaration only changes the default symbol table. For example, in the following code, both the **add** and **subtract** functions are part of the **Basemath** package, even though the **square** function has been inserted within a **Multimath** package:

```
package Basemath;

sub add { $_[0]+$_[1] }

package Multimath;

sub square { $_[0] *= $_[0] }

package Basemath;

sub subtract { $_[0]-$_[1] }
```

This example is probably not a good example of when a **package** is normally defined. Normally, the first statement within a new file would be used to define the package name for a module that would be imported via the **use** or **require** statement. Of course, there is nothing to stop you from using a **package** statement anywhere you would use any other statement.

You can reference a symbol entry from any package by specifying the full package and symbol name. The separator between the package and symbol entry is the double colon. You could refer to the preceding **add** function as **Basemath::add**. If you are referring to a variable, you place the character for the variable type before the package name; for example, **$Basemath::PI**. The main package can either be specified directly, as in **$main::var**, or you can ignore the name and simply use **$::var**.

Note

Perl 4 and below used the ' symbol. This is currently still supported, but for the longer term, you should move to the :: notation. It's easier to read, for a start, and editors that try to match quotes and parentheses don't fall over when you use double colons.

You can also nest package names in order to create a package hierarchy. Using the math module again, you might want to split it into three separate packages. The main **Math** package contains the constant definitions, and it has two nested packages **Math::Base** and **Math::Multi**. The hierarchy does not introduce any additional symbol tables, so the variable **$Math::Multi::var** is simply not accessible as **$Multi::var**. You either need to change the current package with a **package** statement or refer to the variable with its full name.

The symbol table is the list of active symbols (functions, variables, objects) within a package. Each package has its own symbol table, and with some exceptions, all the identifiers starting with letters or underscores are stored within the corresponding symbol table for each package. This means that all other identifiers, including all of the special punctuation-only variables, such as **$_**, are stored within the **main** package. Other identifiers that are forced to be within the **main** package include **STDIN**, **STDOUT**, **STDERR**, **ARGV**, **ARGVOUT**, **ENV**, **INC**, and **SIG**.

Finally, if you name any package with a name matching one of the pattern operators (**m//**, **s///**, **y///**, or **tr///**), you cannot use the qualified form of an identifier as a filehandle, as it will be interpreted as a pattern match, substitution, or translation.

Signals also need special care: when specifying a signal handler, you should ideally qualify the signal handler completely. See Chapter 14 for more information on specifying signal handlers.

Package Symbol Tables

The symbol table for a package can be accessed as a hash. For example, the **main** package's symbol table can be accessed as **%main::** or, more simply, as **%::**. Likewise, symbol tables for other packages are **%MyMathLib::**. The format is hierarchical, so that symbol tables can be traversed using standard Perl code. The **main** symbol table includes a reference to all the other top-level symbol tables, so the preceding nested example could be accessed as **%main::Math::Base**.

The keys of each symbol hash are the identifiers of the symbols for the specified package; the values are the corresponding typeglob values. This explains the use of a typeglob, which is really just accessing the value in the hash for the corresponding key from the symbol table. The following code prints out the symbol table for the **main** package:

```
foreach $symname (sort keys  %main::)
{
    local *symbol = $main::{$symname};
    print "\$$symname is defined\n" if defined $symbol;
    print "\@$symname is defined\n" if defined @symbol;
    print "\%$symname is defined\n" if defined %symbol;
}
```

You can also use the symbol table to define static scalars by assigning a value to a typeglob:

```
*C = 299792458;
```

You now cannot modify **$C**, the speed of light, since the variable **$C** does not really exist—Perl is just allowing us to access a typeglob as a scalar value. Note that uppercase is used for the constant, even though normally the speed of light is specified as "c." This is a convention in Perl. Constants and filehandles are typically in uppercase, variables and functions are lowercase, and package names are specified in title case. Although this is convention, Perl doesn't really care!

Special Blocks

Perl has reserved a number of specially named blocks that provide some additional control over the execution of your script—although these are more complex topics, we'll cover them here, as their execution will help you to understand how modules and importing and exporting objects works.

The four blocks are **BEGIN**, **CHECK**, **INIT**, and **END**, and they are executed in that order. When you execute a Perl script, any **BEGIN** blocks are executed during the parsing process—that is, as soon as the statements within a **BEGIN** block have been parsed and verified. The **CHECK** block is executed as soon as the parsing and compilation stages have been completed, but before the actual execution of the script. The **INIT** block runs before the main flow of the program starts. The **END** blocks execute when the program terminates.

If you specify more than one of these blocks in your script, they are executed in the order in which they are parsed in the case of **BEGIN** and **CHECK**, and in reverse order in the case of **INIT** and **END**, and still in the overall order given above. You can see this better using a simple script:

```
print "Now in the main script\n";
die "Script abnormally terminated!\n";
CHECK { print "1st declared CHECK block\n" }
CHECK { print "2nd declared CHECK block\n" }
END { print "1st declared END block\n" }
BEGIN { print "1st declared BEGIN block\n" }
INIT { print "1st declared INIT block\n" }
BEGIN { print "2nd declared BEGIN block\n" }
END { print "2nd declared END block\n" }
INIT { print "2nd declared INIT block\n" }
```

When executed, the script generates the following:

```
1st declared BEGIN block
2nd declared BEGIN block
2nd declared CHECK block
```

```
1st declared CHECK block
1st declared INIT block
2nd declared INIT block
Now in the main script
Script abnormally terminated!
2nd declared END block
1st declared END block
```

Note that the execution also applies to individual packages and modules. Here, the **BEGIN** and **END** blocks can act as initializers and finalizers for the package. They are defined like this:

```
BEGIN { print "Start!\n" };
END   { print "End!\n"   };
```

A **BEGIN** block is executed as soon as possible after it has been defined. This overrides the parsing of the rest of the package. You can have multiple **BEGIN** blocks that are executed in the order they were defined. You can use a **BEGIN** block to import functions and values from other modules so that the objects required by the rest of the package are defined at the point the block is parsed. This can be especially useful if you are using the function prototyping and declarations seen earlier in this chapter. If a function has been defined such that it is interpreted as an operator, or with a specific prototyping format, then it will need to exist before Perl interprets the rest of the package.

An **END** routine is the opposite: it is executed as late as possible. In practice, this means that an **END** block is executed at the point the parser and interpreter are about to exit to the calling process. This is the case, even if the reason for the failure is a **die** function or the result of an exception raised due to the nonexistence of a required system call. You can use this facility to help print error messages or close filehandles cleanly in the event of an error. Of course, in a well-written Perl script, you should be able to find cleaner ways of handling exceptions and errors.

END blocks are executed in reverse order—that is, the last **END** block specified will be the first to be executed. The following program doesn't do quite what we want, although it's pretty close:

```
BEGIN { print "Eanie\n" }
die "Meanie\n";
END { print "Miney\n" }
END { print "Mo\n" }
```

You should not assume that the main program code has been executed in an **END** block. Care is needed to ensure you don't try to use a variable or function in an **END** block that has not otherwise been defined, although you should be doing this kind of checking in the main body of the script anyway.

Modules

Modules are the loadable libraries of the Perl world. A Perl module is generally just another Perl source file that defines a number of functions and/or variables, although it can also be an interface to an external C library. Modules are the main way for supporting additional functionality in your Perl scripts and for properly dividing up your module into a reusable format. For example, we can import the **CGI** module, which supports a range of web-related functions and tools using

```
use CGI;
```

What actually happens is that during the compilation stage, when Perl sees **require** or **use**, it looks for a file called CGI.pm, first in the current directory, and then in the library directories for the current Perl interpreter (as defined in **@INC**). As soon as it finds the module, it imports the module source and then parses that as part of the main script. We don't need to worry about naming conflicts, because the **package** system explained earlier in the chapter will be able to determine the difference between different objects.

Creating Modules

At the simplest level, a module is just another name for a package that has been moved to a separate file with the same name as the package, and that has the extension .pm attached. Perl doesn't actually know how to magically import the functions defined within the module file; for that we need to use the **Exporter** module, which supplies the necessary intelligence for us.

To explain the process, let's look at a very simple module called **MyMathLib**, which is contained in the file MyMathLib.pm:

```
package MyMathLib;          # Define the package (and module) name
require Exporter;           # Import the functions required to export
                            # functions from our own module
@ISA      = qw/Exporter/;   # Set the inheritance tree so that Perl can
                            # find the function required
@EXPORT   = qw/add/;        # Specify the functions we want to export

sub add                     # The function we want to export
```

```
{
    $_[0]+$_[1];
}

1;                          # Modules must return a true value
```

The important parts here are the **package** line, the **Exporter** module, the **@EXPORT** array, and the final **1;** line.

The **package** definition tells Perl what package the functions we are defining should be belong to. This is required—Perl expects to find the package **MyMathLib** in the file MyMathLib.pm—and it also helps to protect the name spaces between the entities you've defined in your module and those used in your scripts.

The **Exporter** module provides the **import** function, which exposes the list of functions that you specify in **@EXPORT** so that they exist within the name space of the caller. For example, in the script

```
use MyMathLib;
print add(1,2);
```

you can use the **add** function without qualifying it with its full name because the **import** function has made the **add** function available within the **main** name space—see the section on "Packages" earlier in this chapter for more information on packages and name spaces.

The **1;** in the module file is simply used as a return value. The **use** keyword checks when parsing the module to ensure that the return value is true as an indication of whether the module loaded correctly. In most instances, you'll always use a simple value like this to show success, but more advanced uses can use this value to indicate an error somewhere else. For example, a module that relies on a set of configuration files might return false if the files couldn't be found—the **use** statement would identify the error and the execution of your script would terminate because of this.

The Exporter Module

The **Exporter** module supplies the **import** function required by the **use** statement to import functions. The absolute minimum required at the top of your module is this:

```
package ModuleName;
require Exporter;
@ISA = qw(Exporter);
```

The package name should reflect the module's file name—remember that the module **MyGroup::MyModule** equates to a file name of MyGroup/MyModule.pm. The remaining statements import the **Exporter** module, and the **@ISA** array defines the inheritance—it's inheritance that allows the **import** module in **Exporter** to be inherited by the module you are creating.

The **Exporter** module then uses the values in **@EXPORT**, **@EXPORT_OK**, **@EXPORT_FAIL**, and **%EXPORT_TAGS** to determine which objects should or should not be exported from the module.

The **@EXPORT** array should be used to list the objects that should be exported by default from the module. The **@EXPORT_OK** array should list the objects that can be exported if they have been specifically requested. For example, this:

```
use MyModule qw/process regurgitate/;
```

would cause **MyModule** to only export the **process** and **regurgitate** subroutines. You can think of this in a similar way to the public and private methods in object-oriented programming— although Perl's OOP system works slightly differently.

The **%EXPORT_TAGS** is a hash that contains a series of import sets; for example, the definition

```
%EXPORT_TAGS = ('standard' => [process, regurgitate],
                'processing' => [process, parse]);
```

can be used from a caller with

```
use MyModule qw/:standard :processing/;
```

Finally, if you don't want any specific objects to be exported, then the naming convention is to use a preceding underscore, but this is not actually enforced—it's still possible to import an object with that prefix. You can disable this ability by defining those objects within the **@EXPORT_FAIL** array—the **Exporter** will **die** if any objects that appear in this array are explicitly requested.

Comparing use and require

When you import a module, you can use one of two keywords: **use** or **require**. We'll look in more detail at their differences in a moment, but in essence, a **require** statement imports the functions and objects only within their defined packages. The **use** keyword, on the other hand, imports the functions and objects so they are available to the current package as if they had been defined globally.

require

The format of the **require** statement is

```
require Module;
```

The specified module is searched for in the directories defined in **@INC**, looking for a file with the specified name and an extension of .pm. You can also specify the full file name (and path, if necessary) by inserting the file name in single quotes:

```
require 'Fcntl.pl';
```

Furthermore, the **require** function can be used to specify that a particular minimum version of Perl is required. For example, to specify a minimum version of 5.003:

```
require 5.003;
```

This can be especially useful if a module or script you have written requires the features or functions of a specific version of Perl. If the specification does not match the version of Perl being used to execute the script, it will fail at compilation time.

use

The **use** keyword accepts one of two forms:

```
use Module;
```

and

```
use Module LIST;
```

The first format imports all of the symbols that have been specified in the **@EXPORT** array. You can therefore think of the **@EXPORT** array as listing the symbols that should be exported by default. The **@EXPORT_OK** array lists the additional symbols that can only be exported when the user requests them via the second form. For example, the line

```
use MyMathLib qw/add square/;
```

would cause only the **add** and **square** functions to be exported from the **MyMathLib** module.

The Difference Between use and require

What actually happens when you use the **use** statement is that Perl calls the **import** method defined in the specified module. If one has not been defined, the **Exporter** module supplies this method for you. This means that the process you would need to follow in order to support this ability without the **use** statement would look something like this:

```
BEGIN
{
    require "Module.pm";
    Module->import();
}
```

You could, for example, request no functions from the module using

```
use MyMathLib ();
```

which is, in fact, identical to

```
BEGIN { require MyMathLib; }
```

You can see from the preceding example the important difference: the **require** statement reads in the specified module, but it does not call the **import** method. This has the effect that symbols defined within another package do not update the current package's symbol table. For example,

```
require Cwd;
$pwd = Cwd::getcwd();
```

as opposed to

```
use Cwd;
$pwd = getcwd();
```

One other significant difference between **require** and **use** is that **use** statements are interpreted and executed at the time the file is parsed, but **require** statements import modules at run time, which means you can supply a variable name to a **require** statement based on other elements of your program. This can be useful for dynamically selecting a different module to import, outside of the usual dynamic loading capabilities of the Perl module system.

The dynamic loading and autoloading features are generally used when you are extending Perl using external code written in C or Pascal or even Java. It's normally up to the module you import to autoload the external modules it requires. We'll look again at the autoloading process when we look at extending and embedding Perl in Chapter 20.

You'll also notice from many of the latter examples that we are not specifying the full file name. By specifying a file name, we imply the full name and location of the file. If you do not specify the name in quotes, and you leave off the extension, both **require** and **use** imply the .pm extension. The path used to determine the location of the files imported this way is the **@INC** array. This can be updated to allow other paths to be taken into account. The paths specified are the top directories. You can further subdivide modules into other subdirectories for clarity, in which case you must specify the relative pathname for the module you want to import, using the double-colon notation in place of your operating system's pathname separator. For example,

```
use File::Basename;
```

actually imports the **File/Basename.pm** module on a Unix machine.

The **use** function also supports a number of pragmas—small modules (typically with lowercase names) that control the execution and parsing of a Perl script. For example, pragmas exist to switch on warnings or change the contents of the **@INC** array. Generally, pragmas affect the entire execution of a script, but see Chapter 19 for full details.

no

The **no** statement is the complete opposite of the **use** statement. It "unimports" meanings that have been imported via the **use** statement. It does this by calling a corresponding **unimport** method, if one has been defined, for a specified module. If no **unimport** method has been defined, Perl quits with a fatal error. Generally, **no** is only really required to switch off compiler pragmas, and we'll look at the use of the function in Chapter 18.

do

The **do** statement is rather like a cross between **eval** and the **require** and **use** functions, although it is neither as practical nor user friendly as any of those functions. The format for the command is

```
do EXPR
```

where **EXPR** is the name of a file to be executed. The return value is taken as the evaluated value of the last statement in the file. If the file is not in the current directory, then the paths specified in the **@INC** array are searched instead.

The main difference between **do** and **require** is that the file specified by **do** will be executed each time it is called. The **require** function (and **use**), on the other hand, keeps track of the files it has imported and will only import a file once.

Scope

When you create a variable, it's created within the scope of the current package. In the case of the **main** package, it means that you are creating a "global" variable. Although packages allow you to split up the global variables that you create into different sections, many programs would be difficult to work with if we had to keep giving unique names to all the variables we used.

For that reason, Perl also allows us to create variables that are lexically scoped— that is, they are declared as existing only until the end of the innermost enclosing scope, which is either a block, a file, or an **eval** statement. In fact, Perl supports three scoping declarations that enable us to create private variables (using **my**), selectively global variables (using **our**), and temporary copies of selected global variables (using **local**).

At the simplest level, you just prefix the variable with the declaration keyword:

```
my $var;
our $var;
local $var;
```

If you want to specify more than one variable, then supply the names in parentheses,

```
my ($var, @var, %var);
```

and if you want to assign a value as well,

```
my ($var, $string) = (1,'hello');
```

If you forget to use parentheses, you get some strange effects:

```
my $var, $string = 1,'hello';
```

The preceding line actually works like this:

```
my $var;
$string = 1;
'hello';
```

If you have warnings switched on, then you'll get an error, because the **'hello'**
is actually interpreted in a void context (since it doesn't actually do anything).

In general, you'll see and use **my** more than other declarations, because it generally
does what you expect when you declare variables in this way. The **our** declaration is a
relatively new invention (it was only introduced in Perl 5.6), and it allows you to declare
a variable as being global and potentially usable by any other subroutine defined in your
script. Both **my** and **our** are examples of lexically scoped variables—the difference is in
the level at which the lexical scope is applied.

The **local** variable is really a dynamically scoped variable—it effectively creates a
copy of a global variable within the current scope. It operates just like a lexically scoped
variable; its effects disappear when the variable goes out of the current scope, with the
variable returning to its original value instead of simply disappearing.

We'll look at the specific effects of each declaration in the following sections.

Effects of my

The **my** keyword declares a variable to be scoped within the current block. For the
duration of the block, the new variable will take precedence over any previously
scoped variable. When the block ends, the variable goes out of scope. You can easily
demonstrate this with this script:

```
my $string = "We are the world";
print "$string\n";
myfunction();
print "$string\n";

sub myfunction
{
    my $string = "We are the function";
    print "$string\n";
    mysub();
}

sub mysub
{
    print "$string\n";
}
```

This generates

```
We are the world
We are the function
We are the world
We are the world
```

The **my** declaration does exactly what you expect—it defines a variable as existing only within the current block (and is therefore not available to any functions called from within that block). The moment the block terminates, the variable effectively disappears from view—you can't access a variable declared with **my** from outside of the block within which it's defined. This means that from outside of a function, you can't access a variable declared with **my** within that function.

It also means that variables declared with **my** within a module are not accessible outside of that module (since the module is a single block), even when called upon explicitly by using **$MyModule::string**. You also can't export a variable declared with **my** outside of a module; for that you'll need to use the **vars** pragma or, with Perl 5.6 or later, use the **our** keyword to declare a global variable and then place the full name in **@EXPORT** or **@EXPORT_OK**.

Effects of local

When using **local** on a global variable, the variable is given a temporary value each time the **local** statement is executed. The temporary value lasts only for the duration of the block. However, the use of **local** does not affect its accessibility—it's still a global variable; it just has a temporary value while it's being used within that block. For example,

```
{
    local $var = 'newvalue';
    myfunc();
}
```

can be thought of as

```
{
    $oldvalue = $var;
    $var = 'newvalue';
    myfunc();
```

```
}
continue
{
    $var = $oldvalue;
}
```

except that the **continue** block is executed however the block exits, including through a **return**.

Note that the value of a variable modified using **local** is consistent for all functions called from the block in which the variable has been localized. In the preceding examples, the **myfunc** function will access the temporary value of **$var** when called from within that block, but the normal value when outside of it.

Don't use **local** on an exported module variable—the value of the variable will never change.

Effects of our

The **our** keyword (introduced in Perl 5.6) declares a variable to be global, effectively making it the complete opposite of **my**. For example,

```
our $string = "We are the world";
print "$string\n";
myfunction();
print "$string\n";

sub myfunction
{
    our $string = "We are the function";
    print "$string\n";
}
```

produces

```
We are the world
We are the function
We are the function
```

Using **our** within a function, or indeed any form of nesting within any block, on the same variable has no effect; you are *always* referring to the same global variable. The use of **our** on a variable declared with **my** will have no effect.

Scope Within Loops

There is a slightly special case when declaring a variable in a loop statement. In the fragment,

```
foreach my $key (sort keys %hash)
{
...
}
```

the **$key** variable is lexically defined for the duration of the entire statement, which means that it's accessible within the block that makes up the loop (including any **continue** block in a **while** or other statement), but it immediately disappears when the loop terminates.

However, be careful where you define the variable. In the fragment,

```
do {
    my $var = 1;
} while ($var);
```

the **$var** used in the test has no value—only the **$var** in the block has a value.

Autoloading

There are times when what you really want to do is use a subroutine that hasn't been defined. If a subroutine with the magic name **AUTOLOAD** has been defined within a package, then any unknown subroutine calls are sent to this subroutine. The **AUTOLOAD** subroutine is called with all the same arguments as the unknown routine, and the fully qualified subroutine name is placed into the **$AUTOLOAD** variable.

This is traditionally used in combination with the **AutoSplit** module to automatically load functions from external script files where each file contains a single subroutine.

What actually happens is that the **AUTOLOAD** subroutine uses **do, require,** or **eval** to import and parse the external function into the current name space. The **AUTOLOAD** subroutine then calls the special format of the **goto** function to make Perl (and the auto-loaded subroutine) think that it was the function that loaded after all.

This is effectively identical to the process used to load external C functions into the current name space, but this is called dynamic loading and is handled by the **DynaLoader** module. However, the **DynaLoader** imports whole function suites, not single functions, and is generally used to import entire modules (and even base classes) at one time.

The **AUTOLOAD** module can also be used directly within a Perl script to add blanket functionality to a script without requiring you to create many subroutines. Here's an example that employs the **AUTOLOAD** routine as a way of introducing constants looked up from a hash:

```
BEGIN
{
    $constants{"PI"} = 3.141592654;
}

use subs keys %constants;
print "The value of PI is ",PI;

sub AUTOLOAD
{
    my $constant = $AUTOLOAD;
    $constant =~ s/.*:://;
    return $constants{"$constant"};
}
```

We actually use a few tricks here. First of all, we create the **%constants** hash table in a **BEGIN** block to ensure it's defined as early as possible. The main reason for this is that we need to use the keys of this hash as the argument to the **use subs** pragma in order to predeclare the subroutines (or in this case, constants) that we want to use. By predeclaring them, we set up Perl to allow us to use the "functions" without requiring parentheses. See Chapter 16 for more details on this pragma.

Finally, we use the **AUTOLOAD** subroutine to look up the value in the **%constants** hash and return the value.

The
Complete
Reference

Chapter 7

Working with Files

It is almost impossible to make good use of a programming language without at some point having to access information from or about files. Accessing the information in a file is relatively easy, but unless you know the exact name of the file, you are basically stuck. Perl supports a number of ways of extracting the list of files, either by using the familiar wildcard operations that you use within a shell, or by reading individual file names directly from the directory.

You can also glean more information about the file that you are using. You may need to find out the file size or perhaps the file permissions to test whether you can access a file. We will also take a look in this chapter at ways of controlling files, including deleting files, and creating and accessing symbolic and hard links.

It is inevitable that at some point you will need to communicate with the outside world. We will consider three basic outside influences in this chapter: screen, keyboard, and files. In fact, Perl works much like many other languages. The default input and output devices are the screen and the keyboard, but these devices can also be referenced via files.

Unlike C, Perl uses, within reason, the same set of functions for communicating with the terminal, keyboard, pipes (external commands or command input), network sockets, and files. This creates less confusion while you are working and helps optimize the language. This means that many of the functions we will look at can be used not only for accessing files but also for accessing any kind of external data stream outside of the main Perl script.

The basics of handling files are simple: you associate a *filehandle* with an external entity (usually a file) and then use a variety of operators and functions within Perl to read and update the data stored within the data stream associated with the filehandle. This is similar to other languages that use the same structure. In C, for example, a **FILE** structure contains all the information on a data stream and acts as the reference point for using the data stored within that stream.

Using files and filehandles effectively, particularly when using network sockets or providing an interactive user interface, also requires more complex controls on the capabilities and data handling of individual filehandles. This can be achieved using **fcntl** and **ioctl**—two functions that provide an interface to the underlying operating system equivalents. Furthermore, in a complex installation you need to be able to handle data I/O between multiple files simultaneously. This can be achieved using a simple round-robin approach, but a more reliable and efficient method is to use the **select** function, which is examined in some detail in this chapter.

Caution   *All of the functions in this chapter are derived or descended from their operating system equivalents. It is vital that you check the return values of all the functions in this chapter, especially those that modify the execution environment for the script, such as **chdir** and **unlink**. In most cases, if there is an error, the error string is stored in the **$!** variable, which should be used with the **die** or **warn** function to report the error to the user. See Chapter 9 for more information on using these functions.*

Filehandles

A filehandle is a named internal Perl structure that associates a physical file with a name. A filehandle can be reused. It is not permanently attached to a single file, nor is it permanently related to a particular file name. The name of the filehandle and the name of the file are not related.

As far as Perl is concerned, all operating systems support three basic filehandles—**STDIN**, **STDOUT**, and **STDERR**. The exact interpretation of the filehandle and the device or file it is associated with depend on the OS and the Perl implementation. Table 7-1 shows the relationship between Perl filehandles and the underlying C file descriptors.

Note *Perl also supports a number of standard filehandles that provide access to files while in special command line modes (see Chapter 15), and when accessing information appended to a Perl script. See the end of Chapter 4 for a list of standard variables and filehandles.*

All filehandles are capable of read/write access, so you can read from and update any file or device associated with a filehandle. However, when you associate a filehandle, you can specify the mode in which the filehandle is opened. This option prevents you from accidentally updating or overwriting information in a file that you only wanted to read. You can see from Table 7-1 the access modes for the standard filehandles.

All filehandles are by default buffered on both input and output. In most cases, this helps to improve performance by reading more than is needed from the physical device, or by block writing to a physical device. Information is buffered on a block-by-block basis (the underlying OS defines the block size). The only exception to this rule is **STDOUT**, which is buffered on a line basis: appending the newline character to a printed string will automatically flush the buffer. You can switch the buffering for the currently selected filehandle by setting the value of the $| variable to any value other

Perl Filehandle	C File Descriptor	Associated Device	Access Mode
STDIN	0	Keyboard/terminal	Write-only
STDOUT	1	Monitor/terminal	Read-only
STDERR	2	Monitor/terminal	Write-only

Table 7-1. *Standard Perl Filehandles*

than zero. It's also possible to set the buffering on other files if you use the **IO::Handle** module with the **autoflush** method. For example, the following code turns buffering off for the **DOOR** filehandle:

```
use IO::Handle;
open(DOOR,"<file.in") or die "Couldn't open file";
autoflush DOOR 1;
```

To switch it back on again:

```
autoflush DOOR 0;
```

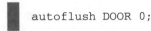

*In the preceding example, the arguments to **open** are placed in parentheses to ensure that the **or** operator checks the entire statement, not the value of the file name. See "Error Handling" in Chapter 9 for more information on error handling skills.*

A filehandle can be referred to by either a static token or an expression. If an expression is specified, then the value of the expression is used as the filehandle name. Note that a filehandle token does not have a special preceding character, as with a variable, and the name is written in uppercase. This is to help separate a filehandle from a normal variable. If the filehandle is referred to by an expression, then the result of the expression is used as the filehandle name.

The only limitation with a filehandle is that it cannot be supplied directly to a user-defined function. In this instance you must use a *typeglob*. This is a special type of identifier that enables you to refer to different types of variables by prefixing the name with an asterisk. This allows a typeglob to refer to all, or any, of **$name**, **@name**, **%name**, or **name** with ***name**. How the typeglob is used, and therefore which interpretation is employed, is at the discretion of the expression or statement using the typeglob. See Chapter 6 for more information on the symbol table and the use of typeglobs in functions.

Opening and Closing Files

A fundamental part of the Perl language is its ability to read and process file data very quickly. In Chapter 1 we saw how the historical development of Perl was geared toward text processing long before it gained the general-purpose status it holds now.

All file data is exchanged through the use of a filehandle, which associates an external data source (a file, network socket, external program, pipe) with an internal data structure (the filehandle). The method with which you associate the filehandle varies depending on the type of external data source, although many of the functions used to access the data available with the filehandle are the same. For files, you use the **open** function to open ordinary files and the **sysopen** function to handle more complex opening procedures. The **close** function is used to close any open filehandle, regardless of how it was opened.

open

The **open** function is almost certainly one of the most complicated to understand when you first approach the Perl language. Once grasped, however, it becomes easy and almost second nature in use, often making the methods employed in other languages seem clumsy and constricting.

```
open FILEHANDLE, EXPR
open FILEHANDLE
```

The first form is the one used most often. The **FILEHANDLE** is a token name that allows you to refer to a file with a specific name. A **FILEHANDLE** in any function can alternatively be an expression, which is evaluated; the value being used as the filehandle name. If the expression supplied does not evaluate to a suitable value, Perl does not make one up for you. You must ensure, therefore, that the expression you supply in place of **FILEHANDLE** evaluates to something identifiable.

The **EXPR** is more complex. Perl takes the value supplied, interpolates the string where necessary, and then strips any leading or trailing white space. The string is then examined for special characters at the start and end of the string that define the mode and type of file to be opened.

The basic operators are the greater-than/less-than signs. The syntax is taken from the shell, which uses a less-than sign to pass file contents to the standard input of a command. Within Perl, this translates to this:

```
open(DATA, "<file.txt");
```

The **EXPR** for the function shows that the file is being opened read-only. If you want to write to a file, you use the greater-than sign:

```
open(DATA, ">file.txt");
```

This example actually truncates (empties) the file before opening it for writing, which may not be the desired effect. If you want to open a file for reading and writing, you can put a plus sign before the > or < characters.

For example, to open a file for updating without truncating it:

```
open(DATA, "+<file.txt");
```

To truncate the file first:

```
open DATA, "+>file.txt" or die "Couldn't open file file.txt, $!";
```

Note that in the preceding example I've combined the **open** function with the **die** function to report an error if the **open** failed. Nearly all functions within Perl return true (a value greater than zero) if the function was a success, so you can easily place it within a test or with the **warn** or **die** functions to report an errors—see Chapter 9 for more information on error trapping in Perl. So, in this example, if the **open** function returns true, then the **die** function will not be executed. However, if it returns **false** (zero), indicating a failure, then the **die** function will be executed. This is quicker and significantly more efficient than using **if** statements to test the success of functions.

This also demonstrates a basic principle of any programming: you must be able to track and trace errors. Perl has a simple but effective method of error checking that we'll see in various examples throughout the rest of the book. In this case, not being able to open a file is a serious problem, so there is little point in continuing.

One final item to mention for this example is that I've left out the parentheses (which is valid in Perl; they are optional for all function arguments, but essential for other lists) and used **or** as the operator, which checks the function's success. Using **or** is safe in a list context because it has a lower precedence than the list supplied to the **open** function. If you wanted to use the | | operator, you would have to enclose the **open** statement in parentheses; otherwise, the operator would act on the **EXPR** and **die** function:

```
open(DATA,"+>file.txt") || die "Couldn't open file file.txt, $!";
```

In both of the previous cases, the file has been opened for updating, but the file pointer that describes the current position within the file is at the start of the file. If you want to append, you can also use shell-style operators:

```
open(DATA, ">>file.txt");
```

A double >> opens the file for appending, placing the file pointer at the end, so that you can immediately start appending information. However, you can't read from it unless you also place a plus sign in front of it:

```
open(DATA, "+>>file.txt");
```

The list of tricks for opening files does not end there. Let's imagine a situation in which you need to read the contents of a compressed file within a script. The normal method would be to use a function to call an external program that uncompresses the file so that you can read it, before recompressing the file once you finish. But this is very time consuming, and on systems that have limited resources (CPU and disk space), it is extremely wasteful.

With Perl, you can open a filehandle that is associated with the output of an external command. The **gzcat** function decompresses Gzipped files on the fly, sending the output to the commands stdout without actually decompressing the file to its full size. You can use Perl to read in this information directly by using a pipe at the end of the **EXPR**:

```
open(GZDATA, "gzcat file.gz|");
```

You can now use one of the many functions that read from a filehandle to process the data being decompressed on the fly. You haven't created a temporary file, nor will you have to recompress the data once you've finished reading it. The opposite is also true. So you could, for example, send an email message by using the **mail** program and opening a filehandle to which you can write the email message:

```
open(EMAIL, "|mail mc@mcwords.com");
```

The only limitation to this is that you cannot open an external program for both reading and writing; the pipes work only one way—read when at the end, write when at the start.

You can also open **STDIN** and **STDOUT** directly by specifying "–" and ">–," respectively.

The next forms allow you to duplicate a filehandle. This is again similar to the shell tradition of being able to redirect information not to just one file, but to multiple files. The duplication can be specified by the existing filehandle name:

```
open(SECOUT,">&STDOUT");
```

This is especially useful if you want to save the information that would normally be printed to **STDOUT** and **STDERR**. You duplicate the two standard filehandles to new filehandles. You can then respecify the destination for **STDOUT** and **STDERR**, perhaps to an external log file. This will force all output and errors to the new location, without losing the ability to report information to the real standard output and error using the duplicated filehandles. For example:

```
open(SECOUT,">&STDOUT");
open(SECERR,">&STDERR");
open(STDOUT,">stdlog.txt");
open(STDERR,">stderr.txt");
```

In the preceding example, all standard prints will go to the stdlog.txt file, while errors will go to stderr.txt. If you needed to, however, you could still report to the real standard output and error by using the **SECOUT** and **SECERR** filehandles.

The penultimate form of the **open** function emulates the functionality of the **fdopen** system function. It associates a filehandle with a specific file descriptor number. For example, the following line opens **STDIN** by file descriptor:

```
open(SECIN,"<&=1");
```

The final two formats are really extensions of the earlier pipe expressions. Instead of starting a new program from the current script, an explicit **fork** is done, creating a new child process. The return value of **open** is the process ID of the child. The filehandle is normal as far as the parent is concerned. However, the input and output to the parent filehandle is piped to the **STDOUT** or **STDIN**, respectively, of the child.

There is little advantage in this method of using a piped command, except that it can be useful in secure situations where you want to control the method used to execute the external command. For example, the earlier **gzcat** example could be rewritten as

```
open(GZDATA,"-|") or exec 'gzcat', 'file.gz';
```

and the email example could be written as

```
open(EMAIL, "|-") or exec 'mail' 'mc@mcwords.com';
```

Note that in both cases communication is still one way: you can still only read from a "-|"-based **open**.

The full list of available expressions for opening files is shown in Table 7-2.

Expression	Result
"filename"	Opens the file for reading only.
"<filename"	Opens the file for reading only.
">filename"	Truncates and opens the file for writing.
"+<filename"	Opens the file for reading and writing.
"+>filename"	Truncates and opens the file for reading and writing.
" | command"	Runs the command and pipes the output to the filehandle.
"command | "	Pipes the output from the filehandle to the input of command.
"-"	Opens **STDIN**.
">-"	Opens **STDOUT**.
"<&FILEHANDLE"	Duplicates specified **FILEHANDLE** or file descriptor if numeric, for reading.
">&FILEHANDLE"	Duplicates specified **FILEHANDLE** or file descriptor if numeric, for writing.
"<&=N"	Opens the file descriptor matching **N**, essentially identical to C's **fdopen()**.
" |-" and "-| "	Opens a pipe to a forked command.

Table 7-2.   *Options for Opening Files*

Note that you need to use the **binmode** function under some systems (notably Windows) to stop Perl from automatically implying input line processing on the file. See "binmode" later in this chapter, and Chapter 24 for more information.

File Disciplines

Perl v5.6 or above allows you to specify the encoding format to be used when reading and writing to and from a filehandle by supplying the format as part of the **EXPR** argument, and supplying the name of the file to be opened in **LIST**, making a three-argument form of the **open** function. To specify the encoding formation, you must supply one of the modes shown in Table 7-3.

Discipline	Meaning
:raw	Binary mode—no line input processing—Equivalent to calling **binmode**.
:text	Text processing—the basic mode supported by versions prior to v5.6.
:def	Default—as declared by the **use open** pragma.
:latin1	Use the ISO-8859-1 format.
:lctype	Use the **LC_CTYPE** format.
:utf8	Use the **UTF-8** (unicode) format.
:utf16	Use the **UTF-16** (unicode) format.
:utf32	Use the **UTF-32** (unicode) format.
:uni	Intuit Unicode (**UTF-***) format.
:any	Intuit **Unicode/Latin1/LC_CTYPE**
:xml	Use the file-specified encoding format.
:crlf	Intuit newlines.
:para	Paragraph mode.
:slurp	Slurp mode.

Table 7-3.   *File Format Encoding Disciplines*

Note   *The exact list of modes supported is dependent on the support in the current release of Perl. Check the Perl documentation for more information on the current list.*

For example, we could open a file that will be used in paragraph mode and interpret carriage returns and line feeds as a single newline by using

```
open(FILE, "<:para:crlf", 'myfile');
```

The default mode (**:def**) is to use **:text**, but you can change the default by using the **open** pragma:

```
use open IN => ":any", OUT => "utf8";
```

sysopen

The **sysopen** function is similar to the main **open** function, except that it uses the system **open()** function, using the parameters supplied to it as the parameters for the system function:

```
sysopen FILEHANDLE, FILENAME, MODE, PERMS
sysopen FILEHANDLE, FILENAME, MODE
```

There are some differences between the **sysopen** and **open** functions. The **FILENAME** argument is not interpreted by **sysopen**. The special codes used with **open** are interpreted as elements of the file name. In essence, the **FILENAME** argument is taken literally. This allows you to take information from a user that specifies the full pathname to a file and use it directly without requiring variable interpolation.

Because of this difference, the format in which a file is opened is taken from **MODE**. The value of **MODE** is a bitset using the constants defined in the system's fcntl.h header file. Perl can either use the numbers directly or use word equivalents if the standard **Fcntl** module has been imported. Because it's a bitset, you'll need to **OR** the values together to produce the final mode. There are some standard values if you want to remain completely portable. A **MODE** of zero opens the file read-only; one, write-only; and two, read/write. These correspond to the constants **O_RDONLY**, **O_WRONLY**, and **O_RDWR**, which are defined in the **Fcntl** module.

Two other standard constants are **O_CREAT**, which creates a file if it does not already exist, and **O_TRUNC**, which truncates a file before it is read or written.

For example, to open a file for updating, emulating the **"+<filename"** format from **open**,

```
sysopen(DATA, "file.txt", O_RDWR);
```

or to truncate the file before updating,

```
sysopen(DATA, "file.txt", O_RDWR|O_TRUNC);
```

The **PERMS** argument specifies the file permissions for the file specified if it has to be created (provided **O_CREAT** has been specified in **MODE**). This should be specified in standard octal notation, and Perl uses a default of **0x666** if **PERMS** are not defined. The values are modified according to your current **umask** if applicable.

close

To close a filehandle, and therefore disassociate the filehandle from the corresponding file, you use the **close** function. This flushes the filehandle's buffers and closes the system's file descriptor.

```
close FILEHANDLE
close
```

If no **FILEHANDLE** is specified, then it closes the currently selected filehandle. It returns **true** only if it could successfully flush the buffers and close the file. If you have been writing to a file, then **close** can be used as an effective method of checking that information has been successfully written. For example:

```
open(DATA,"+<data.txt") || die "Can't open data.txt";
    #do some work
close(DATA) || die "Couldn't close file properly";
```

However, if you are not worried about the file condition (for example, you are reading from a file), you do not need to close a filehandle before reassigning the filehandle to a new file. The **open** function implicitly closes the previous file before opening the new one, but be warned that there is no way of guaranteeing the file status in this way.

When you open a pipe, either via the **pipe** function or via **open,** the function will return **false** if one of the related system calls fails. Alternatively, if the program called via the pipe returns an exit status other than zero, the return value from the called program is placed in **$?**. In either case, closing a pipe waits for the child process to exit before returning.

Reading and Writing Filehandles

Once you have an open filehandle, you need to be able to read and write information. There are a number of different ways of reading and writing data, although it's likely you'll stick to one or two methods that you find you prefer.

The <FILEHANDLE> operator

The main method of reading the information from an open filehandle is the
<FILEHANDLE> operator. In a scalar context it returns a single line from the
filehandle. For example:

```
print "What is your name?\n";
$name = <STDIN>;
print "Hello $name\n";
```

I've used **STDIN** to demonstrate how to read information from the keyboard or
terminal. Since it is already open, I don't have to worry about opening it beforehand.

When you use the **<FILEHANDLE>** operator in a list context, it returns a list of
lines from the specified filehandle. For example, to import all the lines from a file into
an array:

```
open(DATA,"<import.txt") or die "Can't open data";
@lines = <DATA>;
close(DATA);
```

Note   *Although this operation looks dangerous, Perl lets you go ahead and read the entire
contents of a file into a single variable. Perl dynamically allocates all of the memory
it needs. The only limitation is the amount of physical and virtual memory your
machine has.*

Although it appears that **<FILEHANDLE>** only reads in lines from the file, you can
specify a different record separator using the **$/** or **$INPUT_RECORD_SEPARATOR**
variable. This enables you to read in character-separated data files. On the Mac, for
example, a program called TouchBase Pro supports the export of name and address
information using a record separator with an ASCII value of 252; hence you could use
Perl to import this information using a script like this:

```
open(DATA,"+<tbpro.dat") or die "Can't open tbpro.dat, $!\n";
$/ = "\374";
while(<DATA>)
{
    # Process and update a record
}
```

I've introduced two new things here. One is the use of the special **$!** variable to report the error returned by the **open** function if it fails. The other is that I've enclosed the <FILEHANDLE> operator within a **while** loop. Because the <FILEHANDLE> operator returns a single record in a scalar context, you can use it within a **while** loop to work through a file until the end. Each iteration of the loop will return a new record, and the data is placed into the **$_** default input space.

readline

The **readline** function is actually the internal function used by Perl to handle the <FILEHANDLE> operator function.

```
readline EXPR
```

The only difference is that **readline** accepts an expression directly, instead of the usual filehandle. This means you need to pass a typeglob to the **readline** function, instead of the normal filehandle. However, the same rules apply. The function reads in records from the filehandle using the value of **$/** as a record separator. So to duplicate the **while** statement shown earlier, you would use

```
while(readline *DATA)
```

getc

The **getc** function returns a single character from the specified **FILEHANDLE**, or **STDIN** if none is specified:

```
getc FILEHANDLE
getc
```

If there was an error, or the filehandle is at end of file, then **undef** is returned instead. Unfortunately, because of the buffering on filehandles, you can't use it effectively to get nonbuffered single characters. There is a trick for this, and we'll examine some techniques for this in Chapter 13.

read

Whereas the <FILEHANDLE> operator or **readline** function reads data from a filehandle using the input record separator, the **read** function reads a block of information from the buffered filehandle:

```
read FILEHANDLE, SCALAR, LENGTH, OFFSET
read FILEHANDLE, SCALAR, LENGTH
```

The length of the data read is defined by **LENGTH**, and the data is placed at the start of **SCALAR** if no **OFFSET** is specified. Otherwise data is placed after **OFFSET** bytes in **SCALAR**, allowing you to append information from the filehandle to the existing scalar string. The function returns the number of bytes read on success, zero at end of file, or **undef** if there was an error.

This function can be used to read fixed-length records from files, just like the system **fread()** function on which it is based. However, it must be used in combination with **print** and **seek** to ensure that the buffering system works correctly without overwriting existing data. For a more reliable method of reading and writing fixed-length data, and for the equivalent of the system **read( )** function, see the section "**sysread**" later in the chapter.

print

For all the different methods used for reading information from filehandles, the main function for writing information back is the **print** function. Unlike in C, in Perl **print** is not just used for outputting information to the screen; it can be used to print information to any open filehandle. This is largely due to the way Perl structures its internal data. Because scalars are stored precisely, without using the traditional null termination seen in other languages, it's safe to use the **print** function to output both variable and fixed-length information.

```
print FILEHANDLE LIST
print LIST
print
```

Caution   *The most common error a new Perl programmer makes is to place a comma between* ***FILEHANDLE*** *and* ***LIST***. *This often causes undesired results, because to the* ***print*** *function, the comma makes* ***FILEHANDLE*** *the first element of the* ***LIST*** *to be evaluated and printed.*

The **print** function prints the evaluated value of **LIST** to **FILEHANDLE**, or to the current output filehandle (**STDOUT** by default). For example:

```
print "Hello World!\n";
```

or

```
print "Hello", $name, "\nHow are you today?\n";
```

which prints

```
Hello Martin
How are you today?
```

Note that a **LIST** rather than string interpolation is used in the last example. You can achieve the same result using a here document with the **print** function:

```
print <<EOT;
Hello $name
How are you today?
EOT
```

Because the argument to the **print** function is a **LIST**, the individual elements of the list are evaluated before the results are passed to **print**, which then outputs the values. You need to be careful when incorporating a **print** statement within a larger statement, especially one that itself uses a **LIST** context. For example, the line

```
print "Hello ", print "How are you today?";
```

actually prints

```
How are you today?Hello 1
```

The second element to the **print** function is evaluated first, resulting in the message, and then the resulting list values are output by **print**, which explains the 1—the return value from the nested **print** function.

To get around this problem, you can use parentheses to enclose the list of values for **print**,

```
print("Hello "),print "How are you today?";
```

which correctly outputs the message "Hello How are you today?" However, care should be taken with the parentheses, since you can also get unexpected results:

```
print (1+2)*3, "\n";
```

Only the first calculation is printed, since the parser assumes that the parentheses specify the **LIST** to the **print** function. The remaining values are ignored, since they no longer form part of a valid expression. Perl doesn't produce an error because you are still defining valid Perl code—even though the values of the list are never used.

The correct way to write the preceding equation is

```
print(((1+2)*3),"\n");
```

If no **LIST** is specified, the value of **$_** is printed instead. It returns true (1) on success and zero on failure.

printf

Although **print** is incredibly useful, it suffers from a lack of format. The Perl parser decides how a particular value is printed. This means that floating point numbers are printed as such, when you may wish to restrict the number of places past the decimal point that the number is printed. Alternatively, you may wish to left- rather than right-justify strings when you print them.

```
printf FILEHANDLE FORMAT, LIST
printf FORMAT, LIST
```

Within C, the only function available is **printf**, which uses a formatting string as the first element and formats the remaining values in the list according to the format specified in the format string. Each format is called a *format conversion* and is made up of an initial percent sign, followed by some optional flags, and finally a single character that defines how the value in the list is printed. Each format conversion string relates to the corresponding value in the remainder of the argument list.

For example, the statement

```
printf "%d\n", 3.1415126;
```

only prints the number 3. The "%d" conversion format determines that an integer should be printed. Alternatively, you can define a "currency" format like this,

```
printf "The cost is $%6.2f\n",499;
```

which would print

```
The cost is $499.00
```

The **printf** function accepts the format conversions in Table 7-4.

Format	Result
%%	A percent sign.
%c	A character with the given ASCII code.
%s	A string.
%d	A signed integer (decimal).
%u	An unsigned integer (decimal).
%o	An unsigned integer (octal).
%x	An unsigned integer (hexadecimal).
%X	An unsigned integer (hexadecimal using uppercase characters).
%e	A floating point number (scientific notation).
%E	A floating point number (scientific notation using "E" in place of "e").
%f	A floating point number (fixed decimal notation).
%g	A floating point number (%e of %f notation according to value size).
%G	A floating point number (as %g, but using "E" in place of "e" when appropriate).
%p	A pointer (prints the memory address of the value in hexadecimal).
%b	An unsigned integer in binary.
%n	Stores the number of characters output so far into the next variable in the parameter list.
%i	A synonym for %d.
%D	A synonym for C %ld.
%U	A synonym for C %lu.
%O	A synonym for C %lo.
%F	A synonym for C %f.

Table 7-4.   *Conversion Formats for **printf***

Perl also supports flags that optionally adjust the output format. These are specified between the % and conversion letter, as shown in Table 7-5.

FUNDAMENTALS

Flag	Result
space	Prefix positive number with a space.
+	Prefix positive number with a plus sign.
–	Left-justify within field.
0	Use zeros, not spaces, to right-justify.
#	Prefix non-zero octal with "0" and hexadecimal with "0x."
number	Minimum field width.
.number	Specify precision (number of digits after decimal point) for floating point numbers.
l	Interpret integer as C type "long" or "unsigned long."
h	Interpret integer as C type "short" or "unsigned short."
V	Interpret integer as Perl's standard integer type.
v	Interpret the string as a vector of integers (v-string)—output as a series of numbers separated by dots, or by an arbitrary string supplied by the argument list when the flag is preceded by *.

Table 7-5. *Formatting Flags for **printf** Conversion Formats*

The **v** format is useful for displaying ordinal values of characters within strings. For example:

```
printf "Perl's version is v%vd\n",$^V;
```

Note that the **v** format is only a modifier for the true format in which the information will be output. We can also therefore use it to output the information in decimal, or hex, or even as a series of strings:

```
printf "IP address: %vd\n", $addr;
printf "IPv6 address: %vX\n", $addr;
```

The special * format character tells Perl to accept the corresponding argument as the separating character in lieu of the period, so we could print out an Ethernet address using

```
printf "Ethernet address: %*vX\n", %addr;
```

Nonbuffered I/O

Using the standard **read** and **print** functions can cause problems if you want to access fixed blocks of data that are not separated by a recognizable record or if you want to avoid the problems associated with buffered input. In particular, this can cause delayed reads and writes, and, overall, make the system seem inefficient compared to a direct access system.

To get around this, you can use the **sysread** and **syswrite** functions, which emulate the underlying **fread** and **fwrite** functions. They read and write a block of data of a specified size, ignoring the usual field and record boundaries of the **<FILEHANDLE>** operator and the **read** and **print** functions.

sysread

The **sysread** function reads a fixed number of bytes from a specified filehandle into a scalar variable:

```
sysread FILEHANDLE, SCALAR, LENGTH, OFFSET
sysread FILEHANDLE, SCALAR, LENGTH
```

If **OFFSET** is specified, then data is written to **SCALAR** from **OFFSET** bytes, effectively appending the information from a specific point. If **OFFSET** is negative, data is written from the number of bytes specified counted backward from the end of the string.

The function is based on the system **read()** function, and therefore it avoids the normal buffering supported by standard streams-based **stdio** functions.

syswrite

The **syswrite** function is the exact opposite of **sysread**. It writes a fixed-sized block of information from a scalar to a filehandle:

```
syswrite FILEHANDLE, SCALAR, LENGTH, OFFSET
syswrite FILEHANDLE, SCALAR, LENGTH
```

If **OFFSET** has been specified, then **LENGTH** bytes are read from the **SCALAR** and written to **FILEHANDLE**. If the length of the scalar is less than **LENGTH**, the data is padded with nulls.

In both cases, you should avoid using the **sysread** and **syswrite** functions with the functions that do use buffered I/O, including **print**, **seek**, **tell**, **write**, and especially **read**.

If you use these two functions in combination with the **sysseek** function (discussed later in the chapter), you can update a database with a fixed record size:

```
open(DATABASE,"+<datafile") or die "Can't open datafile";
$recloc = 0;
while(sysread(DATABASE,$record,80))
{
    # Find the record we're looking for
    if ($found)
    {
        last; # quit out of the read loop
    }
    $recloc += 80; #Otherwise, record the next record start
}
# Update the information
sysseek(DATABASE,$recloc,SEEK_SET); #Go back to the start of the record
syswrite(DATABASE,$record,80); #Write record back, replacing previous
```

You could use the **tell** function, since that takes into account the usual buffering; so you have to calculate the file position manually by totaling up the bytes read from the database. If you had used **read**, **seek**, and **print**, then the standard buffering used may have affected the results, probably overwriting information. Using **sysread** guarantees that the information read and written from the filehandle is what you received and supplied.

Locating Your Position Within a File

When reading and writing files using the standard line-based or record-based methods, you are normally processing individual records in sequence—outputting or formatting the results as you read in the entire file in sequence. However, if you are accessing fixed-length information—for example, a database—you are likely to require access to the information in a more random fashion. In order to work correctly, you need to be able to discover your current location and set a new location within the file.

tell

The first requirement is to find your position within a file, which you do using the **tell** function:

```
tell FILEHANDLE
tell
```

This returns the position of the file pointer, in bytes, within **FILEHANDLE** if specified, or the current default selected filehandle if none is specified. The function returns **undef** if there is a problem getting the file position information, since a value of zero could just indicate that you're at the start of the file.

seek

The **seek** function positions the file pointer to the specified number of bytes within a file:

```
seek FILEHANDLE, POSITION, WHENCE
```

The function uses the **fseek** system function, and you have the same ability to position relative to three different points: the start, the end, and the current position. You do this by specifying a value for **WHENCE**. The possible values are 0, 1, and 2 for positions relative to the start of the file, the current position within the file, and end of the file. If you import the **IO::Seekable** module, you can use the constants **SEEK_SET**, **SEEK_CUR**, and **SEEK_END**, respectively.

Zero sets the positioning relative to the start of the file. For example, the line

```
seek DATA, 256, 0;
```

sets the file pointer to the 256th byte in the file. Using a value of one sets the position relative to the current position; so the line

```
seek DATA, 128, 1;
```

moves the file point onto byte 384, while the line

```
seek DATA, -128, SEEK_CUR;
```

moves back to byte 256.

A **WHENCE** value of two moves the file relative to the end of the file, and the value of **POSITION** is generally specified as a negative number. You can move to a point 80 bytes from the end of the file using a line like this:

```
seek DATA, -80, SEEK_END;
```

It's worth noting that the **seek** function resets the end-of-file condition. You can use the **SEEK_CUR** constant with a **WHENCE** value of zero to achieve this, since the overall effect is to move nowhere. If you were to use the **SEEK_SET** or **SEEK_END** function, you'd have to use the **tell** function to discover the current location.

FUNDAMENTALS

sysseek

As you already know, the bulk of the functions that use filehandles rely on the buffering provided by the system's **stdio** functions. The **sysseek** function is essentially identical to the **seek** function, except that it ignores the buffering on filehandles:

```
sysseek FILEHANDLE, WHENCE, POSITION
```

In the earlier database example, you might want to move to the last record in a database, which you could do with

```
sysseek DATABASE, -80, 2;
```

Miscellaneous Control Functions

A few functions do not conveniently fall into one of the sections we have already discussed. They are functions that primarily control the operation or control of a filehandle, or they may return some additional information for a specific filehandle.

binmode

On older operating systems, there is a distinction between textual and binary files. The difference occurs because Perl converts automatically between external file formats that contain two characters for line separation. MS-DOS, for example, uses **CR LF** to terminate lines, which Perl translates internally to **LF**, converting them back when information is written.

```
binmode FILEHANDLE
```

This obviously causes a problem when opening files for binary access, since you will lose information in the internal representation and can corrupt the files due to the conversion process. To get around this problem, you can use the **binmode** function, which forces Perl to ignore line termination, thus preventing it from doing any form of conversion. To use it, open a filehandle, and then call the **binmode** function with the new filehandle. For example:

```
open(DATA,"+<input.bin") or die "Couldn't open the file input.bin\n";
binmode(DATA) or die "Couldn't set binary mode on input.bin\n";
...
```

The **binmode** function returns the usual **true/false** on success/failure. Once set, there is no way to unset binary mode short of closing the filehandle and reopening it, although you're unlikely to want to change the format of an open file anyway.

The function has no effect on systems that make no distinction between formats, such as Unix, Mac OS, and Windows.

eof

Although all functions and operators that read information automatically detect the end-of-file condition and return a suitable error code to the user, it is sometimes necessary to check the status outside of such a test. The **eof** function supports this action:

```
eof FILEHANDLE
eof()
eof
```

If **eof** is specified with a **FILEHANDLE**, then it checks whether the next read from the specified filehandle will return an end-of-file condition. The function returns **true** if the end-of-file condition exists, or **undef** otherwise.

When called with parentheses, it returns **true** when the end of file has been reached for the last file within a **while(<>)** loop (see Chapter 9). For example, the following code prints an error message when it realizes it's running out of source text:

```
while(<>)
{
    if(eof())
    {
        print "Running out of data!!\n";
    }
    ...
}
```

When used without a filehandle or parentheses, the function detects the end-of-file condition for the end of file within the current file of a **while(<>)** loop. So the next example prints a separator after each file that is printed:

```
while(<>)
{
    print;
    if (eof)
    {
        print "\n",'=' x 50,"\n\n";
    }
}
```

The actual method used by Perl for discovering the end-of-file condition is to get a byte of information from the required filehandle and then push the character back onto the input stream of the filehandle with the C **ungetc()** function. This makes it useless in an interactive context, so it may catch keystrokes that you are trying to read.

fileno

The **fileno** function returns the underlying operating system file descriptor for the specified filehandle:

```
fileno FILEHANDLE
```

Essentially this function is only used when you require the file descriptor number instead of the filehandle. The **select** function is a classic example that requires the number in order to create the necessary bitsets used to monitor the filehandles. The function can also be used when duplicating filehandles (although you can do that easier by name) and detecting whether two filehandles are duplicated:

```
print "Dupes\n" if (fileno(DATA) == fileno(SRC));
```

select

There are two forms of **select**. One sets the default filehandle, and the other is used for the more complex act of handling multiple I/O effectively. We will deal only with the first in this section.

```
select FILEHANDLE
select
```

The **select** function returns the default filehandle name and sets the default filehandle to **FILEHANDLE**. This is the default filehandle used by functions such as **print** and **read** when the user does not specify a **FILEHANDLE**. If no **FILEHANDLE** is specified, the name of the current filehandle is returned.

For example, to switch buffering off for another filehandle, you could use this code:

```
$stdfh = select DATA;
$| = 1;
select $stdfh;
```

This works because **select** returns the current filehandle before setting it to the new supplied value.

This trick is also sometimes useful when you are formatting and producing reports using the Perl reporting mechanism. In both cases, however, there are now convenient ways of modifying report formats and setting the buffering of filehandles.

If you import the **FileHandle** module, then to switch off buffering, you can use

```
use FileHandle;
autoflush(DATA);
```

Alternatively, using the method syntax, you can set the format options for two separate reports:

```
use FileHandle;
DETAILS->format_top_name("Detailed Phone Statistics");
SUMMARY->format_top_name("Summary Phone Statistics");
```

This virtually eliminates the need for **select** altogether, but it remains for historical compatibility.

truncate

You can truncate (empty) a specific filehandle to trim it down to a specific size:

```
truncate FILEHANDLE, LENGTH
```

For example, to reset the size of an error log, perhaps after the full contents have been printed, you can use this line:

```
truncate LOGFILE, 1024;
```

The function causes a fatal error if your system does not support the underlying **truncate** function, or returns **true** if the operation is successful.

File Management

For most people, the bulk of the data they want to process comes from the contents of a file. However, a significant amount of information is stored along with file data. The most obvious is the file's name, but this is often coupled with additional information about the file. This information is often called *metadata*, since it refers to metaphorical information about a file, rather than the file data itself. The exact specification of this information is reliant on the operating system, but it usually includes permissions (or attributes), ownership, and more trivial information such as modification times and the file size.

Perl provides an entire suite of functions for determining the metadata of a file. We'll start by looking at the basic test operators, **-X**, which return a Boolean response to simple queries about a specific file, such as whether the file can be read or written to. There is also a simple operator for finding the size, in bytes, of a specified file. We then move on to the **stat** and **lstat** functions, which return extended information from the directory entry for the specified file or link.

There is also a series of functions that enable you to create and manage files, including deleting files, creating hard and symbolic links, and obtaining the location of the file or directory that a particular link points to. We will also be examining methods for finding out the list of available files in a particular directory and how to access the entire directory contents.

Finally, we'll look at the more advanced operations available for control filehandles and I/O with a range of files using **fcntl**, **ioctl**, and the **select** function.

File Information

You can test certain features very quickly within Perl using a series of test operators known collectively as **-X** tests. The file test operators take either a file name or a filehandle, returning true, false, or a value, depending on the operator being used. The format of the operator is as follows:

```
-X EXPR
-X FILEHANDLE
-X
```

If you do not specify a file to get the information from, the operator uses the value of **$_** as a file name for all tests except **-t**, which instead uses **STDIN**. The full list of available tests is shown in Table 7-6.

For example, to perform a quick test of the various permissions on a file, you might use a script like this:

```
my (@description,$size);
if (-e $file)
{
    push @description, 'binary' if (-B _);
    push @description, 'a socket' if (-S _);
    push @description, 'a text file' if (-T _);
    push @description, 'a block special file' if (-b _);
    push @description, 'a character special file' if (-c _);
    push @description, 'a directory' if (-d _);
    push @description, 'executable' if (-x _);
    push @description, (($size = -s _)) ? "$size bytes" : 'empty';
    print "$file is ", join(', ',@description),"\n";
}
```

Operator	Description
-A	Age of file (at script startup) in days since modification.
-B	Is it a binary file?
-C	Age of file (at script startup) in days since modification.
-M	Age of file (at script startup) in days since modification.
-O	Is the file owned by the real user ID?
-R	Is the file readable by the real user ID or real group?
-S	Is the file a socket?
-T	Is it a text file?
-W	Is the file writable by the real user ID or real group?
-X	Is the file executable by the real user ID or real group?
-b	Is it a block special file?
-c	Is it a character special file?
-d	Is the file a directory?
-e	Does the file exist?
-f	Is it a plain file?
-g	Does the file have the setgid bit set?
-k	Does the file have the sticky bit set?
-l	Is the file a symbolic link?
-o	Is the file owned by the effective user ID?
-p	Is the file a named pipe?
-r	Is the file readable by the effective user or group ID?
-s	Returns the size of the file, with zero referring to an empty file.
-t	Is the filehandle opened by a TTY (terminal)?
-u	Does the file have the setuid bit set?
-w	Is the file writable by the effective user or group ID?
-x	Is the file executable by the effective user or group ID?
-z	Is the file size zero?

Table 7-6. *File Test Operators*

Note that after the first test, I've used a special character, the underscore, which is a special filehandle. This is a buffer that holds the information from the last file name or filehandle test, or the last **stat** command. Using this special filehandle is more efficient than continually specifying the file, since this special filehandle stores all of the status information for the last file accessed. If you specify each file or filehandle individually, the physical device holding the file will be polled each time for the information.

| **Caution** | *Be careful of foreign language files with high-bit or special characters, such as characters with accents. They can sometimes be misinterpreted as a binary file when using **-B** or **-T**.* |

Beyond this standard set of tests, there is also a separate **stat** command that obtains further information about the file specified, including the physical device, underlying file system parameters such as the inode number, the owner and group permissions, and the access and modification times for the file. The information is returned by the function as a list:

```
($dev,  $inode, $mode,  $nlink, $uid,  $gid,     $rdev
$rdev, $size,  $atime, $mtime, $ctime, $blksize, $blocks) = stat $file;
```

The full list of information supplied is shown in Table 7-7.

The **stat** function uses the operating system **stat()** function to obtain information directly from the inode (see sidebar), returning the list. The information is very raw; for example, it returns user IDs rather than names, but using other functions seen elsewhere in this chapter, it's possible to extract the information to make it more usable.

The most complex procedure is the extraction of the permissions information, which is supplied back to use as a number, but needs to be treated as an octal value that many Unix programmers will be familiar with. The following example shows one

Inodes

An *inode* is the name for a directory entry within a file system. The term "inode" comes from Unix, although all operating systems have a similar term for the inode. Both Macs and NT use the term *directory entry*. Regardless of the operating system or file system type, the primary purpose for an inode or directory entry is to store the information about the physical location of the data that constitutes a file on the physical (or logical) device.

Because this is effectively a mapping structure between the data and the name the user gives the file, an inode is also used to store other information such as the ownership and security information and other data obtainable with the **stat** function. Inodes also play a part in the management of files.

Element	Short Name	Description
0	dev	Device number of file system.
1	inode	Inode number.
2	mode	File mode (type and permissions).
3	nlink	Number of (hard) links to the file.
4	uid	Numeric user ID of file's owner.
5	gid	Numeric group ID of file's owner.
6	rdev	The device identifier (special files only).
7	size	File size, in bytes.
8	atime	Last access time since the epoch.
9	mtime	Last modify time since the epoch.
10	ctime	Inode change time (*not* creation time!) since the epoch.
11	blksize	Preferred block size for file system I/O.
12	blocks	Actual number of blocks allocated.

Table 7-7.   *Data Returned by the* **stat** *Function*

method for extracting the information into a usable form using the logical **and** operator to compare known values against the value returned.

```
for $file (@ARGV)
{
    my ($mode,$nlinks,$uid,$gid,$size,$mtime) = (stat($file))[2..5,7,9];
    printf("%s %2d %-10s %-10s %8d %s   %s\n",extperms($mode),
                                    $nlinks,
                                    scalar getpwuid($uid),
                                    scalar getgrgid($uid),
                                    $size,
                                    scalar localtime($mtime),
                                    $file);
}
```

```perl
sub extperms ()
{
    ($mode) = @_;
    my $perms = '-' x 9;

    substr($perms,0,1) = 'r' if ($mode & 00400);
    substr($perms,1,1) = 'w' if ($mode & 00200);
    substr($perms,2,1) = 'x' if ($mode & 00100);
    substr($perms,3,1) = 'r' if ($mode & 00040);
    substr($perms,4,1) = 'w' if ($mode & 00020);
    substr($perms,5,1) = 'x' if ($mode & 00010);
    substr($perms,6,1) = 'r' if ($mode & 00004);
    substr($perms,7,1) = 'w' if ($mode & 00002);
    substr($perms,8,1) = 'x' if ($mode & 00001);
    substr($perms,2,1) = 's' if ($mode & 04000);
    substr($perms,5,1) = 's' if ($mode & 02000);
    substr($perms,8,1) = 't' if ($mode & 01000);

    $perms;
}
```

The script largely emulates the Unix **ls** command or, indeed, the Windows **dir** command. When run, it produces output similar to this:

```
rwxr-xr-x  7 root   root  512 Fri Jun 12 10:00:50 1998  /usr/local/atalk
rwxr-xr-x  2 root   root 1536 Tue Nov  3 22:17:09 1998  /usr/local/backups
rwxr-xr-x  4 root   root 3584 Wed Feb 17 12:12:32 1999  /usr/local/bin
rwxr-xr-x  3 root   root  512 Fri Jun 12 10:03:19 1998  /usr/local/com
rwxrwxrwx 15 root   root 1024 Sat Feb 20 06:57:26 1999  /usr/local/contrib
rwxr-xr-x  2 root   root  512 Sat Feb 20 07:04:19 1999  /usr/local/cpan
rwxrwxrwx  5 root   root  512 Wed Feb 17 13:08:56 1999  /usr/local/etc
rwxrwxrwx 10 root   root  512 Tue Jan 19 20:56:41 1999  /usr/local/http
rwxr-xr-x  6 root   root  512 Thu Aug 27 21:31:21 1998  /usr/local/include
rwxr-xr-x  2 root   root 4096 Mon Feb  8 10:14:58 1999  /usr/local/info
rwxr-xr-x 11 root   root 1024 Wed Jan 20 16:39:53 1999  /usr/local/lib
rwxr-xr-x  4 root   root  512 Fri Jun 12 10:30:39 1998  /usr/local/libexec
rwx------  2 root   root 8192 Thu Jun 26 13:31:45 1997  /usr/local/lost+found
rwxr-xr-x 16 root   root  512 Wed Jan 20 16:39:35 1999  /usr/local/man
rwxr-xr-x 11 root   root  512 Thu Jan 21 09:56:08 1999  /usr/local/nsr
rwxr-xr-x 10 root   root  512 Wed Feb 17 12:27:15 1999  /usr/local/qmail
rwxr-xr-x  6 root   root  512 Tue Jun 16 22:27:18 1998  /usr/local/samba
rwxr-xr-x  8 root   root  512 Tue Jun 16 23:52:46 1998  /usr/local/share
```

When accessing a symbolic link on a Unix system, the information returned by **stat** is that of the file the link points to, rather than the link itself. To return the information for the link (rather than the file it points to), you need to use the **lstat** function:

```
lstat EXPR
```

This returns exactly the same information as **stat**. (Refer to Table 7-7 for the list of information returned.) If your system does not support symbolic links, a normal **stat** operation is done instead.

Basic File Management

Under Unix, files are created on a file system by creating a link to an inode (see the earlier sidebar), which creates the necessary directory entry that links to the file data. Many of the functions for managing files therefore have a direct effect on the inode information without requiring you to access the file. The **rename** function is the first of these. It changes the registered name for a file:

```
rename OLDNAME, NEWNAME
```

The **OLDNAME** is the specification of the old file, and **NEWNAME** is the new name for the file. The function fails if it is unable to find the file or unable to change the file name (perhaps because it is open).

The next few functions all directly affect the existence, creation, or information about a link. The first is the **link** function. This creates a "hard" link to an existing file. A hard link is a new inode that points to an existing data stream; that is, it's a duplicate directory entry for an existing file. The duplicate has a different name and different permissions and access times. Only the inode field (from the **stat** function) is identical to the original:

```
link OLDNAME, NEWNAME
```

Creation of a new hard link updates the link count (the number of links to a file); the significance of this will be seen shortly. If the function fails, it returns a value of zero and sets the error string in **$!**. Note that you cannot create hard links across file systems, because the new directory entry must refer to the inode of a file on the same file system. Use symbolic links instead.

Since the notion of a duplicate directory entry for an existing file is a Unix feature, other operating systems are unlikely to support this option. They may, however, support symbolic links via the **symlink** function. Certainly Mac OS and Windows support symbolic links in the form of aliases and shortcuts, respectively. A symbolic link is similar in principle to a hard link; however, rather than duplicating the information about an existing inode, a symbolic link contains a reference (the path) to the file you want to link to:

```
symlink OLDNAME, NEWNAME
```

Because a symbolic link is a reference to a file, rather than a physical pointer to a real file, you can create a symbolic link on any file system and have it point to any other file system.

Symbolic links do not update the link count either. This is significant because the link count of an inode is used by the file system to determine whether a file is to be deleted completely. The **unlink** function deletes a link from a file system. If you a delete a link, you are only deleting the directory entry that relates the file name you see in the file list to the physical file. By deleting a link, you effectively remove access to the file.

For most files you create, there will be only one link to the file (the name you originally gave it). Once the link count in the inode reaches zero, the file system deletes the file in question. In effect, therefore, the **unlink** function does not actually delete a file; it only decrements the link count for the inode number to which the directory entry relates.

```
unlink LIST
```

The function accepts a list of files to be deleted, or it uses the value of **$_** if you do not specify a list. Because the file globbing operator and functions return lists, that means all three of these examples will work:

```
unlink $file;
unlink @files;
unlink <*.o>;
```

To delete directories, use the **rmdir** function. Although Perl supports the deletion of a directory via **unlink** (providing you are root and have specified the **-U** option on the command line), it's not advised. Removing the directory entry/inode for a directory without also deleting the files that refer to that directory can cause serious file system problems—probably not the effect you want.

Once you have created (or indeed identified) a symbolic link, any references to the link actually return the file contents that the link points to. This is sensible, since the link itself contains no valid information. However, you can find out the pathname of the file that the symbolic link points to using the **readlink** function:

```
readlink EXPR
```

The function returns the location of the file pointed to by the symbolic link **EXPR**, or **$_** if none is specified. If the value cannot be determined, or if **EXPR** is not a symbolic link, the function returns **undef**.

Also be aware that symbolic links can be relative to the location of the link, rather than a full pathname. The value returned to you will only be of any use if you are currently in the same directory as the link you are reading.

You may remember the access permissions information returned by **stat** earlier in this chapter. The access permissions (mode) of a file can also be set using the **chmod** function:

```
chmod MODE, LIST
```

The **MODE** should be the numerical value associated with a specific file mode. Normally, this information is represented as an octal value (as seen earlier). For example, to change the permissions of a file to be readable by everybody:

```
chmod 0444, $file;
```

The most common mistake when using this command is to specify a decimal rather than octal number. Remember that Perl identifies octal numbers by a leading zero, or you can use the **oct** function to convert a decimal value to its octal equivalent.

The **LIST** is the list of file names whose mode you want to change, and the function returns the number of files that successfully had their modes changed. To find out which files have not been successfully modified, you will either need to use a loop or use the **grep** function to identify the files in a list. For example:

```
@failure = grep { not chmod 0444, $_ } @files;
warn "Unable to change the mode of @failure" if @failure;
```

To change the user and group ownership of a file, you need to use the **chown** function:

```
chown USERID, GROUPID, LIST
```

The **USERID** and **GROUPID** are the numerical IDs of the user and group, and **LIST** is the list of files whose ownership you want to change. For example:

```
chown 1000,1000,@files;
```

Like the **chmod** function, it returns the number of files actually changed. You want to use a similar trick to the earlier **chmod** example if you are modifying a number of files.

Note that the user and group information must be specified numerically. You may want to use the **getpwnam** and **getgrnam** functions to obtain the IDs of user and group names, as in

```
chown scalar getpwnam($user), scalar getgrnam($group), @files;
```

You'll see further examples of obtaining user and group information later in this chapter.

To modify the last access and modification time for a file, you need to use the **utime** function:

```
utime ATIME, MTIME, LIST
```

The **ATIME** and **MTIME** arguments specify the access and modification times you wish to set. The values should be specified as the number of seconds that have elapsed since the epoch. See the section "Time" in Chapter 11 for details on converting between the epoch value and date format.

For the next example, the time specified is taken from the **time** function, which returns the number of seconds since the epoch at the time executed; so this script effectively emulates the Unix **touch** command:

```
$now = time;
utime $now, $now, @files;
```

Note in this example that the time is assigned to a variable before being set. This prevents two different times being set between invocations and also reduces the number of system calls. If you fail to specify a value, the corresponding time for the file is not modified. Like the previous two commands, the function returns the number of files that were successfully modified.

When creating a file using **open**, **sysopen**, or other functions, the mode of the file is determined by a combination of the mode specified and the current umask. The umask is an octal permissions mask that specifies the permissions bits that cannot be set when a file is created. For example, with a umask of 0077, the read, write, and execute bits for group and other users cannot be set, even if the function creating the file specifies them.

```
umask EXPR
umask
```

The function returns the current mode, and if you do not specify **EXPR**, there is no modification of any kind to the umask.

Accessing Directory Entries

If you do not already know the name of the file you are trying to access, or if you want to specify a list of files but don't know where to get the list, you can use one of three methods. The first is similar to the filehandle operator:

```
<*>
```

The pattern between the brackets is matched against the list of files in the current directory, or that specified within the pattern.

The pattern supports the standard file pattern matching of many shells on the Unix platform. Users of Mac and NT platforms may be unfamiliar with these, although they follow guidelines similar to the basic pattern matching supported by Perl regular expressions. The supported formats are very basic, and they only support the use of * as a wildcard for any number of characters and ? as a wildcard for a single character. For example, to get a list of all of the files ending in ".c":

```
@files = <*.c>;
```

Other patterns that you may be familiar with within the shell, such as braces (for multiple options) and square brackets (for a single character from a set), are not supported. However, this is not a problem, since you can use the **grep** function (discussed in the next chapter) to select a more specific list of files.

You can also use the standard variable interpolation to use a scalar variable as the pattern, but don't do

```
@files = <$pattern>;
```

since Perl will assume you're referring to an indirect filehandle (one specified by a variable, rather than a static tag). Instead, either use braces to force interpretation as a file name glob,

```
@files = <${pattern}>;
```

or use the **glob** function, which is actually what calling the **<PATTERN>** operator does anyway. The **glob** function is also clearer: it is obvious to any reader that you are trying to do a file name glob, not access a filehandle.

The format for the **glob** function is identical to the operator. The earlier C source file example can be restated as

```
@files = glob("*.c");
```

Whether you use the operator or the function, the return value in a scalar context is the next entry matching the specified pattern. If you don't assign the value returned to a variable in a **while** loop, the value is assigned to **$_**, so you can do

```
while (<*.c>)
{

}
```

Both the operator and function methods for file name globbing invoke a subshell in order to expand the pattern supplied to a suitable file list. For quick searches, this is not a major issue, but because you are using an external application to produce the list, you may run into a combination of both performance and memory allocation problems. This is definitely the case if your shell does not support large argument lists (and most shells don't).

To get around this problem, you can use the **opendir** function set. This facility is an interface to the underlying routines that the operating system supports, and it functions rather like a directory-specific filehandle. In fact, you access it in a similar way, using a directory handle:

```
opendir    DIRHANDLE, EXPR
readdir    DIRHANDLE
rewinddir  DIRHANDLE
telldir    DIRHANDLE
seekdir    DIRHANDLE, POS
closedir   DIRHANDLE
```

To use **opendir**, first you need to open the directory handle and associate it with the directory you want to examine. The **EXPR** should be a directory name, not a file specification, since the function set does not handle file name globbing. Once opened, subsequent reads to **readdir** on the specified filehandle return the next file name in the directory in a scalar context. In a list context, the entire directory contents are returned. Once you have finished reading the directory names, you need to close the directory handle.

To list the contents of the directory:

```
opendir (DIR, '.') or die "Couldn't open directory, $!";
while ($file = readdir DIR)
{
    print "$file\n";
}
close DIR;
```

This circumvents all of the memory problems associated with the globbing operator and function, since each entry of the directory is retrieved individually.

Because the process of reading in from a directory is associated with a specific directory handle, you can have multiple handles open simultaneously. You can also record your position within a directory handle using the **telldir** function. The return value is an integer representing the current location within the directory list held within the instance of the directory handle. Unfortunately, even over short periods of time, this value is not guaranteed to actually return you to the location it originally indicated. This is because the number of directory entries may increase or decrease in size between the time you obtain the position information and when you attempt to move to that position using the **seekdir** function.

The best solution in these instances is to record not the theoretical position within an arbitrary directory list, but instead the actual pathname and file name you want to store. If all you want to do is start reading the directory entry list again, you can use the **rewinddir** function. This resets the pointer within the directory handle to the start of the list without the file pattern being reevaluated. Due to the nature of the directory handle system, a more reliable method for processing the same list of files a number of times is to use an array—providing, as ever, that the list size is not so great that it starts eating up too much memory in the process.

To emulate the globbing features of the **glob** function, you will need to check each individual file name or pass the list returned by **readdir** through the **grep** function. You can also use the opportunity to sort the list returned, since the **readdir** function does not return a sorted list. For example, to print the list of C source code files, you might use

```
opendir(DIR, '.') or die "Couldn't open directory, $!";
foreach (sort grep(/^.*\.c$/,readdir(DIR)))
{
    print "$_\n";
}
closedir DIR;
```

We'll be looking at the **sort** and **grep** functions in more depth in the next chapter.

Managing Directories

All programs are aware of their current directory. This is either the directory they reside in or the current directory of the application (such as a shell) that called the program. The system **chdir()** function is supported within Perl in order to change the current directory for the current process.

```
chdir EXPR
chdir
```

If you do not specify a directory to change to, Perl changes to the home directory for the current user. Under Unix, this information is derived from the user's entry in the /etc/passwd file, and under NT, it's the home directory defined in the environment variable **%HOME%**. On the Mac, if you do not specify a directory, it simply changes to the current directory (which means that it does nothing!). The function returns false if the function failed, or true if it succeeded:

```
chdir or die "Couldn't change back to the home directory, $!";
```

Perl does not support a function internally for discovering the current working directory. What it does provide, however, is a **Cwd** module as part of the standard distribution:

```
use Cwd;
print getcwd(),"\n";
```

The method used to discover the current working directory is basically the one that works on your system. In practice, most OSs support a **getcwd** function; others support a **pwd** command that returns the current directory. The **Cwd** module simply chooses the one that works each time **getcwd** is called.

For security reasons, it can sometimes be necessary to create your own directory structure that contains a reduced set of devices and utilities, or you may want to restrict a user-defined function or process to a similar environment. Under Unix, you also have the ability to change the root directory—the directory from which all "/" references are taken. This is not implemented under either the Mac OS or Windows versions.

By changing the "root" of the current process to another directory, such as /etc/miniroot, you can guarantee that a call to a program of the form /sbin/shutdown actually executes /etc/miniroot/sbin/shutdown. The user may be unaware of the restricted directory structure and will be unable to access any directories above the one configured as the new root. For example, here's a line taken from a Perl-based web server. Without the restriction of the **chroot** function, it would be possible for a cracker to access the web page /etc/passwd—not the level of access we want to provide.

```
unless (chroot("/users/martinb"))
{
    warn "You are not root!\n" if ($>);
    die "Cannot change to root directory, $!";
}
```

You can only use the **chroot** function if you are root, and once set, there is no way to unset the root directory change (since all new references are relative to the previous

chroot function call). The effect is inherited both by the current function and by any children, including those generated by **fork**, implicitly or otherwise.

You can make a new directory using the **mkdir** function:

```
mkdir EXPR, MODE
```

The **EXPR** argument is the name of the directory you would like to create, with the permissions specified by the octal **MODE**. If your operating system does not support a **mkdir** function within the C library, the command line **mkdir** program will be called, with **EXPR** as the argument; so be wary of creating a large number of directories with this function if this is the case. Calling the external program puts extra overhead on the system, as it executes an additional program.

To remove a directory, use the **rmdir** function:

```
rmdir EXPR
```

The directory must be empty for the function to work. If an error occurs, the return value will be zero, and the **$!** variable will be populated with the error message. If the directory is not empty, the message is usually something like "File Exists"; so you may want to test specifically for this during execution, as in this example:

```
unless (rmdir($dir))
{
    if ($! =~ /File Exists/i)
    {
        warn "Error removing directory: The directory is not empty";
    }
    else
    {
        warn "Error removing directory: $!";
    }
}
```

If you fail to specify an expression, the directory to remove will be taken from the **$_** variable, which may not be the desired result.

File Control with fcntl

The **fcntl** function is the Perl interface to the system **fcntl()** function, which enables certain file control operations on your files that are not supported by other functions.

Typically, these are specific to an operating system, although many features are available across a number of different platforms.

```
fcntl FILEHANDLE, FUNCTION, SCALAR
```

The function performs the function specified by **FUNCTION**, using **SCALAR** on **FILEHANDLE**. **SCALAR** either contains a value to be used by the function or is the variable used to store any information returned by the corresponding **fcntl** function. To use **fcntl** effectively, you will probably want to import the **Fcntl** module with a

```
use Fcntl;
```

For all subfunctions of the **fcntl** function, the return value is slightly different in Perl from that returned by the operating system. A value of **-1** from the operating system is returned as **undef** by Perl, while a value of 0 from the system is returned by Perl as **0 but true**. This equates to true in a test condition, but 0 when evaluated as a number. For all other values the return values are the same for the operating system and Perl.

Since the **fcntl** functions are operating system specific, no details will be given on the **fcntl** function at this stage, but see Table 7-8 for some sample functions and Table 7-9 for a description of many of the constants you will need. You'll need to refer to your operating system documentation for details on the **fcntl()** functions supported on your system, or examine the **Fcntl** module, which will contain a summarized list of the functions as a list of constants for use when using the command. We will be using some of the functions later in this chapter and elsewhere in the book.

If your system does not support **fcntl()**, a fatal error will occur.

Function	Description
&F_DUPFD	Duplicates the supplied file descriptor, returning the lowest numbered file descriptor not currently in use. This is roughly equivalent to the ">&FH" format with the Perl **open** function.
&F_GETFD	Returns the **FD_CLOEXEC** flag (see the next table) for the specified filehandle.
&F_SETFD	Sets the state of the **FD_CLOEXEC** flag on the filehandle.

Table 7-8. *Example Functions for **fcntl***

Function	Description
&F_GETFL	Gets the current flags for the specified filehandle. These flags are identical to those you can specify during a **sysopen** function (see Table 7-9 for more information).
&F_SETFL	Sets the flags for the specified filehandle (see Table 7-9 for suitable values).
&F_GETLK	Gets the lock status for a specified filehandle; used to test whether a particular lock can be set on a file (see "File Locking" later in the chapter).
&F_SETLK	Sets or clears a file segment lock (see "File Locking").
&F_SETLKW	Identical to **F_SETLK**, except that the process will block until a read or write lock can be set on the specified filehandle (see "File Locking").

Table 7-8. *Example Functions for **fcntl** (continued)*

Constant	Description
FD_CLOEXEC	The close-on-exec flag. If set on a filehandle (it's set by default), it will be closed if its file descriptor number is greater than 2 (that is, not **STDIN**, **STDOUT**, or **STDERR**) when a new process is forked.
O_APPEND	File opened in append mode.
O_BINARY	File opened in binary mode.
O_TEXT	File opened in text mode.
O_NDELAY	Non-blocking I/O.
O_NONBLOCK	Non-blocking I/O.
O_RDONLY	File opened in read-only mode.
O_RDWR	File opened in read/write mode.
O_WRONLY	File opened in write-only mode.

Table 7-9. *Filehandle Flags for Use with **fcntl***

I/O Control with ioctl

The **ioctl** function is similar in principle to the **fcntl** function. It too is a Perl version of the operating system equivalent **ioctl()** function.

```
ioctl FILEHANDLE, FUNCTION, SCALAR
```

The **ioctl** function is typically used to set options on devices and data streams, usually relating directly to the operation of the terminal. You will need to include the system **ioctl.h** header file, available in a Perl version, by doing

```
require 'ioctl.ph';
```

This will provide you with the necessary constants to use the **ioctl** function. A value of **-1** from the operating system is returned as **undef** by Perl, while a value of 0 from the system is returned by Perl as **0 but true**. This equates to true in a test condition, but zero when evaluated as a number. For all other values the return values are the same for the operating system and Perl.

As a general rule, calls to **ioctl** should not be considered portable. When using terminals for a Perl interface, you may want to consider using a more portable module such as **Tk** to do the portability work for you. We'll be examining the use of the terminal and the **Tk** module in Chapter 13.

select

The second form of the **select** function (you may remember the first one was defined earlier in this chapter and used to set the "default" filehandle for **print**) is an interface to the system **select()** function. This function is for determining whether the filehandles you have specified are ready to accept input, supply output, or report an exceptional condition.

```
select RBITS, WBITS, EBITS, TIMEOUT
```

The **RBITS, WBITS,** and **EBITS** are bitmasks specifying the file descriptors that you want to monitor for reading, writing, and exceptional status, respectively. You can specify any of these as **undef** if you are not interested in the value. The bitsets are created by placing a value of 1 in each bit, with each bit number being equal to the file descriptor number (obtainable with **fileno**) that you want to monitor. You can create this structure using **vec**, for example:

```
vec($rbits,fileno(DATA),1) = 1;
```

The **TIMEOUT** specifies the interval to wait for the selection to complete. The **select** function will block until the time-out expires. If **TIMEOUT** is 0, the effect is the same as polling in a round-robin fashion—simply returning the current status without waiting.

The return value from the function is the number of filehandles that are waiting to be accessed, or on some platforms, it will return the number of filehandles and the time remaining on the time-out value:

```
($nfound, $timeleft) = select($rout=$rin, $wout=$win, $eout=$ein, $timeout);
```

The function also replaces the supplied scalar bitmasks with bitmasks defining the list of filehandles that require attention. The preceding example shows the best method for using the values of the bitmasks **$rin, $win**, and **$ein** while returning the information into **$rout, $wout**, and **$eout**.

The problem with using most filehandles is that in order to monitor and read or write information from or to them, you need to "poll" each filehandle to see if it's ready. This is time consuming, especially with multiple files when a good proportion of them may not be ready. This is further complicated if your filehandles or network sockets are blocking (the default status). A blocking filehandle will cause a **<FH>** operator or a **sysread** function to halt execution of the program until some data is ready to be read. The opposite is also true: if a filehandle or network socket is not ready to accept data, a **print** or **syswrite** function will also wait until it is ready. In some situations this is ideal; in others, particularly if you are handling multiple filehandles or a user interface, this is far from ideal.

The solution is to use **select**, which reports the status of the filehandle without attempting to access it, thereby ignoring the blocking state. A better alternative is to set a non-blocking operation on the filehandle using **fcntl**. Non-blocking I/O with **select** works as follows: First you need to open one or more filehandles—either genuine files, pipes, or network sockets—and then set them to be non-blocking using **fcntl**:

```
use Fcntl;
open(DATA,"ls|") or die "Couldn't open pipe, $!";
if ((fcntl(DATA,&F_GETFL,0) & O_NONBLOCK) != O_NONBLOCK)
{
    die "Can't set non-blocking status"
        unless fcntl(DATA,&F_SETFL,(fcntl(DATA,&F_GETFL,0) & ~O_NONBLOCK));
}
else
{
    die "Couldn't get non-blocking status";
}
```

Then, once the files are open and ready for access, you need to create the necessary bitsets for use with the **select** function. Since we're only reading from a pipe, we really only need to create the **RBITS** bitset, but this example shows creation of all three for clarity:

```
$rbits = $wbits = $ebits = '';

vec($rbits, fileno(DATA), 1) = 1;
vec($wbits, fileno(DATA), 1) = 1;

$ebits = $rbits | $wbits;
```

You're now ready to start checking the status of the filehandles you want to monitor. Typically of course you'd do this in a loop as part of the main execution process, but for this example, we'll simply check the status once:

```
$nfound = select($rreq = $rbits, $wreq = $wbits, $ereq = $ebits, 0);
print "$nfound filehandle(s) waiting for input\n";
print "Expecting input from 'ls' command\n" if ($rreq && fileno(DATA));
```

If you put the preceding example together, and assuming there are no problems opening the **ls** command or setting non-blocking on the filehandle, you should get a result like this:

```
1 filehandle(s) waiting for input
Expecting input from 'ls' command
```

The **select** function has a much easier to use module, **IO::Select**, which makes it much easier to manage multiple **select** file sets. See Chapter 12, where we'll be looking at the use of this function for handling multiple network sockets.

File Locking

Using files in a single script environment does not often cause any sort of file access problems. But if you want to access a file that may be in use by another process (or another invocation of the same script), you need to support file locking. By "locking" a file, you can prevent it from being updated by another process at the same time you are using it. Furthermore, it can be used to stop other processes' even reading from the file, allowing you to update a file before it needs to be read by another process.

*When locking DBM databases, there is no built-in method for locking in the generic ODBM/NDBM/SDBM implementations. In these situations you must use **flock** or something similar. If you can use GDBM or Berkeley DB, these provide built-in file locking capabilities as part of the implementation. See Chapter 13 for more information.*

The main method for locking within Perl is the **flock** function.

```
flock FILEHANDLE, OPERATION
```

This supports file locking on the specified **FILEHANDLE** using the system **flock()**, **fcntl()** locking, or **lockf()**, in that order of preference. The exact implementation used is dependent on what your system supports. **OPERATION** is one of the static scalar values defined in Table 7-10, which can be obtained from the **Fcntl** module, although you must specify the symbols you want to import:

```
use Fcntl qw/LOCK_SH LOCK_EX LOCK_UN LOCK_NB/;
```

Here is an example of locking a mailbox before writing:

```
use Fcntl;
flock DATA, LOCK_EX;
print DATA $message;
flock DATA, LOCK_UN;
```

Note that **flock** will block process execution until such time as the requested lock can be achieved. The way to get around this is to use **$LOCK_NB**, which attempts to lock the filehandle without blocking. However, caution should be used here: you must

Operation	Result
LOCK_SH	Set shared lock.
LOCK_EX	Set exclusive lock.
LOCK_UN	Unlock specified file.
LOCK_NB	Set lock without blocking.

Table 7-10. *Locking Operations*

make sure you test the result of the lock before you start using the file. When using **$LOCK_NB**, the result from **flock** will be true, irrespective of whether the lock succeeded.

In nearly all cases file locking is generally advisory, that is, the fact the lock has been set does not guarantee that another application will not be able to access or overwrite the file. This is because all applications that use the file need to use the same file locking mechanism. This is especially true if the underlying implementation is through the **flock()** function because of the way in which **flock()** sets its locks. You should also be aware that it is unlikely that **flock** will work over a networked file system. If you want to force the use of **fcntl**, you will need to use it directly; so the equivalent of the earlier example becomes

```
use Fcntl qw/F_SETLK LOCK_EX LOCK_UN/;
fcntl(DATA,&F_SETLK,LOCK_EX);
print DATA $message;
fcntl(DATA,&F_SETLK,LOCK_UN);
```

Another alternative is to use a separate file with a .lck or similar extension and check for that during execution. This only works if all processes are aware of the method of locking you are using. Both **flock** and **fcntl** have the advantage that they are operating system functions, so the information and locks are shared across the whole operating system.

In theory this means that a C program that uses file locking will also be aware of the locks imposed by a Perl script. It also means that all the operating system commands will also be aware of the locks imposed on different files. Of course, the exact system you use will often rely on the supported options for the platform you are using; **fcntl** is the most supported cross-platform solution.

Chapter 8

Data Manipulation

Most software is written to work with and modify data in one format or another. Perl was originally designed as a system for processing logs and summarizing and reporting on the information. Because of this focus, a large proportion of the functions built into Perl are dedicated to the extraction and recombination of information. For example, Perl includes functions for splitting a line by a sequence of delimiters, and it can recombine the line later using a different set.

If you can't do what you want with the built-in functions, then Perl also provides a mechanism for regular expressions. We can use a regular expression to extract information, or as an advanced search and replace tool, and as a transliteration tool for converting or stripping individual characters from a string.

In this chapter, we're going to concentrate on the data-manipulation features built into Perl, from the basics of numerical calculations through to basic string handling. We'll also look at the regular expression mechanism and how it works and integrates into the Perl language.

We'll also take the opportunity to look at the Unicode character system. Unicode is a standard for displaying strings that supports not only the ASCII standard, which represents characters by a single byte, but also provides support for multibyte characters, including those with accents, and also those in non-Latin character sets such as Greek and kanji (as used in the far east).

Working with Numbers

The core numerical ability of Perl is supported through the standard operators that you should be familiar with. For example, all of the following expressions return the sort of values you would expect:

```
$result = 3+4;
$ftoc = (212-32)*(5/9);
$square = 16*2;
```

Beyond these basic operators, Perl also supports a number of functions that fill in the gaps.

Without exception, all of these functions automatically use the value of **$_** if you fail to specify a variable on which to operate.

abs—the Absolute Value

When you are concerned only with magnitude—for example, when comparing the size of two objects—the designation of negative or positive is not required. You can use the **abs** function to return the absolute value of a number:

```
print abs(-1.295476);
```

This should print a value of 1.295476. Supplying a positive value to **abs** will return the same positive value or, more correctly, it will return the nondesignated value: all positive values imply a + sign in front of them.

int—Converting Floating Points to Integers

To convert a floating point number into an integer, you use the **int** function:

```
print int abs(-1.295476);
```

This should print a value of 1. The only problem with the **int** function is that it strictly removes the fractional component of a number; no rounding of any sort is done. If you want to return a number that has been rounded to a number of decimal places, use the **printf** or **sprintf** function:

```
printf("%.2f",abs(-1.295476));
```

This will round the number to two decimal places—a value of 1.30 in this example. Note that the 0 is appended in the output to show the two decimal places.

exp—Raising e to the Power

To perform a normal exponentiation operation on a number, you use the ** operator:

```
$square = 4**2;
```

This returns 16, or 4 raised to the power of 2. If you want to raise the natural base number *e* to the power, you need to use the **exp** function:

```
exp EXPR
exp
```

If you do not supply an **EXPR** argument, **exp** uses the value of the $_ variable as the exponent. For example, to find the square of *e*:

```
$square = exp(2);
```

sqrt—the Square Root

To get the square root of a number, use the built-in **sqrt** function:

```
$var = sqrt(16384);
```

To calculate the *n*th root of a number, use the ****** operator with a fractional number. For example, the following line

```
$var = 16384**(1/2);
```

is identical to

```
$var = sqrt(16384);
```

To find the cube root of 16,777,216, you might use

```
$var = 16777216**(1/3);
```

which should return a value of 256.

log—the Logarithm

To find the logarithm (base *e*) of a number, you need to use the **log** function:

```
$log = log 1.43;
```

Trigonometric Functions

There are three built-in trigonometric functions for calculating the arctangent squared (**atan2**), cosine (**cos**), and sine (**sin**) of a value:

```
atan2 X,Y
cos EXPR
sin EXPR
```

If you need access to the arcsine, arccosine, and tangent, then use the **POSIX** module, which supplies the corresponding **acos**, **asin**, and **tan** functions.

Unless you are doing trigonometric calculations, there is little use for these functions in everyday life. However, you can use the **sin** function to calculate your biorhythms using the simple script shown next, assuming you know the number of days you have been alive:

```
my ($phys_step, $emot_step, $inte_step) = (23, 28, 33);

use Math::Complex;

print "Enter the number of days you been alive:\n";
```

FUNDAMENTALS

```
my $alive = <STDIN>;

$phys = int(sin(((pi*($alive%$phys_step))/($phys_step/2)))*100);
$emot = int(sin(((pi*($alive%$emot_step))/($emot_step/2)))*100);
$inte = int(sin(((pi*($alive%$inte_step))/($inte_step/2)))*100);

print "Your Physical is $phys%, Emotional $emot%, Intellectual
$inte%\n";
```

Conversion Between Bases

Perl provides automatic conversion to decimal for numerical literals specified in binary, octal, and hexadecimal. However, the translation is not automatic on values contained within strings, either those defined using string literals or from strings imported from the outside world (files, user input, etc.).

To convert a string-based literal, use the **oct** or **hex** functions. The **hex** function converts only hexadecimal numbers supplied with or without the **0x** prefix. For example, the decimal value of the hexadecimal string "ff47ace3" (42,828,873,954) can be displayed with either of the following statements:

```
print hex("ff47ace3");
print hex("0xff47ace3");
```

The **hex** function doesn't work with other number formats, so for strings that start with **0, 0b,** or **0x,** you are better off using the **oct** function. By default, the **oct** function interprets a string without a prefix as an octal string and raises an error if it doesn't see it. So this

```
print oct("755");
```

is valid, but this

```
print oct("aef");
```

will fail.

If you supply a string using one of the literal formats that provides the necessary prefix, **oct** will convert it, so all of the following are valid:

```
print oct("0755");
print oct("0x7f");
print oct("0b00100001");
```

Both **oct** and **hex** default to using the **$_** variable if you fail to supply an argument. To print out a decimal value in hexadecimal, binary, or octal, use **printf**, or use **sprintf** to print a formatted base number to a string:

```
printf ("%1b %1o %1x", oct("0b00010001"), oct("0755"), oct("0x7f"));
```

See **printf** in Chapter 7 for more information.

Conversion Between Characters and Numbers

If you want to insert a specific character into a string by its numerical value, you can use the **\0** or **\x** character escapes:

```
print "\007";
print "\x07";
```

These examples print the octal and hexadecimal values; in this case the "bell" character. Often, though, it is useful to be able to specify a character by its decimal number and to convert the character back to its decimal equivalent in the ASCII table.

The **chr** function returns the character matching the value of **EXPR**, or **$_** if **EXPR** is not specified. The value is matched against the current ASCII table for the operating system, so it could reveal different values on different platforms for characters with an ASCII value of 128 or higher. This may or may not be useful.

The **ord** function returns the numeric value of the first character of **EXPR**, or **$_** if **EXPR** is not specified. The value is returned according to the ASCII table and is always unsigned.

Thus, using the two functions together,

```
print chr(ord('b'));
```

we should get the character "b".

Random Numbers

Perl provides a built-in random number generator. All random numbers need a "seed" value, which is used in an algorithm, usually based on the precision, or lack thereof, for a specific calculation. The format for the **rand** function is

```
rand EXPR
rand
```

The function returns a floating-point random number between 0 and **EXPR** or between 0 and 1 (including 0, but not including 1) if **EXPR** is not specified. If you want an integer random number, just use the **int** function to return a reasonable value, as in this example:

```
print int(rand(16)),"\n";
```

You can use the **srand** function to seed the random number generator with a specific value:

```
srand EXPR
```

The **rand** function automatically calls the **srand** function the first time **rand** is called, if you don't specifically seed the random number generator. The default seed value is the value returned by the **time** function, which returns the number of seconds from the epoch (usually January 1, 1970 UTC—although it's dependent on your platform). The problem is that this is not a good seed number because its value is predictable. Instead, you might want to try a calculation based on a combination of the current time, the current process ID, and perhaps the user ID, to seed the generator with an unpredictable value.

I've used the following calculation as a good seed, although it's far from perfect:

```
srand((time() ^ (time() % $])) ^ exp(length($0))**$$);
```

By mixing the unpredictable values of the current time and process ID with predictable values, such as the length of the current script and the Perl version number, you should get a reasonable seed value.

The following program calculates the number of random numbers generated before a duplicate value is returned:

```
my %randres;
my $counter = 1;

    srand((time() ^ (time() % $])) ^ exp(length($0))**$$);

while (my $val = rand())
{
    last if (defined($randres{$val}));
    print "Current count is $counter\n" if (($counter %10000) == 0);
    $randres{$val} = 1;
    $counter++;
}

print "Out of $counter tries I encountered a duplicate random number\n";
```

Whatever seed value you choose, the internal random number generator is unlikely to give you more than 500 numbers before a duplicate appears. This makes it unsuitable for secure purposes, since you need a random number that cannot otherwise be predicted. The **Math::TrulyRandom** module provides a more robust system for generating random numbers. If you insert the **truly_random_value** function in place of the **rand** function in the preceding program, you can see how long it takes before a random number reappears. I've attained 20,574 unique random numbers with this function using that test script, and this should be more than enough for most uses.

Working with Very Small Integers

Perl uses 32-bit integers for storing integers and for all of its integer-based math. Occasionally, however, it is necessary to store and handle integers that are smaller than the standard 32-bit integers. This is especially true in databases, where you may wish to store a block of Boolean values: even using a single character for each Boolean value will take up eight bits. A better solution is to use the **vec** function, which supports the storage of multiple integers as strings:

```
vec EXPR, OFFSET, BITS
```

The **EXPR** is the scalar that will be used to store the information; the **OFFSET** and **BITS** arguments define the element of the integer string and the size of each element, respectively. The return value is the integer store at **OFFSET** of size **BITS** from the string **EXPR**. The function can also be assigned to, which modifies the value of the element you have specified. For example, using the preceding database example, you might use the following code to populate an "option" string:

```
vec($optstring, 0, 1) = $print   ? 1 : 0;
vec($optstring, 1, 1) = $display ? 1 : 0;
vec($optstring, 2, 1) = $delete  ? 1 : 0;
print length($optstring),"\n";
```

The **print** statement at the end of the code displays the length, in bytes, of the string. It should report a size of one byte. We have managed to store three Boolean values within less than one real byte of information.

The bits argument allows you to specify select larger bit strings: Perl supports values of 1, 2, 4, 8, 16, and 32 bits per element. You can therefore store four 2-bit integers (up to an integer value of 3, including 0) in a single byte.

Obviously the **vec** function is not limited to storing and accessing your own bitstrings; it can be used to extract and update any string, providing you want to modify 1, 2, 4, 8, 16, or 32 bits at a time. Perl also guarantees that the first bit, accessed with

```
vec($var, 0, 1);
```

will always be the first bit in the first character of a string, irrespective of whether your machine is little endian or big endian. Furthermore, this also implies that the first byte of a string can be accessed with

```
vec($var, 0, 8);
```

The **vec** function is most often used with functions that require bitsets, such as the **select** function. You'll see examples of this in later chapters.

 Little endian machines store the least significant byte of a word in the lower byte address, while big endian machines store the most significant byte at this position. This affects the byte ordering of strings, but doesn't affect the order of bits within those bytes.

Working with Strings

Creating a new string scalar is as easy as assigning a quoted value to a variable:

```
$string = "Come grow old along with me\n";
```

However, unlike C and some other languages, we can't access individual characters by supplying their index location within the string, so we need a function for that. This same limitation also means that we need some solutions for splitting, extracting, and finding characters within a given string.

String Concatenation

We have already seen in Chapter 3 the operators that can be used with strings. The most basic operator that you will need to use is the concatenation operator. This is a direct replacement for the C **strcat()** function. The problem with the **strcat()** function is that it is inefficient, and it requires constant concatenation of a single string to a single variable. Within Perl, you can concatenate any string, whether it has been derived from a static quoted string in the script itself, or in scripts exported by functions. This code fragment:

```
$thetime = 'The time is ' . localtime() . "\n";
```

assigns the string, without interpolation; the time string, as returned by **localtime**; and the interpolated newline character to the **$thetime** variable. The concatenation operator is the single period between each element.

It is important to appreciate the difference between using concatenation and lists. This **print** statement:

```
print 'The time is ' . localtime() . "\n";
```

produces the same result as

```
print 'The time is ', localtime(), "\n";
```

However, in the first example, the string is concatenated before being printed; in the second, the **print** function is printing a list of arguments. You cannot use the second format to assign a compound string to a scalar—the following line will *not* work:

```
$string = 'The time is ', localtime(), "\n";
```

Concatenation is also useful when you want to express a sequence of values as only a single argument to a function. For example:

```
$string = join($suffix . ':' . $prefix, @strings);
```

String Length

The **length** function returns the length, in characters (rather than bytes), of the supplied string (see the "Unicode" section at the end of this chapter for details on the relationship between bytes and characters). The function accepts only a single argument (or it returns the length of the **$_** variable if none is specified):

```
print "Your name is ",length($name), "characters long\n";
```

Case Modifications

There are some simple modifications built into Perl as functions that may be more convenient and quicker than using the regular expressions we will cover later in this chapter. The four basic functions are **lc**, **uc**, **lcfirst**, and **ucfirst**. They convert a string to all lowercase, all uppercase, or only the first character of the string to lowercase or uppercase, respectively. For example:

```
$string = "The Cat Sat on the Mat";
print lc($string)  # Outputs 'the cat sat on the mat'
print lcfirst($string)  # Outputs 'the Cat Sat on the Mat'
print uc($string)  # Outputs 'THE CAT SAT ON THE MAT'
print ucfirst($string)  # Outputs 'The Cat Sat on the Mat'
```

These functions can be useful for "normalizing" a string into an all uppercase or lowercase format—useful when combining and de-duping lists when using hashes.

End-of-Line Character Removal

When you read in data from a filehandle using a **while** or other loop and the **<FH>** operator, the trailing newline on the file remains in the string that you import. You will often find yourself processing the data contained within each line, and you will not want the newline character. The **chop** function can be used to strip the last character off any expression:

```
while(<FH>)
{
    chop;
...
}
```

The only danger with the **chop** function is that it strips the last character from the line, irrespective of what the last character was. The **chomp** function works in combination with the **$/** variable when reading from filehandles. The **$/** variable is the record separator that is attached to the records you read from a filehandle, and it is by default set to the newline character. The **chomp** function works by removing the last character from a string only if it matches the value of **$/**. To do a safe strip from a record of the record separator character, just use **chomp** in place of **chop**:

```
while(<FH>)
{
    chomp;
...
}
```

This is a much safer option, as it guarantees that the data of a record will remain intact, irrespective of the last character type.

String Location

Within many programming languages, a string is stored as an array of characters. To access an individual character within a string, you need to determine the location of the character within the string and access that element of the array. Perl does not support this option, because often you are not working with the individual characters within the string, but the string as a whole.

Two functions, **index** and **rindex**, can be used to find the position of a particular character or string of characters within another string:

```
index STR, SUBSTR [, POSITION]
rindex STR, SUBSTR [, POSITION]
```

The **index** function returns the first position of **SUBSTR** within the string **STR**, or it returns –1 if the string cannot be found. If the **POSITION** argument is specified, then the search skips that many characters from the start of the string and starts the search at the next character.

The **rindex** function returns the opposite of the **index** function—the last occurrence of **SUBSTR** in **STR**, or -1 if the substring could not be found. In fact, **rindex** searches for **SUBSTR** from the end of **STR**, instead of the beginning. If **POSITION** is specified, then it starts from that many characters from the end of the string.

For example:

```
$string = "The Cat Sat on the Mat";
print index($string,'cat');    # Returns -1, because 'cat' is lowercase
print index($string,'Cat');    # Returns 4
print index($string,'Cat',4);  # Still returns 4
print rindex($string,'at');     # Returns 20
print rindex($string,'Cat');    # Returns 4
```

Note *In both cases, the **POSITION** is actually calculated as the value of the $[variable plus (for **index**) or minus (for **rindex**) the supplied argument. The use of the $[variable is now heavily deprecated, since there is little need when you can specify the value directly to the function anyway. As a rule, you should not be using this variable.*

Extracting Substrings

The **substr** function can be used to extract a substring from another string based on the position of the first character and the number of characters you want to extract:

```
substr EXPR, OFFSET, LENGTH
substr EXPR, OFFSET
```

The **EXPR** is the string that is being extracted from. Data is extracted from a starting point of **OFFSET** characters from the start of **EXPR** or, if the value is negative, that many characters from the end of the string. The optional **LENGTH** parameter defines the number of characters to be read from the string. If it is not specified, then all characters to the end of the string are extracted. Alternatively, if the number specified in **LENGTH** is negative, then that many characters are left off the end of the string. For example:

```
$string = 'The cat sat on the mat';
print substr($string,4),"\n";      # Outputs 'cat sat on the mat'
print substr($string,4,3),"\n";    # Outputs 'cat'
```

```
print substr($string,-7),"\n";    # Outputs 'the mat'
print substr($string,4,-4),"\n";  # Outputs 'cat sat on the'
```

The last example is equivalent to

```
print substr($string,4,14),"\n";
```

but it may be more effective to use the first form if you have used the **rindex** function to return the last occurrence of a space within the string.

You can also use **substr** to replace segments of a string with another string. The **substr** function is assignable, so you can replace the characters in the expression you specify with another value. For example, this statement,

```
substr($string,4,3) = 'dog';
print "$string\n";
```

should print "the dog sat on the mat" because we replaced the word "cat," starting at the fourth character and lasting for three characters.

The **substr** function works intelligently, shrinking or growing the string according to the size of the string you assign, so you can replace "dog" with "computer programmer" like this:

```
substr($string,4,3) = 'computer programmer';
print "$string\n";
```

Specifying values of 0 allows you to prepend strings to other strings by specifying an **OFFSET** of 0, although it's arguably easier to use concatenation to achieve the same result. Appending with **substr** is not so easy; you cannot specify beyond the last character, although you could use the output from **length** to calculate where that might be. In these cases a simple

```
$string .= 'programming';
```

is definitely easier.

Stacks

One of the most basic uses for an array is as a stack. If you consider that an array is a list of individual scalars, it should be possible to treat it as if it were a stack of papers. Index 0 of the array is the bottom of the stack, and the last element is the top. You can put new pieces of paper on the top of the stack (**push**), or put them at the bottom (**unshift**). You can also take papers off the top (**pop**) or bottom (**shift**) of the stack.

There are, in fact, four different types of stacks that you can implement. By using different combinations of the Perl functions, you can achieve all the different combinations of LIFO, FIFO, FILO, and LILO stacks, as shown in Table 8-1.

pop and push

The form for **pop** is as follows:

```
pop ARRAY
pop
```

It returns the last element of **ARRAY**, removing the value from the list. If you don't specify an array, it pops the last value from the **@ARGV** special array when you are within the main program. If called within a function, it takes values from the end of the **@_** array instead.

The opposite function is **push**:

```
push ARRAY, LIST
```

This pushes the values in **LIST** on to the end of the list **ARRAY**. Values are pushed onto the end in the order supplied.

shift and unshift

The **shift** function returns the first value in an array, deleting it and shifting the elements of the array list to the left by one.

```
shift ARRAY
shift
```

Acronym	Description	Function Combination
LIFO	Last in, first out	**push/pop**
FIFO	First in, first out	**unshift/shift**
FILO	First in, last out	**unshift/pop**
LILO	Last in, last out	**push/shift**

Table 8-1.   *Stack Types and Functions*

Like its cousin **pop**, if **ARRAY** is not specified, it shifts the first value from the @_ array within a subroutine, or the first command line argument stored in **@ARGV** otherwise.

The opposite is **unshift**, which places new elements at the start of the array:

```
unshift ARRAY, LIST
```

This places the elements from **LIST**, in order, at the beginning of **ARRAY**. Note that the elements are inserted strictly in order, such that the code

```
unshift @array, 'Bob', 'Phil';
```

will insert "Bob" at index 0 and "Phil" at index 1.

Note that **shift** and **unshift** will affect the sequence of the array more significantly (because the elements are taken from the first rather than last index). Therefore, care should be taken when using this pair of functions.

However, the **shift** function is also the most practical when it comes to individually selecting the elements from a list or array, particularly the **@ARGV** and @_ arrays. This is because it removes elements in sequence: the first call to **shift** takes element 0, the next takes what was element 1, and so forth.

The **unshift** function also has the advantage that it inserts new elements into the array at the start, which can allow you to prepopulate arrays and lists before the information provided. This can be used to insert default options into the **@ARGV** array, for example.

Splicing Arrays

The normal methods for extracting elements from an array leave the contents intact. Also, the **pop** and other statements only take elements off the beginning and end of the array or list, but sometimes you want to copy and remove elements from the middle. This process is called splicing and is handled by the **splice** function.

```
splice ARRAY, OFFSET, LENGTH, LIST
splice ARRAY, OFFSET, LENGTH
splice ARRAY, OFFSET
```

The return value in every case is the list of elements extracted from the array in the order that they appeared in the original. The first argument, **ARRAY**, is the array that you want to remove elements from, and the second argument is the index number that you want to start extracting elements from. The **LENGTH**, if specified, removes that number of elements from the array. If you don't specify **LENGTH**, it removes all elements to the end of the array. If **LENGTH** is negative, it leaves that number of elements on the end of the array.

Finally, you can replace the elements removed with a different list of elements, using the values of **LIST**. Note that this will replace any number of elements with the new **LIST**, irrespective of the number of elements removed or replaced. The array will shrink or grow as necessary. For example, in the following code, the middle of the list of users is replaced with a new set, putting the removed users into a new list:

```
@users = qw/Bob Martin Phil Dave Alan Tracy/;
@newusers = qw/Helen Dan/;
@oldusers = splice @users, 1, 4, @newusers;
```

This sets **@users** to

```
New Bob Helen Dan Tracy
```

and **@oldusers** to

```
Martin Phil Dave Alan
```

join

The normal interpolation rules determine how an array is displayed when it's embedded within a scalar or interpreted in a scalar context. By default, the individual elements in the array are separated by the contents of the **$,** variable which is empty by default, so this:

```
@array = qw/hello world/;
print @array;
```

outputs

```
helloworld
```

To change the separator, change the value of **$,**:

```
@array = qw/hello world/;
$, = '::';
print @array,"\n";
```

Be careful though, because the preceding outputs

```
hello::world::
```

The **$,** variable replaces each comma (including those implied by arrays and hashes in list context). However, remember that when interpolating an array into a scalar string, an array is *always* separated by a space, completely ignoring the value of **$,**.

To introduce a different separator between individual elements of a list, you need to use the **join** function:

```
join EXPR, LIST
```

This combines the elements of **LIST**, returning a scalar where each element is separated by the value of **EXPR** to separate each element. Note that **EXPR** is a scalar, not a regular expression:

```
print join(', ',@users);
```

EXPR separates each pair of elements in **LIST**, so this:

```
@array = qw/first second third fourth/;
print join(', ',@array),"\n";
```

outputs

```
first, second, third, fourth
```

There is no **EXPR** before the first element or after the last element.

The return value from **join** is a scalar, so it can also be used to create new strings based on the combined components of a list:

```
$string = join(', ', @users);
```

The **join** function can also be an efficient way of joining a lot of elements together into a single string, instead of using multiple concatenation. For example, in the following code, I've placed multiple SQL query statement fragments into an array using **push**, and then used **join** to combine all those arguments into a single string:

```
if ($isbn->{rank} < $row[10])
  {
    push @query,"reviewmin = " . $dbh->quote($isbn->{review});
    push @query,"reviewmindate = " . $dbh->quote($report->{date});
}
if ($isbn->{rank} > $row[12])
{
    push @query,"reviewmax = " . $dbh->quote($isbn->{review});
    push @query,"reviewmaxdate = " . $dbh->quote($report->{date});
}
$dbh->do("update isbnlimit set " .
```

```
join(', ',@query) .
" where isbn = " .
$dbh->quote($isbn->{isbn}) .
" and host = " .
$dbh->quote($host->{host}));
```

Note *If you want to join elements using a regular expression, try* ***awk***.

split

The logical opposite of the **join** function is the **split** function, which enables you to separate a string using a regular expression. The result is an array of all the separated elements. The **split** function separates a scalar or other string expression into a list, using a regular expression.

```
split /PATTERN/, EXPR, LIMIT
split /PATTERN/, EXPR
split /PATTERN/
split
```

By default, empty leading fields are preserved, and empty trailing fields are deleted.

If you do not specify a pattern, then it splits $_ using white space as the separator pattern. This also has the effect of skipping the leading white space in $_. For reference, white space includes spaces, tabs (vertical and horizontal), line feeds, carriage returns, and form feeds.

The **PATTERN** can be any standard regular expression. You can use quotes to specify the separator, but you should instead use the match operator and regular expression syntax.

If you specify a **LIMIT**, then it only splits for **LIMIT** elements. If there is any remaining text in **EXPR**, it is returned as the last element with all characters in the text. Otherwise, the entire string is split, and the full list of separated values is returned. If you specify a negative value, Perl acts as if a huge value has been supplied and splits the entire string, including trailing null fields.

For example, you can split a line from the /etc/passwd file (under Unix) by the colons used to identify the individual fields:

```
while (<PASSWD>)
{
    chomp;
    @fields = split /:/;
}
```

You can also use all of the normal list and array constructs to extract and combine values,

```
print join(" ",split /:/),"\n";
```

and even extract only select fields:

```
print "User: ",(split /:/)[0],"\n";
```

If you specify a null string, it splits **EXPR** into individual characters, such that

```
print join('-',split(/ */, 'Hello World')),"\n";
```

produces

```
H-e-l-l-o-W-o-r-l-d
```

Note that the space is ignored.

In a scalar context, the function returns the number of fields found and splits the values into the @_ array using **??** as the pattern delimiter, irrespective of supplied arguments; so care should be taken when using this function as part of others.

grep

The **grep** function works the same as the **grep** command does under Unix, except that it operates on a list rather than a file. However, unlike the **grep** command, the function is not restricted to regular expression searches, even though that is what it is usually used for.

```
grep BLOCK LIST
grep EXPR, LIST
```

The function evaluates the **BLOCK** or **EXPR** for each element of the **LIST**. For each statement in the expression or block that returns true, it adds the corresponding element to the list of values returned. Each element of the array is passed to the expression or block as a localized $_. A search for the word "text" on a file can therefore be performed with

```
@lines = <FILE>;
print join("\n", grep { /text/ } @lines);
```

FUNDAMENTALS

A more complex example, which returns a list of the elements from an array that exist as keys within a hash, is shown here:

```
print join(' ', grep { defined($hash{$_}) } @array);
```

This is quicker than using either **push** and **join** or catenation within a loop to determine the correct list.

In a scalar context, the function just returns the number of times the statement matched.

map

The **map** function performs an expression or block expression on each element within a list. This enables you to bulk modify a list without the need to explicitly use a loop.

```
map EXPR, LIST
map BLOCK LIST
```

The individual elements of the list are supplied to a locally scoped $_, and the modified array is returned as a list to the caller. For example, to convert all the elements of an array to lowercase:

```
@lcarray = map { lc } @array;
```

This is itself just a simple version of

```
foreach (@array)
{
    push @lcarray,lc($_);
}
```

Note that because $_ is used to hold each element of the array, it can also modify an array in place, so you don't have to manually assign the modified array to a new one. However, this isn't supported, so the actual results are not guaranteed. This is especially true if you are modifying a list directly rather than a named array, such as:

```
@new = map {lc} keys %hash;
```

sort

With any list, it can be useful to sort the contents. Doing this manually is a complex process, so Perl provides a built-in function that takes a list and returns a lexically sorted version. For practicality, it also accepts a function or block that can be used to create your own sorting algorithm.

```
sort SUBNAME LIST
sort BLOCK LIST
sort LIST
```

Both the subroutine (**SUBROUTINE**) and block (**BLOCK**, which is an anonymous subroutine) should return a value—less than, greater than, or equal to zero—depending on whether the two elements of the list are less than, greater than, or equal to each other. The two elements of the list are available in the **$a** and **$b** variables.

For example, to do a standard lexical sort:

```
sort @array;
```

Or to specify an explicit lexical subroutine:

```
sort { $a cmp $b } @array;
```

To perform a reverse lexical sort:

```
sort { $b cmp $a } @array;
```

All the preceding examples take into account the differences between upper- and lowercase characters. You can use the **lc** or **uc** functions within the subroutine to ignore the case of the individual values. The individual elements are not actually modified; it only affects the values compared during the sort process:

```
sort { lc($a) cmp lc($b) } @array;
```

If you know you are sorting numbers, you need to use the <=> operator:

```
sort { $a <=> $b } @numbers;
```

Alternatively, to use a separate routine:

```
sub lexical
{
    $a cmp $b;
}
sort lexical @array;
```

You can also use this method to sort complex values that require simple translation before they can be sorted. For example:

```
foreach (sort sortdate keys %errors)
{
    print "$_\n";
}

sub sortdate
{
    my ($c,$d) = ($a,$b);
    $c =~ s{(\d+)/(\d+)/(\d+)}{sprintf("%04d%02d%02d",$3,$1,$2)}e;
    $d =~ s{(\d+)/(\d+)/(\d+)}{sprintf("%04d%02d%02d",$3,$1,$2)}e;
    $c <=> $d;
}
```

In the preceding example, we are sorting dates stored in the keys of the hash **%errors**. The dates are in the form "month/day/year", which is not logically sortable without doing some sort of modification of the key value in each case. We could do this by creating a new hash that contains the date in a more ordered format, but this is wasteful of space. Instead, we take a copy of the hash elements supplied to us by **sort**, and then use a regular expression to turn "3/26/2000" into "20000326"—in this format, the dates can be logically sorted on a numeric basis. Then we return a comparison between the two converted dates to act as the comparison required for the hash.

reverse

On a sorted list, you can use **sort** to return a list in reverse order by changing the comparison statement used in the sort. However, it can be quicker, and more practical for unsorted lists, to use the **reverse** function.

```
reverse LIST
```

In a list context, the function returns the elements of **LIST** in reverse order. This is often used with the **sort** function to produce a reverse-sorted list:

```
foreach (reverse sort keys %hash)
{
...
}
```

In a scalar context, it returns a concatenated string of the values of **LIST**, with all bytes in opposite order. This also works if a single-element list (or a scalar!) is passed, such that

```
print scalar reverse("Hello World"),"\n";
```

produces

```
dlroW olleH
```

Regular Expressions

Using the functions we've seen so far—for finding your location within a string and updating that string—is fine if you know precisely what you are looking for. Often, however, what you are looking for is either a range of characters or a specific pattern, perhaps matching a range of individual words, letters, or numbers separated by other elements. These patterns are impossible to emulate using the **substr** and **index** functions, because they rely on using a fixed string as the search criteria.

Identifying patterns instead of strings within Perl is as easy as writing the correct regular expression. A *regular expression* is a string of characters that define the pattern or patterns you are viewing. Of course, writing the correct regular expression is the difficult part. There are ways and tricks of making the format of a regular expression easier to read, but there is no easy way of making a regular expression easier to understand!

The syntax of regular expressions in Perl is very similar to what you will find within other regular expression–supporting programs, such as **sed**, **grep**, and **awk**, although there are some differences between Perl's interpretations of certain elements.

The basic method for applying a regular expression is to use the pattern binding operators =~ and !~. The first operator is a test and assignment operator. In a test context (called a *match* in Perl) the operator returns true if the value on the left side of the operator matches the regular expression on the right. In an assignment context (substitution), it modifies the statement on the left based on the regular expression on the right. The second operator, !~, is for matches only and is the exact opposite: it returns true only if the value on the left does not match the regular expression on the right.

Although often used on their own in combination with the pattern binding operators, regular expressions also appear in two other locations within Perl. When used with the **split** function, they allow you to define a regular expression to be used for separating the individual elements of a line—this can be useful if you want to divide up a line by its numerical content, or even by word boundaries. The second place is within the **grep** statement, where you use a regular expression as the source for the match against the supplied list. Using **grep** with a regular expression is similar in principle to using a standard match within the confines of a loop.

The statements on the right side of the two test and assignment operators must be regular expression operators. There are three regular expression operators within Perl—**m//** (match), **s///** (substitute), and **tr///** (transliterate). There is also a fourth operator, which is strictly a quoting mechanism. The **qr//** operator allows you to define a regular expression that can later be used as the source expression for a match or substitution operation. The forward slashes in each case act as delimiters for the regular expression (regex) that you are specifying.

Pattern Modifiers

All regular expression operators support a number of pattern modifiers. These change the way in which the expression is interpreted. Before we look at the specifics of the individual regular expression operators, we'll look at the common pattern modifiers that are shared by all the operators.

Pattern modifiers are a list of options placed after the final delimiter in a regular expression and that modify the method and interpretation applied to the searching mechanism. Perl supports five basic modifiers that apply to the **m//**, **s///**, and **qr//** operators, as listed here in Table 8-2. You place the modifier after the last delimiter in the expression. For example **m/foo/i**.

The **/i** modifier tells the regular expression engine to ignore the case of supplied characters so that **/cat/** would also match CAT, cAt, and Cat.

The **/s** modifier tells the regular expression engine to allow the **.** metacharacter to match a newline character when used to match against a multiline string.

The **/m** modifier tells the regular expression engine to let the ^ and $ metacharacters to match the beginning and end of a line within a multiline string. This means that **/^The/** will match "Dog\nThe cat". The normal behavior would cause this match to fail, because ordinarily the ^ operator matches only against the beginning of the string supplied.

Modifier	Description
i	Makes the match case insensitive
m	Specifies that if the string has newline or carriage return characters, the ^ and $ operators will now match against a newline boundary, instead of a string boundary
o	Evaluates the expression only once
s	Allows use of . to match a newline character
x	Allows you to use white space in the expression for clarity

Table 8-2. *Perl Regular Expression Modifiers for Matching and Substitution*

The **/o** operator changes the way in which the regular expression engine compiles the expression. Normally, unless the delimiters are single quotes (which don't interpolate), any variables that are embedded into a regular expression are interpolated at run time, and cause the expression to be recompiled each time. Using the **/o** operator causes the expression to be compiled only once; however, you must ensure that any variable you are including does not change during the execution of a script—otherwise you may end up with extraneous matches.

The **/x** modifier enables you to introduce white space and comments into an expression for clarity. For example, the following match expression looks suspiciously like line noise:

```
$matched =
/(\S+)\s+(\S+)\s+(\S+)\s+\[(.*)\]\s+"(.*)"\s+(\S+)\s+(\S+)/;
```

Adding the **/x** modifier and giving some description to the individual components allows us to be more descriptive about what we are doing:

```
matched = /(\S+)      #Host
           \s+        #(space separator)
           (\S+)      #Identifier
           \s+        #(space separator)
           (\S+)      #Username
           \s+        #(space separator)
           \[(.*)\]   #Time
           \s+        #(space separator)
           "(.*)"     #Request
           \s+        #(space separator)
           (\S+)      #Result
           \s+        #(space separator)
           (\S+)      #Bytes sent
          /x;
```

Although it takes up more editor and page space, it is much clearer what you are trying to achieve.

There are other operator-specific modifiers, which we'll look at separately as we examine each operator in more detail.

The Match Operator

The match operator, **m//**, is used to match a string or statement to a regular expression. For example, to match the character sequence "foo" against the scalar **$bar**, you might use a statement like this:

```
if ($bar =~ m/foo/)
```

Note the terminology here—we are matching the letters "f", "o", and "o" in that sequence, somewhere within the string—we'll need to use a separate qualifier to match against the *word* "foo". See the "Regular Expression Elements" section later in this chapter.

Providing the delimiters in your statement with the **m//** operators are forward slashes, you can omit the leading **m**:

```
if ($bar =~ /foo/)
```

The **m//** actually works in the same fashion as the **q//** operator series—you can use any combination of naturally matching characters to act as delimiters for the expression. For example, **m{}**, **m()**, and **m<>** are all valid. As per the **q//** operator, all delimiters allow for interpolation of variables, except single quotes. If you use single quotes, then the entire expression is taken as a literal with no interpolation.

You can omit the **m** from **m//** if the delimiters are forward slashes, but for all other delimiters you must use the **m** prefix. The ability to change the delimiters is useful when you want to match a string that contains the delimiters. For example, let's imagine you want to check on whether the **$dir** variable contains a particular directory. The delimiter for directories is the forward slash, and the forward slash in each case would need to be escaped—otherwise the match would be terminated by the first forward slash. For example:

```
if ($dir =~ /\/usr\/local\/lib/)
```

By using a different delimiter, you can use a much clearer regular expression:

```
if ($dir =~ m(/usr/local/lib))
```

Note that the entire match expression—that is the expression on the left of **=~** or **!~** and the match operator, returns true (in a scalar context) if the expression matches. Therefore the statement:

```
$true = ($foo =~ m/foo/);
```

Will set **$true** to 1 if **$foo** matches the regex, or 0 if the match fails.

In a list context, the match returns the contents of any grouped expressions (see the "Grouping" section later in this chapter for more information). For example, when extracting the hours, minutes, and seconds from a time string, we can use

```
my ($hours, $minutes, $seconds) = ($time =~ m/(\d+):(\d+):(\d+)/);
```

This example uses grouping and a character class to specify the individual elements. The groupings are the elements in standard parentheses, and each one will match (we hope) in sequence, returning a list that has been assigned to the hours, minutes, and seconds variables.

Match Operator Modifiers

The **match** operator supports its own set of modifiers—the standard five operators shown in Table 8-2 are supported, in addition to the **/g** and **/cg** modifiers. The full list is shown in Table 8-3 for reference.

The **/g** modifier allows for global matching. Normally the match returns the first valid match for a regular expression, but with the **/g** modifier in effect, all possible matches for the expression are returned. In a list context, this results in a list of the matches being returned, such that:

```
@foos = $string =~ /foo/gi;
```

will populate **@foos** with all the occurrences of "foo", irrespective of case, within the string **$string**.

Modifier	Description
i	Makes the match case insensitive
m	Specifies that if the string has newline or carriage return characters, the ^ and $ operators will now match against a newline boundary, instead of a string boundary
o	Evaluates the expression only once
s	Allows use of . to match a newline character
x	Allows you to use white space in the expression for clarity
g	Globally finds all matches
cg	Allows the search to continue even after a global match fails

Table 8-3. *Regular Expression Modifiers for Matches*

In a scalar context, the **/g** modifier performs a progressive match. For each execution of the match, Perl starts searching from the point in the search string just past the last match. You can use this to progress through an array searching for the same string without having to remove or manually set the starting position of the search. The position of the last match can be used within a regular expression using the **\G** assertion. When **/g** fails to match, the position is reset to the start of the string.

If you use the **/c** modifier as well, then the position is not reset when the **/g** match fails.

Matching Only Once

There is also a simpler version of the match operator—the **?PATTERN?** operator. This is basically identical to the **m//** operator except that it only matches once within the string you are searching between each call to **reset**. The operator works as a useful optimization of the matching process when you want to search a set of data streams but only want to match an expression once within each stream.

For example, you can use this to get the first and last elements within a list:

```
@list = qw/food foosball subbuteo monopoly footnote tenderfoot catatonic footbrdige/;

foreach (@list)
{
    $first = $1 if ?(foo.*)?;
    $last = $1 if /(foo.*)/;
}

print "First: $first, Last: $last\n";
```

A call to **reset** resets what **PATTERN?** considers as the first match, but it applies only to matches within the current package. Thus you can have multiple **PATTERN?** operations, providing they are all within their own package.

The Substitution Operator

The substitution operator, **s///**, is really just an extension of the match operator that allows you to replace the text matched with some new text. The basic form of the operator is

```
s/PATTERN/REPLACEMENT/;
```

For example, we can replace all occurrences of "dog" with "cat" using

```
$string =~ s/dog/cat/;
```

The **PATTERN** is the regular expression for the text that we are looking for. The **REPLACEMENT** is a specification for the text or regular expression that we want to use to replace the found text with. For example, you may remember from the **substr** definition earlier in the chapter that you could replace a specific number of characters within a string by using assignment:

```
$string = 'The cat sat on the mat';
$start  = index($string,'cat',0);
$end    = index($string,' ',$start)-$start;
substr($string,$start,$end) = 'dog';
```

You can achieve the same result with a regular expression:

```
$string = 'The cat sat on the mat';
$string = s/cat/dog/;
```

Note that we have managed to avoid the process of finding the start and end of the string we want to replace. This is a fundamental part of understanding the regular expression syntax. A regular expression will match the text anywhere within the string. You do not have to specify the starting point or location within the string, although it is possible to do so if that's what you want. Taking this to its logical conclusion, we can use the same regular expression to replace the word "cat" with "dog" in any string, irrespective of the location of the original word:

```
$string = 'Oscar is my cat';
$string = s/cat/dog/;
```

The **$string** variable now contains the phrase "Oscar is my dog," which is factually incorrect, but it does demonstrate the ease with which you can replace strings with other strings.

Here's a more complex example that we will return to later. In this instance, we need to change a date in the form 03/26/1999 to 19990326. Using grouping, we can change it very easily with a regular expression:

```
$date = '03/26/1999';
$date =~ s#(\d+)/(\d+)/(\d+)#$3$1$2#;
```

This example also demonstrates the fact that you can use delimiters other than the forward slash for substitutions too. Just like the match operator, the character used is the one immediately following the "s". Alternatively, if you specify a naturally paired delimiter, such as a brace; then the replacement expression can have its own pair of delimiters:

```
$date = s{(\d+)/(\d+)/(\d+)}
         {$3$1$2}x;
```

Note that the return value from any substitution operation is the number of substitutions that took place. In a typical substitution, this will return 1 on success, and if no replacements are made, then it will return 0—a false response.

The problem with modifying strings in this way is that we clobber the original value of the string in each case—which is often not the effect we want. The usual alternative is to copy the information into a variable first, and then perform the substitution on the new variable:

```
$newstring = $string;
$newstring =~ s/cat/dog/;
```

You can do this in one line by performing the substitution on the lvalue that is created when you perform an assignment. For example, we can rewrite the preceding as

```
($newstring = $string) =~ s/cat/dog/;
```

This works because the lvalue created by the Perl interpreter as part of the expression on the left of =~ is actually the new value of the **$newstring** variable. Note that without the parentheses, you would only end up with a count of the replacements in **$newstring** and a modified **$string**—not what we wanted!

The same process also works within a loop, for the same reasons:

```
foreach ($newstring = $string)
{
    s/cat/dog/;
}
```

A loop also affords us the ability to perform multiple substitutions on a string:

```
foreach ($newstring = $string)
{
    s/cat/dog/;
    s/sheep/camel/;
}
```

Substitution Operator Modifiers

In addition to the five standard modifiers, the substitution operator also supports a further two modifiers that modify the way in which substitutions take place. A full list of the supported modifiers is given in Table 8-4.

The **/g** operator forces the search and replace operation to take place multiple times, which means that **PATTERN** is replaced with **REPLACEMENT** for as many times as **PATTERN** appears. This is done as a one-pass process, however. The substitution operation is not put into a loop. For example, in the following substitution we replace "o" with "oo":

```
$string = 'Both foods';
$string =~ s/o/oo/g;
```

The result is "Booth foooods", not "Booooooooooooth fooooooooooods" ad infinitum. However, there are times when such a multiple-pass process is useful. In those cases, just place the substitution in a **while** loop. For example, to replace all the double spaces with a single space you might use:

```
1 while($string =~ s/  / /g);
```

Modifier	Description
i	Makes the match case insensitive
m	Specifies that if the string has newline or carriage return characters, the ^ and $ operators will now match against a newline boundary, instead of a string boundary
o	Evaluates the expression only once
s	Allows use of . to match a newline character
x	Allows you to use white space in the expression for clarity
g	Replaces all occurrences of the found expression with the replacement text
e	Evaluates the replacement as if it were a Perl statement, and uses its return value as the replacement text

Table 8-4. *Substitution Operator Modifiers*

The **while** loop will drop out as soon as the substitution fails to find a double space.

The **/e** modifier causes Perl to evaluate the **REPLACEMENT** text as if it were a Perl expression, and then to use the value as the replacement string. We've already seen an example of this when converting a date from traditional American slashed format into the Japanese/Universal format:

```
$c =~ s{(\d+)/(\d+)/(\d+)}{sprintf("%04d%02d%02d",$3,$1,$2)}e;
```

We have to use **sprintf** in this case; otherwise, a single-digit day or month would truncate the numeric digits from the eight required—for example, 26/3/2000 would become 2000326 instead of 20000326.

Translation

Translation is similar, but not identical, to the principles of substitution, but unlike substitution, translation (or transliteration) does not use regular expressions for its search on replacement values. The translation operators are

```
tr/SEARCHLIST/REPLACEMENTLIST/cds
y/SEARCHLIST/REPLACEMENTLIST/cds
```

The translation replaces all occurrences of the characters in **SEARCHLIST** with the corresponding characters in **REPLACEMENTLIST**. For example, using the "The cat sat on the mat." string we have been using in this chapter:

```
$string =~ tr/a/o/;
print "$string\n";
```

this script prints out "The cot sot on the mot."

Standard Perl ranges can also be used, allowing you to specify ranges of characters either by letter or numerical value. To change the case of the string, you might use

```
$string =~ tr/a-z/A-Z/;
```

in place of the **uc** function. The **tr** operator only works on a scalar or single element of an array or hash; you cannot use it directly against an array or hash (see the discussion of **grep** or **map** in Chapter 7). You can also use **tr//** with any reference or function that can be assigned to. For example, to convert the word "cat" from the string to uppercase, you could do this:

```
substr($string,4,3) =~ tr/a-z/A-Z/;
```

Unlike regular expressions, the **SEARCHLIST** and **REPLACEMENTLIST** arguments to the operator do not need to use the same delimiters. As long as the **SEARCHLIST** is naturally paired with delimiters, such as parentheses or braces, the **REPLACEMENTLIST** can use its own pair. This makes the conversion of forward slashes clearer than the traditional regular expression search:

```
$macdir = tr(/)/:/;
```

The same feature can be used to make certain character sequences seem clearer, such as the following one, which converts an 8-bit string into a 7-bit string, albeit with some loss of information:

```
tr [\200-\377]
   [\000-\177]
```

Three modifiers are supported by the **tr** operator, as seen in Table 8-5.

The /c modifier changes the replacement text to be the characters not specified in **SEARCHLIST**. You might use this to replace characters other than those specified in the **SEARCHLIST** with a null alternative; for example,

```
$string = 'the cat sat on the mat.';
$string =~ tr/a-zA-Z/-/c;
print "$string\n";
```

replaces any non-character with a hyphen, resulting in "the-cat-sat-on-the-mat-."

Modifier	Meaning
c	Complement **SEARCHLIST**.
d	Delete found but unreplaced characters.
s	Squash duplicate replaced characters.

Table 8-5. *Modifiers to the **tr** Operator*

The **/d** modifier deletes the characters matching **SEARCHLIST** that do not have a corresponding entry in **REPLACEMENTLIST**. For example,

```
$string = 'the cat sat on the mat.';
$string =~ tr/a-z/b/d;
print "$string\n";
```

deletes any characters from "b-z", whilst translating "a" to "b". This results in

```
b b    b.
```

The last modifier, **/s**, removes the duplicate sequences of characters that were replaced, so

```
$string = 'food';
tr/a-z/a-z/s;
```

returns "fod". This is useful when you want to de-dupe the string for certain characters. For example, we could rewrite our space-character compressing substitution with a transliteration:

```
$string =~ tr/ / /s;
```

If you do not specify the **REPLACEMENTLIST**, Perl uses the values in **SEARCHLIST**. This is most useful for doing character-class-based counts, something that cannot be done with the **length** function. For example, to count the nonalphanumeric characters in a string:

```
$cnt = $string =~ tr/a-zA-Z0-9//cs;
```

In all cases, the **tr** operator returns the number of characters changed (including those deleted).

Regular Expression Elements

The regular expression engine is responsible for parsing the regular expression and matching the elements of the regular expression with the string supplied. Depending on the context of the regular expression, different results will occur: a substitution replaces character sequences, for example.

The regular expression syntax is best thought of as a little language in its own right. It's very powerful, and an incredible amount of ability is compacted into a very small space. Like all languages, though, a regular expression is composed of a number of discrete elements, and if you understand those individual elements, you can understand the entire regular expression.

For most characters and character sequences, the interpretation is literal, so a substitution to replace the first occurrence of "cat" with "dog" can be as simple as

```
s/cat/dog/;
```

Beyond the literal interpretation, Perl also supports two further classes of characters or character sequences within the regular expression syntax: metacharacters and metasymbols. The *metacharacters* define the 12 main characters that are used to define the major components of a regular expression syntax. These are

```
\  |  (  )  [  {  ^  $  *  +  ?  .
```

Most of these form multicharacter sequences—for example \s matches any white-space character, and these multicharacter sequences are classed as *metasymbols*.

Some of the metacharacters just shown have their own unique effects and don't apply to, or modify, the other elements around them. For example, the . matches any character within an expression. Others modify the preceding element—for example the + metacharacter matches one or more of the previous elements, such that .+ matches one or more characters, whatever that character may be.

Others modify the character they precede—the major metacharacter in this instance is the backslash, \, which allows you to "escape" certain characters and sequences. The \. sequence, for example, implies a literal period. Alternatively, \ can also start the definition of a metasymbol, such as \b, which specifies a word boundary.

Finally, the remaining metacharacters allow you to define lists or special components within their boundaries—for example, [a-z] creates a character class that contains all of the lowercase letters from "a" to "z."

Because all of these elements have an overall effect on all the regular expressions you will use, we'll list them here first, before looking at the specifics of matching individual characteristics within an expression, such as words and character classes. In both Tables 8-6 and 8-7, the entries have an "Atomic" column—if the value in that column is "yes", then the metasymbol is quantifiable. A quantifiable element can be combined with a quantifier to allow you to match one or more elements.

Table 8-6 lists the general metacharacters supported by regular expressions.

Character	Atomic	Description
\	Depends	Treats the following character as a real character, ignoring any associations with a Perl regex metacharacter—see Table 8-7.
^	No	Matches from the beginning of the string (or of the line if the **/m** modifier is in place).
$	No	Matches from the end of the string (or of the line if the **/m** modifier is in place).
.	Yes	Matches any character except the newline character.
|	No	Allows you to specify alternative matches within the same regex—known as the OR operator.
()	Yes	Groups expressions together, treating the enclosed text as a single unit.
[]	Yes	Looks for a set and/or range of characters, defined as a single character class, but [] only represents a single character.

Table 8-6. *Regular Expression Metacharacters*

The next table, Table 8-7, lists the metasymbols supported by the regular expression mechanism for matching special characters or entities within a given string. Note that not all entries are atomic—as a general rule, the metasymbols that apply to locations or boundaries are not atomic.

Sequence	Atomic	Purpose
\0	Yes	Matches the null character.
\033	Yes	Matches the specified octal character, up to \377 (255 decimal).
\n	Yes	Matches the *n*th previously captured string (deprecated, use $n instead).
\A	No	Matches only the beginning of a string.
\a	Yes	Specifies alarm (bell).
\b	Yes	Matches the backspace character (within a character class).
\b	No	Matches a word boundary (outside a character class).
\B	No	Matches a non-word boundary.
\cX	Yes	Matches the control character X.
\c	Yes	Matches one byte (8-bit character), even when the **utf8** pragma is in force.
\d	Yes	Matches a digit.
\D	Yes	Matches a nondigit character.
\e	Yes	Matches the escape (ASCII) character.
\E	NA	Ends case (\U, \L) or metaquote (\Q) translation.
\f	Yes	Matches the form feed character.
\G	No	Matches where previous **m//g** operation left off (only works with **/g** modifier).
\l	NA	Translates only the next character to lowercase.
\L	NA	Specifies lowercase until \E.
\n	Yes	Matches a newline (CR on Macs).

Table 8-7.   *Regular Expression Character Patterns*

Sequence	Atomic	Purpose
\N{NAME}	Yes	Matches the named UTF character.
\p{PROP}	Yes	Matches any UTF character with the named property.
\P{PROP}	Yes	Matches any UTF character without the named property.
\Q	NA	Quotes (disables) regex metacharacters until **e**.
\r	Yes	Matches the carriage return character (NL on Macs).
\s	Yes	Matches any white-space character (spaces, tabs, etc.).
\S	Yes	Matches any non-white-space character.
\t	Yes	Matches the (horizontal) tab character.
\u	NA	Translates only the next character to uppercase.
\U	NA	Specifies uppercase until \E.
\w	Yes	Matches any alphanumeric character (including _).
\W	Yes	Matches any nonalphanumeric character.
\x1B	Yes	Matches any two-digit hexadecimal character.
\x{xxxx}	Yes	Matches any multidigit hexadecimal character.
\X	Yes	Matches any Unicode "combining character sequence" string.
\z	No	Matches the end of a string.
\Z	No	Matches the end of a string or before a newline character (except when in multiline-match mode).

Table 8-7.   *Regular Expression Character Patterns* (continued)

Table 8-8 lists the quantifiers supported by Perl. These affect the character or entity immediately before them—for example, **[a-z]*** matches zero or more occurrences of all the lowercase characters. Note that the metasymbols show both maximal and minimal examples—see the "Quantifiers" section later in this chapter for an example of how this works.

Matching Specific Characters

Anything that is not special within a given regular-expression pattern (essentially everything *not* listed in Table 8-2) is treated as a raw character. For example **/a/** matches the character "a" anywhere within a string. Perl also identifies the standard character aliases that are interpreted within double-quoted strings, such as **\n** and **\t**.

In addition, Perl provides direct support for the following:

- **Control Characters** You can also name a control character using **\c**, so that CTRL-Z becomes **\cZ**. The less obvious completions are **\c[** for escape and **\c?** for delete. These are useful when outputting text information in a formatted form to the screen (providing your terminal supports it), or for controlling the output to a printer.

- **Octal Characters** If you supply a three-digit number, such as **\123**, then it's treated as an octal number and used to display the corresponding character from the ASCII table, or, for numbers above 127, the corresponding character within the current character table and font. The leading 0 is optional for all numbers greater than 010.

- **Hexadecimal Characters** The **\xHEX** and **\x{HEX}** forms introduce a character according to the current ASCII or other table, based on the value of

Maximal	Minimal	Purpose
*	*?	Matches zero or more items.
+	+?	Matches one or more items.
?	??	Matches zero or one items.
{n}	{n}?	Matches exactly **n** times.
{n,}	{n,}?	Matches at least **n** times.
{n,m}	{n,m}?	Matches at least **n** times but no more than **m** times.

Table 8-8. *Regular Expression Pattern Quantifiers*

the supplied hexadecimal string. You can use the unbraced form for one- or two-digit hexadecimals; using braces, you can use as many hex digits as you require.

■ **Named Unicode Characters**   Using **\N{NAME}** allows you to introduce Unicode characters by their names, but only if the **charnames** pragma is in effect. See Chapter 19 for more information on accessing characters by their names.

Matching Wildcard Characters

The regular expression engine allows you to select any character by using a wildcard. The **.** (period) is used to match any character, so that

```
if ($string =~ /c.t/)
```

would match any sequence of "c" followed by any character and then "t." This would, for example, match "cat" or "cot", or indeed, words such as "acetic" and "acidification."

By default, a period matches everything except a newline unless the **/s** modifier is in effect, in which case it matches everything including a newline.

The wildcard metasymbol is usually combined with one of the quantifiers (see the "Quantifiers" section later in the chapter) to match a multitude of occurrences within a given string. For example, you could split the hours and minutes from "19:23" using

```
($hours,$mins) = ('19:23' =~ m/(.*?):(.*?)/);
```

This probably isn't the best way of doing it, as we haven't qualified the type of character we are expecting—we'd be much better off matching the **\d** character class.

The **\X** matches a Unicode character, including those composed of a number of Unicode character sequences (i.e. those used to build up accented characters). For example /\X/i would match "c", "ç", "C" and "Ç".

The **\C** can be used to match exactly one byte from a string—generally this means that **\C** will match a single 8-bit character, and in fact uses the C **char** type as a guide.

Character Classes

Character classes allow you to specify a list of values for a single character. This can be useful if you want to find a name that may or may not have been specified with a leading capital letter:

```
if ($name =~ /[Mm]artin/)
```

Within the [] metacharacters, you can also specify a range by using a hyphen to separate the start and end points, such as "a-z" for all lowercase characters, "0-9" for numbers, and so on. If you want to specify a hyphen, use a backslash within the class to prevent Perl from trying to produce a range. If you want to match a right square bracket (which would otherwise be interpreted as a character class), use a backslash or place it first in the list, for example [[]].

You can also include any of the standard metasymbols for characters, including \n, \b, and \cX, and any of the character classes given later in this chapter (class, Unicode, and POSIX). However, metasymbols used to specify boundaries or positions, such as \z, are ignored, and note that \b is treated as backspace, not as a word boundary. The wildcard metasymbols, ., \X, and \C, are also invalid. You also can't use | within a class to mean alternation—the symbol is just ignored.

Finally, you can't use a quantifier within a class because it doesn't make sense. If you want to add a quantifier to a class, place it after the closing square bracket so that it applies to the entire class.

All character classes can also use negation by including a ^ prefix before the class specification. For example, to match against the characters that are not lowercase, you could use

```
$string =~ m/[^a-z]/;
```

Standard (Classic) Character-Class Shortcuts

Perl supports a number of standard (now called Classic) character-class shortcuts. They are all metasymbols using an upper- or lowercase character. The lowercase version matches a character class, and the uppercase versions negate the class. For example, \w matches any word character, while \W matches any non-word character.

The specifications are actually based on Unicode classes, so the exact matches will depend on the current list of Unicode character sets currently installed. If you want to explicitly use the traditional ASCII meanings, then use the **bytes** pragma. Table 8-9

Metasymbol	Meaning	Unicode	Byte
\d	Digit	\p{IsDigit}	[0-9]
\D	Non-digit	\P{IsDigit}	[^0-9]
\s	White space	\p{IsSpace}	[\t\n\r\f]
\S	Non-white space	\P{IsSpace}	[^ \t\n\r\f]
\w	Word character	\p{IsWord}	[a-zA-Z0-9_]
\W	Non-word character	\P{IsWord}	[^a-zA-Z0-9_]

Table 8-9.   *"Classic" Character Classes*

shows the metasymbol, the meaning, and the Unicode- and byte-based interpretations of each metasymbol.

Note that the **\d** sequence is strict, such that if you want to match periods or commas that are often used to separate elements of numbers, then you must specify them additionally within a set:

```
if ('23,445.33' =~ m/([\d,.]+)/)
```

Also note that, as in the preceding example, a character class can be used both outside and inside of a character-class definition.

POSIX-Style Character Classes

The POSIX-style character classes allow you to specify a class according to the **Is...** functions defined by the POSIX standard. For example, you can specify an alphanumeric character class using **[:alnum:]**. However, a POSIX character class must be specified as part of another character class, for example **[[:alnum:]]** or **[[:alpha:][:digit:]]**.

The full list of supported classes is shown in Table 8-10.

 Note *POSIX character classes are only supported in Perl 5.6 and above.*

If the **utf8** pragma is in effect, then the POSIX character classes shown in Table 8-10 are identical to the **Is** properties for Unicode characters given in Table 8-12 later in the chapter.

You can negate a POSIX character class by specifying the **^** character before the class name, as in **[:^digit:]**.

Class	Meaning
alnum	Any alphanumeric (equivalent to **[[:alpha:][:digit:]]**)
alpha	Any letter (upper or lowercase)
ascii	Any 7-bit ASCII character (that is, those with a value between 0 and 127)
cntrl	Any control character—basically those ASCII characters with a decimal value of less than 32, including newlines, carriage returns, and tabs
digit	Any character representing a digit (0–9)
graph	Any alphanumeric or punctuation character

Table 8-10. *POSIX Character Classes*

Class	Meaning
lower	Any lowercase letter
print	Any printable character (equivalent to [[:alnum:][:punct:][:space:]])
punct	Any punctuation character
space	Any white-space character (space, tab, newline, carriage return, and form feed)
upper	Any uppercase letter
word	Any identifier character—basically **alnum** and the underscore
xdigit	Any hexadecimal digit (upper- or lowercase, 0–9 plus a–f)

Table 8-10.   *POSIX Character Classes* (continued)

Unicode Classes

You can use \p{PROP} and its negation, \P{PROP}, to select characters according to their Unicode properties. The braces are optional for classes that use a single character. Perl uses a combination of the formal definitions specified in the Unicode standard, and a number of composites defined purely within Perl that act as equivalents to the classic or POSIX character classes we've already seen.

For the moment, all of the Unicode character classes require the **utf8** pragma to be in effect for the matches to work properly. Table 8-11 lists the standard Unicode properties that are supported by Perl, along with those composites that are defined by Perl only to act as umbrellas for the main categories.

Property	Meaning
IsC	Control codes (Perl defined)
IsCc	Other, control
IsCf	Other, format
IsCn	Other, not assigned
IsCo	Other, private use
IsCs	Other, surrogate

Table 8-11.   *Standard Unicode Character-Class Properties*

Property	Meaning
IsL	Letters (Perl defined)
IsLl	Letter, lowercase
IsLm	Letter, modifier
IsLo	Letter, other
IsLt	Letter, title case
IsLu	Letter, uppercase
IsM	Marks (Perl defined)
IsMc	Mark, combining
IsMe	Mark, enclosing
IsMn,	Mark, non-spacing
IsN	Numbers (Perl defined)
IsNd,	Number, decimal digit
IsNl,	Number, letter
IsNo	Number, other
IsP	Punctuation (Perl defined)
IsPc	Punctuation, connector
IsPd	Punctuation, dash
IsPe	Punctuation, close
IsPf	Punctuation, final quote
IsPi	Punctuation, initial quote
IsPo	Punctuation, other
IsPs	Punctuation, open
IsS	Symbols (Perl defined)
IsSc	Symbol, currency
IsSk	Symbol, modifier
IsSm	Symbol, math
IsSo	Symbol, other

Table 8-11. *Standard Unicode Character-Class Properties* (continued)

Property	Meaning
IsZ	Separators (Perl defined)
IsZl	Separator, line
IsZp	Separator, paragraph
IsZs	Separator, space

Table 8-11.   *Standard Unicode Character-Class Properties* (continued)

Perl uses these classes to define its own unique sets, which are POSIX or classic compatible; these are themselves listed in Table 8-12. For more information on Unicode and how the properties are interpreted and supported in Perl, see the Unicode folder in the main Perl 5.6 library—since the Unicode standard is subject to change and expansion, we'll only deal with the basic classes and Perl composites in this section.

Property	Consists of
IsASCII	[\x00-\x7f]
IsAlnum	[\p{IsLl}\p{IsLu}\p{IsLt}\p{IsLo}\p{IsNd}]
IsAlpha	[\p{IsLl}\p{IsLu}\p{IsLt}\p{IsLo}]
IsCntrl	\p{IsC}
IsDigit	\p{Nd}
IsGraph	[^\pC\p{IsSpace}]
IsLower	\p{IsLl}
IsPrint	\P{IsC}
IsPunct	\p{IsP}
IsSpace	[\t\n\f\r\p{IsZ}]
IsUpper	[\p{IsLu}\p{IsLt}]
IsWord	[_\p{IsLl}\p{IsLu}\p{IsLt}\p{IsLo}\p{IsNd}]
IsXDigit	[0-9a-fA-F]

Table 8-12.   *Perl's Composite Unicode Properties*

For more information on the other properties supported by Perl (which are subject to constant change as new languages, character sets, and Perl composites are produced), check the Unicode documentation that comes with Perl.

Matching the Beginning and End of a String

The ^ metacharacter matches the beginning of the string. The following line would only return true if the character sequence "cat" were present at the beginning of **$string**:

```
if ($string =~ /^cat/)
```

This would match "catatonic", "cat", and "cationic surfactant", but not "polecat". The ^ also matches the beginning of a line, so when it is used within a multiline string (using the **/m** modifier), it will match not only the start of the string, but also the start of each line (matching against a preceding newline character). If you have supplied a multiline string, but want to match only the beginning of that string then use **\A**. For example,

```
$string = "Cats go Catatonic\nWhen given Catnip";
($start) = ($string =~ /\A(.*?) /);
@lines  = $string =~ /^(.*?) /gm;
print "First word: $start\n","Line starts: @lines\n";
```

outputs

```
First word: Cats
Line starts: Cats When
```

The **$** metasymbol matches the end of the string,

```
if ($string =~ /cat$/)
```

so this example only matches when the "cat" character sequence is at the end of the string being matched. However, just like ^, when used in a multiline string with the **/m** modifier, **$** also matches the end of a line (at the point just before the newline character).

The **\z** metasymbol matches at the end of the string, no matter what the contents of the string are. The **\Z** matches just before the newline at the end of the string if there was a newline, or at the end of string if there wasn't a newline. The **\Z** can be useful when reading information from a file that contains newlines, when you want to execute a regular expression on the source string without first using **chomp**.

Boundaries

The **\b** matches at any word boundary, as defined by the difference between the **\w** class and the **\W** class. Because **\w** includes the characters for a word, and **\W** the opposite, this normally means the termination of a word. The boundary also works in reverse; that is, a change from **\W** to **\w**, which indicates the beginning of a word. The **\B** assertion matches any position that is not a word boundary. For example:

```
/\bcat\b/     # Matches 'the cat sat' but not 'cat on the mat'
/\Bcat\B/     # Matches 'verification' but not 'the cat on the mat'
/\bcat\B/     # Matches 'catatonic' but not 'polecat'
/\Bcat\b/     # Matches 'polecat' but not 'catatonic'
```

Note, however, that because **\W** includes all the punctuation characters, you may end up splitting in the middle of a word, such as "can't" and "mc@mcslp.com", which may or may not be what you want.

Selecting Alternatives

The | character is just like the standard or bitwise OR within Perl. It specifies alternate matches within a regular expression or group. For example, to match "cat" or "dog" in an expression, you might use this:

```
if ($string =~ /cat|dog/)
```

You can group individual elements of an expression together in order to support complex matches. Searching for two people's names could be achieved with two separate tests, like this:

```
if (($string =~ /Martin Brown/) ||
    ($string =~ /Sharon Brown/))
```

You could write this more efficiently in a single regular expression, like this:

```
if ($string =~ /(Martin|Sharon) Brown/)
```

The use of grouping here is vital. By using a group, the code looks for "Martin Brown" or "Sharon Brown", because the OR operation simply works on either side of the | metacharacter. Had you written

```
if ($string =~ /Martin|Sharon Brown/)
```

the regular expression would match either "Martin" or "Sharon Brown", which may or may not be what you want. In general, the use of grouping with the | metacharacter follows the same rules as the logical operators elsewhere in Perl.

Grouping

As seen earlier, you can logically group any part of an expression together. Syntactically the groupings have no specific meaning within an expression unless combined with a | operator, as in the example earlier. In fact, from a regular-expression point of view, there is no difference between

```
$string =~ /(\S+)\s+(\S+)/;
```

and

```
$string =~ /\S+\s+\S+/;
```

except, perhaps, that the former is slightly clearer.

However, the benefit of grouping is that it allows us to extract a sequence from a regular expression. Groupings are returned as a list in the order in which they appear in the original. For example, in the following fragment,

```
my ($hours, $minutes, $seconds) = ($time =~ m/(\d+):(\d+):(\d+)/);
```

we've pulled out the hours, minutes, and seconds from a string.

As well as this direct method, matched groups are also available within the special **$x** variables, where **x** is the number of the group within the regular expression. We could therefore rewrite the preceding example as follows:

```
$time =~ m/(\d+):(\d+):(\d+)/;
my ($hours, $minutes, $seconds) = ($1, $2, $3);
```

When groups are used in substitution expressions, the **$x** syntax can be used in the replacement text. Thus, we could reformat a date string using this:

```
$date = '03/26/1999';
$date =~ s#(\d+)/(\d+)/(\d+)#$3$1$2#;
```

Each element of the date is placed into the temporary variables, so the month (group one) is in **$1**, the day is group two, and the year is in group three. To convert to the number format, you just need to specify each element in the desired order—in this example, year, month, day. The resulting string is "19990326". The matched groups are perpetual—that is, you can also access each matched group outside of the substitution expression. Obviously, the next regular expression executed resets all of the values.

Note
Perl also supports \x as a group definition, but it is only valid within the confines of a substitution. It is also limited to just nine groups (\1 to \9), whereas $x is essentially unlimited.

If you nest groups, then you must remember that the numbering system keys on the first opening parenthesis, as demonstrated by the following code:

```
$date = '03/26/1999';
$date =~ s#((\d+)/(\d+)/(\d+))#Date $1 = $4$2$3#;
print "$date\n";
```

which prints this:

```
Date 03/26/1999 = 19990326
```

The first parenthesis matches the whole date string; the nested parentheses then match the individual year, month, and day of the date.

Quantifiers

In many of the preceding examples, you'll see a quantifier—a special character or sequence that defines the number of times the previous sequence or character appears. Using a quantifier, you can specify that a sequence must appear a minimum or maximum number of times, or that a character can repeat indefinitely until the next regex element. Table 8-8 earlier in the chapter shows the supported quantifiers.

The * and + operators match 0 or more, or 1 or more items, respectively. By using a pattern of /.*/, you can match everything including an empty string (although this seems rather pointless), or with /.+/, you must match at least one character. The brace specifications allow you to specify a range of repetitions. Some examples and equivalencies are shown here:

```
m/.{0}/;     #Matches no characters
m/.{1,}/;    #Matches any character at least once, equivalent to /.+/
m/\d{2,4}/;  #Matches any digit at least two and a maximum of four times
```

In Table 8-8, entries in the left-hand (Maximal) column will match preceding expression or class the maximum number of times. This means that the quantifier will soak up all the characters it can before it attempts the next match in the regex. The Minimal column shows the sequence that will match the minimum number of times before the next element of the regular expression is matched. The following code demonstrates the effect:

```
$string = "There was a food shortage in foodham";
print "Maximal:",($string =~ /(.*)foo/),"\n";
print "Minimal:",($string =~ /(.*?)foo/),"\n";
```

If you run this, the result is as follows:

```
Maximal:There was a food shortage in
Minimal:There was a
```

Using the \G Assertion

The **\G** assertion allows you to continue searching from the point where the last match occurred. This is the same as using **pos** (see the "pos" section, later in the chapter), except that you can continue using regular expressions instead of splitting up your string using **substr**.

For example, in the following code we've used **\G** so that we can search to the correct position and then extract some information, without having to create a more complex, single regular expression:

```
$string = "The time is: 12:31:02 on 4/12/00";

$string =~ /:\s+/g;
($time) = ($string =~ /\G(\d+:\d+:\d+)/);
$string =~ /.+\s+/g;
($date) = ($string =~ m{\G(\d+/\d+/\d+)});

print "Time: $time, Date: $date\n";
```

The **\G** assertion is actually just the metasymbol equivalent of the **pos** function, so between regular expression calls you can continue to use **pos**, and even modify the value of **pos** (and therefore **\G**) by using **pos** as an lvalue subroutine:

```
pos($string) = 0;
```

Regular Expression Variables

Regular expression variables include $, which contains whatever the last grouping match matched; $&, which contains the entire matched string; $`, which contains everything before the matched string; and $', which contains everything after the matched string.

Use of the $` and $' variables induces a significant overhead within your program, since the first time you use them Perl then starts to populate the variables for each regular expression executed. Avoid using them if you can. Grouping will often give you the same result without the same overhead. The $& also adds overhead, but since version 5.005, the performance hit is not as high as that induced by $`.

The following code demonstrates the result:

```
$string = "The food is in the salad bar";
$string =~ m/foo/;
print "Before: $`\n";
print "Matched: $&\n";
print "After: $'\n";
```

This code prints the following when executed:

```
Before: The
Matched: foo
After: d is in the salad bar
```

Regular Expression Extensions/Assertions

The regular expression engine also allows you to specify a number of additional extensions, called *assertions*, within the main expression. These extensions enable more specific matches to take place without the match affecting the variables and/or groupings that are in place. These work in combination with the grouping facilities within the regular expression and the global variables that are affected by regular expression matches. The assertions are summarized in Table 8-13.

For example, here's a regular expression match using the **(?{code})** assertion:

```
use re 'eval';
$_ = '<A href="/index.shtml">';
m<
    (?{ $cnt = 0 })
    \<A.*"
    (.(?{ local $cnt = $cnt + 1;}))*
    "\>
    (?{ $res = $cnt })
>x;

print $res," words\n";
```

It counts the number of letters between the double quotes in the HTML reference specified in **$_**. This is a fairly simplistic example, since the likelihood is that you'll want to perform some sort of test (perhaps via a function call) within the **(?{code})** assertion, but you can see the general idea.

Assertion	Meaning
(?#text)	Comment text within the brackets is ignored.
(?:pattern)	Identical to grouping, but does not populate **$1**, **$2**, and so on, on a match.
(?imsx:pattern)	Identical to grouping, but does not populate **$1**, **$2**, and so on, on a match; embeds pattern-match modifiers for the duration of the specified pattern.
(?=pattern)	Matches if the regular expression engine would match **pattern** next, without affecting the result of the match. For example, the expression **\w+(?=\t)/** would match a tab following a word, without the tab being added to the value of **$&**.
(?!pattern)	Matches if the regular expression engine would not match **pattern** next. For example, the expression **\foo($!bar)/** would match only if there was an occurrence of "foo" not followed by "bar".
(?<=pattern)	Matches the next statement only if **pattern** would have matched with the following expression, but without placing the result of **pattern** into the **$&** variable. For example, to test for a word following a tab, but without placing the tab into **$&**, you would use **/(?<=\t)\w+/**.
(?<!pattern)	Matches the next statement only if **pattern** would not have matched with the following expression, but without placing the result of **pattern** into the **$&** variable. For example, to match any occurrence of "foo" that isn't following "bar", you might use **/(?<!bar)foo/**.

Table 8-13. *Regular Expression Assertions*

Assertion	Meaning
(?{ code })	Experimental—the intended use for this is for **code** to be executed, and if it returns true, then the result is considered as a match along the same lines as the **(?:pattern)** assertion. The **code** does not interpolate variables. This assertion only works if you have the **use re 'eval'** pragma in effect.
(?>pattern)	Matches the substring that a stand-alone **pattern** would match if the **pattern** was anchored at the current position. For example, the regex **/^(?>a*)ab/** will never match, because the assertion **(?>a*)** will match all characters "a" at the beginning of the string, effectively removing the "a" required to match "ab."
**(?(condition)yes-pattern	no-pattern)** **(?(condition)yes-pattern)**	Conditional expression—the **(condition)** element should either be an integer in parentheses or an assertion.
(?imsx) **(?-imsx)**	Embedded pattern-match modifiers. Useful when you want to embed an expression modifier within a variable, which may then be used in a general regex that does not specify its own modifiers. Anything following a hyphen, -, switches off the modifier for the duration, or until another embedded modifier is in place.

Table 8-13. *Regular Expression Assertions* (continued)

Precompiling Expressions

One of the pitfalls of the regular expression mechanism is that when interpolating variables into expressions, Perl must recompile the regular expression each time. Most expressions are compiled during the compilation phase of the main script, of course, but in those situations where you are using scalars, you can run into a severe performance problem as each regular expression is compiled and checked.

For simple one-shot expressions that include a variable, you can get around this by using the **/o** modifier, which forces the expression to be compiled only once, even if you do change the variable contents.

However, doing so limits the usefulness of Perl in situations where you want to run a number of regular expressions over a list—something that is easy to do in **sed**. For example, the code:

```
while(<FILE>)
{
    foreach $regex (@expressions)
    {
        print if /$regex/;
    }
}
```

would be incredibly time consuming, because for each line in **FILE**, we have to recompile each of the regular expressions in **@expressions**, even though the contents of **@expressions** don't change between each line.

You can get around this, perhaps, by creating a new script based on **@expressions** that could then be executed through an **eval**. Because the regex entries would be "fixed" within the limits of the subscript, they would only have to be compiled once during the **eval** initialization. This is exceedingly messy, however. A much better solution is to use the **qr//** (quote regex) operator.

The **qr//** operator takes a regular expression and compiles it as normal, returning a regular expression object such that

```
$regex = qr/[a-z]+/is;
s/$regex/nothing/;
```

is the same as

```
s/[a-z]+/nothing/is;
```

Because the returned object is a compiled regular expression, we can solve the earlier problem by precompiling all the expressions before we enter the loop.

That means we could change the preceding example to

```
@regexes = map { qr/$_/ } @expressions;
while(<FILE>)
{
```

```
    foreach $regex (@regexes)
    {
        print if /$regex/;
    }
}
```

Now, because the patterns are precompiled, the regular expressions are executed immediately within the main loop without requiring a new compilation.

The return value of the **qr//** operator can also be embedded into other expressions:

```
print if /start${regex}end/;
```

*Be careful when using **qr//**, as you run the risk of compiling an expression during run time that might cause an exception. You should be embedding the compilation into an **eval** statement:*

```
$regex = eval { qr/$pattern/ } || warn "Cant regex from $pattern";
```

Regular Expression Support Functions

There are three functions that support the regular expression engine. The first, **pos**, is an extension of the **\G** assertion, which we have already seen. The second, **quotemeta**, is useful when you want to include a string within an expression that may contain character sequences that match the regular expression engine's metacharacters or metasymbols. The last, **study**, can improve the speed at which the regular expression engine operates when you are matching against large strings.

pos

When you've performed a match, you can find the location within the string at the point where the regular expression stopped checking for new matches within an **m//g** regex. The basic form is

```
pos [SCALAR]
```

The **pos** function, in scalar context, returns the location immediately after the last successful match for **SCALAR**, or **$_** if no scalar is specified. For example,

```
$string = "The food is in the salad bar";
$string =~ m/foo/g;
print pos($string),"\n";
```

should print a value of 7, the number of characters read before the match operator stopped looking for new entries (because there weren't any). In list context, **pos** returns all of the matches from the previous expression.

As we've already seen, **pos** can also be used as **lvalue** to set the position within an expression:

```
pos($string) = 12;
```

This is useful if you are using the **\G** assertion within your regular expressions and want to explicitly set (or reset) the starting point.

quotemeta

In Table 8-7 you should have noticed the **\Q** sequence, which prevented the regular expression engine from interpreting metacharacters or sequences as special values within a regular expression. This effect is actually achieved by the general Perl function **quotemeta**:

```
quotemeta EXPR
quotemeta
```

The function replaces any nonalphanumeric (not matching **[a-zA-Z0-9]**) character with a backslash version. For example, this string

```
print quotemeta "[Foobar!]";
```

will return

```
\[Foobar\!\]
```

If you do not specify an expression, then the value of **$_** will be quoted instead.

study

If you expect to perform a number of pattern matches on a large scalar, you may find that the regular expression process is very slow. To increase the performance of the regular expression system, you can use the **study** function:

```
study EXPR
study
```

The special **$_** is used if you do not specify a scalar to examine. The **study** function works by building a linked list of all the characters within the scalar. This enables the regular expression engine to identify where all of the "x" characters are, for example. When a search is requested, the character that occurs least in the search string is used to choose the starting point for the pattern search.

You will need to check the speed of the search process with and without the **study** function; for many cases, you may find there is little or no difference. Unfortunately, only one scalar can be studied at any one time. The moment you specify a new scalar for the function to examine, it replaces the information stored on the previous scalar.

Unicode

Some of you may have come across Unicode elsewhere, and if you haven't, then it's highly likely that you will soon. It has long been a part of the Windows operating system (having been officially introduced with Windows 98, although support existed in Windows 95 and NT), and the Mac OS has had Unicode support for many years. Although support under Unix is currently a system-wide issue, most software that thinks it ought to be using Unicode comes with its own support.

Unicode solves an age-old problem relating to the representation of characters on screen. The base format that most people are aware of is ASCII, which officially lists the main Latin letters, numbers, and grammatical marks in their upper- and lowercase versions. Some ASCII extensions are also universally accepted and allow for accented characters that support most of the southern European languages. The actual characters are referred to by a number, using a range of 0–255, which enables us to store the numerical equivalent of the letter into a single 8-bit byte.

However, what happens when you migrate a system that uses the ASCII, and therefore Latin, character set into an environment that doesn't actually use Latin characters? In Greece, for example, they use letters from the Greek alphabet, which are not actually part of the ASCII standard. Traditionally, programmers and designers have got around this issue by developing a font that maps normal Latin characters into their foreign equivalents. In essence, we're still using a single byte to represent each character, but because the software knows that we should be using a Greek rather than a Latin font, it displays the Greek character.

When you move to more complex graphical languages, such as Chinese and Japanese, this method no longer works. The traditional Chinese writing system has over 30,000 characters in it—not directly representable by a single byte that limits us to 256 characters. For these languages, we need to use multibyte characters, a specification that allows us to refer to a character in an alphabet that fits in the range 0 to $(2^{32}-1)$ (or 0 to $(2^{64}-1)$ for 64-bit computers).

It's here that Unicode fits in. The Unicode standard is designed to be the accepted set of rules to allow people to exchange textual information around the world. Because the Unicode standard includes information on the character set and the multibyte format of the data being exchanged, you should be guaranteed that the information you are reading is in the correct format and language.

Unicode is not (yet) a compulsory element of any software, and certainly isn't a required part of Perl, but in these modern times when scripts and information are exchanged between hundreds of different languages, and therefore character sets, around the world during the course of its life, ignoring Unicode is not the smartest move you will ever make!

Perl's Interpretation of Unicode

The problem of Unicode from a programmer's perspective is that because it smudges the line between single-byte-based character sets and multibyte-based character sets, some of the operations that we are used to don't always work as we would expect.

To give a very classic example, consider the **length** function. Working within the standard Latin character set, the **length** function returns the length of a string from two perspectives. First, it gives us the length of the string in terms of characters—that is, the number of letters and numbers that we see on the screen. It also returns the length of the string in terms of bytes—because one character is represented by one byte, the relationship is one to one.

If we use the same **length** function on a Unicode string, the two numbers won't always marry. If the string contains letters using two-byte characters, then we end up with a character length of 10 but a byte length of 20. Things get even more complicated if we work with Unicode strings that contain multibyte characters with different byte lengths!

However, before you panic and expect all of your software to suddenly fail, Perl isn't quite so strict about how it applies the rules of Unicode. In fact, the documentation lists the following goals that were applied when Perl's Unicode system was developed:

- **Goal #1**   Old byte-oriented programs should not spontaneously break on the old byte-oriented data they used to work on.

- **Goal #2**   Old byte-oriented programs should magically start working on the new character-oriented data when appropriate.

- **Goal #3**   Programs should run just as fast in the character-oriented mode as in the old byte-oriented mode.

- **Goal #4**   Perl should remain one language, rather than forking into a byte-oriented Perl and a character-oriented Perl.

Perl's support, like Unicode itself, is still largely a work in progress, so not everything is working perfectly within these guidelines, but the goals will remain the same. Although it's too early to speculate at this stage what the Unicode support in Perl 6 will be like, it's likely that many of the developments being made now to bond Perl's core systems into the Unicode fold will still apply.

Unicode Characters in Perl

Unicode characters are, internally at least, still referred to by a number. The difference is in the size of the number used to represent each character. Perl uses the UTF-8 (Unicode Transformation Format-8) system to support variable-length encoding for Unicode characters. The UTF-8 system allows us to specify a multibyte character by using a string of single bytes without losing any information. This means that for the first 128 characters (0–127), which can obviously be represented by a single byte, the relationship between UTF-8 and ASCII is identical.

Perl automatically switches to using UTF-8 when it thinks that it's required. If you are only using single-byte characters in your scripts, then you have nothing to worry about—Perl will carry on working as normal, and you shouldn't have to make any changes to your scripts. What happens internally is that Perl converts the fixed 8-bit characters you supply into the UTF-8 format as necessary.

On the other hand, if you do use a string that contains characters using numbers larger than 255, the string is converted into UTF-8. Perl uses an extended version of UTF-8 called **utf8**, and there is a pragma of that name that can be used to help specify the UTF-8 characters. Although the **utf8** pragma allows you to use any defined Unicode character, it's limited to supporting the characters officially endorsed by the Unicode consortium.

Your main concern when dealing with Unicode characters should be the interface between the Perl code and the outside world. You need to be aware that, by default, all of Perl's interfaces assume they are working with byte (8-bit) rather than character (Unicode) data.

When communicating with the outside world, you must tell Perl that you are expecting (or exporting) character-oriented, rather than byte-oriented, information. Perl should do this automatically, although occasionally it'll need some help—for example, you'll need to tell the **open** function to expect Unicode source (see Chapter 7).

Unicode's Effects on Perl Code

The general rule to follow with Unicode in Perl is that a typical operator will now operate on characters (including multibyte Unicode ones) unless you've explicitly told it otherwise by using the **byte** pragma. If you are only using 8-bit characters, then there is no difference as far as you or your program is concerned, and you won't have to make any changes to your code.

The **utf8** pragma exists as a compatible way of introducing UTF-8 characters in literals, and allowing Perl to support UTF-8 characters in identifiers. Eventually, the **utf8** pragma will have no effect at all, as all of this functionality will be supported natively by the interpreter.

The **bytes** pragma is there to force sections of code to employ a byte-sized interpretation of contents, instead of characters. This means that outside of **bytes**, the **length** function now returns the length in characters, but inside, it returns the length in bytes. The **bytes** pragma can also be used as a wrapper around certain functions (only **length** at present). For example:

```
use bytes (); # Loads wrappers without enforcing byte
interpretation

$charlen = length($string);
$bytelen = bytes::length($string);
```

Outside of a **bytes** pragma, the interpreter follows these rules:

■ Strings and regular expression patterns may contain characters with values larger than eight bits (**utf8** pragma required).

■ Identifiers may contain alphanumeric characters, including ideographs (**utf8** pragma required).

■ Regular expressions match characters, not bytes.

■ Character classes in regular expressions match characters, not bytes.

■ Named Unicode properties and block ranges can be used as character classes.

■ The regular expression metasymbol **\X** matches any Unicode sequence.

■ The **tr///** operator transliterates characters, not bytes.

■ Case translation operators (**\U**, **\L** and **uc**, **ucfirst**, etc.) use the Unicode translation tables.

■ Functions and operators that deal with position and length within a string use character, rather than byte positions. Exclusions are **pack**, **unpack**, and **vec**, which traditionally work on byte- or bit-based data anyway.

■ The **c** and **C pack**/**unpack** formats do *not* change—they still extract byte-based information. If you want to use characters use the **U** format.

■ The **chr** and **ord** functions work on multibyte characters.

■ The **reverse** function in a **scalar** context reverses by character, rather than by byte.

The whole Unicode implementation within Perl is still a work in progress, and there's lots to do before all of the features and/or functionality within both Unicode and Perl works correctly. The best way to keep up to date is to read the Unicode documentation that comes with the latest Perl distribution (available in the unicode/Unicode3.html document within the main Perl library directory).

The Complete Reference

Chapter 9

Errors and Trapping Them

Despite your best efforts, all programs have the potential to cause problems. We'll be looking at the debugging process and tools available in Perl in Chapter 21, but finding and debugging your programs is only part of the issue. Some statements and function calls in Perl will fail—not necessarily through a fault of yours, Perl's, or the operating system's. For example, when you open a file, what happens if the file doesn't exist? Or if it's a new file, what do you do if the operating system doesn't let you create a new file?

Your first question, though, will be: why actually check for errors in the first place? The reason is quite simple—we need to stop our script from doing something we (or the user) don't expect it to do, or from potentially damaging something we didn't expect. Updating a database from a series of text files when one of those text files may be unreadable could have serious consequences.

It's probably dangerous to continue the script under these circumstances, so we now have two problems to resolve—first, how do you identify an error, and second, what do you do with the error once you've identified it?

In this chapter we'll aim to answer those questions. To that end, we'll be looking at the basics and mechanics of error checking and verification in Perl and at the different tricks and tools that can be used to help in that process.

Adding Error Checking to Your Scripts

We've already seen some examples of error-checking mechanisms in Perl, and you should already be adding error-checking processes to your scripts as you write them. It doesn't take long to get into the habit of always adding even basic error-checking sequences as you type, but you need to know which functions deserve checking and how to check and verify their operation.

Error Checking Methods

Most of the basic functions and keywords within Perl and many of the standard CPAN extension modules follow the same basic format—a value is returned of true if the function completed successfully or of false if there was an error. You can identify and trap an error in a number of different ways.

Using if

The **if** statement is the obvious choice when you need to check the return value from a statement; for example:

```
if (open(DATA,$file))
{
    ...
}
```

```
else
{
    die "Woah: Couldn't open the file $!";
}
```

This procedure is most useful when you want to be able to account for two possible outcomes—if the statement works, then continue and execute *these* statements; if it doesn't succeed, then do *these* statements instead.

Alternatively, we can reduce the statement to one line in situations where it makes sense to do so; for example:

```
die "Woah: Something went wrong\n" if (error());
```

See the upcoming section on "Error Checking Guidelines" for more information on when, and indeed whether, to use this format.

Using *unless*

The **unless** function is the logical opposite to **if**: statements can completely bypass the success status and only be executed if the expression returns false. For example:

```
unless(chdir("/etc"))
{
    die "Can't change directory!: $!";
}
```

The **unless** statement is best used when you want to raise an error or alternative only if the expression fails. The statement also makes sense when used in a single-line statement:

```
die "Can't change directory!: $!" unless(chdir("/etc"));
```

Here we die only if the **chdir** operation fails, and it reads nicely.

Using the Conditional Operator

For very short tests, you can use the conditional operator:

```
print(exists($hash{value}) ? 'There' : 'Missing',"\n");
```

It's not quite so clear here what we're trying to achieve, but the effect is the same as using an **if** or **unless** statement. The conditional operator is best used when you want to quickly return one of two values within an expression or statement.

It's not really an error trapping statement, since there's not enough scope to do anything, but it can be used to help communicate status information back to the user. Consider the following example:

```
chdir("/tmp") ? print "Using /tmp\n" : warn "Can't use /tmp: $!";
```

Here it's a useful way of highlighting a potential problem without actually doing anything about it. The same basic principles can be used from within functions when returning values:

```
return (@results) ? @results : undef;
```

Using Short-Circuit Logic

For many situations, especially when you want to immediately exit the script without actually handling the error, the short-circuit capabilities of the **or** operator work best:

```
mkdir("./tmp",0755) or die "Can't make directory!: $!";
```

See "Symbolic Logical Or" in Chapter 3 for more details on why this works and the related dangers.

The || symbolic logical **or** can also be used as a way to provide alternatives when the first-choice option doesn't work. For example, the line

```
$host = param('host') || $user->{prihost} || 'azus';
```

will use the browser-supplied value, then the user-configured value, and finally a default value if the other options fail.

Error Checking Guidelines

There are some general guidelines for testing for errors in this way. The first guideline is to make it obvious what you are testing and what you are trying to do. For example, the statement

```
if (!open(DATA,$file))
```

will work fine, except that it would make more sense to use the **unless** statement, as in

```
unless(open(DATA,$file))
```

The difference is that the **if** statement reads "If I didn't open," and the **unless** statement reads "Unless I can open." It's a minor difference but will make the code easier to read and, therefore, easier to debug. Here's another example that's difficult to read:

```
die "Couldn't change directory: $!" unless(chdir("/etc"));
```

This should be changed to

```
chdir("/etc") or die "Couldn't change directory: $!";
```

The second guideline is that you should make it obvious what the actual problem was; simply reporting that there was an error isn't enough, either for you to debug the program, or for your user to rectify it. Where relevant, also include information on the system error message, as provided by **$!**. Also remember the **$^E** variable, which contains the extended OS error on non-Unix platforms. For example, the line

```
open(DATA,$file) or die "Can't open";
```

is useless compared to

```
open(DATA,$file) or die "Can't open $file: $!, stopped";
```

Coupled with this, you should always report an error to **STDERR** by using either **warn** or **die**. The exception to this rule is when you working with a GUI or web-based application, for which there is no logical **STDERR** file handle. See the end of this chapter for information on reporting errors when no terminal interface is available.

What to Check

The paranoid would say "everything," and the more relaxed and laid back would say "nothing." There are statements and operations that you should always check, whether you are interested in the return value or not, if only to prevent your script from doing something it shouldn't:

- The **open**, **close**, and related statements that provide a conduit to the outside world (including **socket** and **tie**) and external database connectivity
- Reading from or writing to a file or socket handle other than **STDIN**, **STDOUT**, or **STDERR**
- Reading from or writing to **STDIN**, **STDOUT**, or **STDERR** if they have been reassigned or redirected within the script

- Anything that makes changes to the operating system or file system, including calls like **unlink**

- Anything that changes the environment in which you are operating (for example, **chdir** and **chroot**) or modifies the **%ENV** hash

- Any system call not already covered—system calls *always* return their status, so use it!

- Anything that relies on input or information supplied the user—don't automatically assume that users know what they are doing!

- Any calls to an external program, either through **open**, the **qx** operator, or **system**

- The object type when a reference that points to an internal object is dynamically generated—particularly vital for code references

Beyond the preceding list, it comes down to a case of how the operation will affect the execution of your script. If the operation will affect the following statements, then it needs to be traced and probably trapped to prevent it from it having a knock on effect. As a good example, using zero as a division value will raise an error, so it's a good idea to check the value beforehand.

What Not to Check

This list is obviously the inverse of our previous list. Beyond avoiding things that we don't need to worry about, there are some less obvious elements of our scripts that we can safely ignore. Most of the time, the things to avoid checking are those that will not have an immediate effect on what we are trying to achieve.

We can summarize the limit of your checking procedures as follows:

- **Don't Check Things That Don't Matter**   There are some things in your script that just don't merit checking, either because the return values don't mean anything or because they have little or no relevance for the execution of your script.

- **User Input**   When checking a user-supplied value, whether it's from a simple line input, a command line argument, or a web form, you should check that the information is valid according to what you expect. For example, when accepting a name from standard input, we only need to verify that we received some input; we don't need to worry about whether it's actually a name.

Substitution/Transliteration   When modifying a variable through the substitution or transliteration operators, don't bother checking that the operation completed successfully, unless you specifically want to match or identify regular expression elements.

When to Stop Checking

There are times when you can go too far. In the script we modified, for example, we check the result when **close** is called, but nowhere did we actually check that the number of bytes that we read from the file matched the number of bytes in the file when we started. Checking that information is pointless—either we'll read everything from the file, or an error will be raised at some point (in this instance, probably when we try to close the file). On the other hand, there are situations in which checking to that level of granularity would be vital—transferring data over a network connection, for example.

Don't Check Things Twice

There's no point in checking the same thing twice in two different ways. Usually there is a simpler, one-shot solution that will identify the error for us. Here's a common mistake made by some programmers:

```
die "$file doesn't exist!" unless (-e $file);
open(FILE,$file) or die "Can't open $file: $!";
```

Aside from the fact that the second line would never be reached, the chances of the status of the file changing between the two lines is pretty remote. Furthermore, the first test may well pass if the file exists, even though it might not necessarily be readable. By checking the return value of **open**, we actually verify that the file can be opened and read by Perl, not just the file's status.

Here's another example where the checking is basically verifying the same information, albeit at different levels each time:

```
if ($name)
{
    if (length($name) > 0)
    {
        if ($name =~ /[a-zA-Z0-9 ]+/)
        {
            print "Hello $name\n";
        }
    }
}
```

The regular expression will tell us whether the information that was supplied was valid or not. Should the expression match fail, then we'll already know that either it didn't match or that the supplied value wasn't long enough.

Functions, Return Values, and Nesting

If you've followed the guidelines in Chapter 5, you already know that you can improve your scripts and reduce the number and effects of bugs in them by dividing and debugging the individual components. You know as well that the functions should ideally handle errors by returning the error to the caller and not by using their own error-handling statements to report problems (there are some exceptions; see "Reporting Errors Within Modules" later in this chapter). Therefore, in checking for errors when calling one of your own functions, you should avoid situations like this:

```perl
sub formatmessage
{
    my ($msg) = @_;
    if ($msg)
    {
        return "Hello $msg\n";
    }
    else
    {
        warn "No message!";
        return undef;
    }
}

$message = formatmessage(undef);
if ($message)
{
    print $message;
}
else
{
    warn "Invalid message!";
}
```

If we run this script, we get this:

```
No message! at t.pl line 10.
Invalid message! at t.pl line 22.
```

We've checked the same thing twice, once within the function and again with the returned value in the main script. This procedure could be avoided completely by just allowing the caller to handle the error condition and report the problem.

There are exceptions to this rule. There are occasions when it makes more sense to trap and if necessary report a problem within the function itself, yet still report an error condition back to the caller that could, if necessary, be trapped. In the code that follows, for example, we have a function that reads information from a file and returns it to the caller.

```perl
sub template
{
    my $data = '';
    if (open(DATA,"template"))
    {
        $data .= $_ while (<DATA>);
        close(DATA);
        return $data;
    }
    else
    {
        return '';
    }
}

print template();
```

If the template file can't be opened, an empty string is returned—the error is still reported and indeed logged against the function in which the error occurs, but we ignore the error in the caller. We could have trapped the information and provided an alternative, but in this case it's safe to ignore the error.

Error Messages and Numbers

When reporting an error, it's useful to supply the error that was returned by the operating system so that the problem can be identified. For example, when opening a file, the error could be caused by nonexistence of the file or by the user's privileges not allowing access to the file. Perl uses the special **$!** variable to hold the error number or error string for the last system error that occurred.

For example, we could update our **open** error message to

```
open FILE, 'myfile.txt' or warn "Didn't open the file: $!\n";
```

Whether the variable returns a numerical value or a string depends on the context in which it is used. If Perl is expecting a numerical value, then the variable returns the numerical error code. For example, the modified statement

```
open FILE, 'myfile.txt' or warn "Didn't open the file: ", 0+$!, "\n";
```

will return an error code of 2 if the file doesn't exist.

When called in a string context, the variable returns the corresponding error code string. The information for the error codes comes from the operating system's own headers, and the message contents and corresponding numbers will vary across different systems.

If required, you can set the value of **$!** in order to determine the error messages for a platform. The same trick can also be used if you want to set the error message and exit value for **die**; for example,

```
unless(open(DATA,$file))
{
    $! = 1;
    die "Couldn't open the file!";
}
```

will give an exit value of 1 from the script when it terminates.

For platform-specific error messages or extended error messages from outside Perl's normal execution space, you can use the **$^E** variable. This variable holds errors raised external to Perl or the functions that Perl uses to communicate with the operating system. Under Windows, for example, the **$^E** variable will usually hold the information that would otherwise be returned by the statement

```
Win32::FormatMessage(Win32::GetLastError());
```

However, don't rely on the value of **$^E** always being populated—it's quite possible that the value will always be undefined, regardless of the result of the previous system call.

Reporting Errors Within Scripts

The most obvious solution when you want to report an error is to use the **print** function and either send the output directly to **STDOUT** or redirect it to **STDERR**. One advantage of **print** over the normal **warn** and **die** functions is that the output can also be redirected to another, previously opened file that you are using to log errors.

The more usual method, however, is to report the error directly to **STDERR** using the **warn** and **die** functions. The basic format for both functions is

```
warn LIST
die LIST
```

In essence, the two functions are identical, and they both follow the same basic rules:

- The supplied **LIST** is concatenated and then printed to **STDERR**.
- If the final value to **LIST** does not end with a **\n** character, then the current script name, line number, and input source line number (from an opened file) are appended.
- If **LIST** is empty and **$@** already contains a value (from an earlier **eval** call), then the string "\t...propagated" (for **die**) or "\t...caught" (for **warn**) is appended to **$@** and then printed with the current script name and line number.

We'll be returning to this last item later, as it applies specifically to the use of **warn** and **die** with an **eval** statement.

The major difference between the two functions is that **warn** only raises an error, whereas **die** raises an error and calls **exit**.

The Warn Function

The **warn** function just raises a warning—a message is printed to **STDERR**, but no further action is taken. Aside from the rules already given, the **warn** function adds the following rule:

- If **LIST** is empty and **$@** does not contain a value, then the string "Warning: something's wrong" and the source file and line number are printed.

Otherwise, the function is fairly straightforward:

```
chdir('/etc') or warn "Can't change directory";
```

The Die Function

The **die** function works just like **warn**, except that it also calls **exit**. Within a normal script, this function has the effect of immediately terminating execution. The return code given by the script when **die** is called depends on the context. If the $! error variable contains a value, it is used as the error code. If $! is zero, then the value of $! shifted to the right eight times ($! >> 8) is used. This correctly prints the error number retrieved from an external program execution via backticks. If the value is still zero, a value of 255 is passed to the **exit** function.

Beyond the rules given, the **die** function also adds the following rule:

■ If **LIST** is empty and $@ is undefined, then the string "Died" is printed.

The function can be used in an identical fashion to **warn**:

```
chdir('/etc') or die "Can't change directory";
```

It's generally a good idea to add "stopped" or something similar to a **die** message just to make sure that it's obvious the script has abnormally terminated.

Directives and Tokens

The special tokens __FILE__ and __LINE__ contain the currently executing line number and the file in which the line appears. These tokens are automatically populated by Perl and are the same tokens actually used by the **die** and **warn** functions when you supply a string not terminated by a newline character. For example,

```
chdir('/etc')
    or die "Can't change dir in ",__FILE__," line ", __LINE__, "\n";
```

If you failed to change the directory, this would print

```
Can't change dir in adduser.pl line 35
```

You can change the values that these tokens are populated with by using a special type of comment that includes a "line directive"; for example,

```
# line 200 "Parsing engine"
die "Fatal error";
```

produces the following:

```
Fatal error at Parsing engine line 200
```

FUNDAMENTALS

It is important to note that the line number given here just resets the number for the following line of code—three lines down and an error would be reported as occurring on line 202. The line and file information is unique to the current input/source file, so when using **die** or a similar function, the information will be reported accordingly.

Also, because the line directive updates the __FILE__ and __LINE__ tokens, which are themselves used by **die** and similar functions, the modifications will work across all of the functions and tools used to report errors.

See "Comments" in Chapter 3 for more information on line directives and how they are identified.

Reporting Errors Within Modules

Although I've already stated that you should be using return values from functions to relate errors back to the caller, there are times when you need to raise an error within the confines of the module in which it appears. By highlighting a module-specific error, you can more easily track down the problem and also raise errors within a module that are too significant to be safely trapped through the use of an **if** statement.

There are two different situations we need to be able to handle:

- Reporting an error in a module that quotes the module's filename and line number—this is useful when debugging a module, or when you specifically want to raise a module-related, rather than script-related, error.

- Reporting an error within a module that quotes the caller's information so that you can debug the line within the script that caused the error. Errors raised in this fashion are useful to the end-user, because they highlight the error in relation to the calling script's origination line.

The **warn** and **die** functions work slightly differently than you would expect when called from within a module—the __LINE__ and __FILE__ tokens are populated with the information about the module file, not the calling script. This causes a problem when you want to identify the line within the original script that triggered the problem. For example, the simple module

```
package T;

require Exporter;
@ISA = qw/Exporter/;
@EXPORT = qw/function/;
use Carp;

sub function
{
```

```
    warn "Error in module!";
}

1;
```

when called from a script

```
use T;

function();
```

produces the following error message:

```
Error in module! at T.pm line 11.
```

This is more or less what you might expect, but not necessarily what you want. From a module programmer's perspective, the information is useful because it helps to point to a bug within the module itself. For an end-user, the information provided is fairly useless, and for all but the hardened programmer, it completely pointless.

Assuming that we know the module has only been imported from a calling script, we could use the **caller** function to identify the parent and then report the error. This is messy, and it also requires that you know the level to which the module has been called.

The solution is the **Carp** module, which provides a simplified method for reporting errors within modules that return information about the calling script—not the module. The **Carp** module provides four functions: **carp**, **cluck**, **croak**, and **confess**. With each function, the location of the error is specified relative to the script or package that called the function. For errors more than one level deep, it doesn't return the information on the calling script unless you use the **cluck** or **confess** function to report a stack trace.

The Carp Function

```
carp "Error in module!";
```

The **carp** function is the basic equivalent of **warn** and prints the message to **STDERR** without actually exiting the script. The module actually uses **warn**, so the same basic rules are followed. Thus the preceding example would report the following:

```
Error in module! at test.pl line 3
```

Note that the function will always return the call that originated the error. If the script **test.pl** calls the module **S** which in turns calls the module **T**, and this is where **carp** is called, then **carp** will return the call in **S** that triggered the error.

The Cluck Function

The **cluck** function is a sort of supercharged **carp**, it follows the same basic principle but also prints a stack trace of all the modules that led to the function being called, including information on the original script. The **cluck** function is not exported by default by the module, so you'll need to import it explicitly. Following on from our **test.pl->S->T** example, we'd get this:

```
Error in module! at T.pm line 11
        T::function() called at S.pm line 13
        S::raise() called at test.pl line 3
```

The Croak Function

The **croak** function is the equivalent of **die**, except that it reports the caller one level up:

```
croak "Definitely didn't work";
```

Like **die**, this function also exits the script after reporting the error to **STDERR**:

```
Error in module! at S.pm line 13
```

As with **carp**, the same basic rules apply regarding the including of line and file information according to the **warn** and **die** functions.

The Confess Function

The **confess** function is like **cluck**; it calls **die** and then prints a stack trace all the way up to the origination script.

```
confess "Failed around about there";
```

For example:

```
Error in module! at T.pm line 11
        T::function() called at S.pm line 13
        S::raise() called at t2.pl line 3
```

The
Complete
Reference

Part II

Programming with Perl

The Complete Reference

Chapter 10

Complex Data Structures

P erl's base data types are relatively flexible, and they can be used to store and hold all sorts of information—the hash is by far the most popular and practical, as it often solves many of the problems associated with processing large quantities of information.

However, there are times when what you need is to hold even more complex data types—you need to be able to create your own data types. Perl actually provides this facility through a system of references. A reference points to another data type—scalar, array, hash, etc.—and because a reference is in fact just a scalar variable, you can embed references in arrays and hashes. Within Perl, you have lots of options for creating data structures; and this chapter looks at both the simple base structures of arrays and hashes, and the more complex nested structures, references, and objects.

In this chapter, we'll start by looking at the **pack** function, which can be used to store information into a "packed" structure. We'll be looking at it again in Chapter 13 when we see how it can be used for fixed-length databases. In fact, **pack** is a much more versatile tool that allows us to pack and unpack the structures used in C for defining complex records without resorting to the objectivity offered by C++.

We'll then move on to references—these form the core of any complex data structure and, in turn, also provide the basis for Perl's object system. Objects are an intelligent type of data structure that, through programming, know their own structure and how to manipulate it. Unlike other languages, Perl does not enforce its objectivity, but it is beginning to be a driving force behind the development of the language.

The last part of the chapter looks at the **tie** system—this is an object-based interface that allows you to tie internal data structures, such as arrays and hashes (and by design objects), to external data. For example, suppose you want to tie an internal array to a list of files in a directory, or a hash to the table of an external database. The **tie** system handles the requests and conversion of information from operations, such as assigning values and retrieving values, into the correct commands to operate on the external data source.

Accessing Packed Data Structures

When storing information, and especially when exchanging information, it is essential to use a standardized format. The only recognized standardized format is binary, but converting textual and numerical data into a binary format is a difficult process to get right. Perl supports two functions that will do the conversion for you: **pack** converts a list into a binary structure, and **unpack** converts it back into a list.

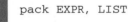
pack EXPR, LIST

The **EXPR** is the template for the binary structure you want to create. The template is composed of characters and numbers that determine the type and count of a specific data type. For example, 'a12 l' would pack a string into a null-padded 12-byte sequence, immediately followed by a packed long integer. The resulting binary string could then be unpacked at a later date. The packing format matches that used by C structures (and unions) and other packed formats, such as IP addresses. The individual data types are specified using the characters shown in Table 10-1.

Character	Description
@	Null fill to absolute position.
a	An ASCII string, will be null padded.
A	An ASCII string, will be space padded.
b	A bitstring (ascending bit order).
B	A bitstring (descending bit order).
c	A signed char (8-bit) value.
C	An unsigned char (8-bit) value.
d	A double-precision float in the native format.
f	A single-precision float in the native format.
H	A hex string (high nibble first).
h	A hex string (low nibble first).
i	A signed integer value.
I	An unsigned integer value.
l	A signed long value (32 bits).
L	An unsigned long value (32 bits).
N	A long (32 bits) in "network" (big-endian) order.
n	A short (16 bits) in "network" (big-endian) order.
p	A pointer to a null-terminated string.
P	A pointer to a fixed-length string.
q	A signed quad (64-bit) value.
Q	An unsigned quad (64-bit) value.
s	A signed short value (16 bits).
S	An unsigned short value (16 bits).

Table 10-1.   *pack Format Characters*

Character	Description
u	A uuencoded string.
U	A Unicode character number (encodes internally to UTF8).
V	A long (32 bits) in "VAX" (little-endian) order.
v	A short (16 bits) in "VAX" (little-endian) order.
w	A BER compressed integer.
x	A null byte (effectively skips forward one byte).
X	Back up a byte.
Z	A null-terminated (and null-padded) string of bytes.

Table 10-1.   *pack Format Characters* (continued)

To use **pack**, you supply a format that lists the data types that you want to pack into a single binary structure. Each element of the supplied list is packed according to the format specification. Specifications are of the form '**X#**', where **X** is one of the characters from Table 10-1, and **#** is a number specifying the length of the format.

Note that each format specification applies to each element within the supplied list, so the format 'a20' packs a single element to a null-padded size of 20 characters. The format 'a20a20' packs two elements, each null padded and each 20 characters in size.

However, the repeat for individual character types applies only to the "a," "A," "b," "B," "h," "H," and "P" types. For "a" and "A," it packs a string to the specified length. For "b" and "B," it packs a string that many bits long; for "h" and "H," that many nibbles (a nibble is 4 bits) long. For all other types, the function gobbles up that number of elements, such that the template 'i20' will pack up to 20 elements from the supplied list as signed integers. If you specify * as the repeat count, then it gobbles up all the remaining elements in the list.

Using the / character within **EXPR** allows you to specify the size of the following value according to **length/string**. For example,

```
pack 'C/a','\04Martin';
```

returns 'Mart'. The leading character (defined by the octal '\04) is extracted by 'C/', which is then used as the repeating value for 'a'. The combination effectively changes the preceding expression to

```
pack 'a4','Martin';
```

Note that the variable-length assertion only works with the **A**, **a**, or **Z** formats; if you supply * (as in **a***), the * will be ignored.

The integer types **s**, **S**, **l**, and **L** may be immediately followed by a ! suffix to signify native shorts or longs. The actual sizes (in bytes) of native **short**, **int**, **long**, and **long long** C data types on the current platform are always available through the **Config** module. For example, to get the length (in bits) of the **int** data type:

```
use Config;
print $Config{intsize},"\n";
```

The floating point packed values are not platform independent, so don't rely on these values for exchanging information between different platforms. You might try using a packed string instead and let Perl handle the conversion of the string into a platform-dependent double value. This eliminates the double interpretation problem when transferring information between different platforms as you are relying on strings and Perl's built-in algorithm for converting scalar values between strings and numbers. Also be aware that Perl uses doubles internally for floating point numbers, so packing a double into a float and then unpacking again may not yield the same value.

Values can be unpacked with the **unpack** function:

```
unpack FORMAT, EXPR
```

This returns a list of values extracted using the specified **FORMAT** from the packed binary string **EXPR**.

The **pack** and **unpack** functions are primarily used for converting between different number formats, for creating fixed-length records for use internally and in external databases, and also for accessing stored C structures within Perl.

The first use, converting between different number formats, makes use of the number formats supported by the **pack** function. For example, to convert a 32-bit binary string into a number:

```
print unpack('I',pack("B32",'0' x 24 . '00001111')),"\n";
```

This should print 15—the value of 1111 in binary.

The second use, creating fixed-length records, makes use of the fact that you can specify field widths and store these fixed-width fields in a file. There are other issues surrounding this, so the information on this and other database methods in Perl are discussed in Chapter 13.

The third use, accessing stored C structures within Perl, is more complex, but it uses many of the core principles you already know. All you need to do is know how to read a C structure, and then use the **pack** and **unpack** functions to convert Perl lists to and from the specified format. For example, the **utmp** structure, which is used to store information about logins, has the following structure definition:

```
struct utmp {
        char ut_user[8];                /* User login name */
        char ut_id[4];                  /* /etc/inittab id */
        char ut_line[12];               /* device name */
        short ut_pid;                   /* process ID */
        short ut_type;                  /* type of entry */
        struct exit_status ut_exit;     /* The exit status of a process */
                                        /* marked as DEAD_PROCESS. */
        time_t ut_time;                 /* time entry was made */
};
```

This can be modeled within a pack template as "a8a4a12ssssl". The following script outputs the information stored in the /var/adm/wtmp file, which uses the native format of the previous structure:

```
my $packstring = "a8a4a12ssssl";
my $reclength = length(pack($packstring));
my @ut_types = qw(EMPTY RUN_LVL BOOT_TIME OLD_TIME
                  NEW_TIME INIT_PROCESS LOGIN_PROCESS
                  USER_PROCESS DEAD_PROCESS ACCOUNTING);

open(D,"</var/adm/wtmp") or die "Couldn't open wtmp, $!";

while(sysread(D,my $rec,$reclength))
{
    my ($user,$userid,$line,$pid,$type,$eterm,$eexit,$time)
        = unpack($packstring,$rec);
    print("$user, $userid, $line, $pid, $ut_types[$type], ",
        "$eterm, $eexit, ", scalar localtime($time),"\n");
}

close(D) or die "Couldn't close wtmp, $!";
```

The **unpack** function takes the binary string created by the C structure and returns it as a list, which you can then use to print out the information.

You can also use the **unpack** function to provide a checksum for a given byte stream. The format is to prefix the packed type with **%number**, where **number** is the number of bits to use for the checksum. For example, to calculate the checksum for a character string:

```
$checksum = unpack("%32C*", $string);
```

The same trick can be used to count the number of set bits in a bit vector (such as that created by **vec**):

```
$bits = unpack("%32b*", $bitset);
```

There are other uses for the **pack** and **unpack** functions, and we'll see some examples of these in the next few chapters.

References

A reference is, exactly as the name suggests, a reference or pointer to another object. That's essentially as complicated as it gets. References actually provide all sorts of abilities and facilities that would not otherwise be available. For C programmers using Perl for the first time, a reference is exactly like a pointer, except within Perl it's easier to use and, more to the point, more practical.

Before we examine the details of references, it's worth covering some of the terminology. There are two types of references: *symbolic* and *hard*. A symbolic reference enables you to refer to a variable by name, using the value of another variable. For example, if the variable **$foo** contains the string "bar", the symbolic reference to **$foo** refers to the variable **$bar**. We'll look at more examples later.

A hard reference refers to the actual data contained in a data structure. However, the form of the data structure to which it points is largely irrelevant. Although a hard reference can refer to a single scalar, it can also refer to an array of scalars, a hash, a subroutine, or a typeglob.

There are several ways to create references to different structures, and we'll examine these later. The act of extracting information from these structures is called *dereferencing*. When you dereference a scalar reference, you are in fact referring to the original data structure. The act of dereferencing information must be explicit. There is no implicit dereferencing supported within Perl on any structure.

A reference is contained within a scalar; and because all other data structures within Perl are essentially based on a scalar or extensions of a scalar, you can create complex data structures. By using references, you can create complex, nested structures, including arrays of arrays, arrays of hashes, hashes of arrays, and hashes of hashes. The structures you create do not have to be two dimensional; you can have as many dimensions as you like. There is no restriction for you to create an array of hashes.

Remember that the array contains references, so individual elements of the array could refer to an array or hash, or indeed, an array of arrays, a hash of hashes, and so on. This enables you to create incredibly complex data structures with relative ease.

Creating Hard References

The unary backslash operator is used to create a reference to a named variable or subroutine, for example:

```
$foo = 'Bill';
$fooref = \$foo;
```

The **$fooref** variable now contains a hard reference to the **$foo** variable. You can do the same with other variables:

```
$array = \@ARGV;
$hash  = \%ENV;
$glob  = \*STDOUT;
```

To create a reference to a subroutine:

```
sub foo { print "foo" };
$foosub = \&foo;
```

Of course, because you are assigning the references to a scalar, there is no reason why you can't place the information into any other scalar-based structure, and that includes arrays and hashes. For example:

```
$foo = 'Bill';
$bar = 'Ben';
$xyz = 'Mary';
@arrayofref = (\$foo, \$bar, \$xyz);
```

The **@arrayofref** array now contains an array of scalars, and each scalar is a reference to the three scalar variables.

Anonymous Arrays

When you create a reference to an array directly—that is, without creating an intervening named array—you are creating an *anonymous array*. The scalar contains a reference that does not have its own name. These are useful for creating complex structures, since you can create an array, a hash, or a combination within the confines of a named variable within a simple statement. This reduces the time it takes to code and also the time it takes for the program to run (although the differences are pretty small for small, simple structures).

Creating an anonymous array is easy:

```
$array = [ 'Bill', 'Ben, 'Mary' ];
```

This line assigns an array, indicated by the enclosing square brackets instead of the normal parentheses, to the scalar **$array**. The values on the right side of the assignment make up the array, and the left side contains the reference to this array. The significance of this description is that you could put other data structures on the left side of the assignment. We'll examine examples of these later in this chapter when we look at more complex data structures.

Remember that the significant element here is the use of square brackets around the list of scalars to indicate an array, not a list. Thus, you can create more complex structures by nesting arrays:

```
@arrayarray = ( 1, 2, [1, 2, 3]);
```

The **@arrayarray** now contains three elements; the third element is a reference to an anonymous array of three elements. Furthermore, you can use the same basic notation to create an array of arrays in a single reference:

```
$arrayarray = [ 1, 2, [1, 2, 3]];
```

This creates a reference to an anonymous array, whose third argument is a reference to another 3-element anonymous array. The resulting reference is placed into **$arrayarray**. Note as well that, as with all other arrays, you could equally have used expressions or variables as elements in the arrays.

Anonymous Hashes

Anonymous hashes are similarly easy to create, except you use braces instead of square brackets:

```
$hash = { 'Man'    => 'Bill',
          'Woman' => 'Mary,
          'Dog'    => 'Ben'
        };
```

The same arguments for the anonymous array composer also apply here. You can use any normal element—a string literal (as in the preceding code), an expression, or a variable—to create the structure in question. Also note that the same principles for arrays of arrays can be applied to hashes, too, but we'll cover the specifics of nested hash and array structures later in this chapter.

Note that this composition procedure only works when Perl is expecting a term—that is, usually when making an assignment or expecting a hash or reference as an element. Braces are not only used for creating anonymous hashes, but they are also responsible for selecting hash subscript elements and for defining blocks within Perl. This means you must occasionally explicitly specify the creation of an anonymous hash reference by preceding the hash creator with a **+** or **return**:

```
$envref = +{ %ENV };
sub dupeenv{ return { %ENV } };
```

Anonymous Subroutines

An *anonymous subroutine* is used in many key situations within Perl. We'll see perhaps the most common examples in Chapter 14 when we examine the methods available or handling signals. Again, the method for creating a reference to an anonymous subroutine is very straightforward:

```
$hw = sub { print "Hello World!\n" };
```

The new **$hw** variable now contains a reference to the anonymous subroutine, which prints the "Hello World!" message on the screen.

The important thing to remember when creating an anonymous subroutine is that you must have a trailing semicolon to end the declaration expression, unlike a typical subroutine definition.

In essence, what this does is create a reference to a piece of code, which you can execute directly using the reference. If you access the reference, then the subroutine code you supplied will be executed, almost as if it was parsed by a **do{}** or **eval{}** block.

To dereference the anonymous subroutine (that is, to actually execute it), we need to use the **&** character to denote the reference type:

```
&$hw;
```

This actually prints the "Hello World!" message. This is an example of dereferencing, and we're getting slightly ahead of ourselves; so we'll take a step back and instead look at another feature of anonymous subroutines, before we look properly at the process of using hard references.

Closures   A *closure* is a Lisp term, where an anonymous subroutine can be created, and the resulting subroutine will execute within the same context as when it was created. This only works with lexically scoped variables (those created with **my**), and the results can provide you with some interesting facilities that provide alternative ways for introducing and using information within an anonymous subroutine.

Consider the following code, in which an anonymous subroutine is created as the return value from a function:

```
sub formatlist
{
    my @list = @_;
    return sub
            {
                my $title = shift;
                print "$title: ", join(' ',@list),"\n";
            }
}

$arguments = formatlist(@ARGV);

&$arguments('Command line');
```

If you run this within a script, you might get this:

```
Command line: -w -o file.txt
```

You'll note that the contents of the **@ARGV** array, which was determined and populated when the anonymous **sub** was created, are also available when you dereference the function later.

Filehandles/Typeglobs

Creating a reference to a filehandle is a case of passing a reference to the corresponding typeglob. This is, in fact, the best way to pass filehandles to or from subroutines, since it has the optical effect of removing the ambiguity of the typeglob:

```
writelog(\*LOG);

sub writelog
{
    my $LOG = shift;
    print $LOG scalar(localtime(time)),":",@_;
}
```

The alternative is to use a filehandle object and pass the object around instead. We'll see more on objects later in the chapter.

Dereferencing

The most direct way of dereferencing a reference is to prepend the corresponding data type character (**$** for scalars, **@** for arrays, **%** for hashes, and **&** for subroutines) that you are expecting in front of the scalar variable containing the reference. For example, to dereference a scalar reference **$foo**, you would access the data as **$$foo**. Other examples are

```
$array = \@ARGV;                     # Create reference to array
$hash  = \%ENV;                      # Create reference to hash
$glob  = \*STDOUT;                   # Create reference to typeglob
$foosub = \&foo;                     # Create reference to subroutine

push (@$array, "From humans");
$$array[0] = 'Hello'
$$hash{'Hello'} = 'World';
&$foosub;
print $glob "Hello World!\n";
```

It's important to get the semantics correct here. In the preceding **$$array[0]** and **$$hash{'Hello'}** lines, the corresponding structures are not actually being dereferenced; in fact, you are dereferencing the scalar to which the corresponding elements refer. We'll return to this in a moment. Also note that you do not have to explicitly dereference a filehandle, since a reference to a typeglob points to an entry in the symbol table—see Chapter 7 for more information on Perl symbol tables.

References and dereferences execute in order. A reference (**$foo**) to a string of the form \\\"hello" can be dereferenced using **$$$$foo**—we need three **$** characters to dereference against each \ character, plus one for the actual reference scalar. However, it's unlikely you'll be using individual scalar references in this form. When it comes to more complex structures, there are different methods available, and these also get around some of the difficulties surrounding the dereferencing of entire structures rather than the individual scalars of which they are composed.

The second alternative for dereferencing a reference is to use **BLOCK** notation. This works in a similar way to quotes, except that you use braces to "quote" the embedded reference. Since the last statement in a block gives the block its return value, by putting a reference as the only statement in a block, you end up returning the data type to which the reference points. All you need to do is instruct Perl on how to interpret the returned data. You can, therefore, rewrite the preceding examples as follows:

```
${$foo} = "Hello World";
push (@{$array}, "From humans");
${$array}[0] = 'Hello';
${$hash}{'Hello'} = 'World';
&{$foosub};
```

Using the block notation is trivial in these cases, but it makes more sense when you want to identify a particular structure as a complete data type, not an element of a data type. For example, the line

```
foreach $key (keys %$hash)
```

looks a bit cryptic compared to

```
foreach $key (keys %{$hash})
```

which is a little clearer.

This notation really comes into its own, however, when you are using nested structures. Let's assume, for the moment, that you have a hash of hashes, created in a similar fashion to

```
$hash = { 'hash' => { 'first' => 1, 'second' => 2 } };
```

If you try to access the keys of the hash reference pointed to by the **'hash'** element in the parent hash reference, you might try

```
foreach $key (keys %$hash{'hash'})
```

However, Perl will report an error—because it interprets the hash element first and, therefore, returns a scalar, not a hash reference. Instead, you need to write it as

```
foreach $key (keys %{$hash->{'hash'}})
```

Finally, the other alternative is to use the arrow operator, **->**. This works only on arrays or hashes, since the arrow operator (more correctly known as the *infix* operator) provides an easier method for extracting the individual elements from both structures.

PROGRAMMING WITH PERL

The benefit of the infix operator is that it does not require you to explicitly dereference the original scalar. Therefore, you can rewrite the statements

```
$$array[0] = 'Hello';
$$hash{'Hello'} = 'World';
```

and

```
${$array}[0] = 'Hello';
${$hash}{'Hello'} = 'World';
```

as

```
$array->[0] = 'Hello';
$hash->{'Hello'} = 'World';
```

This is clearer than the other methods, but as usual, care should be taken to ensure you are actually extracting or using the correct element from the array or hash.

The statements

```
$array[0];
```

and

```
$array->[0];
```

are not equal. The first is accessing the first element of the **@array** variable, while the second is accessing the first element of the array pointed to by **$array**. The **$array** could point to any array, named or anonymous. This makes the infix notation practical and clear when using references directly within a subroutine that potentially needs to access the information for a supplied reference.

To use one of the previous methods, you might use a subroutine like the one that follows to print the first element of an array passed by reference:

```
sub first
{
```

```
    $array = shift;
    print ${$array}[0],"\n";
}
```

This is a little fussy and certainly less than clear, while this

```
sub first
{
    print ${$_[0]}[0],"\n";
}
```

looks suspiciously like line noise, although it achieves the desired result. Using the infix operator, the subroutine looks far clearer:

```
sub first
{
    print $_[0]->[0],"\n";
}
```

Although still a little complex, it's clearer that you are trying to access the first element of the first argument passed to the function.

Determining a Reference Type

You can determine the type of variable that a particular reference points to by using the **ref** function.

```
ref EXPR
ref
```

The function returns a true value (actually a string) if **EXPR**, or **$_**, is a reference. The actual string returned defines the type of entity the reference refers to. The built-in types are

```
REF
SCALAR
```

```
ARRAY
HASH
CODE
GLOB
LVALUE
```

For example, the code

```
$scalar = "Hello World\n";
$ref    = \$scalar;
print ref $ref,"\n";
```

prints

```
SCALAR
```

The actual string value of a reference is a combination of the reference type (as returned by **ref**) and its location in memory. For example, if you print the previous reference, instead of dereferencing it,

```
print "$ref\n";
```

it will print out something like "SCALAR(0xaa472b4)," which doesn't make a lot of sense.

Symbolic References

If you refer back to the start of this section, you will remember that a symbolic reference was defined as the use of a scalar value as a string, which in turn gives a variable its name. For example:

```
$var = "foo";
$$var = "bar";
```

Because **$var** is not a reference, the act of dereferencing a nonexistent reference is to create a new variable with the name of the variable's contents. So in the previous example, you have set the value of **$foo** to "bar". In essence, you've done this:

```
$"$var" = "bar";
```

This statement doesn't work, of course, and the eventual result should be clear. This makes the system very powerful: you can name a variable or subroutine based on a variable piece of information.

However, the problem with symbolic references is that it only takes a simple mistake for you to inadvertently create a symbolic rather than a hard reference. It is, therefore, important (if not imperative) that you check what you are doing or, better still, ask Perl to do it for you. The **use strict** pragma enforces these checks for you. If you only want to check references, then use

```
use strict 'refs';
```

in your script. See Chapter 19 for more information on pragmas.

Hashes and References

You must be careful when using references with hash keys. You cannot use a hard reference as a hash key, because the hard reference will be converted to a string for the benefit of the hash's key. It's unlikely that you will want a hash key of "SCALAR(0xaa472b4)", and even if you do, you cannot dereference the string into the original variable anyway.

The only time this feature is useful is when you want to create a unique key within a hash. The reference is guaranteed to be unique, since you can't have two data types at the same location. What you can't do is dereference the key back to its original variable.

Complex Structures

Beyond the normal constraints of arrays and hashes, you can also create complex structures made up of combinations of the two. These are nested, or complex, structures, and they can be used to model complex data in an easy-to-use format.

What actually happens with a nested structure is that Perl stores the nested data type as a reference to an anonymous variable. For example, in a two-dimensional array, the main array is a list of references, and the subarrays are anonymous arrays to which these references point. This means that an "array of arrays" actually means an array of references to arrays. The same is true of all nested structures; and, although it seems complex, it does provide a suitably powerful method for creating complex, nested structures.

You can create any number of dimensions in an array or hash, simply by extending the existing notation. Perl will handle the rest of the work for you. There are, of course, some complexities and tricks associated with accessing and using these complex structures, and we'll look at the four basic types: arrays of arrays, hashes of hashes, arrays of hashes, and hashes of arrays.

Arrays of Arrays

An array of arrays is a two-dimensional structure and the most basic of those available. We'll be using the array of arrays as a core reference point for many of the nested structures, including how to access them, use them directly, and use arrays and array references to access the entire array and array elements. If you want to use nested structures, you should read this section first. We'll cover the differences and abilities of the other nested structures later.

An array of arrays can be used to hold any list of nested information. For example, users on a system have a list of individual users. The first dimension is the main array, and the second dimension is the array of group members. Another alternative is to think about the classic Battleship game. Individual squares on the battleship grid can be referred to by an X,Y reference. You could use an array of arrays to hold this information.

Populating a list of lists is a case of including anonymous arrays or existing arrays within an existing array structure. For our example, we'll use a tic-tac-toe (or Noughts and Crosses, depending on your nationality) board:

```
@tictactoe = ( ['X','O','O'],
               ['O','O','X'],
               ['O','X','X']
             );
```

This creates a nested set of arrays within a parent array, **@tictactoe**. To print out the bottom-right corner:

```
print $tictactoe[2][2];
```

Alternatively, you can place the array directly into a reference:

```
$tictactoe = [ ['X','O','O'],
               ['O','O','X'],
               ['O','X','X']
             ];
```

Note the use of the square brackets around the nested arrays, which indicates to Perl that you are creating an anonymous array and you need to return a reference to it. You assign the reference to the **$tictactoe** scalar, and to access the bottom-right corner,

```
print $$tictactoe[2][2];
```

Note the semantics here. The leading dollar sign shows that you are dereferencing; and, therefore, Perl knows that the array specification must be to locations within an array reference.

In fact, Perl automatically assumes you are dereferencing if you use pairs of brackets together. Perl knows that this indicates a structure to a list of references, whether that's a hash or an array, so the infix operator (or block names) are implied. This doesn't prevent you from using them if you want to. The following lines are also equal:

```
print $tictactoe->[2][2];
print $tictactoe->[2]->[2];
```

The infix operator here tells Perl that you are dereferencing, so the leading dollar sign is not required. But note that the following are *wrong*:

```
print $tictactoe[2][2];
print $tictactoe[2]->[2];
```

In the first, you haven't specified the return format—you still need to tell Perl that it's a scalar that you're dereferencing. In the second, the dereferencing is implied, but you're trying to dereference the array embedded in a standard array, not an anonymous one.

Like many other similar features, the elimination of the dereference operator is a direct attempt to improve the overall readability of the code. The first form, shown here,

```
print $tictactoe->[2][2];
print $tictactoe->[2]->[2];
```

looks cleaner and should appeal to C programmers, since this is the same format used in C for multidimensional arrays. The other formats would perhaps make more sense to a hardened Perl programmer, and they help if you are particularly bothered about the notation of one reference point to another.

We'll need a more complex source for our next examples. I've used the /etc/passwd file here, since it's the most readily available for most people. However, the principles will apply to any data you want to map into an array of arrays. The individual "rows" of our array (the first dimension) will be each record; the individual fields will form the columns (the second dimension).

The following script populates our database. I've assumed that the file is already open.

```
while(<PASSWD>)
{
    chomp;
```

```
    push @passwd,[ split /:/ ];
}
```

This creates an array **@passwd**, and each field contains a reference to an array, the contents of which is the list of values returned by **split**. Note the notation again here—the square brackets indicate that you are returning a reference to an array.

To put the information directly into an array reference:

```
open(PASSWD,"/etc/passwd");
while(<PASSWD>)
{
    push @{$passwd}, [ split /:/ ];
}
```

You could also set it more explicitly:

```
while(<PASSWD>)
{
    chomp;
    foreach $field (split /:/)
    {
        push @{$passwd[$index]},$field;
    }
    $index++;
}
```

This demonstrates another important point that carries through all nested references. The call to **push** requires an array as its first element, and it must begin with @; so you must quote the reference to the nested array using block notation. Furthermore, note the location of the index for the array reference: it's contained within the block quotes. This is because Perl would see the subscript reference and assume it was returning a scalar, not an array, irrespective of the leading character you have supplied.

What the example does show is the addition of fields, individually, to the row of an array. It uses **push** again, but there's no reason why you can't also track your location in the nested array:

```
while(<PASSWD>)
{
    chomp;
    @fields = ();
    @fields = split /:/;
    foreach $field (0..@fields)
    {
        $passwd[$index][$field] = $fields[$field];
    }
    $index++;
}
```

You make sure you empty the array before you fill it with the information from **split**. This prevents you from putting undefined data into the structure, since the assignment will only update fields, not actually empty them. Then it's a case of assignments to the array of arrays.

Another point to note here is that if you create an entry in an index that doesn't currently exist within the structure (as with any other array), Perl will create the intervening elements, filling them with **undef** as it goes. For example:

```
$passwd[120][0] = 'martinb';
```

Assuming **$passwd** has not already been defined or populated, it now contains a reference to an array 121 elements in size, the first 120 of which contain **undef**.

Now, if you turn to accessing the information, there are also complications. You can't do this

```
print @passwd;
```

for the original form, or

```
print $passwd;
```

because you'll get a list of hash references, and a reference to a hash back as a string value. This is one of the most common mistakes when using nested structures or just references in general. Perl doesn't dereference for you, so you need to use a loop to progress through the parent array.

Try using the simpler array, rather than a reference to an array, first:

```
foreach $array (@passwd)
{
    print join(':',@$array);
}
```

or

```
foreach $array (@{$passwd})
{
    print join(':',@$array);
}
```

Both of these work because the individual elements of the parent array are references, which you can dereference using the correct prefix. If you want to step through the child array as well, then you might use something like this:

```
foreach $x (0..@{$passwd})
{
    foreach $y (0..@{$passwd[$x]})
    {
        print "$x, $y = $passwd[$x][$y]\n";
    }
}
```

The same rules for previous constructs apply here, too. You must use the block notation to ensure you get the correct array returned in the **foreach** statement. The reference to the subarray requires you to insert the subscript operation in the block, not outside of it.

Finally, you need to think about accessing the individual slices of a nested array. If you were to use

```
@new = @passwd[0..4];
```

the **@new** array would contain the first five references contained in **@passwd**. If you want to slice the fields for an individual record, you can either use loops or use a block to indicate the array reference you are extracting from, and then use the normal slice notation to extract the elements from the embedded array reference:

```
print @{$passwd[0]}[4..7];
```

To obtain a slice in the opposite direction—that is, the entire column from your structure—you have to use loops. The following three versions don't work:

```
print @{{$passwd}[0..7]}[0];
print @{$passwd[0..7]}[0];
print @{$passwd}[0..7][0];
```

Instead, you need to use a loop:

```
@users = ();
foreach $x (0..@{$passwd})
{
    push @users,$passwd[$x][0];
}
```

Or, to create a completely nested array of arrays consisting of a two-dimensional slice, you need either to use two nested loops, or use the slice notation used previously:

```
@userhome = ();
foreach $x (5..20)
{
    push @userhome, [ @{$passwd[$x]}[0,6] ];
}
```

The remainder of the nested structures use the same techniques you've seen here, albeit with some minor modifications.

Hashes of Hashes

Earlier in this chapter, you saw how information in a hash could be handled and accessed almost immediately. With some clever use of the key strings, you can also emulate a simple database system internally within a hash, but handling the keys is complex. By using a hash of hashes, you make the structures easier to use and more practical when storing and accessing the information.

The format for creating a hash of hashes is much the same as that for arrays of arrays. In the following example, I've created a hash of hashes that describes a company organization. The primary keys are the departments, and the nested keys are the employee names. The values then contain the corresponding employee's job title.

```
%company = ('Sales'         => {
                                'Brown'   => 'Manager',
                                'Smith'   => 'Salesman',
                                'Albert' => 'Salesman',
                               },
            'Marketing'   => {
                                'Penfold' => 'Designer',
                                'Evans' => 'Tea-person',
                                'Jurgens' => 'Manager',
                               },
            'Production' => {
                                'Cotton' => 'Paste-up',
                                'Ridgeway' => 'Manager',
                                'Web' => 'Developer',
                               },
           );
```

You can also use the nested format, which is also the way you would access the individual data types:

```
$company{'Sales'}{'Brown'}          = 'Manager';
$company{'Sales'}{'Smith'}          = 'Salesman';
$company{'Sales'}{'Albert'}         = 'Salesman';
$company{'Marketing'}{'Penfold'}    = 'Designer';
$company{'Marketing'}{'Evans'}      = 'Tea-person';
$company{'Marketing'}{'Jurgens'}    = 'Manager';
$company{'Production'}{'Cotton'}    = 'Paste-up';
$company{'Production'}{'Ridgeway'} = 'Manager';
$company{'Production'}{'Web'}       = 'Developer';
```

Next is a more practical example, which reads the contents of the file and then outputs the contents in a formatted form using a hash of hashes to store the information. Because you read the entire file into a hash of hashes, you can then sort and manipulate the information before you report. This would be difficult using any of the previous methods you have seen. This example uses the /etc/passwd file, not only because it is easily available, but also because it can be useful to sort the file into a more friendly format. Let's look at the output first:

```
root:x:0:1:Martin Brown:/:/sbin/sh:
smtp:x:0:0:mail daemon user:/::
daemon:x:1:1:0000-Admin(0000):/::
bin:x:2:2:0000-Admin(0000):/usr/bin::
sys:x:3:3:0000-Admin(0000):/::
adm:x:4:4:0000-Admin(0000):/var/adm::
uucp:x:5:5:0000-uucp(0000):/usr/lib/uucp::
nuucp:x:9:9:0000-uucp(0000):/var/spool/uucppublic:/usr/lib/uucp/uucico:
listen:x:37:4:Network Admin:/usr/net/nls::
lp:x:71:8:0000-lp(0000):/usr/spool/lp::
mc:x:1000:1000:Martin C Brown:/users/mc:/usr/local/bin/bash:
martinb:x:1000:1000:Martin C Brown:/users/martinb:/usr/local/bin/bash:
alias:*:7790:2108::/usr/local/qmail/alias:/bin/true:
qmaild:*:7791:2108::/usr/local/qmail:/bin/true:
qmaill:*:7792:2108::/usr/local/qmail:/bin/true:
qmailp:*:7793:2108::/usr/local/qmail:/bin/true:
qmailq:*:7794:2107::/usr/local/qmail:/bin/true:
qmailr:*:7795:2107::/usr/local/qmail:/bin/true:
qmails:*:7796:2107::/usr/local/qmail:/bin/true:
nobody:x:60001:60001:uid no body:/::
noaccess:x:60002:60002:uid no access:/::
```

And here's the script:

```
open(DATA,"</etc/passwd") || die "Couldn't open file properly";
my (%passwd, $ref);

while(<DATA>)
{
    chomp;
    @fields = split /:/;
    $login = shift @fields;
    $passwd{$login}{'passwd'} =  shift @fields;
    $passwd{$login}{'uid'}    =  shift @fields;
    $passwd{$login}{'gid'}    =  shift @fields;
    $passwd{$login}{'name'}   =  shift @fields;
    $passwd{$login}{'home'}   =  shift @fields;
    $passwd{$login}{'shell'}  =  shift @fields;
}

close(DATA) || die "Couldn't close file properly";

foreach (sort { $passwd{$a}{'uid'} <=> $passwd{$b}{'uid'} } keys %passwd)
```

```
{
    print "$_:";
    foreach $field (qw/login passwd uid gid name home shell/)
    {
        print "$passwd{$_}{$field}:";
    }
    print "\n";
}
```

There are some important parts of this script that we need to cover. A standard
sort block statement is used, but you want to sort on the nested hash—not the
numerical sequence used to store each record. The **sort** statement works because the
comparison will return the sorted primary key (as selected via the **$a** and **$b** sort
variables), even though what you are actually sorting on is the value of the nested hash.

If you wanted to sort the primary hash keys, you could use a much simpler statement:

```
foreach $key (sort keys %passwd)
```

And if you wanted to sort on the nested hash keys in the nested loop:

```
foreach $subkey (sort keys %{$passwd{$login}})
```

You must use the block method for selecting a variable name. The statement

```
foreach $subkey (sort keys %passwd{$_})
```

will report an error during compilation because Perl identifies the variable **%passwd**
as a hash, but the fragment **passwd{$_}** as a hash element. Therefore, the entire
%passwd{$_}** is bogus, since you must reference a hash element with a leading **$
to indicate a scalar value.

Here's a different example of the same printing loop that sacrifices sorting for a
more memory-efficient method:

```
while ($key = each %passwd)
{
    print "$key:";
    foreach $field (keys %{$passwd{$key}})
    {
        print "$passwd{$key}{$field}:";
    }
    print "\n";
}
```

Because this example does not use temporary lists, you could safely use it on large structures without fear of running out of memory.

Arrays of Hashes

The previous example used an array of arrays to store information contained in the password file. A hash of hashes was used to access individual information for a specific user without having to search through the hash. As an alternative, an array of hashes could have been used. Each element of the array would be a record and could, therefore, be accessed in the traditional record-number format. The value of the array element is a reference to a hash, and the hash structure consists of the normal key/value pairs, with the key being the field name and the corresponding value the field contents.

Let's take a look at the corresponding array of hashes script for the /etc/passwd file:

```
open(DATA,"</etc/passwd") || die "Couldn't open file properly";
my (%passwd, $ref);

while(<DATA>)
{
    chomp;
    @fields = split /:/;
    $aref = {};
    $aref->{'login'}  =  shift @fields;
    $aref->{'passwd'} =  shift @fields;
    $aref->{'uid'}    =  shift @fields;
    $aref->{'gid'}    =  shift @fields;
    $aref->{'name'}   =  shift @fields;
    $aref->{'home'}   =  shift @fields;
    $aref->{'shell'}  =  shift @fields;
    push @passwd,$aref;
}

close(DATA) || die "Couldn't close file properly";

foreach $ref (sort { $$a{'uid'} <=> $$b{'uid'} } @passwd)
{
    foreach $field (qw/login passwd uid gid name home shell/)
    {
        print $$ref{$field},":";
    }
    print "\n";
}
```

The array of hashes structure is built very simply. You create a new reference to an anonymous hash in **$aref**, and then populate it with the correct key/value pairs.

The new anonymous reference is then pushed onto the global **@passwd** array, just the same as any array element. The result is a fully populated array of anonymous hash references.

For sorting, you have a slightly different problem. You want to sort the records by the **uid** field of the record. Therefore, you need to use a sorting expression that will access the underlying hash element contents, returning a sorted list of array references from the **@passwd** array. You do this by dereferencing the **uid** key from the hash, using the hash references stored in the **$a** and **$b** variables used by the **sort** function.

For a simpler, nonsorted result, you could just use this:

```
foreach $record (@passwd)
{
    foreach $field (qw/login passwd uid gid name home shell/)
    {
        print $record->{$field},":";
    }
    print "\n";
}
```

Again, it's important to remember that the **$record** variable contains a reference to an anonymous hash. If all you did was print that value, Perl would report something like

```
HASH(0xcfaf8)
```

If you wanted to access all the keys of the referenced hashes, you would have to use a slightly different method. Here's the remodeled original:

```
foreach $ref (sort { $$a{'uid'} <=> $$b{'uid'} } @passwd)
{
    foreach $field (keys %$ref)
    {
        print $$ref{$field},":";
    }
    print "\n";
}
```

Unfortunately, for this particular data source, this doesn't take into account the required field order.

Finally, here's a record-number alternative that uses less memory:

```
foreach $id (0..$#passwd)
{
    foreach $field (keys %{$passwd[$id]})
    {
        print $passwd[$id]{$field},":";
    }
    print "\n";
}
```

Note that this example uses a more direct method of accessing an individual within a record, although the eventual result is the same.

Using this method of record organization allows you to have different fields for individual records. You could even use separate keys in the hash, or you could use **pack** and a suitable "packstring" stored in hash keys to store complex structures. See Chapter 13 for more details on planning and using databases with Perl's internal and external structures.

Hashes of Arrays

A hash of arrays is best used when you want to store and use an array, and you want to access it by name. We'll use the /etc/group file, a cousin to the /etc/passwd file, for this demonstration. The file is essentially made up of a list of group names, and against each group name is a list of group members. Here's a sample /etc/group file:

```
root::0:root,dummy,martinb
other::1:dummy,martinb
bin::2:root,bin,daemon
sys::3:root,bin,sys,adm
adm::4:root,adm,daemon
uucp::5:root,uucp
mail::6:root
tty::7:root,tty,adm
lp::8:root,lp,adm
nuucp::9:root,nuucp
staff::10:
daemon::12:root,daemon
sysadmin::14:
nobody::60001:
noaccess::60002:
shared::1000:MC,SLP
qmail:*:2107:
nofiles:*:2108:
```

By modeling the file within a hash of arrays, you can access a list of group members by referring to the group by name. The following script builds the **%group** hash. We'll deal with the printing separately.

```
open(DATA,"</etc/group") || die "Couldn't open file properly";
my (%passwd, $ref);

while(<DATA>)
{
    chomp;
    ($groupname,$members) = (split /:/)[0,3];
    $group{$groupname} = [ split /,/,$members ];
}

close(DATA) || die "Couldn't close file properly";
```

You build the group list by creating an anonymous array, which is generated by the list returned by separating the member list with **split**. You can very quickly print the results because there are no complicated structures to handle, aside from the parent hash:

```
foreach (sort keys %group)
{
    print "$_: ", join(' ' ,@{$group{$_}}),"\n";
}
```

Note, as in previous examples, the most critical part is that the hash value contains a reference to an anonymous array; so to access it as a complete array, you need to use a block reference.

The following example sorts the list of groups by the number of elements in the subarray:

```
foreach (sort { @{$group{$a}} <=> @{$group{$b}} } keys %group)
{
    print "$_: ", join(' ' ,@{$group{$_}}),"\n";
}
```

And for a simpler, structured output, you can access the array by its individual index elements:

```
foreach (sort keys %group)
{
```

```
    print "$_ \n";
    for $i (0..$#{$group{$_}})
    {
        print "  $i = $group{$_}[$i]\n";
    }
}
```

Finally, the following example is a less memory-intensive version, although you lose the ability to sort the list of names.

```
while (($key, $array) = each(%group))
{
    print "$key: ", join(' ', @$array),"\n";
}
```

This time you can dereference the hash value directly, rather than using block quotes.

Beyond Two Dimensions

The preceding examples still assume a relatively strict structure around your data. Depending on your point of view when it comes to data modeling, this may be a good or a bad thing. There is no reason why you can't extend the preceding examples beyond two dimensions. Consider the following nested hash of arrays of hashes, which emulates a database that supports multiple tables.

```
%db = (
    contacts => [
                { 'name'  => 'Martin',
                  'email' => 'mc@mcwords.com' },
                { 'name'  => 'Bob',
                  'email' => 'bob@bob.com' },
                ],
    appointments => [
                { 'Date'  => '22/3/98',
                  'Time'  => '10:30',
                  'Title' => 'Dentist' },
                { 'Date'  => '5/5/98',
                  'Time'  => '00:00',
                  'Title' => 'Birthday' },
                ],
    );
```

To make the process of building complex structures easier, you can also copy references so that a particular element points to some other part of the structure. For example, you might want to create a new appointment and add a new field—an array of contacts who will attend the meeting:

```
%appt = ( 'Date' => '4/5/1999',
          'Time' => '10:30',
          'Title' => 'Production Meeting',
          'Members' => [ $db{'contacts'}[0], $db{'contacts'}[1] ]
          );

push @{$db{'appointments'}}, \%appt;
```

The new 'Members' element of the hash contains an array, which has two references to the two contacts created in the preceding. You can access their email addresses directly with

```
print ${$db{appointments}[2]{Members}[0]}{email},"\n";
```

But note that because it's a reference, an assignation like this

```
${$db{appointments}[2]{Members}[0]}{email} = 'foo@goo.bar';
```

updates the value of the contact's record directly, so that both

```
print ${$db{appointments}[2]{Members}[0]}{email},"\n";
```

and

```
print $db{contacts}[0]{email},"\n";
```

print out the new foo@goo.bar email address.

There isn't any reason to store only literal values, either. Arrays and hashes store lists of scalars, and a scalar can be a reference to a wide range of different entities, including subroutines (anonymous and named), filehandles, other hashes and arrays, and any combination thereof.

Here's another example—this time the creation of a hash with references to subroutines:

```
my %commandlist = (
                    'DISK'  => \&disk_space_report,
                    'SWAP'  => \&swap_space_report,
                    'STORE' => \&store_status_report,
                    'GET'   => \&get_status_report,
                    'QUIT'  => \&quit_connection,
                    );
```

You could now call the function directly, without

```
&{$commandlist->{STORE}};
```

and with these arguments:

```
&{$commandlist->{STORE}}(@values);
```

This type of table is called a *dispatch table* and is often used in situations in which a program receives a string or command from a user or remote process. Perl allows you to call the function desired directly, without having to use a long and complicated **if..elsif..else** statement.

You may have problems with dispatch tables if you are using the **strict** pragma; this is because you are relying on "soft" references—you can get around this limitation by using the provided information to look up the subroutine within the symbol table, and then creating a hard reference to that. For example:

```
my $func = sprintf("%s_%s",$action,$subaction);

*code = \&{$func};
if (defined(&code))
{
    &code($user,$group,$session);
}
else
{
```

```
        display_account($user,$group,$session);
}
```

This example was actually taken from a web script, where **$action** and **$subaction** are actually components extracted from the CGI request. The benefits of using a dispatch table are as follows:

- Allows for multiple function calls based on user input without the need for a multioption **if** statement.

- Allows you to "develop" functions and facilities into the rest of a script, even though the function may not have been created yet. You only need to supply a function definition for the script to work.

- You can extend and expand the script without having to mange that complex **if** statement.

There is really only one downside to using a dispatch table that I've come across:

- The functions you call must be supplied the same list of arguments—you cannot change the argument list based on the function or operation name without introducing another **if** statement.

In a properly designed script, this is unlikely to cause a problem, because you will probably be supplying the same information—just for different processing, in each case.

Finally, here's a filehandle hash. The keys are the names of the files you have open, and the value is a reference to a filehandle, passed, as usual, by a typeglob:

```
%files = { 'source.txt'  => \*SOURCE,
           'report.out'  => \*REPORT,
           'scratch.tmp' => \*SCRATCH
         };
```

You can now print to a filehandle by using the file name, instead of the filehandle directly:

```
print { $files->{'report.out'}} "This is a report\n";
```

Note that you need braces around the typeglob to dereference it properly—otherwise, Perl treats what you return as the text that you want to print out, which is obviously incorrect.

Objects

In the early 1990s, object-oriented programming was seen as heralding a new age in programming methods. Rather than dealing with data and functions as two separate entities, an object combines the two elements into a single entity. An object knows what kind of thing it is and, furthermore, knows what it can do based on what kind of thing it is. In programming terms, an object is a data structure that has a number of functions associated with it that act upon the object's data.

A classic example of object-oriented programming is the definition of animals. You might create a cat object. The object knows it is a cat and, therefore, knows its abilities. When you tell a cat object to move, the object will decide that because it has four legs, it should walk. However, a fish object would know that because it has fins, it should swim when you ask it to move.

In theory, using objects to create programs reduces the amount of code you need to program, promotes code reuse, and allows you to program in terms of "I want to…" rather than "To do…, I need to …." This is certainly the tack applied by C++ and Java—two languages that heavily promote, and even require, the use of objects for programming.

The practice, however, is very different. Many programs do not need object-oriented technology to work effectively. There are instances when it is useful—GUI programming, for example, benefits from object methods. There are also instances when object-oriented programming takes significantly longer than the nonobject method.

Within Perl, the philosophy is simple: use objects when it makes sense to use objects, and avoid them when it doesn't. Within the realm of packages and modules, object-oriented programming in Perl requires that you know how to create packages and modules. Object classes are another form of abstraction that uses the abilities of packages. This means that object classes can cross the boundaries associated with individual files and modules.

Object Basics

Before covering the semantics of objects within Perl, it should be noted that you need to know how to create packages, and how to create and use references. Refer to Chapter 7 and the section on "References," earlier in this chapter for more information. Once again, it's worth covering terminology that will be used in this section before proceeding to the details of creating and using objects. There are three main terms, explained from the point of view of how Perl handles objects. The terms are *object*, *class*, and *method*.

- Within Perl, an *object* is merely a reference to a data type that knows what class it belongs to. The object is stored as a reference in a scalar variable. Because a scalar only contains a reference to the object, the same scalar can hold different objects in different classes. When a particular operation is performed on an object, the corresponding method is called, as defined within the class.

■ A *class* within Perl is a package that contains the corresponding methods required to create and manipulate objects.

■ A *method* within Perl is a subroutine, defined with the package. The first argument to the method is an object reference or a package name, depending on whether the method affects the current object or the class.

Creating and Using Objects

When creating an object, you need to supply a *constructor*. This is a subroutine within a package that returns an object reference. The object reference is created by *blessing* a reference to the package's class. For example:

```
package Vegetable;
sub new
{
    my $object = {};
    return bless $object;
}
```

The preceding code creates a new package, **Vegetable**, with a single method, **new**, which is the default name for an object constructor. The **new** method returns a reference to a hash, defined in **$object**, which has been blessed using the **bless** function into an object reference.

You can now create a new **Vegetable** object by using this code:

```
$carrot = new Vegetable;
```

Note here that a hash is used as the base data type for the object. This is not required. You could use any of the available data types as the base for an object. Hashes are the normal receptacle only because you are usually constructing records in which you want to be able to identify individual fields by name.

The use of **bless** defines the difference between a normal reference and an object reference. An object is a reference that has been blessed into a particular class, whereas a reference is just a reference to another entity.

If you want to initialize the object with some information before it is returned, you can put that into the subroutine itself (the following example takes the data from the supplied arguments),

```
sub new
{
    my $object = {@_};
    return bless $object;
}
```

which can now populate when you create a new object:

```
$carrot = new Vegetable('Color' => 'Orange', 'Shape' => 'Carrot-like');
```

You don't have to use the information supplied to the **new** method as a hash. The subroutine can take any arguments and process them as you require. Here's the same constructor, but this time it assumes you are supplying the information in the arguments to the constructor function:

```
sub new
{
    my $object = {};
    $object->{'Color'  => $_[0],
               'Shape'  => $_[1]
              };
    bless $object;
    return $object;
}
```

Normally, of course, you'd check the contents of the arguments before you started blindly filling in the details; but the process is essentially the same.

To call your own initialization routine on a newly blessed object:

```
sub new
{
    my $object = {};
    bless $object;
    $object->_define();
    return $object;
}
```

The use of a leading underscore on the method **_define** is a convention used to indicate a *private* rather than *public* method. The leading underscore convention is not enforced, however; if someone wants to use the method, they can call it directly if they want to. Here's a quick example of the function:

```
sub _define
{
    my $self = shift;
    $self->{'State'}       = 'Raw';
    $self->{'Composition'} = 'Whole';
}
```

Don't worry too much about the semantics for a second; we'll cover that shortly.

For inheritance purposes, you will need to use a two-argument call to **bless**. The second argument should be the class into which you are blessing the object, and you can derive this from the first argument to the constructor method. For example, to explicitly define the preceding object into the **Vegetable** class:

```
sub new
{
    my $class = shift;
    my $object = {};
    return bless $object, $class;
}
```

The reason you need this is that methods execute within the confines of their base class, not their derived class. Thus, if you were to create a new class **Fruit**, which inherited methods from **Vegetable**, a call to the **new** constructor would bless an object into the **Vegetable** rather than the **Fruit** class. Using the preceding format with the two-argument version of **bless** ensures that the new object is part of the **Fruit** method.

Methods

We'll start with a reminder: an object is a blessed reference, but a reference is just a pointer to a data structure. When writing methods, it's important to understand this distinction. Within the confines of the class package and corresponding methods, you use the object as if it were a reference (which it is), but outside the class package, you use it as an object.

There is no special way within Perl to define a method, since a method is just a function defined within the class package. The only difference between a normal subroutine and a method is that the method should accept at least one argument, the contents of which will be the object you want to manipulate. There are no complications to creating the method. All you need to do is define the function, and Perl will handle the rest. See the later section "Classes and Inheritance" for some exceptions, but, otherwise, this definition stands.

There are two types of methods—*class* and *instance*. A *class* method is one that affects the entire class. You've already seen some examples of this: the constructor subroutine is an example of a class method. The first argument a class method receives is the name of the class. This is ignored by most functions, since they already know to which class (package) they belong. However, as you've already seen in the previous section, it is sometimes necessary to identify the class.

An *instance* method is a function that operates on a specific object. It should accept at least one argument, which is the object on which you want to operate. For example, the **boil** method for our **Vegetable** object modifies the 'State' element of the object's hash to 'boiled':

```
sub boil
{
    my $self = shift;
    $self->{'State'} = 'Boiled';
}
```

You take the first argument off with **shift** and then modify the object's contents. Note that the name of the variable that you store the reference in is **$self**. This is an accepted standard, although there is no reason why you can't call it something else. The use is convention, rather than law. Remember that an object is just a reference to a particular data type, so you can modify the hash "object" just as you would any other reference.

To use this method, you use the infix operator to select the method to use on a particular object, for example:

```
$carrot = new Vegetable('Color' => 'Orange', 'Shape' = 'Carrot-like');
$carrot->boil;
```

The "State" field of the hash has now been updated!

You can also accept arguments to the method,

```
sub boil
{
    my $self = shift;
    $self->{'State'} = 'Boiled';
    if (@_ == 1)
    {
        $self->{'Composition'} = shift;
    }
}
```

thus allowing you to define how the vegetable will be prepared before it's boiled:

```
$carrot->boil('Chopped');
```

You can also create a method that behaves differently based on what information is supplied in that first argument. The way to do this is to use **ref** to identify whether the method was supplied a reference to an object or not.

```
sub new
{
    my $self = shift;
    my $type = ref($self) || $self;
    return bless {}, $type;
}
```

If the return value of the **ref** is a valid reference, then it's safe to assume you should be blessing an object. If **ref** returns false, then the argument is not an object but a class name.

Method Calls

There are two ways of invoking a method. The first format looks like this:

```
METHOD CLASS_OR_INSTANCE LIST
```

This is the format you've used for creating objects, for example:

```
new Vegetable('Color' => 'Orange', 'Shape' = 'Carrot-like');
```

   In this case, **new** is the method, **Vegetable** is the class (and indicates to Perl the package to search for the **new** method), and the list is the optional list of arguments that will be passed to the method after the initial class name. The same format can be used for methods on existing objects:

```
boil $carrot 'Chopped';
```

This actually makes more sense (providing your methods and classes are suitably defined). The preceding line uses the first format (**METHOD CLASS LIST**). The second method-calling syntax is

```
CLASS_OR_INSTANCE->METHOD(LIST)
```

For our carrot, this means using this line to get it chopped and boiled:

```
$carrot->boil('Chopped');
```

   Note that this second method requires parentheses around the arguments to the method because this syntax cannot be used as a list operator. This means you must be careful with the first format. It assumes that the first parenthesis defines the start of the arguments, and the matching closing parenthesis ends the argument list.
   Note also that, in both cases, you can explicitly define the method or class you want to use with the normal qualification:

```
$carrot->Vegetable::boil('Chopped');
```

Finally, you can use a scalar variable to hold the name of a method to call, providing you use the infix operator form of the method call:

```
$method = 'boil';
$carrot->$method('Chopped');
```

It won't work with other constructs, so don't attempt to use a function call or other expression here. It won't be parsed properly, and Perl will report an error.

Accessing Object Data

At the risk of repeating myself yet again, an object is just a reference that knows what class it belongs to. This means you can access an element of the object by using reference notation. For example, to print the status of one of our **Vegetable** objects, you could use a line like this:

```
print $carrot->{'State'},"\n";
```

The same is true of any other data structure you decide to use. There is no need to create a subroutine to do it for you. However, if you want to use this method of accessing fields via methods, then you can use autoloading. See Chapter 6 for more details on autoloading; and for an object-specific example, see the following code:

```
sub AUTOLOAD
{
    my $self = shift;
    my $type = ref ($self) || croak "$self is not an object";
    my $field = $AUTOLOAD;
    $field =~ s/.*://;
    unless (exists $self->{$field})
    {
        croak "$field does not exist in object/class $type";
    }
    if (@_)
    {
        return $self->($name) = shift;
    }
    else
    {
        return $self->($name);
    }
```

So you can print a value,

```
print $carrot->state();
```

or set a value:

```
$carrot->state('Peeled');
```

Classes and Inheritance

A class is just a package. You can inherit methods from a parent class in a new class through the use of the **@ISA** array. Note that you cannot automatically inherit data. Perl leaves that decision to you. Since an object is a reference, you should be able to copy the information over easily, or just copy references in the new object to allow access to the inherited object's data. Since the normal base data type for an object is a hash, copying "fields" is a case of accessing the corresponding hash elements. See the previous sections for more information.

You may remember in the "Modules" section of Chapter 6 that **@ISA** was said to define the list of base classes on which the package relies. This is in fact the array used for inheriting methods. When you call a method on an object, Perl first looks for it within the package class. It then follows the inheritance tree based on the root classes (packages) defined in **@ISA**. For each class (package) defined in the array, Perl follows the inherited classes defined in that package's **@ISA** array, and so on, until the complete tree has been followed. It then moves on to the next one. This allows you to inherit, almost by assumption, the methods defined in the packages specified in the **@ISA** array and, in turn, any methods defined within the base classes of those packages.

This is how you can identify the list of packages specified in **@ISA** as base classes, and how the interpretation of the **@ISA** array becomes "is-a," since a new object is a member of the specified base classes.

The full path followed for method inheritance is actually slightly more complex, and the full list is shown here:

1. Perl searches the class of the specified object for the specified object.

2. Perl searches the classes defined in the object class's **@ISA** array.

3. If no method is found in steps 1 or 2, then Perl uses an **AUTOLOAD** subroutine, if one is found in the **@ISA** tree.

4. If a matching method still cannot be found, then Perl searches for the method within the **UNIVERSAL** class (package) that comes as part of the standard Perl library.

5. If the method still hasn't been found, then Perl gives up and raises a run-time exception.

You can force Perl to examine the base class's **@ISA** list first by specifying the **SUPER** pseudoclass within the base class package, as in

```
$carrot->SUPER::fry();
```

which would automatically force Perl to look in the **@ISA** classes, rather than the local class, for the **fry** method. This can only be used within the base class package. You cannot use it on an object outside of the base class; so it's only of use to object programmers, rather than object users.

Destructors and Garbage Collection

If you have programmed using objects before, then you will be aware of the need to create a "destructor" to free the memory allocated to the object when you have finished using it. Perl does this automatically for you as soon as the object goes out of scope.

You may want to provide your own destruction mechanism, however. This is sometimes necessary if you are using objects to define network connectivity or to update tied persistent data (see the "Using tie" section, later in the chapter), or if you are using other objects that access external information. You will need to close the connections to these external sources politely; and for that, you need to define a special method called **DESTROY**. This method will be called on the object just before Perl frees the memory allocated to it. In all other respects, the **DESTROY** method is just like any other, and you can do anything you like with the object in order to close it properly.

A **DESTROY** method is absolutely essential in situations in which you have objects that refer to nested structures (objects within objects), or when you have inherited information from another class. In these instances, you will need to destroy the nested references, yourself, as part of the special **DESTROY** method.

Comparing Perl Objects to Other Languages

Perl objects have some very specific features and advantages that make them easy to use within a Perl script. The lack of a distinct compartment for object-oriented programs may seem like a problem for programmers used to the confinement of Python or C++. In fact, it makes programming with objects and normal structures much more fluid and intelligent—you can use objects when the need requires it without having to make the decision before starting to program. Let's have a look at some other differences between the object implementation in Perl and other languages.

Python

Python is an object-oriented language. All data structures are created within an object environment and the individual structures, such as lists and dictionaries (which are like Perl's hashes), can all be accessed using a consistent object interface. The external libraries also have an object interface. Although this all appears to be restrictive, in fact Python makes it very easy and straightforward, and you never feel as confined as you do with, say, C++ or Java. As such, Python is an excellent language for learning object-oriented techniques; and although it is more structured than Perl, the fluidity of the environment will appeal to Perl programmers.

The main difference between Python and Perl is that Perl does not impose the structure. Perl also supports objects based on scalars, arrays, and hashes; Python only supports objects using dictionaries (hashes).

C++ and Java

C++ and Java are very similar when it comes to their internal representation and treatment of objects, and so we can comfortably lump the two together when we make a comparison back to Perl.

Perhaps the most significant difference is that Perl is much more relaxed about its object implementation. C++ (and Java) require you to explicitly declare a new class (using the **class** keyword), and you must explicitly specify a function as separate from a method using the **static** keyword. You must declare your classes separately from their implementations; the class goes in a header file and the implementation in a separate file, except in the case of inline definitions.

C++ also requires you to specify the privacy of a method, object, or class explicitly. There is no such feature within Perl; if you need to protect the privacy of a method or function, don't advertise it. If you want to protect a variable, then use a lexically scoped one instead. We can also get away with using a constructor with any name—we don't have to create a constructor with the same name as the class we are creating. Although we typically use **new** in Perl, this is a convention, rather than a restriction.

Finally, because C++ (and indeed Java) are compiled languages, the class information (that is the definition, supported methods, inheritance, etc.) must be known at compile time. Perl allows the definition of everything at run time. We can even modify the inheritance hierarchy by making modifications to the **@ISA** array, while simultaneously making changes to the methods and even format dynamically.

Using tie

Within Perl (versions 5 and up) you can "tie" a variable type to a particular class. The class implements the core methods that create, access, update, and destroy the elements of the underlying data type they are tied to. You can tie a scalar, array, or hash to any external data source. The most obvious use is for DBM files, which are hash-based database files—we'll see more of them in Chapter 13. You can tie a hash to an external DBM file (which uses a hashing system to store data in a physical file) and then use the normal hash constructs to access the keys and values within the external file.

The tie system uses objects and classes to associate a variable with the underlying object methods that support the interface between the Perl data type and the external data source. The base function is **tie**:

```
tie VARIABLE, CLASSNAME, LIST
```

The **VARIABLE** is just a normal variable that you will use to access the information in the tied resource. **CLASSNAME** defines the name of the package that supports the required class methods to tie the variable. Note that **CLASSNAME** is a string, not a bareword or other value. It can come from a variable, but that variable must contain the string to a valid class package.

The package that contains the class definition must have been imported via **use** or **require**. The **tie** function doesn't do this for you. The **LIST** is passed on directly to the class constructor at the point when the variable is tied.

Also note that the underlying class never gets passed the variable. The **tie** function creates the association, not the method class. The actual constructor name is the only way a package can determine what type of variable is being tied. If you **tie** a scalar, then it calls **TIESCALAR** as the constructor. With an array, it's **TIEARRAY**, and **TIEHASH** is used if it's a hash variable. In addition, in each case, the constructors are identical in all other respects to a typical object constructor. They just return a reference to the correct object; the constructor has no way of determining whether it was called from **tie**.

If you want to determine the name of the class to which a variable is tied, you use the **tied** function:

```
tied VARIABLE
```

This returns a reference to the object underlying the tied **VARIABLE**.

Once you have finished with the variable, you need to disassociate the variable from the underlying class methods, and for this you use **untie**:

```
untie VARIABLE
```

This breaks the binding between a variable and a package, undoing the association created by the **tie** function. It calls the **DESTROY** method, if it has been defined.

Creating New tie Classes

In this section we'll look at the creation of new base classes for tying different variable types. In each case, the base class must define a number of methods in order for the **tie** operation to work. Three methods are constant across all three variable types: **FETCH**, for reading the value of a tied variable; **STORE**, for assigning a value to a tied variable; and **DESTROY**, which deletes the tied variable when you call **untie**.

The **FETCH** and **STORE** methods are used to provide an interface to the variable that has been tied, not the underlying object. Accessing the object directly doesn't invoke these methods. The object reference is available either by using **tied** or by capturing the value returned by **tie**, which will be a reference to the underlying object being used.

Tying Scalars

We'll use the methods for tying scalars as our base reference, examining the entire process from start to finish. For this we'll use the example of file ownership, supported by the **FileOwner** package. When you tie a scalar using the methods in the **FileOwner** class, the variable tied contains the name of the file. Accessing the tied variable returns the owner (name, or user ID if the name cannot be resolved). Assigning a value to the tied variable sets the file's ownership, accepting a user ID or name accordingly.

For example, consider this script:

```
use FileOwner;

tie $profile, 'FileOwner', '.bash_profile';

print "Current owner is: $profile\n";
$profile = 'mcslp';
print "New owner is: $profile\n";
```

When the **tie** function is called, what actually happens is that the **TIESCALAR** method from **FileOwner** is called, passing '.bash_profile' as the argument to the method. This returns an object, which is associated by **tie** to the **$profile** variable.

When **$profile** is used in the **print** statements, the **FETCH** method is called. When you assign a value to **$profile**, the **STORE** method is called, with 'mcslp' as the argument to the method. If you can follow this, then you can create tied scalars, arrays, and hashes, since they all follow the same basic model. Now let's examine the details of our new **FileOwner** class, starting with the **TIESCALAR** method:

```
TIESCALAR CLASSNAME, LIST
```

The **TIESCALAR** is a class method and, as such, is passed the name of the class, which you'll use when blessing the new object you create, and the list of additional arguments passed to the **tie** function. For our example, there is only one argument— the name of the file to use for determining and setting file ownership. The method should return an object, blessed accordingly. The content of the scalar object is the name of the file you supplied when the object was created. Thus, you get a method like this:

```
sub TIESCALAR
{
    my $class = shift;
    my $file = shift;

    unless (-e $file)
    {
        carp("File $file does not exist");
        return undef;
    }

    return bless \$file,$class;
}
```

Note that you must make sure the file exists before you continue. You can't create an object that refers to a file that doesn't exist. The method returns an undefined object if the file does not exist, and this will be picked up by **tie**. You also report an error via the **carp** function, defined in the **Carp** module, which supports a more package-friendly way of raising errors.

In essence, the object you have created is anonymous, since you return the reference to the **$file** variable directly. **tie** does what it needs to with the returned object.

FETCH THIS

The **FETCH** method is called every time the tied variable is accessed. It takes only one argument, **THIS**, which is a reference to the corresponding object that is tied to the variable. Because we're working with scalars, the dereferencing is easy. The complex part is the determination of the owner of the file and the resulting resolving process to convert the user ID returned into a user name.

```
sub FETCH
{
    my $self = shift;

    local $! = 0;
    my $userid = (stat($$self))[4];
    if ($!) { croak("Can't get file owner: $!") }
    local $! = 0;
```

```perl
    my $owner = getpwuid($userid);
    $owner = $userid unless (defined($owner));
    return $owner;
}
```

The return value from this method is the user name or user ID. Because of this, you have no way of raising an error exception to the calling script, so you have to use **croak** to indicate a serious problem when determining the owner of the file.

STORE THIS, VALUE

The **STORE** method is called whenever an assignation is made to the tied variable. Beyond the object reference that is passed, **tie** also passes the value you want stored in the scalar variable you are tied to.

```perl
sub STORE
{
    my $self = shift;
    my $owner = shift;

    confess("Wrong type") unless ref $self;
    croak("Too many arguments") if @_;

    my $userid;

    if ($owner =~ /$[a-zA-Z]+/)
    {
        $userid = getpwnam($owner)
    }
    else
    {
        $userid = $owner;
    }

    local $! = 0;
    chown($userid,$$self);
    if ($!) { croak("Can't set file ownership: $!") }
    return $owner;
}
```

The only thing of note here is that you return the new assigned value, since that's the return value of any other assignment.

 DESTROY THIS

The **DESTROY** method is called when the associated object is disassociated, either because it's gone out of scope, or when **untie** is called. Generally, this method shouldn't be used, since Perl will do its own deallocation and garbage collection. However, as mentioned earlier, this method can be used when you want to close opened files, disconnect from servers cleanly, and so on. In the realms of a scalar, this is seldom required.

Tying Arrays

Classes for tying arrays must define at least three methods: **TIEARRAY**, **FETCH**, and **STORE**. You may also want and/or need to define the **DESTROY** method. At the present time, the methods for tied arrays do not cover some of the functions and operators available to untied arrays. In particular, there are no equivalent methods for the **$#array** operator, nor for the **push**, **pop**, **shift**, **unshift**, or **splice** functions.

Since you already know the basics surrounding the creation of tied objects, we'll dispense with the examples and cover the details of the methods required to tie arrays.

 TIEARRAY CLASSNAME, LIST

This method is called when the **tie** function is used to associate an array. It is the constructor for the array object and, as such, accepts the class name and should return an object reference. The method can also accept additional arguments, used as required. See the **TIESCALAR** method in the "Tying Scalars" section earlier.

 FETCH THIS, INDEX

This method will be called each time an array element is accessed. The **INDEX** argument is the element number within the array that should be returned.

 STORE THIS, INDEX, VALUE

This method is called each time an array element is assigned a value. The **INDEX** argument specifies the element within the array that should be assigned, and **VALUE** is the corresponding value to be assigned.

```
DESTROY THIS
```

This method is called when the tied object needs to be deallocated.

Tying Hashes

Hashes are the obvious (and most complete) of the supported **tie** implementations. This is because the **tie** system was developed to provide more convenient access to DBM files, which themselves operate just like hashes.

```
TIEHASH CLASSNAME, LIST
```

This is the class constructor. It needs to return a blessed reference pointing to the corresponding object.

```
FETCH THIS, KEY
```

This returns the value stored in the corresponding **KEY** and is called each time a single element of a hash is accessed.

```
STORE THIS, KEY, VALUE
```

This method is called when an individual element is assigned a new value.

```
DELETE THIS, KEY
```

This method removes the key and corresponding value from the hash. This is usually the result of a call to the **delete** function.

```
CLEAR THIS
```

This empties the entire contents of the hash.

```
EXISTS THIS, KEY
```

This is the method called when **exists** is used to determine the existence of a particular key in a hash.

```
FIRSTKEY THIS
```

This is the method triggered when you first start iterating through a hash with **each**, **keys**, or **values**. Note that you must reset the internal state of the hash to ensure that the iterator used to step over individual elements of the hash is reset.

```
NEXTKEY THIS, LASTKEY
```

This method is triggered by a **keys** or **each** function. This method should return two values—the next key and corresponding value from the hash object. The **LASTKEY** argument is supplied by **tie** and indicates the last key that was accessed.

```
DESTROY THIS
```

This is the method triggered when a tied hash's object is about to be deallocated.

The
Complete
Reference

Chapter 11

System Information

339

There are times when what you need to do is communicate with the host operating system. This can be done at a number of different levels, but there are two core elements that Perl provides built-in support for. The first is the user and group system employed by Unix. The user and group functions are built into Perl, and this is just one of the places where Perl shows its Unix heritage.

The other, more practical, set of functions relates to getting the current time from the system and converting that time into a format that can be used effectively. Once you've got the information, you'll probably want to play with it too, so I've also included information on how to manipulate time values.

Finally, we'll also take this opportunity to look at the generic environment variables available to Perl, how they affect Perl's operation, as well as information on how to determine the information by other means.

Users and Groups

For most situations, the built-in variables initialized at execution time provide the basic user and group information for the current script. To recap, the relevant variables are summarized in Table 11-1. Note that all of this information and the functions in this chapter are only really relevant on a Unix machine. Neither Mac OS nor Windows has the same facilities. However, under Windows you can use the **Win32::AdminMisc** or

Variable	Description
$<	The real user ID (uid) of the current process. This is the user ID of the user who executed the process, even if running **setuid**.
$>	The effective user ID (uid) of the current process. This is the user ID of the current process and defines what directories and features are available.
$(	The real group ID (gid) of the current process contains a space-separated list of the groups you are currently in if your machine supports multiple group membership. Note that the information is listed in group IDs, not names.
$)	The effective group ID (gid) of the current process contains a space-separated list of the groups you are currently in if your machine supports multiple group membership. Note that the information is listed in group IDs, not names.

Table 11-1. *Perl Variables Containing Group and User Membership*

Win32::NetAdmin modules to determine the same information. See Appendix B for more information on the **Win32::NetAdmin** module, and Web Appendix B at **www.osborne.com** for a list of other Win32 modules.

The most basic function for determining your current user name is the **getlogin** function, which returns the current user name (not uid) of the current process.

```
getlogin
```

Getting Unix Password Entries

The next two functions, **getpwuid** and **getpwnam**, return, in a list context, the user information as a list of scalar values. The **getpwuid** function gets the information based on the user's supplied ID number, and **getpwnam** uses the supplied name. These provide an interface to the equivalent system functions, which just return the information stored in the /etc/passwd file (on a Unix system).

```
getpwuid EXPR
getpwnam EXPR
```

This returns the following:

```
($name,$passwd,$uid,$gid,$quota,$comment,$gcos,$dir,$shell)
    = getpwnam('MC');
```

In a scalar context, each function returns the most useful value. That is, **getpwuid** returns the user name, while **getpwnam** returns the user ID. The details of the contents of each element are summarized in Table 11-2. Note that names are advisory; you can assign the details to any scalar.

By using these functions, you can easily print the user name by getting the user's ID from the built-in **$<** variable:

```
print "Apparently, you are: ",(getpwuid($<))[0],"\n";
```

As another example, you can obtain the user name for the current user by using

```
$name = getlogin || (getpwuid($<))[0] || 'Anonymous';
```

Element	Name	Description
0	$name	The user's login name.
1	$passwd	The user's password in its encrypted form. See "Password Encryption" later in this chapter for more details on using this element.
2	$uid	The numerical user ID.
3	$gid	The numerical primary group ID.
4	$quota	The user's disk storage limit, in kilobytes.
5	$comment	The contents of the comment field (usually the full name).
6	$gcos	The user's name, phone number, and other information. This is only supported on some Unix variants. Don't rely on this to return a useful name; use the **$comment** field instead.
7	$dir	The user's home directory.
8	$shell	The user's default login shell interpreter.

Table 11-2. *Information Returned by **getpwent**, **getpwnam**, and **getpwuid***

To read the entire contents of the /etc/passwd file, you could read and process the individual lines yourself. An easier method, however, is to use the **getpwent** function set:

```
getpwent
setpwent
endpwent
```

The first call to **getpwent** returns the user information (as returned by **getpwnam**) for the first entry in the /etc/passwd file. Subsequent calls return the next entry, so you can read and print the entire details using a simple loop:

```
while(($name,$dir)=(getpwent)[0,7])
{
    print "Home for $name is $dir\n";
}
```

In a scalar context, the **getpwent** function only returns the user name. A call to **setpwent** resets the pointer for the **getpwent** function to the start of the /etc/passwd entries. A call to **endpwent** indicates to the system that you have finished reading the entries, although it performs no other function. Neither **setpwent** nor **endpwent** return anything.

Getting Unix Group Entries

Along with the password entries, you can also obtain information about the groups available on the system:

```
getgrgid EXPR
getgrnam EXPR
```

In a scalar context, you can therefore obtain the current group name by using

```
$group = getgrgid($();
```

or if you are really paranoid, you might try this:

```
print "Bad group information" unless(getgrnam(getgrgid($()) == $();
```

The **getgrgid** and **getgrnam** functions operate the same as the password equivalents, and both return the same list information from the /etc/group or equivalent file:

```
($name,$passwd,$gid,$members) = getgruid($();
```

The **$members** variable will then contain a space-separated list of users who are members of the group **$name**. The elements and their contents are summarized in Table 11-3.

There is also a **getgrent** function set for reading the entire group information in a loop:

```
while(($name,$members)=(getgrent)[0,3])
{
    print "$name has these members: $members\n";
}
```

Like the equivalent password functions, **setgrent** resets the pointer to the beginning of the group file, and **endgrent** indicates that you have finished reading the group file.

Element	Name	Description
0	$name	The group name.
1	$passwd	The password for gaining membership to the group. This is often ignored. The password is encrypted using the same technique as the login password information. See "Password Encryption" for more details.
2	$gid	The numerical group ID.
3	$members	A space-separated list of the user names (not IDs) that are members of this group.

Table 11-3. *Elements Returned by the **getgrent**, **getgrnam**, and **getgrgid** Functions*

Password Encryption

All passwords on Unix are encrypted using a standard system function called **crypt()**. This uses an algorithm that is one-way—the idea being that the time taken to decode the encrypted text would take more processing power than is available in even the fastest computer currently available. This complicates matters if you want to compare a password against the recorded password. The operation for password checking is to encrypt the user-supplied password and then compare the encrypted versions with each other. This negates the need to even attempt decrypting the password.

The Perl encryption function is also **crypt**, and it follows the same rules. There are two arguments—the string you want to encrypt and a "salt" value. The salt value is an arbitrary string used to select one of 256 different combinations available for the encryption algorithm on the specified string. Although the rules say the size of the salt string should be a maximum of two characters, there is no need to reduce the string used, and the effects of the salt value are negligible. In most situations you can use any two-character (or more) string.

For example, to compare a supplied password with the system version:

```
$realpass = (getpwuid($<))[1];
die "Invalid Password" unless(crypt($pass,$realpass) eq $realpass);
```

The fact that the password cannot be cracked means the encryption system is useless for encrypting documents. For that process, it is easier to use one of the many encryption systems available via CPAN.

Time

Date and time calculations are based around the standard epoch time value. This is the number of seconds that have elapsed since a specific date and time: 00:00:00 UTC, January 1, 1970 for most systems; 00:00:00, January 1, 1904 for Mac OS. The maximum time that can be expressed in this way is based on the maximum value for an unsigned integer, $2^{31}-1$, which equates to Tue Jan 19 03:14:07 2038.

Although it's a moot point now (I'm writing this in November 2000), Perl was completely Y2K compliant. However, due to the way in which Perl returns the year information, there were a number of problems with scripts returning "19100" on 1st Jan because people added the string "19" to the start of the date, not the integer 1900.

gmtime and localtime

To obtain the individual values that make up the date and time for a specific epoch value, you use the **gmtime** and **localtime** functions. The difference between the two is that **gmtime** returns the time calculated against the GMT or UTC time zones, irrespective of your current locale and time zone. The **localtime** function returns the time using the modifier of the current time zone.

```
localtime EXPR
localtime
```

In a list context, both functions convert a time specified as the number of seconds since the epoch. The time value is specified by **EXPR** or is taken from the return value of the **time** function if **EXPR** is not specified. Both functions return the same nine-element array:

```
#  0    1    2     3      4     5      6     7      8
($sec,$min,$hour,$mday,$mon,$year,$wday,$yday,$isdst) = localtime(time);
```

The information is derived from the system **struct tm** time structure, which has a few traps. The ranges for the individual elements in the structure are shown in Table 11-4.

Since the value returned is a list, you can use subscript notation to extract individual elements from the function without having to create useless temporary variables. For example, to print the current day, you might use

```
print (qw(Sun Mon Tue Wed Thu Fri Sat Sun))[(localtime)][6];
```

Element	Range	Notes
$sec	0–59	Seconds
$min	0–59	Minutes
$hour	0–23	Hours
$mday	1–31	Day of the Month
$mon	0–11	This has the benefit that an array can be defined directly, without inserting a junk value at the start. It's also incompatible with the format in which dates may be supplied back from the user.
$year	0–	All years on all platforms are defined as the number of years since 1900, not simply as a two-digit year. To get the full four-digit year, add 1900 to the value returned.
$wday	0–6	This is the current day of the week, starting with Sunday.
$yday	0–366	
$isdst	0–1	Returns true if the current locale is operating in daylight saving time.

Table 11-4.   *Ranges for the **gmtime** and **localtime** Functions*

In a scalar context, this returns a string representation of the time specified by **EXPR**, roughly equivalent to the value returned by the standard C **ctime()** function:

```
$ perl -e 'print scalar localtime,"\n";'
Sat Feb 20 10:00:40 1999
```

The Perl module **Time::Local**, which is part of the standard distribution, can create an epoch value based on individual values (effectively the opposite of **localtime**):

```
$time = timelocal($sec,$min,$hours,$mday,$mon,$year);
```

In most situations, you should use **localtime** over **gmtime**, since **localtime** probably returns what you want. The only time to use the **gmtime** function is in a situation where a naturalized time is required for comparison purposes across time zones.

time Function

The **time** function returns the number of seconds since the epoch. You use this value to feed the input of **gmtime** and **localtime**, although both actually use the value of this function by default.

```
time
```

In addition, since it returns a simple integer value, you can use the value returned as a crude counter for timing executions:

```
$starttime=time;
for (1..100000)
{
    log(abs(sin($_)))*exp(sin($_));
}
$endtime=time;
print "Did 100,000 calculations in ",$endtime-$starttime, "seconds\n";
```

The granularity here is not good enough for performing real benchmarks. For that, either use the **times** function, discussed later, or the **Benchmark** module, which in fact uses the **times** function.

Comparing Time Values

When comparing two different time values, it is easier to compare epoch calculated times (that is, the time values in seconds) and then extract the information accordingly. For example, to calculate the number of days, hours, minutes, and seconds between dates:

```
($secdiff,$mindiff,$hourdiff,$ydaydiff)
        = (gmtime($newtime-$oldtime))[0..2,7]
```

The **$secdiff** and other variables now contain the corresponding time-value differences between **$newtime** and **$oldtime**.

| Note |

*You should use **gmtime** not **localtime** when comparing time values. This is because **localtime** takes into account the local time zone, and, depending on the operating system you are using, any daylight saving time (DST) too. The **gmtime** function will always return the Greenwich Mean Time (GMT), which is not affected by time zones or DST effects.*

Converting Dates and Times into Epochs

There is no built-in function for converting the value returned by **localtime** or **gmtime** back into an epoch equivalent, but you can use the **Time::Local** module, which supplies the **timegm** and **timelocal** functions to do the job for you. For example, the script:

```
use Time::Local;
$time = time();
($sec,$min,$hour,$mday,$mon,$year) = (localtime($time))[0..5];
$newtime = timelocal($sec,$min,$hour,$mday,$mon,$year);
print "Supplied $time, returned $newtime\n";
```

should return identical values.

Time Arithmetic

There are a number of ways in which you can modify a given time when it's expressed as an epoch value. For example, imagine that you want to determine what the date will be in seven days time. You could use:

```
($mday,$mon,$year) = (localtime($time))[3..5];
$mday += 7;
$mon++;
$year+=1900;
print "Date will be $mday/$mon/$year\n";
```

However, this isn't really very useful, since it doesn't take into account that adding seven to the current day of the month could put us into the next month, or possibly even into the next year. Instead, you should add seven days to the value that you supply to the **localtime** function. For example:

```
($mday,$mon,$year) = (localtime($time+(7*24*60*60)))[3..5];
$mon++;
$year+=1900;
print "Date will be $mday/$mon/$year\n";
```

Here, we've added seven days (7 times 24 hours, times 60 minutes, times 60 seconds); because we're asking **localtime** to do the calculation on the raw value we'll get the correct date. You can do similar calculations for other values too, for example:

```
$time -= 7*24*60*60; # Last week
$time += 3*60*60;    # Three hours from now
```

```
$time -= 24*60*60;   # This time yesterday
$time += 45*60;      # Three quarters of an hour from now
```

The limitation of this system is that it only really works on days, hours, minutes, and seconds. The moment you want to add months or years, the process gets more complicated, as you would need to determine how many days in the month or year in order to get the correct epoch value.

To resolve both problems, you might consider using a function like the one below, which will add or subtract any time value to any other time value. It's based on the Visual Basic **DateAdd** function:

```perl
use Time::Local;

sub DateAdd
{
    my ($interval, $number, $time, $sec,
        $min, $hour, $mday, $mon, $year);

    if (@_ <= 3)
    {
        if (@_ == 2)
        {
            $time = time();
            ($interval, $number) = @_;
        }
        else
        {
            ($interval, $number, $time) = @_;
        }
        ($sec,$min,$hour,$mday,$mon,$year)
            = (localtime($time))[0..5];
    }
    else
    {
        ($interval, $number, $time, $sec,
        $min, $hour, $mday, $mon, $year) = @_;
    }

    $year += $number if ($interval eq 'yyyy');
    if (($interval eq 'q') || ($interval eq 'm'))
    {
```

```
          $mon += $number if ($interval eq 'm');
          $mon += ($number*3) if ($interval eq 'q');
          if ($mon > 11)
          {
              $year += int ($mon/12);
              $mon = $mon % 12;
          }
      }

      $newtime = timelocal($sec,$min,$hour,$mday,$mon,$year);

      $newtime += ($number*24*60*60) if (($interval eq 'y') ||
                                         ($interval eq 'd') ||
                                         ($interval eq 'w'));
      $newtime += ($number*7*24*60*60) if ($interval eq 'ww');
      $newtime += ($number*60*60) if ($interval eq 'h');
      $newtime += ($number*60) if ($interval eq 'n');
      $newtime += $number if ($interval eq 's');
      return $newtime;
  }
```

To use this function, supply the interval type (as shown in Table 11-5) and the number to be added. If you don't supply a time value, then the current time will be used. Alternatively, you can supply either an epoch value or the seconds, minutes, hours, day of the month, month, and year, in the same format as that returned by **localtime**.

For example, the following adds three weeks to the current date (1st April), and then outputs a date/time string of the new value:

```
print scalar localtime(DateAdd('ww',3)),"\n";
```

generates

```
Sat Apr 22 13:50:51 2000
```

Interval	Description
yyyy	Year
q	Quarter
m	Month
y	Day of year
d	Day
w	Weekday
ww	Week
h	Hour
n	Minute
s	Second

Table 11-5. *Interval Conversions*

times Function

The **times** function

```
times
```

returns a four-element list giving the CPU time used by the current process for user-derived and system-derived tasks, and the time used by any children for user- and system-derived tasks:

```
($user, $system, $child, $childsystem) = times;
```

The information is obtained from the system **times()** function, which reports the time in seconds to a granularity of a hundredth of a second. This affords better timing options than the **time** command, although the values are still well below the normal microsecond timing often required for benchmarking. That said, for quick comparisons of different methods, assuming you have a suitable number of iterations, both the **time** and **times** functions should give you an idea of how efficient, or otherwise, the techniques are.

Here's the benchmark example (seen in the "**time** Function" section earlier in this chapter), using **times**:

```
$starttime=(times)[0];
for (1..100000)
{
    log(abs(sin($_)))*exp(sin($_));
}
$endtime=(times)[0];
print "Did 100,000 calculations in ",$endtime-$starttime, "seconds\n";
```

sleep Function

You can pause the execution of a script by using the **sleep** function.

```
sleep EXPR
sleep
```

The function sleeps for **EXPR** seconds, or for the value in **$_** if **EXPR** is not specified.

The function can be interrupted by an alarm signal (see "Alarms," next). The granularity of the functions is always by the second, and the accuracy of the function is entirely dependent on your system's **sleep** function. Many may calculate the end time as the specified number of seconds from when it was called. Alternatively, it may just add **EXPR** seconds to the current time and drop out of the loop when that value is reached. If the calculation is made at the end of the second, the actual time could be anything up to a second out, either way.

If you want a finer resolution for the **sleep** function, you can use the **select** function with undefined bitsets, which will cause **select** to pause for the specified number of seconds. The granularity of the **select** call is hundredths of a second, so the call

```
select(undef, undef, undef, 2.35);
```

will wait for 2.35 seconds. Because of the way the count is accumulated, the actual time waited will be more precise than that achievable by **sleep**, but it's still prone to similar problems.

Alarms

By using signals, you can set an alarm. This is another form of timer that waits for a specified number of seconds while allowing the rest of the Perl script to continue. Once the time has elapsed, the **SIGALRM** signal is sent to the Perl script, and if a handler has been configured, the specified function will execute. This is often used in situations where you want to provide a time-out for a particular task. For example, here's a user query with a default value—if the user does not respond after 10 seconds, the script continues with the default value:

```
print "What is your name [Anonymous]?\n";
eval
{
    local $SIG{ALRM} = sub { die "Timeout" };
    alarm 10;
    chomp($answer = <STDIN>);
    alarm 0;
};
if ($@ and $@ =~ /Timeout/)
{
    $answer = "Anonymous";
}
print "Hello $answer!\n";
```

The **eval** block is required so that the **die** statement that forms the signal handler drops out of the **eval**— setting the value of **$@**—rather than terminating the whole script. You can then test that and decide how to proceed. Of course, if the user provides some input; then the alarm is reset to zero, disabling the alarm timer and allowing you to drop out of the **eval** block normally.

We'll be looking in more detail at signals and signal handlers in Chapter 14, and at the use of the **eval** function in Chapter 15.

Environment Variables

As we saw in Chapter 4, Perl provides an interface to the environment variables of the current Perl interpreter using the **%ENV** built-in variable. For example, to access the **PATH** value, you would use the following:

```
print $ENV{PATH};
```

The environment can affect the operation of different systems in subtle ways. The **PATH** environment variable, for example, contains the list of directories to be searched when executing an external program through **exec**, **system**, or backticks.

As a general rule, it's not a good idea to always rely on the values defined in the environment variables, because they are largely arbitrary. In Tables 11-6 and 11-7, I've listed the environment variables that you are likely to come across under Unix-based and Windows-based operating systems, respectively.

Where relevant, the tables show a probable default value that you can use. The tables also list alternative locations where you can find the same information without relying on an environment variable. Mac OS (but not Mac OS X, which is Unix based) and other non-interactive platforms don't rely so heavily on environment variables for the execution of scripts anyway.

Variable	Description	Alternatives
COLUMNS	The number of columns for the current display. Can be useful for determining the current terminal size when developing a terminal/text interface. However, it's probably better to rely on a user setting or just use the **Term::*** modules and let them handle the effects. If you do need a base value, then use vt100, which most terminal emulators support.	None
EDITOR	The user's editor preference. If it can't be found, then default to **vi** or **emacs** or, on Windows, to **C:/Windows/Notepad.exe**.	None
EUID	The effective user ID of the current process. Use **$>**, which will be populated correctly by Perl, even when using **suidperl**.	**$>**
HOME	The user's home directory. Try getting the information from **getpwuid** instead.	**getpwuid**
HOST	The current hostname. The **hostname.pl** script included with the standard Perl library provides a platform-neutral way of determining the hostname.	**hostname.pl**
HOSTNAME	The current hostname.	**hostname.pl**

Table 11-6. *Environment Variables on Unix Machines*

Variable	Description	Alternatives
LINES	The number of lines supported by the current terminal window or display. See **COLUMNS** earlier in the table.	None
LOGNAME	The user's login. Use the **getlogin** function or, better still, the **getpwuid** function with the $< variable.	**getlogin**, **getpwuid($<)**
MAIL	The path to the user's mail file. If it can't be found, try guessing the value; it's probably **/var/mail/LOGNAME** or **/var/spool/mail/LOGNAME**.	None
PATH	The colon-separated list of directories to search when looking for applications to execute. Aside from the security risk of using an external list, you should probably be using the full path to the applications that you want to execute, or populating **PATH** within your script.	None
PPID	The parent process ID. There's no easy way to find this, but it's unlikely that you'll want it anyway.	None
PWD	The current working directory. You should use the **Cwd** module instead.	**Cwd**
SHELL	The path to the user's preferred shell. This value can be abused so that you end up running a suid program instead of a real shell. If it can't be determined, **/bin/sh** is a good default.	None
TERM	The name/type of the current terminal and therefore terminal emulation. See **COLUMNS** earlier in this table.	None
UID	The user's real ID.	**$<**
USER	The user's login name. See **LOGNAME** earlier in this table.	**getlogin**, **getpwuid($<)**

Table 11-6. *Environment Variables on Unix Machines* (continued)

Variable	Description	Alternatives
VISUAL	The user's visual editor preference. See **EDITOR** earlier in the table.	**EDITOR**
XSHELL	The shell to be used within the X Windows System. See **SHELL** earlier in the table.	**SHELL**

Table 11-6. *Environment Variables on Unix Machines* (continued)

Variable	Platform	Description	Alternatives
ALLUSERS-PROFILE	2000	The location of the generic profile currently in use. There's no way of determining this information.	None
CMDLINE	95/98	The command line, including the name of the application executed. The Perl **@ARGV** variable should have been populated with this information.	**@ARGV**
COMPUTER-NAME	NT, 2000	The name of the computer.	**Win32::Node-Name**
COMSPEC	All	The path to the command interpreter (usually **COMMAND.COM**) used when opening a command prompt.	None
HOMEDRIVE	NT, 2000	The drive letter (and colon) of the user's home drive.	None
HOMEPATH	NT, 2000	The path to the user's home directory.	None

Table 11-7. *Environment Variables for Windows*

Variable	Platform	Description	Alternatives
HOMESHARE	NT, 2000	The UNC name of the user's home directory. Note that this value will be empty if the user's home directory is unset or set to local drive.	None
LOGONSERVER	NT, 2000	The domain name server the user was authenticated on.	None
NUMBER_OF_PROCESSORS	NT, 2000	The number of processors active in the current machine.	None
OS	NT, 2000	The name of the operating system. There's no direct way, but **Win32::IsWin95** and **Win32::IsWinNT** return true if the host OS is Windows 95/98 or Windows NT/2000, respectively.	Win32::IsWin95 **Win32::IsWinNT**
OS2LIBPATH	NT, 2000	The path to the OS/2 compatibility libraries.	None
PATH	All	The path searched for applications within the command prompt and for programs executed via a **system**, **backtick**, or **open** function.	None
PATHEXT	NT, 2000	The list of extensions that will be used to identify an executable program. You probably shouldn't be modifying this, but if you need to define it manually, **.bat**, **.com**, and **.exe** are the most important.	None

Table 11-7.   *Environment Variables for Windows* (continued)

Variable	Platform	Description	Alternatives
PROCESSOR_ARCHITECTURE	NT, 2000	The processor architecture of the current machine. Use **Win32::GetChipName**, which returns 386, 486, 586, and so on for Pentium chips, or Alpha for Alpha processors.	**Win32::GetChip-Name**
PROCESSOR_IDENTIFIER	NT, 2000	The identifier (the information tag returned by the CPU when queried).	None
PROCESSOR_LEVEL	NT, 2000	The processor level: 3 refers to a 386, 4 to a 486, and 5 to the Pentium. Values of 3000 and 4000 refer to MIPS processors, and 21064 refers to an Alpha processor. See the **PROCESSOR_ARCHITECTURE** entry earlier in the table.	**Win32::GetChip-Name**
PROCESSOR_REVISION	NT, 2000	The processor revision.	None
SYSTEMDRIVE	NT, 2000	The drive holding the currently active operating system. The most likely location is **C:**.	None
SYSTEMROOT	NT, 2000	The root directory of the active operating system. This will probably be **Windows** or **Win**.	None
USERDOMAIN	NT, 2000	The domain the current user is connected to.	**Win32::Domain-Name**
USERNAME	NT, 2000	The name of the current user.	None
USERPROFILE	NT, 2000	The location of the user's profile.	None

Table 11-7.   *Environment Variables for Windows* (continued)

Variable	Platform	Description	Alternatives
WINBOOTDIR	NT, 2000	The location of the Windows operating system that was used to boot the machine. See the **SYSTEMROOT** entry earlier in this table.	None
WINDIR	All	The location of the active Windows operating system, this is the directory used when searching for DLLs and other OS information. See the **SYSTEMROOT** entry earlier in this table.	None

Table 11-7.   *Environment Variables for Windows* (continued)

The Complete Reference

Chapter 12

Networking

Before we examine the processes behind using network connections in Perl, it's worth reviewing the background of how networks are supported in the modern world, and from that we can glean the information we need to network computers using Perl.

Most networking systems have historically been based on the ISO/OSI (International Organization for Standardization Open Systems Interconnection) seven-layer model. Each layer defines an individual component of the networking process, from the physical connection up to the applications that use the network. Each layer depends on the layer it sits on to provide the services it requires.

More recently the seven-layer model has been dropped in favor of a more flexible model that follows the current development of networking systems. You can often attribute the same layers to modern systems, but it's often the case that individual protocols lie over two of the layers in the OSI model, rather than conveniently sitting within a single layer.

Irrespective of the model you are using, the same basic principles survive. You can characterize networks by the type of logical connection. A network can either be *connection oriented* or *connectionless*. A connection-oriented network relies on the fact that two computers that want to talk to each other must go through some form of connection process, usually called a handshake. This handshake is similar to using the telephone: the caller dials a number and the receiver picks up the phone. In this way, the caller immediately knows whether the recipient has received the message, because the recipient will have answered the call. This type of connection is supported by TCP/IP (Transmission Control Protocol/Internet Protocol) and is the main form of communication over the Internet and local area networks (LANs).

In a connectionless network, information is sent to the recipient without first setting up a connection. This type of network is also a *datagram* or *packet-oriented* network because the data is sent in discrete packets. Each packet will consist of the sender's address, recipient's address, and the information, but no response will be provided once the message has been received. A connectionless network is therefore more like the postal service—you compose and send a letter, although you have no guarantee that the letter will reach its destination, or that the information was received correctly. Connectionless networking is supported by UDP/IP (User Datagram Protocol/Internet Protocol).

In either case, the "circuit" is not open permanently between the two machines. Data is sent in individual packets that may take different paths and routes to the destination. The routes may involve local area networks, dial-up connections, ISDN routers, and even satellite links. Within the UDP protocol, the packets can arrive in any order, and it is up to the client program to reassemble them into the correct sequence—if there is one. With TCP, the packets are automatically reassembled into the correct sequence before they are represented to the client as a single data stream.

There are advantages and disadvantages to both types of networks. A connectionless network is fast, because there is no requirement to acknowledge the data or enter into any dialogue to set up the connection to receive the data. However, a connectionless network is also unreliable because there is no way to ensure the information reached its destination. A connection-oriented network is slow (in comparison to a connectionless network) because of the extra dialogue involved, but it guarantees the data sequence, providing end-to-end reliability.

The IP element of the TCP/IP and UDP/IP protocols refers to the Internet Protocol, which is a set of standards for specifying the individual addresses of machines within a network. Each machine within the networking world has a unique IP address. This is made up of a sequence of four bytes typically written in dot notation, for example, 198.10.29.145. These numbers relate both to individual machines within a network and to entire collections of machines.

Because humans are not very good at remembering numbers, a system called DNS (Domain Name System) relates easy-to-remember names to IP addresses. For example, the name www.mcgraw-hill.com relates to a single IP address. You can also have a single DNS name pointing to a number of IP addresses, and multiple names point to the same address. It is also possible to have a single machine that has multiple interfaces, and each interface can have multiple IP addresses assigned to it. However, in all cases, if the interfaces are connected to the Internet in one form or another, then the IP addresses of each interface will be unique.

However, the specification for communication does not end there. Many different applications can be executed on the same machine, and so communication must be aimed not only at the machine, but also at a port on that machine that relates to a particular application. If the IP address is compared to a telephone number, the port number is the equivalent of an extension number. The first 1024 port numbers are assigned to well-known Internet protocols, and different protocols have their own unique port number. For example, HTTP (Hypertext Transfer Protocol), which is used to transfer information between your web browser and a web server, has a port number of 80. To connect to a server application, you need both the IP address (or machine name) and the port number on which the server is "listening."

The BSD (Berkeley Systems Division, which is a "flavor" of Unix) socket system was introduced in BSD 4.2 as a way of providing a consistent interface to the different available protocols. A socket provides a connection between an application and the network. You must have a socket at each end of the connection in order to communicate between the machines. One end must be set to receive data at the same time as the other end is sending data. As long as each side of the socket connection knows whether it should be sending or receiving information, then the communication can be two-way.

There are many different methods for controlling this two-way communication, although none is ultimately reliable. The most obvious is to "best-guess" the state that each end of the connection should be in. For example, if one end sends a piece of information, then it might be safe to assume it should then wait for a response. If the opposite end makes the same assumption, then it can send information after it has just received some. This is not necessarily reliable, because if both ends decide to wait for information at the same time, then both ends of the connection are effectively dead. Alternatively, if both ends decide to send information at the same time, the two processes will not lock; but because they use the same send-receive system, once they have both sent information, they will both return to the wait state, expecting a response.

A better solution to the problem is to use a protocol that places rules and restrictions on the communication method and order. This is how Simple Mail Transfer Protocol (SMTP) and similar protocols work. The client sends a command to the server, and the immediate response from the server tells the client what to do next. The response may include data and will definitely include an end-of-data string. In effect, it's similar to the technique used when communicating by radio. At the end of each communication, you say "Over" to indicate to the recipient that you have finished speaking. In essence, it still uses the same best-guess method for communication. Providing the communication starts off correctly, and each end sends the end-of-communication signal, the communication should continue correctly.

Although generally thought of as a technique for communicating between two different machines, you can also use sockets to communicate between two processes on the same machine. This can be useful for two reasons. First of all, communicating between processes on a single machine (IPC—interprocess communication) allows you to control and cooperatively operate several different processes. Most servers use IPC to manage a number of processes that support a particular service.

We'll be looking at the general techniques available for networking between processes, either on the machine or across a network to a different machine. Techniques include those using the built-in Perl functions and those using modules available from CPAN that simplify the process for communicating with existing protocol standards.

If you want more information on networking with sockets and streams under TCP, UDP, and IP, then I can recommend *The UNIX System V Release 4 Programmers Guide: Networking Interfaces* (1990, Englewood Cliffs, NJ: Prentice Hall), which covers the principles behind networking, as well as the C source code required to make it work.

Obtaining Network Information

The first stage in making a network connection is to get the information you need about the host you are connecting to. You will also need to resolve the service port and protocol information before you start the communication process. Like other parts of the networking process, all of this information is required in numerical rather than name format. You therefore need to be able to resolve the individual names into corresponding numbers. This operation is supported by several built-in functions, which are described in the sections that follow, divided into their different types (Hosts, Protocols, Services, Networks, and so on).

Hosts

In order to communicate with a remote host, you need to determine its IP address. The names are resolved by the system, either by the contents of the /etc/hosts file, or through a naming service such as NIS/NIS+ (Network Information Service) or DNS.

The **gethostbyname** function calls the system-equivalent function, which looks up the IP address in the corresponding tables, depending on how the operating system has been configured.

```
gethostbyname NAME
```

In a list context, this returns the hostname, aliases, address type, length, and physical IP addresses for the host defined in **NAME**. They can be extracted like this:

```
($name, $aliases, $addrtype, $length, @addresses) = gethostbyname($host);
```

The **$aliases** scalar is a space-separated list of alternative aliases for the specified name. The **@addresses** array contains a list of addresses in a packed format, which you will need to extract with **unpack**. In a scalar context, the function returns the host's IP address. For example, you can get the IP address of a host as a string with

```
$address = join('.',unpack("C4",scalar gethostbyname("www.mchome.com")));
```

It's more normal, however, to keep the host address in packed format for use in other functions.

Alternatively, you can use a v-string to represent an IP address:

```
$ip = v198.112.10.128;
```

The resulting value can be used directly in any functions that require a packed IP address. If you want to print an IP address, use the **%v** format with **sprintf** to extract that value into a string. See Chapter 4, *V-Strings,* for more information.

In a list context, **gethostbyaddr** returns the same information as **gethostbyname**, except that it accepts a packed IP address as its first argument.

```
gethostbyaddr ADDR, ADDRTYPE
```

The **ADDRTYPE** should be one of **AF_UNIX** for Unix sockets and **AF_INET** for Internet sockets. These constants are defined within the **Socket** module. In a scalar context it just returns the hostname as a string.

The ***hostent** functions allow you to work through the system host database, returning each entry in the database:

```
gethostent
endhostent
sethostent
```

The **gethostent** function iterates through the database (normally the /etc/hosts file) and returns each entry in the form:

```
($name, $aliases, $addrtype, $length, @addresses) = gethostent;
```

Each subsequent call to **gethostent** returns the next entry in the file. This works in the same way as the **getpwent** function you saw in Chapter 11.

The **sethostent** function resets the pointer to the beginning of the file, and **endhostent** indicates that you have finished reading the entries. Note that this is identical to the system function, and the operating system may or may not have been configured to search the Internet DNS for entries. Using this function may cause you to start iterating through the entire Domain Name System, which is probably not what you want.

Protocols

You will need to resolve the top-level names of the transmission protocols used for when communicating over a given service. Examples of transmission protocols include the TCP and UDP protocols that you already know about, as well as AppleTalk, SMTP, and ICMP (Internet Control Message Protocol). This information is traditionally stored on a Unix system in /etc/protocols, although different systems may store it in different files, or even internally.

The **getprotobyname** function translates a specific protocol **NAME** into a protocol number in a scalar context:

```
getprotobyname NAME
```

It can also return the following in a list context:

```
($name, $aliases, $protocol) = getprotobyname('tcp');
```

Alternatively, you can resolve a protocol number into a protocol name with the **getprotobynumber** function.

```
getprotobynumber NUMBER
```

This returns the protocol name in a scalar context, and the same name, aliases, and protocol number information in a list context:

```
($name, $aliases, $protocol) = getprotobyname(6);
```

Alternatively, you can also step through the protocols available using the **getprotoent** function:

```
getprotoent
setprotoent
endprotoent
```

The information returned by **getprotoent** is the same as that returned by the **getprotobyname** function in a list context. The **setprotoent** and **endprotoent** functions reset and end the reading of the /etc/protocols file.

Services

The services are the names of individual protocols used on the network. These relate to the individual port numbers used for specific protocols. The **getservbyname** function resolves a name into a protocol number by examining the /etc/services file or the corresponding networked information service table:

```
getservbyname NAME, PROTO
```

This resolves **NAME** for the specified protocol **PROTO** into the following fields:

```
($name, $aliases, $port, $protocol_name) = getservbyname 'http', 'tcp';
```

The **PROTO** should be either 'tcp' or 'udp', depending on what protocol you want to use. In a scalar context, the function just returns the service port number.

The **getservbyport** function resolves the port number **PORT** for the **PROTO** protocol:

```
getservbyport PORT, PROTO
```

This returns the same fields as **getservbyname**:

```
($name, $aliases, $port, $protocol_name) = getservbyport 80, 'tcp';
```

In a scalar context, it just returns the protocol name.

You can step through the contents of the /etc/services file using **getservent**, which returns the same fields again.

```
getservent
setservent
endservent
```

setservent resets the pointer to the beginning of the file, and **endservent** indicates to the system that you've finished reading the entries.

Networks

A network is a collection of machines logically connected together. The logical element is that networks are specified by their leading IP addresses, such that a network of machines can be referred to by "198.112.10"—the last digits specifying the individual machines within the entire network. This information is stored, mostly for routing purposes, within the /etc/networks file. Just like the hosts that make up the network, a network specification is composed of both a name and a corresponding address, which you can resolve using the **getnetbyname** and **getnetbyaddr** functions.

```
getnetbyname NAME
```

This returns, in a list context:

```
($name, $aliases, $addrtype, $net) = getnetbyname 'loopback';
```

In a scalar context, it returns the network address as a string. You can also do the reverse with the **getnetbyaddr** function:

```
getnetbyaddr ADDR, ADDRTYPE
```

The **ADDRTYPE** should be **AF_UNIX** or **AF_INET**, as appropriate.
As before, you can step through the individual entries within the network file using the **getnetent** function:

```
getnetent
setnetent
endnetent
```

The **getnetent** function returns the same information as **getnetbyaddr** in a list context. The **setnetent** function resets the current pointer within the available lists, and **endnetent** indicates to the system that you have finished reading the entries.

The Socket Module

The **Socket** module is the main support module for communicating between machines with sockets. It provides a combination of the constants required for networking, as well as a series of utility functions that you will need for both client and server socket systems. It is essentially a massaged version of the socket.h header file that has been converted with the **h2ph** script. The result is a module that should work on your system, irrespective of the minor differences that operating systems impose on constants.

The exact list of constants, including those that specify the address (**AF_***) and protocol (**PF_***), are system specific, so it's pointless to include them here. Check the contents of the Socket.pm file for details.

Address Resolution and Conversion

The **inet_aton** and **inet_ntoa** functions provide simple methods for resolving and then converting hostnames and numbers to the packed 4-byte structure required by most of the other socket functions. The **inet_aton** function accepts a hostname or IP address (as a string) and resolves the hostname and returns a 4-byte packed structure. Thus

```
inet_aton("www.mcwords.com");
```

and

```
scalar gethostbyname("www.mcwords.com");
```

return identical values. In fact, **inet_aton** returns only the first IP address resolved; it doesn't provide the facility to obtain multiple addresses for the same host. This function is generally more practical than the **gethostbyname** or **gethostbyaddr** function, since it supports both names and numbers transparently. If a hostname cannot be resolved, the function returns **undef**.

The **inet_ntoa** function takes a packed 4-byte address and translates it into a normal dotted-quad string, such that

```
print inet_ntoa(inet_aton("198.112.10.10"));
```

prints 198.112.10.10.

Address Constants

When setting up a socket for serving requests, you need to specify the mask address used to filter out requests from specific addresses. Two predefined constants specify "all addresses" and "no addresses." They are **INADDR_ANY** and **INADDR_NONE**, respectively. The value of **INADDR_ANY** is a packed 4-byte IP address of 0.0.0.0. The value of **INADDR_NONE** is a packed 4-byte IP address of 255.255.255.255.

The **INADDR_BROADCAST** constant returns a packed 4-byte string containing the broadcast address to communicate to all hosts on the current network.

Finally, the **INADDR_LOOPBACK** constant returns a packed 4-byte string containing the loopback address of the current machine. The loopback address is the IP address by which you can communicate back to the current machine. It's usually 127.0.0.1, but the exact address can vary. The usual name for the local host is **localhost**, and it is defined within the /etc/hosts file or the DNS or NIS systems.

Socket Structures

Socket functions within Perl call the system equivalents, which themselves use structures to store the information for communicating with remote hosts. For Internet communication (that is, within the **AF_INET** domain), the structure is **sockaddr_in**, and for Unix communication (within the **AF_UNIX** domain), the structure is **sockaddr_un**. Although you could create your own Perl versions of the structures using **pack**, it's much easier to use the functions supplied by the **Socket** module.

The primary function is **sockaddr_in**, which behaves differently according to the arguments it is passed and the context in which it is called. In a scalar context, it accepts two arguments—the port number and packed IP address:

```
$sockaddr = sockaddr_in PORT, ADDRESS
```

This returns the structure as a scalar. To extract this information, you call the function in a list context:

```
($port, $address) = sockaddr_in SOCKADDR_IN
```

This extracts the port number and packed IP address from a **sockaddr_in** structure.

As an alternative to the preceding function, you can use the **pack_sockaddr_in** and **unpack_sockaddr_in** functions instead:

```
$sockaddr = pack_sockaddr_in PORT, ADDRESS
($port, $address) = unpack_sockaddr_in SOCKADDR_IN
```

A similar set of functions pack and unpack addresses to and from the **sockaddr_un** structure used for sockets in the **AF_UNIX** domain:

```
sockaddr_un PATHNAME
sockaddr_un SOCKADDR_UN
pack_sockaddr_un PATHNAME
unpack_sockaddr_un SOCKADDR_UN
```

Line Termination Constants

The line termination for network communication should be \n\n. However, because of the differences in line termination under different platforms, care should be taken to ensure that this value is actually sent and received. You can do this by using the octal values \012\012. Another alternative is to use the constants **$CR**, **$LF**, and **$CRLF**, which equate to \015, \012, and \015\012, respectively.

These are exported from the **Socket** module only on request, either individually or with the **:crlf** export tag:

```
use Socket qw/:DEFAULT :crlf/;
```

Socket Communication

There are two ends to all socket connections: the sender and the receiver.

Connecting to a Remote Socket

The process for communicating with a remote socket is as follows:

1. Create and open a local socket, specifying the protocol family (**PF_INET** or **PF_UNIX**), socket type, and top-level protocol number (TCP, UDP, etc.).
2. Determine the IP address of the remote machine you want to talk to.
3. Determine the remote service port number you want to talk to.
4. Create a **sockaddr_in** structure based on the IP address and remote service port.
5. Initiate the connection to the remote host.

This all sounds very complicated, but in fact, it is relatively easy. Many of the functions you need to use have already been discussed in this chapter. To speed up the process, it's a good idea to use something like the function **connectsocket**, shown here:

```
use Socket;

sub connectsocket
{
    my ($SOCKETHANDLE, $remotehost_name, $service_name, $protocol_name) = @_;
    my ($port_num, $sock_type, $protocol_num);
    my ($remote_ip_addr, $remote_socket);

    $protocol_num = getprotobyname($protocol_name);
    unless ($protocol_num)
    {
        $error = "Couldn't find protocol $protocol_name";
        return;
    }
    $sock_type =  $protocol_name eq 'tcp' ? SOCK_STREAM : SOCK_DGRAM;

    unless (socket($SOCKETHANDLE, PF_INET, $sock_type, $protocol_num))
    {
```

```
    $error = "Couldn't create a socket, $!";
    return;
}

if ($service_name =~ /^\d+$/ )
{
    $port_num = $service_name;
}
else
{
    $port_num = (getservbyname($service_name, $protocol_name))[2];
    unless($port_num)
    {
        $error = "Can't find service $service_name";
        return;
    }
}

$remote_ip_addr = gethostbyname($remotehost_name);
unless ($remote_ip_addr)
{
    $error = "Can't resolve $remotehost_name to an IP address";
    return;
}
$remote_socket = sockaddr_in($port_num, $remote_ip_addr);
unless(connect($SOCKETHANDLE, $remote_socket))
{
    $error = "Unable to connect to $remotehost_name: $!";
    return;
}
return(1);
}
```

I've used a variable, **$error**, to indicate the type of error, thus allowing you to return true or false from the function to indicate success or failure. The bulk of the function's code is given over to identifying or resolving names and/or numbers for service ports and other base information. The core of the function's processes is the **socket** function, which associates a filehandle with the relevant protocol family. The syntax of the **socket** function is

```
socket SOCKET, DOMAIN, TYPE, PROTOCOL
```

The **SOCKET** is the name of the filehandle you want to use to communicate over this network connection. The **DOMAIN** is the corresponding domain type, which is typically one of **PF_UNIX** for the Unix domain and **PF_INET** for Internet communication. The **TYPE** is the type of communication, either packet stream or datagram.

A simple test is used in the above function to see if the top-level protocol (TCP, UDP, etc.) is 'tcp', in which case it's safe to assume that you are doing stream communication. Valid values can be extracted from the **Socket** module, but it's likely to be one of **SOCK_STREAM** (for streams-based connections, such as TCP) and **SOCK_DGRAM** (for datagram connections, such as UDP). The final argument, **PROTOCOL**, is the protocol number, as determined by the **getprotobyname** function.

The next part of the function is responsible for looking up the numeric equivalents of the service port and hostname, before you build the **sockaddr_in** structure within the **sockaddr_in** function. You then use the newly created structure with the **connect** function in order to associate the socket you have created with the communications channel to a remote machine. The **connect** function's synopsis looks like this:

```
connect SOCKET, NAME
```

The **SOCKET** is the socket handle created by the **socket** function, and **NAME** is the scalar holding the **sockaddr_in** structure with the remote host and service port information.

Armed with this function, you can create quite complex systems for communicating information over UDP, TCP, or any other protocol. As an example, here's a simple script for obtaining the remote time of a host, providing it supports the **daytime** protocol (on service port 13):

```
use Ssockets;

my $host = shift || 'localhost';

unless(connectsocket(*TIME, $host, 'daytime', 'tcp'))
{
    die $Ssockets::error;
}

$_ = <TIME>;
print "Time on $host is $_";
close(TIME);
```

For convenience the **connectsocket** function has been inserted into its own package, **Ssockets**. This is actually the module used in Chapter 5 of the *Perl Annotated Archives* book (see Web Appendix A at **www.osborne.com**).

PROGRAMMING WITH PERL

The **daytime** protocol is pretty straightforward. The moment you connect, it sends back the current, localized date and time of the remote machine. All you have to do is connect to the remote host and then read the supplied information from the associated network socket.

Listening for Socket Connections

The process of listening on a network socket for new connections is more involved than creating a client socket, although the basic principles remain constant. Beyond the creation of the socket, you also need to bind the socket to a local address and service port, and set the socket to the "listen" state. The full process is therefore as follows:

1. Create and open a local socket, specifying the protocol family (**PF_INET** or **PF_UNIX**), socket type, and top-level protocol number (TCP, UDP, etc.).

2. Determine the local service port number on which you want to listen for new connections.

3. Set any options for the newly created socket.

4. Bind the socket to an IP address and service port on the local machine.

5. Set the socket to the listen state, specifying the size of the queue used to hold pending connections.

You don't initiate any connections or, at this stage, actually accept any connections. We'll deal with that part later. Again, it's easier to produce a simple function to do this for you, and the **listensocket** function that follows is the sister function to the earlier **connectsocket**:

```
use Socket;

sub listensocket
{
    my ($SOCKETHANDLE, $service_name,
        $protocol_name, $queuelength) = @_;
    my ($port_num, $sock_type, $protocol_num, $local_socket);

    $protocol_num = (getprotobyname($protocol_name))[2];
    unless ($protocol_num)
    {
        $error = "Couldn't find protocol $protocol_name";
        return;
    }
    $sock_type = $protocol_name eq "tcp" ? SOCK_STREAM : SOCK_DGRAM ;
```

```perl
if( $service_name =~ /^\d+$/)
{
    $port_num = $service_name;
}
else
{
    $port_num = (getservbyname($service_name, $protocol_name))[2];
    unless($port_num)
    {
        $error = "Can't find service $service_name";
        return;
    }
}

unless(socket($SOCKETHANDLE, PF_INET, $sock_type, $protocol_num))
{
    $error = "Couldn't create a socket: $!";
    return;
}
unless(setsockopt($SOCKETHANDLE,SOL_SOCKET,
                  SO_REUSEADDR,pack("l",1)))
{
    $error = "Couldn't set socket options: $!";
    return;
}
$local_socket = sockaddr_in($port_num, INADDR_ANY);
unless(bind($SOCKETHANDLE, $local_socket))
{
    $error = "Failed to Bind to socket: $!";
    return;
}
unless(listen($SOCKETHANDLE, $queuelength))
{
    $error = "Couldn't listen on socket: $!";
    return;
}
return(1);
}
```

Again, the bulk of this function is given over to determining the numerical versions of the IP addresses, protocols, and service ports that you want to use. Most of the function is therefore identical to the **connectsocket** function. The only difference is the setting of some socket options, which we'll return to later in this chapter, and the use of the **bind** and **listen** functions.

The **bind** function attaches your newly created socket to a local IP interface and service port. This is essentially the same as the **connect** function used to connect to a remote port, except that you are attaching the socket to a local port instead.

```
bind SOCKET, ADDRESS
```

The port definition does not have to be a specific IP address (although it could be). Instead you use the predefined **INADDR_ANY** to allow the connection to be accepted on any of the local configured IP interfaces. On a machine with a single interface, this will obviously mean only one interface, but on a machine with multiple interfaces, it allows you to accept the connection on any of them.

The **listen** function switches the new socket into listen mode. Without this function, the socket will never accept new connections. It accepts two arguments—the socket handle and something called the *queue length*:

```
listen SOCKET, LENGTH
```

The **LENGTH** parameter is the maximum number of connections that will be held in a queue by the operating system before the remote hosts receive an "unable to connect" response. This allows you to control the server loading and response times. It doesn't affect the number of connections that can be open at any one time, since that is controlled (we hope) by the server application. For example, with a web server, since the response time for an individual request is quite small, you may want to specify a relatively high value so the time between individual **accept** calls will be relatively low. Setting the queue length to a low value will affect performance, since the operating system may be refusing connections even when your server is not very busy.

It's also worth keeping in mind the type of communication you expect. With a web server, you tend to get a high number of relatively short requests in a short space of time. If you consider that a typical web page consists of one HTML file and ten images, then you could easily get 11 requests within a few seconds, and you should therefore set the queue length to a higher value. With an FTP server, you tend to get a smaller number of concurrent connections, but with longer times to service the actual requests. This would tend to indicate a lower value, thus helping to reduce the overall loading of your server.

It's always important to remember that your server can run as many child processes as it likes, and so you should also have other safeguards, such as connection counters or load monitors, to ensure that you are not accepting and servicing more requests than you can handle. The queue length will make no difference here. If the time to accept a connection and spawn a new process is one second, you could get 100 requests every second and end up with 100 child processes. This could kill a small server, no matter how small the individual requests might be.

Once your socket is ready and listening, you need to accept new connections as they are made by clients. The **accept** function handles this, blocking the current process until a new connection is made and accepted.

```
accept NEWSOCKET, SOCKET
```

The function monitors **SOCKET**, opening the **NEWSOCKET** filehandle on the accepted connection. It returns the packed address of the remote host that made the connection, or the false value if the connection failed.

This is usually used in combination with **fork** (see Chapter 14) to support multiple simultaneous connections from remote hosts. For example, here is a very simple web server (supporting HTTP) written entirely in Perl. It uses the **listensocket** function and demonstrates the simplicity of the network server once you have gotten past the complexities of creating the original listening socket.

```perl
use Ssockets;
use FileHandle;
use Cwd;
use Getopt::Std;
use Socket;
getopts('d');

$SIG{'INT'} = $SIG{'QUIT'} = \&exit_request_handler;
$SIG{'CHLD'} = \&child_handler;

my ($res);
my ($SERVERPORT) = 80;

unless(listensocket(*SERVERSOCKET, $SERVERPORT, 'tcp', 5))
{
    die "$0: ", $Ssockets::error;
}

autoflush SERVERSOCKET 1;

chroot(getcwd());
die "$0: Couldn't change root directory, are you root?"
    unless (getcwd() eq "/");
```

```perl
print "Changing root to ", getcwd(), "\n" if $opt_d;

print "Simple HTTP Server Started\n" if $opt_d;

while(1)
{
  ACCEPT_CONNECT:
    {
        ($remaddr = accept(CHILDSOCKET, SERVERSOCKET))
            || redo ACCEPT_CONNECT;
    }
    autoflush CHILDSOCKET 1;
    my $pid = fork();
    die "Cannot fork, $!" unless defined($pid);
    if ($pid == 0)
    {
        my ($remip)
            = inet_ntoa((unpack_sockaddr_in($remaddr))[1]);
        print "Connection accepted from $remip\n" if $opt_d;
        $_ = <CHILDSOCKET>;
        print "Got Request $_" if $opt_d;
        chomp;

        unless (m/(\S+) (\S+)/)
        {
            print "Malformed request string $_\n" if $opt_d;
            bad_request(*CHILDSOCKET);
        }
        else
        {
            my ($command) = $1;
            my ($arg) = $2;
            if (uc($command) eq 'GET')
            {
                if (open(FILE, "<$arg"))
                {
                    while(<FILE>)
                    {
                        print CHILDSOCKET $_;
                    }
                    close(FILE);
                }
```

```
                    else
                    {
                        bad_request(*CHILDSOCKET);
                    }
                }
            }
        close(CHILDSOCKET);
        exit(0);
    }
    close(CHILDSOCKET);
}

sub bad_request
{
    my ($SOCKET) = shift;

    print $SOCKET <<EOF;
<html>
<head>
<title>Bad Request</title>
</head>
<body>
<h1>Bad Request</h1>
The file you requested could not be found
</body>
</html>
EOF
}

sub child_handler
{
    wait;
}

sub exit_request_handler
{
    my ($recvsig) = @_;
    $SIG{'INT'} = $SIG{'QUIT'} = 'IGNORE';
    close(SERVERSOCKET);
    close(CHILDSOCKET);
    die "Quitting on signal $recvsig\n";
}
```

The main loop of this program will continue forever, until either a fatal error occurs or the program receives the **SIGINT** or **SIGQUIT** signal. This operation is dealt with by signal handlers, which we'll cover in more detail in Chapter 14.

The main acceptance loop is here,

```
ACCEPT_CONNECT:
    {
        ($remaddr = accept(CHILDSOCKET, SERVERSOCKET))
            || redo ACCEPT_CONNECT;
    }
```

where you just cycle around for as long as it takes until you get a valid connection. Remember that **accept** blocks process execution, so it's not a major concern that you'll be continually looping through this section. In fact, you should only ever **redo** the block if the accepted connection could not be opened properly.

Once you have opened a valid connection, you fork a new child process to handle the communication using the newly created **CHILDSOCKET** filehandle. Since you are forking a new process each time, you don't have to worry about the fact that the filehandle name is identical. You close the filehandle in the parent immediately after the child process has been forked.

There are a couple of other important notes here. First of all, you use a command line option to handle the printout of additional debugging information. Second, you use **chroot** to change the root directory of the script to the current directory. This guarantees the security of the web server by restricting which files can be served to only the files within the current directory and all its subdirectories. Even attempts to access files or directories associated by symbolic links will fail.

Finally, note the communication method employed. Because of the complexities of two-way communication over a single socket, you have to make some assumptions about the process involved. For HTTP, the client sends a single-line request and then waits for the server to send the reply, sending **EOF** or closing the connection as appropriate. The information returned by the server must be text based and can consist of HTTP header information and the actual body of data.

Using IO::Socket

The standard Perl distribution actually includes a module that provides a simpler interface to the built-in socket functions, much like the previous scripts. If you are not designing a custom solution, you might find that the distributed module better suits your needs. It's also more likely to be updated regularly than my own solution, and as part of the standard Perl distribution, it should work on a wide range of platforms without any modifications to your scripts.

Client Side

Initiating a client network connection with the **IO::Socket** module is very simple and actually follows a similar model to the **connectsocket** function:

```
use IO::Socket;
$sock = new IO::Socket::INET (PeerAddr => 'twinspark',
                              PeerPort => 4003,
                              Proto    => 'tcp'
                             );
```

The **$sock** scalar now contains a reference to a filehandle that you can use to transfer information to a remote host.

Server Side

The server side initialization follows a similar model:

```
use IO::Socket;
$sock = new IO::Socket::INET (LocalHost => 'twinspark',
                              LocalPort => 4003,
                              Proto     => 'tcp',
                              Listen    => 5,
                              Reuse     => 1
                             );
```

This follows the same fundamental idea as the **listensocket** function. It creates a socket and binds to the address and port specified by **LocalHost** and **LocalPort**. The **listen** queue is set to the value of the **Listen** element of the passed hash, and you set the **SO_REUSEADDR** option with the **Reuse** hash element.

Once the socket is created, you can use it as before, although many of the functions are now available as methods to the newly created socket object. Thus, you can accept new requests on a server socket with statements like this:

```
$new_sock = $sock->accept();
```

Note how the client- and server-side object-constructing methods are identical. The type of socket to be created is determined by the keys passed to the constructor.

Using IO::Socket and IO::Select

You can employ **IO::Select** in exactly the same way as we saw in Chapter 8 when working with more traditional filehandles. For the record, here's a sample script that uses **IO::Select** and **IO::Socket** to support multiple client connections:

```perl
#!/usr/local/bin/perl -w

use strict;
use IO::Socket;
use IO::Select;
use Socket;

my ($port) = (4000);

my $socket = IO::Socket::INET->new( LocalPort => $port,
                                    Listen => 5,
                                    Reuse => 1 );

die "Can't create server socket: $!" unless $socket;
print "Listening for connections on port $port\n";

my $readable = IO::Select->new;
$readable->add($socket);

while(1)
{
    my ($ready) = IO::Select->select($readable, undef, undef, undef);
    foreach my $s (@$ready)
    {
        if($s == $socket)
        {
            my $new_sock = $socket->accept;
            $readable->add($new_sock) if $new_sock;
            print $new_sock "Status server online!\r\n";
            print STDERR ("Accepted connection from: ", join('.',
            (unpack('C*',$new_sock->peername))[4..7]),
            "\n");
        }
        else
        {
            my $buf = <$s>;
```

```
        if( defined $buf )
        {
            if ($buf =~ /exit/i)
            {
                print $s "Bye!\n";
                $readable->remove($s);
                $s->close;
            }
            elsif ($buf =~ /status/i)
            {
                my $uptime = `/usr/bin/uptime`;
                print $s scalar localtime(time()), ': ',$uptime;
            }
        }
        else
        {
            $readable->remove($s);
            $s->close;
            print STDERR "Client Connection closed\n";
        }
    }
  }
}
```

Getting Socket Addresses

When connecting with a remote socket, you might take it for granted that you know
the remote IP address of the machine you are talking to. In fact, you can't necessarily
guarantee it's the one you expect. It's possible for a single name to resolve to a number
of IP addresses, and the exact one you have connected to may not be obvious.

When you are running a script for use as a server, the same problem occurs if you
forget to use the IP address returned by the **accept** function. In both cases, you can
use the **getpeername** function to return the IP address of the remote machine you are
talking to:

```
getpeername SOCKET
```

The function returns the packed **sockaddr_in** structure of the remote socket
connection. You'll need to extract the real address with something like this:

```
print "Remote: ",inet_ntoa((unpack_sockaddr_in(getpeername SOCKET))[1]),"\n";
```

The opposite is true when a script is acting as a server. If you specified one of the wildcard addresses, such as **INADDR_ANY**, as the address to bind to, then you may not know what you have bound to on a multiple-interface host. You can find out that information with **getsockname**:

```
getsockname SOCKET
```

This returns the same information as **getpeername**, except that it's for the local machine, rather than the remote one.

Note that in both cases, the functions only work on open and connected sockets. You can't create a socket and bind it or connect to it in order to get the current IP address of the local or remote machine. Until a connection has been accepted or connected, the socket is not attached to any local or remote IP address.

Closing Sockets

Because Perl treats a socket just like any other filehandle, the obvious (and natural) way to close a socket is to use the **close** function. However, you can use the **shutdown** function to provide a controlled shutdown of a connected socket.

```
shutdown SOCKET, HOW
```

The **SOCKET** is the filehandle of the open socket. The **HOW** value defines how the socket should be shut down. If **HOW** is 0, you cannot use the socket to receive more information. If **HOW** is 1, you cannot use the socket for sending information. If **HOW** is 2, the socket cannot be used for either sending or receiving information. Note that this doesn't actually close the socket connection; it just indicates to the system that the full-duplex nature of a socket has been modified.

This is perhaps most useful when you are creating a pair of sockets at each end of a connection—one socket purely for sending and one for receiving information. Although **shutdown** doesn't automatically redirect the socket handlers for you, **shutdown** will make sure you do not send data to a remote socket that won't be listening for data, thus preventing deadlocking.

Socket Options

You can specify certain options on individual sockets to improve facilities or performance. For example, the **SO_SNDBUF** option sets the buffer size when sending information via a network socket, whereas the **SO_REUSEADDR** allows you to reuse an existing address/port if a previous connection is still shutting down. Without setting this option, new connections will fail, even if you know that you've closed down the previous socket connection.

To set a particular option, you use

```
setsockopt SOCKET, LEVEL, OPTNAME, OPTVAL
```

The **LEVEL** is the level within the networking model that you want the option to affect. Most of the time this will be **SOL_SOCKET**, to directly affect the BSD network sockets. The **OPTNAME** is one of the constants, exported by the **Socket** module and summarized in Table 12-1. Note that the list here is for guidance only. The exact options available will depend both on your operating system and the level of the connection that you are configuring.

The **OPTVAL** is the value that you want to assign to the particular option. Because each option can have a specific value, you cannot combine multiple options into the same **setsockopt** call; you must set the options individually. For options that can be enabled or disabled, 0 indicates that the option should be disabled, and 1 indicates that it should be enabled.

For example, to switch **SO_REUSEADDR** on:

```
setsockopt(SOCKET, SOL_SOCKET, SO_REUSEADDR, 1);
```

On some systems you may need to pack the setting into a long integer using **pack**:

```
setsockopt(SOCKET, SOL_SOCKET, SO_REUSEADDR, pack('l',1));
```

Option	Description
SO_DEBUG	Enable/disable recording of debugging information.
SO_REUSEADDR	Enable/disable local address reuse.
SO_KEEPALIVE	Enable/disable keep connections alive.
SO_DONTROUTE	Enable/disable routing bypass for outgoing messages.
SO_LINGER	Linger on close if data is present.
SO_BROADCAST	Enable/disable permission to transmit broadcast messages.
SO_OOBINLINE	Enable/disable reception of out-of-band data in band.
SO_SNDBUF	Set buffer size for output.
SO_RCVBUF	Set buffer size for input.

Table 12-1.   *Socket Options Under Solaris 2.4*

PROGRAMMING
WITH PERL

To get the current options, use **getsockopt**:

```
getsockopt SOCKET, LEVEL, OPTNAME
```

This returns the current setting for **OPTNAME** or is undefined if the value cannot be determined. Note that once again you must request each option value individually; it's not possible to request all of the currently set options.

Data Transfer

Transferring information over a network is problematic because of line termination and other issues. However, providing you are careful, you shouldn't have any difficulties while using the normal **print** function and **<FILEHANDLE>** operator. Since Perl treats sockets like filehandles, there is no reason why you shouldn't use any of the available functions and operators that work with filehandles for transferring information.

To avoid getting into a deadlocked situation when communicating between hosts on a single socket, you will need to design a suitable protocol that tells each end of the network link what state it should be in. For simple communication, it should be enough to use a simple flip-flop situation. For example, the server end sits waiting for data while the client sends information, and once transfer is complete, the end toggles. Now the client waits for data while the server sends it. This is the basic idea behind protocols such as HTTP and SMTP. However, if you are using one of these protocols for transfer, then you might find one of the CPAN modules, such as Graham Barr's excellent **libnet** bundle, significantly easier to use.

A possible alternative solution, as already discussed, is to open two sockets at each end of the connection. The client uses **shutdown** to disable sending on socket A while disabling receiving on socket B. The server, on the other hand, disables receiving on socket A while disabling sending on socket B. Although this improves the situation, you can still enter a deadlocked state if you are expecting to receive data on both ends of the connection.

You cannot even use **select** to solve the problem. Many people mistakenly believe that **select** eliminates the deadlocking situation. It doesn't; all it does is provide a method for a single threaded process to communicate on more than one socket semi-simultaneously. If both ends of the connection are listening when one of them should be sending, all **select** does is monitor multiple sockets very efficiently for no data.

If you are transferring fixed blocks of information, particularly binary data or fixed-length records, then you might find the **send** and **recv** functions to be more practical. You may also find that your operating system does not support the use of **print** and other filehandle constructs for sending information. In these instances, you will have to use the **send** and **recv** functions.

The **send** function sends a message on a socket handle, just like the **send()** system function:

```
send SOCKET, MSG, FLAGS [, TO]
```

The **MSG** argument is the data string that you want to send. Since Perl automatically knows the length of a string, you do not need to supply this information. The **FLAGS** specify particular operations to be configured for this transmission. Only two are generally supported—**MSG_OOB** and **MSG_DONTROUTE**. **MSG_OOB** allows you to send the **MSG** as out-of-band data. This is generally only supported on Internet streams. The **MSG_DONTROUTE** flag switches on the **SO_DONTROUTE** option for the duration of the transfer (see the previous "Socket Options" section). The **TO** argument, if specified, should be a suitable **sockaddr_in** structure to send the data to if the socket has not already been connected to a remote socket.

The **recv** function accepts information from **SOCKET**, placing it into **SCALAR**:

```
recv SOCKET, SCALAR, LEN, FLAGS
```

It accepts up to a maximum of **LEN** bytes from the socket, and **SCALAR** will be shrunk or grown accordingly to hold the received information. The function returns the IP address of the host from which the data was received, or **undef** on error.

Graham Barr's libnet Bundle

Graham Barr supports the **libnet** bundle, which consists of a large number of modules that support communication over a network with existing TCP/IP servers and protocols, such as HTTP, FTP, SMTP, and NNTP. Because the complexities of the protocols have been taken care of for you, the difficulties associated with communicating using these protocols is virtually eliminated. The interfaces provided are object based, and if you are familiar with the protocols, then using the modules and the classes provided is very easy. Even if you don't understand the protocols, simplified top-level functions are provided for the most common tasks.

For example, here's a script that expands an email address, first by resolving the MX (mail exchanger) hosts for the email address's domain, and then by communicating directly with the mail server to expand the email address. This script also uses the **Net::DNS** module by Michael Fuhr, which provides an interface to the DNS name-resolving system. Again, it's object based and is very easy to use. (Web Appendix B describes details on the networking modules that are available from CPAN, or use Appendix C to locate your local CPAN mirror.)

```
#!/usr/local/bin/perl5

use Net::SMTP;
use Net::DNS;

while (@ARGV)
{
```

```
my $email = shift;
my ($user, $host) = split '@', $email;
my $res = new Net::DNS::Resolver;
my @mx = mx($res, $host);

if (@mx)
{
    print "Expansions for $email\n";
    foreach my $rr (@mx)
    {
        my ($mxhost) = $rr->exchange;
        print "Checking $mxhost\n";
        my $smtp = Net::SMTP->new($mxhost);
        unless($smtp)
        {
            warn "Couldn't open connection to $host";
            next;
        }
        my $realrecipient = $smtp->expand($email);
        print "$realrecipient\n" if $realrecipient;
        $smtp->quit();
    }
    print "\n";
}
else
{
    warn "Couldn't find any MX hosts for $host\n";
}
}
```

You can see from this sample how easy it is both to resolve an address using DNS and to communicate with an SMTP server. The complexities of opening the remote connection and handling the protocol and communication have been eliminated, and something that would otherwise take hundreds of lines is resolved to just 34 lines. To use it, just specify an address on the command line:

```
Expansions for mc@mcwords.com
Checking mcwords.com
<mcwords@prluk.demon.co.uk>
```

Here's a very simple script using the **Net::FTP** module that uploads all the files from a particular directory to a remote FTP server:

```
use Net::FTP;

my $ftp = Net::FTP->new($collector);
die "Couldn't FTP\n" unless($ftp);
$ftp->login($colluser,$collpass);
$ftp->cwd($remlogdir);
chdir($logdir);
my @list = glob("perf.*");
for my $file (@list)
{
    if ($ftp->put($file,$file))
    {
        unlink $file;
    }
}
$ftp->quit;
```

Gisle Aas' LWP Bundle

Gisle Aas supports the LWP (libwww-Perl) bundle. Unlike the **libnet** bundle, which
is concerned with a number of specific protocols at a protocol level, the LWP bundle
provides you with a number of simple methods for downloading and accessing web
pages. As well as allowing you to download standard pages, you can also use cookies,
passwords, and other entities in your requests, and once downloaded, the links and
images in the files can also be extracted.

At the basic level, you can use the **LWP::Simple** module to download a single page:

```
use LWP::Simple;

$url = "http://www.osborne.com";
$file = "osborne.html";
$rc = mirror($url, $file);

if ($rc == 304)
{
    print STDERR "$progname: $file is up to date\n"
}
elsif (!is_success($rc))
{
    print STDERR ("$progname: $rc ", status_message($rc), "    ($url)\n");
}
```

Replace **$url** and **$file** with a URL and the file to which you want the page downloaded, and the LWP modules will handle everything else for you.

If you want to make use of a cookies file, you need to use the **LWP::UserAgent** module—the same module is actually used by **LWP::Simple**. The next example opens a Netscape cookies file, and then builds a new request consisting of the cookie data and the URL you are requesting before calling the **request** method to download the homepage of BlackStar, a DVD/video seller:

```
use LWP::UserAgent;
use HTTP::Cookies;

my $cookie_jar = HTTP::Cookies::Netscape->new( File =>
"/.netscape/cookies");
my $ua = LWP::UserAgent->new;
$ua->cookie_jar($cookie_jar);
my $request = HTTP::Request->new('GET',"http://www.blackstar.co.uk");
$ua->request($request, "blackstar.html");
```

Chapter 13

Database Systems

U p to now, all of the chapters have concentrated on the process of utilizing information within the Perl environment and the Perl script you have invoked. However, it is often desirable, if not essential, to create, update, and access information for external databases. This process is called *object persistence*, since the data is created and is persistently (or permanently) available.

There are many different types of database systems. Some of them will be familiar to many of you, as you probably already use them, although you may not always realize that you are doing so. Most databases take one of two basic forms: *flat file* and *relational*. With a flat-file database, the information is stored in a fixed format, and the information stored is considered to be isolated or complete. For example, the /etc/passwd file under Unix or an .ini file under Windows could both be considered examples of a flat-file database. The information is stored in its entirety in a format that is easy to understand, and it does not need to be linked to another database for the information to make sense.

A relational database, on the other hand, uses a number of separate "tables." Each table contains a list of information, and links between the tables enable you to store information in a structured and relative way. For example, imagine a music database. It might have two tables—one lists the artists and the other lists the individual recordings they have made. You can access all of the recordings for a particular artist by examining the links between the two tables.

When it comes to accessing and using databases, there are other problems to contend with. First of all, you must decide how you are going to store the information within a file. Using a single- or multicharacter delimiter is a fairly common system and one that Unix uses in many different places. By using a tab or colon or some other character, you can separate the individual fields within a record. The return character is often used to separate the individual records within the entire file.

The problem with this method is that if you want to store information that may possibly contain one of these delimiting characters, you may experience some corruption of data or even complete loss of information. A better solution in this instance is to use a fixed-length record system. Rather than delimiting the individual fields and records, fixed-length systems specify the length of each field. Providing you know the format (field sizes and types), you should be able to read entire records from the file and determine the individual fields by their positions. This is wasteful of space for databases with very large fields. In a database with 16K records, you can easily eat up a lot of space. A record with 1K of useful data still takes up 16K of storage space.

Even once you have solved these problems, there are other considerations. Text databases are great for accessing sequential information or for storing a stream of information that will be processed by a program at a later time. What they are not so good at is random access. Searching through a large text database can be a time-consuming task, since you will need to read in each individual record to determine whether it is the one you want. There are ways around this: you can use an index system to point to the records you want, but the chances are that this also uses a text format, and you end up back at square one.

To get around this particular problem, you need to investigate a system that automatically handles the indexing and searching of your database in a timely manner but still provides you with a simple interface for extracting the individual records and fields from the database files. The easiest solution is to use the DBM system (the precise expansion of the acronym has been lost, but it probably stands for database management). This is a hashing database using the same key/value pair system as Perl's internal hash variable.

The more complex database implementations, especially those relying on relational features, either require more complex use of the text or DBM database systems or require the use of an external database implementation. Perl supports access to all of the major database systems and many of the smaller systems, through a number of extensions provided through the DBI toolkit, a third-party module available from CPAN. Using a series of database drivers (DBDs), the DBI toolkit allows you to create and use databases using Oracle, Sybase, mSQL/mySQL, PostgreSQL, and ODBC (open database connectivity). Under Windows you can use either the DBI interfaces or the **Win32::ODBC** toolkit, which provides direct access to any ODBC-compliant database, including FileMaker Pro, Oracle, and Microsoft's Visual FoxPro, Access, and SQL Server database products.

In this chapter, we'll look at all four solutions—text, DBM, DBI, and ODBC—and at more general methods and practices for creating and using databases within Perl. We'll also look at ways of using DBM databases for storing complex data and at using DBI with text files.

Text Databases

Although they are the most basic of the database systems, text databases provide a reliable and safe location for storing information. Many log systems using either delimited or fixed-length records and many of the files that you take for granted on Unix and Windows systems are actually text based, and are only imported or reported on when required.

If you look at a typical /etc/passwd file, you will notice that it has records—one per line—where the individual fields are separated by colons:

```
root:x:0:1:0000-Admin(0000):/:/sbin/sh
daemon:x:1:1:0000-Admin(0000):/:
bin:x:2:2:0000-Admin(0000):/usr/bin:
sys:x:3:3:0000-Admin(0000):/:
adm:x:4:4:0000-Admin(0000):/var/adm:
lp:x:71:8:0000-lp(0000):/usr/spool/lp:
smtp:x:0:0:mail daemon user:/:
uucp:x:5:5:0000-uucp(0000):/usr/lib/uucp:
nuucp:x:9:9:0000-uucp(0000):/var/spool/uucppublic:/usr/lib/uucp/uucico
listen:x:37:4:Network Admin:/usr/net/nls:
```

```
nobody:x:60001:60001:uid no body:/:
noaccess:x:60002:60002:uid no access:/:
martinb:x:1000:1000:Martin C Brown:/users/martinb:/usr/local/bin/bash
```

There is a problem with the type of layout shown here if you start using this technique for more complex databases. What happens if the data you are trying to store contains a colon? As far as the Perl script is concerned, the colon specifies the end of one field and the beginning of the next. An additional colon would only upset the information stored in the "record." Even worse, what would happen if you wanted to record multiple lines of text in the database? Individual records are often stored on individual lines; multiline fields would confuse the script again. You could use separate record delimiters that don't rely on the newline character, but again, this adds more complexity.

There are ways around these problems. You could use a different character for the field and record separators, although this is still open to the same abuse and possible results. You could just remove the field and record separator characters from the source before you put them in the database, but this reduces the utility of being able to store the information in the first place. The simplest solution is to ignore any field or record separators and instead use fixed-length records to store the information. The use of fixed-length records implies that you know the maximum size of the data that you are storing before you place it into the database, and therefore you need to know the format of the database before you write to and read from it.

Using fixed-length records would allow you to store any sort of information in the database, including multiple-line text, without worrying about how the data may affect the database layout. The only problem with fixed-length databases is that you not only restrict the amount of information you can store, but you also increase the size of the data file for small records, as the individual fields are "padded" to make up the fixed lengths. To complicate matters further, you may have trouble choosing a padding character that won't affect the contents of the fields you are storing. Null characters, for example, produce all sorts of results when they are included as the text within a browser window when writing CGI programs. In these situations, you can usually augment the fixed-length structure by also specifying the field length for each field in each record. But this too increases the size of the database.

To add more complexity, you will also need to overcome the problems of searching the file if you are using it as a random-access database. If you know the record number you want to access, then with either form of text database, you should be able to move to the location relatively quickly. But if you don't know the record number, the time taken to find the data will be a factor of the database size. This is why, practically, text databases are only good for small-scale installations or in situations where the information flow is basically one way.

Using a text database for storing log information is an example of a one-way information flow. One or more programs will add data to the file without referring back to the data they have written. Another script will be responsible for taking in the raw data and producing a summary report of the information contained in it. Again, the information flow is one way: the data comes from the database but is not updated or modified.

In the following sections, we'll look at the techniques for reading from and writing to textual databases, including some example scripts. We'll also examine the methods you will need to employ if you need to update, rather than read from or append, information in a text database.

Delimited Databases

Accessing delimited databases is a case of using the **split** and **join** functions to extract fields from and combine fields into the records used to store the information. For example, to access the password file on a Unix system, which uses colons for the field delimiters and newlines for record delimiters, you can use a very simple script:

```
open(D,"</etc/passwd") || die "Can't open file, $!";
while(<D>)
{
    chomp;
    @fields = split /:/;
    print join(' ', @fields),"\n";
}
close(D) || dir "Couldn't close file, $!";
```

Of course, in this instance it's easier to use **getpwent** and other functions to read the file in a more reliable and safe format, but the principles remain the same.

If you want to import and export records using a different record separator, you can use the **$/** and **$** variables. You can set the values of the input and output field values when you call the **split** and **join** functions. You may also want to investigate the **DBD::CSV** module, which allows you to access a comma separate value file as if it were a SQL database table. See Web Appendix B and the "**DBI**" section later in this chapter for more information.

Many of the remaining technicalities surrounding the use of delimited text files also apply to fixed-length databases, so we'll examine the problems in the next section.

Fixed-Length Records

Using fixed-length records is also a case of using an existing function set that you already know about. The **pack** and **unpack** functions, which you saw in the previous chapter, can be used to create fixed-length records that can be written to a file. Because the bytestring generated by **pack** is (within reason) architecture independent, using **pack** and **unpack** can be a reliable method for storing and exchanging information across platforms.

Following are three simple scripts: one to add data to a task list, one to report from it, and one to update the information in a task list. The first is relatively simple. We will compose the information from that supplied on the command line and append a packed bytestring to the end of the file.

```perl
my ($taskfile) = "tasks.db";
my ($taskformat) = "A40LL";

my ($sec,$min,$hour,$mday,$mon,$year) = (localtime(time))[0..5];
$mon++;
$year += 1900;

die "Usage: $0 title required-date\n" if (@ARGV<2);

($mday,$mon,$year) = split '/',$ARGV[-1];
$reqdate = ($year*10000)+($mon*100)+$mday;

open(D,">>$taskfile") || die "Couldn't open the task file, $!\n";
print D pack($taskformat,$ARGV[0],$reqdate,0);
close(D);
```

The only important note is that we convert the date into a numerical format. The reason for this, which will be more important in the next script, is that the numerical version can be more easily sorted via the standard Perl functions.

Reporting from the database is almost as simple. Once again we employ the **unpack** function to extract the individual records in turn:

```perl
use Getopt::Std;

my $taskfile   = "tasks.db";
my $taskformat = "A40LL";
my $tasklength = length(pack($taskformat,));
my $ref=0;

getopts('drc');

open(D,"<$taskfile") || die "Couldn't open the task file, $!\n";

while(read(D,$_,$tasklength))
{
    ($title,$reqdate,$compdate) = unpack($taskformat,$_);
    $lref{$ref} = $title;
```

```perl
        $lref{$ref} = "$reqdate" if ($opt_r);
        $lref{$ref} = "$compdate" if ($opt_c);
        $ltitle{$ref} = $title;
        $lreqdate{$ref} = $reqdate;
        $lcompdate{$ref} = $compdate;
        $ref++;
    }

close(D);

printf("%-40s  %-10s  %-10s\n","Title","Req. Date","Comp. Date");

foreach $key (sort_values(\%lref))
{
    $lreqdate{$key} =~ s#(....)(..)(..)#$3/$2/$1#;
    if ($lcompdate{$key}>0)
    {
        next if ($opt_d);
        $lcompdate{$key} =~ s#(....)(..)(..)#$3/$2/$1#;
    }
    else
    {
        $lcompdate{$key}="";
    }
    printf("%-40s  %10s %10s\n",
            $ltitle{$key},$lreqdate{$key},$lcompdate{$key});
}

sub sort_values
{
    my $lref = shift;

    if ($opt_r || $opt_c)
    {
        sort {$lref{$a} <=> $lref{$b}} keys %$lref;
    }
    else
    {
        sort {$lref{$a} cmp $lref{$b}} keys %$lref;
    }
}
```

The final script is more complicated. Updating information in either a delimited or fixed-length database requires that you know the location of the data that you want to update. With a delimited database, the data can potentially be of any length, and so you need to copy the existing information from the current database into a new file, substituting the updated information in the new file before continuing the copy process. It's not possible to "insert" data into the file—you cannot move data within a physical file without moving the information somewhere else first. You could do it in memory, but for large databases, this wouldn't be practical. Instead, the better solution is to use external files for the process.

With a fixed-length database, the process is slightly easier. The length of each record in the database is the same, so updating a record is as easy as overwriting the updated and packed record in the same physical location within the file. To do this you use the **seek** and **tell** functions. This is a cyclical process in which you read in each record until you find the one you want, remembering the location of the start of the record in each case. Then, once the information has been updated, you go back to the start of the record and rewrite the packed record.

Here's the script that updates our earlier task file entries:

```perl
use Fcntl;

my ($taskfile) = "tasks.db";
my ($taskformat) = "A40LL";
my $tasklength = length(pack($taskformat,));

die "Usage: modtask.pl title completed-date\n" if (@ARGV<2);

open(D,"+<$taskfile") || die "Couldn't open the task file, $!\n";

while(read(D,$_,$tasklength))
{
    ($title,$reqdate,$compdate) = unpack($taskformat,$_);
    last if (($title eq $ARGV[0]) && ($compdate eq 0));
    $lastseek=tell(D);
}

if ($lastseek >= (-s $taskfile))
{
    die "Couldn't find the task specified\n";
}
```

```
($mday,$mon,$year) = split '/',$ARGV[-1];
$compdate = ($year*10000)+($mon*100)+$mday;

seek(D,$lastseek,SEEK_SET);

print D pack($taskformat,$title,$reqdate,$compdate);

close(D) || die "Couldn't close the database\n";
```

To use all three scripts, first call **addtask.pl** (the first script) to create and add a record to the database, and then update the task you have added by specifying a completion date:

```
$ perl -w addtask.pl 'Phone Richard' 25/3/1999
$ perl modtask.pl 'Phone Richard' 26/3/1999
$ perl listtask.pl
Title                                  Req. Date    Comp. Date
Phone Richard                          25/03/1999   26/03/1999
```

DBM Databases

For simple structures, such as single-record databases, and especially for a sequential series of data, text files are exceedingly practical. However, they suffer from performance issues if you want to access the information on a random basis, or where the amount of information you wish to store becomes unmanageable in a text database. A better solution is to store the information in a real database where the information can be recorded and extracted using identified and unique keys. This enables you to ignore the searching and storage mechanisms that are required for text databases and instead to concentrate on writing the code for using, rather than the code for accessing, the database.

The standard database under Unix is a system called DBM, which is based on a simple key/value pair, much like Perl's own hash data type. Each entry within the database will have a unique key, and attached to this will be the piece of data you want to store. To extract information from the database, you simply request the data associated with a particular key.

Although it sounds complicated, it is really no different from the way hash variables are stored within Perl. You access a hashed variable entry within Perl by specifying a textual key. With some careful programming and the use of well-worded keys, you can store information in a DBM file in the same way you would store information in any off-the-shelf database.

DBM files are an integral part of the Unix operating system. Many of the standard components use DBM files for their own storage. Sendmail, for example, uses DBM to store aliases in a time-efficient manner. The alias file is converted, using the **newalias** command, into a DBM database. This is quicker than manually trawling through the text-based alias file—something that is vitally important when processing a large number of email messages. As a demonstration of the power of the DBM system, it is also the storage format for the Network Information Service (NIS/NIS+, formerly called the Yellow Pages), a networked version of many of the core operating system configuration files for everything from user data to hostnames and IP addresses.

DBM Implementations

Over the years, the original DBM system has been improved and has gone through a number of different incarnations, although the original specification remains the same. Most of the different DBM systems are compatible with each other, but to a greater or lesser extent, compatibility depends on the platform and implementation involved. It should be noted, as well, that DBM files are not portable. The storage format used is specific to a particular hardware platform and operating system. In some cases, even different versions of the same operating system have incompatible DBM systems. Furthermore, the format used by DBM is very wasteful of space compared to even a fixed-length text database. Because of this, copying a DBM file across file systems on the same machine can be problematic because the OS doesn't know how to copy the "empty" space.

Depending on the implementation, a DBM database is composed of either two files or a combined single file. In the two-file combination, one is a directory table containing a bit-based representation of the buckets and their index location and has .dir as its suffix. The second file contains all the data and has .pag as its suffix. The data file is often full of "holes," where storage space has been allocated but not used, or where the key has been deleted. In these instances, the area within the file actually contains no useful information, although it will be reused when new data is added to the file.

The downside to this method is that some implementations allocate too much storage space, thereby generating a file that is reported to be 10, 100, or even 1,000 times the size of the useful information stored within the file. There is, unfortunately, no clear method for compacting the information into a smaller version of the database. Even using Perl to copy the contents of the database into a new database will not necessarily provide you with a suitable solution to the problem. Of course, the flip side to all of this is that the speed of access, even for a very large database, is very quick.

There is a limitation on the storage size of each key/value pair, which is known as the bucket size. Creating entries larger than this will either crash you out of Perl or just truncate the information you attempt to store, depending entirely on how the database has been implemented at C level. The maximum bucket size is dependent on the DBM implementation being used, and the information is summarized in Table 13-1.

Implementation Module	DBM/ODBM ODBM_File	NDBM NDBM_File	SDBM SDBM_File	GDBM GDBM_File	Berkeley DB DB_File
Bucket Limit	1–2K	1–4K	1K (none)	None	None
Disk Usage	Varies	Varies	Small	Big	Big
Speed	Slow	Slow	Slow	Okay	Fast
Data Files Distributable	No	No	Yes	Yes	Yes
Byte-Order Independent	No	No	No	No	Yes
User-Defined Sort Order	No	No	No	No	Yes
Wildcard Lookups	No	No	No	No	Yes

Table 13-1.   *DBM Modules in Perl*

The following sections describe common DBM implementations and their advantages, disadvantages, and differences from the range available.

DBM/ODBM

The generic term for the original DBM toolkit on which all the newer toolkits are based is DBM/ODBM. Although included as standard in most Unix variants, it has been replaced almost entirely by NDBM as the DBM implementation of choice. Perl refers to ODBM as "Old DBM." The supported bucket size is 1K on most platforms, but it may be as high as 2K on some. The database files are created with .dir and .pag extensions, although you only specify the prefix name when opening the file.

NDBM

The "new" replacement for the original DBM, with some speed and storage-allocation improvements, is NDBM. This has replaced the standard DBM libraries and in some cases is the only implementation available. Depending on the operating system, the bucket size is anything from 1K to 4K. The database files are created with .dir and .pag extensions, although you only specify the prefix name when opening the file. NDBM should, in theory, be compatible with files created using the DBM/ODBM implementations, although this isn't guaranteed. You should use this in place of ODBM if it is available.

SDBM

Substitute/Simple DBM is a speed- and stability-enhanced version of DBM. Included as standard with the Perl distribution, it's supported on all Perl platforms except Mac OS. The SDBM system supports a default bucket size of 1K, but this can be modified at compile time. The database files are created with .dir and .pag extensions, although you only specify the prefix name when opening the file.

GDBM

The GNU/FSF implementation of DBM is faster than all implementations except Berkeley DB. GDBM has also been ported to a larger number of platforms than other implementations. Unlike other systems, it also supports an unlimited bucket size and has built-in file locking within the GDBM module. This eliminates a lot of the complexity surrounding the normal responsibilities of file locking. Unlike other DBM implementations, the entire hash table is stored in a single file, rather than two separate files.

Berkeley DB

Berkeley DB is a public domain C library of database access methods, and it supports not only the traditional DBM implementation but also a number of advanced storage and indexing systems that allow you to store and retrieve information in a more efficient fashion. For the technically minded, Berkeley DB supports B+Tree, Extended Linear Hashing, record-number indexing, and both fixed- and variable-length storage records. The **DB_File** Perl module puts a DBM-like wrapper around the B-Tree and hash implementations, enabling them to be used as DBM replacements. The fixed- and variable-length record implementation also has a Perl array wrapper for direct use within Perl scripts.

Berkeley DB libraries also support relational database system facilities such as multiuser updates and transactions and the ability to recover corrupt database files. We'll take a look at using the additional features of Berkeley DB, beyond simulating DBM files, later in this chapter.

DBM Functions

Perl 4 used a system of functions to access DBM files. The process was basically identical to the process used for any normal file, and the result was very similar to the **tie** solution we will see shortly. In each case, the **dbmopen** function creates a relation between a Perl hash and an external DBM database. Using these functions, only one type of DBM implementation is supported, and that's usually the standard for your operating system (NDBM, ODBM) or the Perl-supplied SDBM if these are not available.

```
dbmopen HASH, EXPR, MODE
```

This binds the database file specified by **EXPR** to the hash **HASH**. If the database does not exist, then it is created using the mode specified by **MODE**. The file **EXPR** should be specified without the .dir and .pag extensions.

For example, to associate the aliases database on a Unix machine to a hash called **%aliases**:

```
Use Fcntl;
dbmopen %aliases,'/etc/aliases',O_RDWR;
foreach (keys %aliases)
{
    print "$_: $aliases{$_}\n";
}
```

Once you have finished using the DBM database, you must disassociate the hash from the underlying DBM file with the **dbmclose** function:

```
dbmclose HASH
```

Note   *Use of these functions is heavily deprecated—and it's highly likely that they will be dropped completed in Perl 6.0, due out late in 2001. Use the **tie** method unless you really need to retain compatibility with Perl 4.*

Using Tied DBM Databases

Using the **tie** function, which you saw in the last chapter, provides an object-oriented interface to DBM databases and is now the preferred method within Perl 5. By using **tie**, you can create a connection between a standard Perl hash and a DBM database. Since DBM databases use the same key/value system as Perl hashes, there is no complex handling of the information. Accessing a key in the hash automatically provides you with the correct key/value pair in the DBM database. Creating new entries and deleting them similarly updates the DBM file. The access and control is instantaneous, and it eliminates so much of the complexity of using a DBM database that it's very easy to forget you are even using an external file instead of an internal structure.

The format of the **tie** function with DBM files is as follows:

```
tie %hash, DBMTYPE, FILENAME, MODES, FILEMODE;
```

The **DBMTYPE** element should be the name of a DBM implementation from which to inherit the necessary methods for the **tie** function. For example, to create a new database using GDBM, you might use

```
tie %db, 'GDBM_File', 'database.db', O_CREAT|O_RDWR, 0644;
```

You will need the definitions from the **Fcntl** module for the specification of the different flags when opening and closing the files. The different flags available for all DBM implementations are shown in Table 13-2. Both GDBM and Berkeley DB have their own additional flags, which we will examine separately.

Once opened, the DBM file can be accessed using the hash it has been tied to. For example, the following code fragment opens a text file and creates a DBM database of the contents. The first line of the text file is assumed to be the list of fields to be used as keys in the rest of the database.

Flags	Description
O_APPEND	Appends information to the given file
O_CREAT	Creates a new file if it doesn't already exist
O_EXCL	Causes the open to fail if the file already exists when used with **O_CREAT**
O_NDELAY	Opens the file without blocking; reads or writes to the file will not cause the process to wait for the operation to be complete
O_NONBLOCK	Behaves as **O_NDELAY**
O_RDONLY	Opens the file read-only
O_RDWR	Opens the file for reading and writing
O_TRUNC	Opens the file, truncating (emptying) the file if it already exists
O_WRONLY	Opens the file write-only

Table 13-2.   *File Access Flags*

```perl
#!/usr/local/bin/perl5 -w

use NDBM_File;
use Fcntl;

my ($dbfile,%db,$i,@fieldnames,@fields,$key,$n);

die "Usage:\n$0 source\n" if (@ARGV<1);

$dbfile = $ARGV [0];

open(D,"<$dbfile") || die "Can't open $dbfile, $!";

(tie %db, NDBM_File, $dbfile, O_RDWR|O_CREAT|O_EXCL, 0666)
      || die "$0: Error creating $dbfile: $!\n";
$_ = <D>;
chomp;
s/,//;
@fieldnames = split "\t";

$db{fieldlist} = join(",",@fieldnames);

while(<D>)
{
    chomp;
    @fields = split "\t";

    for($n=0;$n<=@fields;$n++)
    {
        if (defined($fields[$n]))
        {
            $key = $fieldnames[$n] . "-$i";
            $db{$key} = $fields[$n];
        }
    }
    $i++;
}

$db{seqid} = $i;
close(D) || die "$0: Couldn't close source, $!\n";
untie %db || die "$0: Couldn't close db, $!\n";
```

```
print "Read $i records\n";
```

Other hash functions, such as **each**, **keys**, and **delete**, work the same way on a DBM file as on a hash. The changes are immediate: if you delete an entry in the hash tied to the DBM database, it has been deleted forever; recovery is impossible. You can also check for the existence of a key within the database using the normal **exists** function, and you can check the value of a specific key using **defined**. The **tie** object interface performs all the necessary checks and other operations for you on the actual DBM file.

Also note that the **keys** and **values** functions should be used sparingly if the DBM file is particularly large. Perl will quite happily create a large internal temporary array to contain the list of information. Unless you are producing a sorted list of the contents, it's best to avoid the use of functions altogether. In most cases, you will be accessing individual key/value pairs from the database, and this should not then be a problem. However, when searching (perhaps when building a list of records to display), use the **each** function (see Chapter 7) to prevent Perl from creating such large temporary structures.

Converting Between DBM Formats

Because Perl 5 now uses the **Tie** module to create a link between a hash and a DBM object, you can use Perl to convert from one DBM implementation to another. The following example converts an **NDBM_File** database into a **GDBM_File** database:

```perl
use NDBM_File;
use GDBM_File;
use Fcntl;

die "Usage:$0 old new\n" if (@ARGV<2);

my($old,$new) = @ARGV;

tie (%oldhash, 'NDBM_File', $old, O_RDONLY, 0444)
    || die "$0: Error opening source $old: $!\n";
tie (%newhash, 'GDBM_File', $new, O_CREAT|O_RDWR|O_EXCL, 0666)
    || die "$0: Error opening dest $new: $!\n";

%newhash = %oldhash;

untie %oldhash || die "$0: Error closing old DBM file, $!\n";
untie %newhash || die"$0: Error closing new DBM file, $!\n";
```

Given our earlier concerns, you may want to use a less memory-intensive process for copying the records. Here's the same example using **each** to extract the information before writing it into the new database:

```perl
use NDBM_File;
use GDBM_File;
use Fcntl;

die "Usage:$0 old new\n" if (@ARGV<2);

my($old,$new) = @ARGV;

tie (%oldhash, 'NDBM_File', $old, O_RDONLY, 0444)
    || die "$0: Error opening source $old: $!\n";
tie (%newhash, 'GDBM_File', $new, O_CREAT|O_RDWR|O_EXCL, 0666)
    || die "$0: Error opening dest $new: $!\n";

while(($key, $value) = each(%oldhash))
{
    $newhash{$key} = $value;
}

untie %oldhash || die "$0: Error closing old DBM file, $!\n";
untie %newhash || die "$0: Error closing new DBM file, $!\n";
```

Using AnyDBM_File

If you are not worried about the DBM implementation you are using, you can use the **AnyDBM_File** module to include a DBM implementation from those available. It selects a class from the implementations, choosing the first valid one from the following list: **NDBM_File**, **DB_File**, **GDBM_File**, **SDBM_File**, and **ODBM_File**. In the unlikely event that all of these modules are unavailable, the **use** statement will fail.

When using **AnyDBM_File**, you should be aware that the implementation selected may differ from the one you require if you are attempting to open an existing DBM database. If you do not know the format of the database you are trying to open, you will have to try and work it out. In general, any DBM file set ending in .dir or .pag will be an NDBM or ODBM database. If you know these are not supported on your system, then it's probably an SDBM database (except on Mac OS, where SDBM is not supported). If the DBM database is stored in a single file, the most likely implementation is GDBM, but it's possible that Berkeley DB is also supported.

GDBM Features

The **GDBM_File** implementation, if available on your system, provides some additional benefits over the standard DBM implementations. Although the GDBM library supports DBM/NDBM compatibility, you cannot use the **GDBM_File** module to open existing databases. If you need to do this and don't have DBM/NDBM, try the SDBM module that comes with Perl.

The biggest benefit with the GDBM implementation of the DBM database system is that there is no limit on the bucket size. This, theoretically, means you can store arbitrary pieces of data in a single key/value pair. The size of the GDBM files that are created is slightly larger than traditional files—about 24K for a "blank" database is about average. I've successfully used the GDBM system to store large data structures within a database file—even, in one case, the graphics used for a website.

```
use GDBM_File;
tie %db, 'GDBM_File', 'db', &GDBM_WRCREAT, 0640;
untie %db;
```

You can use the modes ordinarily supplied by the **Fcntl** module, or you can instead use a set of modes defined by **GDBM_File**, as listed in Table 13-3.

Mode	Description
GDBM_READER	Open for read-only.
GDBM_WRITER	Open for read/write.
GDBM_WRCREAT	Open for read/write, creating a new database if it does not already exist, using the permissions mode specified.
GDBM_NEWDB	Open for read/write, creating a new database even if one already exists, using the permissions mode specified.

Table 13-3. *GDBM-Specific Modes*

In addition, you can specify the **GDBM_FAST** mode when opening a file for read/write. This forces disk synchronization with the memory version of the hash only when the file is closed. This improves performance, but it may produce unpredictable results if the script exits ungracefully.

Berkeley DB Features

The Berkeley DB system is a more involved and enhanced version of the base DBM implementation. The module provides a number of different database formats, accessed and used by means of the same **tie** function. The modules are the standard key/value pair database supported by other DBM systems (**DB_HASH**); a B-Tree–based system, accessible via a hash (**DB_BTREE**); and a record-number system using arrays (**DB_RECNO**).

Standard Hash Database

A **DB_HASH** is identical in most respects to Perl's internal hash structure, only the key/value pairs are stored in data files, not memory. The functionality provided is basically identical to that provided by the other DBM-style database engines. **DB_File** uses its own hashing algorithm for storing and retrieving the key/value pairs, but you can supply your own system if you prefer.

```
use DB_File ;
[$X =] tie %hash,  'DB_File', $filename, $flags, $mode, $DB_HASH;
```

The value of **$flags** is identical to that of other databases and refers to the mode in which the file will be opened. The **$mode** is the octal mode with which the file should be created or accessible. The final item is actually a reference to a hash; I've used a predefined reference in the synopsis above. We'll return to the configuration options available via this hash shortly.

The **$DB_HASH** argument should be a **DB_File::HASHINFO** object. The object defines the default options that control how the database is configured, and you can change the options by simply updating the hash keys. The supported options are listed in Table 13-4.

Hash Key	Description
bsize	Defines the hash table bucket size. The default is 256 bytes, and you may want to increase this if you know you are storing information larger than this size. Remember that the size defined here will apply to all new entries created in the database. Arbitrarily increasing this may degrade performance and increase the storage space used by the database.
ffactor	Indicates the density of information. The value assigned becomes the number of keys that will accumulate within a single bucket allocation. The default is 8, and therefore a maximum of 8 key/value pairs of 32 bytes each could be stored in a single bucket. Reducing the value to 1 will increase the file size by the bucket size (defined in **bsize**) for each record. Specifying too large a value may decrease performance.
nelem	An estimation of the final size of the hash table (number of buckets or the number of elements divided by **ffactor**). If you know the number of elements you are going to store, you can use this to achieve a slight increase in performance. The value set is not restrictive; the database will automatically grow in size if you set a value that is too low. The default value is 1.
cachesize	The maximum size in bytes of physical memory to allocate as a buffer between the in-memory database and the physical file store. Specifying a large value will increase performance, since more of the database will be kept in memory. However, it may also cause a synchronization error if there is a crash or other problem, since there may still be data in the cache that has not been written to a file. A value of 0 lets the system choose a reasonable value for you.
Hash	A reference to a user-defined function that returns a 32-bit quantity suitable for ordering and referencing a hash.

Table 13-4. *Customizable Elements for **DB_HASH** Databases*

Hash Key	Description
Lorder	The byte order to be used for storing integers within the metadata in the file. The number specified should represent the order as an integer (that is, 4321 is big endian, and 1234 is little endian). If a value of 0 (the default) is specified, the current host order is used instead. If the file you are using already exists, the format used within that file is always used. This can help with compatibility across platforms if you are sharing a database file on multiple systems that support different byte orders.

Table 13-4.   *Customizable Elements for **DB_HASH** Databases* (continued)

For example, to create a database with a bucket size of 1,024 bytes:

```
$options = new DB_File::HASHINFO;
$options->{'bsize'} = 1024;
tie %db, 'DB_File', "file.db", O_RDWR, 0644, $options;
```

The **hash** element should point to a function that you want to use for creating a hash value.

B-Tree Hash Database

The B-Tree hash is architecturally identical to the standard hashing system used on most other DBM systems. The difference is that the keys are stored in an ordered format using a binary tree. This allows you to use a hash database in an ordered form without having to resort to the use of **sort** to order the data before it is used.

```
use DB_File ;
tie %hash,  'DB_File', $filename, $flags, $mode, $DB_BTREE;
```

As before, the **$flags** and **$mode** are identical to other DBM databases. The **$DB_BTREE** argument is another object with a set of base properties that you can modify according to the options listed in Table 13-5.

Hash Key	Description
Flags	A value that should be composed of values **or**'d together. Two values are currently available: **R_DUP** and **R_NOOVERWRITE**. The value **R_DUP** allows duplicate keys to be entered into the database. The **R_NOOVERWRITE** prevents you from overwriting existing keys. You cannot specify the two flags together, since they effectively cancel each other out.
Cachesize	The maximum size in bytes of physical memory to allocate as a buffer between the in-memory database and the physical file store. Specifying a large value will increase performance, since more of the database will be kept in memory. However, it may also cause a synchronization error if there is a crash or other problem, since there may still be data in the cache that has not been written to a file. A value of 0 lets the system choose a reasonable value for you.
maxkeypage	The maximum number of keys that will be stored in a single page. This currently has no effect on the process within Perl.
minkeypage	The minimum number of keys that will be stored in a single page. This value defines which keys will be stored on overflow rather than main pages. The default value is 2, and this value will be selected if you try to define a value of 0.
psize	The size, in bytes, of the pages used to store nodes of the B-Tree structure. The minimum page size is 512 bytes and the maximum is 65,535 (64K). Ideally, you should choose a size that matches your data and the **minkeypage** value, or a value that matches the underlying size of your operating system allocation blocks.

Table 13-5. *Options for **DB_BTREE** Databases*

Hash Key	Description
compare	A reference to a function that operates the comparison between keys that will be used when storing the information. (See the discussion of the comparison function in this section for more information.) If none is specified, or if the **undef** value is used, then a default function that uses lexical comparisons is used instead. This function is basically alphanumeric, with shorter keys considered as being less than longer keys.
prefix	A reference to a function that returns the number of bytes necessary to determine whether the second key supplied is greater than the first key. The basic point behind the function is to optimize the size of the search tree used to find key/value pairs. For lexical comparisons, the built-in function should suffice. See the discussion of the **prefix** option in this section for more information.
lorder	The byte order to be used for storing integers within the metadata in the file. The number specified should represent the order as an integer (that is, 4321 is big endian, and 1234 is little endian). If a value of 0 (the default) is specified, the current host order is used instead. If the file you are using already exists, the format used within that file is always used. This can help with compatibility across platforms if you are sharing a database file on multiple systems that support different byte orders.

Table 13-5.   *Options for **DB_BTREE** Databases* (continued)

The method for defining these flags is identical to the system for standard hash databases:

```
$options = new DB_File::BTREEINFO;
$options->{'cache'} = 16384;
tie %db, 'DB_File', "file.db", O_RDWR, 0644, $options;
```

PROGRAMMING
WITH PERL

The comparison function (defined through the **compare** option) should accept and compare two keys, returning a numerical value depending on how key1 compares to key2. The function should return 0 if the two keys are equal, –1 if key1 is less than key2, and 1 if key1 is greater than key2. For example, to use the default Perl string comparisons, you might use the following functions:

```
sub compare
{
    my ($key1, $key2) = @_;
    return 0  if ("\L$key1" eq "\L$key2");
    return -1 if ("\L$key1" lt "\L$key2");
    return 1  if ("\L$key1" gt "\L$key2");
}
```

More simply, you could just use the **cmp** operator:

```
sub compare
{
    my ($key1, $key2) = @_;
    "\L$key1" cmp "\L$key2";
}
```

Note in both examples that you convert the keys to lowercase to ensure that the comparison works in proper alpha order rather than the normal ASCII order that would be implied otherwise.

The **prefix** option allows you to specify the number of bytes that should be used when making comparisons between keys. The value should simply return the number of bytes used to make the comparison. This works with the comparison function to decide at what size a specific key is given priority over another key in the sorting process.

Record Number Database

The **DB_RECNO** option enables you to store fixed-length or variable-length records within a database file. The format used is basically text based. If you want to open and use a comma-separated file (CSV), you can use the **DB_RECNO** system to open and then use the database. Alternatively, you can make use of the fixed-length approach we looked at, at the start of this chapter.

Unlike the other Berkeley DB databases, the record number database is tied to a standard array rather than a hash, and individual records are accessed by their record number using the standard index you would use with any normal hash:

```
use DB_File ;
tie @array, 'DB_File', $filename, $flags, $mode, $DB_RECNO ;
```

The options for the **$DB_RECNO** object are listed in Table 13-6.

Hash Element	Description
flags	This is a value based on **or**'d predefined flags, and three values are currently defined: **R_FIXEDLEN**, **R_NOKEY**, and **R_SNAPSHOT**. The **R_FIXEDLEN** flag signifies that the records are of fixed length rather than being byte delimited. Use the **reclen** option to specify the length of the record and **bval** to specify the character to be used for padding the record to the specified size. Records are automatically padded if you supply a record with a length less than that specified. The **R_NOKEY** flag forces the routines and methods that are used to access the database not to include the key information. This allows you to access records that are at the end of the database without having to read the intervening records. The **R_SNAPSHOT** flag specifies that a snapshot of the file's contents be taken when the file is opened.
cachesize	The maximum size, in bytes, of physical memory to allocate as a buffer between the in-memory database and the physical file store. Specifying a large value will increase performance, since more of the database will be kept in memory. However, it may also cause a synchronization error if there is a crash or other problem, since there may still be data in the cache that has not been written to a file. A value of 0 lets the system choose a reasonable value for you.

Table 13-6. *Options for **DB_RECNO** Databases*

Hash Element	Description
psize	Records from a **DB_RECNO** database are stored in memory in a B-Tree format. The **psize** specifies the number of pages to be used for the nodes of the B-Tree structure.
lorder	The byte order to be used for storing integers within the metadata in the file. The number specified should represent the order as an integer (that is, 4321 is big endian, and 1234 is little endian). If a value of 0 (the default) is specified, the current host order is used instead. If the file you are using already exists, the format used within that file is always used. This can help with compatibility across platforms if you are sharing a database file on multiple systems that support different byte orders.
reclen	The length, in bytes, of a fixed-length record.
bval	The value of the character to be used to mark the end of a record in a variable-length database, and the character to use for padding in a fixed-length database. If no value is specified, then a newline is used to specify the end of a record in a variable-length database, and spaces are used to pad fixed-length records.
bfname	The name of the B-Tree file to be used for the B-Tree structure of the in-memory record-number database. If none is specified, the hash is stored entirely in memory.

Table 13-6.   *Options for **DB_RECNO** Databases* (continued)

For example, to set the record length in a fixed-length database:

```
$options = new DB_File::BRECNOINFO;
$options->{'reclen'} = 1024;
tie @db, 'DB_File', "file.db", O_RDWR, 0644, $options;
```

If you want, you can use the array as a stack. Versions of Perl newer than 5.004_57 can use the normal **pop**, **push**, **shift**, and **unshift** functions directly with the tied array.

Older versions will need to use the object methods for the object reference returned when the database is first opened, for example:

```
$DBX = tie @db, 'DB_File', "file.db", O_RDWR, 0644, $DB_RECNO;
```

You can then use the methods shown in Table 13-7 to push, pop, shift, and unshift information from the stack.

In-Memory Databases

You can use the features of the Berkeley DB databases for in-memory databases. This can be useful if you want to use a hash with information stored in an ordered format (as with **DB_BTREE**) but don't want to create a file in the process. To do this, you specify the **undef** value as the name of the database file. For example

```
tie %db, 'DB_File', undef, O_CREAT|O_RDWR, 0666, $DB_BTREE;
```

or, for the standard hash:

```
tie %db, 'DB_File', undef, O_CREAT|O_RDWR, 0666, $DB_HASH;
```

If you want to use an in-memory standard hash, the preceding line can be shortened to

```
tie %db, 'DB_File';
```

Method	Description
$DBX->push(list)	Pushes the elements of **list** onto the end of the tied array
$DBX->pop	Pops the last element of the array
$DBX->shift	Removes and returns the first element of the array
$DBX->unshift(list)	Pushes the elements of **list** onto the start of the tied array
$DBX->length	Returns the number of elements in the array

Table 13-7.   *Object Methods for **DB_RECNO** Databases*

Storing Complex Data in a DBM Database

The simplest model for storing information in a DBM database is identical to the model used for a Perl hash. You have a unique key of information and use that key to refer to a single piece of data. However, this is a fairly flat model if you want to store complex pieces of information in a structured format. Instead, you can use the key/value pairs to store the more traditional records used in a database system.

By using a formatted key or value, you can store the information for individual fields within a DBM file. The entire record can be stored either in multiple keys or within a single key with a structure value. For example, imagine the simple record structure below:

```
Firstname, 10 characters
Lastname, 10 characters
Email, 40 characters
```

You could use a formatted key value of the form **field-id**, such that a single record could be entered into the database as

```
$db{'firstname-1'} = 'Martin';
$db{'lastname-1'} = 'Brown';
$db{'email-1'} = 'mc@mcwords.com';
```

The first name of the next person in the table would be stored in the key **firstname-2**, the last name in **lastname-2**, and so on. Although this seems like a practical method, it is a relatively complex system to implement, and it is wasteful of database keys, which will need to be processed individually.

An alternative solution is to use one of the methods described earlier for text-based databases. By using delimiters or fixed-length records, an entire record can be stored within a single key/value pair. Using delimiters, the preceding information could be written into the database and then recovered from it using the following Perl code:

```
use Fcntl;
use GDBM_File;

tie %db, 'GDBM_File', 'Test_GDBM', O_CREAT|O_RDWR, 0644
     || die "Can't open DB File, $!";;

$db{'1'} = join(',',qw/Brown Martin mc@mcwords.com/);
$db{'2'} = join(',',qw/Foo Bar foo@foobar.com/);
$db{'3'} = join(',',qw/Bar Foo bar@barfoo.com/);
```

```
foreach $id (sort keys %db)
{
    ($lastname, $firstname, $email) = split(/,/,$db{$id});
    print "$id: lastname: $lastname\n";
    print "$id: firstname: $firstname\n";
    print "$id: email: $email\n";
}

untie %db || die "Can't close DB File, $!";
```

In this example, the database is populated using a simple numeric key, with the data added via a **join** using a comma as the delimiter. To print the information you've just stored, you work through the database and, using **split**, place each field's data into individual variables, which you then print.

As you know, however, delimited text requires very careful selection of the delimiter to ensure that the information is stored correctly. Here is the same result using **pack** and fixed-length records, which gets around this problem.

```
use Fcntl;
use GDBM_File;

tie %db, 'GDBM_File', 'Test_GDBM', O_CREAT|O_RDWR, 0644
    || die "Can't open DB File, $!";

$db{'email-pstr'}   = 'a10a10a30';
$db{'email-fields'} = join(',', qw/Lastname Firstname Email/);

$db{'email-1'} = pack($db{'email-pstr'},qw/Brown Martin mc@mcwords.com/);
$db{'email-2'} = pack($db{'email-pstr'},qw/Foo Bar foo@foobar.com/);
$db{'email-3'} = pack($db{'email-pstr'},qw/Bar Foo bar@barfoo.com/);

@fieldnames = split(/,/,$db{'email-fields'});

foreach $id (sort grep(/^email-[0-9]+/,keys %db))
{
    @fields = unpack($db{'email-pstr'},$db{$id});
    for($i=0;$i<@fields;$i++)
    {
        $id =~ s/email\-//;
        print "$id: $fieldnames[$i]: $fields[$i]\n";
    }
```

```
}

untie %db || die "Can't close DB File, $!"
```

Note in this example that you also manage to keep track of the field names and sizes by recording this information into keys within the database. This makes the format of the database and its contents completely database defined. Also note that I've used a prefix in the base keys. Although it's relatively useless here, it can be useful if you want to store multiple tables within a single database file. Each table has its own name and, in turn, its own **pack** string, field list, and sequence.

There is still a problem with this particular solution. It is even more wasteful of space than a flat text file using fixed-length records. This is because of the internal storage method used for DBM databases and the problems associated with fixed-length records. In this example, every record will take up at least 60 bytes. A more complex record structure will take up significantly more.

Of course, Perl allows you to do more than just use simple key/value pairs. In Chapter 10 we looked at the complex data structures you can create to model information using nested Perl variables, such as hashes of hashes and arrays of hashes. Unfortunately, you cannot use normal DBM implementations to create nested hashes of hashes and hashes of arrays. If we return to our first solution, we can expand it by using a hash of hashes to store the data in a more structured format:

```
use Fcntl;

use GDBM_File;

tie %db, 'GDBM_File', 'Test_GDBM', O_CREAT|O_RDWR, 0644;
     || die "Can't open DB File, $!";

$db{1} = 'Record';
$db{1}{lastname} = 'Brown';
$db{1}{firstname} = 'Martin';
$db{1}{email} = 'mc@mcwords.com';

$db{2}{lastname} = 'Foo';
$db{2}{firstname} = 'Bar';
$db{2}{email} = 'foo@foobar.com';

$db{3}{lastname} = 'Bar';
$db{3}{firstname} = 'Foo';
$db{3}{email} = 'bar@barfoo.com';
```

```
foreach (sort keys %db)
{
    foreach $field (sort keys %{$db{$_}})
    {
        print "$_: $field: $db{$_}{$field}\n";
    }
}


untie %db || die "Can't close DB File, $!"
```

However, the **MLDBM** module by Gurusamy Sarathay (available from CPAN) uses existing DBM modules and the **Data::Dumper** module to convert such complex references into a simple format that can be stored within an ordinary hash file. It implements the same basic idea, using the **tie** function to associate a hash with a hash file—the **MLDBM** object handles all of the complexity for you:

```
use GDBM_File;
use MLDBM qw(GDBM_File);
use Fcntl;
tie (%db, 'MLDBM', 'Test_MLDBM', O_CREAT|O_RDWR, 0644) || die $!;
```

This overcomes all the previous problems. The data is stored in a structured format, which can be accessed simply using standard hash techniques. Furthermore, the storage space used for this system is significantly lower than the fixed-length database example shown earlier. The storage space is still slightly higher than the delimited system, due to the use of a secondary level key, but it overcomes the problem of choosing a suitable delimiter.

Relational Databases with DBM

The *relational* element of a relational database that most people think of is actually the automatic lookup of information. When you report from a database that is composed of many tables, you can choose to print out the "merged" information from all of the linked tables in order to produce the desired set of results. The clever bit is the linking between the individual tables, and this is something that is actually possible to do manually using any database system—text, DBM, or otherwise. With DBM, you have the advantage over text databases of convenient random access, which is the only practical way of achieving a "flat" relational system.

You can model relational data in any database system. The only requirement for using it is that you are able to access all of the tables simultaneously. The actual method of linking between the tables can be done automatically or manually. With the

tie interface, you can have as many physical DBM databases open at any one time as you like (operating system limits permitting). Through the use of the principles you saw in the previous section, there is no reason why you couldn't actually model the information in a single database with structured key/value pairs.

The most critical part of the development of a relational system is the modeling of the data. Once you have decided on the format of the information and how it is going to be linked, you also need to consider how the links will work. Let's look briefly at a relational system for storing multiple contact information for multiple people using a DBM database.

The first table is the list of contact names—this will be the lynchpin for our database because it contains our contact names. The contact table has three fields—first name, last name, and a list of record numbers for the second table, the numbers table. The numbers table has two fields—the number type and the number itself. "Number" can mean pager, phone, fax, or mobile number, email address, and so on.

The first table might be populated like this:

```
$db{'contact-1'} = "Martin;Brown;1,3,4";
$db{'contact-2'} = "Bob;Smith;2,5";
```

The key is made up of the table name and a unique ID within that table. The information is stored using delimited text fields in the value portion of the key/value pair. Note that semicolons separate the individual fields, but commas separate the link data in the third field.

The numbers table could be populated with the following information:

```
$db{'numbers-1'} = "Email;mc@mcwords.com";
$db{'numbers-2'} = "Email;bsmith@foobar.com";
$db{'numbers-3'} = "Fax;01234 456789";
$db{'numbers-4'} = "Phone;09876 543210";
$db{'numbers-5'} = "Mobile;0789 123456";
```

To access the complete contact information for Martin Brown, you need to access record number one of the contact table and then access the related information listed in field three of that record. In this case, this is records 1, 3, and 4 from the numbers table. To dump the information from the database in a formatted formation, you might use a script like this:

```
use Fcntl;
use GDBM_File;
```

```
tie %db, 'GDBM_File', 'Test_Rel', O_CREAT|O_RDWR, 0644
    || die "Can't open DB File, $!";;

foreach $id (sort grep(/^contact-[0-9]+/,keys %db))
{
    ($lastname, $firstname, $relations) = split(/;/,$db{$id});
    print "$firstname $lastname\n";
    foreach $subid (sort split(/,/,$relations))
    {
        ($type,$num) = $db{"numbers-$subid"}
            if (exists($db{"numbers-$subid"}));
        print "    $type: $num\n";
    }
}

untie %db || die "Can't close DB File, $!";
```

The method is basically very similar to the tricks you saw in the previous section for modeling complex data structures within a DBM database. When run on the database above, it produces the following results:

```
Brown Martin
    Email: mc@mcwords.com
    Fax: 01234 456789
    Phone: 09876 543210
Smith Bob
    Email: bsmith@foobar.com
    Mobile: 0789 123456
```

If you want to use some of the earlier techniques for including information in the database about the database, you can even begin to drive the links using formatted structures. I've developed a simple relational database system, originally designed for complex contact management, using this type of relational system. It needed to be ultimately portable to a variety of platforms, and the client wanted to keep away from proprietary database systems.

Database File Locking

Without at least some form of file locking, it will be possible for two processes, Perl-based or otherwise, to access and update the database file at the same time. When reading from the database, this is not an issue; there is no reason (normally) to lock people out from the database if all they want to do is look up a value. When updating, however, the end results could be disastrous. With more than one person updating different lines, sections, and key/value pairs in the different database types, you could end up with, at best, a corrupt database and, at worst, one that is completely unreadable.

The best solution is to use the Perl **flock** function, which uses the best of the underlying locking mechanisms (**flock**, **lockf**, or **fcntl**). You may also want to consider using a separate file to indicate the lock condition. See the example in Chapter 7 for information on using and checking the file locks with the **flock** function.

You will need to take care about how you implement the locking mechanism. With a text-file database, you can use **flock** directly on the filehandle you use to access the database. With DBM databases, the system is more complex, since the actual file is hidden from you via the **tie** object interface. For the **ODBM_File**, **NDBM_File**, and **SDBM_File**, this will mean checking and imposing locks on both files used to store the DBM data. For **GDBM_File**, you only need to check the locks on one file.

For **DB_File**, you can use a method applied to a **DB_File** object in order to discover the file descriptor, and then use the duplication notation with the **open** function to assign it to a filehandle that can be used with **flock**. For example:

```
use Fcntl qm/:flock:/;
use DB_File;

$dbobj = (tie(%db, 'DB_File', 'dbfile.db', O_RDWR, 0644)
        || die "Can't tie database to hash, $!";

$fileno = $dbobj->fd;
open(DBHANDLE, "+<&=$fileno") || die "Can't open FH, $!";
unless (flock(DBHANDLE, LOCK_EX|LOCK_NB)) { die "Can't lock: $!" }
...
# Update the database
...
flock(DBHANDLE, LOCK_UN);
close(DBHANDLE);
untie %db;
```

This only sets and releases a lock for update. You'll also need to include the necessary tests to ensure that the file is not already locked.

Using the DBI and Win32::ODBC Toolkits

Although text and DBM databases have their place, as the quantity of information starts to grow, even the best organized DBM systems start to degrade in speed and become more difficult to manage and update. Professional, and often commercial, databases have been part of the computing world almost from the start, and using them has a number of advantages over designing your own DBM system. The advantages of a relational database management system (RDBMS) include

- Faster access—because an RDBMS is written in C, and often highly optimized in its routines and storage and indexing methods, it will be much faster than a typical DBM file for databases with large (>5,000) records.

- Easier management—with a DBM or flat-file database, you have a lot of management overhead controlling what you delete, how it's deleted, and the general housekeeping of the files themselves. An RDBMS does it for you.

- Easier access—most, if not all, RDBMSs use SQL to create, modify, and access information, and this makes the entire process much easier as all you have to worry about is writing a suitable query; the RDBMS will do all the actual work.

There are a number of ways to access RDBMS systems from within Perl. Some have their own interfaces and modules, while others have had a number of modules written specifically to access their contents. However, a much better solution is to use either the DBI toolkit, which is available under Unix and Windows, or the **Win32::ODBC** toolkit under Windows. Which you choose will largely depend on the database you are connecting to, your current platform, and how portable and compatible you want your scripts to be with different database systems.

DBI

The DBI toolkit, developed for the most part by Tim Bunce, is a suite of objects and methods that allow you to connect and execute queries to a database. What actually happens is that the **DBI** module talks to a **DBD** (database driver) module, which is usually a C/C++ API to the actual database engine. At all times, you actually communicate with the **DBI** module, so the underlying database becomes a relative non-issue.

This ability to separate the methods for executing queries—and getting back information—from the specifics of talking to the different databases has a number of advantages, and first and foremost is the ease of use and programming. Because there are a fixed number of methods for accessing the database, you will always know how to send a query, check for errors during execution, and get any information back. You don't have to worry about the specifics of the database you are using.

More importantly, though, you can develop a database-driven application that uses one database on your system, but that could be used with just about any database supported by the DBI kit. Since the currently supported database list includes DB2, Informix, Ingres, JDBC, ODBC, Oracle, PostGreSQL, Sybase, Unify, Xbase, mSQL/mySQL, and even flat CSV files, you're not going to be short of a suitable database either for development or production purposes.

Win32::ODBC

The **Win32::ODBC** module comes as part of the standard ActivePerl distribution, and like DBI, it supports a generic interface for accessing databases, providing those databases are accessible through the ODBC system. ODBC, open database connectivity, is a standard now followed by all the major database players, including IBM, Oracle, and Microsoft. Both DBI and ODBC work in essentially the same manner, supporting a single API to the database. The difference is in where the interface sits within the connectivity model.

Under DBI, the **DBI** module talks to a DBD driver that in turn communicates with the database. We're therefore using the RDBMS libraries to access the database; we're just doing it through DBI. ODBC, however, is an API that sits within the RDBMS; we just use a library to talk using ODBC protocols to the ODBC driver supplied by the database vendor.

When communicating with a database over a network, the DBD and the database API that supports it must have network connectivity. The ODBC, on the other hand, includes a network communication layer, so I can talk to an ODBC-compliant database over a network through the ODBC system, whether that data source supports network connectivity or not.

With DBI, I can talk to any database that has had a DBD written for it and to any networked database that has network ability; with ODBC, I can communicate with any ODBC-compliant database over a network.

Under Windows, ODBC connectivity is a standard part of the operating system—if I install an ODBC-capable application, then a driver is installed and I can access that data source from any ODBC client. For example, if I install Microsoft Office, ODBC interfaces are installed for CSV, Excel spreadsheets, and Access databases. Now from within Excel, I can run queries on flat files, excel spreadsheets, or Access databases. I can do the same from Perl too. If I were using DBI, I'd need a DBD to access those sources. In reality, DBI supports CSV databases, and an ODBC DBD exists to communicate with any ODBC-compliant source.

The other point at which the two differ is in the extended support. The DBI toolkit explicitly works on a relatively basic level, providing the necessary interface for communicating with the database and executing queries. The **Win32::ODBC** toolkit is a complete API to the ODBC system, including the ability to control the operation and default data handling of a suitable database. This level of ODBC support is likely to be incorporated into DBI in due course, but for now, if you want to exercise a significant level of control over a Windows RDBMS, especially SQL Server, you'd be better off with **Win32::ODBC**.

Database Mechanics and Compatibility

The basic operation of both databases is more or less identical. A relatively simple process of getting information from the database can be summarized on both systems like this:

1. Open a database connection.
2. Submit a query.
3. Start a loop to retrieve each row.
4. Extract each record.
5. Close the database connection.

Whichever database and interface you decide to use, the query method is the same—you use SQL statements to create tables, add or modify data, and to get it back. Although there are minor differences in the exact SQL implementation (as with all standards) the same statements should return the same information. If you are not familiar with SQL, then see the "SQL Refresher" section later in this chapter.

If you are developing a script that may use a number of different databases, then here are some tips for making the process of moving from one driver to another a bit easier:

■ Check that the return value from a DBD module matches what you expect. The DBI module doesn't normalize all the error codes and values from all database drivers, so check the documentation specific to the DBD module.

■ Write SQL queries as tightly as possible so as to remove ambiguity and reduce the return dataset to only what you need. Also, don't rely too much on engine-specific SQL components, especially data types. Some engines support 20 to 30 different types for different pieces of information. In reality, you could probably get away with the types listed in the *SQL Refresher* section later in the chapter.

■ Don't rely on engine-specific features. Transactions are not supported by all engines, and other features like outer joins, triggers, and persistent sequences are not always available.

■ Avoid making assumptions about what is available. Ensure that your script knows which database interface it's using.

The easiest way to get around the issues raised in the previous tips is to write an extra level of interface between your application and the **DBI** module. From that interface you can make decisions about which tools and tricks to use, according to the database driver. For example, you could create a function called **add** that sits between your script and the DBI interface. If your database supports transactions, **add** would use them, but for databases that do not support transactions, the function would just supply the SQL statement without using transactions.

Connecting to a Database

The act of connecting to a database associates an object with a connection to the database itself, and it's this object through which you communicate with the database.

DBI

Under DBI, you only import the **DBI** module, not the DBD that you want to use to connect to the database, and then you create a DBI object using the **connect** method:

```
use DBI;
my $dbh = DBI->connect(DSN);
```

The DSN, or Data Source Name, defines the DBD driver, and therefore the RDBMS that you want to communicate with. For example, to connect to a mySQL database called **tv**:

```
use DBI;
my $dbh = DBI->connect("DBI:mysql:tv");
```

To connect to a database with the same name using PostGreSQL:

```
use DBI;
my $dbh = DBI->connect("dbi:Pg:dbname=mctv","","");
```

Note here the inclusion of two null arguments after the DSN—under most DBDs, this is the user name and password required to connect to the database.

The object will be undefined if an error occurs.

Win32::ODBC

When using the **Win32::ODBC** module, the process is slightly more complex. You can use the same basic method—import the module and then create a new object using a specific DSN:

```
Use Win32::ODBC;
$database = new Win32::ODBC("DSN" [, CONNECT_OPTION, ...]);
```

The difference is in the DSN specification. It can be either the name of a predefined DSN, created through the ODBC Data Sources control panel, or you can specify the name of the database driver and database within the DSN. The optional **CONNECT_OPTION** arguments set additional options to be enabled when connecting to the database. The available options are ODBC-driver specific, so check the database driver for more information.

To connect to a predefined DSN, just specify the DSN name, in quotes; for example, to connect to our Acronym DSN, you would use the following line:

```
$db = new Win32::ODBC("Acronym");
```

The string form of the DSN allows you to specify additional information when connecting to a DSN. The options are supplied as a list of **keyword=value** pairs, each pair separated by a semicolon. See Table 13-8 for details of the keywords you can use.

Keyword	Value
DSN	The name of an existing, preconfigured DSN.
FILEDSN	The path to a DSN file, which contains the list of configured options to allow you to connect to an ODBC database. A DSN file must have the extension .dsn.
DRIVER	The name of the driver to use for opening this connection. You can get a list of drivers by calling the **Win32::ODBC::Drivers()** function.
UID	The user ID to use to connect to the ODBC database.
PWD	The password to use to connect to the ODBC database.
SAVEFILE	The path to a file in which to save the DSN string information as a DSN file. This file can then be used with the **FILEDSN** option.

Table 13-8. *DSN String Keywords*

For example, to connect to an Access database that requires a login and password:

```
$db = new Win32::ODBC("DSN=Acronym;UID=MC;PWD=Hello");
```

The new object will be undefined if the connection to the database fails. To trap errors, enclose the call in an **if** statement or check the value of the new object after you try to connect.

Executing Simple Queries

Simple queries include the single statement operations that do not return information. For example, the creation of a table, index, or even adding a row of information or updating it are simple queries that return nothing more than their success (or otherwise) to the caller.

DBI

Under DBI, the **do** method will execute a query for you:

```
$dbh->do("create table names (first char(20), second char(20))");
```

Because the query will only return a success or failure, all we need to do is actually check the return value of the whole operation to determine whether it succeeded. The same method can be used for any statement. For example:

```
$dbh->do("insert into names values('Fred','Flintstone')");
$dbh->do("create index names on names (first,second)");
$dbh->do("delete from names where first = 'Fred'");
```

For more **SELECT** statements, you'll need to use the extended query methods.

Win32::ODBC

The **Sql** method handles simple queries under **Win32::ODBC**:

```
$sql->Sql("create table names (first char(20), second char(20))");
```

Again, the return value from the whole operation indicates the success (or otherwise) of the operation.

Executing Extended Queries

When you are performing a **SELECT** or similar query on a database and expect more than just a success/failure return value, then you need to use more advanced methods to get the information back, usually on a row-by-row basis.

DBI

The DBI toolkit provides a number of methods and method sequences for pulling information from the database. You start by defining the query that you want to run on the database and prepare a select table handler; this is a new object, which will be used to access the individual rows returned by the **SELECT** statement. You then execute the statement—this actually sends the query to the database engine. For example:

```
my ($sth) = $dbh->prepare("select * from tv where title LIKE " .
                          $dbh->quote("$title%") .
                          " order by date,time,channel");

    $sth->execute();
```

To access the information, you call one of the **fetch** functions in a **while** or other loop to extract each row of information from the query. For example:

```
while(my $row = $sth->fetchrow_hashref())
```

The **fetchrow_hashref** method is probably the most practical, as it returns the row in the form of a hash reference, with each key being the name of a returned column, and the corresponding value being the value of the field. For example, to extract the date and time:

```
$date = $row->{date};
$time = $row->{time};
```

Other methods include **fetchrow_array**, which returns an array of fields in the order they were specified in the **select** statement, and **fetchrow_arrayref**, which returns a reference to an array on the same basis.

Once you've read all of the rows, you must call **finish** on the select object (**$sth** in the examples above) to complete the sequence.

Win32::ODBC

The **Win32::ODBC** module supports the same basic sequence, although you don't have to explicitly create a handler to operate the query and extraction process:

```
$db->Sql("SELECT Acronym,Expansion from Acronyms");
while($db->FetchRow())
{
    ($acronym,$expansion) = $db->Data();
    print "$acronym: $expansion\n";
}
```

The **FetchRow** method gets a single row as returned by the query—it's the **Data** method that actually extracts and returns the information from the row. By default, it returns an array of the fields in the order they were specified in the **SELECT** statement. You can also extract individual fields by name:

```
$db->Sql("SELECT * from Acronyms");
while($db->FetchRow())
{
    ($expansion, $acronym) = $db->Data('Expansion', 'Acronym');
    print "$acronym: $expansion\n";
}
```

Or, you can return the information as a hash and then access the fields directly:

```
$db->Sql("SELECT * from Acronyms");
while($db->FetchRow())
{
    %row = $db->DataHash();
    print "$row{Acronym}: $row{Expansion}\n";
}
```

The result is the same in each case. Note, however, that you don't have to explicitly finish the process as you do with DBI.

Closing the Connection

Once you've finished using a database, you must formally close the connection from within **DBI** or **Win32::ODBC**. On some databases, including mySQL and PostGreSQL, failing to formally close the connection causes a rollback, undoing any insertions, updates, or deletions that you've conducted within that process.

Using the **DBI** module, it's as simple as

```
$dbh->disconnect();
```

and under **Win32::ODBC**, you use the **Close** method:

```
$sql->Close();
```

Identifying Errors

Both modules work on the same basic premise as the rest of Perl—a false return value from a function or method call indicates a failure, while a true value indicates success. However, to get an error message describing why the process failed, you must use a separate method defined by each module.

DBI

The **errstr** method returns the error string reported by the last statement—you should use it in combination with the result code from an operation to actually report an error. For example:

```
$result = $dbh->do($query);
print $dbh->errstr(),"\n" unless ($result);
```

Win32::ODBC

You can use the **Win32::ODBC::Error** function to get the extended error from the ODBC interface:

```
$db = new Win32::ODBC("Acronym");
if ($db)
{
    # Do some querying
}
else
{
    die "Couldn't connect to DB:" . Win32::ODBC::Error();
}
```

Doing More

Although this has been a fairly quick overview of what's possible, you should be able to do 95 percent of the tasks you need to using the information given in this chapter.

The important part of the equation when talking to a SQL database using either the **DBI** or **Win32::ODBC** module is not how to use the modules themselves—they are actually very simple, and really only support a conduit through which to execute SQL statements.

The real trick and advantages come from understanding, first, how to design the database effectively, and second, how to write SQL statements to create, update, and maintain information in the database. Good database design is beyond the scope of this book, and indeed, good DB design and implementation only comes from experience.

To try and plug at least some of the gap, I've included a SQL refresher course at the end of this chapter that covers most of the SQL statements you will need to use.

SQL Refresher

SQL has been around for many years—it was the standard query language supported by many of the early relational systems and was actually designed and developed by IBM. Other companies, perhaps now better known for their database systems, such as Oracle and Microsoft, have adopted SQL as their main query language. The SQL language is now further developed by a consortium of database developers, led primarily by IBM, Microsoft, and Oracle, the leading players in the database market.

The role of the consortium is to define the SQL language standard. Although some companies have their own extensions to the SQL language, the core operations of creating, updating, and querying tables remain the same across all the different database systems.

Actually, this isn't entirely true. There are some semantics of the language that are optional on some systems, and these can occasionally cause problems when migrating between different database systems. Often, the differences relate to how the databases have been developed over the years. As a classic example, examine these two **CREATE** statements:

```
CREATE table AUDIO (ID numeric (10,0) identity,
                    TITLE varchar (30) not null,
                    ARTIST varchar (30) not null)
```

and

```
CREATE table AUDIO (ID number,
                    TITLE varchar2(30),
                    ARTIST varchar2(30))
```

The two statements create the same table, AUDIO, with a numeric ID field, and two character fields for TITLE and ARTIST. The first is valid on Microsoft SQL Server 7, while the second version works on an Oracle8 database. The differences here are to do with the supported data types. We'll look at data types later in this chapter when we look at creating new tables. We'll also look at other places where there are possible differences as we work through the different basic statements.

Also note, in the examples given above, that certain words are in uppercase. Although SQL is not case sensitive, by convention certain words are typed in uppercase so that you can identify different portions of a SQL statement more quickly. Those that are normally specified in uppercase are leading statement keywords (**CREATE**, **INSERT**, **SELECT**) and any additional keywords for the statement (**WHERE**, **INTO**, **FROM**, etc.). All other elements, such as the file names, are specified in title case or lowercase.

SQL Statements

Although it's difficult to summarize all of the different operations available via SQL into a number of distinct statements, essentially there are four main SQL statements that can be executed on a SQL database. They are **SELECT**, **INSERT**, **UPDATE**, and **DELETE**. You might also want to use a fifth statement, **CREATE**, which creates new objects (tables, indexes) within a database file. We'll look at all five statements before moving on to the topic of executing these statements within Perl.

SELECT

When you want to extract information from the database, you use the **SELECT** statement. The **SELECT** statement retrieves a set of rows and columns from the database, returning a dataset. The basic format of the **SELECT** statement is

```
SELECT [ALL|DISTINCT] field [, field, ...]
FROM table
[WHERE condition]
ORDER BY field [ASC|DESC] [, field [ASC|DESC]]
```

The **field** is the name (or names) of the fields from the **table** that you want to select. Because the **SELECT** statement allows you to specify the individual fields from the table that you want to extract, you can avoid many of the problems normally associated with extracting data from a database. Instead of manually ignoring the fields you don't want to access, you can instead only select the fields you want. You can also specify an asterisk (*) as the **field** name, and this will select all fields within the table.

The optional **ALL** prefix tells the SQL engine to select all of the columns from the table matching the **condition**, and is equivalent to the asterisk specification just mentioned. The optional **DISTINCT** prefix forces the **SELECT** statement to only return a list of distinct (unique) rows from the database. This removes any duplicates from the table column, irrespective of their location in relation to each other. For example, if you wanted a list of all of the acronyms in our database, you could use the following code.

```
SELECT Acronym from Acronyms
```

However, the list returned contains a lot of duplicates:

```
AAMOF
AFAIC
AFAIK
...
RSN
RTFM
RTFM
RTFM
RTFM
RTFMA
...
```

To just get a list of the acronyms, without any duplicates, change the **SELECT** query to include the **DISTINCT** keyword:

```
SELECT DISTINCT Acronym from Acronyms
```

This now returns:

```
AAMOF
AFAIC
AFAIK
...
RSN
RTFM
RTFMA
...
```

The use of the **DISTINCT** keyword is especially useful in situations where you want to give a user a list of possible values, but don't want to use a separate table to hold the information. Instead, just use **DISTINCT** to reduce all of the values already in the table to a list of accepted values.

You can select fields from multiple tables by specifying the table and field names in the query, separated by a single period. For example, to extract the contact name and business from the contact and company tables:

```
SELECT contact.name, company.name FROM contact, company
WHERE contact.company = company.id
```

The **condition** is an expression that refines the selection of rows from the table. If the **WHERE** keyword is not specified, then all rows from the table are selected. Most of the syntax for conditions are identical to those you will find within Perl. See Table 13-9 for a list of valid conditional operators. Note that in all cases in the table, **A** is the name of a field from one of the selected tables, and **B** (or **C**) are either constants or further **SELECT** statements. For example, to select all of the addresses where the city is London, you might use the condition **city = "London"**.

Operator	Description
A = B	**A** is equal to **B**.
A > B	**A** is greater than **B**.
A >= B	**A** is greater than or equal to **B**.
A < B	**A** is less than **B**.
A <= B	**A** is less than or equal to **B**.
A <> B	**A** does not equal **B**.
A [NOT] BETWEEN B AND C	Value of **A** is (is NOT) between the range of values specified by **B** and **C**.
A [NOT] LIKE B	Value of **A** is (is NOT) like the value of **B**. The value of **B** should be a string specifying the string (and wildcard characters) to match against the contents of **A**.
EXISTS (B)	Returns true for every row returned by the subquery specified by **B**.
A IS [NOT] NULL	Value **A** is (is NOT) null (empty).
A [NOT] IN (B, C, ...)	Value **A** is (is NOT) in the list of values specified within the parentheses.
A <operator> {ALL I ANY} (B)	Value **A** is compared to all or any of the records returned by subquery **B**. If the **ALL** keyword is used, then all the returned rows must match the **operator** condition. If **ANY** is specified, then only one of the returned values must match.

Table 13-9. *Condition Operators for the **SELECT** Statement*

For example, to extract the acronym and expansion from out of the acronyms database, but only for acronyms that match "RTFM" we could use the query

```
SELECT Acronym,Expansion from Acronyms
WHERE Acronym = 'RTFM'
```

You can also combine multiple statements using the **AND** and **OR** keywords to perform logical comparisons with individual conditions:

```
SELECT Acronym, Expansion from Acronyms
WHERE Acronym = 'RTFM' AND Expansion = 'Read The Factual Manual'
```

You can also nest logical comparisons using parentheses to group comparisons and conditions together.

We can also get more complex and perform wildcard searches. Imagine you are looking for an acronym that contains the word "Fact"; you might use the following query:

```
SELECT Acronym,Expansion from Acronyms
WHERE Expansion LIKE '%Fact%'
```

The percent (%) character is a wildcard, and it matches zero or more characters, and any character. Think of it as shorthand for the ".*" you would normally use in a regular expression. Conversely, the underscore (_) matches any one character; thus, we can look for all three-letter abbreviations using this query:

```
SELECT Acronym from Acronyms WHERE Acronym LIKE '___'
```

If you want to include either of the two wildcard characters in your queries, you can escape the character with the familiar backslash:

```
SELECT Salespc from Sales WHERE Salespc LIKE '__\%'
```

Not all SQL engines support the escaping of the wildcard characters. You can work out whether the ODBC driver supports escaping and what character to use by using the following script:

```
use Win32::ODBC;
```

```
$db = new Win32::ODBC("Acronym");

if ($db->GetInfo($db->SQL_LIKE_ESCAPE_CLAUSE()) eq 'Y')
{
    print "ODBC Driver supports wildcard escapes\n";
    $char = $db->GetInfo($db->SQL_SEARCH_PATTERN_ESCAPE());
    print "Escape Character is: $char\n";
}
```

SQL accepts single quotes as delimiters to text strings. The single quotes tell SQL to treat anything between them as text, rather than as a keyword. For most queries within Perl, it's best to use the double quotes to specify the query, so that you can use single quotes within the string:

```
$db->Sql("SELECT Acronym from Acronyms WHERE Acronym LIKE '___'");
```

However, be careful when using the single quote in text strings where the quote has its normal apostrophe meaning. The following query would raise an error:

```
SELECT Acronym, Expansion from Acronyms WHERE Expansion LIKE '%I'm%'
```

The error would be raised, even if you embedded the query in a string within Perl, since you are still including three single quotes in the query you are supplying the SQL engine. The trick is to use the escape character for SQL. Confusingly, the escape character for most SQL interfaces is the single quote, so you would rewrite the above query as follows:

```
SELECT Acronym, Expansion from Acronyms WHERE Expansion LIKE '%I''m%'
```

Since you can't always control the query strings that you are supplying to the SQL engine, you should probably create a simple function to replace single quotes in query strings to double quotes:

```
sub SqlEscape($)
{
    $_[0] =~ s/'/''/g;
}
```

Now you can use the function inline to the queries you supply to the database:

```
$db->Sql("SELECT Acronym, Expansion from Acronyms " .
         "WHERE Expansion LIKE " . SqlEscape("%I'm%"));
```

When using the DBI toolkit, the **quote** method of the database connection object will do this for you:

```
$dbh->do("SELECT Acronym, Expansion from Acronyms " .
         "WHERE Expansion LIKE " . $dbh->quote("%I'm%"));
```

The last thing to be aware of is that double quotes can be used to quote identifiers. For example, imagine you have created a table called "Audio Tapes". If you tried to select data from this table using the following query, an error would be raised:

```
SELECT * FROM Audio Tapes
```

Instead, you need to quote the table name by using quoted identifiers. SQL accepts the double quote as a delimiter for quoted identifiers:

```
SELECT * FROM "Audio Tapes"
```

Within a Perl statement, you'll need to escape the double quotes by using the backslash character:

```
$db->Sql("SELECT * FROM \"Audio Tapes\"");
```

The final part of the **SELECT** statement is the **ORDER BY** clause. This allows you to specify the order in which information will be returned, according to the normal sorting orders. You can order the entire dataset by one or more fields within the tables you have selected. The default operation is to sort in ascending order (lowest to highest number, and A–Z) or you can explicitly request ascending order by using the **ASC** keyword. You can also sort in descending order by using the **DESC** keyword. For example, to sort our acronyms, we might use:

```
SELECT Acronym, Expansion FROM Acronyms ORDER BY Acronym
```

Joins   Joins are a critical part of the relational process. A join is where you create a logical connection between two columns in two different tables. For example, in an order processing system, you might have two tables. One contains the list of orders, the other contains a list of order lines. A join between the two would enable you to obtain all of the information from a single order.

You specify a logical join using the **WHERE** clause to the **SELECT** statement, specifying an expression that links the two tables together. For example:

```
SELECT Order.Order_ID, Item.Order_ID, Item.Item_ID, Item.PLU,
Order.Total FROM Order, Item
WHERE Order.Order_ID = Item.Order_ID
```

The join can be to another table, or to the same table in the case of nested information, such as staff and their supervisors. There are other types of joins, such as inner and outer joins, and left, right, and full outer joins. For more information on the different types of joins and the results they produce, see *SQL from the Ground Up*, by M. Pyefinch (Osborne/McGraw-Hill, 1999).

INSERT

The **INSERT** statement adds a row of information to a table. An **INSERT** statement has the following syntax:

```
INSERT INTO table
[(colname [, colname ] ... )]
VALUES (value [, value ] ... )
```

The **table** is the name of a table into which the data will be inserted, and **colname** and **value** are the fields and values that you want to insert. The order of the field names and the data must match, in order for the information to be inserted correctly. The specification of field names is optional if you want to insert information into all the columns of the database.

For example, to add a new record to our acronym database, we might use the following SQL statement:

```
INSERT INTO Acronyms (Acronym, Expansion)
VALUES ('PDQ', 'Pretty Darn Quick')
```

Since we are creating entries in both columns, we can simplify the statement:

```
INSERT INTO Acronyms VALUES ('PDQ', 'Pretty Darn Quick')
```

UPDATE

The **UPDATE** statement updates the information for one or more rows in a table. The syntax for the **UPDATE** statement is

```
UPDATE table
SET column=value
[, column=value ...]
[WHERE condition]
```

The **table** is the name of the table in the database. The **column** and **value** are the column names and values that you want to assign to those columns. If the **WHERE** keyword is included, then the statement will only update those columns that match **condition**. The condition uses the same operators and syntax as the **SELECT** statement. Note that if the condition matches multiple rows, all of the rows will be updated with the given information.

For example, to modify the entry for IIRC in our acronyms database:

```
UPDATE Acronyms SET Expansion='If I Recall Correctly'
WHERE Acronym='IIRC'
```

Note, of course, that this would update all of the IIRC entries in the table—we could supply a more specific statement to ensure we update the correct row:

```
UPDATE Acronyms SET Expansion='If I Recall Correctly'
WHERE Acronym='IIRC' AND Expansion='If I Remember Correctly'
```

DELETE

The **DELETE** statement is essentially identical to the **SELECT** statement, except that instead of returning a matching list of rows from a table, it deletes the rows from the database:

```
DELETE [FROM] table [WHERE condition]
```

The **table** is the name of the table that you want to delete rows from, and **condition** is the expression to use to find the rows to be deleted. Note that the **FROM** keyword is not really optional; some data sources require it, and others do not.

For example, to delete all of the IIRC entries from the Acronyms table:

```
DELETE FROM Acronyms WHERE Acronym = 'IIRC'
```

You can also delete all of the rows in a table by omitting the search condition:

```
DELETE FROM Acronyms
```

CREATE

If you are developing a database system, then there may be times when you need to build your tables pragmatically within Perl. One major benefit of creating databases in this way is that you can transport an application to another machine and have the script create the tables it needs to operate. For turnkey solutions, this is invaluable—it automates the process of installing a new application, right down to the creation of the storage mechanisms required.

Not all databases support the creation of database tables. Many have some constraints or limitations on what can be done with a **CREATE** statement. However, for those that do allow it, the basic format for a **CREATE** statement is shown below. Not all of the options are included here—if you need to use a more complex SQL statement to create your tables, use a guide, such as *SQL from the Ground Up*, by M. Pyefinch (Osborne/McGraw-Hill, 1999).

```
CREATE TABLE table
(field type[(size)] [NOT NULL] [index]
[, field type[(size)] [NOT NULL] [index], ...])
```

The **table** is the name of the table to be created. The **field** is the name of the field to be created in the table, and **type** and **size** define the field's type and width. The **NOT NULL** keywords indicate that the field must contain a value; **INSERT** and **UPDATE** statements that do not populate a **NOT NULL** field will fail.

The valid data types depend on the ODBC driver that you are using, but there are some generic types that should work on most systems. See Table 13-10 for a list of the base types that should be translated by most drivers into the local format.

Data Type	Size Specification	Description
Char	(**x**)	A simple character field, with the width determined by the value of **x**
Integer	N/A	A field of whole numbers, positive or negative
Decimal	(**x,y**)	A field of decimal numbers, where **x** is the maximum length in digits for the number, and **y** is the maximum number of digits after the decimal point
Date	N/A	A date field (see the "Formatting Dates" section that follows)
Logical	N/A	A field that can have only two values: true or false

Table 13-10. *Generic SQL Data Types*

For example, here's how to create a table that will hold the time information for a task:

```
CREATE TABLE Tasktime (TaskID Integer NOT NULL,
                       TaskName Char(40),
                       StartDate Date,
                       CompDate Date,
                       TotalHours Decimal(4.2),
                       Completed Logical)
```

Formatting Dates

Although the SQL language is standardized, the format for storing specific data strings, such as dates, is not. Different systems record dates in different orders (d/m/y, m/d/y, y/m/d, etc.) and to different precisions (2- and 4-digit years). To get around this, the SQL language allows for an escape clause that accepts a standard format that is translated by the ODBC driver into the database's native format.

You use the escape sequence just as you would a quoted text block:

```
SELECT Date, Event FROM Event WHERE Date > {d '1999-03-26'}
```

The SQL language supports three such formats: one for dates, one for times, and a final one for dates and times called the timestamp. The formats for each are as follows:

```
{d 'yyyy-mm-dd'}           # Date
{t 'hh:mm:ss'}             # Time
{ts 'yyyy-mm-dd hh:mm:ss'} # Timestamp
```

Note that the formats are explicit—you must specify all the digits, using zeros to fill the gaps where necessary.

The Complete Reference

Chapter 14

Interprocess Communication

The ability to control or interact with another process is called *interprocess communication* (IPC). It can take many different forms, from reading or writing information from or to another process, through to terminating or restarting processes, all the way to exchanging large volumes of information between two or more processes.

There are many different ways of doing this by using internal methods, such as **open**, and external methods that make use of the networking techniques you saw in Chapter 12. Network communication is expensive resource-wise, and is probably overkill for many solutions that simply require a conduit for exchanging small pieces of discrete data.

Most of the solutions center around the use of pipes, which, as the name suggests, provide the necessary conduit for data exchange. Unix users will be familiar with the use of pipes, and Windows users will probably have used them without realizing. We've also looked at their simplified use once already, back in Chapter 8.

In this chapter, we'll look at all the different facilities built into Perl for interprocess communication. This will include process creation, control, and communication to allow you to interact with other processes. We'll also look at the signal system, supported under most platforms as a way of signaling a specific state to a process, and then look at some IPC-specific techniques.

Processes

Processes are the individual programs that are running on your machine. Some of these are obvious to you, like the applications and utilities that you use. Others are hidden from view and control different parts of the operating system operation. On a Unix machine, these include everything from the core operating system and scheduler right through to the shell you use to run other programs.

Under Windows, the core operating system is hidden, but there are still references to the underlying applications and background processes used to support different services. You can view the individual processes using the Task Manager. The same effect can be seen under Mac OS, although you will be unable to see the background processes without a special application—the normal About This Computer window won't show them.

Note that most of the functions in this section do not work under the Mac OS, but the actual interpretation under Windows NT and Unix should be more or less identical because of the common POSIX support on both platforms. The only feature with processes that does work under Mac OS is the value of the **$$** variable, which is in fact always 1. This makes the use of the **$$** variable when creating unique references—such as for sessions in web programming—untenable.

Controlling Perl Execution

You already know about the statements and the operators that can help to control the execution of a Perl program. You also know about **die** and **warn**. The **die** function reports an error to **STDERR** and quits the program, while **warn** just reports an error to **STDERR**.

However, there are times when you want to exit a program without triggering an error message to **STDERR**, or when you want to trigger an installed signal handler (see the "Signal Handlers" section, later in the chapter). In these instances, the solution is to use the **exit** function:

```
exit 1;
```

This immediately causes the script to exit, passing a value of 1 back to the caller. If you do not specify a value, then a value of 0 is returned, which is generally accepted as indicating a successful completion.

You should really only use **exit** within the main part of a script, because using it within a subroutine is bad practice. What you should do is call **return**, passing a suitable value back to the caller to deal with. Furthermore, if you want to trap the execution of a block, use **die** within **eval** to trap the error.

Process Information

The process ID of the current script is permanently available within the **$$** variable. Since this value will be different for each execution, you cannot rely on this number to store persistent information. On the other hand, the process ID can be used as part of a random identification number if combined with date, time, and even a random number.

If you want to get the process ID of the parent process, you need to use the **getppid** function:

```
print "The parent of $$ is ",getppid,"\n";
```

This information is useful if you want to modify process groups or send the parent process a signal. Under Unix, your parent process ID should be greater than 1; a parent process ID of 1 indicates that the parent has died and that you've been adopted by the **init** process.

Process Groups

A collection of processes is logically grouped into process groups. For example, all the programs run within a shell belong to the same process group, providing they don't elect to change the process group. You can obtain the process group of a process using the **getpgrp** function:

```
print "Group of current($$): ", getpgrp(0),
      ", parent(",getppid,"):", getpgrp(getppid),"\n";
```

If you do not specify a process, or use a process ID of 0, it returns the process group of the current process.

You can "daemonize" a process—that is, make it act like a typical Unix daemon process that runs in the background without a controlling terminal—by calling the **setpgrp** function. A daemon process is one that is running in the background, and by using **setpgrp**, you can emulate a Unix command line like this:

```
$ script.pl &
```

To do this, you need to change the process group for the current process to 0. This needs to be done after forking a new process to ensure that you are not automatically a member of an existing process group:

```
my $childpid = fork;
exit if $childpid;
setpgrp(0, $$);
```

Because you are starting a daemon process, it's also a good idea to ensure that the new process you are creating is safe and well behaved. For example, you should consider redirecting **STDIN**, **STDOUT**, and **STDERR** either to /dev/null or to an external log file. You'll see some more examples of this later in this chapter when we look at the **fork** function in more detail.

Process Priority

You can obtain and set the priority of a given process, process group, or user, using the **getpriority** and **setpriority** functions:

```
getpriority WHICH, WHO
setpriority WHICH, WHO, PRIORITY
```

The value of **WHICH** should be one of **PRIO_PROCESS** for an individual process, **PRIO_PGRP** for a process group, and **PRIO_USER** for an individual user. The **WHO** value should then be the corresponding process ID, process group ID, or user ID (all numerical) that you want to obtain or set the priority for. The current priority will be returned by the **getpriority** function, and you can set it by supplying a new priority value in **PRIORITY**.

Note that the priorities are arbitrary values, and different values will have different meanings on different operating systems. For most instances, however, the priority is in reverse order. The higher the priority number, the lower the actual priority of the process. All users can decrease the priority of a process (just as they can with **nice**), but only the superuser can increase the priority (by setting a lower value).

Note *Under Windows, the **getpriority** and **setpriority** functions don't work. If you want to control the priority of a Windows process, then use the **Win32::Process** module to create the process. This supports two methods on the newly created process object called **GetPriorityClass** and **SetPriorityClass** that allow you to control the process's priority.*

Signals

Signals do exactly what the name suggests. They provide a method for signaling a particular process. Since a single signal is not very practical, there are a whole range of signals that indicate different events to the process. Some signals are generated by the operating system and signify some problem with the current execution process. Other signals can be user generated. Almost all signals can be trapped, both by other processes and by Perl scripts. The list of POSIX signals is shown in Table 14-1.

POSIX Name	Perl Name	Description
SIGABRT	ABRT	Abnormal termination
SIGALRM	ALRM	The timer set by the **alarm** function has expired
SIGFPE	FPE	Arithmetic exceptions; for example, divide overflow or divide by zero
SIGHUP	HUP	Hang-up detected on the controlling terminal or death of a controlling process
SIGILL	ILL	Illegal instruction indicating a program error
SIGINT	INT	Interrupt signal (special character from the keyboard or signal from another application)
SIGKILL	KILL	Termination signal; cannot be caught or ignored
SIGPIPE	PIPE	Attempt to write to a pipe with no application reading from it

Table 14-1. *POSIX Signals*

POSIX Name	Perl Name	Description
SIGQUIT	QUIT	Quit signal (special character from the keyboard or signal from another application)
SIGSEGV	SEGV	Attempt to access an invalid memory address
SIGTERM	TERM	Termination signal (from another application or OS)
SIGUSR1	USR1	Application-defined (user-defined) signal
SIGUSR2	USR2	Application-defined (user-defined) signal
SIGCHLD	CHLD	A child process terminated or stopped
SIGCONT	CONT	Continue the process if currently stopped
SIGSTOP	STOP	Stop signal; stops the specified process
SIGTSTP	TSTP	Stop signal from special character from keyboard
SIGTTIN	TTIN	A read was attempted from the controlling terminal by a background process
SIGTTOU	TTOU	A write was attempted to the controlling terminal by a background process

Table 14-1. *POSIX Signals* (continued)

Different Perl implementations will support a different range of signals. On most Unix systems, the list will be longer than that shown in Table 14-1 to cater to the OS-specific entries supporting features such as threads and resource limits. Under Windows NT, there is a subset of the full POSIX list, which includes most of the POSIX signals. Under the Mac OS implementation, there is a very short subset, since the Mac OS does not treat or handle processes in the same way as Unix or Windows. Mac OS X however works the same as a Unix implementation. For more information on the list of signals supported under your current operating system, use this simple script:

```
foreach $signal (sort keys %SIG)
{
    print "$signal\n";
}
```

Signal Handlers

If you have used signal-handling systems within C before, then you will find the signal-handling abilities of Perl something of a shock. Perl provides an incredibly simple interface to signal handling using a single **%SIG** hash. The individual keys of the **%SIG** hash are the signal names (as seen in the second column of Table 14-1), and the corresponding value indicates the operation that should be performed when that signal is received by the script. For example,

```
$SIG{INT} = { print "Got SIGINT" };
```

This example sets up a signal handler to an anonymous subroutine, which will print a message when an interrupt signal is received. This is a fairly impractical example, as we don't do anything with the signal once we've caught it.

Usually, you'd create a special signal-handling function:

```
sub sig_int
{
    my $signal = shift;
    print "Got the signal $signal\n";
    $SIG{$signal} = \&sig_int;
}

$SIG{INT} = \&sig_int;
```

This example has a number of advantages. First of all, the signal handler is now a separate function, which means you can use the same handler for a number of signals. Furthermore, it ensures that the signal is reset to the current signal handler after it has been received, which guarantees that the handler will always be in place. Also note from this example that the first argument given to a signal handler is the name of the signal received.

It's important to remember that you should be passing a reference to the desired signal-handler function—not simply a bare word, which could be misinterpreted, or the return value from a function call itself. The following are bad examples that you should try to avoid:

```
$SIG{INT} = sig_int;
$SIG{INT} = sig_int();
```

Both could cause problems. The bare word doesn't guarantee that the function will be called correctly. The function call is positively lethal—the value of the signal handler is now the value returned by the **sig_int** function.

Care should be taken with signal handlers. Since a signal can be received at any time, it's possible to receive a signal while another signal handler is executing. It's unusual, for example, to do this:

```
sub sig_int
{
    my $signal = shift;
    print "Got the signal $signal\n";
    do_some_work();
    $SIG{$signal} = \&sig_int;
}


$SIG{INT} = \&sig_int;
```

The obvious solution is to keep the contents of the signal handler as short as possible. Alternatively, you can set the condition of a signal (or signals) to **IGNORE** during the signal handler. This setting will cause Perl to ignore the specified signal until a new signal handler has been installed, thereby allowing you to work uninterrupted (if you'll excuse the pun).

```
sub sig_int
{
    my $signal = shift;
    $SIG{$signal} = IGNORE;
    do_some_work();
    $SIG{$signal} = \&sig_int;
}

$SIG{INT} = \&sig_int;
```

An alternative solution is to use Perl's **local** keyword to inherit the signal hash from the enclosing block. This will allow you to set an alternative handler, or **IGNORE** status on signals within the current handler, while retaining the handler information for the parent block, as in

```
sub sig_int
{
    my $signal = shift;
    local $SIG{$signal} = 'IGNORE';
    do_some_work();
    $SIG{$signal} = \&sig_int;
```

```
    }

    $SIG{INT} = \&sig_int;
```

To reset a signal to its original state (before you started installing your own handlers), you can set the signal value to **DEFAULT**:

```
    $SIG{INT} = 'DEFAULT';
```

A common use for the alarm signal (**ALRM**) is as a time-out system for different operations. This can be used for many things, such as setting file options, file locking, networking communication, or, as in the example below, for accepting input and setting a default value:

```
print "Your name is? :\n";
eval
{
    local $SIG{ALRM} = sub { die "Timeout"; };
    alarm 10;
    $name = <STDIN>;
    chomp $name;
    alarm 0;
};
if ($@ and $@ =~ /Timeout/) { $name = 'Anonymous' }
print "Hello $name!\n";
```

The action you want to place a time-out on is put within the **eval** block, and the signal handler calls **die** when the alarm time has been exceeded. This causes the **eval** block to drop out, and you check the return status with the $@ variable, setting a default name if the user hasn't supplied one.

Note | *Not all signals can be trapped or ignored. You'll need to check your operating system for the exact list. Typical signals that cannot be trapped include* ***KILL*** *and* ***STOP***.

The __WARN__ and __DIE__ Signals

The special signals __WARN__ and __DIE__ can be used to execute statements when **warn** and **die** are called. This allows you greater control over exactly what happens when these two functions are called. Normally, **warn** reports the supplied error to **STDERR** and then continues, while a call to **die** reports the error and then calls **exit()**. This automatic operation causes a problem if you want to close files safely or even to report the problem to the user directly and still use the "standard" error-trapping tools.

You can, of course, use any of the tricks we've seen so far—both the **eval** and exception signals will work in most cases, but they still require micromanagement of your scripts in order for the processes to work effectively. By using these two signals instead, you can trap errors dynamically and even make decisions about how to report the error without making major modifications to your code.

Using $SIG{__WARN__}

The **warn** handler is called whenever the **warn** function is called. The handler is passed any arguments passed to the **warn** function, but the **warn** function does not actually operate—the handler acts as a complete replacement for the operation normally handled by the function. For example,

```
sub warn_handler
{
    print STDERR "Woah - trapped a warning!\n\t",@_;
}

$SIG{__WARN__} = \&warn_handler;

warn "Something went awry\n";
warn "Something went awry again\n";
```

Running this produces the following output:

```
Woah - trapped a warning!
    Something went awry
Woah - trapped a warning!
    Something went awry again
```

You can see that the message is printed out only once—in this case, from the embedded call to **print** in the signal handler.

The **__WARN__** handler is best employed when you want to provide an alternative way of reporting or recording an error. You'll find examples elsewhere in this chapter for reporting information directly to logs; all you need to do is install a handler at the top of your script that traps and handles the warning in an alternative fashion. For example, here's a handler that uses a function called **writelog** to report the error to a file, instead of to the screen:

```
sub warn_handler
{
    writelog("warning: (%s)",join(', ',@_));
```

```
}

$SIG{__WARN__} = \&warn_handler;
```

We don't need to make any further modifications to the code (aside from adding the **writelog** function definition). From now on, all calls to **warn** will trigger this handler and force the output to be written to a file instead of **STDERR**. Similar tricks allow us to report warnings through Tk:

```
sub warn_handler
{
    dialog(undef,"Warning", join(', ',@_),
           'warning',1,"OK");
}
```

Using $SIG{__DIE__}

Unlike __WARN__, the __DIE__ handler merely acts as an interloper in the process—the handler is called, but the **die** continues as normal, both printing out the error and calling **exit()**. Consider the following script:

```
sub die_handler
{
    print "Woah - trapped a call die\nTrying to exit
gracefully...\n";
}

$SIG{__DIE__} = \&die_handler;
die "Something went completely wrong\n";
```

Note that the handler will be passed the text as formatted by **die**—this means we can adapt the text and then call **die** again to actually output the updated version of the text. For example, the line

```
die "Just couldn't do it anymore!";
```

generates

```
Just couldn't do it anymore! at sigdiemod.pl line 7.
```

but add a handler:

```
sub die_handler
{
    my ($error) = @_;
    die "Trapped an error: $error";
}

$SIG{__DIE__} = \&die_handler;
```

and the error becomes:

```
Trapped an error: Just couldn't do it anymore! at sigdiemod.pl line 9.
```

The **die_handler** function will be called only once, as the signal handler is reset after the first call.

The __DIE__ handler is best used when you want to gracefully exit from a script—perhaps providing a simple prompt to the user and safely closing files or network connections before finally allowing the script to die. It's true that you could use an **END** block for this process, but doing so means that the closing statements are executed *after* **die** has actually been called. It also relies on the functions, filehandles, and other artifacts being accessible to the **END** block at the time of termination.

*Currently the __DIE__ (and __WARN__) handler is called even within an **eval** block. This can cause problems, so consider using the $^S variable to check the status of the interpreter at the point the handler is called. The $^S variable will be true if the statements are being called from within an **eval** string or block.*

Sending Signals

You can send signals to other processes using the **kill** function, which actually just calls the Unix **kill()** function. For example, to call the **SIGINT** handler within the function, you could use

```
kill('INT', $$);
```

You can use short names or numbers as the first argument to the function, and the second argument should be the process ID or process group to which you are sending the signal. To send the signal to all of the processes in the specified signal group, prefix the process ID with a minus sign:

```
kill INT => -$$;
```

Note here that the hash notation has also been used to specify the signal. Since the => operator is just an alias for the comma, this works perfectly. It also has the advantage of automatically quoting the signal number to send, which makes more sense if you think about the process logically. In the preceding example, you are sending the signal **INT** to the process group **-$$**.

By sending the signal number 0 to a process, you can determine whether it is currently running, or whether it's possible to send a valid signal. Since you can only send a signal to processes that you own, this is a good way to test whether a specific process is still running and whether it is still yours. It is particularly useful when forking and subsequently monitoring a child process.

For example, the following code checks that the schedule is running on a Solaris (and indeed most other Unix flavors) machine:

```
unless (kill 0 => 0)
{
    die "Panic: Scheduler not running!\n";
}
```

Pipes

Pipes are a one-way communication channel that can be used to transfer information between processes. Because they are one-way, they can only be used to communicate information to or from a process, although there are ways to get around this.

The most typical use of pipes is within the **open** function when you want to read from and write to a particular command, instead of a typical file. This class of pipe is called an anonymous pipe. You can also have named pipes (within Unix only) that provide a method for two unconnected processes to communicate with each other.

There are other methods available using pipes, but these are only practical when used with child processes, so we'll cover them at a later stage. For now, let's concentrate on the basics of opening, reading from, and writing to pipes.

Anonymous Pipes

An *anonymous pipe* is one implied through the use of the pipe symbol at the beginning or end of an **open** statement. For example, to read the output from **gzcat**, which decompresses a Gzipped file to the standard input:

```
open(COMPRESSED, "gzcat file.gz|") or die "Can't fork: $!";
while(<COMPRESSED>)
{
    print;
```

```
}
close(COMPRESSED) or die "Error in gzcat: $!";
```

Alternatively, to write information and have it immediately compressed, you can pass input directly to the **gzip** command:

```
open(COMPRESS, "|gzip - >file.gz") or die "Can't fork: $!";
print COMPRESS "Compressed Data";
close(COMPRESS) or die "Gzip didn't work: $!";
```

When using pipes, you must check the return status of both **open** and **close**. This is because each function returns an error from a different element of the piped command. The **open** function forks a new process and executes the specified command. The return value of this operation trapped by **open** is the return value of the **fork** function. The new process is executed within a completely separate process, and there is no way for **open** to obtain that error. This effectively means that the **open** will return true if the new process could be forked, irrespective of the status of the command you are executing. The **close** function, on the other hand, picks up any errors generated by the executed process because it monitors the return value received from the child process via **wait** (see the "Creating Child Processes" section, later in this chapter).

Therefore, in the first example, you could actually read nothing from the command, and without checking the return status of **close**, you might assume that the command failed to return any valid data.

In the second example, where you are writing to a piped command, you need to be more careful. There is no way of determining the status of the opened command without immediately calling **close**, which rather defeats the purpose. Instead, you can use a signal handler on the **PIPE** signal. The process will receive a **PIPE** signal from the operating system if the piped command fails.

Two-Way Communication

As convenient as it may seem, you can't do the following:

```
open(MORE, "|more file|");
```

This is because a pipe is unidirectional—it either reads from or writes to a piped command. Although in theory this should work, it can result in a deadlocked process where neither the parent nor piped command know whether they should be reading from or writing to the **MORE** filehandle.

The solution is to use the **open2** function that comes as part of the **IPC::Open2** module, which is part of the standard distribution:

```
use FileHandle;
use IPC::Open2;
$pid = open2(\*READ, \*WRITE, "more file");
WRITE->autoflush();
```

You can now communicate in both directions with the **more** command, reading from it with the **READ** filehandle and writing to it with the **WRITE** filehandle. This will receive data from the standard output of the piped command and write to the standard input of the piped command.

There is a danger with this system, however, in that it assumes the information is always available from the piped command and that it is always ready to accept information. But accesses either way will block until the piped command is ready to accept or to reply with information. This is due to the buffering supported by the standard **STDIO** functions. There isn't a complete solution to this if you are using off-the-shelf commands; if you are using your own programs, you'll have control over the buffering, and it shouldn't be a problem.

The underlying functionality of the **open2** function is made possible using the **pipe** function, which creates a pair of connected pipes, one for reading and one for writing:

```
pipe READHANDLE, WRITEHANDLE
```

We'll look at an example of this when we look at creating new child processes with **fork**.

Named Pipes

A *named pipe* is a special type of file available under Unix. It resides, like any file, in the file system but provides two-way communication between two otherwise unrelated processes. This system has been in use for some time within Unix as a way of accepting print jobs. A specific printer interface creates and monitors the file while users send data to the named pipe. The printer interface accepts the data, spools the accepted file to disk, and then spawns a new process to send it out to the printer.

The named pipe is treated as a FIFO (First In, First Out) and is sometimes simply called a FIFO. You create a named pipe using the **mknod** or **mkfifo** command, which in turn creates a suitably configured file on the file system. The following example,

```
system('mknod', 'myfifo', 'p');
```

is identical to this one:

```
system('mkfifo', 'myfifo');
```

Once created, you can read from or write to the file just like any normal file, except that both instances will block until there is a suitable process on the other end. For example, here is a simple script (the "server") that accepts input from a FIFO and writes it into a permanent log file:

```perl
my $fifo = 'logfifo';
my $logfile = 'logfile.txt';

unless (-p $fifo)
{
    unlink $fifo;
    if (system('mkfifo','logfifo'))
    {
        die "Can't create FIFO: $!";
    }
}

open(FIFO, "<$fifo") or die "Can't open fifo for reading: $!";
open(LOG, ">>$logfile") or die "Can't append to $logfile: $!";
while(<FIFO>)
{
    my $date = localtime(time);
    print LOG "$date: $_"\n;
}

close(FIFO) or die "Can't close fifo: $!";
close(LOG) or die "Can't close log: $!";
```

Here's the corresponding log reporter (the "client"), which takes input from the command line and writes it to the FIFO:

```perl
my $fifo = 'logfifo';

die "No data to log" unless @ARGV;

open(FIFO,">$fifo") or die "Can't open fifo for writing: $!";
```

```
print FIFO @ARGV;
close(FIFO) or die "Can't close fifo: $!";
```

If you run the "server" (the first script above) and then call the "client," you should be able to add an entry to the log file. Note, though, that the server will quit once it has accepted one piece of information, because the client closes the pipe (and therefore sends **eof** to the server) when it exits. If you want a more persistent server, call the main loop within a forked subprocess. For more information, see the discussion of **fork** later in the "Creating Child Processes" section.

Named Pipes Under Windows

The Windows named pipe system works slightly differently to that under Unix. For a start, we don't have access to the **mkfifo** command, so there's no immediately apparent way to create a named pipe in the first place. Instead, Windows supports named pipes through the **Win32::Pipe** module.

The **Win32::Pipe** module provides the same pipe communication functionality using Windows pipes as the built-in functions and the **mknod** or **mkfifo** commands do to normal Unix named pipes. One of the biggest differences between Unix and Windows named pipes is that Windows pipes are network compliant. You can use named pipes on Win32 systems to communicate across a network by only knowing the UNC of the pipe—we don't need to use TCP/IP sockets or know the server's IP address or name to communicate. Better still, we don't need to implement any type of communications protocol to enable safe communication across the network—the named pipe API handles that for us.

The Windows implementation also works slightly differently from the point of view of handling the named pipe. The server creates the named pipe using the API, which is supported by Perl using the **Win32::Pipe** module. Once created, the server uses the new pipe object to send and receive information. Clients can connect to the named pipe using either the normal **open** function or the **Win32::Pipe** module.

Creating Named Pipes

When you create a named pipe, you need to use the **new** method to create a suitable **Win32::Pipe** object:

```
$pipe = new Win32::Pipe(NAME);
```

The **NAME** should be the name of the pipe that you want to create. The name you give here can be a short name; it does not have to be fully qualified (see the "Pipe-Naming Conventions" sidebar for more information).

Pipe-Naming Conventions

When you are creating a new pipe, you give it a simple name. For example, you can create a pipe called "Status". Any clients wishing to access the pipe must, however, use the full UNC name of the pipe. Pipes exist within a simple structure that includes the server name and the special "pipe" shared resource. For example, on a machine called "Insentient", our pipe would be available for use from a client via the name "\\INSENTIENT\pipe\Status".

If you do not know the name of the server, then you should be able to use "\\.\pipe\Status", where the single dot refers to the current machine.

You can also nest pipes in their own structure. For example, you could have two pipes: one in "\\INSENTIENT\pipe\Status\Memory" and the other in "\\INSENTIENT\pipe\Status\Disk".

The structure is not an actual directory, nor is it stored on the file system—it's just another shared resource made available by the Windows operating system that is accessible using the UNC system.

There are some limitations to creating and using pipes:

- There is a limit of 256 client/server connections to each named pipe. This means you can have one server and 255 client machines talking to it through a single pipe at any one time.

- There is no limit (aside from the disk and memory) resources of the machine to the number of named pipes that you can create.

- The default buffer size is 512 bytes, and you can change this with the **ResizeBuffer** method.

- All named pipes created using this module are streams, rather than being message based (see note).

Note   *Dave Roth, the original author of this module, has updated the module, but the updated version is not included as standard in the ActivePerl 615 distribution, though it should have been rolled into the 616 distribution. The new version does allow for message-based communication, where client and server communicate using fixed-size messages, with the buffer size determining the message size.*

Opening Named Pipes

The easiest way to open an existing pipe is to use the **open** function:

```
open(DATA, NAME);
```

NAME is the UNC of the pipe to open. For example:

```
open(DATA,"\\\\INSENTIENT\\pipe\\MCStatus");
```

Alternatively, and in my experience more reliably, you can use the **Win32::Pipe** module to open an existing pipe by supplying the UNC name:

```
$pipe = new Win32::Pipe("\\\\INSENTIENT\\pipe\\MCStatus");
```

Note, in both cases, the use of double backslashes—these are required to ensure that the first backslash is not parsed by the Perl interpreter.

Accepting Connections

Once the pipe has been created, you need to tell the server to wait for a connection from a client. The **Connect** method blocks the current process and returns only when a new connection from a client has been received.

```
$pipe->Connect();
```

Once connected, you can start to send or receive information through the pipe using the **Read** and **Write** methods.

Note that you do not need to call this method from a client—the **new** method implies a connection when accessing an existing pipe.

Reading and Writing Pipes

If you have opened the pipe using **open**, then you can continue to use the standard **print** and **<FILEHANDLE>** formats to write and read information to and from the filehandle pointing to the pipe.

If you have used the module to open a pipe, or to create one when developing a server, you need to use the **Read** and **Write** methods. The **Read** method returns the information read from the pipe, or **undef** if no information could be read:

```
$pipe->Read();
```

Note that you will need to call **Read** multiple times until all the information within the pipe's buffer has been read. When the method returns **undef**, it indicates the end of the data stream from the pipe.

To write to a pipe, you need to use the **Write** method. This writes the supplied string to the pipe.

```
$pipe->Write(EXPR);
```

The method returns true if the operation succeeded, or **undef** if the operation failed—usually because the other end of the pipe (client or server) disconnected before the information could be written. Note that you write information to a buffer when using the **Write** method and it's up to the server to wait long enough to read all the information back.

The Pipe Buffer

The information written to and read from the pipe is held in a buffer. The default buffer size is 512 bytes. You can verify the current buffer size using the **BufferSize** method.

```
$pipe->BufferSize()
```

This returns the current size, or **undef** if the pipe is invalid.

To change the buffer size, use the **ResizeBuffer** method. For most situations, you shouldn't need to change the buffer size.

```
$pipe->ResizeBuffer(SIZE)
```

This sets the buffer size to **SIZE**, specified in bytes.

Disconnecting and Closing Pipes

Once the server end of a pipe has finished using the open pipe connection to the client, it should call the **Disconnect** method. This is the logical opposite of the **Connect** method. You should only use this method on the server of a connection—although it's valid to call it from a client script, it has no effect because clients do not require the **Connect** method.

```
$pipe->Disconnect();
```

To actually close a pipe because you have finished using it, you should use the **Close** method. From a client, this destroys the local pipe object and closes the connection. From a server, the **Close** method destroys the pipe object and also destroys the pipe itself. Further client connections to the pipe will raise an error.

```
$pipe->Close();
```

Getting Pipe Errors

You can get the last error message raised by the pipe system for a specific pipe by using the **Error** method.

```
$pipe->Error();
```

When used on a pipe object, it returns the error code of the last operation. An error code of 0 indicates a success. When used directly from the module, that is **Win32::Pipe::Error()**, the function returns a list containing the error code and associated error string for the last operation, irrespective of the pipe on which it occurred.

In general, you should probably use the **$^E** variable or the **Win32::GetLastError** functions to obtain an error from a function. For example,

```
$pipe = new Win32::Pipe('MCStatus') or die "Creating pipe: $^E ($!)";
```

Safe Pipes

You might remember that Chapter 8 briefly discusses the different methods you can use to open pipes with the **open** command. Two of these options are –| and |–, **which imply a fork and pipe, providing an alternative method for calling external programs. For example:**

```
open(GZDATA,"-|") or exec 'gzcat', 'file.gz';
```

This example forks a new process and immediately executes **gzcat**, with its standard output redirected to the **GZDATA** filehandle. The method is simple to remember. If you open a pipe to minus, you can write to the filehandle, and the child process will receive the information in its **STDIN**. Opening a pipe from minus enables you to read information that the child sends to its **STDOUT** from the opened filehandle.

This can be useful in situations where you want to execute a piped command when running as a setuid script. More useful in general, though, is the fact that you can use this in combination with **exec** to ensure that the current shell does not parse the command you are trying to run. Here's a more obvious version of the previous example that also takes care of the setuid permission status:

```
$child = open(GZCAT, "-|");
if ($pid)
{
    while(<GZCAT>)
    {
        print $_;
    }
    close(<GZCAT>);
}
else
{
    ($EUID, $EGID) = ($UID, $GID);
    exec 'gzcat', 'file.gz';
}
```

Here, the **exec**'d program will be sending its output (a decompressed version of file.gz) to the standard output, which has in turn been piped through the **GZCAT** filehandle in the parent. In essence, this is no different from a standard piped **open**, except that you guarantee that the shell doesn't mess with the arguments you supply to the function.

Executing Additional Processes

There are times when you want to run an external program but are not interested in the specifics of the output information, or if you are interested, you do not expect vast amounts of data that needs to be processed. In these situations, a number of avenues are open to you. It's also possible that you want to create your own subprocess, purely for your own use. You've already seen some examples of this throughout this book. We'll look at both techniques in this section.

Running Other Programs

To run an external command, you can use the **system** function:

```
system LIST
```

This **fork**s a new process and then executes the command defined in the first argument of **LIST** (using **exec**), passing the command any additional arguments specified in **LIST**. Execution of the script blocks until the specified program completes.

The actual effect of **system** depends on the number of arguments. If there is more than one argument in **LIST**, the underlying function called is **execvp()**. This bypasses the current shell and executes the program directly. This can be used when you do not want the shell to make any modifications to the arguments you are passing. If there is only one argument, it is checked for shell metacharacters. If none are found, the argument is split into individual words and passed to **execvp()** as usual. If any metacharacters are found, the argument is passed directly to /bin/sh -c (or the current operating system equivalent) for parsing and execution.

Note that any output produced by the command you are executing will be displayed as usual to the standard output and error, unless you redirect it accordingly (although this implies metacharacters). If you want to capture the output, use the **qx//** operator or a piped **open**. For example:

```
system("rm","-f","myfile.txt");
```

The return value is composed of the return status of the **wait** function used on the forked process and the exit value of the command itself. To get the exit value of the command you called, divide the value returned by **system** by 256.

You can also use this function to run a command in the background, providing you are not dependent on the command's completion before continuing:

```
system("emacs &");
```

The preceding example works on Unix, but other operating systems may use different methods.

The **system** function has one other trick. It can be used to let a command masquerade as a login shell or to otherwise hide the process's name. You do this by using a slightly modified version of the command:

```
system PROGRAM LIST
```

The first argument is an indirect object and should refer to the actual program you want to run. The entries in **LIST** then become the values of the called program's **@ARGV** array. Thus, the first argument becomes the masquerading name, with remaining arguments being passed to the command as usual. This has the added benefit that **LIST** is now always treated as a list, even if it contains only one argument. For example, to execute a login shell:

```
system {'/bin/sh'} '-sh';
```

A more convenient method for executing a process, especially if you want to capture the output, is to use the **qx//** quoting operator:

```
my $hostname = qx/hostname/;
```

This is probably better known as the backticks operator, since you can also rewrite this as

```
my $hostname = `hostname`;
```

The two are completely synonymous. It's a question of personal taste which one you choose to use. Backticks will be more familiar to shell users, since the same characters are used. The string you place into the `` or **qx//** is first interpolated, just like an ordinary double-quoted string. Note, however, that you must use the backslash operator to escape characters, such as $and @, that would otherwise be interpreted by Perl. The command is always executed via a shell, and the value returned by the operator is the output of the command you called.

Also note that like other quoted operators, you can choose alternative delimiter characters. For example, to call **sed** from Perl:

```
qx(sed -e s/foo/bar/g <$file);
```

Note as well, in this example, that **$file** will be parsed by Perl, not by the shell.

In the previous examples, for instance, you assigned a variable **$hostname** to the output of the **hostname** command. If the command is called in a scalar context, then the entire output is placed into a single string. If called in a list context, the output is split line by line, with each line being placed into an individual element of the list. The list is split using the value of **$/**, so you can parse the output automatically by changing the value of **$/**.

The return value of the command you called is placed in the special **$?** variable directly. You do not need to parse the contents in any way to determine the true exit value.

The function used to support the **qx//** operator is **readpipe**, which you can also call directly:

```
readpipe EXPR
```

Replacing the Current Script

You can replace the currently executing script with another command using the **exec** function. This works exactly the way the **system** command works, except that it never returns. The command you specify will completely replace the currently executing script. No **END** blocks are executed, and any active objects will not have their **DESTROY** methods called. You need to ensure, therefore, that the current script is ready to be replaced. It will be, and should be treated as, the last statement in your script.

```
exec LIST
```

All the constructs noted for **system** apply here, including the argument-list handling. If the call fails for any reason, then **exec** returns false. This only applies when the command does not exist and the execution was direct, rather than via a shell. Because the function never returns, Perl will warn you (if you have warnings switched on) if the statement following **exec** is something other than **die**, **warn**, or **exit**.

Note that the masquerading system also works:

```
exec {'/bin/sh'} '-sh';
```

Creating Child Processes

It is common practice for servers and other processes to create "children." These subprocesses can be controlled from the parent (see the "Processes" section at the start of this chapter). You do this by using **fork**, which calls the **fork()** system call. **fork** creates a new process that is identical in nearly all respects to the parent process. The only difference is that the subprocess has a new process ID. Open filehandles and their buffers (flushed or otherwise) are inherited by the new process, but signal handlers and alarms, if set, are not:

```
fork
```

The function returns the child process ID to the parent and 0 to the child process. The **undef** value is returned if the **fork** operation fails.

Use of the **fork** function needs some careful consideration within the Perl script. The execution contents of the new process are part of the current script; you do not call an external script or function to initiate the new process (you are not creating a new thread—see Chapter 15 for that). For example, you can see from the comments in the following code where the boundaries of the child and parent lie:

```perl
#Parent Process

print "Starting the parent\n";

unless ($pid = fork)
{
#Start of Child Process
    sleep 2;
    for (1..10)
    {
        print "Child, Count $_\n";
        sleep 1;
    }
    exit 0;
}
#End of Child

#Continuation of Parent
for (1..5)
{
    print "Parent, Count $_\n";
    sleep 2;
}

waitpid($pid,0);

#End of Parent
```

As soon as the **fork** function returns, the child starts execution, running the script elements in the following block. You can do anything within this block. All the functions, modules, and variables are inherited by the child. However, you cannot use an inherited variable to share information with the parent. We'll cover the method for that shortly.

Also note that execution of the parent continues as soon as the **fork** function returns, so you get two simultaneously executing processes. If you run the preceding script, you should get output similar to this:

```
Starting the parent
Parent, Count 1
Child, Count 1
Parent, Count 2
Child, Count 2
Child, Count 3
Parent, Count 3
Child, Count 4
Child, Count 5
Parent, Count 4
Child, Count 6
Child, Count 7
Parent, Count 5
Child, Count 8
Child, Count 9
Child, Count 10
```

You can therefore use **fork** as a quasi-multithreading solution. Many HTTP, FTP, and other servers use this technique to handle more than one request from a client at the same time (see the simple web server example in Chapter 12). Each time a client connects to the server, it spawns a new process solely for servicing the requests of the client. The server immediately goes back to accepting new requests from new clients, spawning additional processes as it goes.

Open filehandles are inherited, so had you redirected **STDOUT** to a different file, the child would also have written to this file automatically. This can be used for parent-child communication, and we'll look at specific examples of this in the "Communicating with Children" section, later in the chapter.

Support for fork Under Windows

As a rule, Windows does not support **fork()** at an operating system level. Historically, the decision was made during development of the Win32 series (Windows 9x/NT/2000) to instead support threads. Rather than duplicating the current process, which is a relatively time-consuming task, you just create a new thread through which to execute the function that you want to run simultaneously.

However, despite this lack of support, the need for a **fork**-like function under Windows was seen as a major part of the cross-platform compatibility puzzle. To that end, a **fork** function has been developed which works under the Windows platform. Support is currently fairly limited, and some of the more useful tricks of the **fork** system are not implemented, but the core purpose of the function—to duplicate the currently executing interpreter—does work. This means that it's now possible to do most operations that rely on the **fork** function within ActivePerl.

Rather than creating a child process in the strict sense, the Windows **fork** function creates a pseudo-process. The pseudo-process is actually a duplication of the current interpreter created within a new thread of the main interpreter. This means that using **fork** does not create a new process—the new interpreter will not appear within the process list. This also means that killing the "parent" kills the parent and all its "children," since the children are just additional threads within the parent.

The Windows **fork** function returns the pseudo-process ID to the parent and 0 to the child process, just like the real **fork** function. The pseudo-process ID is separate from the real process ID given to genuine additional processes. The **undef** value is returned if the **fork** operation fails.

*Although the Windows **fork** function makes use of the threading system built into Windows to create the processes, you don't actually have access to the threads within Perl. If you want to use threads instead of **fork**, see Chapter 15.*

ActivePerl fork Limitations   There are some limitations and considerations that you should keep in mind when using the **fork** function under ActivePerl—all because of the way the system works. A brief list of these issues is given here:

■ Open filehandles are inherited, so had you redirected **STDOUT** to a different file, the child would also have written to this file automatically. This can be used for parent-child communication, and we'll look at specific examples of this in the "Communicating with Children" section, later in the chapter. Note, however, that unlike Unix **fork**, any shared filehandles also share their position, as reported by **seek**. This means that changing the position within a parent will also change the position within the child. You should separately open the file in the child if you want to maintain separate file pointers.

■ The $$ and **$PROCESS_ID** variables in the pseudo-process are given a unique process ID. This is separate from the main process ID list.

■ All pseudo-processes inherit the environment (**%ENV**) from the parent and maintain their own copy. Changes to the pseudo-process environment do not affect the parent.

■ All pseudo-processes have their own current directory.

■ The **wait** and **waitpid** functions accept pseudo-process IDs and operate normally.

- The **kill** function can be used to kill a pseudo-process if it has been supplied with the pseudo-process's ID. However, the function should be used with caution, as killed pseudo-processes may not clean up their environment before dying.

- Using **exec** within a forked process actually calls the program in a new external process. This then returns the program's exit code to the pseudo-process, which then returns the code to the parent. This has two effects. First, the process ID returned by **fork** will not match that of the **exec**'d process. Secondly, the −| and |− formats to the **open** command do not work.

Since the operation of **fork** is likely to change before this book goes to print, you should check the details on the **fork** implementation at the **ActiveState** web site. See Appendix F for details.

Waiting for Children

As you **fork** new processes and they eventually die, you need to wait for the child processes to exit cleanly to ensure they do not remain as "zombies" within the process table. Child processes send the **SIGCHLD** signal to the parent when they exit, but unless the signal is caught, or the processes are otherwise acknowledged, they remain within the process table. They are called zombies because they have completed execution but have not been cleared from the table.

In order to acknowledge the completion of the child process, you need to use one of the two available functions, **wait** and **waitpid**. Both functions block the parent process until the child process (or processes) has exited cleanly. This should not cause problems if the functions are used as part of a signal handler, or if they are called as the last function within a parent that knows its children should have exited, probably because it sent a suitable signal.

```
wait
waitpid PID, FLAGS
```

The **wait** function simply waits for a child process to terminate. It's usually used within a signal handler to automatically reap child processes as they die:

```
$SIG{CHLD} = sub { wait };
```

This should guarantee that the child process completes correctly. The other alternative is to use the **waitpid**, which enables you to wait for a specific process ID and condition.

Valid flags are defined in the **POSIX** module, and they are summarized here in Table 14-2.

Of course, there are times when you specifically want to wait for your children to exit cleanly.

Flag	Description
WIFEXITED	Wait for processes that have exited
WIFSIGNALED	Wait for processes that received a signal
WNOHANG	Non-blocking wait
WSTOPSIG	Wait for processes that received **STOP** signal
WTERMSIG	Wait for processes that received **TERM** signal
WUNTRACED	Wait for processes stopped by signals

Table 14-2. *Flags for* **waitpid**

Communicating with Children

It's possible to do one-way communication between a parent and its children using the |– and –| methods to the **open** command. However, this is a one-way transfer, and the **fork** is implied by the **open** command, which reduces your flexibility somewhat. A better solution is to use the **pipe** function to create a pair of filehandles.

```
pipe READHANDLE, WRITEHANDLE
```

Information written to **WRITEHANDLE** is immediately available on **READHANDLE** on a simple first in, first out (FIFO) basis. Since a forked process inherits open filehandles from the parent, you can use a pair of filehandles for communicating between the child and parent and for reading from and writing to the corresponding filehandle. The following example creates a new subprocess, which accepts calculations that are then evaluated by **eval** to produce a result.

```perl
use IO::Handle;
pipe(PARENTREAD, PARENTWRITE);
pipe(CHILDREAD, CHILDWRITE);

PARENTWRITE->autoflush(1);
CHILDWRITE->autoflush(1);

if ($child = fork)      # Parent code
{
    close CHILDTREAD;   # We don't need these in the parent
```

```
        close PARENTWRITE;
        print CHILDWRITE "34+56;\n";
        chomp($result = <PARENTREAD>);
        print "Got a value of $result from child\n";
        close PARENTREAD;
        close CHILDWRITE;
        waitpid($child,0);
}
else
{
        close PARENTREAD;   # We don't need these in the child
        close CHILDWRITE;
        chomp($calculation = <CHILDREAD>);
        print "Got $calculation\n";
        $result = eval "$calculation";
        print PARENTWRITE "$result\n";
        close CHILDREAD;
        close PARENTWRITE;
        exit;
}
```

You can see that the calculation is sent to **CHILDWRITE**, which is then read by
the child from **CHILDREAD**. The result is then calculated and sent back to the parent
via **PARENTWRITE**, where the parent reads the result from **PARENTREAD**. Note
that you must use newlines as terminators when communicating between the parent
and the child to identify the end of the communication. You could have used any
string (see "Data Transfer" in Chapter 12), but newlines are the natural choice, since
it's what you use elsewhere.

Another alternative is to use sockets, and you saw many examples of this in Chapter 12.
There is, however, one trick particularly relevant to communication between parents
and children. This is the **socketpair** function, which is only supported on a small number
of platforms. It works in a similar way to **pipe**, except that you can use just two
filehandles to communicate between the two processes. Here's another version of the
preceding example, this time using **socketpair**:

```
use IO::Handle;
use Socket;
socketpair(CHILD, PARENT, AF_UNIX, SOCK_STREAM, PF_UNSPEC)
    or die "socketpair failed: $!";

PARENT->autoflush(1);
CHILD->autoflush(1);
```

```
if ($child = fork)       # Parent code
{
    close PARENT;
    print CHILD "34+56;\n";
    chomp($result = <CHILD>);
    print "Got a value of $result from child\n";
    waitpid($child,0);
    close CHILD;
}
else
{
    close CHILD;
    chomp($calculation = <PARENT>);
    $result = eval "$calculation";
    print PARENT "$result\n";
    close PARENT;
    exit;
}
```

Note that this works slightly differently, although the basic theory is the same. The **socketpair** function creates a pair of network sockets where information sent to **CHILD** is readable on **PARENT**, and vice versa. This means you write information to the **CHILD** filehandle in the parent, but read it from **PARENT** in the child. This is the same as the **PARENTWRITE** and **PARENTREAD** filehandles in the previous **pipe** example, except that you have only one filehandle in each to deal with.

Note the importance of the **close** statements in both this and the previous example. The filehandles will remain open if you do not explicitly close them correctly in the child and parent. You must make sure all filehandles in both the parent and child are closed correctly. This is less important in the **pipe** version, since Perl will close them for you, but in the **socketpair** version you run the risk of either child or parent assuming that the connection is still open.

Other Function Calls

Although not strictly a method of IPC, Perl does provide a mechanism for calling functions that are part of the system library, but that are not available as a directly supported function. In order for this to work, you'll need to create the syscall.ph Perl header file using the **h2ph** script:

```
h2ph /usr/include/sys/syscall.h
```

This will install the Perl header file into the Perl library structure so it's available via a normal **require** statement.

```
require syscall.ph;
syscall(&SYS_chown,"myfile",0,0);
```

You can supply up to 14 arguments to be passed to the function, and they are interpreted according to their types. If the scalar is numeric, it is passed to the system function as an **int**; otherwise a pointer to a string is passed. If the system call populates a variable, you may supply a suitable variable, but make sure it's large enough to contain the returned value.

The **syscall** function always returns the value returned by the function you have called. If the call fails, the return value is –1, and the **$!** variable is populated accordingly.

A better solution if you regularly make use of a system function not supported within Perl is to create an XSUB definition for it. See Chapter 17 for more information.

System V IPC

The System V flavor of Unix introduced a number of different methods for interprocess communication. It centers around three basic premises: messages, semaphores, and shared memory. The messaging system operates a simple message queue for the exchange of information. Semaphores provide shared counters across processes and are usually used to indicate the availability of shared resources. Shared memory allows for segments of memory to be shared among processes.

From my point of view, as well as a practical one, network sockets (Chapter 12) provide a much better system for communicating and transferring information between processes, both locally and remotely. For a start, they are supported on many more platforms than the System V IPC. Furthermore, they are far more practical in most instances than the System V IPC functions, which restrict you, necessarily, to a few minor facilities. System V IPC is not supported on many Unix flavors and certainly not under Mac OS or Win32 systems. If you want to use this system, I suggest you refer to the man pages for more information on these functions.

The Complete Reference

Chapter 15

Other Execution Enhancements

Perl code can be executed in a number of different ways. You can execute a script written in a text, supply a miniscript on the command line, or execute Perl scripts within other Perl scripts. Using the embedding techniques we'll see in Chapter 20, you can even execute Perl statements and scripts within the confines of a C program.

The term "advanced" is perhaps a little over the top, but in this chapter we'll look at alternative methods for executing Perl subroutines and scripts beyond the normal direct interpretation of a file.

The first method we'll look at is using Perl on the command line, along with the options you can supply to Perl to change the way it operates. For example, the **-w** command line option turns on *warnings*—a list of problems that may exist in your script. There are other tricks, though: you can use Perl on the command line as a form of scriptable editor and with only a few more keystrokes, it can even operate as a "do it all" utility.

We'll then move on to the use of threads—a sort of miniprocess within the main execution of a script. You can use threads as a way to execute a number of subroutines simultaneously without resorting to the complexities and overheads of the **fork** function we saw in Chapter 14. On suitable operating systems (thread support is very operating-system limited) this allows multiple operations to occur simultaneously—a great way for handling complex GUIs or client/server systems. It can also be used where you are processing many files simultaneously without using the round-robin approach of **IO::Select**.

We have already seen some examples of using the **eval** function, which effectively operates as another Perl interpreter. The **eval** function has many uses, but its primary use is as an exception handler to trap operations that would otherwise cause the main interpreter to fail. A good example here is calling a function that may not be supported on the current platform—you call the function within an **eval**, and it's the embedded Perl interpreter that fails, not the interpreter running your script.

Finally, we'll consider the security implications of using Perl and how to get around them using the standard Perl distribution. Perl has always supported a "tainting" mechanism, which highlights variables and information Perl considers possibly unsafe. For a more secure environment, you can use the **Safe** module to create a new, unique compartment where you can restrict the list of available opcodes (the smallest executable part of a Perl script). This can reduce the resources and methods available to a script, preventing it from using functions, or even operators, that you do not want it to run.

Perl on the Command Line

During the normal execution process, Perl looks for a script in one of the following places, in this order:

1. On the command line (via the **-e** option).

2. Contained in the file specified by the first non-option argument to the Perl interpreter.

3. Piped in to the interpreter via the standard input. This works either if there are no arguments or if there is a command line argument.

Perl supports a number of command line options. These can either be specified on the actual command line, if you are manually executing Perl, or they can be specified within the #! line at the start of the script. The #! line is always processed by Perl, irrespective of how the script is invoked. If you are using this method, be aware that some Unix systems place a limit on the size of the line—usually 32 characters. You will therefore need to make sure you place the most significant of the command line options early in the arguments. Although there are no hard-and-fast rules, the **-T** (taint checking) and **-I** arguments should be placed as early as possible in the command line options, irrespective of where they are specified.

Whether they are specified on the command line or within the #! line, command line options can either be selected individually, as in,

```
$ perl -p -i.bak -e "s/foo/bar/g"
```

or they can be combined:

```
$ perl -pi.bak -e "s/foo/bar/g"
```

-a

Turns on autosplit mode (implies the **split** function); fields are split into the **@F** array. The use of the **-a** option is equivalent to

```
while (<>)
{
    @F = split(' ');
}
```

This is generally used with the **-F**, **-n**, or **-p** option to automatically split and/or summarize a group of input files.

-C

Tells Perl to use the native wide character APIs, currently only implemented on the Windows platform.

-c

Checks the syntax of the script without executing it. Only **BEGIN** and **END** blocks and **use** statements are actually executed by this process, since they are considered an integral part of the compilation process. The **INIT** and **END** blocks, however, are skipped. Executing a program that does not have any syntax errors will report "syntax ok". For example:

```
$ perl -wc myscript.pl
myscript.pl syntax OK
```

If you want to check a number of scripts concurrently, then you will need to use the looping features of your shell to execute each script as follows:

```
for file in *.pl
do
perl -wc $file
done
```

It's also a good idea, as shown here, to switch on warnings while testing.

-d[:module]

Without the optional **module**, this invokes the Perl debugger after your script has been compiled and places the program counter within the debugger at the start of your script. If **module** is specified, the script is compiled and control of the execution is passed to the specified module. For example, **-d:Dprof** invokes the Perl profiling system and **-d:ptkdb** starts the ptkdb debugger interface in place of the normal command line debugger. See Chapter 21 for more information.

-Dflags

Specifies the debugging options defined by **flags**, as seen in Table 15-1. Note that options can be selected either by their letter combination or by specifying the decimal value of the combined options. For example, to switch on taint checks and memory allocation, you would use **-Dmu** or **-D2176**.

You will need to have compiled Perl with the **-DDEBUGGING** compiler directive for these debugging flags to work. See Chapter 21 (and also Appendix C) for more details on debugging Perl scripts, or see my book, *DeBugging Perl* (Osborne/McGraw-Hill) for a complete description of what each of these options provides.

PROGRAMMING
WITH PERL

Number	Letter	Description
1	p	Tokenizing and parsing
2	s	Stack snapshots
4	l	Context (loop) stack processing
8	t	Trace execution
16	o	Method and overloading resolution
32	c	String/numeric conversions
64	P	Print preprocessor command for **-P**
128	m	Memory allocation
256	f	Format processing
512	r	Regular expression parsing and execution
1024	x	Syntax tree dump
2048	u	Tainting checks
4096	L	Memory leaks (you need to have used the **-DLEAKTEST** directive when compiling Perl)
8192	H	Hash dump
16384	X	Scratchpad allocation
32768	D	Cleaning up
65536	S	Thread synchronization

Table 15-1.   *Debugging Flags*

-e commandline

The **commandline** will be interpreted as a single-line Perl script. For example,

```
$ perl -e 'print 4+5,"\n";'
```

will print 9.

-Fregex

Specifies the pattern to use for splitting when the **-a** command line option is in use. By default, the value used is a single space. The **regex** can be specified including any of the normal delimiters allowed by **split**, that is " ", "", and //.

-h

Prints the Perl usage summary but does not execute the Perl interpreter.

-iext

Edits the file "in place"—that is, edits are conducted and written straight back to the file. The optional **ext** defines the extension to append to the old version of the file. Actually, what happens is that the file is moved to the "backup" version, and then the file and edits are written back into the original. If **ext** is not specified, a temporary file is used. Note that you must append the extension, including a period if desired; Perl does not add any characters to the backup file except those specified.

This is generally used with the **-p**, **-n**, and **-e** options to edit a series of files in a loop. For example, the command line

```
$ perl -pi.bak -e "s/foo/bar/g" *
```

replaces every occurrence of "foo" with "bar" in all files in the current directory.

-Idir

Prepends the directory, **dir**, to the list used to search for modules (**@INC**) and the directories used to search for include files included via the C preprocessor (invoked with **-P**). See also the **use lib** pragma in Chapter 19 and the effects of the **PERLLIB** and **PERL5LIB** environment variables later in the chapter.

-l[char]

Sets the character, **char**, that will automatically be appended to all printed output. The specification should be via the octal equivalent. By default, no characters are automatically added to printed lines. If **char** is not specified, this makes the value of the output record separator ($\) equal the value of the input record separator ($/).

-mmodule and -Mmodule

Includes the module specified by **module** before executing your script and allows you to specify additional options to the **use** statement generated. For example, the command line

```
$ perl -MPOSIX=:fcntl_h,:float_h
```

is equivalent to

```
use POSIX qw/:fcntl_h :float_h/;
```

The **-M** form also allows you to use quotes to specify the options. For example, the preceding line could be written as

```
$ perl -M'POSIX qw/:fcntl_h :float_h/'
```

In both cases, a single hyphen as the first character after **-M** or **-m** indicates that **no** should be used in place of **use**.

-n

Causes Perl to assume the following code around your script for each file specified on the command line:

```
while(<>)
{
}
```

Note that the contents of the files are not printed or otherwise output during execution, unless specified within the script itself. Any files in the list of those to be opened that cannot be opened are reported as errors, and execution continues to the next file in the list.

-p

Causes Perl to assume the following code around your script for each file specified on the command line:

```
while(<>)
{
}
continue
{
    print or die "-p destination: $!\n";
}
```

As you can see, an error during printing/updating is considered fatal. The **-p** option overrides the **-n** option.

Any files in the list of those to be opened that cannot be opened are reported as errors, and execution continues to the next file in the list.

-P

Invokes the C preprocessor on the script before it is parsed by the Perl interpreter. Care should be taken when using comments in the original C source, since lines starting with a # character and a keyword, such as **if** or **define**, will be interpreted as a preprocessor directive.

-s

Enables basic command line switching. Once this option has been set, any command line options specified after the script name are interpreted as the names of variables, with their values being set to true within the script. For example,

```
$ perl -s t.pl -true
```

will create a variable **$true** within the current invocation of t.pl.

A more advanced system is to use the **Getopt::Long** or **Getopt::Std** modules.

-S

Uses the **$PATH** environment variable to find the script. It will also add extensions to the script being searched for if a lookup on the original name fails.

-T

Switches on "taint" checking. Variables and information that originate or derive from external sources are considered to be "unsafe" and will cause your script to fail when used in functions such as **system**. This is most often used when a script is executed on behalf of another process, such as a web server. You should specify this option at the start of the command line options to ensure that taint checking is switched on as early as possible. See the "Security" section later in this chapter for more information.

-u

Causes Perl to dump the program core of the interpreter and script after compilation (and before execution). In theory, this can be used with an **undump** program to produce a stand-alone executable, but the Perl-to-C compiler has superseded this option. See Chapter 19 for more information on these and other methods for generating stand-alone Perl binaries.

-U

Allows the Perl script to do unsafe operations. These currently include only the unlinking of directories when you are superuser or when running setuid programs. This option will also turn fatal taint checks into warnings, providing the **-w** option is also specified.

-v

Prints the version and patch level of the Perl interpreter, but does not execute the interpreter.

-V[:var]

Prints the version and configuration information for the Perl interpreter. If the optional **var** is supplied, it prints out only the configuration information for the specified element as discovered via the **Config** module. Here is the default output from the function:

```
$ perl -V
Summary of my perl5 (revision 5.0 version 6 subversion 0) configuration:
  Platform:
    osname=solaris, osvers=2.8, archname=i86pc-solaris-thread-multi
    uname='sunos twinsol 5.8 generic_108529-03 i86pc i386 i86pc '
    config_args='-ds -e -Dcc=gcc -Dthreads'
    hint=previous, useposix=true, d_sigaction=define
    usethreads=define use5005threads=undef useithreads=define usemultiplicity=define
    useperlio=undef d_sfio=undef uselargefiles=define
    use64bitint=undef use64bitall=undef uselongdouble=undef usesocks=undef
  Compiler:
    cc='gcc', optimize='-O', gccversion=2.95.2 19991024 (release)
    cppflags='-D_REENTRANT -fno-strict-aliasing -I/usr/local/include -D_LARGEFILE_SOURCE -D_FILE_OFFSET_BITS=64'
    ccflags ='-D_REENTRANT -fno-strict-aliasing -I/usr/local/include -D_LARGEFILE_SOURCE -D_FILE_OFFSET_BITS=64'
    stdchar='char', d_stdstdio=define, usevfork=false
    intsize=4, longsize=4, ptrsize=4, doublesize=8
    d_longlong=define, longlongsize=8, d_longdbl=define, longdblsize=12
    ivtype='long', ivsize=4, nvtype='double', nvsize=8, Off_t='off_t',
    lseeksize=8
    alignbytes=4, usemymalloc=y, prototype=define
  Linker and Libraries:
    ld='gcc', ldflags =' -L/usr/local/lib '
    libpth=/usr/local/lib /lib /usr/lib /usr/ccs/lib
    libs=-lsocket -lnsl -ldb -ldl -lm -lposix4 -lpthread -lc -lcrypt -lsec
    libc=/lib/libc.so, so=so, useshrplib=false, libperl=libperl.a
  Dynamic Linking:
    dlsrc=dl_dlopen.xs, dlext=so, d_dlsymun=undef, ccdlflags=' '
    cccdlflags='-fPIC', lddlflags='-G -L/usr/local/lib'


Characteristics of this binary (from libperl):
  Compile-time options: MULTIPLICITY USE_ITHREADS USE_LARGE_FILES PERL_IMPLICIT_CONTEXT
  Built under solaris
  Compiled at Nov 17 2000 18:12:25
  @INC:
    /usr/local/lib/perl5/5.6.0/i86pc-solaris-thread-multi
    /usr/local/lib/perl5/5.6.0
    /usr/local/lib/perl5/site_perl/5.6.0/i86pc-solaris-thread-multi
    /usr/local/lib/perl5/site_perl/5.6.0
    /usr/local/lib/perl5/site_perl
    .
```

The specification of **var** can be a specific option; for example:

```
$ perl -V:lns
lns='/usr/bin/ln -s';
```

shows the name of the symbolic link command.

Alternatively, **var** can be a regular expression:

```
$ perl -V:install.*lib
installarchlib='/usr/local/lib/perl5/5.6.0/i86pc-solaris-thread-multi'
installprivlib='/usr/local/lib/perl5/5.6.0'
installsitelib='/usr/local/lib/perl5/site_perl/5.6.0'
installvendorlib=''
```

-w

Prints out warnings about possible typographical and interpretation errors in the script. Note that this command line option can be overridden by using the **no warnings** pragma or adjusting the value of the **$^W** variable in the source script. See Chapter 19 for more information on the Perl warnings system.

-W

Enables all warnings, ignoring the use of **no warnings** or **$^W**. See Chapter 19 for more information on the Perl warnings system.

-X

Disables all warnings, even if **$^W** and **use warnings** have been employed. See Chapter 19 for more information on the Perl warnings system.

-x[dir]

Extracts the script from an email message or other piped data stream. Perl will ignore any information up to a line that starts with **#!** and contains the word **perl**. Any directory name will be used as the directory in which to run the script, and the command line switches contained in the line will be applied as usual. The script must be terminated either by an EOF or an **__END__** marker.

This option can be used to execute code stored in email messages without first requiring you to extract the script element.

-0[val]

Specifies the initial value for the input record separator **$/**.

Special Handling

When running Perl via the command line, there are special treatments for some of the functions and operators we have already seen. In general, these only affect Perl when you have called it with the **-p** and/or **-i** options. For example:

```
$ perl -pi.bak -e "print" *
```

As we already know, this puts a notional loop around the single **print** statement to iterate through the files on the command line. In fact, the loop is slightly more complex, and more correctly actually looks like this:

```
while($ARGV = shift)
{
    open(ARGV, $ARGV) or warn "Can't open $ARGV: $!\n";
    while(<ARGV>)
    {
    }
    continue
    {
        print or die "-p destination: $!\n";
    }
}
```

The special filehandle **ARGV** is attached to the current file within the list of files supplied on the command line.

The effect of the **eof** function is now changed slightly. The statement

```
eof();
```

only returns the end of file of the last file in the list of files supplied on the command line. You have to use **eof(ARGV)** or **eof** (without parentheses) to detect the end of file for each file supplied on the command line.

Perl Environment Variables

The effects of certain elements of Perl and Perl functions can be modified by environment variables. Many of these variables are set automatically by your shell. In the case of MacPerl, these values can be configured within the MacPerl environment.

HOME

The home directory for the script. This is used by **chdir** if no argument is specified.

LOGDIR

Used by **chdir** if no argument is specified and the **HOME** environment variable is not set.

PATH

This is the list of directories searched when invoking a command via **system**, **exec**, backticks, or other external application callers. This is also the directory list searched with the **-S** command line option.

PERLLIB

The colon-separated list of directories used to look for the modules and libraries required for the Perl script. Note that this list overrides the values defined within the interpreter. This variable is ignored if **PERL5LIB** has been set.

PERL5LIB

The colon-separated list of directories used to look for the modules and libraries required for the Perl script. Note that this list overrides the values defined within the interpreter.

The values here can be added to or overridden entirely using the **use lib** pragma (see Chapter 16) and the **-l** command line option (explained earlier in this chapter). Note that only the **use lib** pragma is supported when taint checking is in effect.

PERL5OPT

Allows you to predefine any of the **DIMUdmw** command line switches for every invocation of the Perl interpreter. The variable is ignored when taint checking is in effect.

PERL5DB

The command used to load the debugger code when the **-d** option is specified on the command line. The default value is

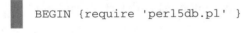

```
BEGIN {require 'perl5db.pl' }
```

You can use this variable to permanently enable profiling or to use an alternative debugger (including those with windowed interfaces). See Chapter 21 for more information on using the Perl debugger.

PERL5SHELL

This is specific to the Win32 port of Perl (see Chapter 22). It specifies the alternative shell that Perl should use internally for executing external commands via **system** or backticks. The default under Windows NT is to use the standard **cmd.exe** with the **/x/c** switches. Under Windows 95 the **command.com /c** command is used.

PERL_DEBUG_MSTATS

This option causes the memory statistics for the script to be dumped after execution. It only works if Perl has been compiled with Perl's own version of the **malloc()** function. You can use

```
$ perl -V:d_mymalloc
```

to determine whether this is the case. A value of **define** indicates that Perl's **malloc()** is being used.

PERL_DESTRUCT_LEVEL

Controls the destruction of global objects and other references, but only if the Perl interpreter has been compiled with the **-DDEBUGGING** compiler directive.

Perl in Perl (eval)

A favorite function of many Perl programmers is **eval**. This function provides a great number of facilities, the most useful of which is the ability to execute a piece of arbitrary Perl source code during the execution of a script without actually affecting the execution process of the main script.

Normally when you run a Perl script, the code contained in the script is parsed, checked, and compiled before it is actually executed. When the script contains a call to the **eval** function, a new instance of a Perl interpreter is created, and the new interpreter then parses the code within the supplied block or expression at the time of execution. Because the code is handled at execution time, rather than compile time, the source code that is executed can be dynamic—perhaps even generated within another part of the Perl script.

Another advantage of **eval** is that because the code is executed in a completely separate instance of the interpreter, it can also be used for checking the availability of modules, functions, and other elements that would normally cause a break during the compilation stage of the script.

The basic format for the execution of an expression or block with **eval** is

```
eval EXPR
eval BLOCK
```

In both cases, the variables, functions, and other elements of the program are accessible within the new interpreter. We'll look at the specifics of each technique in more detail.

Using eval EXPR

When **eval** is called with **EXPR**, the contents of the expression (normally a string or scalar variable) will be parsed and interpreted each time the **eval** function is called. This means that the value of **EXPR** can change between invocations, and it also implies a small overhead because the code contained within the expression is parsed and compiled just like any other Perl script.

For example, the following code attempts to import a module based on the value of a variable, but we already know (from Chapter 6) that **use** statements are interpreted at run time, and therefore the following will not work:

```
if ($windows)
{
    use DBI::W32ODBC;
}
else
{
    use DBI;
}
```

What will actually happen is that Perl will parse both **use** statements, which are interpreted at compile time, rather than execution time, and therefore probably fail.

However, we can use **eval** to do the job for us:

```
$module = $windows ? 'DBI::W32ODBC' : 'DBI';
eval " use $module; ";
```

Because the **eval** statement is evaluating the string in a new instance of the interpreter, the above example will do what we wanted, loading the correct based on the value of a variable. Also, because the new interpreter is a subset of the main interpreter, the newly imported module will also be available to the parent script.

Using eval BLOCK

With the **BLOCK** form, the contents are parsed and compiled along with the rest of the script, but the actual execution only takes place when the **eval** statement is reached. This removes the slight performance delay, but it also reduces the ability to dynamically parse and execute a piece of Perl code.

Because the code is parsed at the time of compilation of the rest of the script, the **BLOCK** form cannot be used to check for syntax errors in a piece of dynamically generated code. You also cannot use it in the same way as the example we used for **EXPR** formats. If you try the previous operation using the **BLOCK** form,

```
$module = $windows ? 'DBI::W320DBC' : 'DBI';
eval { use $module; };
```

the compilation will fail because we're trying to use a variable in a **use** statement. Even if it did work, **$module** doesn't have a value yet—the preceding line has not been executed, so **$module** is undefined.

> **Note** *The **BLOCK** form of **eval** must have a semicolon at the termination of the block. The **BLOCK** you are defining is not the same as that used by **while**, **for**, or **sub**.*

Trapping Exceptions

Because **eval** starts a new instance of an interpreter, any exceptions (serious errors) raised during the parsing of the statement can be trapped without affecting the execution of the main script. The text or error message from an exception raised during the execution of an **eval** statement, either from the parser (in the case of **eval EXPR**) or through an embedded call to a **die** function, is placed directly into the $@ variable, and execution of the expression ends. For example, to check for the existence of a specific module,

```
eval { use DBI; };
print "Error loading DBI: $@" if ($@);
```

Alternatively you can force the error using **die**:

```
eval { die "Quitting..."; };
print "Error: $@" if ($@);
```

In all other respects, the **eval** statement executes a script as normal. The filehandles **STDIN**, **STDOUT**, and **STDERR** are still valid, and calls to **warn** print an error message to **STDERR** as normal. Only a call to **die**, **exit**, or an exception (missing function or module or a syntax error) can cause the termination of an **eval** statement.

You can, however, use the $SIG{__WARN__} signal handler to interrupt the normal **warn** execution and update the $@ variable if necessary. See Chapter 14 for more information on signals, propagation, and the $SIG{__WARN__} signal handler.

Returning Information

The **eval** statement returns information in the same way as a subroutine—the return value (not $@) from **eval** is the value specified in a call to **return**, or it is the last evaluated statement in the block or expression. For example,

```
$retval = eval "54+63";
```

should contain the value 117.

eval and the __DIE__ signal handler

If you have installed the __DIE__ signal handler, you need to take care when using the **die** function within an **eval** block. If you do not want the signal handler to be called when the **die** function is used, you can localize the $SIG{__DIE__} function, which effectively disables the main signal handler for **die** (if installed) for the duration of the **eval** statement. This is as easy as placing the localize statement within the **eval** block.

This becomes even more useful if you actually make use of the localized signal handler within the confines of the **eval** sequence. Since the signal handler is cyclical, once the localized signal handler has completed, you can call **die** again to exit the **eval** block, thereby producing a customized error message. The following example prepends some information to the error message produced:

```
{
    local $SIG{'__DIE__'} =
        sub { die "Fatal Error: $_[0]"; };
    eval { die "Couldn't open...." };
    print $@ if ($@);
}
```

Threads

Threads are a relatively new to Perl, and they have been heavily rewritten under Perl 5.6 to make better use of the facilities offered by the operating systems that support threads, such as Solaris, Linux, and Windows. Before we look at how Perl handles threads, we'll take a look at what threads are and how most operating systems handle and take advantage of the thread facility.

How Multitasking Works

If you look at a typical modern operating system, you'll see that it's designed to handle the execution of a number of processes simultaneously. The method for employing this is either through *cooperative multitasking* or *preemptive multitasking*. In both cases, the actual method for executing a number of processes simultaneously is the same—the operating system literally switches between applications every fraction of a second, suspending the previous application and then resuming the next one in a round-robin fashion. So, if the operating system has 20 concurrent processes, each one will be executed for a fraction of a second before being suspended again and having to wait for 19 other processes to do their work before getting a chance to work again.

The individual processes are typically unaware of this switching, and the effects on the application are negligible—most applications couldn't care less whether they were working as a single process or as part of a multiprocessing environment, because the operating system controls their execution at such a low level.

The two different types of multitasking—cooperative and preemptive—describe how the operating system controls the applications that are executing. With *cooperative* multitasking, all processes are potentially given the same amount of execution time as all others. Some operating systems are more specific and provide the "main" application with the bulk of the processor time (say 80 percent), and the "background" applications with equal amounts of the remainder (20 percent). This is the model used by the Mac OS, and it allows the GUI environment to give the most time to the application the user is currently employing.

Preemptive multitasking is much more complex. Instead of just arbitrarily sharing the processor time between all of the processes that are executing, an operating system with preemptive multitasking gives the most processor time to the process that requires it. The operating system does this by monitoring the processes that are running and assigning priorities to each process; those with higher priorities get more time, and those with the lowest priorities get the least. Because we can control the priorities of the processes, we have much greater control over how different processes are executed. On a database server, for example, you'd want to give the database process the highest priority to ensure the speed of the database. Preemptive multitasking is one of the main features of server-oriented operating systems, including Unix, Linux, and NT-based Windows implementations, including Windows 2000 and NT itself.

The different multitasking solutions also determine the different hardware types that can be used with an operating system. Cooperative multitasking is really only practical on a single-processor system. This is because of the round-robin approach, which requires that the process resides on the same processor for its entire duration.

With preemptive multitasking, multiprocessor solutions are available. Because the operating system knows how much time each process requires, it can assign individual processes to different processors depending on how busy each processor is, in order to make the best use of the available processor capacity and to spread the load more effectively. However, the division of labor is only on a process-by-process basis, so if you have one particularly intensive process, it can only be executed on a single processor, even if it has enough load to be spread across multiple processors.

From Multitasking to Multithreading

With a multitasking operating system, there are a number of processes all executing, apparently, concurrently. In reality, of course, each process is running for a fraction of a second, and potentially many times a second, to give the impression of a real multitasking environment with lots of individual processors working on their own application.

For each process, there is an allocation of memory within the addressing space supported by the operating system that needs to be tracked, and for multiuser operating systems, such as Unix, there are also permission and security attributes and, of course, the actual code for the application itself. Tracking all of this information is a full-time job—under Unix there are a number of processes that keep an eye on all of this information, in addition to the core kernel process that actually handles many of the requests.

If an individual process wants to be able to perform a number of tasks concurrently, then there are two possible solutions. The first solution is a round-robin approach, as used by the main operating system, but without the same level of control. Each function that needs to be executed is called in sequence in a loop, but because we can't arbitrarily terminate a function mid-execution, there are often problems with "lag-time"—if a function has a large amount of information to process, then its execution will hold up the entire loop.

For file processing, you can get around this by using **select** and parsing fixed blocks of information for each file. In this instance, we only process the information from the files that have supplied (or require) more data, and providing we only read a single line, or a fixed-length block of data, the time to process each request should be relatively small.

For solutions that require more complex multitasking facilities, the only other alternative is to **fork** a new process specifically to handle the processing event. Because **fork** creates a new process, its execution and priority handling can be controlled by the parent operating system. This is usually the solution used by network services, such as Apache and IMAP or POP3 daemons. When a client connects to the server, it forks a new process designed to handle the requests of the client.

The problem with forking a new process is that it is a time-consuming and very resource-hungry process. Creating a new process implies allocating a new block of memory and creating a new entry in the process table used by the operating system's scheduler to control each process's execution. To give you an idea of the resource implications, a typical Apache process takes up about 500K—if 20 clients connect all at the same time, it requires the allocation of 10MB of memory and the duplication of the main image into each of the 20 new processes.

In most situations, we don't actually need most of the baggage associated with a new process. With Apache, a forked process doesn't need to read the configuration file—it's already been done for us, and we don't need to handle any of the complex socket handlers. We only need the ability to communicate with the client socket we are servicing.

This resource requirement puts unnecessary limits on the number of concurrent clients that can be connected at any one time—it is dependent on the available memory and ultimately the number of processes that the operating system can handle. The actual code required to service the client requests could be quite small, say 20K. Using multiprocessing on a system with 128MB might limit the number of clients to around 200—not a particularly large number for a busy website. To handle more requests than that, you'd need more memory, and probably more processors—switching between 200 processes on a single CPU is not recommended because the amount of time given to each process during a single pass (executing each process once), would be very small, and therefore it would take minutes for a single process to service even a small request.

This is where threads come in. A thread is like a slimmed-down process—in fact they are often called "lightweight processes." The thread runs within the confines of the parent process and normally executes just one function from the parent. Creating a new thread doesn't mean allocating large areas of memory (there's probably room within the parent's memory allocation) or require additions to the operating system's schedule tables either. In our web server example, rather than forking a new process to handle the client, we could instead create a new thread using the function that handles client requests.

By using multithreading, we can therefore get the multiprocessing capability offered by the parent operating system, but within the confines of a single process. Now an individual process can execute a number of functions simultaneously, or alternatively execute the same function a number of times, just as you would with our web server.

On an operating system that supports preemptive multitasking and multithreading, we get the prioritizing system on the main process and an internal "per-process" multitasking environment. On a multiprocessor system, the operating system will also spread the individual threads from a single process across all of the processors. So, if we have one particularly intensive process, it can use all of the available resources by splitting its operation into a number of individual threads.

Threading is, of course, very OS-specific. Even now, there are only a handful of operating systems that provide the functionality to a reasonable level, and some require additional or different libraries to enable the functionality. Most of the operating systems that support threading are either Unix based (Solaris, AIX, HP-UX, some Linux distributions, BSD, Mac OS X) or Windows based (Windows 98/NT/2000/Me).

Comparing Threads to Multiple Processes

The major difference between multithreaded and multiprocess applications is directly related to the relative resource cost, which we've already covered. Using **fork** to create duplicate instances of the same process requires a lot of memory and processor time. The overhead for a new thread is only slightly larger than the size of the function you are executing, and unless you are passing around huge blocks of data, it's not inconceivable to be able to create hundreds of threads.

The only other difference is the level of control and communication that you can exercise over the threads. When you **fork** a process, you are limited in how you can communicate and control the process. To exchange information, you'll need to open pipes to communicate with your children and this becomes unwieldy with a large number of children. If you simply want to control the children, you are limited to using signals to either kill or suspend the processes—there's no way to reintegrate the threads back into the main process, or to arbitrarily control their execution without using signals.

Comparing Threads to select()

The **select** function provides an excellent way of handling the data input and output from a number of filehandles concurrently, but this is where the comparison ends. It's not possible, in any way, to use **select** for anything other than communicating with filehandles, and this limits its effectiveness for concurrent processing.

On the other hand, with threads you can create a new thread to handle any aspect of your process's execution, including, but not limited to, communication with filehandles. For example, with a multidiscipline calculation you might create new threads to handle the different parts of the calculation.

Threads and Perl

Threads have been heavily updated in Perl 5.6 to form a significant, if still largely experimental, part of the Perl language. In fact, in some circumstances, threads actually form a core part of the language's new architecture, and on the Windows platform threads are used to emulate the operation for **fork**, a function that is missing from the operating system itself.

Within Perl, the thread system is controlled using the **Thread** module, which provides an object-oriented interface for the creation and control of individual threads. To create a new thread, you create a new **Thread** object and supply the name of a predefined subroutine, which forms the basis of the thread's execution sequence. Once started, a thread can be paused, stopped, split into other threads, or bonded with other threads to create a "superthread." In all instances, the threads remain attached to the parent process—it's not possible to convert a thread into a new process, although there's potentially no reason why you couldn't call **fork**!

Creating a New Thread

To create a new thread, import the **Thread** module and then create a new **Thread** object. For example, to create a new thread that uses the subroutine **process_queue**:

```
use Thread;
$thread = new Thread \&process_queue,"/usr/local/queue";
```

The object accepts the name of the subroutine to execute, and any further arguments are supplied as arguments to that subroutine. The **$thread** variable in the preceding example contains a reference to the newly created thread and will provide a link from the main program to the thread.

The thread can obtain a reference to itself with the **self** method:

```
$me = Thread->self;
```

Each thread is given its own unique thread ID. The main program has a thread ID of 0, and subsequent threads are given a sequential thread number up to a current maximum of $2^{32}-1$. You can discover the thread ID using the **tid** method,

```
$tid = $thread->tid;
```

or for a thread to find its own ID:

```
$mytid = Thread->self->tid;
```

You can also get a list of all the running and finished threads (providing the thread has not been **join**ed—see the section on the next page) by using the **list** method:

```
@threads = Thread->list;
```

You'll need to process the information yourself, but the list of object references should be enough for you to determine the current status of each thread using the methods we've already seen.

If all you want is a unique identifier for a thread (perhaps for tracking or logging purposes), the best solution is to use the **Thread::Specific** module, which creates a thread-specific key. To use it, call the **key_create** function within a thread:

```
use Thread::Specific;
my $k = key_create Thread::Specific;
```

Creating a Thread Using an Anonymous Subroutine

You can supply an anonymous subroutine as the first argument to the **new** constructor when creating a new thread, although it looks a little bit like line noise:

```
$t = Thread->new(sub { print "I'm a thread" } );
```

Note that closures work as normal, so this

```
my $message = "I'm another thread";
$t = Thread->new(sub { display $message } );
```

does what you expect, and displays the message using whatever method **display** handles.

As an alternative to the anonymous subroutine form, you can also import the special **async** function from **Thread**, which creates a new anonymous subroutine thread for you. For example, we could rewrite the preceding example as

```
use Thread 'async';
$t = async { display $message; };
```

Note that the block is treated as an anonymous subroutine and must be terminated by a closing semicolon. It returns a thread object, just like the **new** function/constructor.

Controlling a Thread

Once you have created a new thread, it continues running until the subroutine that you supplied terminates. However, there is the issue of what happens to the thread when it returns. Unless the parent process is actually waiting for a return value (which defeats the object!), you need a way of harvesting the threads at some later date, in a similar fashion to harvesting child processes started with **fork**.

The method for handling this is called **join**, and it works in a similar fashion to **waitpid**—if the thread has already terminated, then it returns immediately. If the thread is still running, then **join** blocks the process until it has been completed. For example,

```
$result = $thread->join;
```

Note that the **join** method actually does what it suggests, it joins the thread on which you apply the method to the current process, even if that happens to be another thread. This allows you to spawn a number of threads that can be set to wait for each other's return values—great for cooperative processing tasks where each thread is working on a different part of a calculation.

There are only two exceptions to the use of **join**; you cannot join a thread to itself, and you can't join a thread that has already been joined by another thread.

Note, as well, that the return value from the **join** method is always evaluated in a list context. This means that the return value from the subroutine can be a scalar, array, hash, or other object, but it also means that in a scalar context, the last value of the list is assigned to the scalar.

Trapping join Exceptions

If you want to trap any exceptions raised during the **join** process, you must use the **eval** method instead of **join**. This automatically wraps an **eval** function around the **join** method. Return values from the thread are placed into $@, as usual.

Detaching Threads

If you want a thread to execute, but you are not worried about its return value, then you can call the **detach** method. This effectively relinquishes your control of the thread, although it remains part of the current process. This allows the thread to continue and to die of its own accord without having to call the **join** method to clean up after the thread—Perl will handle the clean-up operation for you.

Note, however, that this doesn't absolve you of all responsibility for the thread. If the thread is still executing when the main parent dies, then execution will wait until the thread has completed—it doesn't actually detach the thread into its own process.

The thread will also continue to consume memory if you neither **join** nor **detach** it. This is because Perl keeps the allocation of memory around just in case it's needed, even though you may have decided to ignore it.

Yielding

The **yield** function is designed to free up processor cycles in use by the calling thread so that they can be used for any child threads. This provides a crude method for prioritizing individual threads and assigning them processor time, but it's not very portable or practical in the long term.

Controlling Variables

Sharing variables across threads is as dangerous and prone to error as sharing a database file across many processes (see Chapter 13). The basis for controlling access to the variables is much the same. You set a "lock" on the variable to indicate its status. Also, like the file locks that are available, the variable locks are advisory. Although you can lock a variable, there is nothing to prevent a thread from accessing or updating it. It is entirely up to the programmer to check the lock status and decide whether the variable should or should not be used. The main function for locking a variable is the **lock** function:

```
lock($var);
```

The lock set on the variable lasts as long as the scope of the current block. If a lock is already set on the variable by another thread, then the **lock** function will block execution of the current thread until the other has finished using it. Note that the lock is on the entity, not the contents, so a call such as

```
lock(@var);
```

only sets the lock on the **@var** variable, not on the individual elements of the array. Therefore, another call to **lock($var[0])** will not block. Also, references are only followed to one level, such that an attempt to lock the reference **\$var** will work, but trying to lock **\\$var** will not work.

Once a variable is locked, you can control the unlocking process with three separate functions: **cond_wait**, **cond_signal**, and **cond_broadcast**. The **cond_wait** function is the main one. It unlocks the variable and blocks until another thread does a **cond_signal** or **cond_broadcast** call for the variable. The function therefore enables you to wait until another process indicates (either through the **cond_signal** or **cond_broadcast** function) that the thread has finished using the variable. Once the **cond_wait** unblocks, the variable is locked again.

The **cond_wait** function takes one argument—a locked variable—and unblocks a random thread that is waiting for the variable via **cond_wait**. It is not possible to specify which thread is unblocked. You can unblock all waiting threads using the **cond_broadcast** function, which also takes a single (locked) variable as an argument.

This is a very complicated description of what is basically a simple process of indicators and signals that allow you to control access to a variable. Consider that you have two threads, A and B, and they both want to update a variable **$var**. Thread A locks the variable with **lock** and then starts its update. Meanwhile, thread B decides that it needs to update the variable, so it calls **cond_wait($var)**, effectively halting the B thread until A has finished.

Once A has completed the update, it calls **cond_signal($var)**, indicating to thread B that it has finished with the variable. The **cond_wait** function called from thread B then locks the variables for its own use and continues execution. This process of waiting and signaling the status of locked variables allows you to control access to them and prevent the corruption that could occur if two threads were to update the variable at the same time.

Fortunately, in the example, there are only two threads, and so the locking method is relatively straightforward. In a multithreaded process, controlling access to a single variable may be more difficult. You may want to try using either the queuing or semaphore methods for divining information about the variables that you want to share among processes.

Controlling Subroutines

Since subroutines are just other objects, you can also lock them using the **lock** function. However, unlike locks on variables, a **lock** on a subroutine is mandatory—no one else but the thread with the lock can use that subroutine.

There are times, however, when you want a subroutine to be locked automatically on execution. You can set this behavior using the **locked** attribute when you define the subroutine. For example:

```
sub process : locked
{
}
```

Queues

Although you can use ordinary variables for exchanging information between running threads, it often requires careful use of the **lock** function to ensure you are using the right value at the right time. If all you want to do is exchange simple information between threads, a better method is to use a simple stack. However, you can't use a simple scalar array, since that will exhibit the same (if not more complex) problems regarding locking and access you already know about regarding the **lock** and other functions.

Instead, the Perl thread system supports a message queue object. This is basically a standard array, except that it is thread compatible and so handles additions and removals from the list safely, without the normal risk to corruption of the variables. To create a new queue:

```
use Thread::Queue;
my $queue = new Thread::Queue;
```

The list operates strictly on a LILO (last in, last out) format, so new entries are added to the end of the list, and entries are removed and returned from the start of list. The **enqueue** method adds a list of values to the end of the queue:

```
$thread->enqueue('Martin', 'Brown');
```

The **dequeue** function returns and removes a single scalar from the beginning of the queue:

```
$value = $thread->dequeue;
```

If the queue is empty, the thread blocks until there is an entry in the queue. To immediately return from a **dequeue** operation, you use **dequeue_nb**, which does not block; it simply returns **undef** if the list is empty.

Finally, you can use the **pending** method to find out how many items are left on the queue. Note that this information is correct at the time the method is called, but it does not guarantee that this is the current value if multiple threads are accessing and using the queue simultaneously. To get around this potential problem, you can use the **lock** function to lock the object so that its state is consistent between the **pending** method and the time you use it.

Semaphores

A *semaphore* is defined in the dictionary as a system of signaling. In the realm of threads, a semaphore can be used to indicate a particular occurrence to a thread. The information is provided in the form of a number, and this number can be increased or decreased as necessary. The method for employing the semaphore is to use the **Thread::Semaphore** module and create a new object:

```
$sema = new Thread::Semaphore;
```

The default value is 1, or you can specify the initial value:

```
$sema = new Thread::Semaphore(256);
```

Two methods, **up** and **down**, then increase or decrease the value, either by the default value of 1, or by the amount specified. The lowest value however is 1, so the code

```
$sema->up;
$sema->down(256);
```

will set the value of the **$sema** semaphore back to 1.

How you use the semaphore value is entirely up to you. The usual method is to create a semaphore that relates to the available quantity of a specific resource.

Signals

Because signals could interrupt the normal execution process of the script, particularly when working with threads, it can be a good idea to create a separate thread just for handling signals. This is practical not only for multithreaded applications, but also for applications that make use of pipes, non-blocking I/O, and even networking. Of course, by creating a new thread for signals, your script is now multithreaded, but it doesn't mean you have to create additional threads for handling the rest of your script.

To create a new signal-handling thread, all you do is import the **Thread::Signal** function:

```
use Thread::Signal;
```

This automatically generates a new thread and causes all signals to the program to be handled within this thread. There is no difference in the way you set up signal handlers. They can be assigned to existing functions or handled by anonymous subroutines, as usual. The difference is that the signal handlers execute within the realm of a new thread. This allows execution of the current process to continue when a signal is received.

There are some traps in using this technique. Using **die** within a signal handler executed in the signal thread will cause the thread to exit, but won't necessarily cause the main thread to quit. This also means you will have problems when using **exit** within an extension, since this too will affect the signal handler thread and not the main program.

Security

The security of the script you are running may be an issue, whether you are running a secure service or when you are using Perl as the CGI interface on a web server. There are two basic threats. The first is of introducing bogus or dangerous information from the outside world into the data structures within a Perl script. The second threat is from the execution of a specific feature of Perl that might otherwise make the script unsafe. These two dangers can potentially cause all manner of problems.

Solving the first problem is a case of checking and marking the information so that it can be recognized as possibly being dangerous. Perl will do this automatically by "tainting" the data that has come from external sources, such as from the command line or the outside environment. Using "tainted" information in functions and statements that run an external program could be dangerous. Imagine, for example, getting an email address from a user, entered on the command line. If you passed this unchecked to the **sendmail** program, it could potentially send back to the cracker any information they wanted or it could even be used to modify information in the system files through the use of pipes. The taint mode gets around this problem.

The second problem is more difficult to solve, but a method is also provided with the standard Perl distribution. Execution of certain functions and even of some operators could be a potential problem. Using the **Safe** module (which also makes use of the **Opcode** module), you can enable and disable different functions and operators, and then execute a Perl script within this restricted environment.

Using Taint Mode

Perl provides a facility called *taint checking*. This option forces Perl to examine the origin of the variables used within a script. Information gleaned from the outside world is tainted, or marked as possibly unsafe, depending on the context in which it's used. Further, variables derived from tainted variables are also tainted. Perl then examines where the variables are used, and in what context, to decide whether the code breaks any of the prebuilt rules.

Some of the checks are relatively simple, such as verifying that the directories within a given path are not writable by other users. Some are more complex and rely on Perl's compiler and syntax checker to accept or reject the statement.

The rule is straightforward: you cannot use any data from the outside world that may directly or indirectly affect something outside of your program. In essence, this means you can use external variables internally for everything except specific system calls, subshell executions, or destinations for data files. The following code fragment shows the results of running some statements with taint checking switched on:

```
$cmd = shift;              # tainted - its origin is the command line
$run = "echo $cmd";        # Also tainted - derived from $cmd
$alsoran = `echo Hello`;   # Not tainted
system "echo $cmd";        # Insecure - external shell with $cmd
system "$alsoran";         # Insecure - until $PATH set
system "/bin/echo", $cmd;  # Secure - doesn't use shell to execute
```

If you try to execute this as a script with taint checking switched on, you will receive errors similar to "Insecure dependency" or "Insecure $ENV{PATH}" for lines 4 and 5.

Also note that anything that implies the use of an external command or function also makes the data insecure. Therefore, anything that accesses the environment (via %**ENV**), that calls to file globbing routines (**glob** or <*.c>), as well as some **open** constructs also returns tainted information. Finally, any system functions, such as **umask**, **unlink**, **link**, and others, when used with tainted variables, are also considered insecure. In each case, there are some exceptions.

If you modify the environment from Perl before accessing it, then the information is not tainted (Perl remembers that you made the modification); so the code

```
$ENV{'PATH'} = '/bin:/usr/bin';
$path = $ENV{'PATH'};
```

does not taint **$path**, since its source was actually internal.

In the case of the **open** command, reads from tainted file names are allowed, since reading is nondestructive. However, writes to files referred to by tainted variables are not allowed; thus the code

```
$file = shift;
open(DATA, ">$file");
```

will generate an error, since the **$file** variable has come from an external source.

Using pipes is also an insecure option if the command or data you are using with a command has come from an external source. Therefore,

```
$file = shift;
open(FOO,"gunzip -c $file|");
```

is considered unsafe, since you must call a shell in order to interpret the entire command line. You can get around this by using the alternative pipe notation,

```
$file = shift;
open(FOO,"-|") or exec 'gunzip', '-c', $file;
```

which is considered safe, because you do not use a shell to execute the command.

To switch on taint checking, you must specify the **-T** option on the command line. This works for Unix and Windows NT. Taint checking with MacPerl is not strictly available, and even if it were, it wouldn't make a huge difference since the Mac OS is not capable of executing external programs. In any case, it is not prone to the same security breaches as a Unix or NT system.

Taint checking is also automatically enabled by Perl if you attempt to run a script that is running with different real and effective user and group IDs. If the setuid or setgid bit has been set on a Unix system, this automatically implies taint checking. Once switched on, taint checking is enabled for the rest of your script; you cannot switch it off until the script ends.

To detect whether a variable is tainted, you can use the function **is_tainted** from the **tainted.pl** script supplied in the standard library of the Perl distribution. The only way to untaint variables is to reference substring regular expression matches. For example, for an email address, you might use the following code fragment to extract an untainted version of the address:

```
If ($addr =~ /^([-\@\w.]+)$/)
{
    $addr = $1;
}
else
{
    die "Bad email address";
}
```

Obviously, running an expression match on every tainted element defeats the object of taint checking in the first place. You can switch this untainting behavior off by using the **re** pragma,

```
use re 'taint';
```

which means that all regular expressions taint data if their source data is already tainted.

Because variables from CGI scripts are tainted (they come from either an external environment variable or the standard input), tainting Perl CGI scripts is a good idea.

The Safe and Opcode Modules

The **Safe** module makes use of Perl's ability to run code within a separate compartment. Normally this is done via the **eval** function. The difference with the **Safe** module is that the compartment can be configured to allow only certain internal Perl functions to execute. This allows you to disable or enable functions that you want to allow or prevent the use of in the script you want to execute.

The new compartment is completely restrictive. You cannot access subroutines or variables outside of the compartment, regardless of the methods you try to use. In fact, the only variables that are shared between the main script and the safe compartment are $_, @_, %_, and the _ special filehandle. You can place variables into the compartment for the main script if you need to.

The method for creating the new compartment is to create a new **Safe** object and then, optionally, create a new opcode mask that limits the list of available opcodes that form the basis of any Perl script (see Chapters 16 and 17):

```
$safe = new Safe;
```

You can create a new name space to use for the new compartment by specifying it as an argument:

```
$safe = new Safe("Compartment");
```

By default, the value is **Safe::Root0**, and it is incremented for each new compartment created within the scope of the current script.

There are five main methods for controlling the compartment once it has been created:

```
$safe = new Safe;
$safe->permit(OP,...);
$safe->permit_only(OP,...);
$safe->deny(OP,...);
$safe->deny_only(OP,...);
$safe->share(NAME,...);
```

The **permit** and **deny** methods add opcodes to the lists of allowed and restricted opcodes for the new compartment, respectively. Thus, additional calls to these methods add or remove the specified opcodes from the list of those that can be used. The **permit_only** and **deny_only** methods explicitly define the entire list of allowed and restricted opcodes for the compartment.

The **share** method specifies the list of variables and subroutines from the enclosing script that can be shared with the compartment. The **NAME** should include the variable type (**$foo**, **@foo**, and so on), and all the main object types are allowed. All the shared items are assumed to be in the calling package. Alternatively, you can use the **share_from** method to specify the package from which you want to share the symbols:

```
$safe = new Safe;
$safe->Share_from('main',['calc_sin', '$PI']);
```

Once you have completed the mask and specified the opcodes that you want to enable (or disable), you run a Perl script either by supplying a text string or by using the **reval** method:

```
$safe = new Safe;
$safe->reval($script);
```

Or you can point execution to an external file with the **rdo** method:

```
$safe = new Safe;
$safe->rdo($file);
```

For the list of available opcodes on your machine, refer to the **Opcode** module for your platform. The available list of opcodes is specific both to your platform and the current version of Perl, so a list here would be useless without the cross-reference of the specific module for your platform.

PROGRAMMING
WITH PERL

The Complete Reference

Perl

Part III

Developing Applications

Chapter 16

User Interface Tools

The title of this chapter is a bit of a misnomer, but the practicalities are clear. All the uses of Perl discussed so far have centered around the specifics of the Perl language. When using Perl in the wide world, however, there are some niceties that can make the use of Perl easier for both the programmer and the user. The most basic of these is to allow the user to supply information and instructions to a Perl script on the command line. Most users will be familiar with command line arguments to programs, under both Windows and Unix. Command line arguments can consist of either straight information (usually a file or hostname) or a series of options, signified by a preceding hyphen. A number of methods, both manual and automatic, can help to extract the information from the command line, and we'll look at them in the beginning of this chapter.

If you are a programmer, you may have already encountered the problems associated with reporting information in a formatted presentation. The most obvious method is to use the **printf** function to arrange the output data into a normalized format, but it suffers from numerous problems. The most fundamental of these is that information may stretch beyond the width of an element specified in the **printf** format definition. This means using regular expressions and/or functions to extract a specific number of characters from the data.

This is all too complex and still doesn't get around the difficulties presented by producing a report, such as accounting for page length and printing headers (and footers) on a page. The solution to this with Perl is to use the Perl reporting mechanism (otherwise known as Formats). This allows you to define a fixed output format for printed information. The format allows you to specify the justification (left, right, or centered) and even the template that should be used when printing floating point numbers. Formats also automatically handle page sizes, line numbers, and headers, although you will need to work out a method for printing footers for yourself.

Processing Command Line Arguments

Command line arguments are available to any script via the **@ARGV** array. You can access this directly, either by referencing individual elements or by using the **shift** and **pop** functions. The important thing to remember about the **@ARGV** array is that unlike many other languages (most notably C/C++), element zero is not the name of the script. This is contained in the **$0** variable. This means that the first argument is at index zero, and therefore you can print out the entire command line argument list by printing the array:

```
print join(' ',@ARGV),"\n";
```

You can also use **shift** to take off individual arguments in sequence:

```
$filein = shift;
$fileout = shift;
```

Note, though, that this technique only works when you use **shift** in the main script block; calling it within a subroutine takes values off the @_ array instead.

It can also sometimes be necessary to put arguments back onto the command line before it is processed, perhaps to insert default or required options. Because the command line arguments are simply available as the **@ARGV** array, you can **push** or **unshift** elements onto the command line. For example:

```
unshift @ARGV,qw/-v --/ if (@ARGV == 0);
```

Refer back to Chapter 2 if you want more information on the manipulation of arrays.

If you want to process command line arguments, rather than doing it yourself, the best method is to use either the standard or extended options supported by the **Getopt::Std** and **Getopt::Long** modules, respectively.

Note   *Both **Getopt::Std** and **Getopt::Long** support functions that process the individual elements of the **@ARGV** array looking for command line options. When the function finds a valid argument, it removes it from the array. Any elements of the **@ARGV** array that cannot be identified as options remain in the **@ARGV** array, so you can continue to use the values supplied in your script.*

Getopt::Std

The **Getopt::Std** module provides a very simple interface for extracting options from the command line arguments. Each option can only be specified with a single letter, for example:

```
$ script.pl -ol file.in
```

There are two functions, **getopt** and **getopts**:

```
use Getopt::Std;

getopt('ol');
getopts('ol:');
```

Both functions require a single argument that specifies the list of single-letter arguments you would like to identify on the command line.

In the case of the **getopt** function, it assumes that all arguments expect an additional piece of information, such that the example above would accept the following line:

```
$ script.pl -o -l
```

DEVELOPING
APPLICATIONS

However, it would incorrectly assume that "-l" was the data for the **-o** option. With the **getopts** function, each character is taken to be a Boolean value. If you want to accept arguments with additional information, then append a colon. This means that the preceding script fragment will accept

```
$ script.pl -o -l file.input
```

correctly identifying the **-l** as a simple switch.

The **getopts** function supports combined options. For example,

```
$ script.pl -eafl
```

which would correctly be recognized as four individual options, setting the values of **$opt_e**, **$opt_a**, **$opt_f**, and **$opt_l** to 1.

Both **getopt** and **getopts** create new variables starting with a prefix of **$opt_**. The preceding script would create two variables: **$opt_o** will have a value of 1, and **$opt_l** will have a value of "file.input." If a letter defined to the function is not found, then no variable will be created. In addition, for either function, you can also supply a second argument, which should be a reference to a hash:

```
getopts('i:',\%opts);
```

Each supplied argument will be used as the key of the hash, and any additional information supplied will be placed into the corresponding values. Thus, a script with the preceding line when called,

```
$ getopts -i Hello
```

will place the string "Hello" into the **$opts{'i'}** hash element.

If you have the **strict 'vars'** pragma in effect (see Chapter 19), you will need to predefine the **$opt_** and hash variables before they are called. Either use a **my** definition before calling the function, or, better still, predeclare them with **use vars**.

Getopt::Long

The **Getopt::Std** module is suitable for simple scripts and argument passing. However, it falls over if you try to do more complex processing or want to place the extracted information into specific variables and structures. The **Getopt::Long** module implements a more advanced system. The function is identical in operation to the one that is defined as part of the POSIX standard, and it is therefore suitable for use in scripts that require POSIX compliance.

POSIX compliance allows not only the standard single-character matching supported by the **Getopt::Std** module, but also string arguments. For example:

```
$ script.pl --inputfile=source.txt
```

The command line option in this case is **--inputfile**. Note that long names as arguments are supported by both the single and double hyphen, although the double hyphen is the **POSIX** default. The older, single-hyphen style is still supported, but you cannot support the combined options, such that,

```
$ script.pl -eafl
```

is interpreted as a single argument, "eafl".

The module uses a different format from the previous functions in the **Getopt::Std** module to support the extended functionality. The specification for the command line arguments is passed to the **GetOptions** functions in one of two ways. The first is to supply a hash. The keys of the hash specify the command line arguments to accept, and the value should be a reference to the variable in which you want to store the value. The following code sets the value of **$verbose** to 1 if the word "verbose" is found as a command line argument:

```
use Getopt::Long;
GetOptions("verbose" => \$verbose);
```

The alternative is to supply a reference to a hash as the first argument. As with the **Getopt::Std** module, each further argument to the function is then treated as a command line argument to match. The name specified will be used as the key, with the value, if supplied, being inserted into the corresponding value:

```
use Getopt::Long;
GetOptions(\%options, "verbose");
```

The default interpretation for all arguments is as Boolean values. However, like the **getopts** function in the **Getopt::Std** module, you can signify that additional values can be supplied on the command line. The module supports two constructs for specifying values: you can either use a space separator or an equal sign. For example:

```
--inputfile source.txt
--inputfile=source.txt
```

Note *The + sign is also supported, but its use is deprecated and not part of the POSIX specification.*

The list of available modifiers, which should be specified, is given in Table 16-1. For example, to set debugging in a script from a value on the command line, you might use

```
use Getopt::Long;
GetOptions("debug:i" => \$debug);
```

This allows you both to use

```
$ script.pl -debug
```

Option	Description
!	The option does not accept an optional piece of information and may be negated by prefixing **no**. For example, **opt!** will set the value of an option **--opt** to 1, and **--noopt** to 0.
+	The option does not accept an additional piece of information. Each appearance in the command line options will increment the corresponding value by one, such that **--opt --opt --opt** will set a value of 3, providing it doesn't already have a value.
=s	The option requires a mandatory additional string argument. The value of the string will be placed into the corresponding variable.
:s	The option accepts an optional string argument. The value of the string will be placed into the corresponding variable.
=i	The option requires a mandatory integer argument. The value will be placed into the corresponding variable.
:i	The option accepts an optional integer argument. The value will be placed into the corresponding variable.
=f	The option requires a mandatory real number argument. The value will be placed into the corresponding variable.
:f	The option accepts an optional real number argument. The value will be placed into the corresponding variable.

Table 16-1. *Options for the **Getopt::Long** Module*

to simply set debugging, or

```
$ script.pl -debug 256
```

to specify a debug level.

The function also allows you to use a single hyphen, which will be treated as a valid argument with the corresponding entry name as the empty string. The double hyphen (--) on its own will be interpreted by the **GetOptions** function as the termination of the command line arguments.

Linkage

When using a hash reference as the first argument to the **GetOptions** function, there are additional facilities available to you for processing more-complex command lines. By default, the operation is identical to the **getopts** function, that is,

```
GetOptions(\%options, "file=s");
```

will perform the equivalent of the following assignment:

```
$options{file} = "source.txt";
```

By using a trailing @ sign,

```
GetOptions(\%options, "files=s@");
```

you can process command lines like this:

```
$ script.pl --files source.txt --files sauce.txt
```

The result is an assignment to the hash, as follows:

```
$options{files} = ['source.txt', 'sauce.txt'];
```

Finally, you can process more complex "name=value" command line assignments by using a trailing % in the definition:

```
GetOptions(\%options, "users=s%");
```

Thus, you can now process a command line,

```
$ script.pl --users Bob=Manager --users Fred=Salesman
```

DEVELOPING
APPLICATIONS

which is roughly equivalent to:

```
$options{users} = { 'Bob' => 'Manager', 'Fred' => 'Salesman' };
```

If you do not specify a hash reference as the first argument, the function will instead create a new variable of the corresponding type, using the argument name prefixed by **opt_**. Thus, the previous examples could be translated as follows:

```
$opt_file = "source.txt";
@opt_files = ('source.txt', 'sauce.txt');
%opt_users = ( 'Bob'  => 'Manager',
               'Fred' => 'Salesman' );
```

Providing you supplied a function call like this,

```
GetOptions("file=s","files=s@","users=s%");
```

you could also use the hash argument feature to update your own variables directly:

```
GetOptions("file=s"   => \$file,
           "files=s@" => \@files,
           "users=s%" => \%users);
```

This last specification method also supports a function that will handle the specified option. The function will receive two arguments—the true option name (see the next section) and the value supplied.

Aliases

You can support alternative argument names by using the pipe character (|) to separate individual names. For example:

```
GetOptions("file|input|source=s");
```

The "true" name would be "file" in this instance, placing the value into **$opt_file**. This true name is also passed to a function if specified (as mentioned previously).

Callback Function

If **GetOptions** cannot identify an individual element of the **@ARGV** array as a true argument, then you can specify a function that will handle the option. You do this by using a value of "<>" as the argument name. For example:

```
GetOptions("<>" => \&nonoption);
```

Remember that the **GetOptions** function removes identifiable arguments from @ARGV and leaves the remainder of the elements intact if you don't use this facility. You can then process the arguments as you wish, after **GetOptions** has completed successfully.

Identifying Errors

The **GetOptions** function returns true (1) if the command line arguments can be identified correctly. If an error occurs (because the user has supplied a command line argument the function wasn't expecting), the function returns false and uses **warn** to report the bad options.

If the definitions supplied to the function are invalid, then the function calls **die**, reporting the error.

Perl's Reporting Mechanism

Using your own custom reporting mechanisms for complex structures, such as arrays and hashes, can be a practical way of outputting information in a formatted fashion. However, if you are reporting simpler structures, or you want to produce reports that would be reported and formatted using the **printf** function, then you can use a specially designed feature of Perl to format the output for you. The Perl mechanism actually inherits much of its functionality from a variety of sources, including FORTRAN and BASIC.

The Perl mechanism (otherwise called Formats) is a complete reporting environment that is very similar to many systems in commercial database-oriented packages, such as those used for accounting and contacts systems. The Perl reporting mechanism keeps track of all the different parameters that affect a report, including the number of lines on the page, the page number you are currently printing to, and even the production of formatted page headers for each generated page. The format for a format definition is as follows:

```
format NAME =
FORMLIST
.
```

A format is treated like another core structure within Perl, and so it can be defined anywhere in your script, just like a subroutine or package declaration. Just like other structures, a format also has its own name space, so a format called **Foo** can coexist with a function called **Foo**. The tradition is for format names to be uppercase and usually have the same name as the filehandle to which they are output. The default format **NAME** is **STDOUT**, for example.

The **FORMLIST** portion is just like a subroutine definition, but without the brace enclosure, and is made up of one of three types of information: a comment, a "picture," or an "argument" line. A comment is signified by a # character in the first column and is treated just like any other comment within Perl.

The picture line is a text string that specifies how the information will be output. It is printed verbatim, apart from the field definitions that are used to print out the information you want to output. Special characters, as summarized in Table 16-2, specify the individual field formats for the pictures.

Using the information in Table 16-2, you can create definitions accordingly. For example,

```
format STDOUT =
@<<<<<<<< @|||||| @####.## @>>>>
$prodid, $type, $cost, $instock
.
```

prints out each line with an eight-character, left-justified product ID; a centered type; a cost, printed as a formatted floating point value; and a right-justified stock level. The repetition of the individual format characters specifies the field width; so in the example of the cost field, it is printed as four digits, a decimal point, and two more digits.

Picture Character	Description
@	Defines a field picture.
<	Specifies left justification; the number of repetitions specifies the field width.
>	Specifies right justification; the number of repetitions specifies the field width.
|	Specifies centered justification; the number of repetitions specifies the field width.
#	Specifies numbered justification; usually used for floating point fields. See the example in the text.
^	Defines a split field; information will be printed at the specified width, but will span multiple lines.
~	Indicates that blank lines in a format should be ignored. This means that if you specify multiple ^ fields but the information does not fill all the lines, then blanks won't be printed instead.

Table 16-2. *Field Formats*

Note that this format is used for *each* line in the printed report. How you treat and refer to this line is entirely dependent on how you decide to use the reporting mechanism. For most uses, the individual line will be a record of information. We'll return to the significance of this shortly.

Note that the previous example also includes the third type of line, the argument line, which specifies the information that will be printed on each line. This is defined quite simply using a list of variables, separated by commas. Each variable is printed using each format, in order. The actual values supplied are evaluated at run time, so the values can also be functions and even arrays and hash references.

You can define multiline records by specifying a multiline format. That means you can modify the above example to

```
format STDOUT =
Product: @<<<<<<<<
         $prodid
   Type: @|||||||
         $type
   Cost: \$@####.##
         $cost
  Stock: @>>>>
         $instock
```

Note that, in each case, for each output line, you have to specify the value you want printed on the next line. This means that although the preceding format is eight lines long, the report will only produce four lines for each record of output.

There are a number of ways of producing reports that output a single variable or record on multiple lines. The first method is to use the ^ field definition. This allows you to specify a justified format for a field, and each invocation of the picture and the variable that goes with it will produce an additional string of information extracted from the variable supplied. Perl puts as much information as possible into the field, removing the information each time the picture format is called.

To get a clearer idea, let's add a description to the preceding example, printed next to the existing details:

```
format STDOUT =
Product: @<<<<<<<<     Description:
         $prodid
   Type: @|||||||      ^<<<<<<<<<<<<<<<<<<<<<<<<<<<<<<<<<<<<<<<<<<
         $type,        $description
   Cost: \$@####.##    ^<<<<<<<<<<<<<<<<<<<<<<<<<<<<<<<<<<<<<<<<<<
         $cost,        $description
  Stock: @>>>>         ^<<<<<<<<<<<<<<<<<<<<<<<<<<<<<<<<<<<<<<<<<<
```

```
$instock,     $description
              ^<<<<<<<<<<<<<<<<<<<<<<<<<<<<<<<<<<<<<<<
              $description
```

Unfortunately, this process means that the variable itself is modified during the reporting procedure. If you want to preserve the contents of the data, you should use a temporary variable to hold the information. The individual lines are correctly separated so that words do not cross line boundaries. You can also change the list of characters that Perl considers it sensible to break a line on by modifying the value of the **$:** variable.

Also note that this method presents a very different problem. The preceding example uses a field width of 44 characters. If the data contained in **$description** is longer than 176 characters (4 SYMBOL 205 \f "Wingdings 2" \s 12 44), then it will be truncated; and if it is shorter, you will get a blank line printed where you probably don't want one.

The latter problem is easier to solve. You just insert a ~ character anywhere on the line. This indicates that the line should be ignored if it contains no useful information. The first problem is more complex, since you have to get around the problem of printing an infinitely long text field. There are two ways to avoid this. The first is to use a double ~ on a line, which indicates that the line should be repeated until the corresponding variable is empty. The other option is to use the special @* format. This prints multiline values without truncating them, but it also reduces your ability to specify a maximum width or any justification for the item and is therefore less useful and practical than the ~~ method.

Once you have written your format, it's then up to you to process the results and call **write** for each set of values that you want to report. To complete the preceding example, you might use something like the following:

```
format STDOUT =
Product: @<<<<<<<<     Description:
         $prodid
Type:    @|||||||      ^<<<<<<<<<<<<<<<<<<<<<<<<<<<<<<<<<<<<<<<
         $type,        $description
Cost:    \$@####.##    ^<<<<<<<<<<<<<<<<<<<<<<<<<<<<<<<<<<<<<<<
         $cost,        $description
Stock:   @>>>>         ^<<<<<<<<<<<<<<<<<<<<<<<<<<<<<<<<<<<<<<<
         $instock,     $description
                       ^<<<<<<<<<<<<<<<<<<<<<<<<<<<<<<<<<<<<<<<
                       $description

open(DATA,"<datafile.db") or die "Can't open database";
```

```
while(<DATA>)
{
    chomp;
    ($prodid, $type, $cost, $instock, $description) = split /:/;
    write;
}
close(DATA);
```

This does the absolute minimum to produce a report from the information supplied in an external file. For each input line from the file, the data is extracted and the **write** function is called. This tells the reporting mechanism to build the line according to the specified format, and then to output it. In this case, the output is **STDOUT**, but it could have been any open filehandle, providing you named the format accordingly.

Headers and Footers

If you want to print a header for each page of output, you can create a format with the same name as the main format, with _**TOP** attached. The information contained in this format will be printed at the top of every page (see the "Format Variables" section that follows). This can be helpful both for printing column headers and for printing titles and page numbers.

For example, the two formats for printing a columnar version of the previous report might look like this:

```
format STDOUT_TOP =
Product    Type     Cost       Stock   Description
-------    ------   --------   -----   ------------------------------------
.
format STDOUT =
@<<<<<<<<  @||||||  @####.##  @>>>>   ^<<<<<<<<<<<<<<<<<<<<<<<<<<<<<<<<<<<<<
$prodid,   $type,   $cost,    $instock,$description
                                       ^<<<<<<<<<<<<<<<<<<<<<<<<<<<<<<<<<<<~~
```

Footers are more difficult, because there is no built-in device for printing a footer on each page. The best method is to check the value of **$-** (**$FORMAT_LINES_LEFT** when the **English** module is used) and then print out the new footer before calling **write**. Note, however, that you will need to update the value of **$-** to account for the number of lines you have added to the current page. Setting **$-** to 0 triggers the generation of a new page.

Format Functions

The format process makes use of three main functions: **format**, **formline**, and **write**. The **format** function you already know about. The **formline** function takes a **PICTURE** specification and a list of values, and places the value into the accumulate variable, **$^A**. It is this variable that is printed to the filehandle when **write** is called. For example, the function call

```
formline "@<<<<<<<< @||||| @####.##", $prodid, $type, $cost;
write;
```

is equivalent to:

```
format STDOUT =
@<<<<<<<< @||||| @####.##
$prodid, $type, $cost
.
write;
```

You can think of **formline** as the reporting mechanism's own version of **printf**. Note, as well, that because the **$^A** variable is populated during the process, you can create a function that returns a **formline** formatted string:

```
sub sformline
{
    my $picture = shift;
    $^A = '';
    formline($picture,@_);
    return $^A;
}
```

Care should be taken, of course, to ensure that you don't unwittingly overwrite the values currently stored in the accumulator using this method.

The **write** function populates the **$^A** accumulator variable (using **formline** and the predefined format). It then writes the contents of **$^A** to the current output filehandle, or to the filehandle specified:

```
write FILEHANDLE
write
```

Note that the format used changes when you specify a different filehandle. This is not normally a problem, since it's unlikely that for most installations you'll be using more than one filehandle with more than one type of format.

Format Variables

The main format variables, including their **English** module names and their descriptions, are shown in Table 16-3.

Use of any of these variables affects the currently selected default filehandle (defined using the **select** function). However, if you want the effects to be felt on a different filehandle, you will either have to change filehandles with the **select** function or use the **FileHandle** module, which provides methods for all of the special variables. For example, to specify the format name for the **REPORT** filehandle:

```
use FileHandle;
REPORT->format_name("Financial_Report");
```

Variable	English	Description
$~	$FORMAT_NAME	Current format name
$^	$FORMAT_TOP_NAME	Current top-of-form format name
$%	$FORMAT_PAGE_NUMBER	Current page number (within current format)
$=	$FORMAT_LINES_PER_PAGE	Number of printable lines on a current page
$-	$FORMAT_LINES_LEFT	Number of printable lines left on the page
$^L	$FORMAT_FORMFEED	String to be output before each top of the page (except the first)

Table 16-3.   *Variables Used by the Format System*

The Complete Reference

Chapter 17

Advanced User Interfaces

Designing an effective user interface is a difficult task. There are the complexities of designing the interface elements: the display boxes, buttons, menus, and the general layout of the interface. More difficult is the implementation. There is no single user-interface toolkit (although **Tk** does a pretty good job), and depending on your platform, you may choose a number of different possible solutions.

For an operating system that supports a text-based interface, the difficulties are even more significant. Many would argue that the number of people actually using text interfaces is very small, and few would disagree. Although Windows and Unix have had windowed environments for many years, both still support a text interface, and many well-known programs rely heavily on that interface as their way of supporting functionality. Two of the best applications under Unix are **emacs**, an editor, and Lynx, a web browser.

Working directly with a terminal to control an interface is not a step to be taken lightly. It only really affects Unix and Win32 systems, since the Mac does not support a text-based interface anyway. Irrespective of the platform, you will need to "drive" the terminal directly. Although toolkits and modules are available (such as **Term::Cap** for Unix and **Win32::Console** for Windows), you will still need to design and manage your own on-screen elements, such as menus, buttons, and text areas, and none of it is easy, even with a simplified toolkit.

Generally, if you're developing a stand-alone (rather than web) application in any programming language, it's highly likely you're planning on building a GUI environment to work with it. There is no standard toolkit for designing GUI interfaces, but Tk is a good choice. It removes a lot of the complexity of implementing an interface, although the individual design is still your responsibility.

Tk is cross-platform compatible and there are systems that work on Unix (through the X Window System), Windows, and Mac OS. Unfortunately, an interface for Perl under Mac OS is not available yet, but that still means we can develop a Tk-based application that will present a consistent user interface to Windows and Unix users.

If you are not worried about cross-platform compatibility, and you want something that looks a little less generic, you can use the **Gtk** interface builder for Unix or the **Win32::GUI** system for Windows. Both support a more natural interface that works in harmony with the host GUI, rather than trying to build its own style of interface on top of an existing solution.

Of course, a traditional GUI doesn't support every type of application, and there's been a significant increase in the number of applications that are actually developed either with the Web in mind, or solely as web-based applications. These require a completely different set of skills, and we'll be looking in more detail at those in Chapter 18.

For this chapter, we'll start by looking at the basis of interface development for terminal-based applications. The main focus, however, will be on using the Tk interface-building system to develop a GUI for your application.

Working with a Terminal

Most terminal interfaces rely on the use of the special escape code sequences that the terminal driver supports for moving the cursor around the screen, changing the text to inverse, and so on. The information is held in a central database, and it's the accessibility of this database that causes problems within Perl.

In the early years of Unix development, editing was handled by **ed**. The **ed** program was advanced for its time, allowing you to edit individual lines of a document. You could even search for text and replace it. Unfortunately, working on a document more than ten lines long when you can only view and edit one line at a time becomes tedious.

Editors progressed in the late 1970s with the introduction of **vi**, the visual version of **ed**. The same basic functionality remained; what was different was that you were able to view multiple lines of the document and move around them in a way never before possible. This presented something of a problem for the developer of **vi**, Bill Joy. The problem was that different terminals used different sets of control characters and control codes to perform even basic tasks like moving the cursor around the screen. Out of the **vi** project grew the termcap terminal-capabilities database. This described the abilities of each terminal, and a set of functions allowed a programmer to access the functions in a standard way.

The termcap system was eventually improved upon and became the curses package. This package offered the same basic functionality, but with some higher-level and more complex functions added to take advantage of the clever features being introduced to the newer terminals. The next development phase was carried out by the Unix Systems Group (USG), which improved upon the curses package to produce terminfo. Like curses before it, terminfo provided the same basic interface to the terminal as termcap, albeit via a different set of functions. Also, like curses, terminfo was intended to eliminate some of the shortcomings of the termcap system.

The result is that we now have two basic systems for using terminals. The termcap system is found largely on BSD-based Unix variants. The terminfo package is found mainly on System V—based Unix variants. Some Unix systems, such as Solaris, SunOS, and HP-UX, supply both termcap and terminfo.

Within Perl, the **Term::Cap** module provides an interface to the termcap system. The processes behind the termcap system and how to make the best use of it are beyond the topic of this book, but the **Term::Cap** module should provide you with everything you need to access and control your terminal. Since the bulk of the development effort concentrates on Tk GUI interfaces, we'll move straight on to using that for building user interfaces.

Under Windows, there is a more extensive solution in the form of the **Win32::Console** module. This sits at essentially the same level as the **Tk** extension that we'll see later in this chapter. The **Win32::Console** module allows you to control the display and output of a typical Windows console—the same environment used when you start a DOS session.

Using **Win32::Console**, it's possible to place text at specific areas, copy, move, and scroll text areas, and control the colors used to display the text. You can even have multiple buffers that you can populate offline and then display into the console at will, making quite complex interfaces possible. We won't go into the details here, as the module itself is quite complex—instead, look at Chapter 10 of the *ActivePerl Developer's Guide*; see Appendix C for more information.

Using Tk

Tk was originally developed by Dr. John Ousterhout, who was at the University of California, Berkeley, before moving to Sun Microsystems. A new commercial development was created by Ousterhout to help develop Tk and Tcl in preparation for a commercial release. Called Scriptics, the company has now been bought by Interwoven, although development of Tcl and Tk continues under the Scriptics name. The original Tcl and Tk projects are still free, while Scriptics also develops commercial products such as TclPro.

The role of Tk is to make the process of designing a user interface significantly easier. The core of the windowing system provides the methods and basis for simple operations and events, such as opening windows, drawing lines, and accepting input and actions from the keyboard and mouse.

Creating even a simple on-screen element, such as a button or even a simple text pane, originally involved hundreds of lines of code. The result was the development of individual elements of a GUI environment called widgets. A single widget can define a core element of the interface, such as a button, scroll bar, and even more complex elements, such as scales and hierarchical lists, which themselves can be composed of other simpler widgets. Within Unix and the X Window System, a number of different widget toolkits have been produced, including Motif, Athena, OpenWindows, and, of course, Tk.

Because of the natural relationship between widgets and objects, developing GUIs within a scripting language is incredibly easy, and Tk was originally developed in cooperation with the Tcl language. Tcl (short for Tool Command Language) is essentially a macro language for making development of complex programs within the shell easier. However, Tcl is itself difficult to use in comparison to Perl, Python, and other scripting languages, so efforts were made to support the Tk widgets directly within these languages.

The first real solution was designed by Malcolm Beattie. He embedded a Tcl interpreter within a Perl layer to enable a connection between Perl and Tk. It was Nick Ing-Simmons who developed the now-standard Perl/Tk interface by stripping the Tk system of its Tcl-specific code. On top of the base Tk functionality was built a generic porting layer, called pTk, which is now the basis for a number of Tk interfaces to scripting languages, including Perl, Python, Scheme, and Guile.

The result is Perl/Tk—an interface system that you access within Perl as the **Tk** module. This has been successfully supported on Unix for a number of years. At Sun, Tcl and Tk were ported to Windows and Mac OS, and although the Windows version of Perl/Tk has been available for some time, a Mac version has yet to materialize.

If you are serious about developing interfaces with Tk, or any other system, I suggest for the benefit of you and your users that you read a suitable human-computer interface book. I can heartily recommend all of Apple's texts; they are the basis for many of the best interfaces you will find. You may also want to check Alan Cooper's *About Face: The Essentials of User Interface Design*, or the excellent introductory guide *The Elements of User Interface Design*, by Theo Mandel.

Installing Tk Under Unix

You should use the **CPAN** module for all of your module installation—see Web Appendix B at **www.osborne.com** for more information on using the **CPAN** module. For the purposes of installing Tk, you should probably use:

```
$ perl -MCPAN -e shell
cpan> install Bundle::Tk
```

This will download and install everything you should need—including the sources for the libraries required by the Perl/Tk interface.

Installing Tk Under Windows

The best way to install Tk under Windows is to use either the basic Perl Package Manager (PPM) or the Visual Package Manager (VPM) that come with ActivePerl and the Perl Development Kit respectively.

Within PPM, just typing:

```
PPM> install Tk
```

should be enough to download and then install everything you need.

Hello from Tk

Developing a user interface with Tk is a case of creating a number of nested objects. The first object you create is the main window for your application. The nested objects are the individual widgets that make up the user interface. A widget is a button, text box, menu, or any of a variety of other components used to build up your interface within your window.

Once you have defined the individual widgets that make up the window, the script then goes into a loop, called the event loop. The script accepts events from the user and performs the commands and actions that were defined when the widgets were created. This is different from most other Perl scripts, which follow a logical process. However, unlike many Perl scripts, users control the execution and choose a number of different options, depending on which button, text box, or other widget they manipulate.

The basic process for creating a Tk-based GUI application is as follows:

1. Create a window to hold all of your objects. The main window is generally known as *main* or *top-level*, although it could be called anything.

2. Create a number of widgets, defining their contents, actions, and other elements. In this example, a label, to hold a simple message, and a button, which when pressed will exit the script, are created.

3. Display and arrange the widgets within the window. This is frequently handled by the Pack geometry manager, although there are other managers available. The geometry manager supplies a function that allows you to control the orientation and spacing of the widgets within the window. Although you can exercise a certain amount of control, the geometry manager actually does a lot of the work for you. It makes decisions, based on your recommendations, about how to lay out the individual components.

4. Start the event loop. The main execution of the script has now finished, and the rest of the script will be driven by the events configured for individual widgets.

Here is a very quick Perl/Tk script that demonstrates this:

```perl
use Tk;

$main = MainWindow->new();
$main->title("Hello World!");

$label = $main->Label(text => 'Hello from Tk!');
$button = $main->Button();

$icon = $button->Photo(-file => 'icon.gif');

$button->configure(image => $icon,
                   command => sub { exit; }
                  );

$label->pack(side => 'left');
$button->pack(side => 'left',
              padx => 5
             );

MainLoop();
```

The result, when run, looks like this on a Windows 98 machine:

You can see the effects of the script quite clearly. As a comparison, you can see the same script executed on a Red Hat Linux machine here:

The insides of the two windows are identical. It is only the window manager dressing for resizing the window, minimizing or maximizing the window, or closing it altogether that are different. The window decorations are specific to the platform and window manager, and any window you create within Tk will have these decorations.

There are five important elements that you should remember when developing Tk interfaces: windows, widgets, nesting, the geometry manager, and callbacks.

Windows

The window is the main container for all widgets and the only way in which you can develop an interface with Tk. Without a window, you cannot create a widget. It's possible to create a number of different "main" windows within the same application; you are not restricted to only one window. This makes Tk much more practical from an application-development point of view—you can actually develop most of the basic artifacts that you would expect from a GUI interface. This includes not just the basic windows, but also floating palettes, pop-up boxes, and warning messages.

Widgets

It's also worth paying attention to how the individual widgets are created. You cannot create a widget outside of a window—a widget must be within a container of some kind. Most containers are windows, although you can have widgets that are containers for others—for example, the **Frame** widget can contain other widgets and is used to help confine one or more widgets within certain areas of your window. Furthermore, because the **Frame** is a widget itself, you can nest multiple frames to produce complex layouts.

Nesting

The nesting of widgets is another important principle. Within Microsoft Windows applications, each application window generally consists of two main areas. The very top of the window contains the menu bar, and the remainder of the window is given to either a single frame of other components, or an interface that allows multiple windows to exist within the larger frame. For example, within Microsoft Word, you can have multiple documents open that all share the same menu bar.

Note *As an aside, the inclusion of a per-window menu bar is different in other environments—Mac OS is a prime example, there is one menu bar at the top of the screen, and all applications share this menu bar. When you switch applications, the contents of the menu bar changes to match the active application. This makes the menu bar a completely separate item to deal with, almost as if it's within its own window.*

The contents of a menu bar within a Windows application are somewhat limited. Although some applications feign certain abilities, most Windows menus are limited to simple lists of options. The menu bar is, in fact, a container widget—there is nothing special about the **MenuBar** object—it's, in fact, largely based on the **Frame** widget. Into that **MenuBar** widget you place **MenuButton**s, and each **MenuButton** is made up of a number of menu items. However, unlike our typical Windows application, a Tk-based application can put anything into the menu item: buttons, checkboxes, radio buttons, and in fact, any other widget you like.

Furthermore, because a **MenuBar** is just another widget, we can place menus anywhere within the window—we're not tied to just producing the menu at the top of the window. The combination of flexible menus and nested widgets within those menus is great for tool and color palettes, or when you want to introduce a complex list of possibilities within a confined space.

I would be willing to argue that the nesting ability of the Tk interface system is perhaps the most powerful feature, after Tk's cross-platform compatibility.

Geometry Manager

Finally, you must not dismiss the need for a geometry manager. The geometry manager actually does a lot more than just organizing the layout of the individual widgets within the window. Because the geometry manager is also ultimately responsible for drawing the widgets on the screen (since only it knows where they should be drawn), it's the geometry manager that actually displays each widget.

If you didn't call the geometry manager, then no widgets would be displayed, because Tk doesn't inherently know where to display them—it only knows how to display them.

Callbacks

In our demonstration script, the main **Button** widget had a **command** property. This pointed to the function **exit** via an anonymous subroutine. This command is what's called a callback—it calls back a piece of code from another part of the script when you perform a certain action. In this case, when you clicked on the button, the scripted ended.

To fully understand callbacks, and how the other elements of the Tk window work, we need to understand event loops.

Event Loops

The **MainLoop** function executes a simple loop that dispatches requests from the underlying windowing system to the corresponding widgets. For each event, the function defined in the **command** property is executed. However, it's the responsibility of the called function to perform its job and relinquish control as soon as possible, so as to allow other waiting events to execute.

For complex systems that are CPU intensive, you will also need to make sure that you can effectively multitask between the different threads of execution so that you don't lock up the process while servicing an earlier event loop. For some applications and some systems, this will require you to manually divide a task into manageable chunks. This will allow the event loop to send requests to other callback functions. An alternative solution is to use a multithreaded application model.

Any system call that blocks is generally a bad idea within a GUI interface, since events in the event stack will not be processed while the system blocks. This is a particular problem on Windows, where the process blocking can actually freeze the whole machine (although it's not supposed to). The best method is to use something like **select**, which will do the job of multiplexing between open filehandles for you. Unfortunately, this doesn't get around the problem of handling GUI and file events for you.

The **MainLoop** function is not configurable; it's impossible to supply your own version. The loop only exits when users click on the close box within their windowed environment, or when a call to **exit** is made. Without multithreaded support, there will be no way for you either to use the **select** function or to handle the data. The solution is to use the **fileevent** function. This notifies a callback function when the specified filehandle is ready to accept or supply data. You use it much like you use any other callback function within the Tk environment:

```
open(DATA, "file.txt) or die "Can't open $!";
$label->fileevent(DATA, "readable", \&accept_data);
```

The callback function will be called, in this instance, when data is waiting to be read from the file and when an end-of-file is identified. The callback function will need to handle both these instances. For example:

```
sub accept_data
{
    if (eof(DATA))
    {
        $label->fileevent(DATA, "readable", undef);
        return;
    }
    else
    {
        $text .= <DATA>;
    }
}
```

Of course, this doesn't guarantee that the operator or function you have chosen will not block the process if there isn't as much information as it was expecting. You should be using non-blocking I/O for this sort of process anyway. See Chapter 8 for more information.

Event Bindings

Beyond the basic event bindings handled by the **command** property, it is possible to bind specific events, such as keypresses and mouse clicks, to other functions. This is how you make keys equate to specific function calls and provide shortcuts to commands and functions. Tk provides the **bind** function, which allows you to map these low-level events to corresponding functions. It is also the method employed by individual widgets when you define the **command** property. The format for the function is

```
$widget->bind(event, callback);
```

The **event** is the name of the event you want to bind and can include keypresses or a mouse click (which is defined as a press and release). The **bind** function also supports more complicated events, such as a mouse click and drag, general mouse motion, the mouse pointer entering or leaving a window, and whole-window events, like resizing and iconifying.

The **event** is defined as a string containing the sequence you want to map, which can be made up of one or more individual events called event sequences. For example, the code

```
$widget->bind("<z>", \&pressed_z);
```

maps the user pressing the Z key, without any modifier, to the function. Other possible values for **event** are

```
$widget->bind("<Control-z>", \&undo);
```

which occurs when the CTRL key and Z are pressed at the same time, and

```
$widget->bind("<Escape><Control-z>", \&redo);
```

which will call **redo** when the ESC key is pressed, followed by CTRL and Z. For mouse clicks, you would use

```
$widget->bind("<Button1>", \&redo);
```

Individual events are grouped into different classes called *modifiers*, *types*, and *details*. A modifier is a special key, such as ESC, CTRL, META, ALT, and SHIFT. Mouse buttons are also grouped into this class, so you get **Button1**, **Button2**, **Double** (for a double click), and **Triple** (for a triple click). There is also a special modifier, **Any**, which matches all of the modifiers, including none.

The type of event is one of **KeyPress**, **KeyRelease**, **ButtonPress**, **ButtonRelease**, **Enter**, **Leave**, and **Motion**. Note that you can identify both a keypress and its release, so you can configure a game, for example, to accept a certain keypress, and only stop processing when the key is finally released. The same is true of button presses and releases. Finally, the **Leave** option identifies when the pointer leaves the confines of a widget (useful for tear-off menus and palettes), and **Motion** identifies when the pointer has been moved whilst a button and/or keyboard combination is pressed.

The detail class is only used for keyboard bindings and is a string defining the character that has been pressed. In addition, it also supports ENTER, **Right**, DELETE, BACKSPACE, ESC, F1, and the basic ASCII characters, A–Z, punctuation, and so on.

To make life easier, the Tk library also allows you to use abbreviations of the most common keypresses so that **<KeyPress-z>** can be specified simply as **<z>** and **<Button1-ButtonPress>** as **<1>**.

In addition, the **Text** and **Canvas** widgets allow an even finer granularity on individual bindings, allowing you to attach a binding to a specific tag. The format of **bind** changes accordingly: the first argument now defines the tag to identify, and the second and third arguments define the binding and function to be called. Thus, you can create a binding for pressing the second button on a piece of tagged text:

```
$text->bind('word', '<2>', \&synonym_menu);
```

Obtaining Event Details

Since it's possible to bind any key or button sequence to a function, it's also possible to assign multiple bindings to a single handler. In these instances, the handler must be able to determine what key or button was pressed and where the cursor was at the time the event occurred. To obtain the event details, you use the **Ev** function, which extracts the information from the event itself, since it is the event that records the information about what was pressed and where.

The **Ev('k')** call returns the keycode that triggered the event, as previously defined, and **Ev('x')** and **Ev('y')** return the x and y coordinates of the mouse pointer when the event was received. To use this, you need to supply an array as the value to the function-binding argument:

```
$widget->bind("<Button1>", [\&redo, Ev('k')]);
```

The first element of the array reference is the function to be called, and further elements are the arguments to be passed to the function.

Widgets

To understand how the Tk system works, we'll take a brief look at the most commonly used widgets. There are many exceptions that are not listed, due to space constraints. If you want more information, check the well-organized and voluminous documentation supplied with the Perl/Tk package.

The Core Widgets

The Tk library comes with a number of predefined widgets. Some are the basic building blocks of your typical GUI application, such as **Button** and **Label**. Others are composites of other widgets. Table 17-1 lists the basic widgets that are supported by the Tk system.

Widget Class	Description
BitmapImage	A subclass of the **Image** widget for displaying bitmap images
Button	A simple push-button widget with similar properties to the **Label** widget
Canvas	A drawing area into which you can place circles, lines, text, and other graphic artifacts

Table 17-1. *The Basic Widget Set*

Widget Class	Description
Checkbutton	A multiple-choice button widget, where each item within the selection can be selected individually
Entry	A single-line text entry box
Frame	A container for arranging other widgets
Image	A simple widget for displaying bitmaps, pixmaps (color bitmaps), and other graphic objects
Label	A simple box into which you can place message text (not editable)
Listbox	A multiline list of selection choices
Menu	A list of menu selections that can be made up of **Label**, **Message**, **Button**, and other widgets
Menubutton	A menu (within a single menu bar) that lists the selections specified in a **Menu** object
Message	A multiline **Label** object (not editable)
OptionMenu	A special type of **Menu** widget that provides a pop-up list of items within a selection
PhotoImage	A subclass of the **Image** widget for displaying full-color images
Radiobutton	A multiple-choice button widget, where you can choose only one of multiple values
Scale	A slider that allows you to set a value according to a specific scale
Scrollbar	A slider for controlling the contents of another widget, such as **Text** or **Canvas**
Text	A multiline text widget that supports editable text that can also be tagged for display in different fonts and colors
Toplevel	A window that will be managed and dressed by the parent window manager
Tributton	An adaptation of the **Button** widget that allows it to support three different states instead of the normal bipolar on/off

Table 17-1.   *The Basic Widget Set* (continued)

One of the advantages of Tk is that because it supports such basic levels of widgets, they can be combined or modified to build other widgets. For example, the **ScrolledText** widget is a combination of the **Scrollbar** and **Text** widgets that allows you to control what part of the **Text** widget's text is displayed, according to the position of the **Scrollbar**.

At first, this makes Tk look far less practical than other more feature-rich toolkits. For example, unlike Windows and some of the Unix-based toolkits, Tk doesn't support a "standard" dialog box widget—you have to make one yourself. On the other hand, because you have to make it yourself, you can produce a custom version, perhaps including an error or reference number—something that the predefined toolkits wouldn't be able to support. The downside is that the development process can take longer—you spend a long time introducing the "standard" artifacts of a good GUI—but the flexibility wins out in the end.

We'll take a closer look at some of the more commonly used widgets as we go through the rest of this chapter.

Generic Widget Properties

The configuration of individual widgets is controlled through a series of properties. All widgets have a set of properties that define everything from the existence of borders and colors, through to font styles and sizes. Individual specialized widgets also have properties for the unique elements that make up that widget. For example, a **MenuButton** widget has a property called **state**, which indicates whether the menu is active or disabled.

When you define a widget, you set the properties by specifying the property name and value as part of the hash that you supply to a widget method called **configure**. For example:

```
$label->configure(text="Hello World!\n", foreground = 'red');
```

The generic properties that are configurable for all widgets are shown in Table 17-2. Note that although the properties shown here are without leading hyphens (as required by Tk normally), you may need to add them. The Perl/Tk interface allows you to use specifications both with and without the hyphen prefix.

All widgets also support a number of methods for controlling and configuring their options. There are two basic methods. The first is **configure**, which allows you to set multiple properties on a widget object at once:

```
$label->configure(text  => 'Hello World!', foreground => 'red');
```

The second, **cget**, returns the value of a specific property:

```
$color =  $label->cget('foreground');
```

Property	Description
font	The font name in X or Windows format
background, bg	The color of the background, specified either by a name or hexadecimal RGB value
foreground, fg	The color of the foreground, specified either by a name or hexadecimal RGB value
text	The string to be displayed within the widget, using the foreground and font values specified
image, bitmap	The image or bitmap file to be displayed within the widget
relief	The style of the widget's border, which should be one of raised, sunken, flat, ridge, or groove
borderwidth	The width of the relief border
height	The height of the widget; specified in the number of characters for labels, buttons, and text widgets, and in pixels for all other widgets
width	The width of the widget; specified in the number of characters for labels, buttons, and text widgets, and in pixels for all other widgets
textvariable	The name of a variable to be used and/or updated when the widget changes
anchor	Defines the location of the widget within the window, or the location of the text within the widget; valid values are **n**, **ne**, **e**, **se**, **s**, **sw**, **w**, **nw**, and **center**

Table 17-2.   *Generic Widget Properties*

DEVELOPING
APPLICATIONS

Specifying Fonts   Font values are traditionally specified in the XLFD (X Logical Font Description) format. This is a complex string consisting of 14 fields, each separated by a hyphen. Each field defines a different property. For example, the font

```
-sony-fixed-medium-r-normal--16-120-100-100-c-80-iso8859-1
```

defines a font from the "sony" foundry, the "fixed" family, of medium weight. It's a regular (rather than italic) font—identified by the "r"—and the width is normal.

The size of the font is 16 pixels or 12 points high (point size is specified in tenths of a point, so the size specified is 120 rather than 12). The next two fields specify the resolution—in this instance 100 pixels wide and 100 pixels high—with an overall character ("c") width of 80. The last field is the registry or character locale name.

Usually, however, you can get away with specifying an asterisk or question mark as wildcards in particular fields so that you can request a more general font, and then let the Tk and windowing interface determine the correct font. You should be able to get away with specifying the foundry, family, weight, slant, and points fields. For example, to use 12-point Helvetica, you might use:

```
$label->configure(font=>'-adobe-helvetica-medium-r-*--*-120-*-*-*-*-*');
```

Obviously this is quite a mouthful, and it doesn't really apply to the Windows font system, which is much simpler. The Tk libraries also accept the simpler Windows style definition, which is also backward compatible with the Unix Tk libraries. This definition includes the font name, point size, and weight; for example:

```
$label->configure(font => 'Helvetica 12 regular');
```

Specifying Colors The X Window System supports a file called rgb.txt, which maps red, green, and blue intensities to color names. This allows you to specify a color with a simple name. Here's a short extract from the beginning of a sample rgb.txt file:

```
255 250 250        snow
248 248 255        ghost white
248 248 255        GhostWhite
 47  79  79        DarkSlateGray
  0 191 255        DeepSkyBlue
 46 139  87        SeaGreen
178  34  34        firebrick
147 112 219        MediumPurple
```

Obviously, Windows does not use X Windows, but it still has access to the core set of colors described here. If you want to be more specific, you can explicitly specify the RGB values precisely in the form **#RGB**, **#RRGGBB**, **#RRRGGGBBB**, and **#RRRRGGGGBBBB**, where the **R**, **G**, and **B** refer to an individual hexadecimal digit of the corresponding color's intensity.

For example, the **GhostWhite** color could be described as "#F8F8FF". For many situations, it may be easier to use **sprintf** to create the string:

```
$color = sprintf("#%02x%02x%02x",142,112,219);
```

Specifying Sizes   When specifying the size for a specific widget parameter, there are a number of choices available to you, depending on the widget you are using. If the widget is of a graphical, rather than textual, base—for example **Canvas**—then the size specification accepted by the **height** and **width** properties is in pixels. This also extends to labels and buttons that have a graphical, rather than textual, value. For all widgets that are text based, the specification is in characters, according to the size of the font being used to display the text.

Images and Bitmaps   Certain widgets support the use of images rather than text. For example, you can use an image in place of the text that would normally appear on a button. There are essentially two types of images—a two-color bitmap and a multicolored pixmap. In an effort to help improve performance, Tk considers an image to be a unique element. If it needs to be displayed in more than one place, you render it once and use the rendered image object as the source for the widget image. This means there are two steps to using an image within a widget.

The first step is to create the rendered image object. You use a different function to render individual image formats, although the return value from each function is always of the same type. To create an image object from X Bitmap (XBM):

```
$image = $label->Bitmap(file => 'icon.xbm');
```

For an X Pixmap (XPM):

```
$image = $label->Pixmap(file => 'icon.xpm');
```

And for a GIF or Portable Pixmap (PPM) format, you need to use the **Photo** constructor:

```
$image = $label->Photo(file => 'icon.gif');
```

When you want to configure a particular widget with an image object, use the **image** property:

```
$label->configure(image => $image);
```

For bitmaps, the **foreground** and **background** properties of the widget control the foreground and background color of the bitmap.

Labels

A **Label** widget is the basic widget and provides a simple way of displaying a small text label within a window. It supports all the basic properties shown in Table 17-2. Because labels are such a basic element, they often form parts, or the basis, of many of the other widgets in the Tk toolkit.

Property	Description
command	A reference to the Perl function to be called when the button is clicked with mouse button 1

Method	Description
flash	Flashes the button briefly by reversing and resetting the foreground and background colors
invoke	Starts the subroutine defined in the **command** property

Table 17-3. *Properties and Methods for Buttons*

Buttons

Button widgets are essentially just labels with an additional property, **command**, which is a pointer to a function that will be called when the button is clicked. The list of additional properties and methods beyond the base list are shown in Table 17-3.

You saw an example of both the label and button in the introductory script.

Radio Buttons

The **Radiobutton** widget is used to provide either a simple on/off button, or to act as a toggle between several different options. The valid properties and methods for a radio button are shown in Table 17-4.

For example, the following script shows a very simple radio button that allows you to choose between different names:

```
use Tk;

$name = 'martin';

$main = MainWindow->new();

$main->Radiobutton(text   => 'Martin',
                   value => 'martin',
                   variable => \$name)->pack(side => 'left');
$main->Radiobutton(text   => 'Sharon',
                   value => 'sharon',
                   variable => \$name)->pack(side => 'left');
```

```
$main->Radiobutton(text   => 'Wendy',
                   value => 'wendy',
                   variable => \$name)->pack(side => 'left');

MainLoop();
```

Note that the same variable is used in each property definition, so the information is shared. A change to the value will update the corresponding radio-button family with the correct selection. The resultant window is shown here:

Property	Description
command	A reference to the Perl function to be called when the button is clicked with mouse button 1. The variable referred to by the **variable** property is updated with the value in the **value** property before the referenced subroutine is invoked.
variable	Takes a reference to a variable and updates it with the **value** property when the button is clicked. When the value of the referenced variable matches the **value** property, the button is selected automatically.
value	Specifies the value to store within the variable pointed to by the **variable** property when the button is selected.
Method	**Description**
select	Selects the radio button and sets the **variable** to **value**
flash	Flashes the button briefly by reversing and resetting the foreground and background colors
invoke	Starts the subroutine defined in the **command** property

Table 17-4.   *Properties and Methods for Radio Buttons*

Check Buttons

A **Checkbutton** widget, perhaps better known as a checkbox, depending on your background, is like a radio button, except that it is normally used to allow the user to select multiple checkboxes for a single option. The possible properties and methods for a **Checkbutton** widget are shown in Table 17-5.

Property	Description
command	A reference to the Perl function to be called when the button is clicked with mouse button 1. The variable referred to by the **variable** property is updated with the value in the **value** property before the referenced subroutine is invoked.
variable	Takes a reference to a variable and updates it with the **value** property when the button is clicked. When the value of the referenced variable matches the **value** property, the button is selected automatically.
onvalue	Specifies the value to store within the variable pointed to by the **variable** property when the button is selected
offvalue	Specifies the value to store within the variable pointed to by the **variable** property when the button is not selected
indicatoron	If false (zero), then rather than displaying the checkbox indicator, it toggles the **relief** base property of the entire widget, effectively making the whole widget the checkbox.
Method	**Description**
select	Selects the check button and sets the **variable** to **value**
flash	Flashes the button briefly by reversing and resetting the foreground and background colors
invoke	Starts the subroutine defined in the **command** property
toggle	Toggles the selection state and values of the button on and off

Table 17-5.   *Properties and Methods for Check Buttons*

DEVELOPING
APPLICATIONS

Text

A **Text** widget is a simple text box used for displaying multiple lines of text, unlike a label, which is really only useful for a small number of words on a single line. A **Text** widget becomes an editable entry box for information. It supports the **emacs** keyboard shortcuts for data entry and for moving around the box. In addition to the editing features of a **Text** widget, you can also "tag" individual pieces of text and change their properties. This allows you to create a fully featured text editor with multiple font, point size, and color support without any additional programming.

Text widget methods take one or more index specifications as arguments. An argument can be an absolute number (base) or a relative number (base and modifier), and both are specified as strings. Supported base index specifications are shown below. Items in italics indicate the components of the index specification that you can modify. Anything else is a keyword.

line.char	Indicates the character at **char** characters across (left to right) and **line** lines down (top to bottom). The specification starts at 0 for characters within a line, and 1 for lines within a text box.
end	The end of the text, as defined by the character just after the last newline
insert	The location of the insertion cursor
mark	The character just after the marker whose name is **mark**
tag.**first**, *tag*.**last**	Used to specify the **first** and **last** characters of a tag

These index specifications can also be qualified with an additional modifier:

+*count* **chars**, -*count* **chars**, +*count* **lines**, -*count* **lines**	Adjust the base index specification by **count** characters or lines.
wordstart, wordend, linestart, lineend	Adjust the index to point to the first character on the word or line specified by the index (**wordstart, linestart**) or to the character immediately after the word or line(**wordend, lineend**).

A sample of supported properties and methods is shown in Table 17-6. For example, to insert a piece of text at the end of a text box:

```
$text->insert('Beginning!', 'end');
```

Property	Description
tabs	The list of tab stops for the **Text** widget. Specification should be as a reference to a list of strings. Each string should be composed of a number defining the character location within the line, followed by **l**, **c**, or **r** for left, center, or right justification for the specified tab.
state	One of **normal** for a standard editable text box, or **disabled** for an unmodifiable text box.

Method	Description
insert(INDEX [, STRING [, TAG]] ...)	Insert **STRING** with an optional **TAG** at the specified **INDEX**.
delete(INDEX1 [,INDEX2])	Delete the character at **INDEX1** or the text from **INDEX1** to **INDEX2**.
get(INDEX1 [,INDEX2])	Get the character at **INDEX1** or the text from **INDEX1** to **INDEX2**.
index(INDEX)	Returns an absolute index for the corresponding **INDEX** supplied
see(INDEX)	Returns true if the text at **INDEX** is visible
markSet(NAME, INDEX)	Gives the text at **INDEX** the bookmark name **NAME**
markUnset(NAME)	Unsets a bookmark **NAME**

Table 17-6. *Properties and Methods for Text Widgets*

Or to insert the same piece of text at character 20 on line 5:

```
$text->insert('Beginning!', '5.20');
```

To specify and configure the tags, you need the methods and properties shown in Table 17-7.

Method	Description
tagAdd(NAME [,INDEX1[.INDEX2]] ...)	Adds the tag **NAME** at the position specified in **INDEX1** or bounded by **INDEX1** and **INDEX2**
tagRemove(NAME [,INDEX1[.INDEX2]] ...)	Removes the tag **NAME** from the character or range specified by **INDEX1** and **INDEX2**, but does not delete the actual tag definition
tagDelete(NAME)	Removes and deletes the tag **NAME**
tagConfigure	Configures one or more properties for a tag

Property	Description
-foreground, -background, -font	Same as for the basic properties
-justify	Justification for the tagged text, one of **center**, **left**, and **right**
-relief, -borderwidth	The border width and relief style
-tabs	Same as for basic text widget properties, but applies only if the first character in that line also belongs to the same tag. You cannot add "subtabs" to a tagged block.
-underline	Underlines the tagged text

Table 17-7. *Tag Methods and Properties*

For example, to create a simple tag:

```
$text->tagAdd('tagged', '1.0', '3.0');
```

This creates a tag called "tagged" from lines 1 through 3 inclusive. The tag name should be unique because you need it when configuring the options on an individual tag. Therefore, to change the text tagged with the name "tagged" to 24-point Times, boldfaced:

```
$text->tagConfigure('tagged', font => 'Times 24 Bold');
```

You can also use the **tie** function with a **Text** widget to tie the text box contents to a filehandle. Once tied, you can print and read from the text widget just like any other filehandle. Thus, you can create a very simple text-file viewer with code like this:

```
use Tk;

$main = MainWindow->new();
$main->title("Text Viewer");

$maintext = $main->Scrolled('Text');

open(SOURCE, "myfile.txt") or die "Can't open source";
tie(*TEXT, 'Tk::Text', $maintext);
print TEXT <SOURCE>;
close (SOURCE);

$maintext->pack();

MainLoop();
```

Entry

An **Entry** widget is essentially a single-line text box, and it inherits many features and methods from the **Text** widget. However, because it's only a single line, the indexing and methods are much simpler. The indexing options are as follows:

number	An index into the widget's contents, starting with zero as the first character
end	The end of the text
insert	The position immediately after the insertion cursor
sel.**first**, *sel*.**last**	Indicates the first and last characters of a tag

The supported properties and methods are shown in Table 17-8.

List Boxes

A **Listbox** widget enables you to create a list, from which you can select an individual item. It displays a list of strings, one per line, and all the strings displayed have the

Property	Description
show	A simple Boolean option. If set, it displays * for each character entered, and is primarily used for password entry. Note that although the characters are displayed in this manner, copying and pasting the contents of a "hidden" field will reveal the real contents.

Method	Description
get(INDEX)	Gets the string starting at INDEX
insert(INDEX, STRING)	Inserts STRING at INDEX
index(INDEX)	Returns an absolute index from a relative one
selectionFrom(INDEX)	Sets the selection from INDEX to the end of the field
selectionTo(INDEX)	Sets the selection from the beginning of the field to INDEX
selection(FROM, TO)	Sets the selection to the characters starting at FROM and ending at TO
selectionClear	Clears the selection
selectionPresent	True if a selection is currently active

Table 17-8.   *Properties and Methods for the Entry Widget*

same characteristics. When creating the list, the easiest way to populate it is to create the widget and then use the **insert** method to add items to the list. The **width** and **height** properties for the **Listbox** widget define the width of the list box and the height in characters. Or you can specify values of zero, which will cause the list box to grow to display all of the objects.

Here is an example of using the **Listbox** widget:

```
use Tk;

$main = MainWindow->new();

$list = $main->Listbox(height => 5,
                       width => 0)->pack();

$list->insert('end', qw/Martin Sharon Wendy Sharon Chris/);

MainLoop();
```

The result is shown here:

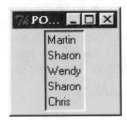

Note that you will need to use the **bind** method shown earlier in this chapter to bind a particular operation, such as a double-click, to a function. Within the function, you'll need to use the **get** method to obtain the current selection.

You can refer to individual elements within a **Listbox** in a similar fashion to selecting text within a **Textbox** widget. Specification is by a string defining the row, row selection, or relative location within the list. The details are shown here.

number	The index of the row, starting with zero for the first element
end	Indicates the end of the current row
active	Where the location cursor is currently positioned, and the active location appears underlined in the list view
anchor	The anchor point of the selection

The properties and methods supported by the **Listbox** widget are shown in Table 17-9.

Menus

Menus are logically split into **MenuButton** widgets, which are the menu names. The **MenuButton** widget then becomes a container that holds the individual menu item widgets, which are split into different types to allow you to add normal menu items (actually just labels), buttons, checkboxes, and radio buttons to your menus.

The normal method for a creating a menu is as follows:

1. Create a menu bar frame, using the **Frame** widget, to hold individual menu buttons.

2. Create the individual menu buttons within the new frame.

3. Use the **MenuButton** widget methods to create the individual menu items.

Property	Description
height, width	The height and width of the list in rows and characters. If either is zero, then the widget resizes to incorporate all of the list elements.
selectMode	Defines the selection mode of the list; one of **single**, **browse**, **multiple**, or **extended**

Method	Description
get(INDEX)	Gets the string, starting at **INDEX**
insert(INDEX, STRING)	Inserts **STRING** at **INDEX**
delete(INDEX [, LAST])	Deletes the row at **INDEX**, or the rows between **INDEX** and **LAST**
see(INDEX)	Brings the element **INDEX** into the current view
selectionFrom(INDEX)	Selects all the rows from **INDEX** to the end of the list
selectionTo(INDEX)	Selects all the rows from the beginning of the list to **INDEX**
selection(FROM, TO)	Selects the rows starting at **FROM** and ending at **TO**
selectionClear( )	Clears the selection
selectionPresent( )	Returns true if there is an active selection
curselection( )	A list of the index values of all the selected items

Table 17-9.   *Properties and Methods Supported by the Listbox Widget*

Every method of the **MenuButton** widget supports the now familiar index format, although the index refers to the individual menu item:

number   The index of the menu item, starting at zero for the first item. When the menu is configured for tear-off, the first entry is a separator automatically inserted by the widget.

end, last   Indicates the last entry

active   Where the location cursor is currently active

none   Indicates that none of the menu options are active

pattern   A pattern to be matched against all entries. This only matches exactly; regular expressions are supported.

Properties and methods for the **MenuButton** widget are shown in Table 17-10.

Property	Description
indicatorOn	If true, shows a small diamond to the right of the menu
state	The state of the menu—one of **normal**, **active**, or **disabled**
Method	**Description**
menu	Returns the underlying menu associated with this menu button
command(OPTIONS)	Creates a standard menu item using the properties in **OPTIONS**
separator(OPTIONS)	A separator
radiobutton(OPTIONS)	A radio button menu item using the properties in **OPTIONS**
checkbutton(OPTIONS)	A check button menu item using the properties in **OPTIONS**
cascade(OPTIONS)	Inserts a new cascading (hierarchical) menu using the properties in **OPTIONS**
add(TYPE, OPTIONS)	Adds a new menu of **TYPE** with **OPTIONS**
delete(INDEX1 [, INDEX2])	Deletes the menu item **INDEX1** or the items from **INDEX1** to **INDEX2**
insert(INDEX1, TYPE, OPTIONS)	Inserts a menu item of **TYPE** with **OPTIONS** into the location **INDEX1**
entryconfigure(INDEX, OPTIONS)	Changes the properties of the menu item according to **OPTIONS** pointed to by **INDEX**
entrycget(INDEX)	Gets the configuration options for the menu item at **INDEX**

Table 17-10. *Menu Item Methods*

The configurable **options** supported for the methods in Table 17-10 work like all other properties and are listed in Table 17-11. Note that because you can have hierarchical menus, individual items can use further methods from Table 17-10.

Property	Description
indicatorOn	If true, places a small diamond next to the menu option, which allows an option to be toggled on and off by a menu
selectColor	The color of the indicator, if **indicatorOn** is true
tearOff	If true, the first element of the menu is a separator. Clicking on the separator "tears off" the menu into a separate top-level window. This is not always supported on all implementations.
label	The text to use for the menu item. This should be used in place of the normal **text** property.
underline	The index of a character to underline. This is used in combination with the **accelerator** property to indicate which keyboard shortcut should be used for this menu.
accelerator	Shows the string to be displayed, right justified, as the keyboard equivalent for the menu option. This doesn't bind the key to the command for you—you'll have to do that separately.
state	Status: **normal**, **active**, or **disabled**
command	The reference of a subroutine to call when the menu item is selected
value	The value of the attached radio button (see Table 17-4)
variable	The variable used to store **value**
onvalue, offvalue	Identical to the options in Table 17-5 for check button style entries

Table 17-11.   *Menu Item Properties*

DEVELOPING
APPLICATIONS

For example, to create a simple Help menu, you might use a script like this:

```perl
use Tk;

$main = MainWindow->new();

$menu = $main->Frame()->pack(side => 'top');

$help_menu = $menu->Menubutton(text        => 'Help',
                               relief       => 'raised',
                               borderwidth => 2,
                               )->pack(side => 'left',
                                       padx => 2
                                      );

$help_menu->command('-label'   => 'About',
                    accelerator => 'Meta+A',
                    underline   => 0,
                    command     => sub { print "All about me\n" }
                    );

$help_menu->separator();

$help_menu->command('-label'   => 'Help Index',
                    accelerator => 'Meta+H',
                    underline   => 0,
                    command => \&draw_help_window(),
                    );

$help_menu->command('-label' => 'Help on Help',
                    command   => sub { print "Try Help Index\n" }
                    );

MainLoop();
```

The result can be seen here:

Frame

A **Frame** widget is simply a container for other widgets. It's used when you need to create a complex layout that requires more advanced geometry management than you can normally do with the available tools. The way it works is that you divide individual areas of the window into frames and pack the collection of objects into the frame. For example, you might create a new frame that contains the menu bar, which you gravitate to the top of the window, while the actual menu buttons within the menu bar are arranged horizontally. We'll see an example later in this chapter when we look at the **Scale** widget.

Scroll Bars

Scroll bars are available either as separate widgets, in which case you are responsible for managing the corresponding widget you are scrolling, or they can be automatically added to any suitable widgets.

We'll deal with the automatic scroll bars first. To create an automatically scrolled widget, you use the special **Scrolled** widget method, and then specify the type of widget to create with a scroll bar. For example, here's the line from the text viewer that creates a scrolled **Text** widget:

```
$maintext = $main->Scrolled('Text');
```

Internally, this creates a **Frame** widget that contains the main **Text** widget and the horizontal (and vertical) scroll bars. The reference returned actually refers to the newly created **Frame** widget.

Alternatively, you can create and manage your own scroll bars using the methods and properties in Tables 17-12 and 17-13. The methods in Table 17-13 allow you to set the current view within the widget to which you want to associate the scroll bar. The **set** function controls the current view, and the **command** property is called when the scroll bar is moved.

All widgets that are scrollable also support the methods and properties shown in Table 17-13. The properties define the functions and increments that the scroll bars control. The scroll bar widget automatically calls the correct method (**xview** or **yview**) to modify the display of the linked widget.

Scale

Scales are like thermometers. You define a size and range, and the widget displays a horizontal or vertical slider. The slider automatically has a label (if you've defined one) and tick marks to indicate individual divisions. You can see a sample in Figure 17-1, and we'll look at the code required to build this application shortly.

Property	Description
command	A reference to a subroutine used to change the view in the widget
Method	**Description**
set(FIRST, LAST)	Indicates the current view. The **FIRST** and **LAST** elements should be fractions between 0 and 1. For example, a value of 0.1 and 0.2 should indicate that the area between 10 percent and 20 percent of the item should be shown.
get	Returns the current scroll bar settings

Table 17-12. *Properties and Methods for Scroll Bars*

Property	Description
xscrollincrement, yscrollincrement	The scrolling in the x and y axis will be according to the supplied increment.
xscrollcommand, yscrollcommand	A reference to the function used to reposition the widget when the scroll bar is moved
Method	**Description**
xview('moveto', FRACTION) **yview('moveto', FRACTION)**	Moves the scrollbar to the location specified by **fraction**; the new value will indicate the leftmost, or topmost, character or pixel of the scrollbar tab. Note that the first argument is a constant.
xview('scroll', NUMBER, WHAT) **yview('scroll', NUMBER, WHAT)**	Indicates that the view should be moved up or down, or left or right, for **NUMBER** increments. If **WHAT** is "units," then it is scrolled according to the increment in the **xscrollincrement** and **yscrollincrement** properties. If **WHAT** is "pages," then the widget is scrolled **NUMBER** pages.

Table 17-13. *Properties and Methods for Scrollable Widgets*

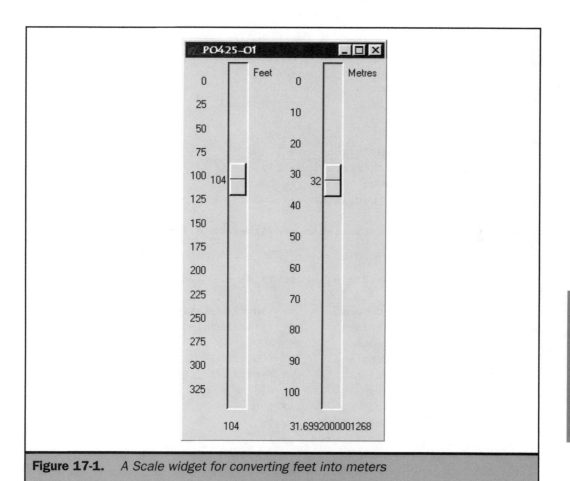

Figure 17-1. *A Scale widget for converting feet into meters*

The supported properties and methods are shown in Table 17-14.

Here's the script that generated Figure 17-1. It provides a simple tool for converting feet into meters and vice versa.

```
use Tk;

my ($feetscale, $metrescale) = (0,0);

$main = MainWindow->new();

$feetframe = $main->Frame()->pack(side => 'left');
```

```perl
$feetframe->Scale(command       => \&update_feet,
                  variable      => \$feetscale,
                  width         => 20,
                  length        => 400,
                  orient        => 'vertical',
                  from          => 0,
                  to            => 328,
                  resolution    => 1,
                  tickinterval  => 25,
                  label         => 'Feet'
                  )->pack(side => 'top');

$feetframe->Label(textvariable => \$feetscale)->pack(side => 'top',
                                                     pady => 5);


$metreframe = $main->Frame()->pack(side => 'left');

$metreframe->Scale(command       => \&update_metre,
                   variable      => \$metrescale,
                   width         => 20,
                   length        => 400,
                   orient        => 'vertical',
                   from          => 0,
                   to            => 100,
                   resolution    => 1,
                   tickinterval  => 10,
                   label         => 'Metres'
                   )->pack(side => 'top');

$metreframe->Label(textvariable => \$metrescale)->pack(side => top,
                                                       pady => 5);


MainLoop();

sub update_feet
{
    $metrescale = $feetscale/3.280839895;
}

sub update_metre
{
    $feetscale = $metrescale*3.280839895;
}
```

Property	Description
command	Reference to a subroutine, which will be called when the scale's value is changed
variable	Reference to a variable to be updated whenever the slider moves. Works like the **variable** base property; updating this value will also set the slider position.
width, length	The **width** and **length** of the scale in pixels (not characters)
orient	Allows you to select **horizontal** or **vertical** orientation
from, to	The real range of values that the widget should scale **from** and **to**
resolution	The value displayed and set into **variable** will always be a multiple of this number. The default is 1.
tickinterval	The spacing, in real values, between tick marks on the scale
label	The label to be displayed to the top (horizontal) or left (vertical) of the scale
Method	**Description**
set(VALUE)	Identical to modifying the value of **variable**

Table 17-14.   *Properties and Methods for Scale Widgets*

A **Frame** widget is used to specify two frames, side by side, and then within each frame, the scale and the floating-point value are shown one above the other.

Controlling Window Geometry

Throughout this chapter, you've seen examples of the **pack** function, and you already know it is a required element of the window-building process. However, there are some tricks you can do with **pack** to aid in the arrangement of individual widgets within a window. Tk also supports two other methods of arranging widgets: the placer and the grid. You must use the same geometry manager within a single parent, although it's possible to mix and match individual geometry managers within multiple frames within a single window to suit your needs.

The placer requires some careful planning to use properly, since you must specify the location of each widget within the window using x and y coordinates. This is the same system used within the **Bulletin Board** widget under Motif and Visual Basic, so people moving from those systems may be more comfortable with this system.

The grid geometry manager uses a simple table layout, as you might use within a word processor or when designing web pages with HTML. Each widget is placed into a table cell, and you specify its location by defining the row and column in which the widget should appear. Individual widgets can span multiple rows and columns if necessary. As with the placer geometry manager, you will need to give some careful thought to how to lay out your widgets in this system.

The packer geometry manager is the one we've been using in this chapter, and it's the most practical if you do not want to think too much about the geometry management process. As such, it's the one we'll pay the most attention to in this chapter. If you want details on the systems, please see the documentation that comes with the Perl/Tk module.

Packer

The packer geometry manager is similar to Motif's **Form** widget and uses a much simpler system for defining the location of widgets within a frame of a window. Remember that the **pack** function is just that—it only provides the algorithm used to organize the layout of widgets. Individual calls to the **pack** method pack the corresponding widget into the next available space within the frame or window. This means that widgets are added to the window or frame in the order in which they are packed. This is similar to how you would pack a bag or fill a shelf: you start from a single point and add items until the space is all used up.

The algorithm works like this:

1. Given a frame, the packer attaches a widget to a particular side (top, bottom, left, or right).

2. The space used up by the widget is taken off from the space available in the frame, an area called the parcel. If the widget does not fill the parcel completely (if the parcel is wider or taller than the area sliced for the widget), then that space is essentially wasted. This is, in fact, the reason for supporting additional **Frame** widgets to make the best use of the space.

3. The next widget is then placed into the remaining space, and once again the widget can attach itself to the top or bottom or one of sides to use up the available space.

4. Note that all widgets that specify a particular anchor point will be grouped together and share that space. Thus, if you specify multiple widgets with "left" anchor, they will be organized left-to-right within the frame. Once again, if you want to do more complex layouts (as in the **Scale** widget example), you will need to create separate frames.

The available options to the packer method are shown in Table 17-15. Like other elements of the Tk system, options are specified as a hash to the **pack** method. If you do not specify an option, the packer geometry manager inserts widgets from top to bottom.

Property	Description
side	The side of the frame to which the widget should be added. Should be one of **left**, **right**, **top**, or **bottom**
fill	Specifies whether the widget should fill up the space in the parcel in the **x** or **y** direction. You can also specify **both**, to fill in both directions, or **none**, to prevent filling altogether. The **ipadx** or **ipady** options can be used to specify some additional blank padding space around the widget within the parcel.
expand	Specifies whether the widget should expand to take up all of the remaining space after the other widgets have been placed. This is useful for **Textbox** widgets where you are defining an outer menu and toolbar and want the main widget to take up all the remaining space.
padx, pady	The spacing between widgets, specified in pixels, millimeters, inches, or points (see also Table 17-16)
ipadx, ipady	The spacing around a widget that is "filling" the space provided by the parcel; specified in pixels, millimeters, inches, or points (see also Table 17-16)

Table 17-15. *Options to the **pack** Function*

The **padx**, **pady**, **ipadx**, and **ipady** properties accept a string, rather than a numeric value. Depending on the value's suffix, the value is interpreted either as pixels, centimeters, inches, millimeters, or points. For values other than pixels, the geometry manager will interrogate the window manager and determine the screen resolution and density to decide how many actual pixels to use—for example, on a typical Windows screen running at 96dpi, a specification of "1i" would introduce padding of 96 pixels. The valid suffixes are shown in Table 17-16.

Grid

The grid geometry manager works in an identical fashion to tables within HTML. Individual widgets are placed into a grid of rows and columns. Individual widgets are confined to each cell within the grid, but individual cells can be made to span more than one row or column, if required.

The **grid** function/method is the interface to the grid manager. You specify the location of each widget according to the row and column in which it should appear.

Suffix	Description
none	Size is calculated in pixels.
c	Size is interpreted as onscreen centimeters.
i	Size is interpreted as onscreen inches.
m	Size is interpreted as onscreen millimeters.
p	Size is interpreted as printer's points (1 point is approximately 1/72 inch). This is the same unit as the point size used when specifying font sizes.

Table 17-16. *Padding Character Suffixes*

The final size of the grid is based on the maximum row and column that you specify. The properties for the **grid** function are shown in Table 17-17.

Property	Value
column	The column in which to insert the widget
columnspan	The number of columns that the widget should span within the grid
row	The row in which to insert the widget
rowspan	The number of rows that the widget should span within the grid
sticky	Defines the side of the parent widget to which the widget will stick. Should be specified as zero or more of the characters **n**, **s**, **e**, or **w**. If none are specified, the widget becomes centered within its cell. If both **n** and **s** (or **e** and **w**) are specified, then the widget will stretch to fill the height (or width) of the cell. If all four are specified, then the widget grows to fill the entire cell.
padx, pady	The spacing between widgets; specified in pixels, millimeters, inches, or points (see Table 17-16)
ipadx, ipady	The spacing around a widget that is "filling" the space provided by the parcel; specified in pixels, millimeters, inches, or points (see Table 17-16).

Table 17-17. *Properties for the Grid Geometry Manager*

Placer

The placer works slightly differently than the other two geometry managers. Whereas the packer and grid work on the basis of aligning widgets according to the other widgets on the page, the placer allows you to specify very precisely where you want a widget to be placed. The specification is based on the location and size of the window into which the widget is placed. If you consider each window to be similar to a cell with the grid manager, you should get the idea. The widget is then placed into the window that is created.

The specification for the size of the window, itself, is defined in relation to the widget's parent (either a **Window** or **Frame** or other container widget). Armed with this principle, you can specify:

- The location (in pixels) and size of the window within the parent.
- The location and size of the window in relation to the parent.
- A combination of the two, so you can have a fixed size, but a variable location, or a fixed location, but a variable size.

Thus, you can have a widget centered within a parent that expands with the parent, increasing both the border and widget size. These options are incredibly useful for **Canvas**, **Text**, and other widgets where you want to expand the display area without affecting the other widgets within the window.

The interface to the placer manager is via the **place** method to your widgets. The key/value pairs accepted by the function are shown in Table 17-18.

Note *The x, relx, y, and rely settings can be combined. A value of 0.5 for relx and 5 for x would place the widget 5 pixels to the right of the center of the parent. The same is true for width, relwidth, height, and relheight, where a specification of 1.0 for relwidth and 5 for width would produce a window 5 pixels smaller than the parent.*

Easing the Process

If you are designing a relatively static window for your Perl script rather than one with many dynamic elements, you may find the **SpecTcl** application of some use. **SpecTcl** is a GUI designer, which is itself written in Tcl and Tk. The newer versions include the ability to design Tk-based user environments that generate the necessary code for Tcl, Java, HTML, and Perl. The Java 1.1, HTML, and Perl extensions are still experimental, but they will allow you to generate most of the required code to build your application.

SpecTcl will particularly appeal to people who have had experience using a visual interface development environment, such as Access or Visual Basic. You lay out widgets of static pages by simply dragging and dropping the individual elements into a window and configuring the properties, such as fonts and colors, from lists of suitable values. **SpecTcl** creates all the Perl/Tk code for you; all you need to do is supply the callback functions and the rest of the support code to go with it.

DEVELOPING
APPLICATIONS

Property	Description
in	The widget (object) that the widget should be placed relative to. The value must be a valid widget object, and must either be the window parent or a descendant of the window parent. You must also ensure that the widget and its parent are both descendants of the same window.
x, y	The *x* (horizontal) and *y* (vertical) coordinates to use as the anchor point for the widget. See Table 17-16 for a list of valid qualifiers for the number.
relx, rely	The relative *x* (horizontal) coordinate within the parent window. The number should be specified as a floating point number, where 0.0 refers to the left edge of the parent, and 1.0 to the right edge; thus, the setting 0.5 would center the widget in the parent.
anchor	Defines which point of the window should be treated as the anchor point. Uses the normal **n**, **ne**, **e**, **se**, **s**, **sw**, **w**, **nw** values.
width, height	Specifies the width or height of the window. See Table 17-16 for a list of valid qualifiers for the values. Note that in both cases the measurement defines the outer width of the window, including any border.
relwidth, relheight	The relative width or height of the window compared to the size of the parent, where 0.5 means the window is half as big as the parent, and 1.0 means that the window and parent are the same width or height
bordermode	One of **inside** (default), **outside**, or **ignore**. If set to **inside**, then the area for the window is calculated less any border on the parent. If **outside**, it includes the area set by the parent's border. If set to **ignore**, then the calculations are taken irrespective of the border size, making the entire parent window available for use.

Table 17-18.   *Properties for the Placer Geometry Manager*

For example, Figure 17-2 shows the **SpecTcl** application in action, in this case developing the basic layout for a calculator (actually based on a Python application, although **SpecTcl** doesn't currently support Python). When you have finished drawing and configuring all of the individual components, then you click on the "build" icon, and the Perl code is generated.

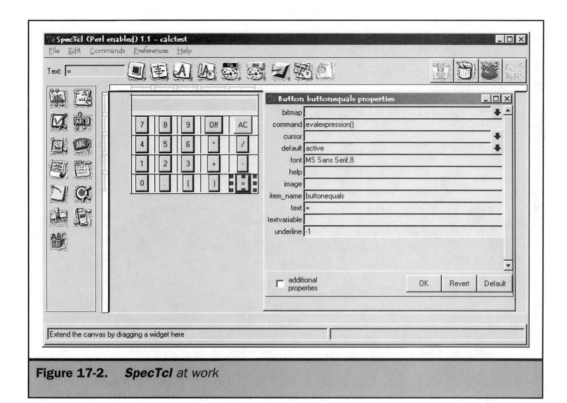

Figure 17-2.   *SpecTcl* at work

The code generated for our calculator application can be seen here.

```perl
use Tk;

my $expression ='Welcome';

# interface generated by SpecTcl (Perl enabled) version 1.1
# from C:/Program Files/SpecTcl1.1/demo/calctest.ui
# For use with Tk400.202, using the gridbag geometry manager

sub evalexpression
{
    my $result;
    $result = eval($expression);

    if ($@)
```

```perl
    {
        $expression = $@;
    }
    else
    {
        $expression = $result;
    }
}

sub all_clear
{
    $expression = '';
}

sub insert
{
    $expression .= $_[0];
}

sub calctest_ui {
    my($root) = @_;

    # widget creation

    my($expression) = $root->Entry (-textvariable => \$expression,);
    my($button7) = $root->Button (-text => '7',);
    my($button8) = $root->Button (-text => '8',);
    my($button9) = $root->Button (-text => '9',);
    my($buttonoff) = $root->Button (-text => 'Off',);
    my($buttonAC) = $root->Button (-text => 'AC',);
    my($button4) = $root->Button (-text => '4',);
    my($button5) = $root->Button (-text => '5',);
    my($button6) = $root->Button (-text => '6',);
    my($buttontimes) = $root->Button (-text => '*',);
    my($buttondivide) = $root->Button (-text => '/',);
    my($button1) = $root->Button (-text => '1',);
    my($button2) = $root->Button (-text => '2',);
    my($button3) = $root->Button (-text => '3',);
    my($buttonplus) = $root->Button (-text => '+',
    my($buttonminus) = $root->Button (-text => '-',
    my($button0) = $root->Button (-text => '0',);
    my($buttonperiod) = $root->Button (-text => '.',);
```

```
my($buttonleft) = $root->Button (-text => '(',);
my($buttonright) = $root->Button (-text => ')',);
my($buttonequals) = $root->Button (-text => '=',);

# widget commands

$button7->configure(-command => sub { insert '7'; });
$button8->configure(-command => sub { insert '8'; });
$button9->configure(-command => sub { insert '9'; });
$buttonoff->configure(-command => sub { exit(); });
$buttonAC->configure(-command => \&all_clear);
$button4->configure(-command => sub { insert '4'; });
$button5->configure(-command => sub { insert '5'; });
$button6->configure(-command => sub { insert '6'; });
$buttontimes->configure(-command => sub { insert '*'; });
$buttondivide->configure(-command => sub { insert '/'; });
$button1->configure(-command => sub { insert '1'; });
$button2->configure(-command => sub { insert '2'; });
$button3->configure(-command => sub { insert '3'; });
$buttonplus->configure(-command => sub { insert '+'; });
$buttonminus->configure(-command => sub { insert '-'; });
$button0->configure(-command => sub { insert '0'; });
$buttonperiod->configure(-command => sub { insert '.'; });
$buttonleft->configure(-command => sub { insert '('; });
$buttonright->configure(-command => sub { insert ')'; });
$buttonequals->configure(-command => \&evalexpression);

# Geometry management

$expression->grid(-in => $root,
                  -column => '1',
                  -row => '1',
                  -columnspan => '5');
$button7->grid(-in => $root,
               -column => '1',
               -row => '2');
$button8->grid(-in => $root,
               -column => '2',
               -row => '2'
                    );
$button9->grid(-in => $root,
               -column => '3',
```

```
                         -row => '2');
$buttonoff->grid(-in => $root,
                 -column => '4',
                 -row => '2');
$buttonAC->grid(-in => $root,
                -column => '5',
                -row => '2');
$button4->grid(-in => $root,
               -column => '1',
               -row => '3');
$button5->grid(-in => $root,
               -column => '2',
               -row => '3');
$button6->grid(-in => $root,
               -column => '3',
               -row => '3');
$buttontimes->grid(-in => $root,
                   -column => '4',
                   -row => '3');
$buttondivide->grid(-in => $root,
                    -column => '5',
                    -row => '3');
$button1->grid(-in => $root,
               -column => '1',
               -row => '4');
$button2->grid(-in => $root,
               -column => '2',
               -row => '4');
$button3->grid(-in => $root,
               -column => '3',
               -row => '4');
$buttonplus->grid(-in => $root,
                  -column => '4',
                  -row => '4');
$buttonminus->grid(-in => $root,
                   -column => '5',
                   -row => '4');
$button0->grid(-in => $root,
               -column => '1',
               -row => '5');
$buttonperiod->grid(-in => $root,
                    -column => '2',
```

```
                                -row => '5');
    $buttonleft->grid(-in => $root,
                    -column => '3',
                    -row => '5');
    $buttonright->grid(-in => $root,
                    -column => '4',
                    -row => '5');
    $buttonequals->grid(-in => $root,
                    -column => '5',
                    -row => '5');

    # Resize behavior management

    # container $root (rows)
    $root->gridRowconfigure(1, -weight  => 0, -minsize  => 30);
    $root->gridRowconfigure(2, -weight  => 0, -minsize  => 17);
    $root->gridRowconfigure(3, -weight  => 0, -minsize  => 8);
    $root->gridRowconfigure(4, -weight  => 0, -minsize  => 7);
    $root->gridRowconfigure(5, -weight  => 0, -minsize  => 2);

    # container $root (columns)
    $root->gridColumnconfigure(1, -weight => 0, -minsize => 2);
    $root->gridColumnconfigure(2, -weight => 0, -minsize => 13);
    $root->gridColumnconfigure(3, -weight => 0, -minsize => 13);
    $root->gridColumnconfigure(4, -weight => 0, -minsize => 30);
    $root->gridColumnconfigure(5, -weight => 0, -minsize => 30);

    # additional interface code
    # end additional interface code

}

$main = MainWindow->new();
$main->title("Calculator");

calctest_ui($main);

MainLoop();
```

The amount of code generated is quite high when compared to that generated manually, because the properties are created in separate sections (basic, then commands), but otherwise the code generated works. The three functions used by the buttons have been added at the top, in addition to the glue code required to generate a window and then call the **MainLoop** function to kick the process off, but it works. You can see the finished calculator here:

It's primarily aimed at producing simple form-based windows for data entry and other similar static window development, but it may also provide you with enough base code to start you on your way with Tk development.

Development of the SpecTcl system has now stopped, since it was actually developed at Sun whilst the Tcl and Tk projects were being developed at the company. Even so, the package still remains solid, and for projects that require very quick development, it may provide an immediate solution without the manual labor.

You can download SpecTcl from Scriptics, www.scriptics.com. The SpecPerl portion of the development is handled by Mark Kvale, and you can download the latest version from **http://www.keck.ucsf.edu/~kvale/specPerl**.

Chapter 18

Developing for the World Wide Web (WWW)

Despite the recent and historical criticisms of the web (too slow, too passive, not interactive enough), the fact remains that more and more people are using it and more and more companies are developing web-related products and services. Right now, you can log on to the web and order a pizza, buy the latest book, video, jacket, and a million other items, send an email to your friends around the world, and even become part of a virtual community.

Most hardware and operating system companies will tell you that the equipment that runs the web is theirs. What they often don't tell you is that one of the main languages that runs web applications is Perl. Although it's unfair (but not uncommon) for people to class Perl as an "Internet" language, it does have some benefits not found (easily) within other languages.

Perl's biggest advantage over many other languages, especially C and Visual Basic, is that it handles raw text and the textual information returned from a database so well. Since most of the web applications rely in one form or another on processing text (from web forms) and then processing, reformatting, and regurgitating that content back out, it's all text in one form or another.

In this chapter, we're going to have a look at most of the issues that surround working with web applications in Perl, starting from the basics of web mechanics (HTML and URLs), through to the interfaces and mechanisms required for Perl to communicate with the web server and ultimately with the user. Along the way, we'll also look at methods for post-processing HTML (using the **HTML::TreeBuilder** module), using cookies, and parsing and reformatting XML documents into HTML format.

HTML

The core of any web application is HTML (Hypertext Markup Language). Despite what design agencies and professional web authors tell you, it is not difficult to learn and use. What is difficult, however, is ensuring that the HTML you have generated does what you want and displays correctly. A lot of the complexity comes from the coding required to produce the format and layout of the HTML you are writing; a much smaller, but perhaps more significant, proportion comes from the semantics of the HTML itself.

I don't really want to get into the precise details of how HTML is formed. If you want more information on how to write good HTML, refer to the www.w3c.org website, which gives full details. Alternatively, visit a bookstore and select almost any HTML title off the shelf. HTML is a simple text format that uses tags to format text in different point sizes and type styles. For example,

```
<b>Hello World!</b>
```

would produce a boldfaced "Hello World!" within a web browser window. The tags are the **** at the beginning of the text section and the **** at the end.

This format is used throughout HTML coding, so the fragment

```
<i>Hello World!</i>
<u>This is a test message</u>
```

would produce "Hello World!" in italics and "This is a test message" underlined. This tagging technique has developed over the years, and actually borrows a lot from the principles of typesetting systems, where they used tags within a document to indicate how it should be laid out to the manual typesetter. It's interesting to see that the old techniques are still practical, even though the technology that uses them has moved on.

One very useful tag is **<a>**, which is short for "anchor" or "address." It denotes the hypertext links that allow you to jump from one HTML document to another (that is, the sections of a WWW document that are often underlined and allow you to jump to other documents).

```
<a href="about_us.html">About us</a>
```

Another significant tag is **<img...**, which allows you to incorporate graphics into your pages. Unlike the other links discussed so far, there is no closing tag, since you are simply inserting another element into the web page.

Generating HTML code within Perl is normally a case of using **print** or a "here" document to embed the HTML tags and accompanying text in the page that is output. The danger with this very manual solution is that you could generate HTML that is missing tags or contains badly formed tags that don't produce what you expect. For example, forgetting to place the **</table>** tag at the end of an HTML table will stop it from being displayed (although the precise interpretation of a missing tag depends on the browser).

There is an alternative that allows you to generate HTML that will automatically have the correct start and end tags. The **CGI** module, which is part of the standard Perl library, can generate HTML tags through a series of functions. For example:

```
h1('All About Me');
```

correctly produces

```
<H1>All About Me</H1>
```

You can even use it to introduce more complex elements—for example, a table row. The following line is taken from a script that displays a website directory using Perl to get and then format a list of files:

```
print Tr({-valign=>TOP},
        [th(['Mode','File/Directory',
            'User', 'Group', 'Mod Time', 'Size'])]);
```

Obviously this is only outputting the header row for the table, but you can see how easy it is to introduce the information. The first argument to the **Tr** function (which generates a matching **<tr></tr>** tag) is a hash reference that contains the table row properties. The second argument is a table header function, embedded in an array reference, whose first argument is an array reference—each element in this array will appear as a separate table header cell in the single row. Further elements within the embedded array reference in **Tr** would have become additional rows, and we could have embedded the entire sequence into a **table** function to have everything output as a table with all the correct start and end tags.

Uniform Resource Locators

Before we continue, we need to take a slight detour to ensure that you understand the basic principles of how the Internet, and more specifically, the World Wide Web, is used. Everybody who uses the Internet uses Uniform Resource Locators (URLs). A URL is an address for a resource on the Internet that consists of the protocol to be used, the address of the server, and the path to the file that you want to access. For example, the address

```
http://www.mcwords.com/index.shtml
```

indicates that you want to use the HTTP protocol, that you are connecting to the machine known as **www.mcwords.com**, and that you want to retrieve the file index.shtml.

URLs can also incorporate login names, passwords, and optional service port number information:

```
http://anonymous:password@ftp.mcwords.com:1025/cgi/sendme.pl?sendme=info.zip
```

The preceding example shows downloading information from the server **ftp.mcwords.com**, using service port **1025**, with a login of **anonymous** and a password of **password**.

Also shown in the preceding example is the feature that we are particularly interested in with respect to Perl. Although it's difficult to tell with any certainty from the URL here, it looks like you're accessing a Perl script called sendme.pl. It's actually up to the web server to identify a file's type. In this example, the **/cgi** path is the default name given to CGI scripts—the web server will treat files in this directory as being as being executable.

When the web server sees a URL requesting a path that refers to a script, rather than the server returning the contents of the Perl script, it will instead be executed. You've supplied it some information—in this case a list of field/value pairs. Each field and value is separated by the "=" character, and pairs are separated by ampersands. In this case, we have a field called **sendme** that contains the name of a file (info.zip)—although exactly what the script does is not clear.

This demonstrates, from the browser end, how an end-user executes a script on a server. The user accesses a URL. The file path that is supplied is parsed by the web server, which identifies the file that the user has requested as, in fact, a script, and the web server executes that script. What the script is, what it does, or indeed what language it is written in are completely hidden from the user (and, normally the web server). Incidentally, although by convention Perl scripts terminate in .pl, this does not guarantee that the script you are accessing is a Perl script.

Now let's take a wider look at the whole process, including how the script interacts with the web server software.

Web Operation Overview

At the start of this chapter, I stated that a web-based application using a Perl script is not really a client/server application. In fact, a web application (written in Perl or any other language) exhibits many traits of a client/server application, even though the connection is not permanent. The definition of a client/server application is one that makes use of the client to act as a user interface to a server, which hosts the information and runs the application. The client does not store any data, and the server does not provide any user interface.

In some systems, both ends can do some form of processing on the information. In the case of a web application, the browser supports a certain amount of processing. You can select checkboxes and pop-up lists. If you need more complex systems, you can use JavaScript or even Java to provide a more interactive client interface.

What the server provides is a communications channel for exchanging information between the stored information and the client. With a web server, the information includes the HTML files, graphics, animations, and other downloadable elements. It also includes any other data sources that can be accessed via an application, and this is where CGI scripts are used.

Here's the normal execution sequence of a user accessing a script on a web server:

1. The user's browser (the client) opens a connection to the server.

2. The user's browser requests a URL from the server.

3. The server parses the URL and determines whether a file is to be returned or whether it needs to run an external application. For this run-through we'll assume the latter.

4. The external application is called. This can be a binary executable, a batch file, a shell script, an **awk** script, or perhaps one written in Python. In our case, we're only interested in Perl scripts.

5. Any additional information supplied by the user's browser, such as that from a form, is supplied to the application, either by using an environment variable or by passing the data as a stream to the application's standard input.

6. Any output produced by the application is sent back directly to the user's browser.

This is a very simplified outline of how the process works, but it does show the basic process. The steps we are interested in are 4, 5, and 6.

In step 4, you need to think about the environment in which an application is executed. The environment defines the physical and logical confines of the Perl script you want to run. In addition to the standard environment variables, such as **PATH**, there is also some web-specific information. In step 5, you have to extract any information supplied by the browser, either from one of the environment variables, which requires the **GET** method, or from the standard input, using the **POST** method. These names, **GET** and **POST** are the commands sent by the browser—according to the configuration of the form—when it sends the form data to the server. In step 6, you have to know how to communicate information back to the user's browser.

We'll take a look at each of these issues separately in the next few sections of this chapter.

The Environment

The environment in which a script is executed does not normally affect the script's operation, except where otherwise noted in the general operation of Perl. For example, a Perl script executed within an environment that defines an alternative **PATH** will affect which programs the script has direct access to. The environment doesn't change how the script executes.

However, the environment does act as a useful conduit for exchanging information about the browser and web server with an executing script. What you really need to know is the environment variables that are available within the confines of your script. You can see a list of the most useful environment variables in Table 18-1.

The exact list of environment variables supported depends on your web server, and also on the instance in which the URL was requested. For pages that are displayed as the result of a referral, you will also get a list of "referrer" information—the site from which the reference to the requested URL was made. You can find out this information using a CGI script like the one that follows. Don't worry too much about the details of this script at this stage.

Environment Variable	Description
DOCUMENT_ROOT	The root document directory for this web server
GATEWAY_INTERFACE	The interface name and version number
HTTP_ACCEPT	The formats accepted by the browser. This information is optionally supplied by the browser when it first requests the page from the server. In our example, the default types accepted include all of the major graphics types (GIF, JPEG, X bitmap), as well as all other MIME types (*/*).
HTTP_ACCEPT_CHARSET	The character sets accepted by the browser
HTTP_ACCEPT_ENCODING	Any special encoding formats supported by the browser. In our example, Netscape supports Gzip-encoded documents; they will be decoded on the fly at the time of receipt.
HTTP_ACCEPT_LANGUAGE	The languages accepted by this browser. If supported by the server, then only documents of a specific language will be returned to the browser.
HTTP_CONNECTION	Any HTTP connection directives. A typical directive is Keep-Alive, which forces the server to keep a web-server process and the associated network socket dedicated to this browser until a defined period of inactivity.
HTTP_HOST	The server host (without domain)
HTTP_USER_AGENT	The name, version number, and platform of the remote browser. In our preceding example output, this was Mozilla (actually Microsoft Internet Explorer) v4.5b2, for Macintosh PPC. Don't be fooled into thinking that the name Mozilla applies only to Netscape Navigator; other browsers, including Microsoft Internet Explorer, also report themselves as being Mozilla browsers—this helps with compatibility identification, even though all browsers render HTML differently.

Table 18-1. *Web Server Environment Variables for CGI Scripts*

Environment Variable	Description
PATH	The path for the CGI script
CONTENT_LENGTH	The length of the query information. It's available only for **POST** requests, and it can help with the security of the scripts you produce.
QUERY_STRING	The query string, used with **GET** requests
REMOTE_ADDR	The IP address of the browser
REMOTE_HOST	The resolved name of the browser
REMOTE_PORT	The remote port of the browser machine.
REQUEST_METHOD	The request method; for example, **GET** or **POST**
REQUEST_URI	The requested URI (Uniform Resource Identifier)
SCRIPT_FILENAME	The full path to the CGI script
SCRIPT_NAME	The name of the CGI script
SERVER_ADMIN	The email address of the web-server administrator
SERVER_NAME	The fully qualified name of the server
SERVER_PORT	The server port number
SERVER_PROTOCOL	The protocol (usually HTTP) and version number
SERVER_SOFTWARE	The name and version number of the server software that is being used. This can be useful if you want to introduce a single script that makes use of specific features of multiple web servers.
TZ	The time zone of the web server

Table 18-1. *Web Server Environment Variables for CGI Scripts* (continued)

```perl
print "Content-type: text/html\n\n";

print "<font size=+1>Environment</font><p>\n";

foreach (sort keys %ENV)
{
    print "$_: $ENV{$_}<br>\n";
}
```

On my web server, which is Apache 1.3.14 running under Solaris 8, the following ends up being displayed within a browser window (Microsoft Internet Explorer for Mac 5.01):

```
DOCUMENT_ROOT: /export/http/webs/test
GATEWAY_INTERFACE: CGI/1.1
HTTP_ACCEPT: */*
HTTP_ACCEPT_LANGUAGE: en
HTTP_CONNECTION: Keep-Alive
HTTP_EXTENSION: Security/Remote-Passphrase
HTTP_HOST: test
HTTP_IF_MODIFIED_SINCE: Tue, 05 Dec 2000 13:48:09 GMT
HTTP_UA_CPU: PPC
HTTP_UA_OS: MacOS
HTTP_USER_AGENT: Mozilla/4.0 (compatible; MSIE 5.0; Mac_PowerPC)
PATH: /usr/sbin:/usr/bin
QUERY_STRING: data=sometestinfo
REMOTE_ADDR: 198.112.10.134
REMOTE_PORT: 52566
REQUEST_METHOD: GET
REQUEST_URI: /test.cgi?data=sometestinfo
SCRIPT_FILENAME: /export/http/webs/test/test.cgi
SCRIPT_NAME: /test.cgi
SERVER_ADDR: 198.112.10.1
SERVER_ADMIN: mc@test.com
SERVER_NAME: test.mchome.com
SERVER_PORT: 80
SERVER_PROTOCOL: HTTP/1.1
SERVER_SIGNATURE:
Apache/1.3.14 Server at test.mchome.com Port 80

SERVER_SOFTWARE: Apache/1.3.14 (Unix)
TZ: GB
```

You can glean lots of useful information from this that you can use in your script. For example, the **SCRIPT_NAME** environment variable contains the name of the CGI script that was accessed by the client. The most important fields as far as a CGI program are concerned, however, are the **REQUEST_METHOD**, which defines the method used to transfer the information (request) from the browser, through the web server, to the CGI application.

The **CONTENT_LENGTH** defines the number of bytes contained in the query when using the **POST** method. This is useful primarily for verifying that some data has been supplied (and therefore needs processing). The **CONTENT_LENGTH** environment variable is not provided by all web servers and shouldn't be your only way of verifying whether any query has been sent. However, if used properly, it can also aid in the security of your web scripts. See the "Security" section later in this chapter for more information. The **QUERY_STRING** is the environment variable used to store the data from the client's browser when using the **GET** method.

The Common Gateway Interface

The Common Gateway Interface, or CGI, is a set of standards that define how information is exchanged between the web server and a script. In fact, web applications are often called CGI scripts, but don't make the mistake of calling a CGI script simply "CGI." The term *CGI* refers to the standards and isn't the name of an application.

The part of the process you need to worry about at this stage is the transfer of information from the browser, through the web server, to the CGI script. The reason you need to accept information is to enable you to process information entered into an HTML form. For example, the form shown in Figure 18-1 comes from my own site and is used to accept book errors.

Each of the fields in the form can contain free-form data or, in the case of the Type and Book Title fields, the information in the pop-up menus. The information and definition of the form is done in HTML. Although in this case a static file supplies the definition, there is no reason why it couldn't be script driven.

When the user clicks the Send button, the information will be transferred to the web server and then on to the CGI script. The CGI script to be used is defined within the HTML definition for the form. The information is transferred using one of two main methods, **GET** and **POST**. The difference between the two methods is directly attributable to how the information is transferred. With the **GET** method, the information is placed into the **QUERY_STRING** environment variable, and with the **POST** method, the information is sent to the standard input of the application that has been called. There are other methods supported for transferring information, but these are the main two that are used.

There are advantages and disadvantages to both methods. The **GET** method supports two ways of transferring information from the client. With **GET**, you can supply information either through HTML forms or through the use of an extended URL. If you remember, back at the start of this chapter we looked at the following URL:

```
http://anonymous:password@ftp.mcwords.com:1025/cgi/sendme.pl?sendme=info.zip
```

The **sendme.pl** is the name of a script, and the question mark at the end of the script's name indicates the start of the information that you want to supply to the script. This has major benefits because you can generate new URLs and include the information as links in normal HTML pages, thus saving time. The limitation is that

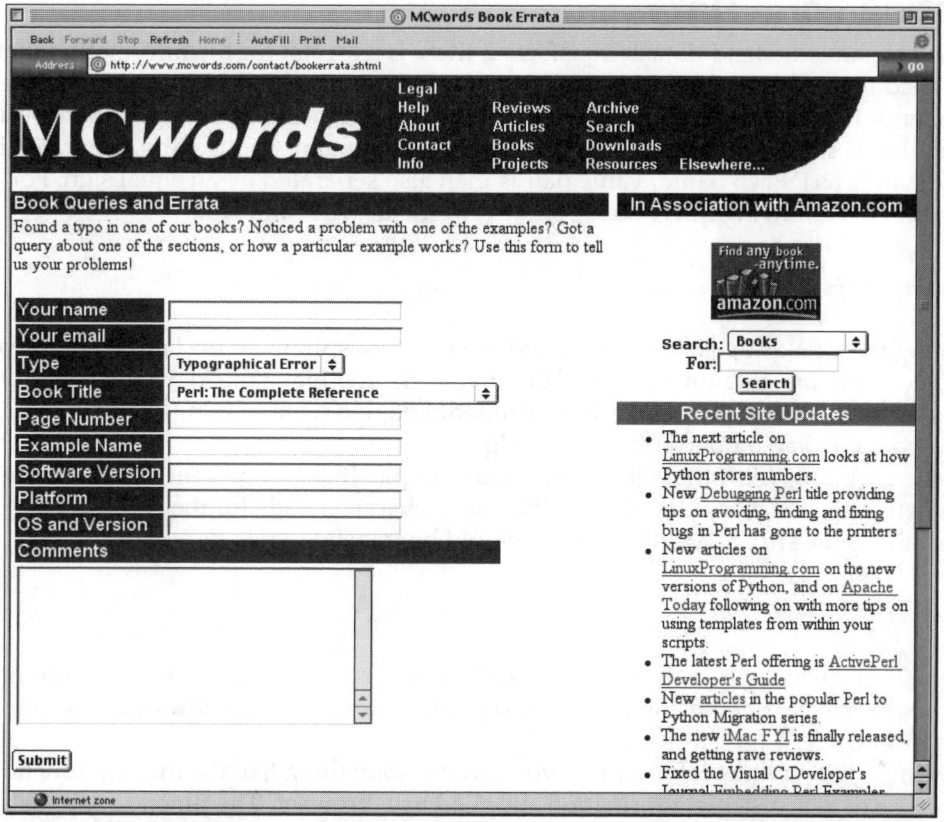

Figure 18-1. *The Book Bug Report form from* ***www.mcwords.com***

the **GET** method has a limited transfer size. Although there is officially no limit, most people try to keep **GET** method requests down to less than 1K (1,024 bytes). Also note that because the information is placed into an environment variable, your operating system might have limits on the size of either individual environment variables or the environment space as a whole.

The **POST** method has no such limitation. You can transfer as much information as you like within a **POST** request without fear of any truncation along the way. However, you cannot use a **POST** request to process an extended URL. For the **POST** method, the **CONTENT_LENGTH** environment variable contains the length of the query supplied, and it can be used to ensure that you read the right amount of information from the standard input.

Extracting Form Data

No matter how the field data is transferred, there is a format for the information that you need to be aware of before you can use the information. The HTML form defines a number of fields, and the name and contents of the field are contained within the query string that is supplied. The information is supplied as name/value pairs, separated by ampersands (**&**). Each name/value pair is then also separated by an equal sign. For example, the following query string shows two fields, **first** and **last**:

```
first=Martin&last=Brown
```

Splitting these fields up is easy within Perl. You can use **split** to do the hard work for you.

One final note, though—many of the characters you may take for granted are encoded so that the URL is not misinterpreted. Imagine what would happen if my name contained an ampersand or equal sign!

The encoding, like other elements, is very simple. It uses a percent sign, followed by a two-digit hex string that defines the ASCII character code for the character in question. So the string "Martin Brown" would be translated into,

```
Martin%20Brown
```

where 20 is the hexadecimal code for ASCII character 32, the space. You may also find that spaces are encoded using a single **+** sign (the example that follows accounts for both formats).

Armed with all this information, you can use something like the **init_cgi** function, shown next, to access the information supplied by a browser. The function supports both **GET** and **POST** requests:

```perl
sub init_cgi
{
    my $query = $ENV{QUERY_STRING};      # get the query string
    my $length = $ENV{CONTENT_LENGTH};   # get the content length
    my (@assign, %formlist);             # create some temporaries

    if ($query =~ /\w+/)                 # Check if GET query contains data
    {
        @assign = split('&',$query);     # Extract the field/value pairs
    }
    elsif (defined($length) and $length > 0 ) # GET is empty, POST instead
    {
        sysread(STDIN, $_, $length);            # Read in CONTENT_LENGTH bytes
        chomp;
        @assign = split('&');                   # Extract the field/value pairs
    }
```

```
    foreach (@assign)                      # Now split field/value pairs to hash
    {
        my ($name,$value) = split /=/;
        $value =~ tr/+/ /;
        $value =~ s/%([a-fA-F0-9][a-fA-F0-9])/pack("C", hex($1))/eg;
        if (defined($formlist{$name}))     # If the field exists, append data
        {
            $formlist{$name} .= ",$value";
        }
        else                               # Otherwise, create new hash key
        {
            $formlist{$name} = $value;
        }
    }
    return %formlist;                       # Return the hash to the caller
}
```

The steps are straightforward, and they follow the description. First of all, you access the query string—either by getting the value of the **QUERY_STRING** environment variable or by accepting input up to the length specified in **CONTENT_LENGTH**—from standard input using the **sysread** function. Note that you must use this method rather than the **<STDIN>** operator because you want to ensure that you read in the entire contents, irrespective of any line termination. HTML forms provide multiline text entry fields, and using a line input operator could lead to unexpected results. Also, it's possible to transfer binary information using a **POST** method, and any form of line processing might produce a garbled response. Finally, **sysread** acts as a security check. Many "denial of service" attacks (where too much information or too many requests are sent, therefore denying service to other users) prey on the fact that a script accepts an unlimited amount of information while also tricking the server into believing that the query length is small or even unspecified. If you arbitrarily imported all the information provided, you could easily lock up a small server.

Once you have obtained the query string, you split it by an ampersand into the **@assign** array and then process each field/value pair in turn. For convenience, you place the information into a hash. The keys of the hash become the field names, and the corresponding values become the values as supplied by the browser. The most important trick here is the line

```
$value =~ s/%([a-fA-F0-9][a-fA-F0-9])/pack("C", hex($1))/eg;
```

This uses the functional replacement to a standard regular expression to decode the **%xx** characters in the query into their correct values.

To encode the information back into the URL format within your script, the best solution is to use the **URI::Escape** module by Gisle Aas. This provides a function,

uri_escape, for converting a string into its URL-escaped equivalent. You can also use **uri_unescape** to convert it back. See Appendix D for more information.

Using the above function (init_cgi), you can write a simple Perl script that reports the information provided to it by either method (this uses the **init_cgi** script shown earlier, but it's not included here for brevity):

```
#!/usr/local/bin/perl -w

print "Content-type: text/html\n\n";

%form = init_cgi();
print("Form length is: ", scalar keys %form, "<br>\n");

for my $key (sort keys %form)
{
    print "Key $key = $form{$key}<br>\n";
}
```

If you place this on a server and supply it a URL such as this:

```
http://www.mcwords.com/cgi/test.cgi?first=Martin&last=Brown
```

the browser window reports this back:

```
Form length is: 2
Key first = Martin
Key last = Brown
```

Success!

Of course, most scripts do other things besides printing the information back. Either they format the data and send it on in an email, or search a database, or perform a myriad of other tasks. What has been demonstrated here is how to extract the information supplied via either method into a suitable hash structure that you can use within Perl. How you use the information depends on what you are trying to achieve.

The process detailed here has been duplicated many times in a number of different modules. The best solution, though, is to use the facilities provided by the standard **CGI** module. This comes with the standard Perl distribution and should be your first point of call for developing web applications. We'll be taking a closer look at the **CGI** module in the next chapter.

Sending Information Back to the Browser

Communicating information back to the user is so simple, you'll be looking for ways to make it more complicated. In essence, you print information to **STDOUT**, and this is then sent back verbatim to the browser.

The actual method is more complex. When a web server responds with a static file, it returns an HTTP header that tells the browser about the file it is about to receive. The header includes information such as the content length, encoding, and so on. It then sends the actual document back to the browser. The two elements—the header and the document—are separated by a single blank line. How the browser treats the document it receives is depends on the information supplied by the HTTP header and the extension of the file it receives. This allows you to send back a binary file (such as an image) directly from a script by telling the application what data format the file is encoded with.

When using a CGI application, the HTTP header is not automatically attached to the output generated, so you have to generate this information yourself. This is the reason for the

```
print "Content-type: text/html\n\n";
```

lines in the previous examples. This indicates to the browser that it is accepting a file using **text** encoding in **html** format. There are other fields you can return in the HTTP header, which we'll look at now.

HTTP Headers

The HTTP header information is returned as follows:

```
Field: data
```

The case of the **Field** name is important, but otherwise you can use as much white space as you like between the colon and the field data. A sample list of HTTP header fields is shown in Table 18-2.

The only required field is Content-type, which defines the format of the file you are returning. If you do not specify anything, the browser assumes you are sending back preformatted raw text, not HTML. The definition of the file format is by a MIME string. MIME is an acronym for Multipurpose Internet Mail Extensions, and it is a slash-separated string that defines the raw format and a subformat within it. For example, text/html says the information returned is plain text, using HTML as a file format. Mac users will be familiar with the concept of file owners and types, and this is the basic model employed by MIME.

Field	Meaning
Allow: list	A comma-delimited list of the HTTP request methods supported by the requested resource (script or program). Scripts generally support **GET** and **POST**; other methods include **HEAD**, **POST**, **DELETE**, **LINK**, and **UNLINK**.
Content-encoding: string	The encoding used in the message body. Currently the only supported formats are Gzip and compress. If you want to encode data this way, make sure you check the value of **HTTP_ACCEPT_ENCODING** from the environment variables.
Content-type: string	A MIME string defining the format of the file being returned.
Content-length: string	The length, in bytes, of the data being returned. The browser uses this value to report the estimated download time for a file.
Date: string	The date and time the message is sent. It should be in the format 01 Jan 1998 12:00:00 GMT. The time zone should be GMT for reference purposes; the browser can calculate the difference for its local time zone if it has to.
Expires: string	The date the information becomes invalid. This should be used by the browser to decide when a page needs to be refreshed.
Last-modified: string	The date of last modification of the resource
Location: string	The URL that should be returned instead of the URL requested
MIME-version: string	The version of the MIME protocol supported
Server: string/string	The web server application and version number
Title: string	The title of the resource
URI: string	The URI that should be returned instead of the requested one

Table 18-2. *HTTP Header Fields*

Other examples include application/pdf, which states that the file type is application (and therefore binary) and that the file's format is pdf, the Adobe Acrobat file format. Others you might be familiar with are image/gif, which states that the file is a GIF file, and application/zip, which is a compressed file using the Zip algorithm.

This MIME information is used by the browser to decide how to process the file. Most browsers will have a mapping that says they deal with files of type image/gif so that you can place graphical files within a page. They may also have an entry for application/pdf, which either calls an external application to open the received file or passes the file to a plug-in that optionally displays the file to the user. For example, here's an extract from the file supplied by default with the Apache web server:

```
application/mac-binhex40        hqx
application/mac-compactpro      cpt
application/macwriteii
application/msword              doc
application/news-message-id
application/news-transmission
application/octet-stream        bin dms lha lzh exe class
application/oda                 oda
application/pdf                 pdf
application/postscript          ai eps ps
application/powerpoint          ppt
application/remote-printing
application/rtf                 rtf
application/slate
application/wita
application/wordperfect5.1
application/x-bcpio             bcpio
application/x-cdlink            vcd
application/x-compress
application/x-cpio              cpio
application/x-csh               csh
application/x-director          dcr dir dxr
```

It's important to realize the significance of this one, seemingly innocent, field. Without it, your browser would not know how to process the information it receives. Normally the web server sends the MIME type back to the browser, and it uses a lookup table that maps MIME strings to file extensions. Thus, when a browser requests myphoto.gif, the server sends back a Content-type field value of image/gif. Since a script is executed by the server rather than sent back verbatim to the browser, it must supply this information itself.

Other fields in Table 18-2 are optional but also have useful applications. The Location field can be used to automatically redirect a user to an alternative page without using the normal **RELOAD** directive in an HTML file. The existence of the Location field automatically instructs the browser to load the URL contained in the field's value. Here's another script that uses the earlier **init_cgi** function and the Location HTTP field to point a user in a different direction:

```perl
%form = init_cgi();

respond("Error: No URL specified")
    unless(defined($form{url}));

open(LOG,">>/usr/local/http/logs/jump.log")
    or respond("Error: A config error has occurred");

print LOG (scalar(localtime(time)),
          " $ENV{REMOTE_ADDR} $form{url}\n");
close(LOG)
    or respond("Error: A config error has occurred");

print "Location: $form{url}\n\n";

sub respond
{
    my $message = shift;
    print "Content-type: text/html\n\n";
    show_debug();
    print <<EOF;
<head>
<title>$message</title>
</head>
<body>
$message
</body>
EOF
    exit;
}
```

This is actually a version of a script used on a number of sites I have developed that allows you to keep a log of when a user clicks onto a foreign page. For example, you might have links on a page to another site, and you want to be able to record how many people visit this other site from your page. Instead of using a normal link within your HTML document, you could use the CGI script:

```
<a href="/cgi/redirect.pl?url=http://www.mcwords.com">MCwords</a>
```

Every time users click on this link, they will still visit the new site, but you'll have a record of their leap off of your site.

Document Body

You already know that the document body should be in HTML. To send output, you just print to **STDOUT**, as you would with any other application. In an ideal world, you should consider using something like the **CGI** module to help you build the pages correctly. It will certainly remove a lot of clutter from your script, while also providing a higher level of reliability for the HTML you produce. Unfortunately, it doesn't solve any of the problems associated with a poor HTML implementation within a browser.

However, because you just print the information to standard output, you need to take care with errors and other information that might otherwise be sent to **STDERR**. You can't use **warn** or **die**, because any message produced will not be displayed to the user. While this might be what you want as a web developer (the information is usually recorded in the error log), it is not very user friendly.

The solution is to use something like the function shown in the previous redirection example to report an error back to the user. Again, this is an important thing to grasp. There is nothing worse from a user's point of view than this displayed in the browser:

```
Internal Server Error

The server encountered an internal error or misconfiguration and was
unable to complete your request. Please contact the server administrator,
webmaster@mchome.com and inform them of the time the error occurred,
and anything you might have done that may have caused the error.
```

Smarter Web Programming

Up until now, we have been specifically concentrating on the mechanics behind Perl CGI scripts. Although we've seen solutions for certain aspects of the process, there are easier ways of doing things. Since you already know how to obtain information supplied on a web form, we will instead concentrate on the semantics and process for the script contents. In particular, we'll examine the **CGI** module, web cookies, the debug process, and how to interface to other web-related languages.

The CGI Module

The **CGI** module started out as a separate module available from CPAN. It's now included as part of the standard distribution and provides a much easier interface to web programming with Perl. As well as providing a mechanism for extracting elements supplied on a form, it also provides an object-oriented interface to building web pages and, more usefully, web forms. You can use this interface either in its object-oriented format or with a simple functional interface.

Along with the standard CGI interface and the functions and object features supporting the production of "good" HTML, the module also supports some of the more advanced features of CGI scripting. These include the support for uploading files via HTTP and access to cookies—something we'll be taking a look at later in this chapter. For the designers among you, the **CGI** module also supports cascading style sheets and frames. Finally, it supports server push—a technology that allows a server to send new data to a client at periodic intervals. This is useful for pages, and especially images, that need to be updated. This has largely been superseded by the client-side **RELOAD** directive, but it still has its uses.

For example, you can build a single CGI script for converting Roman numerals into integer decimal numbers using the following script. It not only builds and produces the HTML form, but also provides a method for processing the information supplied when the user fills in and submits the form.

```perl
#!/usr/local/bin/perl -w

use CGI qw/:standard/;

print header,
      start_html('Roman Numerals Conversion'),
      h1('Roman Numeral Converter'),
      start_form,
      "What's the Roman Numeral number?",
      textfield('roman'),p,
      submit,
      end_form,p,hr,p;

if (param())
{
    print(h3('The value is ',
          parse_roman(uc(param('roman')))),p,hr);
}

sub parse_roman
```

```
{
    $_ = shift;
    my %roman = ('I' => 1,
                 'V' => 5,
                 'X' => 10,
                 'L' => 50,
                 'C' => 100,
                 'D' => 500,
                 'M' => 1000,
                 );
    my @roman = qw/M D C L X V I/;
    my @special = qw/CM CD XC XL IX IV/;
    my $result = 0;

    return 'Invalid numerals' unless(m/[IVXLXDM]+/);

    foreach $special (@special)
    {
        if (s/$special//)
        {
            $result += $roman{substr($special,1,1)}
                        - $roman{substr($special,0,1)};
        }
    }
    foreach $roman (@roman)
    {
        $result += $roman{$roman} while s/$roman//;
    }
    return $result;
}
```

The first part of the script prints a form using the functional interface to the **CGI** module. It provides a simple text entry box, which you then supply to the **parse_roman** function to produce an integer value. If the user has provided some information, you use the **param** function to access that information. To access the data within the **username** field, for example, you would use

```
$name = param('username');
```

Note that it doesn't do any validation on that information for you; it only returns the raw data contained in the field. You will need to check whether the information in the field matches what you were expecting. For example, if you want to check for a valid email address, then you ought to at least check that the string contains an @ character:

```perl
if ($name =~ /.*\@.*/)
{
    # Do something...
}
else
{
    raise_error("Didn't get a valid email address");
}
```

You can see what a sample screen looks like in Figure 18-2.

Because you are using the functional interface, you have to specify the routines or sets of routines that you want to import. The main set is **:standard**, which is what is used in this script. See Appendix B for a list of other supported import sets.

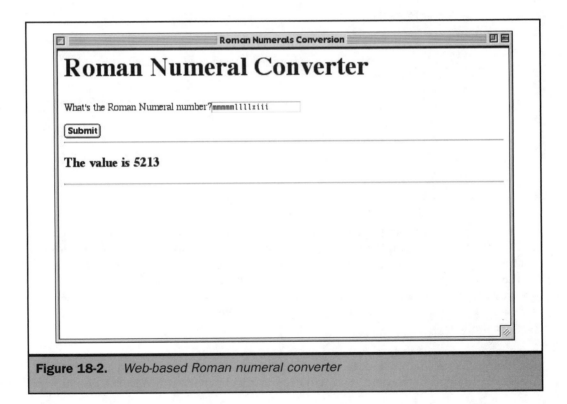

Figure 18-2. *Web-based Roman numeral converter*

Let's look a bit more closely at that page builder:

```
print header,
      start_html('Roman Numerals Conversion'),
      h1('Roman Numeral Converter'),
      start_form,
      "What's the Roman Numeral number?",
      textfield('roman'),p,
      submit,
      end_form,p,hr,p;
```

The **print** function is used, since that's how you report information back to the user. The **header** function produces the HTTP header (see Chapter 14). You can supply additional arguments to this function to configure other elements of the header, just as if you were doing it normally. You can also supply a single argument that defines the MIME string for the information you are sending back; for example:

```
print header('text/html');
```

If you don't specify a value, the text/html value is used by default. The remainder of the lines use functions to introduce HTML tagged text. You start with **start_html**, which starts an HTML document. In this case, it takes a single argument—the page title. This returns the following string:

```
<HTML><HEAD><TITLE>Roman Numerals Conversion</TITLE>
</HEAD><BODY>
```

This introduces the page title and sets the header and body style. The **h1** function formats the supplied text in the header level-one style.

The **start_form** function initiates an HTML form. By default, it assumes you are using the same script—this is an HTML/browser feature rather than a Perl CGI feature, and the **textfield** function inserts a simple text field. The argument supplied defines the name of the field as it will be sent to the script when the Submit button is clicked. To specify additional fields to the HTML field definition, you pass the function a hash, where each key of the hash should be a hyphen-prefixed field name; so you could rewrite the previous **start_form** code as

```
textfield(-name => 'roman')
```

Other fields might include **-size** for the size of the text field on screen and **-maxlength** for the maximum number of characters accepted in a field.

Other possible HTML field types are **textarea** for a large multiline text box, or **popup_menu** for a menu field that pops up and provides a list of values when clicked. You can also use **scrolling_list** for a list of values in a scrolling box, and checkboxes and radio buttons with the **checkbox_group** and **radio_group** functions. Refer to Appendix C for details.

Returning to the example script, the **submit** function provides a simple Submit button for sending the request to the server, and finally the **end_form** function indicates the end of the form within the HTML text. The remaining functions, **p** and **hr**, insert a paragraph break and horizontal rule, respectively.

This information is printed out for every invocation of the script. The **param** function is used to check whether any fields were supplied to the script, either by a **GET** or **POST** method. It returns an array of valid field names supplied. For example:

```
@fields = param();
```

Since any list in a scalar context returns the number of elements in the list, this is a safe way of detecting whether any information was provided. The same function is then used to extract the values from the fields specified. In the example, there is only one field, roman, which contains the Roman numeral string entered by the user.

The **parse_roman** function then does all the work of parsing the string and translating the Roman numerals into integer values. I'll leave it up to the reader to determine how this function works.

This concludes our brief look into the use of the **CGI** module for speeding up and improving the overall processing of producing and parsing the information supplied on a form. Admittedly, it makes the process significantly easier. Just look at the previous examples to see the complications involved in writing a non-**CGI**-based script. Although you can argue that it works, it's not exactly neat. But to be fair, the bulk of the complexity centers around the incorporation of the JavaScript application within the HTML document that is sent back to the user's browser.

Cookies

A cookie is a small, discrete piece of information used to store information within a web browser. The cookie itself is stored on the client, rather than the server, end, and can therefore be used to store state information between individual accesses by the browser, either in the same session or across a number of sessions. In its simplest form, a cookie might just store your name; in a more complex system, it provides login and password information for a website. This can be used by web designers to provide customized pages to individual users.

In other systems, cookies are used to store the information about the products you have chosen in web-based stores. The cookie then acts as your "shopping basket," storing information about your products and other selections.

In either case, the creation of a cookie and how you access the information stored in a cookie are server-based requests, since it's the server that uses the information to provide the customized web page, or that updates the selected products stored in your web basket. There is a limit to the size of cookies, and it varies from browser to browser. In general, a cookie shouldn't need to be more than 1,024 bytes, but some browsers will support sizes as large as 16,384 bytes, and sometimes even more.

A cookie is formatted much like a CGI form-field data stream. The cookie is composed of a series of field/value pairs separated by ampersands, with each field/value additionally separated by an equal sign. The contents of the cookie is exchanged between the server and client during normal interaction. The server sends updates back to the cookie as part of the HTTP headers, and the browser sends the current cookie contents as part of its request to the server.

Besides the field/value pairs, a cookie has a number of additional attributes. These are an expiration time, a domain, a path, and an optional secure flag.

- The expiration time is used by the browser to determine when the cookie should be deleted from its own internal list. As long as the expiration time has not been reached, the cookie will be sent back to the correct server each time you access a page from that server.

- The definition of a valid server is stored within the domain attribute. This is a partial or complete domain name for the server that should be sent to the cookie. For example, if the value of the domain attribute is ".foo.bar", then any server within the foo.bar domain will be sent the cookie data for each access.

- The path is a similar partial match against a path within the web server. For example, a path of /cgi-bin means that the cookie data will only be sent with any requests starting with that path. Normally, you would specify "/" to have the cookie sent to all CGI scripts, but you might want to restrict the cookie data so it is only sent to scripts starting with /cgi-public, but not to /cgi-private.

- The secure attribute restricts the browser from sending the cookie to unsecure links. If set, cookie data will only be transferred over secure connections, such as those provided by SSL.

The best interface is to use the **CGI** module, which provides a simple functional interface to updating and accessing cookie information. For example, here's a function that builds a cookie based on a username and password combination:

```
sub set_cookie
{
    my ($query,$login,$password) = @_;

    print STDERR "Setting a cookie\n";
    my %cookie = (
```

```
                        -name => 'bookwatch',
                        -value => $login . '::' . $password,
                        -path => '/',
                        -domain => $host,
                        -expires => '+1y',
                        );

        return join("\n",
                    "Date: " . CGI::expires(0, 'http'),
                    "Set-Cookie: " . $query->cookie(%cookie));
    }
```

To actually send the cookie back to the browser, you need to print it out as part of the
HTTP header:

```
print set_cookie($query,param('email'),param('password')),"\n";
```

Alternatively, you can do it as part of the **header** function from the **CGI** module:

```
print header(-cookie => $cookie);
```

We can fetch a cookie back from the browser by using the **fetch** function:

```
my %cookies = fetch CGI::Cookie;
```

This actually returns all of the cookies set for this host or domain and path, so to pick
out an individual cookie, you need to access it by name, as I do here by passing the
cookie information to my own **validate_cookie** function, which takes the information
and checks it against the site's login database:

```
my ($ret,$userid,$password) = validate_cookie($cookies{bookwatch});
```

The value of the specified cookie is a cookie object, so you need to use methods to
extract the information—here's the **validate_cookie** used above:

```
sub validate_cookie
{
    my ($cookie) = @_;

    if ($cookie)
```

```
    {
        my ($login,$password) = split /::/,$cookie->value();
        return (1,$login,$password);
    }
    return 0;
}
```

Parsing HTML

There are times when what you want to do is not generate new HTML, but modify some existing HTML. This is often a requirement both for managing the sites and HTML that you produce, and also sometimes to parse the contents of an HTML page before it's sent back to the user. For example, I have scripts that download the cartoons and comics I like to read in the morning and others that access the TV listing pages so that I always know what's on TV for the next week—useful when setting the video recorder!

Processing HTML from another site to extract information from it is generally done by regular expressions and just requires you to key on the elements you want, and as such it's a fairly monotonous task. (See *Perl Annotated Archives*, the scripts for which are available on my website, for some examples. More information on the book is available in Appendix C.)

Modifying existing HTML is more difficult. Although we could use regular expressions, there are complex issues that need to be addressed. For example, how do you cope with the fact that tags can cross multiple lines, or that some tags may not have been closed properly?

The simple answer is that you need to parse the HTML. In short, you need to be able to understand the HTML as if it were a language, just as if you were writing a web browser. There are some third-party modules, available from CPAN, that handle this. The **HTML::Element** and **HTML::TreeBuilder** modules allow you to do this by parsing the HTML and allowing you to work through the HTML by element, or you can search for specific elements and make modifications.

For example, the following code is a script that allows you to modify an HTML tag's properties with a source HTML file:

```
use HTML::Element 1.53;
use HTML::TreeBuilder 2.96;

my $root = HTML::TreeBuilder->new;

my ($source,$destination,$tag,@attr) = @ARGV;
```

```
$root->parse_file($source) or die "Couldn't parse source: $source";
open(OUTPUT,">$destination")
    or  die "Couldn't output destination: $destination";

foreach $elem ($root->find_by_tag_name($tag))
{
    print "Found: ",$elem->as_HTML();

    my ($attr,$value);
    my @my_attr = @attr;
    while (@my_attr)
    {
        $attr = shift @my_attr;
        $value = shift @my_attr;

        $elem->attr($attr,$value);
    }
    print "Found: ",$elem->as_HTML();
}

print OUTPUT $root->as_HTML(),"\n";
```

For example, using the preceding script, we can add alignment and background colors to table cells using:

```
$ cvhtml.pl source.html dest.html td align right bgcolor \#000000
```

The modules do all the work for this, including updating the tags if they already contain alignment and color specifications.

Parsing XML

XML (eXtensible Markup Language) is a side-set of SGML, the same father of the HTML standard. Unlike HTML, however, which has a restricted set of tags and properties that control a document's format and how it should be displayed, XML is extensible. With XML, you can create a completely new set of tags and then use those tags to model information.

XML is not really a web technology, although a lot of its development and design has actually relied on and learnt from the mistakes and restrictive nature of HTML. Strictly, XML is seen as a way of modeling complex, text-based data in a format that frees the information from the constraints of a normal type-driven (integers, floats, strings, dates, etc.) database. For example, here's an XML document that contains two "records":

```
<contact>
    <name>Martin C Brown</name>
    <email>mc@mcwords.com</email>
    <company>MCwords</company>
    <title>MD</title>
</contact>
<contact>
    <name>Joe Foobar</name>
    <email>joe@foobar.com</email>
</contact>
```

It's actually become clear over the past year that XML can also be used as a practical way of storing any type of information and can even be used to exchange information. If you take the humble contacts database, for example, exchanging data between your desktop contacts and those in Palm or other handheld organizers requires a certain amount of mental gymnastics on the part of the integration tool. What do you do about the fields not supported by one database, and what happens if you have more than one email address?

XML should hopefully get around this by supporting a set of extensible fields for a given contact. Each database can then make up its own mind, at the time of import, what to use and what to ignore, and should even be able to modify itself to handle the data stored in the XML document. In all likelihood, we'll probably see a move to a suite of applications that reads an XML contact document directly—when you want to exchange the information between programs, you'll exchange the XML document directly, and then all the application has to do is format it nicely!

However, we can also use the same basic process to allow us to model information in XML and then convert that XML format into the HTML required for display on the web. Again, there is a suite of XML-related modules in Perl that will allow us to process XML information. There's even a parser that allows us to approach an XML document by its individual tags.

The following script will take an XML contacts database and format it for display through a web browser by first identifying each XML tag, and then applying an HTML format to the embedded information.

```perl
#!/usr/local/bin/perl -w
use strict;
use XML::Parser;

print "Content-type: text/html\n\n";
```

```perl
print <<EOF;
<HTML>
<HEAD>
<Title>Contacts</title>
<head>
<body bgcolor="#ffffff" fgcolor="black">
<table>
EOF

my $parse = new XML::Parser();

$parse->setHandlers(Start => \&handler_start,
                    End => \&handler_end,
                    Char => \&handler_char,);

my %elements = ('contact' => [{ tag => 'tr'}],
                'email'   => [{ tag => 'td', attr => 'align=left'},
                              { tag => 'b'}
                              ],
                'name'    => [{ tag => 'td', attr => 'align=right'},
                              ],
                );

$parse->parsefile('contacts.xml');

print <<EOF;
</table>
</body>
</html>
EOF

sub handler_start
{
    my ($parser, $element) = @_;

    if (defined($elements{$element}))
    {
        foreach my $tag (@{$elements{$element}})
        {
            print '<',$tag->{'tag'}, ($tag->{'attr'} ? ' ' . $tag->{'attr'} : ''), '>';
        }
    }
}

sub handler_end
{
    my ($parser, $element) = @_;
```

```
    if (defined($elements{$element}))
    {
        foreach my $tag (reverse @{$elements{$element}})
        {
            print '</',$tag->{'tag'},'>';
        }
    }
}

sub handler_char
{
    my ($parser,$data) = @_;

    print $data;
}
```

The core of the process is the **%elements** hash, which maps the XML document tags into the corresponding HTML tags and attributes to make it suitable for display.

This is just a simple example of what you can do—the **XML::Parser** module provides the basis for extracting XML data; all you need to do is work out what you want to do with those tags and the information they delimit.

Debugging and Testing CGI Applications

Although it sounds like an impossible task, sometimes you need to test a script without requiring or using a browser and web server. Certainly, if you switch warnings on and use the **strict** pragma, your script may well **die** before reporting any information to the browser if Perl finds any problems. This can be a problem if you don't have access to the error logs on the web server, which is where the information will be recorded.

You may even find yourself in a situation where you do not have privileges or even the software to support a web service on which to do your testing. Any or all of these situations require another method for supplying a query to a CGI script, and alternative ways of extracting and monitoring error messages from your scripts.

The simplest method is to supply the information that would ordinarily be supplied to the script via a browser using a more direct method. Because you know the information can be supplied to the script via an environment variable, all you have to do is create the environment variable with a properly formatted string in it. For example, for the preceding phone number script, you might use the following lines for a Bourne shell:

```
QUERY_STRING='first=Martin&last=Brown'
export QUERY_STRING
```

This is easy if the query data is simple, but what if the information needs to be escaped because of special characters? In this instance, the easiest thing is to grab a **GET**-based URL from the browser, or get the script to print a copy of the escaped query string, and then assign that to the environment variable. Still not an ideal solution.

As another alternative, if you use the **init_cgi** from the previous chapter, or the **CGI** module, you can supply the field name/value pairs as a string to the standard input. Both will wait for input from the keyboard before continuing if no environment query string has been set. It still doesn't get around the problem of escaping characters and sequences, and it can be quite tiresome for scripts that expect a large amount of input.

All of these methods assume that you cannot (or do not want) to make modifications to the script. If you are willing to make modifications to the script, then it's easier, and sometimes clearer, just to assign sample values to the form variables directly; for example, using the **init_cgi** function:

```
$SCGI::formlist{name} = 'MC';
```

or, if you are using the **CGI** module, then you need to use the **param** function to set the values. You can either use a simple functional call with arguments,

```
param('name','MC');
```

or you can use the hash format:

```
param(-name => 'name', -value => 'MC');
```

Just remember to unset these hard-coded values before you use the script; otherwise you may have trouble using the script effectively!

For monitoring errors, there are a number of methods available. The most obvious is to use **print** statements to output debugging information (remember that you can't use **warn**) as part of the HTML page. If you decide to do it this way, remember to output the errors *after* the HTTP header; otherwise you'll get garbled information. In practice, your scripts should be outputting the HTTP header as early as possible anyway.

Another alternative is to use **warn**, and in fact **die**, as usual, but redirect **STDERR** to a log file. If you are running the script from the command line under Unix using one of the preceding techniques, you can do this just by using the normal redirection operators within the shell; for example:

```
$ roman.cgi 2>roman.err
```

Alternatively, you can do this within the script by restating the association of **STDERR** with a call to the **open** function:

```
open(STDERR, ">>error.log") or die "Couldn't append to log file";
```

Note that you don't have to do any tricks here with reassigning the old **STDERR** to point elsewhere; you just want **STDERR** to point to a static file.

One final piece of advice: if you decide to use this method in a production system, remember to print out additional information with the report so that you can start to isolate the problem. In particular, consider stacking up the errors in an array by just using a simple **push** call, and then call a function right at the end of the script to dump out the date, time, and error log, along with the values of the environment variables. I've used a function similar to the one that follows to dump out the information at the end of the CGI script. The **@errorlist** array is used within the bulk of the CGI script to store the error lines:

```perl
sub error_report
{
    open (ERRORLOG, ">>error.log") or die "Fatal: Can't open log $!";
    $old = select ERROR;
    if (@errorlist)
    {
        print scalar localtime,"\n\n";
        print "Environment:\n";
        foreach (sort %ENV)
        {
            print "$_ = $ENV{$_}\n";
        }
        print "\nErrors:\n";
        print join "\n",@errorlist;
    }
    select $old;
}
```

That should cover most of the bases for any errors that might occur. Remember to try and be as quick as possible though—the script is providing a user interface, and the longer users have to wait for any output, the less likely they are to appreciate the work the script is doing. I've seen some, for example, that post information to other scripts and websites, and even some that attempt to send email with the errors in them. These can cause both delays and problems of their own. You need something as plain and simple as the **print** statements and an external file to ensure reliability; otherwise you end up trying to account for and report errors in more and more layers of interfaces.

Remember, as well, that any additional modules you need to load when the script initializes will add seconds to the time to start up the script: anything that can be avoided should be avoided. Alternatively, think about using the **mod_perl** Apache module. This provides an interface between Apache and Perl CGI scripts. One of its major benefits is that it caches CGI scripts and executes them within an embedded Perl interpreter that is part of the Apache web server. Additional invocations of the script do not require reloading. They are already loaded, and the Perl interpreter does not need to be invoked for each CGI script. This helps both performance and memory management.

Security

The number of attacks on Internet sites is increasing. Whether this is due to the meteoric rise of the number of computer crackers, or whether it's just because of the number of companies and hosts who do not take it seriously is unclear. The fact is, it's incredibly easy to ensure that your scripts are secure if you follow some simple guidelines. However, before we look at solutions, let's look at the types of scripts that are vulnerable to attack:

- Any script that passes form input to a mail address or mail message
- Any script that passes information that will be used within a subshell
- Any script that blindly accepts unlimited amounts of information during the form processing

The first two danger zones should be relatively obvious: anything that is potentially executed on the command line is open to abuse if the attacker supplies the right information. For example, imagine an email address passed directly to **sendmail** that looks like this:

```
mc@foo.bar;(mail mc@foo.bar </etc/passwd)
```

If this were executed on the command line as part of a call to **sendmail** line, the command after the semicolon would mail the password file to the same user—a severe security hazard if not checked. You can normally get around this problem by using taint checking to highlight the values that are considered unsafe. Since input to a script is either from standard input or an environment variable, the data will automatically be tainted. See Chapter 11 for more details on enabling and using tainted data.

There is a simple rule to follow when using CGI scripts: don't trust the size, content, or organization of the data supplied.

Here is a checklist of some of the things you should be looking out for when writing secure CGI scripts:

- Double-check the field names, values, and associations before you use them. For example, make sure an email address looks like an email address, and that it's part of the correct field you are expecting from the form.

- Don't automatically process the field values without checking them. As a rule, come up with a list of ASCII characters that you are willing to accept, and filter out everything else with a simple regular expression.

- It's easier to check for valid information than it is to try to filter out bad data. Use regular expressions to match against what you *want*, rather than using it to match against what you *don't want*.

- Check the input size of the variables or, better still, of the form data. You can use the **$ENV{CONTENT_LENGTH}** field, which is calculated by the web server to check the length of the data being accepted on **POST** methods, and some web servers supply this information on **GET** requests too.

- Don't assume that field data exists or is valid before use; a blank field can cause as many problems as a field filled with bad data.

- Don't ever return the contents of a file unless you can be sure of what its contents are. Arbitrarily returning a password file when you expected the user to request an HTML file is open to severe abuse.

- Don't accept that the path information sent to your script is automatically valid. Choose an alternative **$ENV{PATH}** value that you can trust, hardwiring it into the initialization of the script. While you're at it, use **delete** to remove any environment variables you know you won't use.

- If you are going to accept paths or file names, make sure they are relative, not absolute, and that they don't contain **..**, which leads to the parent directory. An attacker could easily specify a file of ../../../../../../../../../etc/passwd, which would reference the password file from even a deep directory.

- Always validate information used with **open**, **system**, **fork**, or **exec**. If nothing else, ensure any variables passed to these functions don't contain the characters **;**, **|**, **(**, or **)**. Better still, think about using the **fork** and piped **open** tricks you saw in Chapter 10 to provide a safe interface between an external application and your script.

- Ensure your web server is not running as **root**, which opens up your machine to all sorts of attacks. Run your web server as **nobody**, or create a new user specifically for the web server, ensuring that scripts are readable and executable only by the web server owner, and not writable by anybody.

- Use Perl in place of **grep** where possible. This will negate the need to make a system call to search file contents. The same is true of many other commands and functions, such as **pwd** and even **hostname**. There are tricks for gaining information about the machine you are on without resorting to calling external commands. For a start, refer back to Table 18-1. Your web server provides a bunch of script-relevant information automatically for you. Use it.

■ Don't assume that hidden fields are really hidden—users will still see them if they view the file source, and don't rely on your own encryption algorithms to encrypt the information supplied in these hidden fields. Use an existing system that has been checked and is bug free, such as the **DES** module available from your local CPAN archive.

■ Use taint checking, or in really secure situations, use the **Safe** or **Opcode** module. See Chapter 11 for more details.

If you follow these guidelines, you will at least reduce your risk from attacks, but there is no way to completely guarantee your safety. A determined attacker will use a number of different tools and tricks to achieve his goal.

Again, at the risk of repeating myself, don't trust the size, content, or organization of the data supplied.

Chapter 19

Controlling Execution
with Pragmas

611

All languages and their compilers and interpreters have rules about how the language operates and its semantics, and a similar set of rules that govern how the compiler looks for libraries and how it treats different sequences. In Perl these operations are controlled by a series of pragmas—really just a set of Perl modules that change the way the interpreter parses your script.

Most languages have some form of checking sequence before the code is actually compiled or executed. In the case of a language like C or C++, the checking happens before the source is compiled into its binary format, but no checks are done during execution. With Perl, things are slightly more complicated.

Perl is not a compiled language in the true sense like C/C++. There is a compilation stage, and before this there is also a parsing stage where the code is checked. All of this happens in the milliseconds before the code is actually executed. Perl also supports run-time errors. These are errors or potential problems that Perl identifies while the code is executing; they include simple warnings like undefined values, and more serious problems like attempts to divide by zero.

The level of information provided by these two stages (compile-time and run-time) can be controlled using the Perl warnings feature. Normally, Perl only reports serious errors or severe warnings—those events that Perl feels would cause the script to fail or that fail to pass the standard language semantics. You can also enable a number of nonfatal warnings that may highlight potential problems in your script, including potential naming and typographical errors.

You can also use the **strict** pragma. Unlike the **warnings** pragma (or in older versions the **-w** command line option), the **strict** pragma directly deals with how Perl interprets certain elements of the source code. In particular, it directly addresses the problems relating to Perl's Do What I Mean (DWIM) philosophy.

As a general rule, to prevent many of the problems that users experience with Perl, you should have both warnings and the **strict** pragma enabled at all times. This will help to ensure that your scripts are written to as tight a definition of the Perl language as possible, and as such we'll give these two systems extended attention in this chapter.

The last part of the chapter deals with the other Perl pragmas. These change the way in which Perl operates, such as by adding additional library directories to the search path, signal trapping, and Unicode support.

Warnings

Warnings are one of the most basic ways in which you can get Perl to check the quality of the code that you have produced. As the name suggests, they just raise a simple warning about a particular construct that Perl thinks is either potentially dangerous or ambiguous enough that Perl may have made the wrong decision about what it thought you were trying to do.

There are actually two types of warning, mandatory warnings and optional warnings:

- *Mandatory warnings* highlight problems in the lexical analysis stage.

- *Optional warnings* highlight occasions where Perl has spotted a possible anomaly.

As a rough guide, the Perl warnings system will raise a warning under the following conditions:

- Filehandles opened as read-only that you attempt to write to
- Filehandles that haven't been opened yet
- Filehandles that you try to use after they've been closed
- References to undefined filehandles
- Redefined subroutines
- Scalar variables whose values have been accessed before their values have been populated
- Subroutines that nest with recursion to more than 100 levels
- Invalid use of variables—for instance, scalars as arrays or hashes
- Strings used as numerical values when they don't truly resolve to a number
- Variables mentioned only once
- Deprecated functions, operators, and variables

These errors in your code are not serious enough to halt execution completely, but you can make Perl worried enough about them that it will raise a warning during compilation. For example, the code

```
$string = "Hello";
```

will pass the compiler checks if warnings are switched off, but if you turn warnings on, you get an error about a term that has only been used once:

```
Name "main::string" used only once: possible typo at -e line 1.
```

The traditional way of enabling warnings was to use the **-w** argument on the command line:

```
perl -w myscript.pl
```

You can also supply the option within the "shebang" line:

```
#/usr/local/bin/perl -w
```

But be careful about using command line options on operating systems that restrict the length of the shebang line you can use or that restrict the number of arguments that can be supplied.

You can also enable warnings using the **$^W** special variable. Older versions of Perl include the **warnings** pragma, which enables warnings within the script without needing the command line option. The pragma has been updated in Perl 5.6 to be more flexible—it even allows you to determine which type of warnings are displayed.

The $^W Variable

The **$^W** variable allows you to change—or discover—the current warnings setting within the script. If set to zero, the variable disables warnings; if set to one, they are enabled. In general, though, the use of the variable is not recommended—although it could be used to enable warnings on a lexical basis, it is open to far too many potential problems. It's possible, for example, to accidentally reset the warnings setting without realizing what you're doing. It is also difficult to differentiate between compile-time and run-time warnings.

Ideally you should either use the command line options or use the **warnings** pragmas outlined here.

The Old warnings Pragma

Older versions of Perl (before 5.6) supported a simple pragma that allowed you to switch warnings on and off within your script without the use of the command line. The options were fairly limited; in fact, you could only choose three options, **all**, **deprecated**, and **unsafe**, as detailed in Table 19-1.

You can switch on options with

```
use warnings 'all';
```

Warnings Option	Description
all	All warnings are produced; this is the default if none are specified.
deprecated	Only deprecated feature warnings are produced.
unsafe	Lists only unsafe warnings

Table 19-1. *Options for the **warnings** Pragma*

or you can switch off specific sets with **no**:

```
no warnings 'deprecated';
```

Lexical Warnings in Perl 5.6

Perl 5.6, released at the beginning of April 2000, has changed slightly the way warnings are handled with the **warnings** pragma. This new method is actually now the preferred way of enabling warnings and has a few advantages over the traditional command line switch or the **$^W** variable:

- Mandatory warnings become default warnings and can be disabled.
- Warnings can now be limited to the same scope as the **strict** pragma—that is, they are limited to the enclosing block and propagate to modules imported using **do**, **use**, and **require**.
- You can now specify the level of warnings produced.
- Warnings can be switched off, using the **no** keyword, within individual code blocks.
- Both mandatory and optional warnings can be controlled.

Note *If you've got Perl 5.6, use the **warnings** pragma instead of the -w command line switch for your warnings, and get used to using it alongside the **strict** pragma, which we'll look at later in this chapter. However, if you are creating a script that requires backward compatibility with older versions of Perl, then use -w instead.*

For example, the code

```
use warnings;
$a;
{
    no warnings;
    $b;
}
$c;
```

produces the following output:

```
Useless use of a variable in void context at t2.pl line 2.
Useless use of a variable in void context at t2.pl line 7.
Name "main::a" used only once: possible typo at t2.pl line 2.
Name "main::c" used only once: possible typo at t2.pl line 7.
```

The use of **$b** in line 5 does not raise an error.
To enable warnings within a block, use

```
use warnings;
use warnings 'all';
```

and to switch them off within a block,

```
no warnings;
no warnings 'all';
```

More specific control of warnings is described in the remainder of this section.

Command Line Warnings

The traditional **-w** command line option has now been replaced with those shown in Table 19-2.

The switches interact with the **$^W** variable and the new lexical warnings according to the following rules:

- If no command line switches are supplied, and neither the **$^W** variable nor the **warnings** pragma is in force, then default warnings will be enabled, and optional warnings disabled.

- The **-w** sets the **$^W** variable as normal.

- If a block makes use of the **warnings** pragma, both the **$^W** and **-w** flag are ignored.

- Lexical warnings enabled/disabled with the **warnings** pragma can be overridden only by the **-W/-X** command line switches.

Option	Description
-w	Works just like the old version—warnings are enabled everywhere. However, if you make use of the **warnings** pragma, then the **-w** option is ignored for the scope of the **warnings** pragma.
-W	Enables warnings for all scripts and modules within the program, ignoring the effects of the **$^W** or **warnings** pragma
-X	The exact opposite of **-W**, it switches off all warnings, ignoring the effects of the **$^W** variable or the **warnings** pragma.

Table 19-2. *Command Line Switches for Enabling Warnings*

Warning Options

Beyond the normal control of warnings, you can now also define which warnings will be raised by supplying warning names as arguments to the pragma. For example, you can switch on specific warnings:

```
Yes. MCuse warnings qw/void syntax/;
```

or turn off specific warnings:

```
no warnings qw/void syntax/;
```

The effects are cumulative, rather than explicit, so you could rewrite the preceding as

```
no warnings 'void';      # disables 'void' warnings
no warnings 'syntax';    # disables 'syntax' warnings in addition to 'void'
```

The **warnings** pragma actually supports a hierarchical list of options to be enabled or disabled; you can see the hierarchy in the list that follows. For example, the **severe** warning includes the **debugging**, **inplace**, **internal**, and **malloc** warnings options:

all	chmod	
	closure	
	exiting	
	glob	
	io	closed
		exec
		newline
		pipe
		unopened
	misc	
	numeric	
	once	
	overflow	
	pack	
	portable	

recursion

redefine

regexp

severe   debugging
                    inplace
                    internal
                    malloc

signal

substr

syntax   ambiguous
                    bareword
                    deprecated
                    digit
                    parenthesis
                    printf
                    prototype
                    qw
                    reserved
                    semicolon

taint

umask

uninitialized

unpack

untie

utf8

void

y2k

Making Warnings Fatal

Normally warnings are reported only to **STDERR** without actually halting execution
of the script. You can change this behavior, marking the options as "FATAL" when
importing the **pragma** module:

```
use warnings FATAL => qw/syntax/;
```

Getting Warning Parameters Within the Script

When programming modules, you can configure warnings to be registered against the module in which the warning occurs. This effectively creates a new category within the warnings hierarchy. To register the module within the warnings system, you import the **warnings::register** module:

```
package MyModule;

use warnings::register;
```

This creates a new warnings category called MyModule. When you import the module into a script, you can specify whether you want warnings within the module category to be enabled:

```
use MyModule;
use warnings 'MyModule';
```

To actually identify if warnings have been enabled within the module, you need to use the **warnings::enabled** function. If called without arguments, it returns true if warnings have been enabled. For example,

```
package MyModule;

sub test
{
    if (warnings::enabled())
    {
        warnings::warn('deprecated',
                       'test is deprecated, use the object io');
    }
}
```

The **warnings::warn** function actually raises a warning—note that it raises an error even if warnings are disabled, so make sure you test that warnings have been enabled. Also note that the **warnings::warn** function accepts two arguments—the first is the word used to describe the warning, and the second is the additional text message printed with the warning. So, the line

```
warnings::warn('deprecated','test is deprecated, use the object io');
```

actually produces

```
test is deprecated use the object io at t2.pl line 5
```

The function name is inserted first—or the package or file name if it's within the global scope—just as in the core **warn** function.

You can also be more specific about the warnings that you want to test for; if you supply arguments to the **warnings::enabled** function, for instance, it returns true only if the warning type specified has been enabled:

```
if (warnings::enabled('deprecated'))
...
```

The strict Pragma

The **strict** pragma restricts those constructs and statements that would normally be considered unsafe or ambiguous. Unlike warnings, which raise errors without causing the script to fail, the **strict** pragma will halt the execution of the script if any of the restrictions enforced by the pragma are broken. Although the pragma imposes limits that cause scripts to fail, the pragma generally encourages (and even enforces) good programming practice. For some casual scripts it does, of course, cause more problems than you might be trying to solve.

Tip *As with warnings, you should have the **strict** pragma enforced at all times. It will help you to pick more of those ambiguous instances where your script may fail without warning. It is no replacement for a full debugger, but it will highlight problems that a normal debugging process might overlook.*

The basic form of the pragma is

```
use strict;
```

The pragma is lexically scoped, so it is in effect only within the current block. This means you must specify **use strict** separately within all the packages, modules, and individual scripts you create. If a script that uses the **strict** pragma imports a module that does not, only the script portion will be checked—the pragma's effects are not propagated down to other modules.

By using the pragma, you should be able to identify the effects of assumptions Perl makes about what you are trying to achieve. It does this by imposing limits on the definition and use of variables, references, and barewords that would otherwise be interpreted as functions (subroutines). These can be individually turned on or off using the **vars**, **refs**, and **subs** options to the pragma. You supply the option as an argument to the pragma when the corresponding module is imported. For example, to enable only the **refs** and **subs** options, use the following:

```
use strict qw/refs subs/;
```

The effects are cumulative, so this could be rewritten as

```
use strict 'refs';
use strict 'subs';
```

The pragma also supports the capability to turn it off through the **no** keyword, so you can temporarily turn off strict checking:

```
use strict;

no strict 'vars';

$var = 1;

use strict 'vars';
```

Unless you have any very special reason not to, I recommend using the basic **strict** to enable all three levels of checking.

The vars Option

The **vars** option requires that all variables be predeclared before they are used, either with the **my** keyword, with the **use vars** pragma, or through a fully qualified name that includes the name of the enclosing package in which you want the variable to be defined.

When using the pragma, the **local** keyword is not sufficient because its purpose is only to localize a variable, not to declare it. Therefore the following examples work,

```
use strict 'vars';
$Module::vara = 1;
my $vara = 1;
use vars qw/$varb/;
```

but these will fail:

```
use strict 'vars';
$vars = 1;
local $vars = 1;
```

One of the most frustrating elements of the **vars** option is that you'll get a list of errors relating to the use of variables. For example, the script

```
use strict;

%hash = ('Martin' => 'Brown',
         'Sharon' => 'Penfold',
         'Wendy'  => 'Rinaldi',);

foreach $key (sort keys %hash)
{
    print "$key -> $hash{$key}\n";
}
```

raises these errors when executed:

```
$ perl -w t2.pl
Global symbol "%hash" requires explicit package name at t2.pl line 3.
Global symbol "$key" requires explicit package name at t2.pl line 7.
Global symbol "%hash" requires explicit package name at t2.pl line 7.
Global symbol "$key" requires explicit package name at t2.pl line 9.
Global symbol "%hash" requires explicit package name at t2.pl line 9.
Global symbol "$key" requires explicit package name at t2.pl line 9.
Execution of t2.pl aborted due to compilation errors.
```

The obvious solution to the problem is to declare the variables using **my**:

```
use strict;

my %hash = ('Martin' => 'Brown',
            'Sharon' => 'Penfold',
            'Wendy'  => 'Rinaldi',);

foreach my $key (sort keys %hash)
{
    print "$key -> $hash{$key}\n";
}
```

When developing modules, the use of **my** on variables that you want to export will not work, because the declared variables will be lexically scoped within the package. The solution is to use the **vars** pragma:

```
package MyModule;

use vars qw/@ISA @EXPORT/;

require Exporter;
@ISA = qw/Exporter/;
@EXPORT = qw/
    open_db
/;
```

As a general rule, you should always use the **vars** option, even if you neglect to use the other **strict** pragma options.

The refs Option

The **refs** pragma generates an error if you use symbolic (soft) references—that is, if you use a string to refer to a variable or function. Thus, the following will work,

```
use strict 'refs';
$foo = "Hello World";
$ref = \$foo;
print $$ref;
```

but these do not:

```
use strict 'refs';
$foo = "Hello World";
$ref = "foo";
print $$ref;
```

Care should be taken if you're using a dispatch table, because the traditional solutions don't work when the **strict** pragma is in force. The following will fail, because you're trying to use a soft reference to the function that you want to call:

```
use strict refs;
my %commandlist = (
```

```
                       'DISK'  => 'disk_space_report',
                       'SWAP'  => 'swap_space_report',
                       'STORE' => 'store_status_report',
                       'GET'   => 'get_status_report',
                       'QUIT'  => 'quit_connection',
                       );
...
my ($function) = $commandlist{$command};
die "No $function()" unless defined(&$function);
&$function(*CHILDSOCKET, $host, $type);
```

To get around this, find a reference to the subroutine from the symbol table, and then access it as a typeglob and call it as a function. This means you can change the last three lines in the preceding script to

```
if (defined($main::{$commandlist{$command}}))
{
    *code = \$main::{$commandlist{$command}};
    &code($user,$group,$session);
}
```

> **Note** *You can also use the **exists** function to determine if a function has been created, but it will return true even if the function has only been forward-defined by the **subs** pragma or when setting up a function prototype, not just when the function has actually been defined.*

The subs Option

The final option controls how barewords are treated by Perl (see Chapter 2 for a description of barewords). Without this pragma in effect, you can use a bareword to refer to a subroutine or function. When the pragma is in effect, then you must quote or provide an absolute reference to the subroutine in question.

Normally, Perl allows you to use a bareword for a subroutine. This pragma disables that ability, best seen with signal handlers. The examples

```
use strict 'subs';
$SIG{QUIT} = "myexit";
$SIG{QUIT} = \&myexit;
```

will work, since we are not using a bareword, but

```
use strict 'subs';
$SIG{QUIT} = myexit;
```

will generate an error during compilation because **myexit** is a bareword.

Other Perl Pragmas

Beyond the **warnings** and **strict** pragmas, there are others that can help to control and change the way Perl treats different aspects of your script. Although not always useful when debugging, the effects of pragmas can cause unexpected problems in scripts if you fail to notice that the pragma is in effect. Others help you get by the effects of the **strict** pragma, such as the **vars** and **subs** pragmas.

You've already seen how the **strict** pragma works, and other pragmas operate in exactly the same fashion. Pragmas are in fact just modules, which by convention have their names in lowercase. You enable them with the **use** keyword, supplying any optional parameters as a string or array after the pragma name. For example,

```
use vars qw/$var $string/;
```

To turn off a specified pragma, you need the **no** keyword, which is the logical opposite of the **use** keyword. If you specify **no** at the same level as a previous **use** statement, it acts as a toggle, switching off the earlier pragma until a new **use** statement is seen, or until the end of the block. If you use **no** within an enclosed block (a function or loop) inside a block with the corresponding **use** statement, the pragma is disabled only for the duration of the enclosed block. For example,

```
use integer;
function intdivide
{
    print "67/3","\n"; #Uses integer math
}

function divide
{
    no integer;
    print "67/3","\n"; #Uses floating point math
}

print "67/3","\n"; #Integer math
no integer;
print "67/3","\n"; #Floating point math
```

Other pragmas work in similar ways, although some of the effects are dependent on other pragmas or on the specific implementation.

attributes

The **attributes** pragma (new in 5.6) replaces the old **attrs** pragma and allows you to get or set the subroutine and variable attributes. The new pragma works in conjunction with the new attributes system for subroutines (heavily expanded in Perl 5.6) and will work with other systems, such as the planned variable attribute system. The pragma itself has two purposes, creating attribute lists and obtaining the attribute lists during run time. Because the attribute system is largely an internally declared system, such as that used to create lvalue subroutines, the pragma is really only useful for the getting attribute lists.

To obtain the attribute list for a given object you use the **attributes::get** function. The basic usage is

```
sub func : method;
my $closure = sub : method {};

use attributes;
@attributes = attributes::get(\&func);
```

The pragma also defines the **attributes::reftype** function. This works like the built-in **ref**, except that it always returns the real data type of the reference, as used internally by Perl. This means it ignores any package that the object might have been blessed into, and just returns the base type.

autouse

The **autouse** pragma postpones the loading of the module until a specified function has actually been called. This allows you to delay the loading of a module for functions that are used only infrequently, thereby improving the loading and overall execution time. For example, to delay the loading of **Module** until one of **funca** or **funcb** is actually used,

```
use autouse 'Module' => qw(funca funcb);
```

This is similar in principle, but not identical, to the **Autoload** module. Note that you must specify the functions that will trigger the **autouse** process; otherwise, there is no way for the Perl interpreter to identify the functions that should be imported. The preceding example is therefore equivalent to the method for importing selected functions from a module:

```
use Module qw(funca funcb);
```

You can also supply function prototypes to the **autouse** pragma to trap errors during the compilation, rather than execution, stage:

```
use Module qw(funca($$) funcb($@));
```

The effect of the **autouse** pragma is to reduce the loading and compilation time for a script and also to reduce the number of modules that are loaded at startup in scripts where specific external functions are used only in certain execution trees. Unfortunately, the pragma also has the effect of delaying the loading of the module until execution time, thus bypassing the usual checks that are made when importing a module and shifting the responsibility of reporting any errors to the execution stage, rather than the compilation stages.

Problems can occur when there are bugs or typographical errors in the modules being **autouse**d, because your program will not fall over when the module is imported, but when a function is actually used. Additionally, any module that relies on early initialization (say, within a **BEGIN {}** block) may fail because it expects the initialization to occur during the initial compilation of the whole script.

You can get around the bugs in **autouse** modules during the development phase by placing a genuine **use** statement for the **autouse** modules. For example,

```
use File::Basename
use autouse 'File::Basename' => qw(basename dirname);
```

The first line masks the second; when you come to release your script and/or module to the public, just comment out the first line and let the **autouse** pragma do its work.

base

The **base** pragma establishes a relationship with a base class at compile (rather than execution) time. In effect, this operation is equal to adding the specified classes to the **@ISA** array during the module initialization, such that

```
package Object;
use base qw(Foo Bar);
```

is effectively equal to

```
BEGIN
{
    require Foo;
    require Bar;
    push @ISA, qw(Foo Bar);
}
```

Because of this, any base class not yet loaded but explicitly listed to the **base** pragma will be loaded automatically via **require**. Note, however, that the normal inheritance rules are not followed and the **%INC** hash is not used to determine whether a base class has already been loaded. This is because use of **base** could cause Perl to enter a cycle where it tries to load a class from a file that has already been imported with **require**. Instead, **base** sets the value of **$VERSION** in the base class to the string "–1, defined by base.pm".

Note that in addition to setting the inheritance, the **base** module also causes any special field attributes for the classes named to be initialized, providing they use the **fields** pragma to set the attributes. See the entry for **fields** later in this chapter.

blib

The **blib** pragma forces Perl to look for modules in the blib directory structure, as created by the **MakeMaker** module. This feature is especially useful for testing modules before they are finally installed when using ExtUtils::MakeMaker (see Chapter 25 for more information). Ideally, it should be used only on the command line with the **-M** option:

```
perl -Mblib script
perl -Mblib=dir script
```

If **dir** is specified, it looks in that directory (and subdirectories) for the **blib** structure. If you do not specify **dir**, it assumes you want to include the current directory.

You can also use

```
use blib;
use blib 'dir';
```

but this is not the preferred solution, because it requires modification of the script to disable the behavior.

bytes

The **bytes** pragma forces Perl to consider information in terms of individual bytes, rather than characters (which could be multibyte) for data sources that imply character semantics. See Chapter 9 for more information on Unicode and multibyte character sets.

The **bytes** pragma is lexically scoped, and you can use **no** to reverse the effects:

```
use bytes;
no bytes;
```

charnames

The **charnames** pragma allows you to embed characters by name into any interpolated string. For example:

```
use charnames ':short';
print "\N{greek:Sigma}";
```

The actual format of the pragma is

```
use charnames HOW;
print "\N{CHARSPEC}";
```

Here, **HOW** is an argument that defines either how you refer to the characters you want (using either ":full" or ":short"), or by supplying the name of a specific character script (for example Roman or Greek), as defined by the Unicode Consortium.

If **HOW** is specified as ":full," then **CHARSPEC** is assumed to be a full Unicode character specification, for example "GREEK SMALL LETTER SIGMA". If **HOW** is specified as ":short," then **CHARSPEC** is taken as **SCRIPT:CHARNAME**, where **SCRIPT** is the Unicode script, and **CHARNAME** is the character within that script.

If **HOW** is any other string, then it's taken as the script name, and **CHARSPEC** becomes the name of the character within that script.

The character name, in its long form, can be defined using

```
SCRIPTNAME CAPTIAL LETTER CHARNAME
SCRIPTNAME SMALL LETTER CHARNAME
SCRIPTNAME LETTER CHARNAME
```

The **CAPITAL, SMALL,** and **LETTER** components are merely modifiers to change whether the upper- or lowercase letter is inserted. If **CHARNAME** is specified entirely in lowercase, then **CAPITAL** is ignored.

See the unicode directory installed with the standard Perl library for the files that contain the character scripts. See also Chapter 9 for information on Unicode and how it operates within Perl.

constant

Although there are other techniques for introducing constant variables, the most practical solution is the **constant** pragma. The advantages of a constant are obvious: if you use the same constant value throughout all your calculations and programs, you can be guaranteed that the values calculated will also remain constant.

The rule applies even when the constant is used over many different platforms. For example, the value of <<Unicode: 70>> can be endlessly calculated, and there are varying methods and degrees of precision used for the value. You can create a constant value to be used in all calculations like this:

```
use constant PI => 3.141592654;
```

The value can be any normal Perl expression, including calculations and functions such that the following also work:

```
use constant PI   => 22/7;
use constant USER => scalar getpwuid($<);
```

However, you can't define more than one constant at the same time, so

```
use constant PI   => 22/7, USER => scalar getpwuid($<);
```

will *not* work.

Once it's defined, you can use a constant directly; there is no need for a preceding character to denote the variable type:

```
$zero = (cos(PI/2));
```

The values supplied are evaluated in a list context, allowing you to define constant lists as well as scalars. Note that constants are lists, so you must use subscript, not array, notation. Therefore, the statement

```
$quota = USERDATA[5];
```

will not work; you must use

```
$quota = (USERDATA)[5];
```

Also note that constants can be directly interpolated, although you must use indirect notation:

```
print "I want to eat some @{[PI]}\n";
```

It's also worth noting that, because constants are actually just subroutines, you cannot use them in contexts where a bareword is automatically quoted, such as hashes.

Instead, use an empty parenthesis or the **+** operator in front of the constant to force Perl to identify it as a function:

```
$hash{PI()};
$hash{+PI};
```

Although it is not essential, constants should have names composed only of uppercase characters to help distinguish them from normal variables. All constants must begin with a letter.

Constant definitions are package-scoped rather than block-scoped, so you can have different constant values within the confines of different packages, and you can also refer to constants using fully qualified names.

 Be careful when using constants; the uppercase convention can interfere with filehandles.

diagnostics

The **diagnostics** pragma inserts additional diagnostic capabilities into the Perl script. Although Perl normally outputs a fair number of errors and warnings when it discovers a problem, at both compile time and run time, the messages are often terse single-line descriptions. Even if you know what the error message signifies, the exact cause of the problem may be difficult to determine.

The **diagnostics** pragma prints out not only the terse one-line warnings that you normally see when a warning is displayed, but also the additional descriptive text that you find in the perldiag main page. Although you still don't have the further benefit of a more in-depth description of the problem, the description can often highlight things you have overlooked.

To use, insert the **diagnostics** pragma at the top of the script you want to examine for problems, and then run the script (preferably with warnings switched on) and examine the extended output. This program will produce a few errors:

```
use diagnostics;
print DUMMY 'Wont work';
```

When it's run, you get the following:

```
$ perl -w nodiag.pl
Name "main::DUMMY" used only once: possible typo at t.pl line 2 (#1)

    (W) Typographical errors often show up as unique variable names.
    If you had a good reason for having a unique name, then just mention
    it again somehow to suppress the message.  The use vars pragma is
```

```
    provided for just this purpose.

Filehandle main::DUMMY never opened at t.pl line 2 (#2)

    (W) An I/O operation was attempted on a filehandle that was never
    initialized. You need to do an open() or a socket() call, or call
    a constructor from the FileHandle package.
```

Alternatively, leave your script as it is and pipe the error output to a file. The **splain** program (installed with Perl) can then be used to analyze the errors and produce the full descriptions for the error messages and warnings:

```
perl -w nodiag.pl 2> nodiag.err
./splain <nodiag.err
```

Note *Under MacPerl there is no separate **splain** application, but the **diagnostics** pragma still works if specified within the script.*

If you specify the **-verbose** option when specifying the pragma, the introduction from the perldiag main page will be printed out before the diagnostic warnings and extended information:

```
use diagnostics -verbose;
```

Once they are imported, you can control the behavior of individual elements of the script by switching the diagnostics messages on and off using the **enable** and **disable** functions:

```
enable  diagnostics;
disable diagnostics;
```

These changes affect only any run time errors. It's not possible to switch off the diagnostics process during the parsing/compilation stage.

If your program is making use of the **$SIG{__WARN__}** and **$SIG{__DIE__}** handlers to trap errors in your program (see Chapter 21), you can still use them in conjunction with the **diagnostics** module. However, the **diagnostics::splainthis** function will be executed first, so you'll get the extended warning information before your own extensions are executed. See Chapter 9 for information on using signals for error trapping.

If you want to examine exactly what the **diagnostics** module is doing, you can switch on "debugging" for the **diagnostics** module by defining

```
BEGIN { $diagnostics::DEBUG =1 }
```

before the script starts the rest of the execution process.

fields

The **fields** pragma affects the compile-time error checking of objects. Using the **fields** pragma enables you to predefine class fields, such that a call to a specific class method will fail at compile time if the field has not been specified. This is achieved by populating a hash called **%FIELDS**. When you access a hash with a typed variable holding an object reference, the type is looked up in the **%FIELDS** hash, and if the variable type exists, the entire operation is turned into an array access during the compilation stage. For example,

```
{
    package Foo;
    use fields qw(foo bar _private);
}
...
my Foo $var = new Foo;
$var->{foo} = 42;
```

If the specified field (in this case "foo") does not exist, a compile time error is produced.

For this to work, the **%FIELDS** hash is consulted at compile time, and it's the **fields** and **base** pragmas that facilitate this. The **base** pragma copies fields from the base class definitions, and the **fields** pragma adds new fields to the existing definitions. Field names that start with an underscore character are private to a class; they are not even accessible to subclasses.

The result is that objects can be created with named fields that are as convenient and quick to access as a corresponding hash. You must access the objects through correctly typed variables, or you can use untyped variables, providing a reference to the **%FIELDS** hash is assigned to the 0th element of the array object. You can achieve this initialization with the following:

```
sub new
{
    my $class = shift;
    no strict 'refs';
    my $self = bless [\%{"$class\::FIELDS"}], $class;
    $self;
}
```

filetest

The **filetest** pragma improves on the standard file testing techniques offered by Perl and the **-X** operators. By default, the built-in **-r**, **-w**, **-x**, **-R**, **-W** and **-X** operators actually check only the permissions bitset that is normally returned by **stat**. These do not take into account the facilities of some operating systems that support access control lists (ACLs) or other extended permission systems. Use of the **filetest** pragma overloads these operators so that the tests return true values under these conditions.

```
use filetest;
```

The pragma is lexically scoped, so the effects are only felt until the end of the current block. You can also use **no** to disable the effects.

integer

Perl does all its calculations in floating point by default. Although you can normally force integer results from specific calculations using the **int** function, it can be more useful to specify that all calculations are performed with integers only. For example,

```
use integer;
print 67/3,"\n";
```

The **use integer** pragma lasts only as long as the current block, so it can safely be used within individual functions without affecting the rest of the script. In addition, you can switch off the **integer** pragma with the **no** keyword:

```
use integer;
print 67/3,"\n";
no integer;
print 67/3,"\n";
```

You can also use **no** within an enclosed block to temporarily turn off integer math, as seen earlier in the introductory example under "Other Perl Pragmas."

less

The **less** pragma is currently unimplemented.

```
use less;
```

The intention is to allow you to specify reductions for certain resources, such as memory or processor space. This capability might be useful in situations where you want to ensure that the effects of the script do not upset the rest of your system.

lib

When importing modules with **use**, the interpreter examines the **@INC** array for a list of directories to search for the modules to be imported. Since **use** statements are evaluated during the compilation process, you cannot insert additional directories in the main part of the script. You can, of course, use a **BEGIN {}** block:

```
BEGIN { unshift @INC, LIST }
```

or you can use the **lib** pragma. The equivalent of the preceding block would be

```
use lib LIST;
```

Note that the directories are added before (using **unshift**) the standard directories to ensure that you use the local modules in preference to the standard ones. For all directories added in this way, the **lib** module also checks that a **$dir/$archname/**auto exists, where **$archname** is the name of the architecture of the current platform. If it does exist, it is assumed to be an architecture-specific directory and is actually added to **@INC** before the original directory specification.

Once added, it is not normally necessary to remove directories. Furthermore, you shouldn't ever remove standard directories from the array. It's also worth remembering that you may affect the future operation of a later module if you remove a directory that contains a module on which it relies. Although you could argue that it is the module's responsibility to make sure it has access to the modules it needs, it's also sensible to assume that in the interests of good relations you shouldn't be removing directories anyway. There is no advantage to removing them; it doesn't take a considerable amount of extra memory or processing power for the interpreter to search for what it's looking for.

With all this in mind, you remove directories with a **no lib** pragma, which removes the first instance of the named directory from **@INC**. If you want to remove multiple instances, you will need to call **no lib** multiple times. You can also remove all the specified names from **@INC** by specifying ":ALL" as the first parameter of **no lib**. For example,

```
no lib qw(:ALL .);
```

For each directory, the opposite of the earlier process is executed. The architecture-specific directories are also searched for in the **@INC** array before they too are removed.

Although in practice you shouldn't need to, if you want to reinstate the original (standard) list of directories in **@INC**, you need to use

```
@INC = @lib::ORIG_INC;
```

locale

The **locale** pragma tells the compiler to enable the use of POSIX locales for built-in operations. This has the effect of enforcing the case conversion and pattern matching semantics according to the punctuation and characters used within the current setting. The environment variables **LC_CTYPE** and **LC_COLLATE** should define the locale to be used for regular expression and string comparison respectively. Note that it only applies where your system and C libraries are POSIX compliant.

```
use locale;
```

The pragma is lexically scoped, so the effects are only felt until the end of the current block. You can also use **no** to disable the effects.

open

The **open** pragma works in conjunction with the **open** (and other) function to change the default character conversion discipline. When used, any **open** or **readpipe** (such as backticks) operation within the current lexical scope will be subject to the defaults set. For example

```
use open IN => "crlf", OUT => ":raw";
```

would set the input discipline to **crlf** and the output discipline to **raw**. At the time of writing, these were the only two supported. See Chapter 8 for more information on the disciplines used with **open**.

Also planned is a special **:DEFAULT** discipline, which can be specified to an **open** call to use the default values defined by the enclosing **open** pragma.

ops

The **ops** pragma switches off specific opcodes during the compilation process. The synopsis is as follows,

```
perl -Mops=:default
```

which enables only reasonably safe operations, or you can specify that opcodes be removed from those available, using

```
perl -M-ops=system
```

Note that the best way to use this option is via the command line incorporation; otherwise, you open yourself up to abuse before the compilation process starts through the use of **BEGIN {}** statements. Alternatively, you can use the **Safe** and **Opcode** modules (see Chapter 15), which provide a more comprehensive method for executing Perl code using a restricted set of opcodes.

overload

The **overload** pragma allows you to overload the built-in operators when used with objects to instead use local functions. For example, in your class definition:

```
package SomeThing;
use overload
        '+' => \&myadd,
        '-' => \&mysub;
```

Then in your script:

```
use SomeThing;
$a = new SomeThing 57;
$b=5+$a;
```

Overloading is a complex process, and more details on this pragma, and overloading functions in general, are given in Chapter 7.

re

The **re** pragma alters regular expression behavior. The pragma has three options: **taint**, **debug**, and **eval**. One additional pragma is really just a modification of an earlier one, called **debugcolor.** The only difference is in the color of the output. In all cases the **re** pragma applies to the entire file (it is not lexically scoped), and the effect is felt at both compile and execution time.

The **taint** option ensures that variables modified with a regular expression are tainted in situations where they would otherwise be considered cleaned during the regular expression exercise:

```
use re 'taint';
```

That is, in situations where matches or substitutions on tainted variables would ordinarily produce an untainted result, the results are in fact marked as tainted. Information that is already untainted remains unchanged—the use of the taint option does not taint all regular expression data.

The **debug** and **debugcolor** options force Perl to produce debugging messages during the execution of a regular expression:

```
use re 'debug';
use re 'debugcolor';
```

This is equivalent to using the **-Dx** switch during execution if the **-DDEBUGGING** option was specified during the build process. The information provided can be very large, even on a relatively small regular expression. The **debugcolor** option prints out a color version if your terminal supports it. See Chapter 21 for more information on the effects of the **-D** switch.

The **eval** option enables regular expressions to contain the **(?{...})** assertions, even if the regular expression contains variable interpolation,

```
use re 'eval';
```

Ordinarily this is disabled because it's seen as a security risk, and the pragma is ignored if the **use re 'taint'** pragma is in effect.

Individual pragmas can be switched off with **no re**.

sigtrap

The **sigtrap** pragma enables simple signal handling without the complexity of the normal signal handling routines.

```
use sigtrap;
```

The pragma supports three handlers: two are supplied by the module itself (one provides a stack trace and the other just calls **die**), and the third is one that you supply yourself. Each option supplied to the module is processed in order, so the moment a signal name is identified, the signal handler is installed.

Without any options specified, the module defaults to the **stack-trace** and **old-interface-signals** options. The individual options are listed here.

```
use sigtrap qw/stack-trace HUP INT KILL/;
```

Generates a Perl stack trace to **STDERR** when the specified signals are received by the script. After the trace has been generated, the module calls **dump** to dump the core.

```
use sigtrap qw/die HUP INT KILL/;
```

Calls **croak** (see Chapter 9), reporting the name of the message that was caught.

```
use sigtrap 'handler' => \&my_handler, HUP, INT, KILL;
```

Installs the handler **my_handler** for the specified signals.

The pragma defines some standard signal lists. If your system does not support one of the specified signals, the signal is ignored rather than producing an error.

```
normal-signals
```

These are signals that might ordinarily be trapped by any program: **HUP, INT, PIPE**, and **TERM**.

```
error-signals
```

These are the signals that indicate a serious error: **ABRT, BUS, EMT, FPE, ILL, QUIT, SEGV, SYS**, and **TRAP**.

```
old-interface-signals
```

The list of signals that were trapped by default by the old **sigtrap** pragma. This is the list of signals that are used if you do not specify others; they include **ABRT, BUS, EMT, FPE, ILL, PIPE, QUIT, SEGV, SYS, TERM**, and **TRAP**.

```
untrapped
```

This special option selects from the list of signals that follows or specifies all the signals that are not otherwise trapped or ignored.

```
any
```

applies handlers to all subsequently listed signals; this is the default.

subs

The **subs** pragma predeclares a function so that the function can be called without parentheses even before Perl has seen the full definition.

```
use subs qw(func);
```

This option can also be used to override internal functions by predefining the subroutines you want to override:

```
use subs qw(chdir);
chdir $message;
sub chdir
{
...
}
```

The overriding versions can be defined in the local file (as in the preceding example), or they can be imported from an external module, although it's possible to override functions from external modules by defining the function specifically to the import process, as in

```
use MyBuiltin 'chdir';
```

Obviously, you will need to define the **chdir** function in the **@EXPORT_OK** array as part of the module initialization. See Chapter 6 for more information on creating modules and using the **Exporter** module for creating Perl modules.

The **subs** pragma is not block scoped, so the function definitions are global to the entire execution—as you'd expect.

vars

The **vars** pragma predeclares the variables defined in the list, which has the effect of preventing typographical warnings for variables not yet created. It is also the best way to declare variables that are to be shared with other modules if you do not want to use the **local** keyword. The use of **my** variables won't work, since the variables will be localized strictly to the module. Because the variables are declared globally, it's also the easiest way to declare global variables that would otherwise trip up the **use strict** pragma.

```
use vars qw($scalar @array %hash);
```

Note that **vars** is not block-scoped. The variables are truly global within the current file.

The use of **vars** is now deprecated in favor of the **our** keyword for declaring variables, but is retained for backward compatibility. See Chapter 6 for more information on **our**.

Chapter 20

Extending and Embedding Perl

Many people's understanding of Perl comes to the point we have already reached (if you have followed this book sequentially). However, there is a lot more to the language, even within the realms of writing a simple program. Some of it has been hinted at already—pragmas, the different processes in the execution of a Perl script, and some of the internal structures used by Perl to represent information.

In this chapter, we'll lift the hood of the Perl engine and have a look at how the language works at its lowest level and how we can affect that behavior. Our first goal is to examine the individual components that make up the Perl interpreter. By examining each component of the system, you should gain insight into how the entire application works. Armed with this information, we'll then dig further and follow the execution process of a script from the time it is finished being written to the point at which it completes its execution cycle, including all the intervening steps.

The bulk of the chapter, however, is given to communicating with functions and extensions that extend beyond the capabilities or accessibility of Perl. This process, called *extension programming*, provides a method for writing a simple mapping file that equates Perl functions with external C functions.

This is, in fact, how much of the functionality we take for granted is provided in Perl. The Perl distribution uses this system to provide an interface between Perl and network sockets, threads, and DBM databases (such as **GDBM_File** and **DB_File**), and also the more advanced elements (such as the Perl compiler).

For the end user, extension programming provides you with unlimited flexibility to interface your Perl scripts with external C functions, whether self-written or provided by external libraries and systems. The CPAN archives contain countless examples of this sort of interface, from simple math libraries up to some of the more complex systems you have already seen. The DBI toolkit, for example, provides access to a wide range of external database systems through the use of C functions and the Perl extension interface.

For others, the practicalities and facilities provided by Perl are too attractive, and they want or need to embed the Perl interpreter within their C programs. This has some advantages, such as the ability to parse regular expressions within a C program more easily than is possible with many of the available libraries. Other people have also made good use of the features provided by embedding to improve facilities within their software. On CPAN, for example, there is a module called **mod_perl** that embeds a Perl interpreter within the Apache web server, enabling you to execute Perl CGI scripts much faster than you otherwise could by calling an external Perl interpreter.

Finally, Perl also provides facilities for cooperating with other languages, either through the coercive use of Perl as a language producer or through the supplied scripts that provide you with facilities for converting programs written in other languages, such as **awk** and **sed**, into Perl scripts.

Perl Internals

There comes a time for most programmers when they want to understand how a particular application works. For many commercial applications, this information is just not available. But for open-source projects, such as Perl, anybody can read the source code for the application. The more inquisitive may even take the code and go off and do their own thing (see the upcoming sidebar, "Every Hacker's Goals"). In this chapter, the aim is really to take a step back from that level of detail, and instead look at the architecture and process involved in interpreting and executing a script.

My intention is not to dissuade you from examining the source code if you want to. The code is available; and despite the fact that it's largely uncommented and is composed of a number of complex macros and optimizations, it's still readable by a hardened C programmer. My best suggestion is to get the latest source and start by examining the source code for the different variable types (hv.c for hash values, and so on). Once comfortable with the concepts there, you should then move on to op.c and doop.c, which handle the opcode (see the "Opcodes" section, later in the chapter), before finally examining the execution process in run.c, preferably with a debugger such as **gdb** or the debugger that comes with Microsoft's Developer Studio Product.

Every Hacker's Goals

It has been said, by others as well as me, that the ultimate dream of all serious computer programmers is to achieve three simple goals in their lifetime:

- Write their own computer language
- Write their own operating system
- Build their own computer from individual components (microchips, resistors, and so on)

I'm pleased to say that I've managed to achieve all three—although for the last two, I'm not sure that an embedded computer for controlling a model lift is what one would call a real achievement.

I should probably add at this point that you should not confuse the term "hacker" with the term "cracker." A *hacker* is someone who enjoys toying with computers and, often, programming them. A *cracker* is a malicious individual who tries to break in (crack) a secure program, website, nuclear facility, and so on. Don't get the two mixed up; you'll offend a hacker by calling him a cracker!

If you want to skip the technicals and examine the lexical process of converting the written Perl script into the internal structures and opcodes, then look at perly.y. This is a **yacc** definition file that outlines the main components and structures for the Perl language. Some of the more complex lexical analysis is hand coded within the other source files, most notably toke.c. For regular expressions, Perl uses a modified standard regular-expression library, although all of the functionality has actually been written from scratch. The regular expression compiler and Executor are in the regcomp.c and regexec.c files, respectively.

If you want to avoid the source code, or perhaps just cannot follow it, three tools are available on CPAN (see Appendix A) that provide access to the internal structures within Perl. The **Devel::Peek** module allows you to dump the internal information associated with a variable, while **Devel::Symdump** will dump the symbol table. The **Devel::RegExp** module can examine and monitor regular expressions.

We'll be examining other ways of monitoring the execution process of a Perl script in the coming sections, but first you need to understand how the Perl interpreter works.

Architecture

You can see in Figure 20-1 the basic architecture for the entire Perl interpreter. The shaded blocks show the internal components of the Perl interpreter, including the internal data structures and the execution components. Some of the components can have multiple instances (we'll cover this later). The unshaded blocks on the diagram are the compiled C source code.

You may recognize the diagram as looking mildly similar to the virtual machine diagram often used to describe the operation of the Java language. There are some similarities between the two languages: Perl uses the optimized opcodes (the smallest executable component of a compiled Perl script) in combination with the Executor component to actually run the Perl script. We'll look at these similarities more closely as we examine the execution process.

Internal Objects

The Perl object API in Figure 20-1 represents the functions and structures used to support the four main internal data structures for any Perl program: variables, symbol tables, stacks, and external data streams.

The data formats supported by Perl are familiar by now. We'll examine the gory details of these variable types and how to use them later in this chapter. For now, a summary of the supported types is all we'll need. Each variable can be identified by a two-letter acronym, as seen in Table 20-1.

The scalar value can also be further subclassed as an **IV** (integer value), **PV** (string value), or **DV** (double value). Other internal data structures, such as the symbol tables and stacks, are also represented by these core value types, which are strictly managed and controlled with efficient memory management.

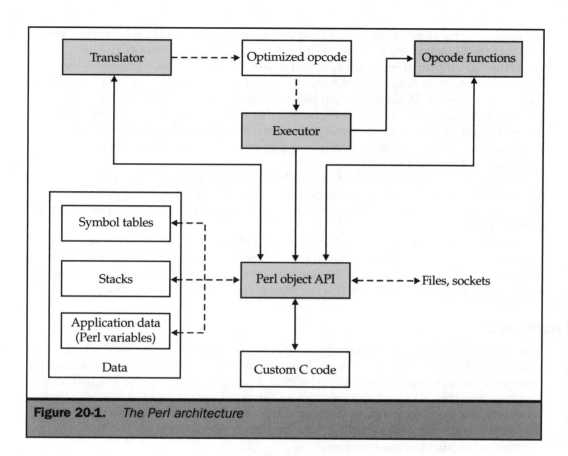

Figure 20-1.   *The Perl architecture*

Acronym	Full Name
SV	Scalar value
AV	Array value
HV	Hash value
CV	Code value
GV	Glob value (typeglobs)
RV	Reference value

Table 20-1.   *Internal Perl Data Type Acronyms*

Perl's internal symbol tables (see Chapter 6) are actually just **HVs**. Identifiers are stored as the keys, and the corresponding data value is a pointer to a **GV**.

Temporary information (including that passed to functions as arguments), the current location within a script, and variables used to store temporary data are all held on stacks. These are **AVs**, which are treated as simple stacks similar to the principles you saw in Chapter 8. When function **foo** wants to call function **bar** with arguments, the arguments are pushed onto the argument stack and the **bar** is called. The first operation performed by **bar** internally is to pop the arguments off the stack and populate the function's @_ array.

Other individual stacks are used to hold the other temporary variables, such as local variables, loop iterators, and control information for the Perl interpreter. We'll be examining the stack and how it can be accessed and modified within a C program later in the chapter.

External data streams are handled by the I/O abstraction API. This is a suite of functions that provide a thin porting layout for the standard **stdio** and **sfio** libraries. For most people, there is no need to refer to the I/O abstraction, even when producing new C-derived Perl functions, but it can be useful background information.

Translator

The translator converts the Perl script into a series of opcodes, which we'll take a closer look at shortly. The opcodes are listed in a tree format to allow for branching, for argument passing, and for a structured logical progression through the original script. The translator is made up of a combination of the **yacc**-based parser file, a hand-coded lexical analyzer, and the actual opcode generator. This is also the point at which regular expressions are compiled (assuming they can be compiled at compilation time) using a customized regular-expression engine.

Multiple Simultaneous Interpreters

When embedding Perl into a C program, you can create multiple instances of **PerlInterpreter()**—the main interpreter function. Each instance will have its own "global" name space, rather than the normal shared name space that uses global C variables to store the main data structures. Unless you have a real need for multiple interpreter instances, you should use the single instance. This is faster (because the data structures do not need to be copied around), and you can create separate packages to separate most user variables.

In a secure installation, there may well be a need for isolating instances of the Perl interpreter in your programs. You can also use the **Safe** module to create a secure environment for script execution. See Chapter 15 for more information on **Safe** and its companion **Opcode** module.

Opcodes

An opcode is the smallest executable component within a Perl program. There are opcodes for all of the built-in functions and operators in the Perl language. During the execution stage, it is the opcodes and the functions on which they rely that are executed by the Perl interpreter. It is at this point that Perl begins to resemble the Java-style virtual machine.

However, within Java, all operations are resolved down a machine-code–like format, not vastly dissimilar to the assembly language for a RISC (Reduced Instruction Set Computing) processor. RISC processors use a small number of instructions, with more complex operations being based on collections of the reduced set of instructions. When you execute a Java program, you are effectively emulating a RISC processor and all of the baggage that goes with it. This has some advantages, since it makes building a hardware-based Java processor as easy as building any other processor.

However, this is where the similarities between Java and Perl end. In Perl, the level of abstraction is much higher. Many of the functions in Perl that you use at a scripting level are, in fact, entire opcodes (much like CISC—Complex Instruction Set Computing—processors). Even functions as seemingly complex as the **grep** function are handled by a single opcode. The current distribution defines 350 opcodes. The source code for the opcode is hand optimized, which explains why Perl code executes so fast. When you "interpret" a Perl script, you are almost running native C code, just written (nay, translated) from Perl.

The use of such high-level opcode abstraction, and the hand-coded and optimized C source code that executes it, is why building a Perl compiler, which creates very fast stand-alone executables, is so easy. It also explains why the difference between interpreted Perl scripts and the generated executables is often minimal; in fact, I've often seen the so-called interpreted version working faster than the compiled version. This could be due to the effects of loading the wrapper that sits around the opcodes in order to make the run, or it could just be a complete fluke.

An opcode is defined by a C structure called **op** in the op.h header file. The important fields for any opcode are defined as follows:

```
OP*         op_next;
OP*         (*op_ppaddr)();
OPCODE      op_type;
```

The **op_next** field is a pointer to the next opcode to be executed when the current opcode has completed. The **op_type** field defines the type of opcode that will be executed. Different opcodes require different additional fields in order to define their execution. The list of opcode types can be determined from the **opcodes.pl** script, which is itself executed during the compilation of the interpreter. This file also conveniently lists all of the opcodes.

The **op_ppaddr** field contains the pointer to the function that will actually be executed. The functions are defined in the pp.c, pp_ctl.c, pp_sys.c, and pp_hot.c source files in the Perl distribution. The first three define a range of opcode functions that support the standard operators and functions, but the last is the most important from a speed point of view.

The pp_hot.c file contains all of the opcode functions that are hand optimized and are expected to be executed a number of times in a typical Perl script. The opcodes defined in this file include those related to assignments, regular expressions, conditional operators, and functions related to handling and converting scalar and list values.

It's also worth noting that there are opcodes for defining and obtaining different variables and constants. Even the definition of a constant within a Perl script is actually handled by an opcode. The significance of this will become apparent very shortly.

Remember that I described the opcode sequence as being a tree? This is because certain opcode functions require calls to additional opcodes for their information. Consider the following Perl script:

```
$a = $b + 2;
```

There are four opcodes in this statement. There are two operators—one is the assignment of the expression to the **$a** scalar, and the other is the addition of the **$b** scalar and the constant. There are also two values—one, the **$b** scalar; and the other, the constant value of 2. Each of these items—operators and values—is an opcode.

You can view the opcodes produced by the statement if your version of Perl has been built with the **-DDEBUGGING** option. The opcode tree is reproduced when you execute a Perl program using the **-Dx** command line option. For example, the command

```
perl -Dx -e '$a = $b +2;'
```

produces

```
{
8    TYPE = leave   ===> DONE
     FLAGS = (VOID,KIDS,PARENS)
     {
1        TYPE = enter   ===> 2
     }
     {
2        TYPE = nextstate   ===> 3
         FLAGS = (VOID)
         LINE = 1
```

```
      }
      {
7       TYPE = sassign  ===> 8
        FLAGS = (VOID,KIDS,STACKED)
          {
5           TYPE = add  ===> 6
            TARG = 1
            FLAGS = (SCALAR,KIDS)
              {
                TYPE = null  ===> (4)
                  (was rv2sv)
                FLAGS = (SCALAR,KIDS)
                  {
3                   TYPE = gvsv  ===> 4
                    FLAGS = (SCALAR)
                    GV = main::b
                  }
              }
              {
4               TYPE = const  ===> 5
                FLAGS = (SCALAR)
                SV = IV(2)
              }
          }
          {
            TYPE = null  ===> (7)
              (was rv2sv)
            FLAGS = (SCALAR,KIDS,REF,MOD,SPECIAL)
              {
6               TYPE = gvsv  ===> 7
                FLAGS = (SCALAR)
                GV = main::a
              }
          }
      }
    }
}
```

You can follow the execution through the opcode tree by following the opcode numbers. Each pair of braces defines the information about a single opcode, and nested braces show the parent-child relation between the opcodes. Execution starts at opcode number one, which simply passes execution to opcode number two, which actually just passes execution to number three after initializing the statement as being part of the first line (and only line) of the script. Opcode number three gets the scalar value of the **main::b** variable and places it onto the stack.

Execution is then passed to opcode number four, which places the static integer value of 2 onto the stack, which then passes execution to opcode number five, the "add" opcode. It takes the two arguments from the stack and adds them together, placing the result back on the stack for opcode six, which obtains the reference for the variable named **main::a** and places it on the stack. Then opcode seven assigns **main::a** the value of addition placed on the stack in opcode five. This is the end of the script.

The tree structure can be understood from this description. The assignation opcode has two siblings: the variable to which the value is to be assigned, and the value. The value is calculated from the result of the addition, which as a binary operator has two children: the values it is adding together. You can see this opcode structure more clearly in Figure 20-2.

Obviously, the more complex the statement, the more complex the opcode tree. Once you examine the output from a multiline script, you'll begin to identify just how efficient and complex the Perl opcode system is.

Compilation

The actual compilation stage is a multipass process that first processes the basic Perl script using the **yacc** parser. Language parsed by **yacc** is actually processed from the bottom up—the most complex expressions within single statements are processed first.

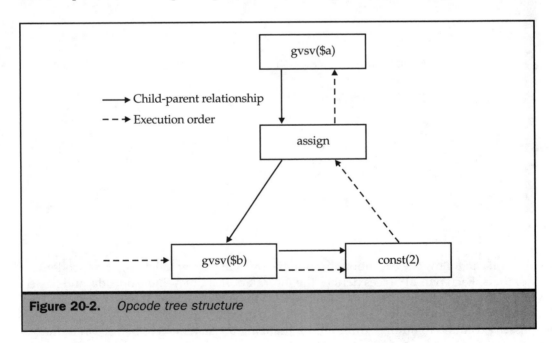

Figure 20-2.   *Opcode tree structure*

Therefore, the nodes at the deepest points (leaves) of an execution tree are populated first, before the higher opcodes (twigs and branches) are finally produced. Once all of the entire statements have been parsed, you can follow the execution line by line, by examining the trunk of the opcode tree.

Once all the opcodes have been produced, the compiler then goes over a number of optimization processes. The first is called *constant folding* and identifies entries that can be executed at the point of compilation. For example, the statement

```
$a = 4 + 5;
```

can be reduced from four opcodes to three by instead creating a parent opcode that assigns a value of 9 to the **$a** variable:

```
$a = 9;
```

You can see the effect of this by comparing the opcode tree for the more complex statement with the variable and constant tree you saw earlier:

```
{
6    TYPE = leave   ===> DONE
     FLAGS = (VOID,KIDS,PARENS)
     {
1        TYPE = enter   ===> 2
     }
     {
2        TYPE = nextstate   ===> 3
         FLAGS = (VOID)
         LINE = 1
     }
     {
5        TYPE = sassign   ===> 6
         FLAGS = (VOID,KIDS,STACKED)
         {
3            TYPE = const   ===> 4
             FLAGS = (SCALAR)
             SV = IV(9)
         }
         {
             TYPE = null   ===> (5)
               (was rv2sv)
             FLAGS = (SCALAR,KIDS,REF,MOD,SPECIAL)
```

```
                {
4                   TYPE = gvsv  ===> 5
                    FLAGS = (SCALAR)
                    GV = main::a
                }
            }
        }
    }
```

The next optimization process is *context propagation*, which is the act of defining the context to a specific opcode and its children. You are used to the terms *scalar context* or *list context* when creating and using functions. Internally, Perl also supports contexts for void, Boolean, and lvalue statements. Context propagation works top down—that is, parent opcodes are examined first, and the context requirement is then propagated down to child opcodes.

The final optimization stage is a process of reduction and is handled by the *peephole optimizer*. This process effectively executes the opcode tree, but without actually doing anything. The purpose is to look ahead to future opcodes in the tree and reduce them as much as possible. In Perl, the lookahead is currently only two statements, which means that a maximum of three statements could be reduced to just one statement.

Any larger figure would slow down the optimization process to the point that any gains made in optimizing the opcode tree would be lost in the optimization process itself. Remember that Perl is still essentially an interpreter, and—unlike C or Java—the opcode tree is regenerated each time a script is executed. When you execute a Perl script, Perl doesn't simply reexecute the previously optimized opcode tree. Perl assumes the source file has changed (probably a good idea).

Ultimately, this makes individual executions of the same script slower than they might be if the peephole optimization were allowed to look ahead further. On the other hand, it ensures that every execution of a script is optimized to a reasonable point, even if you change just one character in the original script each time.

Unfortunately, there is no way of controlling the peephole process. You cannot specify, for example, that when creating a stand-alone executable, the peephole lookahead value be greater than two, although this would be a great idea.

Execution

Once all three stages of the optimization have taken place, it's time to execute the code. The actual path of execution is not as sequential as it may have appeared earlier. All opcodes are numbered, and it's the value of the **op_next** (from the **op** structure) that defines the actual execution path. Since Perl supports conditional statements like **if** and loops like **while**, some opcodes may never be executed, or may be executed several

Opcodes and Safety

Many of the various methods for executing Perl in a safe manner rely on the ability of a single opcode to derive the source of its information. The taint-checking mechanism uses opcodes to ensure that any variable derived from data external to the current program is marked as possibly dangerous. Because you can trace the flow of data within a program via the opcode tree, it's easy for the taint-checking module to track external information.

If you want a very secure environment, you can use the **Safe** module, which we looked at briefly in Chapter 15 (see also Web Appendix B), to restrict the execution of code (rather than data) in a script. The **Opcode** module even allows you to restrict execution to a specific number of opcodes and then to execute a program within a safe compartment. If the compilation process creates an opcode tree that falls outside the environment you have specified, then an error is returned.

Without opcodes, the tracking and filtering at this level would not be possible, and it's one reason Perl is considered a secure environment for many development and e-commerce applications.

times. Perl, therefore, relies on the value of **op_next** returned by each opcode to decide which opcode to execute next.

For each opcode, Perl calls the corresponding function with the information on any child opcodes that are also required to call what the programmer recognizes as the original statement. Once all the opcodes in the desired execution path have been executed, the process ends, and Perl quits.

Perl's Internal Structures

For writing extensions to Perl and for embedding Perl within your C programs, you will need to understand the different structures used internally by the Perl interpreter. Although it's possible to skip this section, proper extension development requires that you know at least the basis of the different Perl data types and how they can be used with C functions rather than Perl functions and operators.

There are two core data structures that you need to consider: variables and the stack. The variables are the data-storage entities that you are accustomed to using within Perl. The stack is a special type of array that is used to pass information to functions and pass return values from functions back to the calling statement.

Note that the information here assumes you know C, at least well enough to know the basic structure of the program and how to call functions and handle variables. For some of the more complex elements, you will also need to understand C pointers. Although we are still talking about Perl, we will not be dealing with Perl source, only C.

If you prefer, you can skip this section now and just use it as a reference for the later parts of this chapter.

Variables

You already know that a number of different variables are available in Perl. At a base level, these are scalars, arrays, and hashes. You're probably also aware that there are references, typeglobs, and objects. A *reference* is essentially just a scalar variable that refers to a particular entity. A *typeglob* is a special structure that is mapped to all of the variables of different types with the same common name. An *object* is a special, or "magic," variable type and is treated separately, even though it's essentially a scalar value.

In each case, the value is stored internally as a structure that has been created as a new variable type with the **typedef** keyword. The name of each type is the two-letter acronym for the Perl data type; so a scalar value is stored in an **SV** structure, an array in an **AV** structure, and so on. There are two basic value types used in all the definitions: The **I32** is a signed integer that is guaranteed to be at least 32 bits wide, irrespective of the host platform. The **U32** value is an unsigned integer, also 32 bits wide. On a 64-bit machine, the values will be 64 bits wide.

In this section, we'll look at the macros that are defined within the Perl environment for accessing, modifying, and converting between the different variable types in their raw C format. We'll leave the use of these different functions to the remainder of this chapter.

Scalar Values

A scalar value, abbreviated **SV**, contains the contents of a scalar variable. Since a scalar variable can contain many different types of information, **SV**s are subclassified as integer values (**IV**s), doubles (**NV**s), strings (**PV**s), and references (**RV**s). The functions for using **AV**s are shown in Table 20-2.

Mortals   If you create an **SV**, it is up to you to automatically delete it once you have finished using it. If you set a variable to be mortal with **sv_2mortal** or one of the other mortal functions, Perl will delete it at the end of the current scope, unless it is used by a reference. Once the reference count reaches 0, Perl will call **sv_free** for you to free the **SV**.

 Do not call sv_free yourself; rely on the internal functions to do it for you.

References   You can reference a reference using the **SvRV()** function, and this can be used in combination with the **SvTYPE()** function to obtain the type of value that is referenced. The following code fragment will return a number relating to the value type. Refer to Table 20-1 for a list of definitions to use when identifying the type.

```
SvTYPE(SvRV(SV*)
```

Function/Macro	Description
SV* newSViv(I32)	Creates a new **SV** from an integer value.
SV* newSVnv(double)	Creates a new **SV** from a float or double value.
SV* newSVpv(char *str, int len)	Creates a new **SV** from a string of length **len**. The length will be calculated if **len** is 0.
SV* newSVsv(SV *)	Duplicates the scalar value. Creating a new empty scalar value requires the use of the special **sv_undef** global scalar.
SV* newSVrv(SV* rv, char *pkgname)	Creates a new **SV** and points **rv** to it. If **pkgname** is not null, then it blesses **rv** into that package. This is the method used to create references to scalars.
SV* newRV_inc(SV* other)	Creates a reference pointing to any type of value, specified by **other**, incrementing the reference count of the entity referred to. Can be used to create references to any type of value.
SV* newRV_noinc(SV* other)	Creates a reference pointing to any type of value, specified by **other**, without incrementing the reference count of the entity referred to. Can be used to create references to any type of value.
SvIOK(SV*)	Returns true if the **SV** is an **IV**.
SvNOK(SV*)	Returns true if the **SV** is an **NV**.
SvPOK(SV*)	Returns true if the **SV** is a **PV**.
SvROK(SV*)	Returns true if the **SV** is a reference (**RV**).
SvOK(SV*)	Returns true if the **SV** is not **undef**.
SvTRUE(SV*)	Returns true if the **SV** is true.

Table 20-2.   *Functions for Accessing and Using **SV**s*

DEVELOPING
APPLICATIONS

Function/Macro	Description

SVTYPE(SV*)	Returns a value referring to the **SV** type. Macros exist for the following:
	    SVt_IV (integer)
	    SVt_NV (double)
	    SVt_PV (string)
	    SVt_RV (reference)
	    SVt_PVAV (array)
	    SVt_PVHV (hash)
	    SVt_PVCV (code)
	    SVt_PVGV (glob)
	    SVt_PVMG (magic/blessed scalar)

IV SvIV(SV*)	Converts an **SV** to an **IV**. Returns 0 if the **SV** contains a non-numeric string.
double SvNV(SV*)	Converts an **SV** to a **double**.
char* SvPV(SV*, int len)	Converts an **SV** to a pointer to a string and updates **len** with the string's length.
SV* SvRV(SV*)	Dereferences a reference, returning an **SV**. This can then be cast to an **AV** or **HV** as appropriate.
sv_setiv(SV*, int)	Gives **SV** an integer value, converting **SV** to an **IV** if necessary.
sv_setiv(SV*, double)	Gives **SV** a double value, converting **SV** to an **NV** if necessary.
sv_setsv(SV* dest, SV* src)	Copies **dest** to **src**, ensuring that pointers **dest** != **src**.
sv_setpv(SV*, char *)	Gives **SV** a string value (assuming a null-terminated string), converting **SV** to a string if necessary.
sv_setpvn(SV*, char *, int len)	Gives **SV** a string value of length **len**, converting SV to a string if necessary.
sv_catpv(SV*, char*)	Concatenates the string to the **SV**.

Table 20-2. *Functions for Accessing and Using **SV**s (continued)*

Function/Macro	Description
svcatpvn(SV*, char*, int len)	Copies **len** characters from the string, appending them to the **SV**.
svcatsv(SV* A, SV* B)	Concatenates the **SV B** to the end of **SV A**.
sv_setref_iv(SV* rv, char *classname, int value)	Creates a new **IV** with the value of **value**, and points **rv** to it. If **classname** is non-null, then it blesses **rv** into that package.
sv_setref_nv(SV* rv, char *classname, double value)	Creates a new **NV** with the value of **value**, and points **rv** to it. If **classname** is non-null, then it blesses **rv** into that package.
sv_setref_pv(SV* rv, char *classname, char* value)	Creates a new **PV** with the value of **value**, and points **rv** to it. If **classname** is non-null, then it blesses **rv** into that package.
svREFCNT_dec(SV*)	Decrements the reference count for **SV**, calling **sv_free** if the count is 0.
SV* sv_bless(SV *rv, HV* stash)	Blesses **rv** within the package represented by **stash**.
int sv_isa(SV*, char *pkgname)	Returns 1 if the **SV** inherits from the class **pkgname**.
int sv_isobject(SV*)	Returns 1 if the **SV** is an object.
SV* sv_newmortal()	Creates a new blank mortal **SV**. See the section "Mortals."
SV* sv_2mortal(SV*)	Marks an existing **SV** as mortal. See the section "Mortals."
SV* sv_mortalcopy(SV*)	Duplicates an existing **SV** and makes the duplicate mortal. See the section "Mortals."
SV* perl_get_sv(char *varname, int create)	Gets the variable name within a Perl script specified by **varname**, which should be a fully qualified reference. If **create** is set to 1, then it creates a new scalar variable of that name.
sv_dump(SV*)	Pretty-prints a Perl variable (**SV**, **AV**, **HV**, etc.).

Table 20-2.   *Functions for Accessing and Using SVs* (continued)

Accessing Perl Variables by Name   The **perl_get_sv** function obtains an **SV** by its fully qualified name within the script. For example, to get the value of **$foo** in the **main** package:

```
SV *foo = perl_get_sv("main::foo",0);
```

There shouldn't be any need to create a variable of a specified name using this function, although it is possible. If you want to pass information back to a Perl script, you should probably be using return values from a function anyway.

Array Values

An array is just a sequential list of scalar values. This is stored within Perl as an array of pointers to **SV**s. Entries in an **AV** can be referenced with an index, and adding new entries beyond the current maximum index number automatically increases the size of the **AV**. The functions for accessing **AV**s are summarized in Table 20-3.

Function/Macro	Description
AV* newAV()	Creates a new, empty **AV**.
AV* av_make(int num, SV **ptr)	Creates a new **AV** populated with the **SV**s contained in ****ptr**.
I32 av_len(AV*)	Returns the highest index of the array. Note that this is not the number of elements in the array; indexes start at 0, so the value is equivalent to **scalar(@array)–1**, or **$#array**.
SV** av_fetch(AV *, I32 index, I32 lval)	Returns a pointer to the **SV** at location **index** from an **AV**. Because a pointer is returned, you can use the reference to update as well as access the value stored. If **lval** is non-zero, then it replaces the value at **index** with **undef**.
SV** av_store(AV*, I32 index, SV* val)	Stores an **SV val** at **index** within an **AV** and returns the pointer to the new element.

Table 20-3.   *Functions for Handling AVs*

Function/Macro	Description
void av_clear(AV*)	Deletes the references to all the SVs in an AV, but does not delete the AV.
void av_undef(AV*)	Deletes the AV.
void av_extend(AV*, int num)	Increases the size of the AV to **num** elements. If **num** is less than the current number of elements, it does nothing.
void av_push(AV*, SV*)	Pushes an SV onto the end of the AV. This is identical to the Perl **push** function.
SV* av_pop(AV*)	Pops an SV off the end of an AV. This is identical to the Perl **pop** function.
SV* av_shift(AV*)	Returns the first SV from an AV, deleting the first element. This is identical to the Perl **shift** function.
void av_unshift(AV*, I32 num)	Adds **num** elements to the end of an AV, but does not actually store any values. Use **av_store** to actually add the SVs onto the end of the AV. This is not quite identical to the operation of the **unshift** function.
AV* perl_get_av(char* varname, int create)	Gets the AV called **varname**, which should be a fully qualified name, without the leading @ sign. Creates an AV with the specified name if **create** is 1.

Table 20-3. *Functions for Handling AVs* (continued)

DEVELOPING APPLICATIONS

Hash Values

Hashes are only slightly more complex than AVs. A hash is a list of paired data consisting of a string key and a pointer to an SV. You cannot have two entries in a hash with the same key; trying to store a new value with an existing key will simply overwrite that value. The functions for accessing HVs are summarized in Table 20-4.

Function/Macro	Description
HV* newHV()	Creates a new, empty **HV**.
SV** hv_store(HV* hash, char* key, U32 klen, SV* val, U32 hashval)	Stores the pointer to **SV** against the **key**. You must supply the length of the key in **klen**. The value of **hashval** is the hash value used for storage. If it is 0, then the value is computed for you. The return value is a pointer to the location of the new value within the hash.
SV** hv_fetch(HV* hash, char* key, U32 klen, I32 lval)	Fetches an entry from an **HV**, returning a pointer to the value.
SV* hv_delete(HV* hash, char* key, U32 klen, I32 flags)	Deletes the element specified by **key**, returning a mortal copy of the value that was stored at that position. If you don't want this value, then specify **G_DISCARD** in the **flags** element.
void hv_clear(HV* hash)	Empties the contents of the hash, but does not delete the hash itself.
void hv_undef(HV* hash)	Empties the contents of the hash and then deletes it.
I32 hv_iterinit(HV* hash)	Returns the number of elements in the **HV**, and prepares for iteration through the hash.
SV* hv_iternextsv(HV* hash, char** key, I32* pkeylen)	Returns the value for the next element in the hash. The key is placed into the variable pointed to by **key**, the physical length of which is placed into the variable pointed to by **pkeylen**. This is the function used with the **keys**, **values**, and **each** functions within Perl.
HV* perl_get_hv(char* varname, int create)	Gets the hash named **varname**, which should be a fully qualified package name. If **create** is 1, the hash is created.

Table 20-4. *Accessing HVs*

Glob Values

A typeglob or glob value (**GV**) relates real value types with a symbol table entry. This enables you to pass a typeglob in a Perl script and have the function use the correct type of value. Normally, this is used for passing filehandles, but it can also be used for scalars, arrays, hashes, functions, and even formats. The result is that a single identifier, such as **value**, can be used as **$value**, **@value**, **%value**, and so on. What in fact happens is that the main identifier is referenced to each of the different value types through the glob value, which is an element in the symbol table hash. Strictly speaking, it's a "stash," short for symbol table hash.

Some of the stash values are available directly within the C environment. These are **$_**, **$@**, **$&**, **$`**, and **$'**, and they relate to the C variables **defgv**, **errgv**, **ampergv**, **leftgv**, and **rightgv**, respectively.

The functions for accessing glob values are a modified subset of those used to access hash values, with functions closely tailored to the glob process. The functions are summarized in Table 20-5.

Function/Macro	Description
GvSV	Returns a pointer to an **SV**.
GvAV	Returns a pointer to an **AV**.
GvHV	Returns a pointer to an **HV**.
GvIO	Returns a pointer to a filehandle.
GvFORM	Returns a pointer to a format.
HV *gv_stashpv(char* name, int create)	Gets the corresponding **HV** for the glob named **name**, and creates it if **create** is equal to 1.
HV *gv_stashsv(SV *, int create)	Gets the corresponding **HV** for the glob named by the **SV**, and creates it if **create** is equal to 1.
HV *SvSTASH(SV* sv)	Gets the stash from a blessed object **sv**. You will need to use **SvRV(sv)** to dereference **sv** if it's a reference.
char* HvNAME(HV* stash)	Given a stash entry, returns the package name.

Table 20-5.   *Accessing Glob Values*

Other Values

Perl also supports objects and code values (**CV**) within the C environment. However, the methods for accessing these different elements are handled separately in this chapter. A **CV** can be accessed using a number of special functions, which are actually the functions used when you want to call Perl functions; therefore, they are covered under the "Embedding Perl" section later in the chapter.

The Stack

In Chapter 8, we looked at the use of a list or array as a stack. Data was pushed onto the top of the stack using **push**, and data was taken back using **pop**. The **push/pop** stack was classed as a LIFO stack (last in, first out). The same principle is used within Perl to store the arguments that are passed to a function during a function call.

This is better understood with an example. When the **print** function is called with arguments, the strings and variables that are passed to it are pushed onto a stack. The internal function for **print** is then called, and its first action is to take the variables from the stack.

The actual sequence is slightly longer, since the Perl interpreter and the stack-handling system need to know when a function wants to examine the stack, and how many elements of the stack are actually destined for the function. The result is that there are two stacks. One is the real stack where the data is stored. The other is a stack of pointers, called the *markstack*, that shows where within the main stack the elements for a particular function start. You can see a sample diagram that demonstrates a simple function call, **add(2,2)**, in Figure 20-3.

You can see from the diagram that the arguments to the **add()** function are stored in order from bottom to top. The function can determine how many arguments it has been passed by calculating the difference between the top of its stack and the stack pointer information for the function in markstack.

The result is that the @_ array to the **add()** function is populated with the contents of the stack. Within the realms of the Perl interpreter, this happens automatically. Perl populates the stack when the **add()** function is called, and populates the contents of @_ within the context of the **add()** function for you to do with what you will. When the function exits, any return values are placed back on the Perl stack, so that the calling function can use the returned values. If the caller does not use the values, a special function is called, which removes the return values from the stack and also the corresponding markstack pointer.

When you are accessing the internals of the Perl interpreter via C, you need to do this stack manipulation manually. This is true whether you are calling Perl functions or creating Perl extensions. In both instances, you will need to be able to exchange information between the Perl environment and the functions that make up the Perl interpreter.

There are some differences between the two environments that imply the need for this interface. Most significant of these is that Perl supports multiple values to be passed both to and from a function. Within C, a function can only return a single entity.

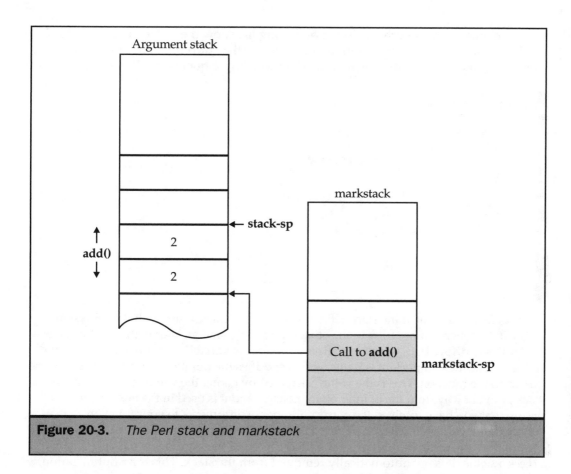

Figure 20-3. *The Perl stack and markstack*

Although this can include structures and unions, this feature is not supported in Perl. The use of a stack to hold the variables going in and out of a function supports the multiple value syntax that is one of the powerful features of Perl.

We'll deal with the use of the stack within a Perl extension first and then look at the effects of embedding Perl on the stack.

Stack Access Within Extensions

When a C function is called from Perl, the Perl stack is used to pass any arguments to the function. The process for retrieving arguments within the C code and then passing return values back is as follows:

1. Initialize the stack interface (**dXSARGS**).
2. Retrieve an argument from the stack into a variable (**ST**).
3. Place the return values back on the stack (**XSRETURN***).

The elements in parentheses in the preceding list show the function macro that is used to achieve the desired operation. Returning to the **add()** function discussed previously, the C function incorporating the preceding sequence can be seen here:

```
XS(XS_StatVFS_add)
{
    dXSARGS;
    if (items != 2)
        croak("Usage: StatVFS::add(a,b)");
    SP -= items;
    {
        int     a = (int)SvIV(ST(0));
        int     b = (int)SvIV(ST(1));
                XSRETURN_IV(a+b);
        PUTBACK;
        return;
    }
}
```

The **XS()** statement at the start defines a new C function for use with the XS system. This will be covered more fully in the "Extending Perl" section, later in this chapter. The next call is to **dXSARGS**, which initializes a number of variables for use in the rest of the function. The most important is **items**, which specifies the number of arguments that were passed to the function. This is the value calculated by taking the value of the top of the stack pointer away from the pointer on markstack, and it is used in the next line to ensure that you have received the correct number of arguments to your function.

Next, the value of the stack pointer is reset to the beginning. You need to do this to ensure that any return values are not added on top of the arguments passed. When you access a value, it is not automatically removed from the stack. This is an optimization, since doing this deletion would add overhead that just isn't required if you manage the stack properly in the first place.

The next two lines actually extract the arguments from the stack. **ST()** is a special macro that accesses the stack directly. The first element, **ST(0)**, is equivalent to **$_[0]** within a Perl function. Note that the values are accessed in order, rather than popping them from the stack. This is to ensure that you receive the variables in the order that they were supplied in the code, not in the order they were pushed onto the stack.

The next line does the calculation by calling the **XSRETURN_IV()** macro. This macro places a new **IV** (integer) value onto the stack, ready to be returned to the caller. You can only use this and its related functions for passing back single variables to the caller. For returning lists, you need to use a different method. See the "Extending Perl" section for more details.

The next line is not required. The **PUTBACK** macro is used to specify that you have finished placing values onto the stack. The **XS** stubs insert this function automatically—although if you are hand coding the function, you can get away without using it.

That's it. The function has been defined and the arguments have successfully been taken from the stack and then put back. The available macros that you can use in this process are summarized in Table 20-6.

If you want to place more than one variable onto the stack to return to the caller, you will need to use a different method from the previous example. Instead, you will need to push values onto the stack, either with a push function or by accessing the stack elements directly using **ST()**. Either way, you should still, ideally, specify the number of elements you have pushed back onto the stack by calling **XSRETURN()**. For example, the following lines push both an addition and a subtraction calculation onto the stack:

```
XPUSHs(sv_2mortal(newSViv(a+b)));
XPUSHs(sv_2mortal(newSViv(a-b)));
XSRETURN(1);
```

Macro	Description
dXSARGS	Defines the local variables used by other macros. Defines the **items** variable, which contains the number of items passed to the function via the stack.
SV* ST(*n*)	Retrieves element *n* from the stack as an **SV**. The first parameter is **ST(0)**.
XSRETURN(*n*)	Specifies the number of elements, *n*, you have left on the stack, adjusting the reference stored on the markstack.
XSRETURN_NO	Returns a value of **0**, and calls **XSRETURN(1)**.
XSRETURN_YES	Returns a value of **1**, and calls **XSRETURN(1)**.
XSRETURN_UNDEF	Returns a value of **undef**, and calls **XSRETURN(1)**.
XSRETURN_EMPTY	Returns a value of **0**, and calls **XSRETURN(1)**.
XSRETURN_IV()	Places a mortal **integer** on the stack, and calls **XSRETURN(1)**.
XSRETURN_NV()	Places a mortal **float** on the stack, and calls **XSRETURN(1)**.
XSRETURN_PV()	Places a mortal **char*** on the stack, and calls **XSRETURN(1)**.

Table 20-6.   *Macros for Using the Stack Within Extensions*

DEVELOPING APPLICATIONS

The specification of these as mortal ensures that the values will be automatically freed at the end of the scope. See the earlier "Scalar Values" section for more information on marking them as mortal.

Stack Access for Embedded Perl

The process for calling a single Perl function with arguments is more or less identical to the previous extension example, except that the process is done in reverse. The process is as follows:

1. Initialize the environment (**dSP**).

2. Start the scope (**ENTER**).

3. Set up the environment such that temporary variables will be automatically deleted at the end of the scope (**SAVETMPS**).

4. Remember the current top of the stack (**PUSHMARK**).

5. Push arguments onto the stack (**XPUSHs**).

6. Signify the end of the arguments (**PUTBACK**).

7. Call the Perl function.

8. Signify the start of return value reclamation (**SPAGAIN**).

9. Get the values from the stack (**POP***).

10. Signify the end of return-value reclamation (**PUTBACK**).

11. Free the temporary variables.

12. End the scope (**LEAVE**).

The same **add()** function example will be used to demonstrate this sequence in practice. We'll assume the **add()** function has already been defined within the Perl environment.

```
void perl_add(int a, int b)
{
    int retval;
    dSP;
    ENTER;
    SAVETMPS;
    PUSHMARK(sp);
    XPUSHs(sv_2mortal(newSViv(a)));
    XPUSHs(sv_2mortal(newSViv(b)));
    PUTBACK;
    retval = perl_call_pv("add", G_SCALAR);
    SPAGAIN;
    if (retval == 1)
```

```
     printf("Returned: %d\n",POPi);
PUTBACK;
FREETMPS;
LEAVE;
}
```

If you followed the sequence at the start of this section, you should be able to follow the sequence in the code. The important parts are the calls to **XPUSHs**, which place the mortal values of the two arguments passed to the **perl_add** function onto the stack, and the **POPi** call. This pops the values placed onto the stack by the call to the Perl **add()** function off the stack. In this example, it's used in a **printf()** statement.

The values popped off the stack in this way come off in the inverse order in which the values were placed onto the stack. That is, the last value in a list will be returned first. You'll need to account for this if you are accepting multiple values back from the Perl function.

The macros available when embedding Perl are summarized in Table 20-7.

Macro	Description
dSP	Sets up the environment for the following macros.
ENTER	Starts the scope of the call.
SAVETMPS	Marks all mortal variables created after this call to be deleted when **FREETMPS** is called.
PUSHMARK	Defines the start of the arguments to be pushed onto the stack.
XPUSHs	Pushes a scalar value onto the stack, extending the stack if necessary.
XPUSHn	Pushes a double onto the stack, extending the stack if necessary.
XPUSHp	Pushes a string onto the stack, extending the stack if necessary.
XPUSHi	Pushes an integer onto the stack, extending the stack if necessary.
XPUSHu	Pushes an unsigned integer onto the stack, extending the stack if necessary.
PUSHs	Pushes a scalar value onto the stack. The stack must have room to accept the new value.
PUSHn	Pushes a double onto the stack. The stack must have room to accept the new value.

Table 20-7. *Macros Used When Embedding Perl Statements*

Macro	Description
PUSHp	Pushes a string onto the stack. The stack must have room to accept the new value.
PUSHi	Pushes an integer onto the stack. The stack must have room to accept the new value.
PUSHu	Pushes an unsigned integer onto the stack. The stack must have room to accept the new value.
PUTBACK	Defines the end of the arguments placed on the stack.
SPAGAIN	Defines the start of the process for obtaining return values.
POPi	Pops an **int** value from the stack.
POPl	Pops a **long** value from the stack.
POPn	Pops a **double** value from the stack.
POPp	Pops a **pointer** value from the stack.
POPs	Pops a **char*** (string) value from the stack.
PUTBACK	Defines the end of the process for obtaining return values.
FREETMPS	Clears the variables marked as mortal.
LEAVE	Ends the scope.

Table 20-7. *Macros Used When Embedding Perl Statements* (continued)

Stack Size

The size of the stack is finite. Although you can normally add values to the stack without having to worry about its size, you may run into problems if you are passing a large number of variables between the C and Perl environments. The quickest way to increase the size of the stack is to use the **EXTEND** macro, as in

```
EXTEND(sp,10);
```

If you use the **XPUSHs** macro to place values onto the stack, and you remember to reset the stack pointer to the beginning, you shouldn't need to use this macro, since **XPUSHs** increases the stack automatically. The XS interface resets the stack pointer for you when it creates the C code for the individual functions.

In practice, I've never had to use the **EXTEND** macro; but as a general rule, if you are returning or accepting more than ten elements, you may want to use this function to increase the available stack space. Remember, however, that increasing stack space also increases the memory footprint of your application.

Internals Summary

You should now be armed with all of the information that (in fact, more information than) you will need for interfacing between C and Perl. The next two sections deal with the specifics of developing extensions to the Perl environment and the different methods for embedding Perl within an application.

Extending Perl

Writing a Perl extension is seen by many as a black art, only to be conducted by senior programmers in the recesses of their programming environments. Unlike modules, which only require a modicum of Perl knowledge to create, extensions require not only knowledge of C or C++, but also knowledge of the internals in order to make your extensions work within the Perl interpreter.

The process of creating an external C extension is actually more straightforward than you think. An understanding of the internals of the Perl interpreter is not required, even by a relatively advanced extension programmer. You can write complex extensions using a small subset of the range that is available. That said, the introductory material provided in this and the previous chapter should prove invaluable to the understanding of the processes and conversions involved.

Once you are comfortable with the process we'll examine—or just because your curiosity gets the better of you—you can examine the Perl documentation for more in-depth detail. For reference, all the internals of the extension process and of the Perl interpreter itself are in the perlxs, perlxstut, and perlguts man pages. For further information, you might also want to refer to the perlcall and perlembed man pages, which contain information on the data interface between Perl and C, as well as details of how to embed a Perl interpreter into your C programs, which is also the next major topic in this chapter.

The process of developing the interface is made easier by two tools that eliminate much of the complexity involved: one is called the XS interface, and the other is called SWIG. The XS interface system is part of the standard Perl distribution and actually refers to the language used to define the interface. The Simplified Wrapper and Interface Generator (SWIG) is a third-party system written by Dave Beazley. It's also based on an intermediary language that defines the interface between the two language environments.

You will notice, as we progress through this section, that much of the information here is not actually specific to producing extensions. The functions and methods explained will also apply to the process of calling the Perl interpreter from a C program. Conversion of information from C variables to the variable types used by the Perl interpreter—and, therefore, the Perl language—make up the bulk of the information provided, and the processes are vital for either extending or embedding Perl using C and C++.

DEVELOPING
APPLICATIONS

The Extension Interface

The Perl interpreter has the ability to call external C functions. This is the basis of many of the built-in functions. When you call a function within Perl, it looks for the definition of the function. If it's a Perl function, it just jumps execution of the opcode tree to the start of the function definition. If it's a built-in function, it makes a call to the underlying C function, if necessary, or uses one of the data-handling functions you saw at the start of this chapter. If the function is neither built in nor a Perl-defined function, then it can be loaded from an external dynamic library. The development of an extension, therefore, requires you to build the library that Perl loads in order to execute your customized C function.

The actual process is slightly more complex than just creating a new function in C and installing it in the Perl directory hierarchy. There are some fundamental differences between the format of Perl data types and their C counterparts. C, for example, does not by default support hashes, whereas Perl does.

The development process must also create some code that interfaces between the internals of the Perl interpreter and the internals of a C function. This is called *glue code*, and it solves the two main differences between Perl and C—data types and memory management.

Data types in Perl are actually complex C structures. Some of the structure and complexity can be found at the beginning of this chapter where we looked at the different Perl variable types and the functions that enable you to access them. Most of the base data types, such as integers and strings, are handled automatically by both XS and SWIG. More complex structures and data types, including C structures and Perl objects, must have special typemapping code written for them so that both sides of the interface are able to access and use the information stored within them.

Perl handles all of its memory management automatically. When you create new variables and delete or undefine them, Perl automatically allocates and deallocates the necessary storage for each variable. C, on the other hand, expects you to do all of this explicitly. For simple variables, this means specifying their size at the initialization stage; but for more complex or large variables, you have to use the **calloc()** or **malloc()** function to allocate the memory, and **free()** to deallocate it when you've finished.

In addition, both interfaces solve two further problems—that of the specializations available in Perl and the necessary glue code to make the functions work. Specializations include the use of objects, packages, and multiple return values, which a Perl programmer takes for granted. The glue code is all of the necessary wrapper and interface code that makes a simple C function accessible within Perl.

XS Overview

The XS interface is part of the standard Perl distribution; and, as such, it is given more attention here than the third-party SWIG interface. XS, or XSUB, stands for eXternal SUBroutine. The term "XS" is usually taken to refer to the interface system, while "XSUB" specifies an individual function within the XS definition. Using the special language called XS, you specify the interface between a Perl module and the C functions you want access to. The actual layout is not hugely different from a typical C header file, except that the information is organized and structured to include the necessary links for the Perl side of the equation.

The XS file is then parsed by the **xsubpp** script, which processes the contents and spits out the C source code ready for compilation. The code includes all the necessary glue code and initialization procedures. You are expected to supply a suitable module for communicating between Perl and the underlying library; but, otherwise, the process is completed.

Because of the similarity of the XS file to a header file, there is a tool, **h2xs**, that will convert existing header files into the XS format. This greatly simplifies the process of manually writing an interface to a C library by doing most of the work for you. In most cases, the converted file can be passed immediately onto **xsubpp**, and the resulting C source file is compiled without any further intervention.

SWIG Overview

The SWIG system takes a slightly different tack. SWIG, itself, was designed as an interface builder between C functions and a number of scripting systems. At the time of this book's writing, they include Perl, Python, Tcl, Guile, and Eiffel. A Java extension has also just been released that provides yet another tool for bringing Java to the desktop.

Like XS, SWIG uses an intermediary file that defines the interface between the C code and the high-level language at which the SWIG definitions are aimed. The result is two files—the glue code in a C file and the Perl module file that can be used to access it. This is more automated than the XS system, which requires you to develop your own module file if you are producing the XS file manually. With **h2xs**, of course, this is not an issue.

One big difference between SWIG and XS is that SWIG is capable of providing the necessary code to support the complex structures within C and objects within C++. The **h2xs** tool, on the other hand, is fairly dumb and can only handle simple data types and functions. Although you can design your own interface and typemap systems, it adds overhead to what is already a complex process.

On the other hand, I very rarely find myself passing back structures or objects to Perl. Instead, I use the other features, such as hashes and multiple return values, to return the information. If you consider **getpwent** and similar functions, they all supply information back to the caller as structures when used in the C environment; but within Perl, the values are returned as a list.

Because of this generalized approach, SWIG is a much more practical solution if you are developing extensions to many scripting languages simultaneously. I've used it before for providing the same basic interface to a C library for both Python and Perl, to suit the needs of two different clients at the same time. On a personal level, I actually prefer to use the XS system for Perl and SWIG for other languages if I'm developing for them in isolation. If I have to develop a library that will be practical for many languages, I use SWIG, if only to cut down on the headaches from developing with two different systems.

There is a school of thought that says XS is better than SWIG because it's a Perl-derived tool and can, therefore, take advantage of the Perl environment better than SWIG. I've never once found that to be the case. The two systems produce code that is almost identical, and unless you are doing something very Perl specific, it's likely that either tool will suit you well. The other thing to consider is that all of the modules on CPAN are provided as XS rather than SWIG extensions. If you ever plan to provide your module to the Perl community, use XS.

Using XS

For the process of designing an extension, we'll be examining the creation of two sample modules. The first is our own interface to the standard C math library, which will help us cover the basics of the XS process. The other is more complex and will demonstrate the advanced features of the XS interface as we develop a simple module that obtains the size of a file system using the **statvfs()** function that is available on many Unix platforms. The result will be a new Perl function. You supply the directory or file name, and the function will provide a list of scalars, detailing the total size of the file system, and the amount of space used and available.

Although this example could be classed as platform specific (it was generated on a Sun Solaris 2.4 machine), the principles learned here will easily translate to other functions and modules. Where necessary, we'll also be sidetracking to look at the other features and capabilities of the XS system.

The h2xs Converter

For all libraries there is a corresponding header file that contains the definitions of any constant values, structure definitions, and the prototypes of any functions contained within the library. Although the XS system does not handle C structures, you can use the **h2xs** utility to convert an existing header file into an XS file, suitable for producing the interface.

The **h2xs** command reads in the contents of the header file and produces an XS file that consists of all the basic definitions and function-interface components to make the C functions available as an extension in Perl. The file produced is very basic and is only suitable for functions that return one of the basic data types. You will need to modify the file if you want to do more complex conversions or if you want to return, say, the contents of a structure as a list of return values. The modification and production of this information makes up the bulk of this section of the chapter.

In addition, **h2xs** produces a module file with all the necessary code required to import the external C function and provide the necessary constants and other values to a Perl script. The module file also includes a bare template of some POD (Plain Old Documentation)–formatted documentation that you should modify if you plan to distribute the module to other people.

The other major component is a Perl makefile called Makefile.PL. This contains the absolute minimum of definitions required to ensure that the **MakeMaker** module produces a makefile suitable for building and installing the extension. This takes a lot of the guesswork out of the process of compiling the extension, as you will see. It's also the method used in the CPAN modules to automatically extract, build, and install the extension on any destination machine. See Chapter 2, for more information.

Finally, **h2xs** produces a test script and two documentation files. The test.pl file just calls each of the functions mentioned to make sure they could be loaded. Again, this file should be modified to include more complex tests to ensure that the extension can be used properly. By default, it's the script used to test the distribution when a **make test** command is run. The Changes file is provided for you to record any modifications, and the MANIFEST file lists the files that make up the core files required for the extension. These files are vital components of a typical CPAN module, because they provide additional information to the user about the expected contents of the package they have downloaded.

The **h2xs** script is very straightforward to use:

```
$ h2xs /usr/include/sys/statvfs.h
Writing Statvfs/Statvfs.pm
Writing Statvfs/Statvfs.xs
Writing Statvfs/Makefile.PL
Writing Statvfs/test.pl
Writing Statvfs/Changes
Writing Statvfs/MANIFEST
```

The file name and package name are title case, as per the usual Perl standards; and, depending on the source content, the files are written into a separate subdirectory. In theory, the files produced should be ready for compilation and installation. If you need to include additional libraries when using the functions, you should append the library names to the command line you supply.

There are also some options to the **h2xs** command, but refer to the man page for more information. The core of the XS system is the XS file; and, although one is produced by the **h2xs** system, it is much more likely that you will want to build in some form of customization.

The .xs File

The XS file is the core of the XS system. It defines the interface between Perl and the underlying C functions you are providing an interface to. Although in some cases the file will be automatically produced by the **h2xs** utility, it's unlikely that it will perfectly match either the desired results or the interface you have come to expect between callers and functions in the Perl language.

DEVELOPING
APPLICATIONS

Once the XS file has been created, it is parsed by a Perl script, **xsubpp**, which takes the information provided and produces the C source file with the necessary statements required to build the interface library.

The format of the file is as follows:

```
C includes

MODULE: Name PACKAGE: Name

OPTIONS

function definitions
```

The top section is passed verbatim onto the C source file that is generated. The headers you include at this point should consist of all the headers required for the functions you are using. The **PACKAGE** and **MODULE** definitions set the module and package names. There are then a number of **OPTIONS** that affect the whole interface process, before you proceed to the function definitions.

The format of the **function definitions** is very strict. The return type is specified first, on its own line, followed by the name of the function and a list of argument names that can be supplied. Then, one per line, come the data type declarations for the argument names. These type declarations are also very strict. If you are defining a pointer to an argument (as in **char* string**), the asterisk must remain with the type, not the argument name. Finally, there are a number of function-specific options. We'll cover all these different aspects as we examine the different XS file complexities.

If we look at a real function definition for our math interface, you can see the format more clearly:

```
double
tan (value)
        double value
```

As you can see, the return value is specified on its own line, and the function's only argument is specified on its own line. This is actually all you need to do if the function is simple. In this case, the **tan()** function accepts and returns a simple value, so there is no need to do any conversion between, say, a structure and a list of return values for Perl. The XS interface system will handle everything else during the compilation process. It really is that simple and straightforward.

You need to understand that the functions you "define" within the XS file are merely function mappings between the function as it will appear in Perl, and the function call and arguments accepted within the C environment. In the preceding example, a map is created between the **tan** function in Perl and the **tan()** function in C.

The definition of the passed and returned values helps the XS process identify the arguments supported by the Perl function and determine how they translate to the underlying C function. The actual conversion of the values is handled automatically by the XS system in conjunction with a predefined typemap.

Let's look at a more complex example—this time the **StatVFS** module, which we'll use to discuss the more advanced components of the XS file structure. The full file can be seen next. It defines two functions: **fsavail** and **fsstat**. The **fsavail** function is a simple one-shot function to find out the number of bytes available on a file system. It returns a long integer specifying the number of bytes. The **fsstat** function returns a list of values containing the total size, space used, and space available for a file system. In both cases, the functions take a single argument—a string containing a file path. The internal **statvfs** function uses this to determine which file system to return the space for.

```
#include "perl.h"
#include "XSUB.h"

#include <sys/types.h>
#include <sys/statvfs.h>


MODULE = StatVFS    PACKAGE = StatVFS


PROTOTYPES: DISABLE

long
fsavail (path)
        char *  path
        CODE:
                struct statvfs vfsrec;
                int statreturn;
                statreturn = statvfs(path,&vfsrec);
                if (statreturn == 0)
                {
                    RETVAL = (vfsrec.f_frsize * vfsrec.f_bavail);
                }
                else
                {
                    RETVAL = -1;
                }
        OUTPUT:
        RETVAL

void
```

```
fsstat (path)
        char *   path
        PPCODE:
        {
                struct statvfs vfsrec;
                int statreturn;
                statreturn = statvfs(path,&vfsrec);
                if (statreturn == 0)
                {
                    PUSHs(sv_2mortal(
                            newSViv(vfsrec.f_frsize *
                                    vfsrec.f_blocks)));
                    PUSHs(sv_2mortal(
                            newSViv((vfsrec.f_frsize *
                                    (vfsrec.f_blocks
                                    -vfsrec.f_bavail))))));
                    PUSHs(sv_2mortal(
                            newSViv((vfsrec.f_frsize *
                                    vfsrec.f_bavail))));
                }
        }
```

The important things to note with this file are the function definitions. For both functions, you are no longer mapping directly between the supported C function, **statvfs()**, and its identical cousin in Perl, **statvfs**. Instead, you are creating brand-new functions that act as wrappers around the underlying calls to the **statvfs()** C function. You no longer rely on XS to do the translation, because the underlying function you are calling returns a C structure, not a single value. C doesn't support multiple return values, so you need to do some manipulation of the information returned in order to translate it into a simple list of values.

For the **fsavail** function, you rely on the XS system to convert between the **long** that you've stated as the return value, and a normal integer value within Perl. You assign the return value to a special variable, **RETVAL**, and then mark that variable with the **OUTPUT:** keyword as the value to be returned to Perl when this function is called.

For the **fsstat** function, you do this conversion within a **PPCODE** block, which tells the XS interface builder that you are manipulating the contents of the Perl stack directly, rather than supplying a return value. The first few steps create the required C structures and then call the **statvfs()** library function to populate the structure with the information you want. In addition to the **PPCODE:** definition, you also need to ensure that the function is defined as **void**, since you are not directly returning any values from the function.

Then you push values onto the Perl argument stack with the **PUSHs** function, which you saw in the section "Stack Access for Embedded Perl," earlier in this chapter. This pushes a scalar value—in this case, an integer—onto the stack. You could (and perhaps should) have used the **XPUSHs** function, to ensure that the stack was extended accordingly. For only three values, we're probably safe with **PUSHs**.

Note that the calculated values are encapsulated within a call to **newSViv**, which creates a new integer scalar value; and **sv_2mortal**, which marks the scalar value as mortal, allowing it to be deleted when the whole process has finished. This helps prevent memory problems by freeing up values after they have been used—you have no need for those temporary values in the calculation.

Also note that error checking is supported in the **fsstat** by returning an empty list, the default return value on an error; **fsavail** returns –1 on an error, also the default operation when calling external system functions. Remember that you can't use 0 as a return value, because that could equally indicate that there was no available space on the drive.

For reference, the format for the **statvfs** C structure is shown here:

```
typedef struct statvfs {
        u_long  f_bsize;          /* fundamental file system block size */
        u_long  f_frsize;         /* fragment size */
        u_long  f_blocks;         /* total # of blocks of f_frsize on fs */
        u_long  f_bfree;          /* total # of free blocks of f_frsize */
        u_long  f_bavail;         /* # of free blocks avail to non-root */
        u_long  f_files;          /* total # of file nodes (inodes) */
        u_long  f_ffree;          /* total # of free file nodes */
        u_long  f_favail;         /* # of free nodes avail to non-superuser */
        u_long  f_fsid;           /* file system id (dev for now) */
        char    f_basetype[FSTYPSZ]; /* target fs type name */
        u_long  f_flag;           /* bit-mask of flags */
        u_long  f_namemax;        /* maximum file name length */
        char    f_fstr[32];       /* filesystem-specific string */
        u_long  f_filler[16];     /* reserved for future expansion */
} statvfs_t;
```

Again, the process is relatively straightforward. If you know how to program in C, you should be able to create and access the necessary structures and use the techniques shown here to produce a customized interface to a C function. Of course, there is no reason to use and translate values determined by an external function; you could use the **CODE** or **PPCODE** block to define your C function without requiring an external function at all.

XS Keywords

You've already seen some of the keywords used by the XS system to indicate different operations and situations. The full list is given here, including all the currently supported keywords and operations.

As a general rule, all keywords with a trailing colon expect some form of argument, statement, or code block following them. Keywords without a trailing colon are generally assigned to (as with **RETVAL**), or assign values or options to an existing statement (as in **NO_INIT**). The exact location and use of these varies, so ensure you understand the descriptions and locations given.

ALIAS: You can specify additional unique Perl names for the current **XSUB** using the **ALIAS:** keyword. The format used is a simple assignation statement, where each individual name should be given an incremental integer value. When the subroutine is called, you can identify which name was used by the value of the **ix** variable, which will contain the number defined in the **XSUB**. If **ix** contains 0, then it was called by its original name. The following example shows that **fsavail** is also available as **spaceavail** and **fileavail**:

```
long
fsavail (path)
        char *  path
        ALIAS:
        spaceavail = 1
        fileavail  = 2
        CODE:
                struct statvfs vfsrec;
                int statreturn;
                statreturn = statvfs(path,&vfsrec);
                if (statreturn == 0)
                {
                    RETVAL = (vfsrec.f_frsize * vfsrec.f_bavail);
                }
                else
                {
                    RETVAL = -1;
                }
        OUTPUT:
        RETVAL
```

BOOT: This keyword defines the code to be added as part of the extension's bootstrap function, which is used to register the **XSUB** within the current Perl interpreter. The **xsubpp** program actually generates the bootstrap function, and the statements added with the **BOOT:** keyword will be appended to the standard bootstrap code. The keyword can be used at any time after the **MODULE** keyword, and a blank line will terminate the bootstrap code.

C_ARGS: This keyword allows you to define an alternate sequence for passing the arguments received to the underlying function. For example, if you were providing an interface to a program that calculated the power of a number,

```
int power(raise, number);
```

you might want to provide the function within Perl as

```
power(number, raise);
```

The definition you would use might be

```
int
power(number, raise)
    int number;
    int raise;
C_ARGS:
    raise, number
```

This negates the need to use the **CODE:** or **PPCODE:** keyword.

CASE: The **CASE:** keyword allows you to set up a multiple-choice option list within an **XSUB**. The **CASE:** statement can switch via an **XSUB** parameter, via the **ix** variable, via the **ALIAS:** keyword, or through the **items** variable (see the "Accepting Variable-Length Argument Lists" section, later in the chapter). The **CASE:** keyword must be the first entry in the **XSUB** definition, and it will swallow all remaining arguments to the current **XSUB**, regardless of their contents.

The format of **CASE:** is very similar to a typical **switch** statement within the standard Unix shell. For example, the following is an alternative to the **ALIAS:** and **C_ARGS:** keywords. This time, the **CASE:** keyword is used to allow both **power** (which raises **a** to the power of **b**) and **r_power** (which raises **b** to the power of **a**):

```
int
power(a, b)
CASE: ix == 1
    ALIAS:
    r_power = 1
```

```
    INPUT:
    int a
    int b
    CODE:
        RETVAL = power(a,b)
    OUTPUT:
    RETVAL
CASE:
    int a
    int b
    CODE:
        RETVAL = power(b,a)
    OUTPUT:
    RETVAL
```

Note that you place a conditional statement after the **CASE:** keyword to act as the matching value; the last **CASE:** becomes the default if you do not specify a conditional statement.

CLEANUP: This keyword enables you to define additional code to be called before the **XSUB** terminates. This keyword must follow a **CODE:**, **PPCODE:**, or **OUTPUT:** block. The defined code will be appended to the end of these blocks as the last statements within the **XSUB**.

CODE: The **CODE:** keyword supports the inclusion of additional wrapper code to be used when calling the function. See the earlier **fsavail** definition for an example. Note that the **RETVAL** is not automatically assumed to be the return value; you explicitly define this via the **OUTPUT:** keyword.

INCLUDE: You can use this keyword to specify the name of another file from which to import XS code:

```
INCLUDE: AddFuncs.xsh
```

You can also import the information from an external command by appending a pipe symbol (I):

```
INCLUDE: generatedXS.pl |
```

INIT: The **INIT:** keyword allows you to insert initialization code before the destination function is called. This can be used for initializing variables, allocating memory, or inserting debugging statements. Unlike when using **CODE:**, **RETVAL** works as you expect.

INPUT: This keyword causes the input parameters to be evaluated later than normal within the function initialization. This is usually used in conjunction with the **PREINIT:** keyword and may be included multiple times within the **XSUB** definition.

INTERFACE: The **INTERFACE:** keyword allows you to define a mapping for a number of functions simultaneously. For example, when developing an interface to a suite of functions that all have the same argument list—such as **sin**, **cos**, and **tan**—you could define them as

```
float
interface_s(value)
        float value
INTERFACE:
    sin cos tan
```

All three functions are now available as individual functions, but you have saved some time processing the directory.

INTERFACE_MACRO: This keyword allows you to define an **INTERFACE** (as defined earlier in the chapter) using a predefined macro to extract a function pointer for the **XSUB** definition. The text following this function should be the names of the preprocessor macros that would extract and set a function pointer. The default macros (used if you don't explicitly specify them) are **XSINTERFACE_FUNC** and **XSINTERFACE_FUNC_SET**. The extractor macro is given the return type, the **CV***　code value pointer, and the **XSANY.any_dptr** pointer for the **CV***. The macro for setting the function is given **cv** (the code value) and the pointer to the correct function.

MODULE   The **MODULE** keyword starts the XS definition section of the XS file:

```
MODULE = StatVFS
```

Everything before the **MODULE** keyword is taken as raw C code to be passed on to the C file created by **xsubpp**. The name specified will be used as the basis of the bootstrap function that will form the interface between Perl and the C functions. It will also be the name of the package that will use the function unless you specify differently with the **PACKAGE** keyword.

NO_INIT   This keyword indicates that a function parameter is being used only as an output value, as in the case of a passed parameter being populated by the function and

DEVELOPING
APPLICATIONS

then used as the return value. This option prevents Perl from taking all the arguments from the argument stack and assigning them to C variables upon entry. For example:

```
bool_t
rpcb_gettime(host, timep)
    char *host;
    time_t &timep = NO_INIT
    OUTPUT:
    timep
```

OUTPUT: The **OUTPUT:** keyword indicates that a particular value within the function arguments has been updated, and the new values should be made available to Perl when the function terminates. This is useful for functions when you are passing the address of a structure to the C function. The C function updates the contents of the array or structure directly, but may actually return an unrelated value (usually an error code). By defining the passed variable or structure as the **OUTPUT:** value, Perl knows this is the information to return to the calling Perl script.

You should also use this keyword when it is unclear what value Perl should be returning. When you use a **CODE:** block, the **RETVAL** variable is not recognized as an output variable, and you would need to pass **RETVAL** to the **OUTPUT:** keyword to ensure that the XS interface returns the correct information.

Finally, an **OUTPUT:** keyword can be used to create an in-line typemap; so the output parameter can be mapped to a particular piece of code, just as it would in the standard typemap.

PACKAGE   You can specify an alternative package name or the specific package name if it's part of a package hierarchy, using the **PACKAGE** keyword:

```
MODULE = StatVFS PACKAGE = StatVFS
```

It is always used with the **MODULE** keyword.

PPCODE: This defines a block of code, just like the **CODE:** block. However, the XS system expects you to update the contents of the Perl stack directly, rather than relying on return values. You also need to make the call to the underlying function yourself, which allows you to use a different function name from that of the **XSUB**. You will also need to handle errors and conversions within the **PPCODE:** block. This is also the only way you can support a function that returns multiple values.

PREFIX   The **PREFIX** keyword should follow the **MODULE** and/or **PACKAGE** keywords, and specifies a string that should be removed from the C function when it is requested within Perl:

```
MODULE = StatVFS PREFIX = prefix
```

For example, if the function is **rpcb_gettime()**, then you might specify a **PREFIX** of **rpcb_** so that function is available within Perl as **gettime()**.

PREINIT: The **PREINIT:** keyword enables you to declare additional variables before they are parsed through the typemap. This prevents the ordinary parsing of the supplied variable through the typemap when it is used within a **CODE:** block. You can use this keyword one or more times within the **XSUB** definition.

PROTOTYPE: You can specify a particular prototype for an individual function with this keyword. This overrides all other prototypes and keywords for the current **XSUB**. The prototype format follows the normal Perl conventions. See Chapter 5 for more details.

```
long
fsavail (path)
        char *  path
        PROTOTYPE: $
        CODE:
                struct statvfs vfsrec;
                int statreturn;
                statreturn = statvfs(path,&vfsrec);
                if (statreturn == 0)
                {
                    RETVAL = (vfsrec.f_frsize * vfsrec.f_bavail);
                }
                else
                {
                    RETVAL = -1;
                }
        OUTPUT:
        RETVAL
```

PROTOTYPES: This keyword creates Perl prototypes for the **XSUB** functions. This overrides the **-prototypes** and **-noprototypes** options to the **xsubpp** compiler. Prototypes are enabled by default, so to explicitly enable them,

```
PROTOTYPES: ENABLE
```

or to disable them (permanently):

```
PROTOTYPES: DISABLE
```

REQUIRE: This keyword allows you to specify the minimum version number of the XS interface and, more specifically, the **xsubpp** compiler that you want to use:

```
REQUIRE: 1.9507
```

SCOPE: This keyword enables scoping for a particular **XSUB**. To enable scoping:

```
SCOPE: ENABLE
```

This will cause the **ENTER** and **LEAVE** macros to be called automatically (see the "The Stack" section, earlier in the chapter). You can switch it off with

```
SCOPE: DISABLE
```

VERSIONCHECK   This enables or disables version checking and overrides the command line options to the **xsubpp** program. With version checking switched on (the default), the XS module will verify that its version number matches the version number of the host Perl module. To enable version checking,

```
VERSIONCHECK: ENABLE
```

and to disable it:

```
VERSIONCHECK: DISABLE
```

XS Tricks

Using the keywords just described and some other tricks, there are ways in which you can easily get around problems without resorting to additional C code within the **XSUB** definition.

Initializing Parameters   When an argument from Perl is supplied to the underlying function you are mapping within XS, a typemap entry is used to convert the supplied Perl value (**IV**, **NV**, **SV**, etc.) into a suitable C data type. You can override the conversions supported within a typemap (see the "Typemaps" section, later in the chapter) by supplying your own initialization code as part of the **XSUB** definition. The method required is to use typemap code directly within the **XSUB** definition, as shown here:

```
long
fsavail (path)
        char *  path = (char *)SvPV($arg,PL_na);
```

```
CODE:
        struct statvfs vfsrec;
        int statreturn;
        statreturn = statvfs(path,&vfsrec);
        if (statreturn == 0)
        {
            RETVAL = (vfsrec.f_frsize * vfsrec.f_bavail);
        }
        else
        {
            RETVAL = -1;
        }
OUTPUT:
RETVAL
```

The supplied code will be **eval**'d before it is parsed by the compiler, so care should be taken to ensure you backslash-quote any Perl variables. The special variables supported by the typemap system are also supported here, so you can use **$var**, **$arg**, and **$type** directly within the initialization code.

For more-complex operations, you can also use initialization strings that begin with **;** or **+**, rather than the **=** used in the preceding code. In the **=** and **;** cases, the supplied code overrides the code supplied by the typemap; while the **+** form is in addition to the typemap code, which is executed before the supplied code. Both the **;** and **+** forms output the initialization code after the arguments have been declared, in deference to the **=** format, where the initialization is placed on the same line.

Default Values   Many Perl functions allow you to use them without specifying any arguments. For example, with the **fsavail** function, it might be handy to use it like this:

```
$rootfree = fsavail;
```

In order to do this, you need to set a default value for this instance of a function call. The normal operation, of course, is for Perl to accept values of the argument stack and pass them to the **XSUB**. The value you assign will be used if the caller does not supply any values. The method for doing this is to specify the default value within the **XSUB** definition:

```
long
fsavail (path="/")
        char *  path
        CODE:
```

```
            struct statvfs vfsrec;
            int statreturn;
            statreturn = statvfs(path,&vfsrec);
            if (statreturn == 0)
            {
                RETVAL = (vfsrec.f_frsize * vfsrec.f_bavail);
            }
            else
            {
                RETVAL = -1;
            }
        OUTPUT:
        RETVAL
```

Returning undef Implicitly   You can return **undef** from the C function by using a
CODE: block and setting the first return value to that returned by **sv_newmortal()**,
which returns the undefined value default. You could, therefore, rewrite the **fsavail**
function as follows:

```
SV *
fsavail (path)
        char *  path
        CODE:
            struct statvfs vfsrec;
            int statreturn;
            statreturn = statvfs(path,&vfsrec);
            ST(0) = sv_newmortal();
            if (statreturn == 0)
            {
                sv_setnv( ST(0),(vfsrec.f_frsize * vfsrec.f_bavail));
            }
```

Note the other changes to the function definition. You are returning a scalar value
directly, rather than relying on the XS system to do the conversion for you. This means a
change to the return type, which is now a pointer to a scalar value, and a modification to
the return value. You now have to set the value of **ST(0)**, the "top" entry within the stack,
explicitly to an integer value with the **sv_setnv()** function.

Returning undef Explicitly   You can explicitly (rather than implicitly) return an
undefined value by setting the return value to the address of **&PL_sv_undef**; so you
can rewrite the preceding code as follows:

```
SV *
fsavail (path)
        char *  path
        CODE:
            struct statvfs vfsrec;
            int statreturn;
            statreturn = statvfs(path,&vfsrec);
            ST(0) = sv_newmortal();
            if (statreturn == 0)
            {
                sv_setnv( ST(0),(vfsrec.f_frsize * vfsrec.f_bavail));
            }
            else
            {
                ST(0) = &PL_sv_undef;
            }
```

Returning Empty Lists   You have already seen an example of returning an empty list. It requires the use of a **PPCODE:** block to ensure that the XS system recognizes that you are manipulating the stack directly. To empty an empty list, you just neglect to push any values onto the stack.

Accepting Variable-Length Argument Lists   To accept a variable length of arguments from Perl to a C function, you need to specify ... (an ellipsis) in the parameter list. This is the same structure as used by ANSI C to define a multiargument function within Perl. Once you have specified this within the function definition, you can examine the value of the **items** variable, supplied to all **XSUB**s, which specifies the number of arguments supplied.

Once you have determined how many arguments have been supplied, you can then take them off the stack directly using **ST()**. You will need to convert the supplied argument yourself, using the correct function to convert from the internal Perl data type to the C equivalent.

Typemaps

The XS system handles the translation of most of the basic data types used in C and Perl automatically. For more complex entities, such as structures and objects, you need to tell the XS system how to convert and translate between the different formats. The Perl distribution installs its own basic typemap, which is composed of, and converts between, most of the data types used as part of the standard libraries. For nonstandard libraries, you will need to supply your own typemaps if you want XS to convert between structures and objects transparently. Obviously, if you are using a **CODE:** or **PPCODE:** block, then chances are that you are doing your own conversion by returning a specific value or list of values to the caller; the typemap is only used for automatic conversions.

The default typemap is contained within the **ExtUtils** directory within your Perl library. Any typemap you define within the local XS directory will override the conversions available in the default typemap.

A typemap is split into three parts: **TYPEMAP**, **INPUT**, and **OUTPUT**. The **TYPEMAP** section contains instructions on how to translate between formats, using the definitions in the **INPUT** and **OUTPUT** sections. The **INPUT** section tells the XS system how to translate Perl values into C variables, and the **OUTPUT** section tells the XS system how to translate C values into Perl values.

The file is parsed by Perl, so the constructs and code should be Perl friendly, even though the resulting code within the typemap will be compiled as C source to perform the conversions. The value to be converted is in the **$arg** variable, and the **$var** variable is the destination of the translated value. Thus, you can generate a simple typemap for converting integer values into Perl scalars and back again like this:

```
int                     T_IV
unsigned                T_IV
unsigned int            T_IV
long                    T_IV
unsigned long           T_IV
short                   T_IV
unsigned short          T_IV
INPUT
T_IV
        $var = ($type)SvIV($arg)
OUTPUT
T_IV
        sv_setiv($arg, (IV)$var);
```

The top of the example is the **TYPEMAP** section, which is implied if no section is specified. The definitions show the C type on the left and the corresponding **INPUT** or **OUTPUT** map to be used on the right. The definition, **T_IV** in this case, is then looked up in the corresponding section, depending on whether you are passing an argument to a C function or returning a value from a C function. The corresponding code is then **eval**'d by Perl and used within the **XSUB** to do the conversion. Note that you can use the same definition for multiple **TYPEMAP** entries.

If you want to convert structures, you can use the predefined **T_PTROBJ** and **T_PTRREF**, which convert a structure to and from a blessed reference, or an unblessed reference, respectively. This allows you to interface directly, both to normal C structures and to C++ objects; the XS interface will handle the conversion for you.

For most situations, the use of a **PPCODE:** block, where you can return a list of values, is generally the best method, since it fits in with the style of the core Perl functions—such as **getpwnam** and others.

The Extension Module

Providing you have used **h2xs** to create a base XS file and module, you should rarely need to make any modifications to it. However, it's worth looking at the code to understand the processes involved in loading and using your extension after it has been compiled.

```perl
package StatVFS;

use strict;
use Carp;
use vars qw($VERSION @ISA @EXPORT @EXPORT_OK $AUTOLOAD);

require Exporter;
require DynaLoader;
require AutoLoader;

@ISA = qw(Exporter DynaLoader);
# Items to export into callers namespace by default. Note: do not export
# names by default without a very good reason. Use EXPORT_OK instead.
# Do not simply export all your public functions/methods/constants.
@EXPORT = qw(
            fsavail
            fsstat
            );

$VERSION = '0.02';

sub AUTOLOAD {
    # This AUTOLOAD is used to 'autoload' constants from the constant()
    # XS function.  If a constant is not found then control is passed
    # to the AUTOLOAD in AutoLoader.

    my $constname;
    ($constname = $AUTOLOAD) =~ s/.*:://;
    croak "& not defined" if $constname eq 'constant';
    my $val = constant($constname, @_ ? $_[0] : 0);
    if ($! != 0) {
        if ($! =~ /Invalid/) {
            $AutoLoader::AUTOLOAD = $AUTOLOAD;
            goto &AutoLoader::AUTOLOAD;
        }
        else {
```

```
                    croak "Your vendor has not defined StatVFS macro $constname";
        }
    }
    *$AUTOLOAD = sub () { $val };
    goto &$AUTOLOAD;
}

bootstrap StatVFS $VERSION;

# Preloaded methods go here.

# Autoload methods go after =cut, and are processed by the autosplit program.

1;
_ _END_ _
```

The most obvious items you will need to change in the module file are the names of the functions you have defined within the XS file. Of course, there is nothing to stop you from adding more Perl functions, variables, or statements to the generated file—it is, after all, just an ordinary module.

Two elements are omitted from the example. One is the list of constants that may or may not be defined within the header file from which the extension and module were produced. There are no constants required for the **StatVFS** module, so there was no **constant()** function to define within the XS file. However, for an example, see the following XS interface file from a typical math.h header file. The method used is to create a function called **constant()**, which accepts the name of the constant to look up. You then use C code and a **switch()** statement to identify the constant that was requested and return the correct value, which is itself taken from the macro values defined in the header file.

```
#include "EXTERN.h"
#include "perl.h"
#include "XSUB.h"

#include <math.h>

static int
not_here(char *s)
{
    croak("%s not implemented on this architecture", s);
    return -1;
}

static double
constant(char *name, int arg)
```

```
{
    errno = 0;
    switch (*name) {
    case 'A':
  break;
    case 'B':
  break;
    case 'C':
  break;
    case 'D':
    if (strEQ(name, "DOMAIN"))
#ifdef DOMAIN
        return DOMAIN;
#else
        goto not_there;
#endif
    break;
    case 'E':
    break;
    case 'F':
    break;
    case 'G':
    break;
    case 'H':
    if (strEQ(name, "HUGE"))
#ifdef HUGE
        return HUGE;
#else
        goto not_there;
#endif
    if (strEQ(name, "HUGE_VAL"))
#ifdef HUGE_VAL
        return HUGE_VAL;
#else
        goto not_there;
#endif
    break;
    case 'I':
    break;
    case 'J':
    break;
    case 'K':
    break;
    case 'L':
    break;
    case 'M':
    if (strEQ(name, "MAXFLOAT"))
```

```
#ifdef MAXFLOAT
        return MAXFLOAT;
#else
        goto not_there;
#endif
    if (strEQ(name, "M_1_PI"))
#ifdef M_1_PI
        return M_1_PI;
#else
        goto not_there;
#endif
    if (strEQ(name, "M_2_PI"))
#ifdef M_2_PI
        return M_2_PI;
#else
        goto not_there;
#endif
    if (strEQ(name, "M_2_SQRTPI"))
#ifdef M_2_SQRTPI
        return M_2_SQRTPI;
#else
        goto not_there;
#endif
    if (strEQ(name, "M_E"))
#ifdef M_E
        return M_E;
#else
        goto not_there;
#endif
    if (strEQ(name, "M_LN10"))
#ifdef M_LN10
        return M_LN10;
#else
        goto not_there;
#endif
    if (strEQ(name, "M_LN2"))
#ifdef M_LN2
        return M_LN2;
#else
        goto not_there;
#endif
    if (strEQ(name, "M_LOG10E"))
#ifdef M_LOG10E
        return M_LOG10E;
#else
        goto not_there;
#endif
```

```
   if (strEQ(name, "M_LOG2E"))
#ifdef M_LOG2E
      return M_LOG2E;
#else
      goto not_there;
#endif
   if (strEQ(name, "M_PI"))
#ifdef M_PI
      return M_PI;
#else
      goto not_there;
#endif
   if (strEQ(name, "M_PI_2"))
#ifdef M_PI_2
      return M_PI_2;
#else
      goto not_there;
#endif
   if (strEQ(name, "M_PI_4"))
#ifdef M_PI_4
      return M_PI_4;
#else
      goto not_there;
#endif
   if (strEQ(name, "M_SQRT1_2"))
#ifdef M_SQRT1_2
      return M_SQRT1_2;
#else
      goto not_there;
#endif
   if (strEQ(name, "M_SQRT2"))
#ifdef M_SQRT2
      return M_SQRT2;
#else
      goto not_there;
#endif
   break;
    case 'N':
   break;
    case 'O':
   if (strEQ(name, "OVERFLOW"))
#ifdef OVERFLOW
      return OVERFLOW;
#else
      goto not_there;
#endif
   break;
```

```
    case 'P':
   if (strEQ(name, "PLOSS"))
#ifdef PLOSS
       return PLOSS;
#else
       goto not_there;
#endif
   break;
    case 'Q':
   break;
    case 'R':
   break;
    case 'S':
   if (strEQ(name, "SING"))
#ifdef SING
       return SING;
#else
       goto not_there;
#endif
   break;
    case 'T':
   if (strEQ(name, "TLOSS"))
#ifdef TLOSS
       return TLOSS;
#else
       goto not_there;
#endif
   break;
    case 'U':
   if (strEQ(name, "UNDERFLOW"))
#ifdef UNDERFLOW
       return UNDERFLOW;
#else
       goto not_there;
#endif
   break;
    case 'V':
   break;
    case 'W':
   break;
    case 'X':
   break;
    case 'Y':
   break;
    case 'Z':
   break;
```

```
     case '_':
   if (strEQ(name, "_POSIX_C_SOURCE"))
#ifdef _POSIX_C_SOURCE
       return _POSIX_C_SOURCE;
#else
       goto not_there;
#endif
   break;
     }
     errno = EINVAL;
     return 0;

not_there:
     errno = ENOENT;
     return 0;
}



MODULE = Math       PACKAGE = Math


double
constant(name,arg)
   char *      name
   int       arg
```

The other element missing from our module is the documentation, written in POD format, for using the function. This is extracted and used to create man or HTML-formatted pages, depending on the platform. See Chapter 23 for more information on the documentation format, and see Chapter 25 for details on the installation process of a module.

Compiling and Testing Your Code

Assuming you've used **h2xs**, either on a genuine header file or a dummy one, the process for compiling your extension should be as easy as this:

```
$ perl Makefile.PL
$ make
```

The Makefile.PL is essentially just a Perl script that uses the **MakeMaker** module to produce a makefile for use with the **make** system. The **MakeMaker** module is complex and is the topic of Chapter 25. Chapter 25 also includes a good walk-through of the process of building and installing an extension, and the locations and methods used for the extension system.

Testing your extension is more critical. The rule often given is that if you divide up the amount of time to develop and test a program, then 80 percent of that total time should be used for the testing process. In practice, this is not always possible. A two-month project would take a further eight months just to test the result, making the total development time almost a year. What you can do, however, is test the ranges of the values that your extension accepts. By this, I mean that you should test the function at the limits of its capabilities. For example, a mathematical function that returns true if the supplied value is even should be tested with values of zero, -**LONG_MAX**, and **UNSIGNED_LONG_MAX**, the two definitions for the lowest and highest possible values within the confines of a **long int** and an **unsigned long int**.

For other more complex functions, you need to ensure that suitable test data is supplied that will stress the function to its limits. If you have written the extension (or indeed, any program) correctly, it should trap errors before they cause problems, or process the arguments supplied as it should.

Once again, the **h2xs** system builds you a sample test file, but all it does is test that the module or extension you have tried to load actually loads and imports correctly. You will need to add custom tests to really stress your function.

The format to follow should match that of the test suite that comes with the Perl distribution. You need to print "OK" or "not OK" for each test you perform, remembering to sequentially number the tests so any errors can be identified. Here's the test script for the **StatVFS** module:

```
# Before 'make install' is performed this script should be runnable with
# 'make test'. After 'make install' it should work as 'perl test.pl'

######################### We start with some black magic to print on failure.

# Change 1..1 below to 1..last_test_to_print.
# (It may become useful if the test is moved to ./t subdirectory.)

BEGIN { $| = 1; print "1..3\n"; }
END {print "not ok 1\n" unless $loaded;}
use StatVFS;
$loaded = 1;
print "ok 1\n";


######################### End of black magic.

# Insert your test code below (better if it prints "ok 13"
# (correspondingly "not ok 13") depending on the success of chunk 13
# of the test code):

# If we don't get any sort of space reading from /
# we're probably in trouble
```

```
my ($total, $used, $free) = fsstat("/");

print ((($total+$used+$free) ? '' : 'not'),"ok 2\n");

# We should get a number >= 0

print (((fsavail("/")>=0) ? '' : 'not'), "ok 3\n");
```

The first thing you should do is check that the module—and, therefore, the XS library—can be loaded correctly. You do this by printing the preamble in a **BEGIN** block and printing an error via the **END** block if the module didn't load. This will be automatically generated for you if you use the **h2xs** script. Each individual test is then executed, printing "OK" or "not OK" accordingly.

Remember to create tests that are compatible. I could have equally requested the space on the /users file system, which is perfect for my system but may not appear on other people's systems. This would have caused the functions to fail, even though the functions may be working perfectly.

Automating the Production/Compilation/Installation Process

The **h2xs** utility, which was covered near the start of the extension-making process covered in this chapter, created a number of files, including one called Makefile.PL. This file is a Perl makefile, similar in principle to the file used by **make** to build Perl in the first place. The content of the file produced by the **h2xs** program is very basic, but it provides enough configuration information to the **MakeMaker** module to generate a makefile for automatically building your extension.

In fact, the file produced will split your module into any component parts, generate the C source from your XS definition file, and compile the source code into a library suitable for use within your Perl scripts. It takes all the guesswork and trials out of the compilation process, automatically specifying the correct location of headers and libraries so that the extension compiles correctly. If you've written any documentation for your module, it will create the man file for the module, suitable for inclusion with the man pages for other modules and extensions.

Finally, **MakeMaker** provides all the necessary installation routines for copying your module, extension libraries, and documentation into the platform-specific directory of the machine you want to install the extension on. Better still, because the source definition for the makefile is written in Perl, you can package the raw files—that is, the Makefile.PL, Module.pm, Module.xs, and any typemap file—and send them to another machine, or even other users, and they can install and compile the module for their machines. The process accounts for all of the platform specifics, such as file locations and the available C compiler, and installs your module and extension in the right place.

This is the way most of the modules on CPAN are supplied. Even some of the Perl extensions, such as **NDBM_File**, are supplied in this way within the Perl distribution. During the build process, the main Perl makefile runs the necessary commands to extract the makefile for the module in question, before asking **make** to parse the file and produce and build the extension.

I frequently use the **h2xs** command on an empty header file. It provides a complete set of skeleton files for any XS development. All you have to do is fill in the blanks—something many people would argue is the complex part. This only adds more weight to the use of **h2xs**, as it takes all the guesswork out of the development process. Make a change to the XS file, and then just type **make** to produce and compile the library. Then use **make install** to install the library, ready for use.

Because the format of the Makefile.PL file can be customized to incorporate all sorts of features and abilities, it is the subject of Chapter 25 at the end of Part IV. Before you refer to that chapter, I should explain that the reason it is at the end is because it should be the last thing you do before supplying your extension to the world at large. Before then, you should ensure that your module is debugged (see Chapter 21), and you might want to investigate the Perl compiler, which provides other useful information and abilities (see Chapter 22).

Embedding Perl

In the previous chapter, you saw how the core of the Perl interpreter was actually handled by a single function call within Perl. The interpreter is obviously made up of a number of other functions; but at the frontend, the interface between the outside world and the interpreter is handled by a single function. Indeed, the main loop of the Perl binary actually calls this function itself. If you separate the idea of the Perl binary being the same as the Perl interpreter, then you could almost argue that the **perl** command has a Perl interpreter embedded within it. This is a feature of the "new" version 5 of Perl, and it provides the ability to embed a Perl interpreter within any C application.

There are a number of different ways and situations in which you may want to incorporate a feature from Perl, or the whole Perl interpreter, within your application. For example, you may want to make use of the regular expression features within Perl to parse certain statements. Another alternative is that you have created an extension to the Perl environment using the **XSUB** interface discussed earlier in this chapter. However, when an error occurs within the extension function, you want it to call not a C error handler, but a Perl one instead. Both of these situations can be achieved by using a function that calls the internal Perl function directly.

A much more obvious reason is to provide an internal scripting system to an existing application. Many different applications already provide this functionality, albeit in many different forms. Microsoft applications use Visual Basic for Applications, a specialized version of the Visual Basic environment. Emacs, the editor of choice for many programmers, supports an internal scripting mechanism based on Lisp.

Other benefits also spring to mind. The text-processing features of Perl are difficult to achieve directly within C without a lot of work. Using Perl to process a configuration file provides you with an instant configuration system without all the hassles normally associated with parsing a text file.

Strangely, the development of an embedded Perl environment is raw compared to the development of extensions. You are, more or less, left to your own devices when embedding Perl within your C programs. We'll look quickly at the methods both for embedding an entire interpreter into your C programs and for calling an individual function, whether built into the Perl interpreter or defined within the script or an external module.

Embedding the Perl Interpreter

Earlier in this chapter, Figure 20-1 showed the basic layout of the Perl interpreter. At the time, I mentioned that the possibility exists to embed a Perl interpreter within a C program. For a simple program, try the following:

```
#include <EXTERN.h>
#include <perl.h>

static PerlInterpreter *my_perl;

int main(int argc, char **argv, char **env)
{
    my_perl = perl_alloc();
    perl_construct(my_perl);
    perl_parse(my_perl, NULL, argc, argv, (char **)NULL);
    perl_run(my_perl);
    perl_destruct(my_perl);
    perl_free(my_perl);
}
```

This creates a simple Perl interpreter that accepts options from the command line. If you don't specify a Perl script on the command line, then just like the Perl interpreter, it reads the script from the standard input. That means you can now do something like this within the shell:

```
$ myperl <<EOF
> print 56*35,"\n";
> EOF
1960
```

The individual components of the C source are quite straightforward. The **PerlInterpreter** is a structure that holds all of the vital information required for an instance of the Perl interpreter. The **perl_alloc()** and **perl_construct()** functions create an interpreter object. The **perl_parse()** function then does some initializations, including supplying the arguments supplied to the C program on the command line. The second argument is **NULL**, but you could equally put **xs_init** in there so it initializes the XS interface, or indeed any other initialization code you think you need. It also parses the script supplied on the command line (via **-e**) or from the standard input. The **perl_run()** function then executes the script, before you finally shut down and deallocate the memory allocated to the embedded interpreter with **perl_destruct()** and **perl_free()**.

To compile the preceding file, you can use the information provided via the **ExtUtils::Embed** function:

```
$ cc -o myperl myperl.c 'perl -MExtUtils::Embed -e ccopts -e ldopts'
```

The embedded call to **ExtUtils::Embed** introduces all of the definitions, libraries, and header file locations for you so that the program will compile properly. The exact output will depend on how your Perl was compiled—the following sample was taken from a Solaris 8 x86 installation:

```
-L/usr/local/lib
/usr/local/lib/perl5/5.6.0/i86pc-solaris-thread-multi/auto/DynaLoader/DynaLoader.a
-L/usr/local/lib/perl5/5.6.0/i86pc-solaris-thread-multi/CORE -lperl
-lsocket -lnsl -ldb -ldl -lm -lposix4
-lpthread -lc -lcrypt -lsec -D_REENTRANT
-fno-strict-aliasing -I/usr/local/include
-D_LARGEFILE_SOURCE -D_FILE_OFFSET_BITS=64
-I/usr/local/lib/perl5/5.6.0/i86pc-solaris-thread-multi/CORE
```

If you want, there is nothing to stop you from placing this into a makefile for building the program; just use the preceding embedded statement. Remember, though, that if you move the makefile to another platform, it's unlikely to work—you should always be compiling an embedded Perl program using the same format as the Perl interpreter was built with.

Using a Specific Perl Function

If what you want to do is call a specific function, you need to use a slightly more complex method, and there are many different options available. The easiest method is to use the **perl_call_argv** function, which calls a specified function with an array of string arguments, as in this example:

```
#include <EXTERN.h>
#include <perl.h>
```

```
static PerlInterpreter *my_perl;

main(int argc, char **argv, char **env)
{
  char *print_args[] = {"Hello ", "World!\n", NULL};
  my_perl = perl_alloc();
  perl_construct(my_perl);
  perl_parse(my_perl, NULL, argc, argv, env);

  perl_call_argv("print", G_DISCARD, print_args);

  perl_destruct(my_perl);
  perl_free(my_perl);
}
```

This calls the **print** function with the arguments supplied in **print_args**. The **G_DISCARD** option to the **perl_call_argv** function indicates that you want to discard any values returned by the Perl function. The list of possible C functions you can call is shown in Table 20-8.

Function	Description
perl_call_argv(char *sub, I32 flags, char **argv)	This calls a subroutine, **sub**, using the **flags** (see Table 20-9, coming up), passing the arguments to the called functions specified in **argv**.
perl_call_va(char *sub, [char *type, arg,] * ["OUT",] [char *type, arg,] * NULL)	Calls the subroutine **sub**, passing the arguments supplied by the argument pairs **type** and **arg**, which specify the argument type and value. If an argument **"OUT"** is seen, then all the arguments following that are taken to be return value pairs of type and variables.
perl_eval_va(char *str, [char *type, *arg], NULL)	Evaluates an arbitrary Perl statement, **str**, instead of calling a specific function. The **type** and **arg** arguments are pairs of return argument types and values.

Table 20-8.   *C Functions for Calling Perl Subroutines*

You have already seen an example of the **perl_call_argv** function. The equivalent in **perl_eval_va** would be

```
perl_eval_va("print (qw/Hello World!\n/)", NULL);
```

Note the use of **qw** to quote the individual arguments, thus saving you from quoting quotes. You can do the same thing with **perl_call_va**:

```
perl_call_va("print","s","Hello","s","World!\n",NULL);
```

In all cases, the functions return the number of items returned by the Perl subroutine called, or **-1** on error.

The possible values for the **flags** argument of **perl_call_argv** are listed in Table 20-9.

Flag	Description
G_SCALAR	Calls the Perl subroutine in a scalar context.
G_ARRAY	Calls the Perl subroutine in a list context.
G_DISCARD	Forces Perl to remove any information placed onto the stack by the Perl subroutine.
G_NOARGS	Indicates that you are not passing parameters to the subroutine you are calling. This has the effect of not building or initializing the @_ array for the subroutine being called.
G_VOID	Calls the Perl subroutine in a void context, and removes any values placed onto the argument stack.
G_EVAL	This places an **eval{}** around the subroutine call. This enables a basic form of error checking around the subroutine you are calling, and also handles **die** calls accordingly. You will have to examine the value of the $@ variable, just as you would within Perl, to ensure that the function executed correctly.
G_KEEPERR	This flag is meant to be used in conjunction with the **G_EVAL** flag. It indicates that the value of $@ should be updated and/or reset by code that executes after the **eval{}** block. Setting this flag ensures that the contents of $@ contain the return status of the **eval{}** block.

Table 20-9. *Execution Flags for Called Subroutines*

In all the cases so far, we have casually ignored any return values from the functions we have been calling. Using the **perl_call_argv** or **perl_call_va** functions, you could take off the values returned by using the stack-manipulation functions that were covered at the start of this chapter. That said, you could also put argument values onto the stack in the same way and use a different method of calling the Perl subroutine.

If you look at the following code, it's complete C source for calling a Perl function called **add** that adds two numbers together:

```c
#include <EXTERN.h>
#include <perl.h>

static PerlInterpreter *my_perl;

void perl_add(int a, int b)
{
    int retval;
    dSP;
    ENTER;
    SAVETMPS;
    PUSHMARK(sp);
    XPUSHs(sv_2mortal(newSViv(a)));
    XPUSHs(sv_2mortal(newSViv(b)));
    PUTBACK;
    retval = perl_call_pv("add", G_SCALAR);
    SPAGAIN;
    if (retval == 1)
        printf("Returned: %d\n",POPi);
    PUTBACK;
    FREETMPS;
    LEAVE;
}

int main (int argc, char **Argv, char **env)
{
    char *my_argv[] = { "", "add.pl" };
    my_perl = perl_alloc();
    perl_construct(my_perl);

    perl_parse(my_perl, NULL, 2, my_argv, (char **)NULL);
    perl_add(35, 53);

    perl_destruct(my_perl);
    perl_free(my_perl);
}
```

The **perl_add** C function calls a very simple function, **add**, defined in a file called add.pl. The bulk of the **perl_add** function is given over to the process of initializing and populating the Perl argument stack before calling the Perl function and then taking the single value returned by the Perl function back off the stack again.

Note that the **perl_parse** function has also been used with our own set of arguments. This is because you need to get the Perl interpreter to load the file that contains the Perl source, which looks like this:

```
sub add
{
    my ($a, $b) = @_;
    return(a+b);
}
```

The whole process runs like this:

1. Initialize a Perl interpreter.
2. Parse the external Perl script that contains the subroutines you want to call from the C source code.
3. Call the C function that calls the actual Perl function you want to use. The execution path of that function performs the following steps:
   a. Initialize the stack.
   b. Push the first argument onto the stack.
   c. Push the second argument onto the stack.
   d. Call the Perl subroutine.
   e. Pop the returned value back off the stack.
   f. Return to the **main** function within Perl.
4. Destruct and free the Perl interpreter object.

Multiplicity

In some rare cases, it may be necessary to create multiple instances of the Perl interpreter within your C code. This is something that was mentioned back in Chapter 16 when we looked at the internal organization of the Perl interpreter. The problem with doing this normally is that the act of initializing any Perl interpreter may actually overwrite some of the values and structures created and required by the first interpreter.

To get around this, you need to set the value of the global variable **PL_perl_destruct_level** to 1, just by placing the following statement into your C code:

```
PL_perl_destruct_level = 1;
```

This is set automatically when you compile Perl using **configure** with the **-Dmultiplicity** directive. Once set, you can create as many **PerlInterpreter** structures as you require, memory permitting, within your C source. Since all the functions you have already seen accept a first (and sometimes only) argument, which is the name of the **PerlInterpreter** object, it should be obvious that each instance should have its own name and object and be called accordingly.

XS Initialization

If you want to call external **XSUB** functions from C via a Perl interpreter, then you need to supply some initialization code. We touched on this briefly earlier. The reason you need to specify it manually is that, by default, the embedded interpreter does not know how to import the extensions—you have to tell it what extensions you expect to use.

To do this, you must create a C function, traditionally called **xs_init()**, which calls the bootstrap function that the **xsubpp** script builds for you from the XS file you supply during the extension-development process. For example, the following code imports the **DynaLoader** extension, so that we can import our dynamically loaded modules, and the **Socket** extension:

```
#ifdef __cplusplus
#  define EXTERN_C extern "C"
#else
#  define EXTERN_C extern
#endif

static void xs_init (void);

EXTERN_C void boot_DynaLoader (CV* cv);
EXTERN_C void boot_Socket (CV* cv);

EXTERN_C void
xs_init()
{
    char *file = __FILE__;
    newXS("DynaLoader::boot_DynaLoader", boot_DynaLoader, file);
    newXS("Socket::bootstrap", boot_Socket, file);
}
```

Although you can write this yourself, a much easier method is to use the **ExtUtils::Embed** module to do it for you:

```
$ perl -MExtUtils::Embed -e xsinit - -o xsinit.c
$ cc -c xsinit.c 'perl -MExtUtils::Embed -e ccopts'
```

```
$ cc -c myperl.c 'perl -MExtUtils::Embed -e ccopts'
$ cc -o myperl myperl.o xsinit.o 'perl -MExtUtils::Embed -e ldopts'
```

Once you've created your **xs_init()** function, you then need to supply it as the second argument to the **perl_parse()** function:

```
perl_parse(my_perl, xs_init, argc, argv, env);
```

Cooperating with Other Languages

Interfacing with other languages is more complex. Since Perl is written in C, the interpreter and extension interface are closely integrated. Without this level of integration, and especially without the tools provided via the **XSUB** interface and the Perl internals, integration is difficult, but not impossible.

The Perl distribution comes with a number of tools that allow other languages and tools to be converted into a Perl script. Recent versions of Perl also enable you to convert the Perl script in a number of different formats, including some C source code that can be compiled into a stand-alone executable.

Of course, if you need to interact with another language, there are a number of options available. Perl makes an excellent source code producer; and with some work, you can create quite complex systems that interact with a program or language.

Converting Other Languages to Perl

As has been repeated in this and many other pieces of documentation over the years, Perl owes a lot of its functionality to the ideas and functionality of other programs. Because of its Unix roots, Perl used features from some of the most common and useful Unix command line utilities. It's no accident that the regular expression system looks like the one available within **sed**, or that some of the operators and semantics of the Perl language look similar to the **awk** language. Of course, Perl provides all the features of a great number of programs built into a single application.

If you have previously been developing with one of these applications, then conversion to Perl can be a long and complex process. To speed up the process, the Perl distribution comes with three programs to convert **sed**, **awk**, and **find** programs and statements into Perl script. This can then either be used natively or modified to fit into an existing application or environment.

sed

Although not strictly a programming language, **sed** does provide a way of modifying files in a programmable fashion. The most significant part of the **sed** environment is the regular expression matching and substitution engine. This is similar to the same regular expression system in Perl, and many of the commands are identical in operation between **sed** and Perl.

The format of a **sed** "script" is a series of lines. Each one starts with a letter defining the operation that should take place, followed by a number of arguments. The name **sed** is short for "stream editor," and each command is executed on each input line. The functionality can be modeled in Perl using a simple **while** loop.

The **s2p** command is a Perl script that takes a **sed** program and converts it into a Perl script using the **while** loop and some corresponding code to account for other features within the **sed** environment. The script is capable of turning any **sed** script into a Perl equivalent; it supports all of the functions and constructs of the **sed** language.

To use **s2p**, specify the name of a **sed** script to the **s2p** command, or enter the script during standard input. The resulting Perl script is sent to the standard output. For example,

```
$ s2p
s/foo/bar/g
```

produces

```
#!/usr/local/bin/perl
eval 'exec /usr/local/bin/perl -S $0 ${1+"$@"}'
        if $running_under_some_shell;

while ($ARGV[0] =~ /^-/) {
    $_ = shift;
  last if /^-/;
    if (/^-n/) {
        $nflag++;
        next;
    }
    die "I don't recognize this switch: $_\\n";
}
$printit++ unless $nflag;

$\ = "\n";                # automatically add newline on print

LINE:
while (<>) {
    chop;
    s/foo/bar/g;
    print if $printit;
}
```

The **s2p** command provides three options, supplied as arguments, as shown in Table 20-10.

It's true to say, of course, that the resulting script is less than friendly, and it's likely that many of the features in Perl provide quicker and cleaner ways of achieving the same goal. In general, therefore, rewriting a **sed** script is probably more efficient than using the conversion program. Since most **sed** programs involve regular expression substitution, matching, or transliteration, the process should be relatively easy.

awk

The **awk** language was one of the few programming environments (other than the shell) that was provided as standard with the Unix operating system. Its original incarnation was fairly basic, and it was replaced with **nawk**. Most people come across the language as **gawk**, the GNU version developed solely by Arnold Robbins. Like Perl, it exists on many different platforms; and also like Perl, its primary purpose is for parsing and processing text files. Some of the features of **awk**, and especially those of **nawk** and **gawk**, are not supported by Perl. They are too numerous to list here; but in general, the more complex regular expressions and the use of regular expressions within certain functions (such as **join**) are not supported in Perl—although you do, of course, get an easily extensible programming language so you can hack these abilities if you need to.

The **a2p** command that can be used to convert from an **awk** script is only compatible with **awk**, and your mileage may vary with **nawk** and **gawk**. Unlike the

Option	Description
-D*x*	Sets debugging, using a value of *x*. Depending on the value specified, it adds a number of additional statements to the Perl script that is produced to enable you to trace possible bugs and problems.
-n	Specifies that the **sed** script was always invoked with the **-n** switch. Functionality for this argument is normally built into the Perl script that is produced, but this option removes this code and sets the option on permanently.
-p	Specifies that the **sed** script was never invoked with the **-n** switch. Functionality for this argument is normally built into the Perl script that is produced, but this option removes this code and sets the option off permanently.

Table 20-10.   *Options to the s2p Converter*

sed converter, **a2p** is written in C, although the basic operation is the same. It accepts the **awk** script, either from a file or from the standard input, and generates Perl script to the standard output. For example, this **awk** script sums up the values of the first column of an input file:

```
{ s += $1 }
END  { print "sum is", s, " average is", s/NR }
```

Looking at this, you can see some of the similarities between Perl and **awk**. The first line adds the value of **$1**, which **awk** has automatically interpreted as the first field in the input file, into a variable. The loop that proceeds through the input file is implied within **awk**, as is the automatic splitting of the input source into individual fields. Once the main block has completed, the **END** block is executed, and this prints out the sum and average of the numbers.

Running this through the converter produces

```
#!/usr/local/bin/perl
eval 'exec /usr/local/bin/perl -S $0 ${1+"$@"}'
    if $running_under_some_shell;
                        # this emulates #! processing on NIH machines.
                        # (remove #! line above if indigestible)

eval '$'.$1.'$2;' while $ARGV[0] =~ /^([A-Za-z_0-9]+=)(.*)/ && shift;
                        # process any FOO=bar switches

$, = ' ';               # set output field separator
$\ = "\n";              # set output record separator

while (<>) {
    ($Fld1) = split(' ', $_, 9999);
    $S += $Fld1;
}

print 'sum is', $S, ' average is', $S / $.;
```

Once again, the output produced is filled with a number of compatibility elements, including the ability to create new variables for use within the script's command line using an **eval** function. The main bulk of the actual script is the last five lines.

Also, like the **sed** converter, the Perl produced in this manner should be classed as compatible, rather than optimal. Rewriting the code in Perl, rather than using a converter, will produce better results, albeit at a slower pace.

The **a2p** program accepts four command line options that affect the script generated, as shown in Table 20-11.

Option	Description
-D*x*	Sets debugging, using a value of *x*. The value affects the output produced by the conversion process, and adds a number of additional statements to the script to output debugging information during the script's progress.
-F*c*	Specifies that the **awk** script was always invoked with a -**F** switch, which changes the default input field separator to **c**.
-n*fields*	Specifies the names of the input fields, rather than automatically using a value of **$Fld1**, **$Fld2**, and so on. Fields can be separated by any of the normal separation characters.
-*number*	Forces **a2p** to assume that the input is always made up of the number of fields specified by **number**.

Table 20-11.   *Command Line Options to the* **awk** *Converter*

find

The **find** command does not really have a language, but it does have a complex array of command line options that can specify, fairly expertly, the definition of the files you want to find. The **find2perl** script takes the command line options you would normally supply to the **find** command, and generates a Perl script that will perform the same function. The script produced actually makes use of the **File::Find** module, which provides a mechanism for parsing a directory tree, following all the subdirectories. For each file or directory found, a user-specified function is called, with the name and location of the current file being available via the **$_** variable and via some variables located within the **File::Find** module.

The result is that Perl has the ability not only to locate a file within the current directory structure, but also to do any number of other operations to convert, translate, summarize, and so on, the contents of the files found.

The **find2perl** script does the basics of the file specification process for you, producing a script that you can modify to your own ends. If you know how to use the **find** command, then using the **find2perl** script should be easy. The command

```
$ find2perl / -name '*bin*' -type d -print
```

produces

```
#!/usr/local/bin/perl
```

```
    eval 'exec /usr/local/bin/perl -S $0 ${1+"$@"}'
        if $running_under_some_shell;

require "find.pl";

# Traverse desired filesystems



&find('/');

exit;
sub wanted {
    /^.*bin.*$/ &&
    (($dev,$ino,$mode,$nlink,$uid,$gid) = lstat($_)) &&
    -d _ &&
    print("$name\n");
}
```

You can also specify more complex constructs directly to the **find2perl** script without having to modify the code. There are two options: one to create a **tar** file and the other to specify a Perl-specific evaluation for the file.

The **-tar** option takes a file name and adds the necessary code to the Perl script to generate a file list to a piped **tar** command that then generates the **tar** file.

The **-eval** option takes a string that will be evaluated as a Perl statement; if it returns true, the file will be considered as a match.

Converting Perl to Other Languages

With Perl 5, the facilities have been put in place to resolve a Perl script to its lowest common denominator—the string of optimized opcodes that are executed by the Perl interpreter proper. At the moment, two modules (**B** and **O**) provide a Perl interface to the internals of a Perl script. The result is that the internal opcode tree can be converted and parsed into a number of different formats to provide a range of different pieces of information.

At present, this is limited to more extensive debugging features and the cross-referencing abilities that are often available to other languages. The same interface also provides you with the ability to generate a file in binary format called *bytecode*. This binary code can then be executed directly by a special Perl interpreter. The code has already been parsed and optimized, and much of the typical interpretation process has already taken place. This makes the code execution much faster and also ensures, to a greater or lesser extent, that the Perl source is hidden from casual view.

The most interesting feature of the **B** and **O** modules, however, is that they can generate raw C code, which can then be compiled into a stand-alone executable. The final executable does not require Perl and cannot be reverse engineered. The performance benefits are debatable, but the distribution and security offered by the process are obvious advantages.

Because this is a significant part of the entire Perl environment, it's discussed more fully in Chapter 22.

Calling Other Languages from Perl

You have seen many times how Perl can call and interact with an external program. In some cases, the level of interaction has been as simple as calling the program with some specified options. There is no reason why, with the use of dual pipes, you couldn't call and interact with another program, or even another programming language.

The most obvious road to cooperating with another language from Perl, however, is to use Perl as a high-level environment that generates an optimized or customized program that can then be executed via a separate language. Perl has many features that make the manipulation of data, particularly strings, significantly easier; and if you want to produce customized or optimized code automatically, it makes sense to use a textual development environment to produce it.

When dealing with a CGI or other web-based system, you can generate the JavaScript code that's embedded into pages—you can even dynamically generate the code to enable different features in the final page. What follows from this is the general ability of Perl to generate the code for any language—it's perfectly possible to create a Perl application that generates, and even compiles, C source code into a final application. In fact, this is exactly what some parts of the XS language and the Perl compiler (see Chapter 22) actually do.

The trick is to make the best use of the Perl environment and, especially, make use of the here document to create customized source code to be passed to the program or language interpreter in question. Although it is possible to make use of pipes, most languages accept an input file as their source. Remember that "compiled" languages—such as C, C++, and Pascal—will require an external compiler, as well as additional processes between code production and the final execution stages; but this should not present too much difficulty.

If it truly is interaction with another language that you require, then the obvious method is to set up some form of communication channel over which you can exchange requests and requirements. All modern languages, including Java, Python, Rebol, and Perl—provide the ability to open a network socket and exchange information.

Some platforms provide an interface through a Perl module for communicating with other languages. For example, the **Win32::OLE** module allows you to communicate with Windows objects, which in turn means that you can control the operation of Word, Excel, and other Windows applications using Visual Basic semantics. Under Mac OS, you can communicate directly with AppleScript, which in turn allows you to communicate with the operating system and the applications, and through an application like Word to Visual Basic again. See Appendix B in this book and Web Appendix B on the Web at **www.osborne.com** for details on some of the platform-specific capabilities and the modules that support them.

The Complete Reference

Perl

Part IV

Fine-Tuning Applications

Chapter 21

Debugging and Tuning

O nce you have completed your application, there are a number of things that you might want to do before finally releasing your code to the world. One of the most obvious procedures is to debug your code. Despite your best efforts, there are bound to be bugs and problems in your code that you probably didn't realize were there, and certainly never intended to introduce.

Debugging under Perl can be handled in a number of different ways. There are command line switches to output different levels of information, there's the output from the Perl compiler, which can be a useful addition to the debugger's toolkit, and there's even an interactive debugger that you can use to execute and monitor the progress of your Perl script's execution.

There are also other steps that you need to take before you can release your code. Documentation is always a good idea, not only as pointers for your end-users, but also as a tool for you, so that when you go back to the code a few months later, you know what it does, how, and why.

If your script is a general purpose tool, then you can make it appeal to a larger user group by making it cross-platform aware, and if possible, compatible. Knowing which functions, facilities, and systems are available on each platform is a good start, but there are also tricks that you can apply to make the process easier.

Finally, Perl includes some tools that make the distribution and installation of modules and applications easier. Learning how to make the best use of these modules can dramatically increase the ease of use and installation by your end-users.

The other chapters in this section cover these latter parts of the application development process. In this chapter, we're going to concentrate purely on the processes and tools available for debugging and optimizing the applications, scripts, and modules that you write.

Debugging is a time-consuming and laborious process. When I was at college, I was taught that the proper ratio was 80 percent testing and 20 percent development time, and after many years in the programming business, I can affirm that that ratio is about right. Even in a very simple piece of code, it's possible to introduce some potential bugs and problems. For every bug you find and eliminate, I can guarantee that two more will be waiting in the wings. Furthermore, the solution to one bug may well introduce new bugs that you aren't aware of.

There is, however, more to debugging than simply finding the bugs and squishing them. A good programmer will take a more pragmatic approach, and try to develop a system that will trap most of the errors before they cause any problems. Remember that the purpose of debugging, and in turn, error trapping, is to ensure that the software does what it is supposed to do, while simultaneously ensuring that it doesn't do anything it shouldn't. A simple log-processing script should not delete or corrupt the log in the process, for example.

We've already seen some examples of basic error trapping in Chapter 9—you should use Chapter 9 as a guide to isolating potential problems before they become real ones. In this chapter, we'll look at two basic procedures for debugging. The second is the use of more simplified debugging processes, such as using **print** and **caller** to provide a history of a script's execution, and therefore to help you to identify where things have gone wrong. The final, but certainly not least important, option that we will look at is the use of the Perl built-in debugger.

The final stage of any debugging process is probably the one least followed—optimization. Although many people do not consider it a bug, a badly optimized script is as much a danger as one that overwrites files it shouldn't have access to. A simple CGI script that processes a form shouldn't take hours doing so—monitoring the execution time can often give you a good idea of where the problems lie. Within Perl, there are a few solutions to that particular problem, including an extension to the core debugging extensions, the Perl Profiler. This monitors the execution time of each subroutine in your script and gives you an excellent idea of where there could be problems.

We'll also look at some of the manual techniques available for improving performance, and at some of the more obvious resource sinks that can slow execution.

| Tip | *It's impossible in a single chapter to cover everything you need to know about trapping errors and debugging. For a more detailed look at debugging with Perl, see my* Debugging Perl: Troubleshooting for Programmers *(Osborne/McGraw-Hill, 2000), from which a lot of the material in this chapter comes. See Appendix C for more information.* |

Debugging Techniques

There are three basic methods for debugging a script. The first two are modifications on a single theme—the primary tool is just to use **print** to output the information. The second uses **caller**, which returns more extended information about the caller of the subroutine, and then uses **print** to output the information. The last is to use one of the full-blown debuggers. Perl actually comes with its own debugger, which is basically a script and module combination called when you use the **-d** command line option to Perl. If you use the ActiveState version of Perl under Windows, then you also have a GUI-based debugger.

Just to add to the confusion, there is a fourth debugging system built into Perl—the **-D** command line option—but this doesn't often give any useful information to the "end-user programmer." Most of the detail given by **-D** is intended for those dealing with the internal workings of the Perl compiler and interpreter. See Chapter 15 for more information on the available options supported by the **-D** option. For a more detailed look at what each of the options does, check out the *Debugging Perl* title (see Appendix C for more information on this book).

Using print

To me, **print** statements have always seemed easy, and, providing you're careful, they can usually provide enough information for you to trace the bug without having to resort to a full-blown debugger. In fact, the easiest way to use the humble **print** statement is during the development of a script—just inserting a quick "this variable has this value" is an easy way for you to check that your script is doing what you think.

You can also use the **print** statement as a way of reporting debugging information in the final version of the script. You usually use this method in combination with a global variable, perhaps set via the script's command line, to enable or disable some simple debugging. The benefits of a script that outputs debugging information in this way is that it allows both the user and programmer to perform a post-mortem debug on the script. The only place where they are often useless is within a loop, because they produce a voluminous amount of information that needs to be processed manually after the execution is complete. On occasion, the loop mechanism can prove useful if you want to continually monitor a single variable as it is processed, or when you want to monitor the input or output to a filehandle.

Usage is pathetically simple. By using a statement such as this,

```
print "Got here!\n";
```

you can trace the execution path of a program. You can use the same basic layout for any valid piece of data that you want to output.

Because you can print whatever you like, you can be quite explicit about the information:

```
print "Data before processing: $data\n";
#process some data
print "Fieldname: $field, data: $data, leftovers: $leftover\n";
```

More usually, though, you'll want to be a bit more explicit about the location in which the debug report occurred. Here you can use the **__LINE__** and **__FILE__** directives, which insert the line number and current file in which the message was printed, respectively. For example,

```
print __FILE__,'(',__LINE__,"): Data before processing $data\n";
```

might print out like this:

```
process.pl(19): Data before processing Name: Martin
```

Note that the **__FILE__** and **__LINE__** tokens must be outside of quotes in order for them to be included in the printed line.

Quoting Information

When using **print** to output data, it's a good idea to delimit the information that you are outputting. This limit helps to make it clear *exactly* what the actual data was. For example, this report line:

```
process.pl(19): Data before processing Name: Martin
```

doesn't tell us if there are any trailing tabs or spaces to the information, which may or may not be important. A simple set of braces on either side of the data highlights the full data string:

```
process.pl(19): Data before processing [Name: Martin          ]
```

Here it's obvious that we have some trailing spaces.

Tip *Don't use angle brackets, <>, to delimit information, especially when displaying debugging data within a CGI or other HTML script. The HTML parser may either identify the entry as a proper HTML tag or simply ignore the data entirely!*

You can also go one stage further and quote the special characters. The following script defines two functions—the interface to the whole thing is the **mapascii** function. This takes a string and then converts the special characters into their equivalent sequence:

```
sub mapasciichar
{
    my ($char) = @_;

    @map = qw/
        \0 [SOH] [STX] [ETX] [EOT] [ENQ] [ACK] \a \b \t \n \v \f \r
        [SO] [SI] [DCE] [DC1] [DC2] [DC3] [DC4] [SYN] [ETB] [CAN]
        [EM] [SUB] [ESC] [FS] [GS] [RS] [US]
            /;

    return $map[ord($char)] if (exists($map[ord($char)]));
    return $char;
}
```

```
sub mapascii
{
    my ($string) = @_;
    join('',map { $_ = mapasciichar($_) } split //,$string);
}

print mapascii("Hello\nThis is a raw test\t\r\n"),"\n";
```

When you run the script as a whole, you get this:

```
Hello\nThis is a raw test\t\r\n
```

Other control characters will also be printed out with their ASCII names or in the format that you would normally use when interpolating special characters into strings.

Tracing Execution

The line and file directives that we saw earlier provide a useful way of isolating the exact script position that raised a particular error. Of course, it makes more sense to include a more detailed report, such that the output produced is as detailed as necessary and describes exactly what the script was doing at the point of the error. Here's the output from a **print**-debugged script that processes a file. The output includes the contents of the variables that we are using to process the data:

```
$ foo.pl
Opened file (input.dat)
Read data (hello)
Read data (world)
Closed file
```

Remember at all times that when producing a debug report in this way, you should be producing an annotated sequence of events. Doing this will help you and your users to understand what is going on without having to look back at the script.

Note *It's a good idea to switch off the file buffering when outputting this information, so that it's updated in real time, rather than in chunks. The easiest way to do this is*
```
use IO::Handle;
autoflush FILEHANDLE 1;
```

Using caller

Printing your own debug information requires a lot of manual entry if you are trying to trace the execution path through a program. For each **print** statement you include in your source, you will need to include a reference about the location of the statement in order for your debug output to make sense.

To ease the process, you can use the **caller** function, which returns the current context information for a subroutine. The information includes details about the subroutine (or **eval** or **require**) statement:

```
caller EXPR
caller
```

In a scalar context, it simply returns the package name. In a simple list context, the function returns the package name, file name, and line of the caller of the current subroutine or **eval** or **require** statement:

```
($package, $filename, $line) = caller;
```

If **EXPR** is specified, **caller** returns extended information. The value of **EXPR** should be the number of frames on the stack to go back to before the current one. That is, if you specify a value of 1, the parent subroutine information will be printed, a value of 2 will print the grandparent subroutine, and so forth. The information returned is

```
($package, $filename, $line, $subroutine,
 $hasargs, $wantarray, $evaltext, $is_require) = caller($i);
```

The **$evaltext** and **$is_require** values are only returned when the subroutine being examined is actually the result of an **eval()** statement. As an example, examine this script:

```
sub bar
{
    Top::top();
}

bar();
```

```
package Top;

sub top
{
    my $level = 0;
    print "Top of the world, Ma!\n";
    while ((($package, $file, $line,
            $subname, $hasargs, $wantarray) = caller($level++)))
    {
        $hasargs   = $hasargs   ? 'Yes' : 'No';
        if (defined($wantarray))
        {
            $wantarray = 'Yes';
        }
        else
        {
            $wantarray = 'No';
        }
        print <<EOF;
Stack:
        Package: $package
           File: $file
           Line: $line
     Subroutine: $subname
  Has Arguments?: $hasargs
    Wants Array?: $wantarray
EOF
    }
}
```

When the code is executed, the resultant information shows the stack trace for the **top** function, including its original call from **main** and from the **bar** function:

```
Top of the world, Ma!
Stack:
        Package: main
           File: ././t.pl
           Line: 5
     Subroutine: Top::top
  Has Arguments?: Yes
    Wants Array?: No
```

```
Stack:
            Package: main
               File: ././t.pl
               Line: 8
         Subroutine: main::bar
     Has Arguments?: Yes
       Wants Array?: No
```

The information provided should enable you to pinpoint the location within a script. If you want to report the information to a log, you may want to introduce a wrapper function, like this one:

```
sub callerlog
{
    my $reference = shift;
    open(DATA,">>caller.log") || return;
    print DATA join(' ',@_),":$reference\n";
    close(DATA);
}
```

Then to call the function, you would use a line such as

```
callerlog("Writing data",caller());
```

to report the information for the current stack trace. Note that you can't directly use the information from **callerlog**, since doing so would introduce its own frame of information at location zero within the stack. You could, however, use a modified form of the **callerlog** function that returns the stack trace from frame one onward:

```
sub callerlog
{
    my $reference = shift;
    my $level = 1;
    while ((($@data) = caller($level++)))
    {
        print join(' ',@data),":$reference\n";
    }
}
```

The information provided by **caller** is actually used by the Perl debugger to provide the tracing information used in the debugging environment.

Using eval

The **eval** function provides a very simple way of checking certain events without affecting the overall execution of your script. In essence, the **eval** function just initiates a new instance of the Perl interpreter in order to evaluate a particular string or block. It's used in all sorts of places within Perl—including in the debugger where it allows you to execute those arbitrary statements—but it can also be employed as a debugging tool.

Because **eval** evaluates a Perl statement or block within its own interpreter, we can use it in situations that might otherwise cause the Perl interpreter to fail. This process works because an embedded **eval** block reports any errors raised by a call to **die** through the **$@** variable. In fact, any exit is reported through **eval** to the **$@** special variable.

We can demonstrate this with a simple **eval** block used to test the existence of a particular module:

```
eval
{
    require Net::FTP;
}
print "Error: Module failed to load ($@)" if $@;
```

This outputs the following:

```
$ perl eval.pl
Failed to load Net::FTP: Can't locate Net/LICK.pm in @INC (@INC contains:
/usr/local/lib/perl5/5.6.0/i686-linux /usr/local/lib/perl5/5.6.0
/usr/local/lib/perl5/site_perl/5.6.0/i686-linux
/usr/local/lib/perl5/site_perl/5.6.0 /usr/local/lib/perl5/site_perl .) at
eval.pl line 1.
```

Armed with this information, we can now check anything (except statements executed at compile time, such as **use**) that might raise an error, and we can trap and report the problem.

The same operation can be followed for simpler statements, such as for checking a possible divide-by-zero error. You could do this:

```
if ($b == 0)
{
    print "Can't divide by zero\n";
}
else
{
    print "Result is ", $a/$b,"\n";
}
```

But it's slightly more convenient to do this:

```
eval { $a/$b };
print $@ if $@;
```

Here's another example, this time of a function that uses an **eval** to execute its statements so that it can return a single error back to the caller instead of simply calling **die** and executing the script completely:

```
if ($error = writedata("debug", "some error text\n"))
{
    print("Raised an error writing to the log: \n",$error,
          "Continuing...\n");
}


sub writedata
{
    my ($file, $data) = @_;

    eval
    {
        open (FILE, ">$file") or die "Can't open file ($file): $!";
        print FILE $data or die "Can't write to file ($file): $!";
        close(FILE) or die "Can't close file ($file): $!";
    };
    return $@ if ($@);
}
```

Here we've got essentially three places where we could potentially drop out of the script. By embedding all three statements into an **eval** block and then checking the return value from the whole function, we've managed to trap what might otherwise be a critical failure into something that we can safely recover from. This capability becomes incredibly useful in situations where you need to continue working even if a particular option fails, but you want to avoid producing your own exception- and error-handling system.

In this example, just running the script produces the following:

```
Raised an error writing to the log:
Can't open file (debug): Permission denied at eval.pl line 15.
Continuing...
```

In this case, we've just ignored the error, but you could redirect the sequence and error report to a Tk widget or another HTML page if this was a CGI script.

Note
*The same trick also provides an ideal way of converting an existing script from a command-line basis to a CGI or Tk basis without having to make major changes to the code. For example, we could take out the embedded **eval** from the **writedata** function and instead move it to surround the function call:*

```
eval
{
    writedata("debug", "some error text\n")
}
print("Raised an error writing to the log: \n",$error,
      "Continuing...\n") if $@;
```

*The **writedata** function remains unchanged, but the basic result is the same.*

Writing a Log

There are times when you'll need to write debugging-style information to something other than the standard output and error filehandles. In these situations, you can redirect the information directly to another file—we've already seen examples of this with the **caller** function earlier in this chapter.

There are a number of different ways in which we can do this. At the simplest level, you can just use **print** to send the output somewhere else. For a more comprehensive solution, you should think about redirection. This approach will ensure that **warn** and **die** also output their information to the log, rather to than to the real **STDERR**. The final solution is to report information to the **syslog** daemon on a Unix machine, or to the Event Log on a Windows machine. This procedure is useful for scripts that play a vital role in an administration environment, where you need the information to be reported to a central, rather than an application-specific, log.

Redirecting STDOUT/STDERR

The simplest way of creating a log without seriously affecting the output of your script is to simply redirect the default **STDOUT** and **STDERR** to somewhere else, which you can do like this:

```
open(SECOUT,">&STDOUT");
open(SECERR,">&STDERR");
open(STDOUT,">stdlog.txt");
open(STDERR,">stderr.txt");
```

Now, to print to the real standard output, you need to send output to **SECOUT**.

Note   *If you're going to redirect the complete output of a script, consider placing the redirection statement into a **BEGIN** block, so that everything is redirected to the log files, even if an error is raised by an imported module.*

In fact, it's probably best to follow those statements with

```
select SECOUT;
```

to ensure that standard **print** and other calls send their output to the real **STDOUT** and not the redirected one.

Note   *It's a good idea to switch off the file buffering when sending information to a log; doing this prevents overruns and ensures that data is written, even if the script crashes.*

Since you will have control over the filehandle on which you provide the user interface, but not the filehandle used to print the debugging information from the contributed module, redirecting only **STDERR** is often a more practical solution.

It's also possible, using this method, to create a log file of the debug output you create. This file is especially useful when using an indirectly accessed script, such as that used on a web server. Here, printing the debug information to the standard output will cause the information to be included as part of the document that is sent back to the user's web browser.

Using a Logging Function

If you don't want to redirect the **STDOUT** and **STDERR** filehandles, the other solution is to create a function that opens and then writes the information you supply directly to a log file.

```
sub writelog
{
    my ($format,@rgs) = @_;
    open(LOGFILE,">>debug.log")
        or die "Can't open debug log!: $!\n";
    printf LOGFILE ($format,@args);
    close LOGFILE;
}
```

Now you can just make calls to the **writelog** function:

```
writelog("Had an error in the line %s from %s", $line, $file);
```

FINE-TUNING
APPLICATIONS

Debug Logs in the Real World

It's probably a good idea to keep some form of logging system in a major application. By logging the output of your application, you can track problems as the application is used by the end-users. Then, when it comes to tracking a reported problem, you have all of the information to hand.

To get the best use out of a debug log, make sure you also record the time that the error was reported, the process ID, and, if relevant, the machine and/or user name. When the user reports the error, get them to email you the log. That way, when you examine the log, it should be easier to determine why the error occurred.

A more efficient solution is to use a global variable as the filehandle and then change the function so that it only opens the file if it isn't already open:

```perl
my $logfile = undef;

sub writelog
{
    my ($format,@rgs) = @_;
    unless(defined($logfile))
    {
        open($logfile,">>debug.log")
            or die "Can't open debug log!: $!\n";
    }
    printf $logfile ($format,@args);
}
```

Now the file will be opened once—when the first call to **writelog** is made—and log information will then just be appended for each subsequent call.

Note that we've removed the call to **close**; I suggest that you instead put it into an end block:

```perl
END
{
    close($logfile) if (defined($logfile));
}
```

Doing this will ensure that the file is properly closed when the script terminates.

Reporting to syslog

Perl comes with the **Sys::Syslog** module, which provides a very simple interface for reporting information to the syslog system, which in turn is written to the system logs, often held at /var/log/syslog (or similar). The best way to use the system if you intend to log information in this way is to call the **openlog** function at the start of your script, and then use **syslog**, which actually writes log entries, as a replacement for **warn** or **die**. Remember to call **closelog** at the end to close the connection to **syslogd** (the **syslog** daemon). A full example looks like

```
use Sys::Syslog;

openlog('perl', 'cons,pid', 'user');
syslog('warning' ,'Something happened');
closelog();
```

The preceding example produces the following entry on a Solaris system:

```
Jul 19 11:13:57 twinspark perl[2686]: Something happened
```

See Appendix B and the **Sys::Syslog** module for more information.

Reporting to the Windows NT/2000 Event Log

The Windows NT Event Log is a central logging system similar in principle to the syslog system, but slightly more advanced. Primarily, the Event Log is used to record errors and warnings, but it can also be used just to store simple informational messages and also audit events—that is, those events configured by the administrator to be specifically tracked and recorded.

The Event Log also stores a lot more information than syslog does in its standard format. For example, the syslog system can be configured and set to report the computer and user information, but it's not enforced. With the Event Log, this information is automatically recorded. In addition, you can include any data that was being processed at the time, extended message strings, categories, and event types.

For example, this snippet

```
use Win32::EventLog;

my $eventlog = new Win32::EventLog('Application');

%event = (Data => 'Some data',
          Source => 'Perl',
```

```
            EventID => 1,
            EventType => EVENTLOG_WARNING_TYPE,
            Strings => 'I failed to get the info I was expecting',
            Category => 0);

$eventlog->Report(\%event);
```

will log an Application error into the Event Log. Note here that I've used a hash and then called the **Report** method instead of embedding the information directly—it's quicker and easier to use the same hash and update only the relevant information when you need to report a new error.

Using a Debugger

There are three basic tools available to you when you are using a debugger: watches, stepping, and breakpoints. We'll have a look at each of these tools and describe how they can best be used to help you when debugging your scripts.

Watches

Watches are the variables that you want to monitor as you execute a script. You set a watch on a variable, and then, for each statement that is executed, you are shown the corresponding value of the variable. By using watches, you can monitor how a variable is updated and isolate those instances where a variable is modified without you realizing it.

Stepping

Stepping is the action of executing Perl statements, either individually or as a group (as when you execute an entire function call in one go). By stepping, you can monitor the execution and variables used and affected by a statement on a line-by-line basis. There are three basic step commands, although some debuggers will offer some additional options:

- **Step Into** executes the current statement, following the execution of any functions or methods found within the statement. Execution goes as far as calling the function or method, bypassing any variable initialization, and stopping at the first executable statement within the called function.

- **Step Over** executes the current statement. Any functions or methods that are called are executed without being processed by the debugger, so execution stops on the next executable statement within the current file.

■ **Step Out** continues execution until the current function or method ends. Execution stops at the next executable statement, either within the next function call of the current line from the calling script or on the next statement from the caller.

The advantage of stepping over breakpoints is that it allows you to monitor each line individually. This capability is particularly useful when you want to study a sequence or each iteration of a loop in detail.

Breakpoints

Breakpoints offer a different approach. Instead of laboriously stepping through each line of a script, you can set a breakpoint at a future point in the script and then start execution. The debugger will execute all of the lines up until the given breakpoint. In addition, you can also set a breakpoint to be triggered only when a variable matches a certain condition.

For example, imagine you are having trouble within a loop, but only when the loop counter reaches 1,000; you can set a breakpoint to be triggered when the counter value is greater than or equal to 1,000. The loop will parse and execute 1,000 times, and then the debugger will halt to allow you to process each individual line until you trace the problem.

The Perl Debugger

The name Perl Debugger is a bit of a misnomer. The debugger is in fact just a suite of modules and a script that ends up sitting almost simultaneously between and behind the script you are attempting to run and the Perl interpreter that will execute it. By sitting in this position, the debugger script can extract the individual lines of your source file and incrementally execute each one—the stepping process.

In addition, the debugger allows you to set watches and breakpoints and provides you with a way of directly executing Perl statements that can interface with the underlying script. For example, when reaching a breakpoint, you might want to perform a simple calculation on a value generated by the script.

The main difference between Perl and many other languages is that you can run the debugger directly—in fact, straight from the command line. There isn't a separate application for doing the debugging, and there's no reason to make any changes to your code.

The User Interface

To start the debugger, you need to specify the **-d** option on the command line to the Perl interpreter:

```
perl -d t.pl
```

Alternatively, it can be used with a dummy **-e** statement to drop you straight into a dummy debugger environment:

```
perl -de 1
```

Once the debugger is invoked, you are placed into it at the first executable statement within the defined script:

```
Loading DB routines from perl5db.pl version 1.0401
Emacs support available.

Enter h or `h h' for help.

main::(-e:1):    1
  DB<1>
```

The value in the angle brackets—1, in this example—is the number of the debugger command. This can be recalled with the **!** debugger command. The number of angle brackets shows the current depth of the debugger. Calling a new subroutine via an **s**, **n**, or **t** command will introduce a new set of brackets as a new execution path is created within the script. You can specify multiline commands by using the \ character, which has the effect of escaping the newline that would ordinarily end the command.

Rather confusingly, the line that is displayed before the prompt is the line that is *about* to be executed, rather than the line that has been executed. Therefore, on first entry into the debugger, no lines (other than compiler directives and package imports) have actually been executed.

The normal operation is to set a breakpoint on a line or statement that you want to monitor, and then use the **T** command to produce a stack trace. For example:

```
  DB<4> b 16
  DB<5> r
Top of the world, Ma!
main::callerlog(t.pl:16):              print join(' ',@data),":$reference\n";
  DB<6> T
. = main::callerlog('Printed Message') called from file 't.pl' line 23
. = main::top() called from file 't.pl' line 5
. = main::bar() called from file 't.pl' line 8
```

The actual execution process for each line in the script is as follows:

1. Check for a breakpoint.

2. Print the line, using tracing if the **AutoTrace** option has been set.

3. Execute any actions defined.

4. Prompt the user if there is a breakpoint or single step.

5. Evaluate the line.

6. Print any modified watchpoints.

Once the execution has halted, you can step through the script, either by every line, using the **s** command, or by each line, stepping over subroutine calls, using the **n** command.

Note that compile-time statements are not trapped by the debugger, which means that those enclosed in a **BEGIN** block, or statements such as **use**, are not stopped by the debugger. The best method for trapping them is to specify the value of the **$DB::single** variable that is part of the Perl debugger. Although it requires modification of the code, it does not affect anything if the debugger is not running. A value of 1 for the **$DB::single** variable is equivalent to having just typed **s** to the debugger. A value of 2 indicates that **n** should be used. Alternatively, you can monitor the status of the commands using the **AutoTrace** option.

You can set watchpoints, which display the value of a variable if it has been modified in the just-executed statement. For example, in the script,

```
while (<DATA>)
{
    chomp;
...
}
```

you could set a watchpoint for $_, which would print the value of $_ for each iteration of the loop.

Debugger Commands

The debugger supports a wide range of commands that are outlined next. As a general rule, anything that is not immediately identified as a command, or alternatively any input line beginning with a space, is interpreted as a Perl statement that is executed via an **eval** function.

 Any debugger command can be piped through an external program by using the pipe symbol, just as at a Unix shell prompt. This feature is primarily useful for parsing output through a pager, but could be used for anything.

h

```
h COMMAND
h
```

Prints out help information for **COMMAND** or general help if **COMMAND** is not specified. If you use the special **h h** command, a condensed version of the general help is printed—it should fit onto a standard screen without scrolling. See the **O** command later for details on how to change the default paging program.

p

```
p expr
```

Prints the evaluated value of **expr** using the standard **print** built-in function. The value of **expr** can include variables and functions defined within the current script being debugged.

The usual rules for the **print** function apply—nested structures and objects will not be printed correctly. (See the **x** command for a more useful version of this command.)

x

```
x expr
```

Evaluates its expression in list context and dumps out the result in a pretty printed fashion. Nested data structures are printed out recursively, unlike with the **print** function. See the options in Table 21-1, further on in the chapter.

V

```
V PACKAGE VARS
V PACKAGE
V
```

Displays the list of variables specified in **VARS** within the package **PACKAGE** if both are specified. If **VARS** is omitted, all variables for **PACKAGE** are printed. If no arguments are specified, it prints out all the variables for the **main** package. Information is intelligently printed, with the values of arrays and hashes and nested structures being formatted before being output. Control characters are also converted into a printable format.

If you specify the variables, you should omit the variable type characters (**$**, **@**, or **%**). You can also specify a pattern to match, or a pattern not to match, using **~PATTERN** and **!PATTERN** arguments.

X

```
X VARS
X
```

Same as **V VARS** for the current package.

T

```
T
```

Prints a stack backtrace, as determined by the **caller** function and the value of the current stack frame array.

s

```
s EXPR
s
```

Executes only the next statement (single step), following subroutine calls if necessary. If **EXPR** is supplied, it then executes **EXPR** once, descending into subroutine calls as necessary. This process can be used to drop directly into a subroutine outside of the normal execution process.

n

```
n EXPR
n
```

Single-steps the next statement, but steps over the subroutines instead of stepping into them. If **EXPR** is specified, then any subroutines are stepped into.

Carriage Return   Repeats the last **n** or **s** command.

c

```
c LINE
c SUB
c
```

Continues execution (all statements) until the next configured breakpoint or the end of the script. If **LINE** or **SUB** is specified, then a breakpoint, active for one break only, is inserted before **LINE** or the subroutine **SUB**.

l

```
l
```

Lists the next page of lines for the current script from the current line.

```
l MIN+INCR
```

Lists **INCR+1** lines from the line specified by **MIN**.

```
l MIN-MAX
```

Lists the lines from line **MIN** to **MAX**.

```
l LINE
```

Lists the line **LINE**.

```
l SUB
```

Lists the first page of lines for the subroutine **SUB**.

— Lists the previous page of lines.

w

```
w LINE
w
```

Lists a page of lines surrounding the current line, or **LINE** if specified.

. Returns the line pointer to the last line executed and prints it out.

f

```
f FILENAME
```

Changes the file currently being viewed to **FILENAME**. The value of **FILENAME** should match either the main script or the name of a file identifiable within the **%INC** variable. If still not found, then it is interpreted as a regular expression that should resolve to a file name.

/PATTERN/   Searches forward within the current file for the regular expression **PATTERN**.

?PATTERN?   Searches backward within the current file for the regular expression **PATTERN**.

L   Lists all the currently set breakpoints and actions.

S

```
S PATTERN
S !PATTERN
S
```

Lists all subroutines matching the regular expression **PATTERN**. If **PATTERN** is preceded by an exclamation mark, then lists those not matching the regular expression **PATTERN**.

t

```
t EXPR
t
```

Toggles trace mode. Trace mode enables the printing of each statement as it is executed. If **EXPR** is specified, traces the execution of **EXPR**. See also the **AutoTrace** option in Table 21-1.

For example, this script

```
sub one { 1 };
sub two { 2 };
print one()*two();
```

prints out only the final value of 2. With trace mode switched on, it also prints the statements:

```
DB<1> r
main::one(t2.pl:1):   sub one { 1 };
```

FINE-TUNING
APPLICATIONS

```
main::two(t2.pl:2):        sub two { 2 };
2
```

b

```
b LINE CONDITION
b LINE
b CONDITION
b
```

Sets a breakpoint on the current line when no arguments are specified. If **LINE** is specified, then the breakpoint is set on the specified line. If **CONDITION** is specified, then each time the breakpoint is reached, it breaks execution only if the condition resolves to true. The **CONDITION** does not use an **if** statement; it is purely the test. If you use **/PATTERN/**, then the breakpoint breaks only if the statement matches the regular expression **PATTERN**.

```
b SUB CONDITION
b SUB
```

Sets a breakpoint on subroutine **SUB**, using **CONDITION** if specified.

```
b postpone SUB CONDITION
b postpone SUB
```

Sets a breakpoint on subroutine **SUB** only after it has been compiled.

```
b compile SUB
```

Sets a breakpoint on the first executable statement of the subroutine **SUB** after it has been compiled.

```
b load FILENAME
```

Sets a breakpoint at the first executed line of **FILENAME**.

d

```
d LINE
d
```

Deletes the breakpoint specified on **LINE**, or the breakpoint on the line that is about to be executed if **LINE** is omitted.

D   Deletes all the currently set breakpoints.

a

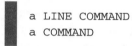

```
a LINE COMMAND
a COMMAND
```

Sets the action specified by **COMMAND** to be executed before the current line, or the line specified by **LINE**, is executed. For example, this can be used to print the value of a variable before it is used in a calculation.

A   Deletes all currently installed actions.

W

```
W EXPR
W
```

Sets a watch on the variable specified by **EXPR**. A change to the specified variable will be printed before the next line to be executed is printed. If **EXPR** is not specified, then all watchpoints are deleted.

O

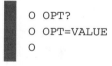

```
O OPT?
O OPT=VALUE
O
```

The first form, **O OPT?**, prints the value of the option named **OPT**. The second format specifies the value for **OPT**; if no value is specified, it defaults to 1. If no arguments are given, then the values of all the current options are printed. The option name can be abbreviated to the minimum identifiable name; for example, the **pager** option can be reduced to **p**.

A list of the most commonly used options is shown in Table 21-1. For others, refer to the perldebug man page.

Option	Description
RecallCommand	The character(s) used to recall a command.
ShellBang	The character(s) used to spawn a shell.
Pager	The program to use for paging the output using the | command within the debugger. The value of the **PAGER** environment variable will be used by default.
TkRunning	Run Tk when prompting. (See the "Alternative Interfaces" section later in this chapter for a discussion of the Tk interface to the Perl debugger.)
SignalLevel	The level of verbosity applied to signals. Default operation is to print a message when an uncaught signal is received. Set to 0 to switch this off.
WarnLevel	The level of verbosity applied to warnings. Default operation is to print a backtrace when a warning is printed out. Set to 0 to switch this off.
DieLevel	The level of verbosity applied to warnings. Default operation is to print a backtrace when a warning is printed out. Set this option to a value of 2 to enable messages to be printed by surrounding **eval** statements. Set to 0 to switch this off.
AutoTrace	Trace mode, identical to the **t** option on the command line. Set to 0 to disable tracing.
LineInfo	The file or pipe to print line-number information to. This is used by debugger interfaces with a pipe to enable them to obtain the information.
inhibit_exit	When set to 0, allows you to step to a point beyond the normal end of the script.

Table 21-1.   *Internal Options for the Debugger*

Option	Description
PrintRet	When set to 0, does not print the return value resolved when the **r** command is used. When set to 1 (the default), the return value is printed.
Frame	Controls how messages are printed during the entry and exit process from subroutines. The value is numeric, based against a bitset. If the value is 0, then messages are printed only on entry to a new subroutine. If bit 1 (value of 2) is set, then both entry and exit to the subroutine is printed. If bit 2 (value of 4) is set, then the arguments to the subroutine are printed, and bit 4 (value of 8) prints the values parsed to **tied** functions and methods. Bit 5 (value of 16) also causes the return value from the subroutine to be printed.Thus, a value of 18 prints the entry and exit to a subroutine with the returned value.
MaxTraceLen	The maximum number of arguments printed when bit 4 of the **frame** option is set.
ArrayDepth	The maximum number of elements printed from an array. An empty string prints all elements.
HashDepth	The maximum number of keys and values printed from a hash. An empty string prints all keys.
CompactDump	Sets the style of the array or hash dump. Short arrays may be printed on a single line.
VeryCompact	Sets the style of the array or hash dump to be very compact.
GlobPrint	Sets whether the resolved file name globs are printed.
TTY	The TTY device to use for debugging I/O.
NoTTY	If set, goes into a nonstop debugging mode, as if there were no controlling terminal. See the examples under the **O** command for more information.
ReadLine	When set to 0, disables **readline** support within the debugger, so that scripts that use **ReadLine** can be debugged.
NonStop	Automatically set by **noTTY**; sets the debugger to non-interactive mode.

Table 21-1.   *Internal Options for the Debugger* (continued)

The default values for the options can be obtained by typing **O** into a new debugger process:

```
perl -de 1

Loading DB routines from perl5db.pl version 1.0401
Emacs support available.

Enter h or `h h' for help.

main::(-e:1):    1
  DB<1> O
              hashDepth = 'N/A'
              arrayDepth = 'N/A'
            DumpDBFiles = 'N/A'
           DumpPackages = 'N/A'
             DumpReused = 'N/A'
            compactDump = 'N/A'
            veryCompact = 'N/A'
                  quote = 'N/A'
                HighBit = 'N/A'
             undefPrint = 'N/A'
              globPrint = 'N/A'
               PrintRet = '1'
              UsageOnly = 'N/A'
                  frame = '0'
              AutoTrace = '0'
                    TTY = '/dev/tty'
                  noTTY = ''
               ReadLine = '1'
                NonStop = '0'
               LineInfo = '/dev/tty'
            maxTraceLen = '400'
          recallCommand = '!'
              ShellBang = '!'
                  pager = '|more'
              tkRunning = ''
              ornaments = 'us,ue,md,me'
            signalLevel = '1'
              warnLevel = '1'
               dieLevel = '1'
            inhibit_exit = '1'
```

```
        ImmediateStop = 'N/A'
        bareStringify = 'N/A'
```

<

```
< EXPR
<
```

Sets a Perl command, specified in **EXPR**, to be executed before each debugger prompt.
If **EXPR** is omitted, the list of statements is reset.

<<

```
<< EXPR
```

Sets a Perl command, specified in **EXPR**, to be executed before each debugger prompt.

>

```
> EXPR
>
```

Sets the Perl command **EXPR** to be executed after each debugger prompt and after any
command on the prompt has been executed. If **EXPR** is not specified, the list of
commands is reset.

>>

```
>> EXPR
```

Sets the Perl command **EXPR** to be executed after each debugger prompt and after any
command on the prompt has been executed.

{

```
{ EXPR
{
```

Sets a debugger command, specified in **EXPR**, to be executed before each debugger
prompt. If **EXPR** is omitted, the list of statements is reset.

{{

```
{{ EXPR
```

Sets a debugger command, specified in **EXPR**, to be executed before each debugger prompt.

!

```
! EXPR
!
```

Redoes the previous command specified by the number **EXPR** (as shown in the debugger prompt), or the previous command if **EXPR** is not specified.

```
! -EXPR
```

Redoes the **EXPR** to the last command.

```
! PATTERN
```

Redoes the last command starting with **PATTERN**.

!!

```
!! EXPR
```

Runs **EXPR** in a subprocess.

H

```
H -EXPR
```

Displays the last **EXPR** commands—if **EXPR** is omitted, then it lists all of the commands in the history.

q or ^D   Quits from the debugger.

r   Returns immediately from the current subroutine. The remainder of the statements are ignored.

R   Restarts the debugger. Some options and history may be lost during the process, although the current specification allows for histories, breakpoints, actions, and debugger options to be retained. Also, the command line options specified by **-w**, **-I**, and **-e** are also retained.

|

```
|EXPR
```

Runs the command **EXPR** through the default pager.

||

```
||EXPR
```

Runs the command **EXPR** through the default pager, ensuring that the filehandle **DB::OUT** is temporarily selected.

=

```
= ALIAS EXPR
ALIAS
```

Assigns the value of **EXPR** to **ALIAS**, effectively defining a new command called **ALIAS**. If no arguments are specified, the current aliases are listed. Note that the aliases do not accept arguments, but you can simulate the effects of arguments by defining **EXPR** as a regular expression:

```
$DB::alias{'strlen'} = 's/strlen(.*)/p length($1)/';
```

This effectively reexecutes the original **strlen** command as **print length($1)**, where **$1** is the value within the first matching parentheses.

m

```
m EXPR
```

Evaluates **EXPR** and lists the currently valid methods that could be applied to it.

```
m PACKAGE
```

Lists the available methods defined in **PACKAGE**.

Using Noninteractive Mode

The interactive interface is great if you're trying to locate a very specific bug or problem, but it may be overkill if all you want is a quick guide or overview of the execution path of a particular script. There are other, perhaps better, tools—for example, the Perl Compiler in Chapter 22 provides some other, often useful, information.

You can get around this by using a "noninteractive" mode, which is basically just a trick using the **PERLDB_OPTS** environment variable to get Perl to execute a series of debugger commands when the debugger is started. It's not officially a way of executing the debugger, but it is a solution when you want to print a stack trace or watch variables during execution without having to manually introduce **print** statements or having to drop into the interactive debugger interface.

To do this, you need to set the value of the **PERLDB_OPTS** environment variable before running the debugger. The following example, which assumes you have the **bash** shell, switches on full frame information for called subroutines and runs the debugger without human intervention, outputting the full trace to the standard output:

```
$ export set PERLDB_OPTS="N f=31 AutoTrace"
$ perl -d t.pl
Package t.pl.
8:        bar();
in   .=main::bar() from t.pl:8
 5:           top();
 in   .=main::top() from t.pl:5
   22:         print "Top of the world, Ma!\n";
Top of the world, Ma!
   23:         callerlog("Printed Message");
   in   .=main::callerlog('Printed Message') from t.pl:23
   12:         my $reference = shift;
   13:         my $level = 1;
   14:         while ((($data) = caller($level++)))
   15:         {
   16:             print join(' ',@data),":$reference\n";
main t.pl 5 main::top 1 :Printed Message
   14:         while ((($data) = caller($level++)))
   15:         {
   16:             print join(' ',@data),":$reference\n";
main t.pl 8 main::bar 1 :Printed Message
```

```
 14:        while (((@data) = caller($level++)))
 15:        {
 out .=main::callerlog('Printed Message') from t.pl:23
out .=main::top() from t.pl:5
out .=main::bar() from t.pl:8
```

The **PERLDB_OPTS** environment variable is actually part of the customization system for the debugger, which we'll have a look at separately.

Customization

There are two ways of customizing the Perl debugger. The first is to specify the internal debugger options within the value of the **PERLDB_OPTS** environment variable, as you have already seen. The other option is to specify options and aliases and commands to be executed when the debugger starts, by placing commands into the .perldb file, which is parsed at the time of execution by the debugger module.

The normal use for this file is to specify new aliases to the debugger, which you do by specifying the keys and values of the **%DB::alias** hash. The key is the name of the alias, and the value is the command that should be executed. See the = command in the earlier "Debugger Commands" section for details.

You can change options to the debugger by calling the **parse_options** function, which takes a single argument—a string such as would be specified in the **PERLDB_OPTS** variable. Note, however, that the definitions in .perldb are parsed before the string defined in the environment **PERLDB_OPTS** variable.

Alternative Interfaces

The **emacs** editor provides an interface to the Perl debugger that enables you to use the **emacs** editor as a complete development and debugging environment. There is also a mode available that allows **emacs** to understand at least some of the debugger commands that can be used during the debugging process.

There are also a number of modules available on CPAN that provide Windows-based interfaces to the Perl debugger. The most friendly of the interfaces I have come across is the **ptkdb** interface.

The **ptkdb** debugger interface uses the **Tk** interface system to provide a windowed interface to the Perl debugger. All of the normal interface elements are available, with buttons and entry points for the most regularly used items. You invoke the **ptkdb** interface (once it has been installed) using the debug extension command line option:

```
$ perl -d:ptkdb t.pl
```

You can see in Figure 21-1 a sample window for the chapter's example debug script. The left side of the window shows the listing of the original Perl script. The right panel displays variables, expressions, subroutines, and breakpoints for the current debugger invocation. The information printed is the same as that produced within the normal text-based debugger interface, albeit within a nice preformatted and windowed environment.

The ActivePerl Debugger

While there is actually nothing wrong with the text-based debugger, for many Windows-based programmers used to tools like CodeWarrior and Visual Studio, it will feel a little restrictive and complicated to use. The ActiveState Perl Debugger (APD), which comes with the Perl Development Kit (a chargeable extra), provides a GUI interface to a debugger that will be familiar to users of Visual Studio and other integrated development environments.

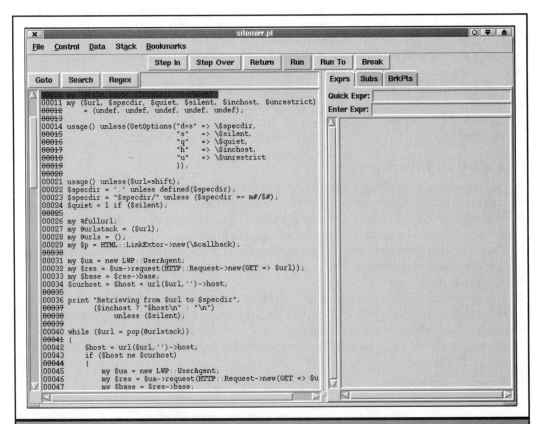

Figure 21-1. *The ptkdb debugger interface*

The basic features of the ActivePerl debugger are essentially identical to those of the core Perl debugger, but it's augmented with a nice GUI in a similar way to the **ptkdb** interface. You can actually see a sample of some of the options in Figure 21-2. In use, there is little real difference between the standard and ActivePerl debuggers—you have access to the same Step Into and Step Over features, and the Watches panel displays a list of the variables that you want to monitor.

Because it's not a standard part of either the Perl or ActivePerl distributions, I won't go into any more detail here. For more information on the ActivePerl debugger, see the online documentation that comes with the Perl Development Kit, the *Debugging Perl* book, or the *ActivePerl Developer's Guide* book—see Appendix C for more information.

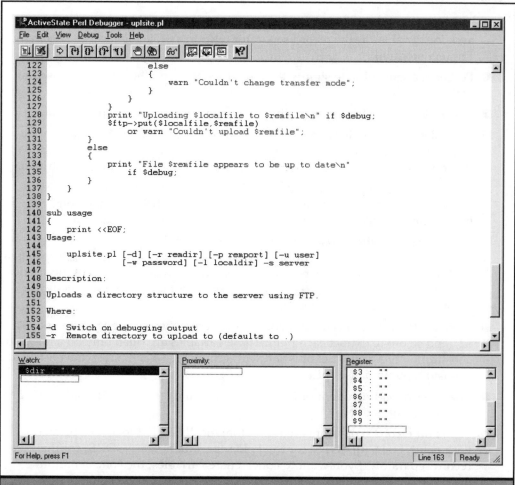

Figure 21-2.   *The ActivePerl Debugger*

FINE-TUNING
APPLICATIONS

Traps for Programmers of Other Languages

Most of the traps listed in this section are the common things that trip up the majority of people. I've done my best to be as comprehensive as possible, but it's difficult to account for all situations. The errors or traps that are covered here will probably solve any remaining errors—the simple traps like missing quotes and termination generate more errors than are probably necessary.

Differences from awk/gawk

Most of the differences between Perl and **awk/gawk** relate to the built-in variables and regular expression systems in each language.

- The **English** module in Perl allows you to use the full variable names used by **awk** for variables as the record separator (**$RS** in **awk** is identical to **$RS** in the **English** module).

- Perl uses a semicolon to signify the end of a statement; the newline as used in **awk** is not sufficient.

- All blocks require braces, including those used with **if** and **while** statements.

- Variables in Perl begin with a prefix character—$ for scalars, @ for arrays (numeric indices), and % for hashes (string indices). Indices in arrays and subscripts begin at zero, as do references to specific characters within strings.

- Numeric and string comparisons are different in Perl. Numeric comparisons use special characters, such as != for "not equal to." String comparisons use letters; the equivalent of "not equal to" when comparing strings is **ne**.

- Input lines from files must be manually split using the **split** function. The results will go to the array you specify, or to the global @_ if you don't specify a destination (this also clobbers any function arguments). The current input line (or default pattern space) is $_ in Perl; if you want the newline stripped, you must use **chop** or **chomp** (better).

- Once the fields have been split, you cannot access them using the variables **$1**, **$2**, (and so on) to extract each field. These variables are filled only on a match or substitution of a regular expression with grouping. To actually extract the fields from an input line, use **split**.

- The pattern binding operator is =~ in Perl, and the range operator is .. not ,. The exponential operator is ******.

- Field and record separators are not automatically added to arrays printed with **print**. Use $ (or **$OFS**) for the field separator and $\ (**$ORS**) for the record separator. If you want to concatenate variables, the concatenation operator is the period.

- Files must be opened before you can print to them—use the **open** function to assign a filehandle to the open file and then use **print FILEHANDLE**.

- Within loop control, the keywords **next**, **exit**, and **continue** work differently. For **next**, Perl always proceeds to the next iteration of the enclosing loop, or the next iteration of the named loop if a name is supplied. The **exit** keyword in Perl terminates the entire script. The **continue** statement indicates a **BLOCK** of code that should be executed before the conditional test for the loop is reevaluated.

The variables in **awk** are equivalent to those in Perl, as shown in Table 21-2.

awk	Perl
ARGC	$#ARGV or scalar @ARGV
ARGV[0]	$0
FILENAME	$ARGV
FNR	$. is only valid for the current/last used filehandle.
FS	No equivalent; use **split** to split fields.
NF	No equivalent; you could count the number of fields returned by **split**.
NR	$.
OFMT	$#
OFS	$,
ORS	$\
RLENGTH	length($&)
RS	$/ can only be set to a string; regular expressions are not supported when using this variable. Use **split** if you need to separate by an expression.
RSTART	length($`)
SUBSEP	$;

Table 21-2.   *awk*/Perl Variable Differences

C Traps

Within C, most of the traps relate to variable types and conversions. Perl does not support separate variable types for numbers and strings. Perl supports only a scalar type that can contain virtually any data:

```
$value = 99;
$value = "String";
```

Also, you cannot access the individual characters of a string using a subscript. The following will not work:

```
$char = $value[0];
```

What it will try to do is access the first element of the array **@value**, which is probably not defined. Use the **substr** function to access individual characters or slices; for example:

```
$char = substr($value,0,1);
```

Alternatively, if you need to iterate over the characters within an array, use **split**:

```
foreach $char (split //,$string)
```

This also highlights a performance issue. When working through the elements of an array, don't use indexing. For example, you might iterate over an array using

```
for($index=0;$index<scalar @array;$index++)
```

Instead, use **foreach**:

```
foreach $element (@array)
```

All code blocks require curly brackets, {}. The statement

```
if (1) print "Hello";
```

will fail in Perl. You can, however, do

```
print "Hello" if (1);
```

if the statement you want to execute fits on one line.

There is no **switch** statement in C, although you can emulate it in a number of different ways in Perl. The most obvious is a messy **if..elsif..else** conditional block. Note that the secondary test is **elsif** in Perl, not **else if**. A better alternative for the **switch** statement, and also one that will look familiar, is

```
SWITCH:
{
    ($date == $today) && do {
                            print "Happy Birthday!\n";
                            last SWITCH;
                        };
    ($date != $today) && do {
                            print "Happy Unbirthday!\n";
                            last SWITCH;
                        };
    ($date == $xmas)  && do {
                            print "Happy Christmas!\n";
                            last SWITCH;
                        };
}
```

Note from this example that the keyword to break out from the statement is **last**, not **break**. The **last** and **next** keywords are direct replacements for the C **break** and **continue** keywords. However, be aware that the Perl versions do not work within a **do { } while** loop.

Here are some other differences between C and Perl to watch out for:

■ Perl uses special characters to identify a variable (and its type). Variables start with **$**, **@**, and **%** in Perl and relate to scalars (normal variables), arrays, and hashes.

■ The **&** symbol in C takes the address of an object, but this is not supported in Perl, although you can use **** to pass a reference to an object instead of the object itself.

■ Arguments to a Perl script, which are accessed via **$ARGV[0]**, start at zero. This rule refers to the first *argument* to the script, not the name of the script, which can instead be found in the **$0** special variable.

■ The Perl **printf** function does not accept the * character in a format definition for inserting a variable field width. However, since Perl does support variable interpolation, you can insert the variable directly into the format and let Perl interpolate the value into the format string.

■ Comments in Perl start with the hash sign and continue until the end of line. They do not need to be terminated as in the C /*..*/ construct.

- The system call functions built into Perl (and indeed most functions) return non-zero for success and 0 for failure. In cases where a 0 would be a valid return result, the function returns **0 but true**, which evaluates to 0 when interpreted as a number.

- When using a signal handler, Perl allows you to use the signal name (without the prefix **SIG**) instead of the signal numbers.

sed Traps

Much of the functionality for Perl, including a large bulk of the regular expression syntax, was inherited from **sed**. There are some minor differences that relate mostly to the way in which **sed** and Perl expect to take in and process data.

Logical groupings of regular expression elements are specified using unbackslashed brackets. The line

```
s/\([A-Z]+\)/\1/;
```

in **sed** should be written like this in Perl:

```
s/([A-Z]+)/$1/;
```

The same is true for the logical **or** operator, which is also unbackslashed. A backslashed bracket **or** | operator within a regular expression will be interpreted by Perl as a literal. Group references in substitutions should use **$1** instead of **\1**. Also note that in Perl, the **$1..$xx** variables are populated generally—their values are present after the regular expression.

Finally, when specifying a range of values in Perl, the **...** operator should be used instead of the comma.

Note that a translator is available (**s2p**) which will convert **sed** programs into Perl equivalents.

emacs Traps

The regular expression syntax in **emacs** is more or less identical to the **sed** syntax. Refer to the preceding "sed Traps" section for details on the differences.

Shell Script Traps

The most fundamental difference between any shell and the Perl interpreter is that Perl compiles the program into a series of opcodes before execution, whereas a shell interprets lines (and sometimes blocks) at once, ignoring the remainder of the code until it reaches it.

The interpolation of variables is different. Perl always interpolates variables into backticked and double-quoted strings, and into angle brackets and search patterns, and the interpolation is done only once (not recursively).

Variables in Perl start with **$**, **@**, and **%**. You must specify the prefix character in Perl. You cannot get away with

```
var = "Hello"
```

as you can in shell script. To confuse matters, you can't do the reverse in shell script either. The example

```
$var = "Hello"
```

will fail in most shells.

Three more differences are worth noting:

- All statements in Perl must end with a semicolon (except when the last statement is in a block).

- The command line arguments in Perl are available via the **@ARGV** array, and not in the variables **$1**, **$2** (and so on) that the shell uses; Perl uses these for grouped regular expression matches.

- With particular reference to **csh**, return values from backticks in Perl are not parsed in any way.

Python Traps

Python and Perl are two very different languages, and since both are available on identical platforms, which one you use is likely to be driven by personal choice or the requirement of a client. However, necessity dictates all sorts of things, so here is a list of differences that may trip up a Python programmer trying to work in Perl. It's intended as a quick checklist of things you may have done wrong, not a list of all the differences, which would probably take up an entire book!

- All statements in Perl end in a semicolon, unlike in Python, which effectively doesn't have a statement terminator other than the newline, and even then it's only implied as the statement terminator.

- Variables in Python are free-form: there is no difference between creating a scalar, array, or hash. You must remember to specify your Perl variables by their type and to use the prefix of **$** for scalars (strings or numbers), **@** for arrays, and **%** for hashes (the Perl term for Python dictionaries).

■ Accessing an element from an array or a hash changes the prefix character to a **$** within Perl. For example, this would access the sixth element of an array:

```
print $array[5];
```

Note that square brackets are still used to refer to the individual elements. With a hash, you use braces:

```
print $hash{elem};
```

■ When splicing elements from an array in Perl, you can either use the **splice** function or use commas and list operators in the square brackets to define the elements to splice (similar to, and identically named as, the subscript operator in Python). The **splice** function is the preferred option on named arrays; the subscript option should be used on the return values from lists.

■ You must specify lists in Perl in surrounding brackets. The Python statement

```
a, b = 1, 2
```

will not work in Perl, even if you add the semicolon and **$** prefix to make

```
$a, $b = 1, 2;
```

What actually happens is that Perl sees three separate expressions in one large statement; only **$b** will actually be assigned a value. It should be rewritten as

```
($a, $b) = (1, 2);
```

■ Variables within Perl are the actual storage containers of the data. Within Python all data storage is via a reference to an object. If you want to pass a variable reference to a function in Perl, you need to prefix the variable with a backslash to indicate to Perl that it is a reference. When dereferencing a variable, you need to specify the type of variable you are attempting to dereference.

■ Perl supports a number of internal functions that provide a lot of the functionality that Python requires external modules for. These functions include those for reading and writing files, using network sockets, handling arrays and hashes, and many other things.

■ Perl includes most of the operating system information within the main interpreter. You can access the environment through the **%ENV** hash and the command line arguments via the **@ARGV** array without having to import them from an external module.

■ External modules are imported via the **use** function in Perl, which is effectively equivalent to the **import** keyword in Python. Note that when you **use** a module, the function is imported into the calling package:

```
use Cwd;
print getcwd();
```

The **from** construct in Python to import specific functions is supported by appending a list of functions, variables, and other objects after the module name. For example,

```
use Cwd qw/getcwd/;
```

is synonymous with the Python construct:

```
from Cwd import getcwd
```

- If you are using objects in Perl, then to call a method, you use the **->** operator:

```
FILEHANDLE->autoflush(1);
```

- Strings are concatenated in Perl using a single period; the Python statement

```
"Hello" "World" "\n";
```

in Perl would become

```
"Hello" . "World" . "\n";
```

Also, Perl interpolates variables and escape sequences (such as the preceding newline) only in certain quotes, excluding, unfortunately, single quotes; in Perl the value of

```
'\n'
```

is a string composed of a backslash and the lowercase character "n". However, this aspect does make **print** statements easier. You can place the variables straight into the double quotes without having to specify a print format. If you want a formatted version of a string, use the **printf** function.

- Perl does not automatically append a new line to a **print** statement; you must add the string **\n** within double quotes somewhere to your **print** statement.
- Code blocks in Perl must be enclosed in braces. An **if** statement looks like this:

```
if ($test)
{
}
```

The block starts after the opening brace and ends before the last brace.

Optimization

Optimization is all about squeezing the last few processor cycles out of your scripts. There are some obvious resource sinks that will affect your script that you can't ignore or optimize away—for example, when you have a script that processes the lines of an Apache log, it's difficult to improve upon the line-reading mechanism built into Perl. However, you could change the way you track the information, so that instead of calling a subroutine hundreds if not thousands of times to add some data to a hash, you just add the information within the main loop.

Spotting these and other sinks is not easy, which is where the Perl Profiler comes in. An extension to the basic debugging API, the profiler tracks the execution of every single subroutine and counts up how long it takes to execute each call to the subroutine. The information is nested, so you can also trace the subroutines called by other subroutines, and the whole report is printed out in a nice easy-to-digest format.

For a quicker view, or perhaps an in-line view, of the execution time of a piece of code, you can use the **time** function to count the seconds between two points, or you can use the **Benchmark** module to get a finer level of detail.

Once you've found the problem, you need to know how you can improve on your algorithm, and I've included some ideas and pointers for you to try.

The Perl Profiler

The Perl Profiler takes a typical script and, using the debugging backend, monitors the execution of individual subroutines within the script. The profiler monitors both the functions or methods defined within the confines of the script itself and any subroutines or methods imported from outside—including the **import** method employed during a **use** statement.

The actual process is in two stages:

- Run the script using the **DProf** debugging extension. Doing this produces a separate file called tmon.out.
- Run the **dprofpp** script, which analyzes the information within tmon.out and produces a variety of reports based on that information.

The first stage is easy—just supply the **DProf** extension as the name of the debugger to use when you execute the script. For example:

```
$ perl -d:DProf slow.pl
```

The tmon.out file contains information for each individual subroutine call, including how long it took to execute and the name of the subroutine that called it. From this information, you can gain a fairly clear understanding of precisely what was executed, and when, and how long it took. Although you can analyze and process this information yourself, Perl comes prepared with its **dprofpp** script.

The **dprofpp** script is installed when you install Perl and should exist within your execution path, ready to use to post-process the profiling. It takes the tmon.out file, collates all of the information, and then outputs a summary of the timing information as a straight list, a nested tree, or in a variety of other formats.

The options for the **dprofpp** script are shown in Table 21-3. If you regularly use a specific set of options, you can use the **DPROFPP_OPTS** environment variable to store the list of default options. The default value would be **-z -O 15 -E**.

Option	Description
-a	Sorts the list of subroutines alphabetically.
-A	Reports the time for functions loaded via the **AutoLoad** module as *::AUTOLOAD, showing the total time for all autoloaded modules. The default is for individual functions (autoloaded or otherwise) to have their own time calculated.
-E	This is the default option, displaying all subroutine times exclusive of child subroutine times.
-F	Generates fake exit time values. This gets around the problem introduced by subroutines calling **exit** or **exec**, which causes the normal execution process of the script to end prematurely.
-g subroutine	Shows the results only for **subroutine** and the subroutines it calls.
-I	Displays child as well as parent execution times.
-l	Sorts the list of subroutines by the number of times each subroutine has been called.
-O count	Displays only the first **count** subroutines.
-p script	Executes **script** and then outputs report.
-Q	Quits after profiling the script with **-p** without producing a report.
-q	Displays report without headers.
-R	Counts anonymous subroutines within the same package scope individually. The normal operation is to count each invocation separately.
-r	Displays only elapsed real times. Individual user and system times are not displayed.
-s	Displays only system times. User times are not displayed.

Table 21-3.   *Options for the **dprofpp** Profiling System*

Option	Description
-S	Displays merged subroutine call tree, with statistical information for each branch, to **STDOUT**. Making multiple calls to the same function within the same branch creates a new branch at the next level. Repeat counts are displayed for each function within each branch. Sort order is by total time per branch.
-T	Displays subroutine call tree to **STDOUT**. Statistics are not printed.
-t	Displays subroutine call tree to **STDOUT**, and subroutines called multiple consecutive times are simply displayed with a repeat count. Statistics are not printed.
-U	Do not sort subroutine list.
-u	Displays only user times. System times are not displayed.
-V	Prints the version number of the **dprofpp** script and prints the **Devel::Dprof** version number stored in the statistics file if found or specified.
-v	Sorts by the average time elapsed for child calls within each call.
-z	Sorts the subroutine list by the amount of user and system time used.

Table 21-3. *Options for the dprofpp Profiling System* (continued)

The default output of the **dprofpp** script is shown here:

```
Total Elapsed Time = 40.28038 Seconds
  User+System Time = 40.18038 Seconds
Exclusive Times
%Time ExclSec CumulS #Calls sec/call Csec/c  Name
 100.   40.21  40.215   1001   0.0402 0.0402  First::foo
 0.31   0.125  40.291      1   0.1254 40.290  Second::foo
 0.00   0.000  40.340      1   0.0000 40.340  main::bar
```

By default, the information output shows the total amount of time elapsed to produce the script. Note that this might give a slightly extended figure, since it will depend on the other processes running on your machine. The user and system time is the total time spent actually executing your script. User time is that spent by Perl actually processing, and the system time is that spent by the system servicing requests—for example, reading data from a file or outputting information to the screen.

The remainder of the figures relate to the individual functions in a columnar format, and the descriptions for each column are summarized here:

- **%Time**   The amount of time relative to the other functions spent in this single function.

- **ExclSec**   The amount of time spent executing this function—this figure does not include the time taken by other functions called by this one.

- **CumulS**   The amount of time spent executing this function and any functions called by this function.

- **#Calls**   The number of calls to this function.

- **Sec/call**   The average number of seconds spent executing each invocation of this function—this figure does not include the time taken by other functions called by this one.

- **Csec/c**   The average number of seconds spent executing each invocation of this function and any other functions called by this one.

You can see from this example that the function called most often, and the one that soaks up the most amount of time, is the **foo** function in the **First** package.

You can also produce a report that shows the nesting and relative execution times of the individual functions and how they were called:

```
main::bar x 1    40.34s = (0.00 + 40.34)s
  Second::foo x 1        40.29s = (0.13 + 40.17)s
    First::foo x 1000    40.17s
  First::foo x 1         0.05s
```

The remainder of the command line options essentially just modify these two basic reports, either changing the order, the calculation parameters, or the tree display.

Sample Script Profile
Let's have a look at a sample script which we'll use to demonstrate the features of the Perl profiler. We're going to use a simplified version of an HTTP log processor.

It extracts a single field (the date/time string) and then produces a list of the unique entries. The log file used is about 8MB in size—consisting of 90,300 lines. It's actually a 180K file duplicated many times—this is deliberate, both to stress-test the script and provide us with enough samples to get a good idea of the relative execution times. The first version of the script looks like this:

```
#!/usr/local/bin/perl -w

use strict;
my @datetime;
process();

sub process
{
    open(DATA,"../access.log") or die "can't open log: $!";
    while(<DATA>)
    {
        chomp;
        my @fields = split;
        process_fields(@fields);
    }
}

sub process_fields
{
    my (@fields) = @_;
    add_to_datetime($fields[3]);
}

sub add_to_datetime
{
    my ($datetime) = @_;
    foreach (@datetime)
    {
        return if ($datetime eq $_);
    }
    push @datetime,$datetime;
}
```

The profiler doesn't pick up on the **main** section of the script, aside from lumping it all into the overall execution time; we've therefore split out the main processing loop into its own function to get a precise timing value. Those who've followed the tips in the last chapter should already be able to spot the two obvious resource sinks in the preceding example.

Running the profiler on this script and then calling **dprofpp** without any arguments gives the following output:

```
Total Elapsed Time = 91.55104 Seconds
  User+System Time = 91.79165 Seconds
Exclusive Times
%Time ExclSec CumulS #Calls sec/call Csec/c  Name
 72.4   66.47  65.511  90300   0.0007 0.0007  main::add_to_datetime
 23.7   21.84  95.886      1  21.841 95.885  main::process
 11.5   10.58  74.044  90300   0.0001 0.0008  main::process_fields
 0.01   0.010   0.010      1   0.0100 0.0099  main::BEGIN
 0.00   0.000  -0.000      1   0.0000      -  strict::import
 0.00   0.000  -0.000      1   0.0000      -  strict::bits
```

The biggest sink is the **add_to_datetime** function, which is responsible for adding a unique entry to the **datetime** array. This is a lengthy process, because it means stepping through the array each time (in fact, 90,300 times). Although there's only about 405 unique items, there's still a lot of iterations to go over before we either pick up the one we need or determine that we need to add the current entry to the list. This particular resource sink is a good example of where using an array is a really bad idea—we could replace it with a hash and eliminate the loop.

The main **process** function we can ignore for the moment—there's not a lot we can do to speed up the parsing of the individual lines that we read from the file. Actually, there is the fact that we call an external function to process. This final execution sink, the **process_fields** function, accepts a relatively large array from the **process** function, and in turn calls the **add_to_datetime** function.

Again, according to the last chapter, calling a function repetitively, especially when there are a number of different arguments, is a resource sink. This is because Perl has to copy the arguments onto the stack before calling the function. We could try using references or a global variable, but, in conjunction with the other sink, there's probably a better solution.

If we fix both of these problems, we can produce a new script that uses a hash rather than two functions and an array. The new version of the script looks like this:

```
#!/usr/local/bin/perl -w

use strict;
my %datetime;

process();
```

```
sub process
{
    open(DATA,"../access.log") or die "can't open log: $!";
    while(<DATA>)
    {
        chomp;
        my @fields = split;
        $datetime{$fields[3]} = 1;
    }
}
```

Running the script with the profiler enabled, and then reporting on it using **dprofpp**, we get:

```
Total Elapsed Time = 19.75992 Seconds
  User+System Time = 19.68992 Seconds
Exclusive Times
%Time ExclSec CumulS #Calls sec/call Csec/c  Name
 99.6   19.62 19.620      1   19.620 19.620  main::process
 0.00   0.000 -0.000      1   0.0000      -  main::BEGIN
 0.00   0.000 -0.000      1   0.0000      -  strict::import
 0.00   0.000 -0.000      1   0.0000      -  strict::bits
```

A big difference—we've managed to reduce the execution time from 91 seconds down to less than 20, just by using a hash. We've also eliminated two function calls—because we don't need them anymore—and ended up with just one function that does all of the work.

This is a great demonstration of why hashes are faster for these sort of summary calculations. The hashing algorithm has done all of the nasty work for us. For a description of the hashing algorithm and why it is so much faster than a normal progressive array lookup, see Chapter 10 of *Debugging Perl*, under "Command-Line Debugging: Hash Dump" (see Appendix C of this book for more information about the *Debugging Perl* book).

One-Hit Profiling

If all you want to do is produce a profile for a single hit of a script, you can use the **dprofpp** script directly:

```
$ dprofpp -S -p t.pl
```

However, if what you want is to continually probe the original results for different combinations and different reports, perhaps targeting a different selection of functions each time, then you should run the script through the profiler to create the tmon.out file. You can then compile reports based on the raw data without having to run the script again. Comparing the results of multiple executions of the script is often a waste of time, since the minor differences between each execution may introduce wildly different figures for certain functions.

Also, be aware of the size of the raw data file created. For this small script, a 16K data file is generated. Larger scripts with more functions and, more importantly, more function calls will generate significantly more data. Our previous slow script example produces a 1.6MB data file for processing.

Profiling by Hand

You can profile areas of your script by hand by simply recording the time before and after a section of code that you want to test. At the simplest level, just record the timings given by **time** before and after calling a function:

```
$before = time();
myfunction();
$after = time();
$duration = $before-$after;
```

The only problem with this solution is that you get to know the duration only in seconds—useful when you are calling a function that will take a long time, but not fine enough if you want to profile the individual calls to functions.

A better solution is the **Benchmark** module, which is part of the standard Perl distribution. This works in the same basic fashion as the previous **time** example, except that we get a granularity of milliseconds (through the use of the **times** function). For example, the code:

```
$t = timeit(1000000,'cos(3.141)');
print "Calculation time: ", timestr($t), "\n";
```

will place the timing information for a million iterations of the calculation into **$t**, which will be a reference to a **Benchmark** object. The **timestr** function then prints out a suitably formatted message:

```
Calculation time:  1 wallclock secs ( 1.70 usr + -0.07 sys =  1.63
CPU) @ 6134969.33/s (n=10000000)
```

Alternatively, you can calculate the timings for an arbitrary set of statements:

```
$ta = new Benchmark;
&render_object();
$tb = new Benchmark;
print "Calculation time: ", timestr(timediff($ta,$tb)), "\n";
```

The problem with both of these solutions is that they require you to modify your scripts before you get any useful data. While this is not a huge problem, it adds to the development time. The profiler doesn't have this problem—you can just get the information instantly.

The tricks are, on the other hand, useful either if you want to provide information directly to your users or if you want to monitor a sequence of statements as a whole. The profiler will deal only with functions, so without splitting your code into a number of subroutines (which will, of course, slow it down) there's no way to identify the timing information for small sections of code.

Optimization Guide

Manually optimizing scripts is not the perfect solution. It will take a significant amount of time to manually trawl through your scripts and make all of the changes suggested here. However, once you've located a problem, either using the manual tricks or **dprofpp**, these tips should give you enough information to at least start the process.

The two areas we will be looking at are ways to increase the speed of execution and ways to reduce memory usage. As in all things, there is usually a trade-off for both sides of the equation. It *is* possible to increase speed—but often at the risk of increasing memory usage. Reading a large file into memory, for example, will reduce the number of calls to the system for more data, but on the other hand, it will also mean allocating a large chunk of memory to hold the file content.

There is no hard-and-fast rule for which to choose. In the modern world, speed is more important than memory, especially when disk and RAM storage is so cheap. However, keep in mind that large memory usage will slow down the execution of web-based solutions, where the possibility of multiple instances of a script executing simultaneously is a reality.

There's also a certain amount of crossover—some of the techniques that are listed as purely speed improvements will actually also help to reduce memory usage. I've tried to note both the crossover and complimentary techniques where possible.

Increasing Speed

Increasing the speed of execution relies on your ability first to produce a good algorithm and second to make the best use of Perl's abilities to help the algorithm along. Simple things like keyword lists are much better handled by a hash than an array because the internal hashing algorithms have already been optimized. We can go straight to a hash value, and even using hashes as a way of de-duping material is still more efficient than using arrays and iteration.

Program Structure   The program structure is the general layout of the script and some of the generic statements that you'll use in all parts of the application.

- Avoid using **goto** when a function or loop-control statement will achieve the same result. Any call to **goto** causes the parser to search for the specified label; Perl doesn't keep an internal table.

- Don't use **eval** when you can use braces to expand information (such as variable names) inline. You can use something like this:

```
${$prefix . $var} = "String";
```

- Also, avoid using **eval** inside a loop, since doing so will cause Perl to run the parser over the **eval** statement for each iteration. Instead, put the iteration inside the **eval** so the block will only have to be parsed once.

- Within the context of a loop, always place control statements as early as possible to prevent Perl from executing statements it then never uses. For example, the following code is wasteful:

```
while (<DATA>)
{
    chomp;
    next if /^#/;
...
}
```

You don't have to take the newline off the end of the string in order for the regular expression test to match.

- Replace **if..else** statements used to select from a range of single values with a logical **or**. You can always use

```
$login = getlogin || (getpwuid($<))[0] || "Anonymous";
```

- Avoid calling complex subroutines in large loops, especially those with few other steps. The overhead in copying arguments to the stack and back again will slow the process down. If you can, use references rather than static lists; or, if that becomes a real problem, rewrite the function in C.

- Use lists to functions that accept them in place of concatenating a string. Using concatenation with **print**, for example, involves copying each value into a new string before returning the concatenated version and moving on to the next element. Using a list speeds up the process considerably. Alternatively, try using **join** with a null separator value, since **join** will add each string to a new string, instead of performing multiple copies on each element.

Variables and Constants   Good variable design should help to reduce most of the overhead—for example, using arrays instead of lists of individual variables. Other tips are listed here:

- Avoid using default values for variables. Perl always initializes variables to 0 or empty anyway.

- Preextending an array or string can save time, as it preallocates memory that Perl would otherwise attempt to allocate on the fly.

- Use hashes instead of arrays to hold information like keywords (for which you would otherwise use an array and a search mechanism to find). Also, remember that you can use hashes to remove duplicates from a list.

- Don't waste time doing the manual math on static expressions:

```
$day_seconds = 24*60*60;
```

  Perl will optimize this away into a single value during compilation for you. Even better, use the expression where it's needed and don't waste time introducing yet another variable.

- Use **my** instead of **local**.

- Don't **undef** variables you may want to use again later for a different purpose. More specifically, don't create multiple variables when a single temporary variable will do. Better still, use **$_** if you can get away with it.

Printing, Interpolation, and Manipulation   The display and interpolation of text can be quite a time-consuming process, especially within a script that makes heavy use of text output—for example, parsers or CGI scripts.

- Avoid using quotes that interpolate on text that doesn't require interpolation. Although doing this won't save you much time, it will mean that Perl has to investigate fewer strings when interpolating data.

- Use **print** in place of **printf** unless you absolutely have to print a specific format. Remember that variables can be interpolated directly into certain quoted strings.

- Avoid using **substr** many times on a long string when a regular expression could perform the conversion or extraction quicker. For example, to extract the elements from a date in the form "19980326" using **substr**, this

```
$date = '19980326';
$year = substr($date,0,4);
$month = substr($date,4,2);
$day   = substr($date,6,2);
```

is almost certainly quicker using a regular expression:

```
$date = '19980326';
($year, $month, $day) = $date =~ /(\d{1,4})(\d{1,2})(\d{1,2})/;
```

Better still, use **pack** and **unpack** for strings. You could rewrite the preceding example as

```
($year, $month, $day) = unpack("c4c2c2",$date);
```

- Use **substr** to modify a string, rather than extracting the elements and concatenating the new version. Better still, use a regular expression substitution.

- Use **tr///** instead of **s///g** to delete characters from a string.

- When working with multiple filehandles, especially if they are network sockets, use **select** rather than a round-robin approach. Better still, consider using **fork** or the new **Thread** module so that you can service requests asynchronously. Remember, though, that **fork** implies an overhead as the process is copied, and threads imply a memory overhead.

Regular Expressions   Regular expressions can be huge resource sinks. The backtracking process used to match groups and repeating elements implies a large overhead as it requires a number of iterations over the same section of text. Other traps and solutions are outlined here:

- Optimize regular expressions by reducing the number of quantifiers and assertions in a single expression. Doing this is especially useful when using expression groups, since this causes the regular expression engine to backtrack and populate the $# variables each time.

- Avoid using the $&, $\`, and $' variables. At the first point of use, Perl starts to track the information for every regular expression used afterward.

- Using a logical **or**, | |, outside of a regular expression can sometimes be quicker than using the alternate within a regular expression. So use

```
$found = if /one/ || /two/;
```

instead of

```
$found = if /one|two/;
```

- When testing a string for a number of times with many regular expressions, group all the a's, all the b's, and so on. Perl works faster this way because the internal tables will have already been built.

- If the string is large and the regular expressions are complex, use the **study** function to improve performance.

Files and File Systems   Because they are external, many people neglect to consider the effects of a file or file system call in the overall equation. Although such a call won't affect the Perl script execution, it does take time for the operating system to process the request. Reducing the number of calls, or the size of such calls, will help both performance and memory usage.

- Use **sysread** to get information in blocks, not **getc**.
- Use **grep** and **opendir** for reading directory listings to avoid large lists being returned from the **glob** function.
- Use the operating system **mkdir** command (if supported) when creating multiple directories, instead of using multiple calls to the built-in **mkdir**.
- Don't use **eof** when operators and functions detect **eof** automatically.

Calling External Applications   You don't have any control over the execution time and sequence of an external program, but you can reduce the effects by using internal functions or by forcing direct, rather than shell-based execution.

- Avoid making calls to operating system functions when the predefined variables built into every Perl script at execution time are likely to contain the information you want.
- Use the **Cwd** module instead of making an external call to **pwd**. Using **system** creates a subprocess and possibly a shell, involving a lot of extra instructions and processor time.
- Use lists with **system** and **exec** instead of using one big string that you have to quote and format in order to get the right information.

Reducing Memory

When we're talking about reducing the memory footprint for Perl, we're really talking about reducing the RAM footprint, rather than disk space. Internally, Perl will allow you to do all sorts of things that potentially increase the memory footprint without your being aware that this is happening. The obvious instances are loading entire files into memory for processing, but less obvious problems can be caused by creating temporary arrays and lists.

The places where we can reduce the memory footprint are few and far between. Perl's practicality comes from its automatic handling of things like memory and variable allocation, and garbage collection when variables go out of context. There is no way to control Perl's memory usage beyond the tips given here, although such control is planned for a future version.

Variables and Data   It's very easy to let Perl use a lot of memory without considering the consequences. The following tips should help you to reduce the memory footprint of your variables:

- Use the **vec** function to store very small numbers in a single variable, rather than individual variables for each.

- Use **pack** and **unpack** to store information efficiently in external files.

- Use **substr** to store small fixed-length strings in one larger string.

You can also follow this through to arrays and hashes, which can be stored in a file if memory space is really tight. If necessary, use temporary files to store very large arrays. In addition, consider using a DBM file to store hash and list information out of memory. If you want to store small pairs of information in hashes, consider using the **Tie::SubstrHash** module, which will compact hash data much more tightly than the normal 1K (or larger) key/value pair size.

Iteration and Program Control   Certain Perl statements automatically imply large memory overheads. The more significant ones are listed here:

- Use **each** in place of **keys** for iterating through hashes when order is not important. It reduces the size of the temporary list passed to the loop-control statement.

- Try to avoid creating large temporary lists; for example:

```
foreach (0..$#array)
{
    #Do something with $array[$_];
}
```

  Although this has been optimized in recent versions of Perl, it's still best avoided if possible. Use a **while** or **for** loop with a simple variable and test.

- In general, try to avoid any list operations that can be avoided; creating an array and then using it frequently uses a lot of temporary storage space, even on relatively small arrays.

- Use **undef** and **delete** to remove variables or hash elements that you no longer need.

- Pass around references to variables, especially lists and hashes, rather than supplying lists to the function each time.

■ Avoid creating temporary lists that are used solely to support a sequence for a hash; for example:

```
@sort = keys %hash;
foreach (sort @sorted)
...
```

Sort the list inline:

```
foreach (sort keys %hash)
```

If the list is complex, and you need to process each element in order to sort, remember that you can supply your own sorting function to **sort**. This process can even be used on complex data—for example, to sort dates, you could use:

```
foreach (sort sortdate keys %errors)
{
    print "$_\n";
}


sub sortdate
{
    my ($c,$d) = ($a,$b);

    $c =~ s{(\d+)/(\d+)/(\d+)}{sprintf("%04d%02d%02d",$3,$1,$2)}e;
    $d =~ s{(\d+)/(\d+)/(\d+)}{sprintf("%04d%02d%02d",$3,$1,$2)}e;

    $c <=> $d;
}
```

Here we've copied the values of **$a** and **$b** supplied to the function and then compared the modified values—doing this prevents us from modifying the originals, since **$a** and **$b** are really references to the list contents. In this instance the space optimization means a decrease in speed!

The
Complete
Reference

Chapter 22

Perl Compiler

P erl is, in the strict sense at least, an interpreted rather than a compiled language. Unlike languages such as C/C++ and Java, you don't have to compile Perl code into a separate binary format before you can actually execute the program you have written. Instead, the Perl interpreter takes the "raw" textual script code and then executes each statement.

In fact, Perl does work in a similar fashion to C/C++ and other compiled languages—there is, in fact, a compilation stage in the execution process. What actually happens is that Perl takes the raw script, parses and then compiles it into a special binary code called bytecode, and then uses the Perl engine to execute the binary code. The bytecode is in many ways similar to the machine code used by the CPU in your computer, but it's highly optimized for executing Perl statements.

In effect, Perl works just like C/C++, except that instead of compiling the source file into a machine-dependent form, the Perl interpreter does the compilation and execution on the fly each time you run the script. Because Perl, its parser and compiler, and the virtual machine that executes the final code are all very heavily optimized, the entire process, from starting the interpreter to actually running the compiled code, takes milliseconds on most modern machines. Even on a 20-year-old machine, Perl takes only a second to compile an average-length script into a form ready to be executed.

There are advantages to this approach—Perl can execute raw source code at a speed not vastly different to executing a compiled program. But because it's executing the source code, that code can be edited and reexecuted in seconds. You don't have to recompile and then reexecute the code first. Comparing even a fairly simple program shows just how optimized Perl is. Taking the simple "Hello World" example, it takes 0.158 milliseconds on my Linux machine to compile and execute the C version, but just 0.013 milliseconds to execute the Perl alternative.

The more astute of you will have recognized a potential bottleneck in the whole process, however. For scripts that don't actually change very regularly, such as those on a website, there is a massive overhead of reading, parsing, and compiling the source code each time Perl is asked to execute the script. There's also the issue of the libraries and modules used by Perl—these change even less frequently, and yet they are imported, parsed, and compiled in exactly the same way as the original script.

Other languages, including C/C++, Java, and Python, get around the library problem by always making use of a precompiled library—if I change the main script, only the script source needs to be recompiled. With Perl, it recompiles everything.

Currently, there are no solutions to the library problem, but there are ways of improving the execution speed of a script by taking the script in its compiled form and using that as the basis of the new script during execution. This is the approach used by extensions such as **mod_perl** and the **PerlEx** extension for ActivePerl—they both store the bytecode and execute that using a built-in interpreter. This avoids both the compilation stage and the requirement to **fork()** a new process and load the Perl interpreter each time the script is called.

These are web solutions, however, and not all problems are web based. They also don't resolve the need by some people to supply a "static" binary file that cannot be modified, mangled, or hacked by a third party.

This is where the Perl compiler comes in. It can convert a raw script into a C file that can then be compiled into a final binary. It's not combining the Perl interpreter and the raw source code; it's combining the Perl interpreter and the compiled bytecode into a single file. The bytecode is embedded into the C source and just becomes the data stream employed by the Perl interpreter to execute the "script."

In actual fact, the Perl compiler is much more useful than that. Because it's looking at the Perl code in its parsed and compiled form, it can also provide information about the source script—such as cross-referencing variable and subroutine references, or regurgitating the script in its parsed form—accounting for any optimization and precedence rules that have been implied during the parsing and compilation process.

In this chapter, we're going to take a detailed look at the Perl compiler and what it can do before we look at the interface, which allows you to take Perl scripts and turn them into stand-alone executables. We'll also do a speed comparison between a C and a Perl version of the same application that shows both the speed of the Perl interpreter and the advantage of an optimized language with advanced data-handling techniques. Before all that, however, we'll look at how not to create Perl executables—using **dump**.

Using dump

Perl—in combination with some operating systems—provides a method for dumping the core image of the current executable, that is, the currently executing Perl interpreter and its current script. The function that supports this is **dump**. Its use is very operating-system specific, since it relies on a separate operating system command to turn the dumped core into an application. The file that is actually produced is a core image, identical to that produced when an application crashes; when used with the **undump** command, this can be translated back into an executable.

```
dump LABEL
dump
```

If specified, execution will start from **LABEL** (by doing a **goto LABEL** when executed), or execution just starts from the beginning of the script.

What actually happens is that Perl calls the **abort** function, which causes a core dump. The contents of the core dump consist of all the current application data and code (core dumps are usually used when debugging an application). The state of the program, including any initialization in the original code, will be in place, so a script of the form

```
$message = "Hello World\n";
dump START;

START:
    print $message;
```

will already have the value of **$message** set when it is executed after being dumped. If you do not specify a label to the **dump** function, the program will just execute from the start.

Once dumped, you need to use the **undump** program to convert the dumped core into an executable. The **undump** program is not available on all platforms; and, in fact, on some systems it is not even possible. Most notably, any system that uses ELF (Executable and Linking Format) for its object format will not be able to use **undump**, and this includes Solaris and Linux. ELF is incompatible with the principle of the **undump** process, although it does support the creation of an executable directly (see the discussion of **unexec()** further on in this section).

In order to get the system working with Perl, you will need to have a version of **undump** installed on your system (it's available within the TeX distribution) and a copy of Perl compiled with static rather than dynamic libraries. You use the static version of Perl in combination with the dumped core file to produce an executable, for example:

```
$ dumpscript.pl
$ undump perl core
$ b.out
```

This example runs the **dumpscript.pl** script, which calls **dump**, and then uses **undump** and the static Perl executable to create a new application, **b.out**, using the core file.

Although **dump** is very clumsy, it does provide the facility for creating a "saved state" of an executable program. Of course, without an easy way to return the execution to this state, the function is virtually useless.

In fact, **dump** can also be used in the debugging process, since it causes a core dump that could be used by an external symbolic debugger, such as **dbx** or **gdb**. You'll need to know the internals of Perl pretty well for it to be of any specific use, since no C-level debugger will be able to understand the opcode format used internally by Perl scripts.

You can also use **dump** with the **unexec()** function (which is part of **emacs**) if you compile Perl with the **-DUNEXEC** flag. Unlike **dump**, **unexec()** attempts to make an executable directly, instead of relying on an external program to produce the final executable. In theory, any platform that supports a "dumped" version of **emacs** should be able to use this method of producing executable Perl scripts.

Irrespective of which method you use to produce the executable, dumping an image of a running program is not very reliable. With the introduction of a Perl compiler, there seems little need for such convoluted methods.

Using the Compiler

The Perl compiler is a relatively new inclusion in the Perl distribution and is still considered largely experimental. It's been updated and improved upon heavily in

Perl 5.6, to the point where most of the features of the compiler now work more or less as expected; but there is still lots of work to do to make it as easy to use and efficient as something like a C or Java compiler.

When producing a stand-alone executable, the opcode tree is embedded along with some C-based wrapper code into a C source file. This, in turn, can be compiled using a standard C compiler, such as **gcc**, to produce the final executable. Because the source file includes the Perl source code and is linked to the Perl interpreter, we get a fully stand-alone application. Further, because the Perl source is taken after the normal Perl parsing and optimization procedures have taken place, we end up with an already optimized version of the original script.

The entire system works using a series of backend modules, such as **B::C** for the C source code creator, or **B::Xref** for the cross-reference backend. When producing a stand-alone executable, you can also use the **perlcc** frontend, which does the conversion and compilation stages for you. We'll have a look at the backends first.

The Backends

There are two parts to the compiler backends. The **B** modules actually contain the backend code itself—these modules turn the raw opcode tree into a number of different formats. The **O** module just provides a nice friendly frontend to enable us to use the available backends.

We will examine nine backends with respect to both optimization and debugging: **C**, **CC**, **Bytecode**, **Terse**, **Debug**, **Xref**, **Lint**, **Deparse**, and **Showlex**. All backends work in the same basic way. You call the **O** module as part of the command line to a normal Perl interpreter, and then specify the backend and any options you want to define:

```
$ perl -MO=Backend[,OPTIONS] foo.pl
```

Most backends support three options. The **-v** option forces the backend to report extensive information about the compilation process. The **-D** option enables debugging—different backends support a number of different debugging options, so check the individual backends for more information on how to use these. The **-o** option (followed by a file name) redirects the output of the backend to another file. Multiple options to the frontend can be separated by commas.

C Backend

The **C** backend is the fundamental part of the conversion of a Perl script into its **C** opcode equivalent. The backend produces code based on the state of the Perl script just before execution begins—that is, the compilation, parsing, and optimization processes normally conducted by the interpreter have already been completed. The compiled program can, therefore, execute more or less identically to the original interpreted version. Unfortunately, this process also means that the speed of execution is identical.

The basic options, shared with the **CC** backend, are shown in Table 22-1. There are also a number of options specific to the **C** backend, shown in Table 22-2.

Option	Description
-	End of options.
-uPackname	Include functions defined in **Packname** to be compiled if they have not otherwise been selected. Normally, only functions that are identified as being used are included in the opcode tree. Unused functions are ignored. Using this option allows functions that are used via an **eval** to be compiled with the rest of the Perl script. Obviously, this also increases the size of the source code created, as well as the eventual size of the executable.

Table 22-1. *Basic C Backend Options*

Option	Description
-Do	Debug opcodes; prints each opcode as it is processed.
-Dc	Debug construct opcodes (COPs); prints COPs as they are processed, including file and line number.
-DA	Debug; prints array value information.
-DC	Debug; prints code value information.
-DM	Debug; prints magic variable information.
-fcog	Copy-on-grow; string values are declared and initialized statically. Can have an effect on speed, since each time the string grows in size, a new string variable is created and the information is copied over. The opposite action, **-fno-cog**, incurs less of a penalty but may also cause memory-related failures during execution of the final application.
-fno-cog	No copy-on-grow; string values are initialized dynamically.
-On	Set optimization to the value of **n**. Values of 1 and higher set **-fcog**.

Table 22-2. *Options Specifically for the C Backend*

For example, the following creates the C source code of the **foo.pl** Perl script to the file **foo.c**, with optimization:

```
$ perl -MO=C,-O1,-ofoo.c foo.pl
```

You can then compile the **foo.c** program using any C compiler, remembering to link to the Perl library in order to produce a final executable. It's quicker and easier to use the **perlcc** frontend to the whole process, which will not only produce the source, but also compile the file for you.

CC Backend

The **CC** backend produces C code equivalent to the tree that would be executed at run time. This is, in effect, like writing the script as it would be executed. The optimization and reduction stages have taken place already, allowing for much better performance. See the "Compilation" section in Chapter 20 for an explanation of the sort of optimizations that take place during the compilation of a Perl script.

At present, the compiler still deals with the raw bytecode of the script directly. This is not as efficient as it could be. For example, when using an integer within a Perl script, we still actually deal with a Perl scalar variable object, instead of just using a genuine C integer—which obviously affects performance.

The **CC** backend supports the basic options of the **C** backend that are shown in Table 22-1. The **CC**-specific options are shown in Table 22-3.

For example, to create the C source code of the **foo.pl** Perl script to the file **foo.c**:

```
$ perl -MO=CC,-ofoo.c foo.pl
```

Again, it's probably better to use the **perlcc** frontend, which we'll look at shortly, to produce and compile your script into its executable format.

Bytecode Backend

We can produce a permanently optimized version of a Perl script by storing the bytecode produced during the normal parsing and optimization stage. That way, when we execute the produced bytecode, we've already gone through the parsing and optimization process, thus saving us some time. This is the solution offered by web accelerators like **mod_perl** and **PerlEx**; they store the compiled version and execute it using an already loaded interpreter.

The easiest interface for producing a bytecode version of a script is to use **perlcc** with the **-b** option:

```
$ perlcc -b foo.pl
```

Option	Description
-mModulename	Generates source code for an XSUB, creating a hook function named **boot_Modulename**, suitable for identification by the **DynaLoader** module.
-Dr	Debug; outputs debugging information to **STDERR**. If **STDERR** is not specified, the debugging information is included as comments in the C source code produced.
-DO	Debug; prints with opcode as it's processed.
-Ds	Debug; prints the shadow stack of the opcode as it's processed.
-Dp	Debug; prints the contents of the shadow pad of lexical variables as loaded for each block (including the main program).
-Do	Debug; prints the name of each fake PP function just before it is processed.
-D	Debug; prints the source file name and line number of each line of Perl code as it is processed.
-Dt	Debug; prints the timing information for each compilation stage.
-ffreetmps-each-bblock	Forces the optimization of freeing temporaries to the end of each block until the end of each statement.
-ffreetmps-each-loop	Forces the optimization of freeing temporaries to the end of each enclosing loop, instead of the end of each statement. You can set only one of the **freetmps** optimizations at any one time.
-fomit-taint	Disables the generation of the tainting mechanism.
-On	Sets the optimization to level **n**. A level of **-O1** implies -ffreetmps-each-bblock, and -O2 implies -ffreetmps-each-loop.

Table 22-3. *Options Specifically for **CC** Backend*

This will produce a file, **foo.plc**, that is actually ready-to-run Perl script. It includes the bytecode and the **ByteLoader** module, which reads and executes the bytecode for you. The produced file is platform independent—it's still essentially a Perl source file, just in its compiled, rather than raw, state. To execute it, just run the script as normal:

```
$ perl foo.plc
```

Alternatively, you can produce a bytecode file, without the **ByteLoader** preamble, by using the backend directly:

```
$ perl -MO=Bytecode,-ofoo.bc foo.pl
```

Note that, by default, the bytecode file is sent to **STDOUT**, which will most likely upset your terminal. You should always use the **-ofilename** option to specify an alternative file in order to store the compiled program. Other options are listed in Table 22-4.

Terse Backend

The **Terse** backend is useful when you want to examine the exact execution path of a script in its opcode-compiled format. The information output is, as the name suggests, very terse, but it should provide you with a basic idea of the process that is taking place when a script executes. By default, the information is formatted and printed in syntax order; for example:

```
$ perl -MO=Terse -e '$a = $b + 2;
-e syntax OK
LISTOP (0x13c530) pp_leave
    OP (0x1349a0) pp_enter
    COP (0x13c5f0) pp_nextstate
    BINOP (0x1435a0) pp_sassign
        BINOP (0x12eb40) pp_add [1]
            UNOP (0x12eb00) pp_null [15]
                GVOP (0x12eae0) pp_gvsv   GV (0xc9864) *b
            SVOP (0x1435c0) pp_const   IV (0xbc9d8) 2
        UNOP (0xbf6c0) pp_null [15]
            GVOP (0xbf660) pp_gvsv   GV (0xc6ba0) *a
```

Option	Description
-Do	Debug; prints out each opcode as it is processed.
-Dt	Debug; prints out the compilation progress.
-Da	Debug; includes source assembler lines in the bytecode as comments.
-DC	Debug; prints each code value as taken from the final symbol tree.
-S	Produces bytecode assembler source instead of the final bytecode binary.
-m	Compiles the script as a module.
-fcompress-nullops	Completes only the required fields of opcodes that have been optimized by the compiler. Other fields are ignored (saves space). Can be switched off with **-fno-compress-nullops**.
-omit-sequence-numbers	Ignores the code normally produced that populates the **op_seq** field of each opcode (saves space). This is normally used only by Perl's internal compiler. Can be switched off with **-fno-omit-sequence-numbers**.
-fbypass-nullops	Ignores null opcodes; the code skips to the next non-null opcode in the execution tree (saves space and time). Can be switched off with **-fno-bypass-nullops**.
-f-strip-syntax-tree	Does not produce the internal pointers that compose the syntax tree. This does not affect execution, but the produced bytecode cannot be disassembled. This has the effect of rendering **goto LABEL** statements useless. It also works as a suitable security measure to stop bytecode-compiled scripts from being reverse engineered. Can be switched off with **-fno-strip-syntax-tree**.
-On	Sets optimization to level **n**. Currently, **-O1** implies **-fcompress-nullops** and **-fomit-sequence-numbers**. **-O6** implies **-fstrip-syntax-tree**.

Table 22-4. *Options Specifically for the **Bytecode** Backend*

The **Terse** backend supports only one option, **exec**, which outputs the opcodes in execution order. Unfortunately, it removes much of the formatting available in the default mode:

```
$ perl -MO=Terse,exec -e '$a = $b + 2;'
-e syntax OK
OP (0x1349a0) pp_enter
COP (0x13c5f0) pp_nextstate
GVOP (0x12eae0) pp_gvsv   GV (0xc9864) *b
SVOP (0x1435c0) pp_const   IV (0xbc9d8) 2
BINOP (0x12eb40) pp_add [1]
GVOP (0xbf660) pp_gvsv   GV (0xc6ba0) *a
BINOP (0x1435a0) pp_sassign
LISTOP (0x13c530) pp_leave
```

Debug Backend

For a more detailed view of the execution of opcodes than that provided by the **Terse** backend, you can use the **Debug** backend instead, which works in a similar way but provides more detailed information. By default, the information is output in syntax order:

```
$ perl -MO=Debug -e '$a = $b + 2;'
-e syntax OK
LISTOP (0x133530)
        op_next          0x0
        op_sibling       0x0
        op_ppaddr        pp_leave
        op_targ          0
        op_type          177
        op_seq           7065
        op_flags         13
        op_private       0
        op_first         0x151bf8
        op_last          0x141dc0
        op_children      3
OP (0x151bf8)
        op_next          0xcf1d0
        op_sibling       0xcf1d0
        op_ppaddr        pp_enter
        op_targ          0
        op_type          176
```

```
        op_seq          7058
        op_flags        0
        op_private      0
COP (0xcf1d0)
        op_next         0x12eae0
        op_sibling      0x141dc0
        op_ppaddr       pp_nextstate
        op_targ         0
        op_type         173
        op_seq          7059
        op_flags        1
        op_private      0
        cop_label
        cop_stash       0xbc87c
        cop_filegv      0xbca50
        cop_seq         7059
        cop_arybase     0
        cop_line        1
...
```

This output has been trimmed for brevity. The full list from this simple statement is 173 lines long!

Like the **Terse** backend, **Debug** also supports the output in execution order (**exec**), but once again the formatting is lost:

```
$ perl -MO=Debug,exec -e '$a = $b + 2;'|more
-e syntax OK
OP (0x151bf8)
        op_next         0xcf1d0
        op_sibling      0xcf1d0
        op_ppaddr       pp_enter
        op_targ         0
        op_type         176
        op_seq          7058
        op_flags        0
        op_private      0
COP (0xcf1d0)
        op_next         0x12eae0
        op_sibling      0x141dc0
```

```
op_ppaddr          pp_nextstate
op_targ            0
op_type            173
op_seq             7059
op_flags           1
op_private         0
cop_label
cop_stash          0xbc87c
cop_filegv         0xbca50
cop_seq            7059
cop_arybase        0
cop_line           1
```

The information provided here is probably only of real use to someone who is investigating the internal opcodes of a script.

Xref Backend

During the development of a project with Perl, it's sometimes difficult to see the wood for the trees. Looking for that elusive function definition, or trying to find where a particular function is used, can be a time-consuming process. Sure, we could use the debugger, or perhaps even **grep**, but there is an easier way that also gives us a useful document that we can keep with the Perl source code and use for future reference.

The **Xref** backend produces a report that details the use of all the variables, subroutines, and formats in a program. The report includes cross-references (including line numbers) indicating where the variables are used and which subroutine uses which variable, along with other valuable cross-referencing details.

The level of detail includes not only the subroutines and variables from the original file, but also all of the modules and files the original script relies upon. This means that even a relatively short script can produce a huge amount of information. The format of the report is as follows:

```
File filename1
  Subroutine subname1
    Package package1
      object1        C<line numbers>
      object2        C<line numbers>
      ...
    Package package2
    ...
```

Here's an example from a five-line script that prints the contents of a DBM file:

```
File dbmdump.pl
  Subroutine (definitions)
    Package UNIVERSAL
        &VERSION              s0
        &can                  s0
        &isa                  s0
  Subroutine (main)
    Package main
        $!                    11
        $0                    3, 11
        $datafile             7
        $df                   i5, 11, 11
        $key                  15, 15
        %db                   11, 13, 15, 17
        &O_RDONLY             &11
        *key                  13
        @ARGV                 3
```

The output has been trimmed for brevity; the full report runs to 246 lines.

The information can prove invaluable if you are trying to optimize the original source or find out which functions rely on certain variables. Normally, this information should be obtainable through the use of the internal debugger or by using one of the debugging methods outlined in Chapter 21. There are instances, however, when a cross-reference report is quicker, and it provides ancillary information that can help trace other bugs.

The function supports only two options, **-r** and **-D**. The **-r** option produces raw output. Rather than the formatted version shown previously, a single line is printed for each definition or use of a function, package, or variable. Here's a fragment from the same script used to produce the previous report:

```
dbmdump.pl (main)     3 main     @ ARGV          used
dbmdump.pl (main)     3 main     $ 0             used
dbmdump.pl (main)     5 main     $ df            intro
dbmdump.pl (main)     7 main     $ datafile      used
dbmdump.pl (main)    11 main     % db            used
dbmdump.pl (main)    11 main     $ df            used
dbmdump.pl (main)    11 main     & O_RDONLY      subused
dbmdump.pl (main)    11 main     $ 0             used
dbmdump.pl (main)    11 main     $ df            used
dbmdump.pl (main)    11 main     $ !             used
```

```
dbmdump.pl  (main)          13  main         %  db          used
dbmdump.pl  (main)          13  main         *  key         used
dbmdump.pl  (main)          15  main         $  key         used
dbmdump.pl  (main)          15  main         %  db          used
dbmdump.pl  (main)          15  main         $  key         used
dbmdump.pl  (main)          17  main         %  db          used
```

I've stripped the full pathname from this example and, once again, trimmed it for size. Otherwise, this is identical to the output produced. The columns are, in order, file, full package name (includes references to functions included via **AutoLoad**), line number, short package name, object type, object name, and how it was used in the specified line. Once the information is produced, it is quite voluminous. Using a suitable Perl script, it should be possible to summarize the information in a more readable form, perhaps by selectively excluding those modules you are not interested in. I'll leave that particular exercise to you.

The **-D** option supports two sub-debugging flags, both of which are best used in combination with the **-r** option. Using **-Dt**, the object on top of the object stack is printed as it is tracked, allowing you to trace the object as it is being resolved in each of the packages. The **-DO** function prints each operator as it is processed during the cross-referencing process.

Remember that much of the information that can be gleaned from the data supplied is also available via more traditional debugging methods. By the same token, a similar proportion of the information is also only available via this backend.

Lint Backend

Under many C environments, there is a program called **Lint**, which checks C source code for any parsing errors, including those that may not normally have been picked up by the C compiler. The **Lint** backend is a similar module for Perl. It can pick up many errors that may not be identified by the Perl interpreter, even with warnings switched on.

You can see from the options shown in Table 22-5 the errors that **Lint** attempts to identify.

Note that the use of this module is not intended as a replacement for either the **-w** command line option or the **strict** pragma (see Chapter 19 for more information). It augments the options available for finding possible performance and/or parser problems.

Deparse Backend

We've already seen some examples of the **Deparse** engine. It takes in a script and regurgitates it in its optimized form; but, unlike the **Bytecode** backend, the regurgitated

Option	Description
context	Warns when an array is used in an implied scalar context, such as **$foo = @bar**. Ordinarily, the Perl interpreter ignores this and just sets the value of **$foo** to the scalar value of **@bar** (the number of elements in the array). You can prevent the error from being reported by explicitly using the **scalar** function.
implicit-read	Warns whenever a statement implicitly reads from one of Perl's special variables, such as **$_**.
implicit-write	Warns whenever a statement implicitly writes to a special variable.
dollar-underscore	Warns when the **$_** variable is used, either explicitly or implicitly, as part of a **print** statement.
private-names	Warns when a variable, subroutine, or method is used when the name is not within the current package, or when the name begins with an underscore.
undefined-subs	Warns when an undefined subroutine is called.
regexp-variables	Warns when one of the special regular expression variables, **$'**, **$&**, or **$`**, is used.
All	Turns on all warnings.
None	Turns off all warnings.

Table 22-5. *Options for the **Lint** Backend*

script is in its source format. This means that we can use the **Deparse** engine to get an idea, in source format, of what the Perl interpreter thinks it is executing, rather than what you wrote. When debugging and optimizing code, it picks out the following:

- Statements and expressions that can be folded or optimized away
- Ambiguous statements, and how Perl interpreted them
- Badly formed expressions that didn't take into account the precedence rules

The specific options for the **Deparse** backend are shown in Table 22-6.

Option	Description
-p	Prints additional parentheses that would otherwise have been optimized away. Many parentheses can be ignored (or are implied) in the source code. For example, parentheses are not necessarily required around function arguments. This option ensures that all locations where parentheses are implied are actually printed. This can be useful when you want to discover how Perl has interpreted your implied parentheses in a statement. (See the examples that follow for more information.) Perl will reduce away any constant values, which will appear as **???** in the resulting output.
-uPACKAGE	Includes subroutines from **PACKAGE** that are not called directly (that is, those loaded by **AutoLoad** or those that are not resolved to subroutines during run time). Normally, these are ignored in the parsed output.
-l	Adds **#line** declarations to the output, based on the source code line and file locations.

-sC	"Cuddle" **elsif**, **else**, and **continue** blocks, for example,
	
	if ( )
	{
	}
	else
	{
	}
	
	will be printed as
	
	if ( ) {
	} else {
	}

Table 22-6.   *Options for the **Deparse** Backend*

The parentheses option is useful for demystifying the operator precedence that Perl uses. For example, here's a deparsed calculation:

```
$ perl -MO=Deparse,-p -e '$a + $b * $c / $d % $e;'
-e syntax OK
($a + (((($b * $c) / $d) % $e));
```

See Chapters 3 and 6 for the list of operators and their precedence.

Showlex Backend

The **Showlex** backend shows the lexical variables (those defined by **my** rather than **local**) used by a subroutine or file. Any options to the backend are assumed to be the names of the subroutines whose list of lexical variables you want to summarize.

For example, to summarize the lexical variables in the **uplsite.pl** script:

```
$ perl -MO=Showlex uplsite.pl
Pad of lexical names for comppadlist has 30 entries
0: PV (0x810af00) "@_"
1: PVNV (0x8315e48) "$debug"
2: PVNV (0x8339de8) "$remserver"
3: PVNV (0x8339dc4) "$remport"
4: PVNV (0x8339db8) "$user"
5: PVNV (0x8339ecc) "$password"
6: PVNV (0x8339ef0) "$dir"
7: PVNV (0x8339f14) "$localdir"
8: PVNV (0x8339f38) "$curxfermode"
9: SPECIAL #1 &PL_sv_undef
10: SPECIAL #1 &PL_sv_undef
11: SPECIAL #1 &PL_sv_undef
12: PVNV (0x8339ff8) "$ftp"
13: SPECIAL #1 &PL_sv_undef
14: SPECIAL #1 &PL_sv_undef
15: SPECIAL #1 &PL_sv_undef
16: SPECIAL #1 &PL_sv_undef
17: SPECIAL #1 &PL_sv_undef
18: SPECIAL #1 &PL_sv_undef
19: SPECIAL #1 &PL_sv_undef
20: SPECIAL #1 &PL_sv_undef
21: SPECIAL #1 &PL_sv_undef
22: SPECIAL #1 &PL_sv_undef
23: SPECIAL #1 &PL_sv_undef
24: SPECIAL #1 &PL_sv_undef
25: SPECIAL #1 &PL_sv_undef
26: SPECIAL #1 &PL_sv_undef
27: SPECIAL #1 &PL_sv_undef
28: SPECIAL #1 &PL_sv_undef
29: PVNV (0x833a154) "$currentdir"
etc/mcslp/books/paa/ch07/uplsite.pl syntax OK
```

The perlcc Frontend

The main method for compiling a Perl script into a final executable is the **perlcc** script. This takes a number of command line options that control the generation process. It also automates the entire process from the generation of the C source code right through to the compilation and linking stages. Using it at its simplest level, the command

```
$ perlcc foo.pl
```

will compile the **foo.pl** script into the executable **foo**.

When converting a script into a stand-alone executable, the process assumes you have installed Perl and have a C compiler on your system. The **perlcc** script (which is written in Perl) should account for the specific file locations of your Perl installation and the required tools for building.

    *The Perl compiler is not currently supported under Windows or Mac OS. Under
    Windows, you can use the PerlApp extension supplied with the Perl Development Kit
    from ActiveState to convert an application into a stand-alone executable.*

The **perlcc** frontend supports a number of command line arguments. These control the compilation, code generation, and linking process for translating a Perl source script into an executable program. Most of the options are actually passed on to the underlying backend modules. The command line options also control the calls to the compiler and linker used to build the final executable. Certain options simplify both the process of compiling large programs consisting of many Perl scripts and modules, and the compilation of multiple scripts into multiple executables.

Using perlcc

The basic way of using **perlcc** is just to supply the name of the script on the command line:

```
$ perlcc foo.pl
```

Doing this will convert and compile **foo.pl** into the ready-to-run executable **foo**. Note that, because it converts and compiles the full version of the script (including any imported modules), we don't need any other options. It will determine any required modules, extensions, or libraries, and either incorporate the extensions into the executable or provide the necessary hooks so that dynamic libraries can be loaded.

If you supply a Perl module, then it gets converted into a shared library that you can use directly within Perl using **use Module**:

```
$ perlcc Bar.pm
```

This produces the library **Bar.so**.

Finally, you can produce a stand-alone bytecode script using the **-b** option:

```
$ perlcc -b foo.pl
```

which produces **foo.plc**, ready for running directly through Perl.

Command Line Arguments

The frontend also supports a number of additional arguments that control different aspects of the compilation process. They are outlined here for reference.

```
-L DIRS
```

adds the directories specified in **DIRS** to the C/C++ compiler. Each directory should be separated by a colon.

```
-I DIRS
```

adds the directories specified in **DIRS** to the C/C++ compiler. Each directory should be separated by a colon.

```
-C FILENAME
```

gives the generated C code the file name specified by **FILENAME**. Only applicable when compiling a single source script.

```
-o FILENAME
```

gives the generated executable the file name specified by **FILENAME**. Only applicable when compiling a single-source script.

```
-e LINE
```

is identical to the Perl **-e** option. Compiles **LINE** as a single-line Perl script. The default operation is to compile and then execute the one-line script. If you want to save the executable generated, use the **-o** flag.

```
-regex NAME
```

NAME should specify a regular expression to be used when compiling multiple source files into multiple executables. For example, the command

```
$ perlcc -regex 's/\.pl/\.bin/' foo.pl bar.pl
```

would create two executables, **foo.bin** and **bar.bin**.

```
-verbose LEVEL
```

sets the verbosity of the compilation process to the level specified by **LEVEL**. This should be in the form of either a number or a string of letters. Except where specified via the **-log** option, the information is sent to **STDERR**. The available levels are given in Table 22-7.

For example, to set the maximum verbosity level, you might use

```
$ perlcc -v 63 -log foo.out foo.pl
```

Note that some options require that the name of a suitable file be given via the **-log** option (described next). If the **-log** tag has been given, and no specific verbosity level has been specified, the script assumes a verbosity level of 63. If no verbosity or log file is specified, a level of 7 is implied.

```
-log NAME
```

Numeric	Letter	Description
1	g	Code generation errors to **STDERR**.
2	a	Compilation errors to **STDERR**.
4	t	Descriptive text to **STDERR**.
8	f	Code generation errors to file (**-log** flag needed).
16	c	Compilation errors to file (**-log** flag needed).
32	d	Descriptive text to file (**-log** flag needed).

Table 22-7.   *Verbosity Levels for the* **perlcc** *Command*

logs the progress of the compilation to the file **NAME**. Note that the information is appended to the file; the contents are not truncated before more information is added. The effect of this option is to make the entire process of compilation silent—all output is redirected to the specified file.

```
-argv ARGS
```

must be used with the **-run** or **-e** option. Causes the value of **@ARGV** to be populated with the contents of **ARGS**. If you want to specify more than one argument, use single quotes and separate each argument with a space.

```
-sav
```

causes the intermediate C source code that is generated during the compilation to be saved in a file with the same name as the source with ".c" appended.

```
-gen
```

tells **perlcc** to generate only the C source code—the file will not be compiled into an executable.

```
-run
```

immediately runs the executable that was generated. Any remaining arguments to **perlcc** will be supplied to the executable as command line arguments.

```
-prog
```

specifies that all files supplied are programs. The option causes Perl to ignore the normal interpretation that .pm files are actually modules, not scripts.

```
-mod
```

specifies that the files should be compiled as modules, not scripts. The option overrides the normal interpretation that files ending in .p, .pl, and .bat are Perl scripts.

Environment Variables

You can change some of the implied logic of the **perlcc** process by using environment variables. These modifications will affect all compilation, unless you use the command line arguments to override the new defaults.

The **PERL_SCRIPT_EXT** variable contains a list of colon-separated regular expressions. These define the extensions that **perlcc** automatically recognizes as scripts. For example, the default value is

```
PERL_SCRIPT_EXT = '.p$:.pl$:.bat$';
```

Note the use of **$** to define that the extension should be at the end of the file name.

The **PERL_MODULE_EXT** variable operates in the same way, only for those files that should be recognized as modules. The default value is .pm$.

During the compilation process, the **perlcc** module creates a number of temporary files. All of these files' names are based on the value of the **$$** Perl variable, which refers to the current process ID. Thus, the temporary file for the **-e** option is perlc$$.p, the file for temporary C code is perlc$$.p.c, and a temporary executable is stored in perlc$$.

Differences Between Interpreted and Compiled Code

Because of the methods used to produce an executable version of a Perl script, there are minor differences between interpreted and compiled code. For the most part, the differences are related to the behavior of the compilation process, and in time they should be able to be modified such that the compiled and interpreted versions of the same script work identically. Unfortunately, other bugs are directly related to the way the compiler operates, and it's unlikely that these will be able to be changed.

The currently known list of differences is as follows:

- Compiled Perl scripts calculate the target of **next**, **last**, and **redo** loop control statements at compile time. Normally, these values are determined at run time by the interpreter.

- The decision of Perl to interpret the .. operator as a range or flip-flop operator is normally decided at run time, based on the current context. In a compiled program, the decision is made at compile time, which may produce unexpected results.

- Compiled Perl scripts use native C arithmetic instead of the normal opcode-based arithmetic used in interpreted scripts. This shouldn't cause too many problems (in fact, it makes things quicker); but it may affect calculations on large numbers, especially those at the boundaries of the number ranges.

- Many of the deprecated features of Perl are not implemented in the compiler.

Comparing Script and Executable Speeds

Many factors affect the speed of execution of a typical program. The platform on which you are running obviously has an effect, including the memory, hard disk, and other application requirements at the time the program is run. When considering a Perl script, there are additional overheads to the execution process.

With a C program, the time to execute a program can be split into three elements:

- The time to load the program, including any dynamic loading of libraries.

- The execution of any user-defined components.

- The execution of any system functions. These include any access to the operating system proper, such as files and network sockets, and any access to the memory system. Depending on the implementation, you can also add the library loading time to this figure.

With a Perl script that is interpreted, the list is longer; and, as such, the equivalent process should take longer, even for a very simple statement:

- The time to load the Perl interpreter

- The time for Perl to load the Perl script

- The time taken for the Perl interpreter to parse the script and translate it into the opcode tree

- The execution of the Perl opcode tree

- The execution of any system functions

It should be obvious that Perl should, in theory, be a lot slower than a compiled version of the same program written in C. When a Perl script is compiled into a binary executable, two of the preceding elements can be removed. The script is already in the format of a binary executable; all you need to do is load the binary and execute it. This is where the speed advantage becomes apparent.

When comparing times, you need to compare the following operations:

- Time taken to compile the C program

- Time taken to execute the C program

- Time taken to execute the interpreted Perl script

- Time taken to compile the Perl script into a binary

- Time taken to execute the Perl binary

It's also worth considering the overall time taken to do the following:

- Compile the C program and then execute it 100 times.

- Execute the Perl script 100 times with the interpreter.

- Compile the Perl script into a binary and then execute it 100 times.

These figures will show the difference in total execution time between the C program, interpreted Perl, and compiled Perl. Remember that when a Perl script is interpreted, it must be compiled before it is executed, which takes a finite amount of time.

Usually, the reason for using a compiled binary is to increase the speed of execution. By checking the combined times for running the script 100 times, you should get a rough idea of how much of a speed increase you can expect. Obviously, it's likely that the script will be run significantly more than 100 times, but the same calculation can be applied to any number of executions.

Tests

We'll be comparing three basic programs. The first performs a repetitive calculation on an ascending number for a specific number of iterations. This tests the relative speed of calculations and loops, something we already know is slower in Perl than in a compiled C program. Here is the C version used in the tests:

```c
#include <math.h>

int main()
{
    int i;

    for(i=0;i<10000;i++)
        {
            sqrt(abs(sin(i)+cos(i)));
        }
}
```

The following code shows the Perl version. Note that it's much shorter; it shows the brevity with which programs can be written in Perl. You don't have to worry about any of the initialization that the C equivalent requires. Also notice that, otherwise, the two versions are very similar.

```perl
for(my $i=0;$i<10000;$i++)
{
    sqrt(abs(sin($i)+cos($i)));
}
```

The next test is a simple text-processing test. We'll count the number of lines in a document. The document in question is actually a list of all the words in a public domain dictionary that begin with "a" (for reasons that will become apparent in the next script). This tests basic I/O in the two languages. Essentially, the performance of the two should be largely identical, since Perl will optimize the process down to an almost identical structure.

```c
#include <stdio.h>

int main()
{
  char *line;
  FILE *data;
  long count=0;

  data = fopen("wordlist","rw");

  while(!feof(data))
    {
       fgets(line,255,data);
       count++;
    }
  printf("%d lines\n",count);
}
```

The Perl version of the second test can be seen next. Once again, note that the overall structure is largely identical, although Perl's **<FH>** operator makes reading in the information much easier.

```perl
open(DATA,"<wordlist")

while(<DATA>)
{
    $lines++;
}
close(DATA);

print "$lines lines\n";
```

The final test is an advanced version of the second test. We'll read in the words from the file and then calculate the number of unique lines. Within C, we'll use a simple keyword table stored in the **words** array. This will hold the list of words we have already recorded. To identify whether the word has already been seen, we just compare the new word against every entry in the array. This process is slow and inefficient, but it is the shortest (in lines) of the methods available. We could have used a binary tree or even a hashing system, but doing so would have added significantly more lines to an already long C program.

```c
#include <stdio.h>

char words[32000][260];
long wordidx=0;

void addtolist(char word[255])
{
  int i=0;
  for(i=0;i<wordidx;i++)
    {
      if (strcmp(word,words[i]) == 0)
          return;
    }
  strcpy(words[++wordidx],word);
}

int main()
{
  char line[255];
  FILE *data;
  long count=0;

  data = fopen("wordlist","rw");

  while(!feof(data))
    {
      fgets(line,255,data);
      addtolist(line);
    }
  printf("%ld unique lines\n",wordidx);
}
```

The Perl script for the third test is significantly shorter, but only because we can directly use hashes, instead of having to use a separate function and loop to search an array.

```perl
open(DATA,"<wordlist") || die "Can't open file";

my %words;
```

```
while(<DATA>)
{
    $words{$_} = 1;
}
close(DATA);

print scalar keys %words," unique lines\n";
```

Summary Results

Each test was run three times, and the **times** command that is standard with the **bash** shell was used to test the execution of each item. This calculates the elapsed time, and the user and system time for each command. The times shown are the elapsed amount of time for the program to load, execute, and quit.

The tests show a significant difference in execution times both between the C and Perl programs, and also between the interpreted and compiled versions of the Perl scripts. The times (in seconds) are shown in Table 22-8. The figures show two things: first, the difference in execution time between a C program and a Perl script and, second, the performance gain between executing a Perl script in its interpreted form

Operation	Test 1	Test 2	Test 3
Compile C to binary	0.201	0.174	0.181
Execute C program	0.018	0.051	128.81
Compile C program once, execute 100 times	2.001	5.274	12.881
Execute interpreted Perl script	0.048	0.174	0.456
Compile Perl script to binary	3.164	3.213	3.214
Execute Perl script as binary	0.058	0.18	0.489
Execute interpreted Perl script 100 times	4.8	17.4	45.6
Compile Perl program once, execute 100 times	8.964	21.21	52.114

Table 22-8. *Summary Times for Comparison Tests (in Seconds)*

and then its compiled form. For additional comparison, the table also shows the time taken to perform 100 C, interpreted Perl, and compiled Perl executions.

Irrespective of the values, it should be noted that these are fairly immature benchmark tests, although they do show many of the advantages of compiling a Perl script into an executable. It's also worth remembering why the time taken to compile the Perl script into a binary is relatively high. Creating a Perl binary involves not only the compilation of the script into its native Perl format, but also a significant amount of translation to make that into a C source that can be compiled. It also needs to be linked to the Perl library that supplies all of the core Perl functions and the Perl interpreter.

The most obvious difference is the drop in speed from a raw C program to a Perl version. In the case of the interpreted version of the script, some of this difference can be attributed to the time taken to compile the script into opcodes, optimize it, and then execute the opcode tree. However, it could equally be related to the speed of the mathematical calculations in Perl.

The compiled version of the Perl script does at least narrow the gap. It is likely that a good deal of the overhead here is related to loading a binary that is about 820K, compared to the 12K for the C version. The Perl binary is large because we used a static, rather than a dynamic, Perl library. With a dynamic Perl library, the size is much smaller—about 11K—but many of the functions from the dynamic library will also need to be loaded.

For the second test, both the Perl and C versions are incredibly quick; the program is very simple, and probable differences between the cores of both programs are likely to be very small. The biggest difference is, of course, in the last test, in which the Perl version is significantly quicker than the C equivalent. The main reason is that we've cheated and used a hash to do the deduping operation. Within the C source we had to use a different method to achieve the same result. The C version is also much longer, by source lines, and the algorithm used here is not ideal. Had I coded a binary tree or even a hash system in the C program, there might have been a smaller difference in the speed tests between the two. However, to add a C-based hashing system or binary tree system would have increased the length of the C program considerably.

The figures comparing the execution of the interpreted Perl script 100 times and the compiled and then interpreted version are much more telling. You can see very clearly that executing the compiled Perl script is much faster than executing the interpreted version. This difference is significant if you are expecting to install a script in a live environment where it may be called a large number of times, as, for example, on a website.

The other benefit of a compiled executable is that you can continue to develop and test with the interpreted version while using a final compiled production version in the live environment. You can be guaranteed that the interpreted and compiled versions will work identically, and they will both retain the same compatibility. They can even use the same configuration and data files without requiring any modifications.

This is a much more efficient development environment than using C or some other language that requires a separate compilation each time you want to test a feature or bug fix. As you saw in the last chapter, when debugging a Perl program, you only need to change the source and run the interpreter again. A C program needs to be recompiled and relinked between each test of a bug fix.

As a further comparison, let's imagine the program in the second test is riddled with 100 bugs, and we recompile the program between each fix. Ignoring the time to edit the source, the C version would take 129 seconds for each compilation and execution, and a total of 214 minutes for the entire process. The Perl version would take 52 seconds, including a final compilation to an executable binary. That's an efficiency gain of 247 percent!

Chapter 23

Perl Documentation

An application is next to useless without documentation. The current trend is not to supply the hefty multipage manuals that used to be supplied with the software that you bought. But even here, you're not bereft of information—even if the single slip of paper just directs you to a README or other document on the supplied CD. This move to online documentation has sparked a completely new range of software purely dedicated to the task of displaying documentation on screen.

These applications can stretch from very simple text viewers to complex help systems, and, more usually these days, a set of HTML documents that can be viewed, searched, and bookmarked just as with any other HTML-based document.

There are some advantages to using online documentation—the obvious one is that the documentation can normally be searched much more effectively than using a contents page or index. Another advantage, and one of the reasons that it's so popular with shareware and free software (including Perl), is that it can be provided along with the software as part of the downloaded package. However, the main problem with online documentation is that it's never easily available if you're having a problem with your machine!

If you're going to supply online documentation, then you have to choose a suitable format, and in the case of Perl, it needs to be something that is ultimately cross-platform compatible and practical for use while you are programming. Perl's development predates the invention of HTML by a few years, and at the time there wasn't a truly cross-platform documentation solution. There still isn't one now—HTML is not really designed to be used for "documents" in the true sense of the word, but it would have filled the gap nicely.

Instead, a new document format was invented, called POD—Plain Old Documentation. This actually works much like HTML, using a combination of tags and raw text to build up the document. Unlike HTML, POD was designed purely with online documentation in mind. This means you are limited to two levels of header, lists, and inline italic, bold, and link elements.

The advantage of POD over all the other formats is that it can be easily translated into HTML, the Unix man pages, plain text, and even word processor formats such as RTF (Rich Text Format). Once you've gone as far as converting to one of these base formats, you've got free reign to go from there and convert to PostScript, Microsoft Word, or Adobe Acrobat PDF (Portable Document Format). Furthermore, POD documents can be embedded into Perl source code, so as you write a function, you can also document it.

In this chapter, we'll concentrate on three aspects of the documentation process. First is understanding how to use the documentation that is supplied with Perl in its different distributions. Next we'll look at how to write and include your own documentation in your applications. The last part of the chapter looks at converting a POD document into an alternative format, including plain text and HTML, and a trick for converting the installed documentation into HTML through a web browser.

Using the Supplied Documentation

Perl comes with its own extensive documentation that covers virtually every angle of the language, from the core components and language descriptions through to the information on the internals. All of the modules that come with the standard distribution also include their own documentation.

You can see a list of the main Perl POD documentation in Table 23-1. The table lists the core documents, loosely referred to as *perlpod*, that make up the core documentation for the Perl language. They don't document any of the individual modules that come with Perl, only the built-in functions, language syntax, and other language-specific (rather than library-specific) information.

Document	Description
perl	The main Perl document that describes the core language and the contents of the other POD documents
perldelta	Perl changes since the previous version
perl5005delta	Perl changes in version 5.005
perl5004delta	Perl changes in version 5.004
perlfaq	The root document of the Perl "Frequently Asked Questions" documents tree
perltoc	Perl documentation table of contents
perldata	Description of the built-in data formats
perlsyn	Guide to Perl's syntax
perlop	Perl operator list, descriptions, and precedence
perlre	Details on the Perl regular-expression engine syntax
perlrun	Perl command line execution options and operations
perlfunc	Core reference for the Perl built-in functions
perlopentut	Tutorial for the **open** function
perlvar	List/description of the predefined Perl variables
perlsub	Design and method guidelines for Perl subroutines

Table 23-1.   *Perl POD Documents*

Document	Description
perlmod	Information on how Perl modules work
perlmodlib	How to write and use Perl modules
perlmodinstall	Installing Perl modules from CPAN
perlform	The Perl **format** system
perlunicode	Perl Unicode support
perllocale	Perl locale support
perlreftut	Perl reference tutorial
perlref	Perl references
perldsc	Perl data structures introduction
perllol	"List of lists" data structure examples
perlboot	Object orientation tutorial for beginners
perltoot	Object orientation tutorial, part 1
perltootc	Object orientation tutorial, part 2
perlobj	Perl objects
perltie	Using **tie** for providing object-based interfaces to complex external data sources
perlbot	Object orientation tricks and examples
perlipc	Perl interprocess communication
perlfork	Perl **fork** information
perlthrtut	Perl threads tutorial
perllexwarn	Perl warnings and their control
perlfilter	Perl source filters
perldbmfilter	Perl DBM filters
perlcompile	Perl compiler suite introduction
perldebug	Perl debugging, including guide to the debugger
perldiag	Perl warning, error, and other diagnostic messages
perlnumber	Perl number semantics

Table 23-1. *Perl POD Documents* (continued)

Document	Description
perlsec	Perl security
perltrap	Perl traps for the unwary
perlport	Perl portability guide
perlstyle	Perl style guide
perlpod	Perl plain old documentation definition
perlbook	List of suggested Perl books
perlembed	Details on how to embed **perl** in your C or C++ application
perlapio	Perl internal I/O abstraction interface
perldebguts	Perl debugging guts and tips
perlxs	XS application programming interface for extensions
perlxstut	XS tutorial
perlguts	Perl internal functions for use with XS extensions
perlcall	Perl calling conventions from C
perlapi	Perl API listing (autogenerated)
perlintern	Perl internal functions (autogenerated)
perltodo	Perl things to do
perlhack	Perl hackers guide
perlhist	Perl history records
perlamiga	Perl notes for Amiga
perlcygwin	Perl notes for Cygwin
perldos	Perl notes for DOS
perlhpux	Perl notes for HP-UX
perlmachten	Perl notes for Power MachTen
perlos2	Perl notes for OS/2
perlos390	Perl notes for OS/390
perlvms	Perl notes for VMS

Table 23-1.   *Perl POD Documents* (continued)

The library modules both from the original distribution and those that you download and install from elsewhere, should include their own POD documentation embedded into the module files themselves.

How you view this documentation is entirely dependent on the platform you are using Perl on. Different platforms also have some tools that can be used to make browsing and finding the right documentation easier. We'll look at the three main operating systems, Unix, Windows, and Mac OS, in this section. If you are using Perl on another platform, then either try the README document that came with your distribution, or see the "Converting POD to Other Formats" section later in this chapter to convert POD documents into a format you can read more easily.

Unix

Under Unix, Perl documentation is converted into *man page* format, accessible through the **man** command. The initial installation procedures convert all of the perlpod and standard library files into manual pages installing them within the **man** directory structure under the main installation directory. For example, if the install directory is /usr/local, then the pages are installed under /usr/local/man. The **perlpod** documentation is put into section 1, and module documentation into section 3. The MakeMaker system will also force the installation of new modules so that their documentation is installed into the same location.

The primary tool for viewing the perlfunc document under Unix is therefore

```
$ man perlfunc
```

To view a library module, such as **Net::Ping**, supply the module name instead:

```
$ man Net::Ping
```

If you use **emacs** or **xemacs**, then you have access to a man-mode. This allows you to view a manual page within a buffer, providing the usual scrolling and cut and paste facilities available in any read-only buffer. To use it, type **M-x man**, and then enter the name of the manual page to view. It'll be located, parsed, and then displayed. Once within a buffer with man-mode, you can press **m** to open a linked document. You can see a sample of the main **Perl** manual page as viewed within **emacs** in Figure 23-1.

As an augmentation to the **man** tool, Perl installs the **perldoc** command. This allows you to view more than just entire documents, it'll also display components of the **perlpod**

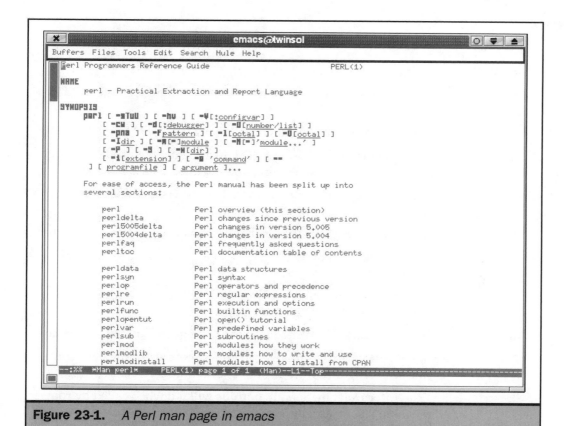

Figure 23-1.   *A Perl man page in emacs*

documentation set, which makes it exceedingly useful for picking out specific elements, especially from the perlfunc document, which includes every single function in one long document. For example, to view only the **localtime** function, you'd use

```
$ perldoc -f localtime
```

The output format is in **man (nroff)** format, so it should be displayed using the appropriate highlights. You can see a list of the full command line options for **perldoc** in Table 23-2.

FINE-TUNING
APPLICATIONS

Option	Description
-h	Prints out a help message.
-v	Annotates the process followed when looking for an individual item.
-t	Displays using plain text, instead of **nroff**.
-u	Outputs the raw POD-formatted documentation; useful if you want to convert to something other than nroff or plain text.
-m	Displays the entire module, including the code and unformatted POD documentation.
-l	Displays the name of the file that contains what you're looking for.
-F	Uses the next argument as a file name, and disable searching of the standard directories.
-f function	Displays the documentation for the built-in **function**, as contained within the perlfunc page.
-q perlfaq	Displays the FAQ entries matching the regular expression **perlfaq**.
-X	Tells **perldoc** to use an index, if one is present, for the item you are searching for.
-U	Run insecurely. By default, **perldoc** will fail when called by **root** because it's not strictly secure. Using **-U** sets the real and effective user IDs to nobody, nouser, or -2.

Table 23-2.   *Command Line Options for **perldoc***

Windows

Windows installations always convert the documentation into HTML format. With the ActiveState distributions, you'll get a very well organized set of HTML documents, as well as Win32-specific documentation and a separate ActiveState/Win32 FAQ. You can see a sample in Figure 23-2. You also have access to the **perldoc** command, but it outputs a text version in the command window, rather than opening a browser and displaying the formatted version.

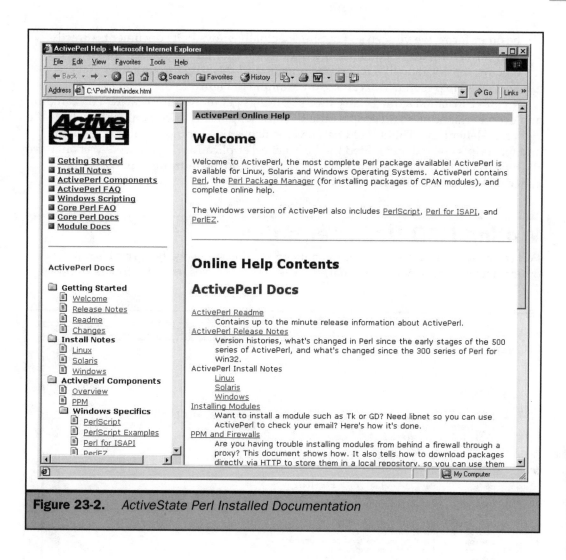

Figure 23-2. *ActiveState Perl Installed Documentation*

Installed modules should install HTML versions of their documentation. The PPM and VPM tools both work this way, and if you use the **CPAN** module, then MakeMaker will install HTML versions of the documentation as well.

Mac OS/Mac OS X

Because the Mac OS doesn't have a command line or a convenient place to install a suite of documentation, MacPerl comes with its own POD viewer called Shuck. Unlike all the other forms we've seen so far, Shuck actually views POD documents directly, without converting the documents into another format. You can access the core Perl documents, the additional MacPerl documents, and the FAQ through the MacPerl application's Help menu. You can see an example in Figure 23-3.

If you've installed a third-party module, things get more complicated. You can drag and drop Perl modules and scripts onto the Shuck application, but only if they have the right four-letter type. This should be TEXT, which is fine for most editor documents and for scripts created and edited by the MacPerl application. If you need to change the file type, then try using FileTyper, which you can download from **http://www.ugcs. caltech.edu/~dazuma/filetyper/**.

Writing POD Documentation

Perl is a cross-platform language, so using an architecture-specific format is not an option. Using a more neutral format, such as HTML, causes its own problems on

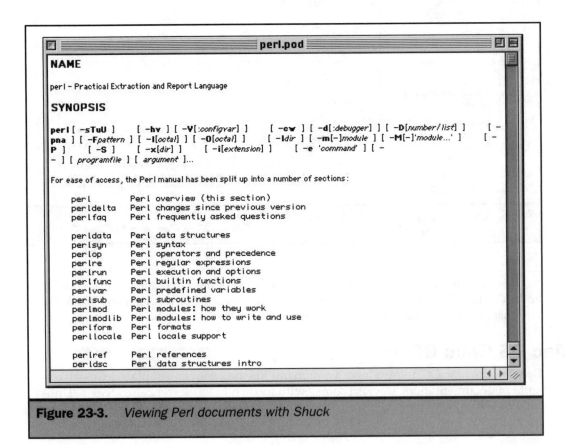

Figure 23-3.   *Viewing Perl documents with Shuck*

machines where it may be possible, but not necessarily practical, to have an HTML browser around all the time. Instead, Perl documentation is written in POD format, which uses a similar tag-based system to HTML, but the overall format is much simpler and straightforward.

Because POD is very simple, it can also be easily translated into other formats—this is done automatically into nroff under Unix and HTML under Windows. Perl even comes with the tools to allow you to convert the documentation yourself.

POD Components

The POD format works slightly different than HTML, even though it uses the same basic premise of simple text tabs. A POD document is made up of three different types of paragraphs: verbatim, command, and ordinary text. The purpose of each paragraph type is fixed in terms of the POD documentation but unique when translated.

The translation of the paragraph information is up to the translation script that turns the original POD documentation into its final state. For example, ordinary paragraphs are turned into justified text paragraphs when converted to text but are embedded into paragraph tags when converted to HTML.

Each element can also have embedded escape sequences, which allow you to specify an alternative printed format for a word or sentence. This includes boldfacing and underlining text, for example, as well as introducing references and links to other documents or other parts of the same document, just like HTML. Again, it's up to the translation scripts to convert the embedded tags into the corresponding format: for HTML, they become a clickable link, and for Unix manual pages (as available through the **man** command), they are underlined references.

There is no standard format or layout for a POD document, but different translators place certain levels of significance on different elements within the source POD file; for example, the text translator ignores links. We'll have a look at a sample document shortly, but it's worth remembering that all of the different encoding samples can be used to create some very simple documentation with little effort.

Command Paragraph

Command paragraphs specify that some special element or formatting should be applied to the supplied word, sentence, paragraph, or section. It allows you to insert headings, subheadings, and lists into the document. All command paragraphs start with an equal sign and a keyword that specifies the formatting to be applied. The paragraph may include an additional keyword or reference. For example, the paragraph

```
=head1 This is a main heading
```

creates a level-one heading, the text of which is "This is a main heading". Other command paragraphs are shown in Table 23-3.

Command	Result
=head1 text	Applies first-level heading, using **text** as the description.
=head2 text	Applies second-level heading, using **text** as the description.
=over n	Starts indentation of paragraphs with **n** specifying the number of characters to use for indentation. Ends the indentation with **=back**.
=item text	Specifies the title for an item in a list. The value of **text** will be interpreted differently, according to the translator.
=back	Ends a list or indentation.
=for format	Allows you to specify that the following paragraph should be inserted exactly as supplied, according to the specified format. For example, **=for html <font size=+1>Heading</font>** would be inserted into the translated file only by an HTML translator.
=begin format **=end format**	Acts similarly to **=for**, except that all the paragraphs between **=begin** and **=end** are included by the specified format translator as preformatted text.
=pod	Specifies the start of a POD document. It is best used when the documentation is included as part of a script. The **=pod** command paragraph tells the compiler to ignore the following text.
=cut	Specifies the end of a **=pod** section.

Table 23-3.   *Command Paragraphs*

Of all the command paragraphs, the head paragraphs are the most important, as they help to define the major and minor headings within the document.

There are some accepted standards for laying out the individual components of your document. At the top level (indicated by **=head1**) are the major sections of the document, such as the title or synopsis of the POD document. At the second level are the subheadings, perhaps major components or functions. If you need an additional

Element	Description
NAME	Mandatory comma-separated list of the functions or programs documented by the man page
SYNOPSIS	Outline of the function's or program's purpose
DESCRIPTION	Longer description or discussion of the program's purpose
OPTIONS	The command line options or function arguments
RETURN VALUE	What the program returns if successful
ERRORS	Any return codes, errors, or exceptions that may be produced
EXAMPLES	Examples of the program's or function's use
ENVIRONMENT	The environment or variables used by and modified by the program
FILES	The files used
SEE ALSO	Other entries to refer to
NOTES	Any additional commentary
CAVEATS/WARNINGS	Anything to be aware of during the program's use
DIAGNOSTICS	Errors or messages produced by the program and what they mean
BUGS	Things that do not work as expected
RESTRICTIONS	Items that are built-in design features and limitations
AUTHOR	Who wrote the function or program
HISTORY	The source or origin of the program or function

Table 23-4. *POD Document Section Names*

FINE-TUNING
APPLICATIONS

level beyond those two, you can use **=item** entries to add new levels: just use in combination with the **=over** command paragraph to indent each additional heading.

Table 23-4 lists, in the rough order in which they should appear, the major headings that you should include for all POD documentation. You don't have to include all of the elements—don't include a **BUGS** heading if there aren't any—but you should include the **NAME**, **SYNOPSIS**, **DESCRIPTION**, and **AUTHOR** sections, especially if you are aiming to release the code and its document to the public.

Ordinary Text Paragraph

Ordinary paragraphs of text are justified and filled during the translation process, according to the destination format. How the justification takes place is entirely dependent on the translator and the reader of the file that it creates.

Verbatim Paragraph

A verbatim paragraph will be reproduced within the final document exactly; you cannot use formatting escapes, and the translator won't make any assumptions about the contents of the paragraph. A verbatim paragraph is identified by indentation in the source text, either with spaces or tabs. The best use for a verbatim paragraph is to reproduce code within the document to ensure that it appears as working code within the final document. Without this facility, the code would be justified and filled just like any other paragraph.

Escape Sequences

Escape sequences are recognized within both ordinary text and command paragraphs. The escape sequences allow you to specify that a block of text is to be displayed as italicized, boldfaced, underlined, and so on. An escape sequence consists of a single letter and a pair of angle brackets that contain the text to be modified. For example, the POD fragment

```
B<Hello World!>
```

specifies that the string should be boldfaced, producing **Hello World!**

Other escape sequences include linking to other types of documents and inserting literal (non-translated) text elements. How the escape sequences are interpreted is again up to the translation and destination format—some will be ignored and others will imply that additional information be added to the embedded sequence.

Table 23-5 provides a list of the escape sequences supported by the POD format, and Table 23-6 lists the link-specific interpretations.

Embedding Documentation

Unlike most other forms of documentation, Perl allows you to embed POD-formatted sequences directly into your Perl source code. This is not necessarily new; other systems have allowed this, but generally only as part of the header or footer to the script or module. Perl allows you to embed sequences at will anywhere within your code, so

Sequence	Description
I<text>	Italic text
B<text>	Boldface text
S<text>	Text with non-breaking spaces (spaces within text that will not be used to wrap or split lines)
C<code>	Literal code fragment (for example, **C <printf()>**)
L<name>	A link or cross reference to another section, identified by name. See Table 23-6.
F<file>	Used for file names
X<index>	An index entry
Z<>	A zero-width character
E<escape>	A named character (similar to HTML escapes)
E<lt>	A literal <
E<gt>	A literal >
E<n>	Character number (in ASCII)

Table 23-5.   *POD Escape Sequences*

Sequence	Description
L<name>	Manual page
L<name/ident>	Item or section within a manual page
L<name/"sec">	Section in other manual page
L<"sec">	Section within the current manual page (quotes are optional, as in **L<name>**)
L</"sec">	Same as above
L<text | name> L<text | name/ident> L<text | name/"sec"> L<text | "sec"> L<text | /"sec">	Same as above, but destination is identified by name but displayed as text; the text element cannot contain | or >

Table 23-6.   *Link Escape Sequences*

you can document a function where the function is defined within the code, which is useful as a cross reference.

The embedding process keys on a command paragraph, and all text after that is taken as POD documentation until the interpreter sees the **=cut** command paragraph. The opposite of this approach is used by the POD translators: they ignore the Perl script and only work on the POD documentation sequences.

For example, when documenting two functions, we might use the following:

```
=item * add function

Adds two numbers together.

=cut

sub add
{
    $_[0]+$_[1];
}

=item * subtract function
Subtracts the second number from the first.

=cut

sub subtract
{
    $_[0] - $_[1];
}
```

This does nothing when executed as a Perl script (except defining two functions that we never use!). However, if you convert it to another format and view the document, you get a nicely formatted document.

Converting POD to Other Formats

It should be obvious by now that POD documentation on its own is fairly useless. Without a great deal of effort, it can't be viewed and easily understood directly, and there is no POD reader (unless you have a Mac, in which case you can use the Shuck application).

Before POD documents can be useful, we therefore need to use a translator to convert them into something we can read. The base Perl distribution comes with stand-alone tools for converting POD documentation into text, HTML, and Unix man pages (nroff), all of which are actually supported by a series of modules.

You can also download a number of additional modules from CPAN that help convert to other formats or provide POD-related utilities. You can see a sample in Table 23-7.

Text

If you do not want to view formatted output from a POD document, you can convert it into textual format. The resulting output is not completely without formatting—the capabilities of your display are taken into account during the translation process. The

Module	Description
Pod::DocBook	Translates to the SGML-based DocBook format.
Pod::Html	The supplied translation module for HTML documents.
Pod::Man	The supplied conversion module to the **man**-based **nroff** format.
Pod::PlainText	Translates to raw plain text, essentially stripping all of the formatting from the POD document—paragraphs are justified and attempts are made to make the conversion clear, but it doesn't attempt the same sort of formatting as **Pod::Text**.
Pod::RTF	Converts to RTF (Rich Text Format) files. RTF files can be imported and formatted in most word processors, including Microsoft Word, Sun's StarOffice, and Lotus WordPro.
Pod::SimpleText	Converts to the SimpleText format used on the Mac for README files.
Pod::Text	The supplied text conversion module; this supports terminal formatting on suitable devices.
Pod::Text::Color	An extension that allows POD documents to be formatted and viewed using color-based formatting.
Pod::Text::Termcap	An extension that makes use of the terminal abilities for bold and underlining on terminals that support it.

Table 23-7. *Conversion Formats*

Pod::Text module provides the capabilities you need, and the base distribution includes a command line interface to the module in the form of the **pod2text** script.

```
$ pod2text [-a] [-width] script.pl
```

The script takes only one argument—the name of the file to translate. The resulting text will be sent to **STDOUT** after it has been converted. There are two additional, optional arguments. The **-a** argument assumes an alternative, and in fact less capable, terminal, which removes more of the POD formatting, but it is useful on terminals that don't support formatting (see also the **Pod::PlainText** module).

The **-width** argument specifies the width of the output device, where **width** is the width in characters of the output device.

HTML

The most compatible destination format (especially across platforms) is HTML. The **pod2html** script works in the same way as the **pod2text** script:

```
$ pod2html script.pl
```

Output is also sent to the standard out, so you will need to redirect the generated HTML to a file if you want to install it on a web server or view it with a browser.

You can also write your own script using the **Pod::Html** module, which exports a single function, **pod2html**, which accepts the same arguments as the stand-alone script; you just supply them as you would on the command line:

```
pod2html("--infile=Module.pm","--netscape");
```

You can see a list of the supported arguments in Table 23-8.

Unix man Pages

The online documentation on Unix is stored in *roff format, using the **man** macro extensions. This is a special formatting system that has been part of Unix and, many years ago, part of full-scale print production systems. To create a man page from raw POD source, you use the **pod2man** script:

```
$ pod2man script.pl
```

The formatted output is sent to **STDOUT**, so you will need to redirect the output. The conversion process will highlight different entities correctly. Headings, page headers and footers, and formatting will all be translated to the manual pages. The

Option	Description
--flush	Flush the contents of the item and directory caches created during the parsing of a POD document.
--help	Print out a help message.
--htmlroot	The base directory from which you reference documents relatively. This is required if you expect to install the generated HTML files onto a web server. The default is /.
--index	Generate an index of **=head1** elements at the top of the HTML file generated (default).
--infile	The file name to convert. You don't have to use this element; the first nonhyphenated argument is taken as a file name. If you don't specify a file by either method, then it will accept input from standard input.
--libpods	A colon-separated list of pages searched when referencing **=item** entries. These are not the file names, just the page names as they would appear in **L<>** link elements.
--netscape	Use Netscape-specific browser directives when necessary.
--nonetscape	Prevent the use of Netscape-specific browser directives (default).
--outfile	The destination file name for the generated HTML; it uses standard output if none is specified.
--podpath	A colon-separated list of directories containing POD files and libraries.
--podroot	The base directory prepended to each entry in the **podpath** command line argument. The default is **.** (dot) and the current directory.
--noindex	Don't generate an index at the top of the HTML file generated.
--norecurse	Don't recurse into the subdirectories specified in the **podpath** option.
--recurse	Recurse into the subdirectories specified in the **podpath** option (this is the default behavior).
--title	The contents of the **<TITLE>** tag in the created HTML document.
--verbose	Produces status and progress messages during production.

Table 23-8.   *Arguments When Converting POD to HTML*

script converts the references to other manual pages, such that interactive man-page readers, such as emacs, can access the linked pages correctly.

Manual pages are stored according to a series of sections that help to isolate and identify individual pages; for example, the **mkdir** command is in section 1, while the **mkdir** function is in section 3, sometimes 3C. The actual section names are dependent on the variety of Unix you are using, although the major sections of 1–8 are unchanged on most systems.

If your POD documentation relates to a command, put it in section 1, and a extension module should be in section 3. A full list of the sections supported under System V Release 4 based Unix variants is shown in Table 23-9.

Section	Contents
1	User commands
1C	Basic networking commands
1F	FMLI commands
1M	Administration commands
2	System function calls
3	BSD routines
3C	C library functions
3E	ELF library functions
3G	Libgen functions
3M	Math functions
3N	Network services functions
3S	Standard I/O functions
3X	Specialized libraries
4	File formats
5	Miscellaneous
6	Games
7	Special files
8	System maintenance procedures
9	Device-driver interface/driver-kernel interface (DDI/DDK)

Table 23-9. *Unix Manual Sections*

Typically, the Perl-specific manual pages are installed in the man directory of the main Perl library directory. The location of this depends on the version of Perl you are using and on the platform. Again, you should let MakeMaker (see Chapter 25) sort this out for you.

PostScript/PDF

If you can convert to HTML, you should be able to view the HTML in a browser and then output to PostScript format. To do this under Unix versions of Netscape/Mozilla, just select the PostScript file option, instead of printing through the **lp** or **lpr** filter. Under Windows, you'll need to set up a printer that uses **FILE:** as the output device. Use the Apple LaserWriter II/IIg driver—this produces some of the cleanest PostScript, which should be compatible with any PostScript printer, and with other tools such as GhostScript and Acrobat for conversion to PDF format.

Under Mac OS, you can select the Output to File pop-up within the Print dialog box and then send the file straight to a PostScript file, or if you have Adobe Acrobat installed, straight to an Acrobat PDF file.

Converting POD to HTML On The Fly

I've written a script that works in a similar fashion to the **perldoc** tool, but instead of outputting the information in man or text format, it's designed to work as a CGI script through a web server so that you can browse the Perl documentation directly through your browser. The script uses **pod2html** and sets the options so that links to other documents in the Perl tree are marked up as normal hyperlinks in the displayed document.

Because it converts the POD documentation on the fly, you don't need to install a set of HTML documents separately. It uses the installed files, so you can even view HTML versions of third-party installed modules without having to convert the documents to HTML format separately.

You can download the tool from the **http://www.mcwords.com** website.

FINE-TUNING
APPLICATIONS

The Complete Reference

Perl

Chapter 24

Cross-Platform Migration Traps

Perl is a cross-platform language—it runs on a myriad of different Unix flavors, all the different Windows versions from 3.1 up to 2000 and Millennium Edition, and on Mac OS. It's also available less widely for operating systems like VMS and BeOS, and there are lots of ports for different devices, including one for the Psion Series 5/7—there's even a version under production for Palm OS!

When programming Perl on a number of different platforms, you tend to take some things for granted. Although Perl is pretty platform independent, there are some differences that will trip you up if you're not concentrating. Most of the problems are relatively obvious, but some are obscure and difficult to treat.

The problem with Perl is that it owes a lot of its history to the Unix world. Many of the built-in functions like **chmod** and **getpwuid** are Unix specific and rely on functions found only under Unix. It's also a textually driven language, from the production and development of the scripts to many of the interfaces that are used. This means that certain elements of Perl are not compatible across platforms.

Just to add to the complexity, not all platforms are the same either. The Mac OS doesn't have a command line interface, and Microsoft is slowly trying to remove the command line interface from their operating systems, which can make using Perl interesting. Other problems, such as line termination (the newline/carriage-return and carriage-return/newline issue) just add to the confusion. As a general rule, don't assume that Perl supports all functions on all platforms, and don't use data without considering where it might have come from.

In this chapter, we'll take a quick look at all of the factors that affect the development of Perl scripts under the different platforms and at some of the solutions we can use to correct them. (For a recap of how Perl works and is available under the different platforms, refer back to Chapter 2.)

Function Support

The most obvious difference between platforms is the support for different functions and operators. The Perl porters are responsible for keeping things as flexible as possible across different platforms. However, Perl's Unix roots show through all too often, and you should keep the following points in mind if you find you have problems on a different platform:

- Functions that involve looking up details in one of the Unix files contained in /etc (generally these functions start with **set** or **get**) are pretty Unix-centric. They include network information routines and also those routines related to group and/or password information. There are usually equivalents in a platform-specific module.

- All the basic file interfacing options will work; but others, such as **–X**, **stat**, and more Unix-centric functions such as **chmod** and **chgrp**, are unsupported. You should also remember that although Mac OS and Windows support the notion of links via aliases and shortcuts, respectively, the **link** and **lstat** functions often do not work.

■ Access to the internals of the operating system tables are also unsupported on many other platforms, particularly those that return unique process and group IDs, or those that return parent group and parent owner information for a process ID. Most of the time, however, the **$$** variable should provide you with a reasonable amount of information.

■ Unix-specific utility functions are also generally unimplemented, such as the IPC systems **shm***, **msg***, and **sem***.

■ Functions and operators that rely on the ability to run an application by name through a command line–like interface may not work on all platforms. In particular, the Mac OS, which doesn't have a command line interface, does not natively support functions like **system** and the backticks or **qx** operator. However, you can use the shell provided with the MPW (Macintosh Programmer's Workshop) environment to run some commands in this manner.

You can get a more up-to-date list in the perlport manual page supplied with the Perl distribution.

Constant Compatibility

If you have problems with the operation of a function that normally uses a constant, make sure that you use the generic name rather than a fixed number. Although in theory the constants used for setting options with functions like **fcntl** and **ioctl** should be the same, some platforms use different values. Make sure you import the **POSIX** module and use the constant names defined there, rather than your own values.

Also, make sure you use the **POSIX** module when using the **seek** function—although the function itself is supported on nearly all platforms, the numbers used to search forward and backward, and to move to the start and end of the file, can differ between platforms.

Execution Environment

The environment in which Perl is executed can have a significant effect on your script. Many problems can arise because you rely on information or capabilities outside of Perl, but that may be directly available internally. Some examples are listed here:

■ Try not to rely on the Unix environment variables or Perl's built-in variables to get certain pieces of information. In particular, avoid using things like **$>** and **$<** and other user and group ID variables, which are not set on all platforms. This advice is especially pertinent if you decide to use one of these variables in a unique ID or other identification string.

■ Related to the preceding point, don't rely on hostnames—or user names, either— especially if you intend to use them to store unique or identification information.

- Don't rely on commands that you want to execute being available within the **PATH** environment variable—set it yourself or, better still, use a full path to the application.

- Don't rely on signals unless you have to. Some platforms support signals and signal handlers, others don't, and those that do may only support a reduced set.

- Use shared files, network sockets, or a platform-specific module, such as **Win32::Pipe**, to exchange information. The **shm***, **msg***, and **sem*** functions are not supported on all platforms.

Errors

Perl reports most errors using the **$!** variable, but platform-specific errors on platforms other than Unix may not be included. Remember to report the information from **$^E** on platforms other than Unix, or use a platform-specific error function, such as **Win32::GetLastError**.

Line Termination

One of the most fundamental problems of using Perl on multiple platforms is the line termination when reading and writing files. Different operating systems use different characters for line termination. In particular, Unix uses a newline (the **\n** or **\012** character) to terminate, whereas Mac OS uses a carriage return (the **\r** or **\015** character). To complicate matters, DOS/Windows uses the carriage return, newline sequence (**\r\n** or **\015\012**).

Perl will automatically account for this difference under most conditions; but if you are transferring data as well as scripts between platforms, then beware. Perl will automatically interpret **\n** as the correct character or character sequence for the current platform. Under Mac OS, Perl simply interprets **\n** as **\015**; but under DOS/Windows, it is interpreted as **\015\012** when a file is accessed in text mode.

Under platforms other than Unix, you will need to use the **binmode** function on an open filehandle to read and write raw data and prevent Perl from doing the conversion automatically. Also, be careful when using **seek**, **tell**, and similar functions—the line termination is not taken into account automatically when calculating **seek** values.

When used with network sockets, more direct specification is required. In all communication between sockets, you should use numerical values instead of their character versions to ensure that **\012** can be identified correctly. Otherwise, the interpretation of **\n** on the two platforms may differ. See the discussion on character sets next. To make the process easier, the **Socket** module, which is part of the standard Perl distribution, can supply the values for you.

```
use Socket qw(:DEFAULT :crlf);
print "Message$CRLF";
```

These import tags provide three constant variables—**$CR**, **$LF**, and **$CRLF**—which map to **\015**, **\012**, and **\015\012**, respectively, and are identical irrespective of the platform on which you are running.

Character Sets

Another popular misconception is that all platforms use the same character set. Although it's true that most use the ASCII character set, you can rely only on the first 128 characters (values 0 to 127, or **\00** to **\0177**) as being identical. Even with this consideration, you shouldn't necessarily rely on the values returned by **chr** or **ord** across different platforms. The actual values of the character set may include all manner of characters, including those that may have accents and may be in any order.

Since version 5.6, Perl is completely Unicode compliant, so you should be able to guarantee that the first 128 characters match the ASCII table, with each character being represented by a single byte. Further characters are represented by one or more bytes, and include many of the accented and special characters. See the perlunicode documentation supplied with Perl.

Data Differences

Different physical and operating system combinations use different sequences for storing numbers. This characteristic affects the storage and transfer of numbers in binary format between systems, either within files or across network connections. The solution to the problem is either to use strings, which will, of course, be displayed in standard form, or to use the **n** and **N** network orders with the **pack** and **unpack** functions (see Chapter 7).

All times are represented in Perl by the number of seconds since the epoch. On nearly all systems, the epoch is 0:00:00, 1 January 1970. However, other platforms define other values (Mac OS, for example). If you want to store a date, use a format that is not reliant on the epoch value, such as a single string like **YYYYMMDDHHMMSS**.

Files and Pathnames

The main three platforms show the range of characters used to separate the directories and files that make up a file's path. Under Unix, it is **/**; but under DOS/Windows it is ****, and on the Mac it is **:**. The Windows and DOS implementations also allow you to use the Unix **/** to separate the elements. To further complicate matters, only Unix and a small number of other operating systems use the concept of a single root directory.

On Windows and DOS, the individual drives, or partitions thereof, are identified by a single letter preceded by a colon. Under Mac OS, each volume has a name that can precede a pathname, using the standard colon separator. The **File::Spec** module can create paths that use the appropriate character set and separator for you. Also be aware that different platforms support different file names and lengths. The following is a rough guide:

- DOS supports only names of no more than eight characters and extensions of three characters, and ignores case.

- Under Windows 95/NT, the definition is slightly more complex: the full pathname has a maximum length of 256 characters and is case conscious.

- Under Mac OS, any element of a path can have up to 31 characters, and names within a directory are case insensitive—you cannot have two files called "File" and "file."

- Older versions of Unix support only 31 characters per path element; but newer versions, including Solaris and HP-UX 10.*x* and above, as well as Linux, support a full 256 characters per path element.

You should also try to restrict file names to use only standard alphanumeric characters.

Modules

Be careful when using modules that contain platform-specific elements or that require the use of a C compiler when the module is built. You cannot guarantee that the module will be supported on all platforms or even that a C compiler will be available if you need it.

Performance and Resources

Not all platforms have the seemingly unlimited resources of the Unix operating system available to them. Although Windows provides a similar memory interface, the available memory on a Windows machine may be significantly less in real terms (physical/virtual) than that available under a typical Unix implementation, although this condition is changing as RAM becomes cheaper. MacPerl must be allocated its own block of memory; and, once exhausted, it cannot automatically gain new memory, even if there is some available. You should, therefore, take care with statements that arbitrarily create large internal structures; for example,

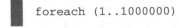
```
foreach (1..1000000)
```

creates a list with one million elements, which will take up a significant amount of memory. This has been fixed in Perl 5.005; but earlier versions, including MacPerl, which is currently based on 5.004, will generate the huge list.

Also remember that other operating systems do not provide the same protected memory spaces or the multitasking features of Unix.

Platform Migration Tricks

There are a few things we can do within a script to identify where, and on what, the script is being executed. Most of the information is available as standard to the Perl interpreter; other pieces of information are available through the use of a supplied Perl module.

Knowing the following will help you identify and trap some problems before they occur:

- Platform and operating system
- Perl version
- Supported function lists

You can also use the information that is generated by Perl during the build process to help identify supported functions and abilities. Alternatively, you can use the **eval** function to trap and test for functions before you try to use them properly.

As a final trick, we'll look at the function-overloading system that allows us to implement locally a built-in function that is not supported by the current Perl version.

Determining Your Platform

The **$^O** variable contains the name of the current platform. The information provided may not be very descriptive if you don't know the significance of the name returned, but it should at the very least enable you to identify the main platform. Alternatively, you can use the value of the **$Config{'archname'}** variable (available via the **Config** module), which contains the name of the architecture on which the current Perl interpreter was compiled. The architecture string returned includes the platform name and the hardware architecture on which the binary was built.

Note the difference here: the build and the current platform are not essentially identical, although it may be safe to assume they are compatible. For example, a Perl binary built on Solaris 2.4 will also run on Solaris 2.6, or even Solaris 7. However, a Perl binary for the Intel version of Solaris will not run on the SPARC version. The value of **$Config{'osname'}** will tell you the name of the operating system on which the binary was built.

Some sample operating system names and **$^O** and **$Config{'archname'}** values are shown in Table 24-1.

On many platforms (particularly those derived from Unix), the value is extracted from that returned by **uname**. In all cases, the value of **$^O** is probably of more use than the architecture name for writing cross-platform scripts.

OS	$^O/$Config{'osname'}	$Config{'archname'}
MS-DOS	dos	
Windows 95	MSWin32	MSWin32-x86
Windows NT	MSWin32	MSWin32-x86
Mac OS	MacOS	
Linux	linux	i686-linux
SunOS 4	sunos	sun4-sunos
Solaris	solaris	sun4-solaris

Table 24-1. *Operating Systems and Their Internal Equivalents*

Determining the Perl Version

The Perl version relates very little to the level of support on different platforms. However, it can sometimes be a useful indicator of whether an official release exists for a platform, as well as a useful reference point for a specific feature, irrespective of the platform on which you are working.

If all you want to do is find out what version of Perl you are using, the obvious solution is to check the version of Perl using the $] variable. This is the version number of the Perl interpreter added to the patch level divided by one thousand. For example, v5.004 is Perl version 5, patch level 4. Sub-version numbers to the patch level are included for the maintenance and development releases of Perl and are indicated as the release number divided by 100,000: a value of 5.00553 is made up of Perl version 5, patch level 5, and development release 53. The maintenance release number increases from 1 to 49 and developmental releases from 50 to 99.

Since Perl 5.6, the information returned is much easier to determine. For a start, the location of the version number has changed. An old-style version number can still be found in $], but the new, post-5.6 version number is stored in $^V. It's also stored as a v-string, so you need a different way to print the version:

```
printf("Perl Version: %vd\n",$^V);
```

There are actually three components to the new-style version number: the major version number, the minor version number, and the patch level. For example, the first version of Perl 5.6 was actually 5.6.0.

You can use the contents of the perldelta man page to determine what functions and abilities are available within each version of the Perl interpreter. The next section presents specific ways of determining the supported functions without requiring prior knowledge.

If you want to restrict a script so it runs only on certain versions, you should use the **require** keyword with a numerical or v-string value. When you supply a numerical value, the comparison is made against the **$]** special variable—if the value of **$]** is numerically higher than the value supplied, the script is allowed to continue:

```
require 5.005_03;
```

However, if you supply a v-string, the value of the string is compared with **$^V**:

```
require v5.6.1;
require 5.6.1;
```

Thus, to ensure the script runs only on the very latest stable version of Perl, you might want to try,

```
require v5.6;
```

although this will probably be out of date by the time you read this. If the value specified does not match the current Perl interpreter, a run-time error will be produced:

```
perl -e 'require 6;'
Perl 6 required—this is only version 5.00553, stopped at -e line 1.
```

Checking for Supported Functions

The **Config** module we used earlier to determine the architecture and operating system name used to build the current Perl interpreter actually contains all the information discovered during the configuration process. You can use this information to determine the functions and the extensions supported within the current Perl interpreter. The data is stored in the form of a hash, **%Config**; so, to determine all of the values, you might use

```
use Config;
foreach (sort keys %Config)
{
    print "$_ : $Config{$_}\n";
}
```

The values output are not cryptic, but also are not obvious. The keys for underlying operating system functions start with **d_**, such that the existence of **chown** can be determined by

```
print "Have chown\n" if ($Config{'d_chown'} eq 'define');
```

Other features, such as extension modules to Perl (**NDBM** or **Socket**, for example), are in other keys within the same hash:

```
print "Extensions: $Config{extensions}\n";
```

To check for a specific function, use an **eval** block to execute the function within its own interpreter. If the call fails, the **eval** block will drop out, setting **$@** in the process. For example, to check once again for the **chown** function, you might use

```
eval { chown() };
warn "chown() $@" if $@;
```

Because **eval** blocks are executed within their own space at run time, this will report a suitable error.

Function Overloading

When you want to support a particular operation within a script that is not supported under multiple platforms, you may want to consider developing a special module that provides a personal interface to the built-in Perl functions. Another alternative is to provide your own set of "built-in" functions, and then overload the real built-in functions with your own versions. You can do this through the use of a **BEGIN** block in your script and the **use subs** pragma.

The code fragment that follows shows the method required to determine which functions are supported:

```
BEGIN
{
    eval { chown() };
    push @functions,'chown' if $@;
}

use subs @functions;
use MyBuiltin @functions;

chown();
```

Note that the actual test must be done within the **BEGIN** block so that it is executed at compile rather than run time; then, by the time compilation reaches the **use subs** pragma, the contents of **@functions** has already been populated with the required information.

The definition for **chown** is then placed into the **MyBuiltin** package, which is defined just like any other:

```
package MyBuiltin;

require Exporter;
@ISA = qw/Exporter/;
@EXPORT = ();
@EXPORT_OK = qw/chown/;

sub chown
{
    print "Changed mode!";
    return 1;
}
```

The contents of **@EXPORT** should be empty, since you don't want to import anything as standard. The value of **@EXPORT_OK** contains the list of built-in functions that you want to support and overload, if necessary. Thus, when you call **use MyBuiltin** with a list of unsupported built-in functions, you import your own list of replacements. In this example, a simple **print** statement is used to show that the overloading is working. In an actual case, you'll probably want to put some real functionality into the functions you want to overload.

If you are testing a lot of functions, you will need to use loops and references to test the functions you want to overload:

```
BEGIN
{
    @subtest = qw/chown exec/;
    foreach $function (@subtest)
    {
        eval { &$function };
        push @functions,$function if $@;
    }
}
```

It's not possible in this to optimize the loop by placing the **foreach** loop within the **eval** block, since you're using each **eval** invocation to test the existence of each function. This is a performance hit, but the overall process improves compatibility, and it's one of the trade-offs examined at the beginning of the chapter.

Chapter 25

Distributing Modules and Applications

Once you've written your Perl module or application, there are a few more steps you need to follow before it can finally be unleashed on the public. Although there's no fixed route to this process, it will probably go something like this:

- Debug and optimize the module or application
- Optionally compile the script into a stand-alone application or library
- Document the script and update the comments to reflect any changes
- Ensure cross-platform compatibility, providing you want to support multiple platforms

We've actually covered all these stages in the past chapters in this section, but there is one final stage—that of packaging up and making your module or application for distribution to the rest of the world.

In this last chapter, we're going to concentrate purely on the process behind packaging up your module or application for distribution. The core of this process centers around the **ExtUtils::MakeMaker** module and Perl makefiles. These are essentially the same as normal makefiles as used by **make**, but are parsed by the **MakeMaker** utility into the real thing, substituting the correct directories, command names, and other information to allow easy installation of your module or application.

We'll also look at some examples of using Perl makefiles, how to package a module up for distribution to CPAN, and how to package up modules for use with the ActiveState Perl Package Manager (PPM) format.

Perl Makefiles and ExtUtils::MakeMaker

We looked at the use of Perl makefiles in Chapter 20, when we set up and built an extension. The makefile system is an integral part of the XS extension system, and a makefile is automatically built for you when you use the **h2xs** utility. Although its primary use is for building and installing modules and extensions, it can actually be used for practically any installation that requires some form of automatic process.

The Perl makefile is, like many other parts of the Perl environment, just a Perl script. It uses a module, **ExtUtils::MakeMaker**, and a configuration supplied in the form of a hash to work out how to build and install the different elements of a package. When the script executes, it loads the **ExtUtils::MakeMaker** module, determines the local configuration parameters, such as the location of the active Perl binary, the library directories, and other information, and then builds a makefile that can be used in combination with the standard **make** command to actually extract, compile (if necessary), and install the module or application into its correct location.

In this section, we're going to look at how the **ExtUtils::MakeMaker** module works and how to configure the system for your own uses above and beyond the default files produced by **h2xs**.

The **ExtUtils::MakeMaker** module actually splits the task of makefile generation into several subroutines, and the overall configuration that is used with these subroutines is infinitely configurable. In each case, the subroutines provided by the module return the text that is required to be written to the makefile. The whole system is object oriented, and the production of individual files within the **MakeMaker** system is possible at all levels. Each file created is treated as a single object, and therefore a single **MakeMaker** configuration can generate a number of makefiles both for the original target and for subdirectories and their targets.

Perl Makefiles and CPAN

To the untrained eye, it might appear that the **CPAN** module and the **MakeMaker** module are closely linked, since we can use **CPAN** to download and automatically install these modules for us. In fact, the two items are relatively independent. The **MakeMaker** tool works just as well if used "manually" at the command line—it still produces a makefile that needs to be parsed by **make** before it does anything.

The **CPAN** module knows the required sequence of downloading, extracting, running the **MakeMaker** tool, and then running **make**—if it wasn't for the ease of use provided by **MakeMaker**, **CPAN** would be difficult to write because the process would be different for each module.

If you want to supply your module to CPAN, then check **www.cpan.org** for the precise submission details. You'll need to package up your source files and the **Makefile.PL** script using **tar** and **gzip**. If you want to support the module under Windows, then check the "Packing for PPM/VPM" section later in this chapter.

For more information on CPAN, see Chapter 2, Appendix B, and Web Appendix B.

Perl Makefiles and PPM

The Perl Package Manager (PPM) and the Visual Package Manager (VPM) are part of ActivePerl and the Perl Developer's Kit, respectively. These work in a similar way to **CPAN**, downloading an extension or application automatically from a central repository and then installing the extension for you. However, unlike **CPAN**, extensions supplied through PPM are precompiled and ready to install, rather than requiring the usual **make** step.

ActivePerl was, up until Perl 5.6, a Windows-only solution, but since the 5.6 release, other versions are now available for a number of Linux and Unix platforms. The main advantage of PPM over **CPAN** is that it doesn't require the end-user to have access to a compiler and development environment to install the extension. See Chapter 2 for more information on how to use PPM, and see the "Packing for PPM/VPM" section later in this chapter.

Extension Building and Installation Overview

Most of this process will be familiar; we've seen a lot of it already in Chapter 20.
However, the build and installation process is slightly more complex than the
examples we have already seen. You should already be aware that the extension uses
the **AutoLoader** module to decide which function should be included. The **AutoLoader**
module is actually capable of a number of different operations. Depending on the
context and requirements, it can do one of the following:

- Perform the function itself; the caller will never know that the **AutoLoader** has
  been used.
- Create the function on the fly using an **eval** statement.
- Use the **system** function to launch an external program of the same name.
- Dynamically load a library using the **DynaLoader** module.

It is the last option that is used to load an external C library extension. The
AutoSplit module is used to separate the original Perl module file into separate files,
one per function, and a mapping within the split file then tells **DynaLoader** which
library to load in order to implement the function. This loading mechanism requires
a bootstrap file and an autoload file, which are both used to select the correct library
location for the function, based on the library that was built and the split module.
The whole system uses a specialized structure within the Perl module directory that
accounts for both site and architecture differences.

The entire process for the makefile produced by **MakeMaker** (under Solaris) is
shown here. Entries taken from the **StatVFS** module we saw in Chapter 20 are used for
reference:

1. A directory structure is created within the extensions directory that will hold
   the files produced during the build process before they are installed:

   ```
   mkdir blib
   mkdir blib/lib
   mkdir blib/arch
   mkdir blib/arch/auto
   mkdir blib/arch/auto/StatVFS
   mkdir blib/lib/auto
   mkdir blib/lib/auto/StatVFS
   mkdir blib/man3
   cp StatVFS.pm blib/lib/StatVFS.pm
   ```

2. The module is split into individual functions. Each function is placed into the
   auto/StatVFS directory:

   ```
   AutoSplitting blib/lib/StatVFS.pm (blib/lib/auto/StatVFS)
   ```

3. The XS file is parsed by **xsubpp**, producing the C file that contains the necessary functions:

```
/usr/bin/perl -I/usr/local/lib/perl5/5.00553/sun4-solaris
              -I/usr/local/lib/perl5/5.00553
              /usr/local/lib/perl5/5.00553/ExtUtils/xsubpp
              -typemap
              /usr/local/lib/perl5/5.00553/ExtUtils/typemap
              StatVFS.xs >xstmp.c && mv xstmp.c StatVFS.c
```

4. The source code is compiled into object format:

```
gcc -B/usr/ccs/bin/ -c  -I/usr/local/include
              -DDEBUGGING -O -DVERSION=\"0.01\"
              -DXS_VERSION=\"0.01\" -fPIC
              -I/usr/local/lib/perl5/5.00553/sun4-solaris/CORE
              StatVFS.c
```

5. The bootstrap code required for **DynaLoader** is produced. The StatVFS.bs file contains the necessary information to enable **DynaLoader** to relate the Perl call to the C function:

```
Running Mkbootstrap for StatVFS ()
chmod 644 StatVFS.bs
```

6. The library file is generated in its dynamic format:

```
LD_RUN_PATH="" gcc -B/usr/ccs/bin/
              -o blib/arch/auto/StatVFS/StatVFS.so
              -G -L/usr/local/lib StatVFS.o
```

7. The library and the bootstrap code are copied into the correct location ready for installation, and the file modes are set to their correct values:

```
chmod 755 blib/arch/auto/StatVFS/StatVFS.so
cp StatVFS.bs blib/arch/auto/StatVFS/StatVFS.bs
chmod 644 blib/arch/auto/StatVFS/StatVFS.bs
```

8. The POD format documentation in the Perl module is extracted and converted into a man page, ready for installation:

```
Manifying blib/man3/StatVFS.3
```

The main process is now finished. The installation process just copies the structure below the blib directory into the site- or architecture-specific directories within the Perl library directory. At this point, if you want to test the module, you can use the **make test** command. The test files will need to include the just-built version of the library. See the **blib** pragma in Chapter 19 for more information on this.

The actual installation process has its tricks too. The following sample is a continuation of the **StatVFS** module example.

1. The files are copied to the specified installation directory. This is defined as a whole by the **PREFIX** option and individually with the **INSTALL*** options.

```
Installing /usr/local/lib/perl5/site_perl/5.00553/sun4-
solaris/auto/StatVFS/StatVFS.so
Installing /usr/local/lib/perl5/site_perl/5.00553/sun4-
solaris/auto/StatVFS/StatVFS.bs
Files found in blib/arch -> Installing files in blib/lib into
architecture dependent library tree!
Installing /usr/local/lib/perl5/site_perl/5.00553/sun4-
solaris/auto/StatVFS/autosplit.ix
Installing /usr/local/lib/perl5/site_perl/5.00553/sun4-solaris/
StatVFS.pm
Installing /usr/local/lib/perl5/5.00553/man/man3/StatVFS.3
```

2. A list of the files installed during the installation process is written in a special file, called .packlist in the module's AutoLoader directory. The actual location will depend on whether you have installed an architecture or site version. See the **INSTALLDIRS** option later in the chapter.

```
Writing /usr/local/lib/perl5/site_perl/5.00553/sun4-
solaris/auto/StatVFS/.packlist
```

3. The installation information, including the configuration details, is written to a general file that can later be consulted (preferably via a POD file viewer) to study which packages and extensions have been installed and when. This can also be a helpful starting point for tracing problems when a script or module suddenly stops working.

```
Appending installation info to /usr/local/lib/perl5/5.00553/sun4-
solaris/perllocal.pod
```

The rest of this chapter is devoted to describing the configurable parameters to the **MakeMaker** module. We'll also take the opportunity to look at some of the other modules that are used by the **MakeMaker** module to do its work.

MakeMaker Overview

The basic use of the **MakeMaker** module is very simple. The synopsis for the module is

```
use ExtUtils::MakeMaker;
WriteMakefile( ATTRIBUTE => VALUE [, ...] );
```

The basic method of operation is to create a simple file that imports the module and then calls the **WriteMakefile** function. You need to specify at least one attribute to the function, which is the name of the module. For example, to create the makefile for building the **StatVFS** module we created in Chapter 20, you could get away with as little as the following in **Makefile.PL**:

```
use ExtUtils::MakeMaker;
WriteMakefile('NAME' => 'StatVFS');
```

When run through a Perl interpreter, like this,

```
$ perl Makefile.PL
```

it automatically produces a makefile capable of building and installing the extension. It accounts for the location of all the necessary libraries and include files, and it selects the correct C compiler and definitions in order to ensure that the extension is compiled properly. This information is selected from the information produced at build time and is specific to the platform on which you use the **MakeMaker** file. Thus, the Perl makefile is completely platform independent. Any platform on which you can build Perl should be able to produce a suitable makefile for the platform for building an extension. The resulting makefile produced is, of course, platform- and build-specific, even though the original **Makefile.PL** file is completely platform independent. It's the **MakeMaker** module that provides the platform-independent information required to build the module.

The resulting makefile is big—751 lines long. It is too long, and completely pointless, to reproduce here. The point about **MakeMaker** is that it hides all the complexity of the makefile production from the user and just ensures that the file produced should work on whatever platform Perl is installed on.

Start with h2xs

It doesn't matter what sort of module, extension, or application you are dealing with—it's almost certainly easier to create the makefile using **h2xs**. The **h2xs** tool is actually designed to convert a header file into a suitable set of stub XS extensions ready for integrating into Perl. However, it can also be used to create a simple MakeMaker template. The command line options for the tool are shown in Table 25-1.

If you want just to create a dummy MakeMaker template, then you should use

```
$ h2xs -f -n MyModule -X
Writing MyModule/MyModule.pm
Writing MyModule/Makefile.PL
Writing MyModule/test.pl
Writing MyModule/Changes
Writing MyModule/MANIFEST
```

Option	Description
-A	Omit the autoloading definitions (implies the **-c** option).
-F	Additional flags for C preprocessor (used with **-x**).
-O	Allow overwriting of a preexisting extension directory.
-P	Omit the stub POD section.
-X	Omit the XS portion.
-c	Omit the **constant()** function and specialized **AUTOLOAD** from the XS file.
-d	Turn on debugging messages.
-f	Force creation of the extension.
-n	Specify a name to use for the extension—defaults to a title case version of the header file's base name.
-p	Specify a string that will be removed from the start of the C functions when they are reproduced as Perl functions.
-s	Create subroutines for specified macros.
-v	Specify a version number for this extension.
-x	Autogenerate XSUBs using **C::Scan**.

Table 25-1. *Command Line Options for h2xs*

Note that it creates most of the files that you need, including a blank module, test script, MANIFEST file (which lists the files that make up your module), and the MakeMaker template in **Makefile.PL**. The default template looks like this:

```
use ExtUtils::MakeMaker;
# See lib/ExtUtils/MakeMaker.pm for details of how to influence
# the contents of the Makefile that is written.
WriteMakefile(
    'NAME'            => 'MyModule',
    'VERSION_FROM'    => 'MyModule.pm', # finds $VERSION
    'PREREQ_PM'       => {}, # e.g., Module::Name => 1.1
);
```

Now it's up to you to populate the module and the rest of the directory contents. Of course, there are times when you want to support a more complex system, and in those situations you need to know how to configure **MakeMaker**.

MakeMaker Configurable Options

The bulk of the information that is produced by **MakeMaker** is gleaned from the configuration and environment of the machine on which the makefile is extracted. **MakeMaker** uses a number of additional modules, including **Config**, which contains all of the information gained at the configuration of the Perl version.

All of the options can be modified to specify alternative installation locations, installation procedures, and even the architecture and version of Perl that you want to install. The usual method is to specify the alternative values within **Makefile.PL** as part of the hash argument passed to **WriteMakefile**; for example:

```
use ExtUtils::MakeMaker;
WriteMakefile('NAME'  -> 'StatVFS',
              'PREFIX' -> '/usr/lib',
              'VERSION' -> '1.01');
```

Alternatively, they can be specified as **NAME=VALUE** pairs on the command line; for example:

```
$ perl Makefile.PL PREFIX=/usr/lib
```

What follows is a list of all the configurable options for the field names supported by the **WriteMakeFile** function from **ExtUtils::MakeMaker**.

AUTHOR   The name and email address of the package author(s)—this information is used by the PPD file used by the PPM/VPM system (see "Packing for PPM/VPM" later in this chapter).

ABSTRACT   A one-line description of the module—used by the PPM/VPM systems in the PPD file.

ABSTRACT_FROM   The name of the file that contains the package description. This overrides **ABSTRACT** and is extracted from a POD file, normally taking the first **=head1 NAME** section.

BINARY_LOCATION   Defines the location of the binary package of the actual module, relative to the PPD that is created when building a PPM file.

C   This should be a reference to an array of C source-file names. The information is not currently used by **MakeMaker**, but it can be a handy reference if you want to use some of the extensions available within **MakeMaker** and other modules. See the "Related Modules" section later in this chapter.

CCFLAGS   The string that will be passed to the compiler between the **INC** and **OPTIMIZE** options on the command line. You might want to include debugging options or special format handling (such as **-traditional** to **gcc**).

CONFIG   An array reference to a list of configuration elements to be incorporated from the configuration information built at Perl's compile time. The following values are added to **Config** by **MakeMaker**: **ar, cc, cccdlflags, ccdlflags, dlext, dlsrc, ld, lddlflags, ldflags, libc, lib_ext, obj_ext, ranlib, sitelibexp, sitearchexp**, and **so**.

CONFIGURE   Should contain a reference to a section of code (anonymous or named function), which in turn should return a reference to a hash. The hash can contain the list of configurable elements for the **MakeMaker** module.

DEFINE   A string containing the definitions required to compile the extension. For example, you may need to specify **-DHAVE_STRING_H**.

DIR   A reference to an array containing a list of subdirectories that have their own **Makefile.PL**. The list will be used to determine the list of subdirectories and extensions that need to be included when each makefile is written, and also when the main makefile is parsed by the **make** command.

DISTNAME   The distribution name of the package that will be created when the directory is packaged by **tar** or **zip**—defaults to the value of **NAME**

DL_FUNCS   A hash reference to a list of symbol names for functions that should be made available as universal symbols at compile time. This is currently only used under AIX and VMS.

DL_VARS   An array reference to a list of symbol names for variables that should be made available as universal symbols at compile time. This is currently only used under AIX and VMS

EXCLUDE_EXT   An array reference to a list of extension names to be excluded when creating a new static Perl binary

EXE_FILES   An array reference to a list of executable files that will be installed into the **INST_SCRIPT** directory

FIRST_MAKEFILE   A string defining the name of the makefile to be produced for the MAP_TARGET—defaults to the value of the **MAKEFILE** option

FULLPERL   A string defining the name of the Perl binary able to run this extension

H   A reference to an array of the header files within the extension distribution

HTMLLIBPODS   Reference to a hash of .pm and .pod files to be converted into HTML format and installed with the other HTML files—defaults to all .pod and .pm files that contain any POD directive

HTMLSCRIPTPODS   Reference to a hash of files containing POD-based documentation that should be converted to HTML and installed—defaults to the value of the **EXE_FILES** configuration option

IMPORTS   Valid only on the OS/2 version of Perl

INC   A string listing the names of the directories to be searched for header files during extension compilation, for example, **-I/usr/local/include**

INCLUDE_EXT   A reference to an array of extension names to be included in the Perl binary when creating a new statically linked Perl. Normally, **MakeMaker** automatically includes the list of currently installed extensions. This allows both the new extension and all the extensions already installed to be incorporated into the new static Perl binary. However, if you specify a list of specific options in **INCLUDE_EXT**, then only the extensions listed will be included in the final binary.

The **DynaLoader** extension (if supported) will always be included in the binary. If you specify an empty array, only the current extension (and **DynaLoader**) will be included.

INSTALLARCHLIB   A string defining the name of the directory in which to install the files contained in **INST_ARCHLIB** if the value of **INSTALLDIRS** is **perl**

INSTALLBIN   A string defining the directory in which executable binaries should be installed

INSTALLDIRS   A string specifying in which of the two directory sets to install the extension. The options are **perl**, which specifies that the extension should be installed into the architecture-specific **INSTALLPRIVLIB** and **INSTALLARCHLIB** directories, and **site**, which installs the extensions into the site-specific **INSTALLSITELIB** and **INSTALLSITEARCH** directories.

FINE-TUNING
APPLICATIONS

INSTALLHTMLPRIVLIBDIR   The directory into which library documentation in HTML format will be installed during compilation time—defaults to **$Config{installhtmlprivlibdir}**

INSTALLHTMLSCRIPTDIR   The directory into which script documentation in HTML format will be installed during compilation time—defaults to **$Config{installhtmlscriptdir}**

INSTALLHTMLSITELIBDIR   The directory into which site-specific library documentation in HTML format will be installed during compilation time—defaults to **$Config{installhtmlsitelibdir}**

INSTALLMAN1DIR   A string specifying the directory to be used for the section 1 (commands) man pages during installation. The value defaults to the value contained in **$Config{installman1dir}**.

INSTALLMAN3DIR   A string specifying the directory to be used for the section 3 (functions/extensions) man pages during installation. The value defaults to the value contained in **$Config{installman3dir}**.

INSTALLPRIVLIB   A string specifying the directory in which to install the built libraries; see **INSTALLDIRS**.

INSTALLSCRIPT   A string specifying the directory in which to install any scripts. The contents of the directory specified by **INST_SCRIPT** is copied to this directory during installation.

INSTALLSITELIB   A string specifying the directory in which to install the built libraries; see **INSTALLDIRS**.

INSTALLSITEARCH   A string specifying the directory in which to install the contents of **INST_ARCH** during installation; see **INSTALLDIRS**.

INST_ARCHLIB   A string specifying the local directory to be used for storing architecture-dependent libraries during build and before installation

INST_BIN   A string specifying the local directory to be used for storing binaries during build and before installation.

INST_EXE   Deprecated; use the **INST_SCRIPT** option instead.

INST_HTMLLIBDIR   The directory that will hold the HTML documents during build time; they will be copied from here into **INSTALLHTMLPRIVLIBDIR** during a **make install**.

INST_HTMLSCRIPTDIR   The directory that will hold the HTML documents during build time; they will be copied from here into **INSTALLHTMLSCRIPTDIR** during a **make install**.

INST_LIB   A string specifying the local directory to be used for storing libraries during build and before installation

INST_MAN1DIR   A string specifying the local directory to be used for storing section 1 man pages during build and before installation

INST_MAN3DIR   A string specifying the local directory to be used for storing section 3 man pages during build and before installation

INST_SCRIPT   A string specifying the local directory to be used for storing binaries and other executables during build and before installation—defaults to blib/bin

LDFROM   A string specifying the list of files to be used to build the final library—defaults to the value of **$OBJECTS**

LIBPERL_A   A string defining the name of the Perl library to be used with the extension—defaults to libperl.a

LIB   A string specifying the directory into which the libraries will be installed—has the effect of setting the values of **INSTALLPRIVLIB** and **INSTALLSITELIB**

LIBS   A reference to an anonymous array listing the library specifications to be searched for, in order, until a suitable library is found. Each element should contain the full list of libraries to be searched. This can be used in situations where the functions required may be in any number of files. For example, DBM interfaces can exist in compatible forms in GDBM, NDBM, ODBM, and SDBM libraries. Other examples include compatibility libraries (such as BSD on an SVR4 platform) and extension libraries such as Tk and Tcl.

    Note that because each element specifies the whole list, you will need to specify the same library a number of times if you are looking for other compatibility; for example:

```
'LIBS' => ["-ltk -lgdbm", "-ltk -lndbm", "-ltk -lodbm"]
```

If you only want to supply one list of libraries, you can supply a scalar, and **MakeMaker** will turn it into an array with only one element. Note that the specifications can also include a library path, as in **-L/usr/local/lib**, in addition to the library list.

LINKTYPE   A scalar specifying the type of linking to be used when creating the extension. This is usually **dynamic** unless your operating system does not support it. For a static build, use **static**.

MAKEAPERL   A scalar; a value of 1 indicates that **MakeMaker** should incorporate the rules to make a new Perl binary.

MAKEFILE   A scalar specifying the name of the makefile to be produced.

MAN1PODS   A reference to a hash of files containing documentation in POD format to be converted to man pages during installation—defaults to **EXE_FILES**

MAN3PODS   A reference to a hash of files containing documentation in POD format to be converted to man pages during installation—defaults to **EXE_FILES**

MAP_TARGET   A string containing the name of the new Perl binary to be produced if **static** linking is requested—defaults to "perl"

MYEXTLIB   A string containing the name of a custom library file built by the extension that should be included when linking the extension.

NAME   A string specifying the name of the extension. If left unspecified, it will default to the name of the directory containing **Makefile.PL**.

NEEDS_LINKING   If set, it indicates to **MakeMaker** that there is linkable code in one of the subdirectories. If not specified, **MakeMaker** will try to work it out and set this value as necessary.

NOECHO   A string specifying the prefix to be placed in front of commands in the produced makefile. By default, it is set to @, which hides all the commands as they are executed. You can set this to an empty string to force the **make** process to output all of its commands, which can be useful for debugging.

NORECURS   If set, **MakeMaker** will not recurse into subdirectories to create additional makefiles. The default behavior is for **MakeMaker** to both create the makefiles and ensure that the parent makefile is capable of recursing into subdirectories to build additional targets.

NO_VC   Normally **MakeMaker** will check the current version of **ExtUtils::MakeMaker** against the version used to create the makefile and fail if it determines that there could be an incompatibility. Setting this disables the version check, but you should use the option on the command line, rather than setting the value directly in the script.

OBJECT   A string defining the list of object files to be created into a single library. Defaults to the single file specified by **$(BASEEXT)$(OBJ_EXT)**.

OPTIMIZE   A string containing the flag to be passed to the compiler to make it optimize the code during compilation. Defaults to **-O**. Other options you may want to try are **-g**, to switch on debugging, and **-g -O**, to switch on debugging and optimization for the compilers that support it (GNU C does).

PERL   A string containing the location of a Perl binary capable of doing the tasks normally executed by the **miniperl** binary created during a Perl build.

PERLMAINCC   A string defining the program to use for compiling the perlmain.c file. The default is to use the value of **$(CC)**.

PERL_ARCHLIB   A string defining the libraries to be used for building the Perl binary.

PERL_LIB   A string specifying the directory containing the Perl library.

PERL_MALLOC_OK   Should be set to true if you are happy to have the extension built using the Perl **malloc()**, rather than the system's own implementation. Defaults to false (0).

PERL_SRC   A string specifying the location of the Perl source code. Normally unnecessary, since the Perl source code is not required to build extensions or a new Perl binary.

PERM_RW   A string defining the octal mode to be used for files that should be available for reading and writing. Defaults to 0644, or read/write for the owner and read-only for everybody else.

PERM_RWX   A string defining the octal mode to be used for files that should be executable. Defaults to 0755, or read, write, and execute for the owner and read and execute for everybody else.

PL_FILES   A reference to a hash that specifies the list of files to be processed as Perl scripts rather than native commands. The default is to use any files in the directory structure for the extension that end in .PL. The keys should be the full file name, and the corresponding value should be the base name of the file. This can be used to create custom installation routines.

PM   A reference to a hash specifying the list of .pm and .pl files to be installed. The key should be the name of the file, and the corresponding value should equal the final installation location. By default, this will be all the matching files found in **PMLIBDIRS**.

PMLIBDIRS   A reference to an array of subdirectories containing library files to be installed. Defaults to [**'lib'**, **$(BASEEXT)**]. The entire contents of the directories are installed into the corresponding location according to their file type. The **libscan** method can be used to alter this behavior. See the section "Customizing Commands" for more details.

POLLUTE   Pollutes the name space with the preprocessor macros used for installing extensions—shouldn't be required under Perl 5.6 and later.

PPM_INSTALL_EXEC   The name of the executable to be used when installing a package using PPM.

PPM_INSTALL_SCRIPT   The name of the script to be executed after the module has been installed using PPM.

PREFIX   A string defining the default prefix to be used in front of installation directories. The default is to use the value determined at configuration time.

PREREQ_PM   A reference to a hash defining the list of modules that need to be available to run this extension. The key for the hash is the module or extension name, and the corresponding value is the minimum version number. If the value of the version number is 0, then **MakeMaker** only checks that the module or extension has been installed.

SKIP   A reference to an array listing the parts of the makefile that should be skipped during production—should be avoided in nearly all cases

TYPEMAPS   A reference to an array of alternative typemap files to be used with **xsubpp**. This should only be used when you want to use a typemap file that is either not in the current directory or isn't called typemap. A typemap file in the current directory has the highest precedence, followed by the last element of **$(TYPEMAPS)**. The system typemap has the lowest precedence.

VERSION   A string containing the version for this distribution of the package. This is gleaned from an alternative file if **VERSION_FROM** is defined.

VERSION_FROM   A string specifying the name of a file to be searched to define the version number of the package distribution. The regular expression /([\$*])(([\w\:\']*)\bVERSION)\b.*\=/ is used to find the version number in the file. This allows for unqualified definitions in the file, for example:

```
$VERSION = '1.00';
```

The result is parsed with **eval** to get the final value, which means you can also use arrays, hashes, and even functions if referenced by **$VERSION** or something similar. Variables qualified with **my** or **local**, or those specified with their full package name, will not be found. If you are using the **strict** pragma, then use the **vars** pragma to predeclare the **VERSION** variable before assigning it a value.

XS   A reference to a hash of XS files to be processed into C files. The key to the hash should contain the XS file name, and the value should contain the corresponding C source file name.

XSOPT   A string specifying the options to be passed to **xsubpp**. Use the **TYPEMAP** option if you want to specify typemap files and the **XSPROTOARG** option for including prototypes.

XSPROTOARG   A string that defines whether prototypes should be included (see Chapter 20). If blank (default), it assumes prototypes should be included; a value of **-noprototypes** specifies that prototypes should not be created.

XS_VERSION   A string defining the version number for the XS file in the current package. Defaults to **VERSION**.

Creating a Dummy Makefile

Not all **Makefile.PL** files are intended to create a makefile suitable for creating an extension module. In these cases, you can get **MakeMaker** to create a dummy makefile that just does nothing. It will succeed for all the specified targets, but otherwise achieve nothing. To do this, you use a different function in the **MakeMaker** module:

```
ExtUtils::MakeMaker::WriteEmptyMakefile();
```

In most instances, this is really only useful for creating a dummy makefile that will be used by some automated process, such as the **CPAN** module. The **CPAN** module tries to determine which packages and modules are required, automatically downloading and installing them as necessary. However, if the functionality of the module is supported by some other method on the current platform, you need some way to "trick" **CPAN** into believing that the installation was a success.

Default Makefile Targets

The makefile created by **MakeMaker** produces a set of standard targets to be used during the build process. The default target always triggers the build process up to, but not including, the installation process. Other default targets are shown in Table 25-2. Other targets deserving special mention are covered in the following sections.

Target	Description
test	Runs the defined test script(s)
testdb	Runs the defined test script(s) within the Perl debugger
install	Installs the extension, modules, and support files, including documentation. The values of the **INSTALL*** options are used to define the final locations for the specified files.

Table 25-2. *Default **make** Targets*

Creating a New Perl Binary

The default operation for the produced makefile is to create a library suitable for dynamic loading. A library file ending with .so on a Unix system and .dll on a Windows system signifies a dynamic library. However, not all systems support dynamic loading, and in these and other situations you may wish to create your own statically linked Perl executable that includes the new extension. If this is the case, you can use a special target, **perl**, to the makefile produced by the **MakeMaker** module. The operation is then slightly different from the normal build process:

1. The extension is recompiled into a static rather than a dynamic library.
2. A new makefile is created—Makefile.aperl, although the exact name is system dependent. This contains the definitions for building a new Perl binary.
3. The new makefile is used to produce the new binary, first by creating a new file with a modified **main()** function, and then by linking the resulting object file with the main Perl library and the extension library.

The new Perl binary is created within the current directory and can be installed over the existing binary using

```
$ make -f Makefile.aperl inst_perl
```

The final binary actually includes all the extensions specified in the **INST_ARCHLIB**, **SITELIBEXP**, and **PERL_ARCHLIB** options defined within the main **MakeMaker** definition.

You can create a Perl binary with a different file name by defining the value of **MAP_TARGET** in the Perl makefile. The best way to do this is on the command line, because that overrides any options defined in the makefile itself, which might well specify the default. For example, to change the name to **vfsperl**:

```
$ perl Makefile.PL MAP_TARGET=vfsperl
$ make vfsperl
```

As a final alternative, you may want to build a static Perl version on a dynamically capable system. In this instance, you use the **LINKTYPE** value to specify the destination type:

```
$ perl Makefile.PL LINKTYPE=static
```

Targets for Package Builders

The built makefile provides for some standard targets primarily aimed at developers. The targets are designed to test and package the final distribution file. Note that the tests are aimed at verifying that all of the required files are in the current directory structure. This is achieved by checking the contents of the MANIFEST file, which contains a list of all the files required before the package can be distributed.

The packaging process uses the defined archiving and compression programs to produce a final distributable package file. This is normally a combination of **tar** and **gzip**, but you can modify this if the file is aimed at Windows (which uses **zip**) or Linux (which occasionally uses **bzip2**). The list of "package" targets is summarized in Table 25-3.

Target	Description
distcheck	Provides a list of files that appear in the current directory structure, but not in MANIFEST, and vice versa. See the section on "ExtUtils::Manifest" later in this chapter for more details.
skipcheck	Provides a list of files that are skipped due to the list provided in MANIFEST.SKIP. See the section on "ExtUtils::Manifest" later in this chapter for more details.
distclean	Executes the **realclean** target and then the **distcheck** target. The result should be a set of files suitable for building a new distribution file or for returning the current directory to its distributed (supplied) state.

Table 25-3.   *Extension Developers' Targets*

Target	Description
manifest	Re-creates the MANIFEST file using the list of files found in the current directory
distdir	Creates a new directory in the parent called **$(DISTNAME)-$(VERSION)** and copies the files listed in MANIFEST to the new directory. This does all of the steps necessary to create a new version-specific directory for the extension.
disttest	Does a **distdir** first and then runs **perl Makefile.PL**, **make**, and **make test** in the new directory. This should perform all of the steps necessary to create and test a new version of an extension.
tardist	Does a **distdir**, and then runs **$(PREOP)** followed by **$(TOUNIX)**. Then it runs **$(TAR)** on the new directory (using **$(TARFLAGS)**) before deleting the directory and running **$(POSTOP)**. This target is intended to create, package, and delete a new version directory for the extension as a **tar** file, suitable for use by Unix machines. You can modify **$(TAR)** and the other options according to taste. See the following section, "Customizing Commands."
dist	Defaults to **$(DIST_DEFAULT)**, which in turn defaults to **tardist**
uutardist	Runs a **tardist** first and then uuencodes the **tar** file (using **uuencode**)
shdist	Does a **distdir**, and then runs **$(PREOP)** followed by **$(TOUNIX)**. Then it runs **$(SHAR)** on the new directory before deleting the directory and running **$(POSTOP)**. This target is intended to create, package, and delete a new version directory for the extension as a **shar** file, suitable for ASCII transmission. You can modify **$(SHAR)** and the other options according to taste. See the following section, "Customizing Commands."
zipdist	Does a **distdir**, and then runs **$(PREOP)**. Then it runs **$(ZIP)** on the new directory (using **$(ZIPFLAGS)**) before deleting the directory and running **$(POSTOP)**. This target is intended to create, package, and delete a new version directory for the extension as a **zip** file, suitable for use by Windows machines. You can modify **$(ZIP)** and the other options according to taste. See the following section, "Customizing Commands."
ci	Checks in a version of each file in MANIFEST (using the value of **$CI**) and updates the RCS label (using **$RCS_LABEL**).

Table 25-3. *Extension Developers' Targets* (continued)

Customizing Commands

The developer targets default to use a number of commands that are expected to be on the host machine. The options can be configured where the destination or source requires a different format. For example, Linux often uses the **bzip2** command for compression, rather than **gzip** or **compress**.

The options in Table 25-4 should be passed as a hash reference to the special **dist** option to the **WriteMakefile** function.

Option	Default	Description
CI	ci -u	Program for "checking in" a revision
COMPRESS	gzip -best	Program for compression
POSTOP	@ :	Commands to be run after archive creation
PREOP	@ :	Commands to be run before archive creation
RCS_LABEL	rcs -q -Nv$(VERSION_SYM):	Extract the RCS label for a file.
SHAR	shar	Program to use for creating a **shar** file
SUFFIX	.gz	Default suffix for compressed files
TAR	tar	Program to use for creating a **tar** format archive
TARFLAGS	cvf	Command line options to use for creating the **tar** file
TO_UNIX	System dependent	Program used to convert the files into Unix format
ZIP	zip	Command to use for **zip** files
ZIPFLAGS	-r	Command line options to use for creating a **zip** file

Table 25-4.   *Options for Extension Developers' Targets*

Related Modules

A number of different modules are used and can help in the process of creating a makefile using **MakeMaker**. It's unlikely that you will need to delve into the bowels of any of these modules, even when creating quite complex extensions. The information provided is merely background detail.

Config

The **Config** module exports a hash, **%Config**, that lists all of the configurable options that were calculated when Perl was built, with the values containing the necessary information. The **MakeMaker** module uses this information to select the correct C compiler and installation directories, among many other things.

ExtUtils::Command

This function is used under Win32 implementations. It defines a list of alternative functions to be used by the building and installation process in place of the usual Unix command line utilities.

ExtUtils::Embed

This module provides the necessary command line options and other information for use when you are embedding a Perl interpreter into an application. See Chapter 20 for more information.

ExtUtils::Install

This module defines two functions, **install** and **uninstall**, which are used during the installation and uninstallation process.

ExtUtils::Installed

This module defines a suite of functions that can be used to query the contents of the .packlist files generated during module installation. If you call the **new** function, it constructs the internal lists by examining the .packlist files. The **modules** function returns a list of all the modules currently installed. The **files** and **directories** both accept a single argument—the name of a module. The result is a list of all the files installed by the package. The **directory_tree** function reports information for all the related directories. In all cases, you can specify **Perl** to get information pertaining to the core Perl installation.

The **validate** function checks that the files listed in .packlist actually exist. The **packlist** function returns an object as defined by **ExtUtils::Packlist** for the specified module. Finally, **version** returns the version number of the specified module.

ExtUtils::Liblist

This module defines the libraries to be used when building extension libraries and other Perl-based binaries. The information provided here broaches much of the complexity involved in getting an extension to work across many platforms; the bulk of the code relates to the information required for individual platforms.

ExtUtils::Manifest

This module provides the functions that produce, test, and update the MANIFEST file. Five of the functions are the most useful, beginning with **mkmanifest**, which creates a file based on the current directory contents. The **maincheck** function verifies the current directory contents against the MANIFEST file, while **filecheck** looks for files in the current directory that are not specified in the MANIFEST. Both **maincheck** and **filecheck** are executed by the **fullcheck** function, and **skipcheck** lists the files in the MAINFEST.SKIP file.

ExtUtils::Miniperl

This module provides the list of base libraries and extensions that should be included when building the **miniperl** binary.

ExtUtils::Mkbootstrap

This module makes a bootstrap file suitable for the **DynaLoader** module.

ExtUtils::Mksymlists

This module produces the list of options for creating a dynamic link library.

ExtUtils::MM_OS2

MakeMaker specifics for the OS/2 operating system are produced by this module.

ExtUtils::MM_Unix

MakeMaker specifics for the Unix platform are produced by this module. It also includes many of the core functions used by the main **MakeMaker** module, irrespective of the host platform.

ExtUtils::MM_VMS

This module produces **MakeMaker** specifics for VMS.

ExtUtils::MM_Win32

This module produces **MakeMaker** specifics for Windows 95/98/NT.

ExtUtils::Packlist

This module supplies the **Packlist** object used by the **ExtUtils::Installed** module.

MakeMaker Tricks

Beyond the basics of generating a simple makefile, **MakeMaker** can be made to perform some more complex operations for those times when the basic **MakeMaker** configuration just doesn't seem flexible enough. It's worth remembering at all times that a Perl makefile is just a script that often (but not always) makes use of the **ExtUtils::MakeMaker** module. Anything that you can do in a script can be done with a Perl makefile.

Checking for Prerequisites

Some modules that you develop may require the preinstallation of other modules that are not included in the standard Perl distribution. The **PREREQ_PM** configuration option can be used to list the modules and version numbers that are required. For example, here's the configuration line used in the LWP bundle:

```
PREREQ_PM       => { 'URI'               => "1.03",
                     'MIME::Base64'      => "2.1",
                     'Net::FTP'          => "2.4",
                     'HTML::HeadParser'  => 0,
                     'Digest::MD5'       => 0,
                   },
```

Sometimes, however, you want a more interactive and informative method for reporting these problems. To do this, you need to add your own set of tests before the call to **MakeMaker** to test for the existence of the modules. For example, you might place some code like this to check for an individual module:

```
print "Checking for My::Module ..";
eval
{
    require My::Module;
};
if ($@)
{
    print " failed\n";
    $missing_modules++;
    print <<EOT;
```

```
$@
You need the My::Module in order to ensure that you have
the right modules installed for installation
EOT
}
else
{
    print " ok\n";
}
```

Because **eval** uses its own interpreter, it'll raise an exception if the module you need can't be found without actually interrupting the current script. In this case, we report an error and also increment the **$missing_modules++** variable. Using this method, you could insert multiple tests just like this and then fail the installation script if **$missing_modules** is greater than 0.

Application Installation

Installing an application is really just a case of supplying the configuration options to **MakeMaker** to copy the scripts into the correct location. This is as simple as

```
use ExtUtils::MakeMaker;

WriteMakefile(
            NAME => 'mctest',
            EXE_FILES => [qw/ping.pl/],
            );
```

The **EXE_FILES** option specifies the list of scripts that should be copied first into the directory pointed to by **INST_SCRIPT** (defaults to ./blib/scripts) during the build phase, and then into the **INSTALLSCRIPT** directory (usually /usr/local/bin) during the installation phase.

If you want to do something more complex during the build phase, you need to configure **MakeMaker** to write the commands you want to execute directly into the makefile. Because these are module specific, there is no "automatic" way of getting **MakeMaker** to do this stage for you. Remember that the process needs to be completed during the call to **make**, not when actually creating the makefile itself.

The way to do this is to override one of the methods used by **MakeMaker** during the production of the makefile. You can override methods used in **MakeMaker** by defining the methods within the **MY** package. For modifying what happens after the main build process, you need to override the **postamble** method, which by default is undefined. The return value from your **postamble** subroutine should be the string containing the **make** target and commands. For example, here's another extract from LWP's Perl makefile:

```perl
package MY;

sub postamble
{
    my @m;
    if (@request_aliases && grep($_ eq 'lwp-request', @programs_to_
install)) {
        push @m, "all ::\n";
        if ($^O eq 'MSWin32') {
          push @m, "\t\$(FULLPERL) -e \"use Config; chdir q[\$(INST_EXE)
          ]; "
                    ."foreach (qw(@request_aliases)) { \" \\\n";
          push @m, <<'EOT';
        -e "unlink \"$$_\"; " \
        -e "system(\"copy lwp-request $$_\") && die; }"
EOT
        } else {
          push @m, "\t\$(FULLPERL) -e 'use Config; chdir q{\$(INST_EXE)}; "
                    ."foreach (qw(@request_aliases)) {' \\\n";
          push @m, <<'EOT';
        -e 'unlink "$$_";' \
        -e 'system("$$Config{\"lns\"} lwp-request $$_") && die; }'
EOT
        }
    }
    join "", @m;
}
```

What's happening here is that we are building a string that will create symbolic links to the **lwp-request** script so that users can type **GET url** or **POST url** at the command line. The output produced in the makefile under Unix looks like this:

```
# --- MakeMaker postamble section:
all ::
        $(FULLPERL) -e 'use Config; chdir q{$(INST_EXE)}; foreach (qw(GET
HEAD POST)) {' \
        -e 'unlink "$$_";' \
        -e 'system("$$Config{\"lns\"} lwp-request $$_") && die; }'
```

You can see here the Perl code to install links for GET, HEAD, and POST. The **$Config{"lns"}** is the name of the link command determined by Perl during the build process, and the rest is just a **foreach** loop that first deletes and then creates the link. The links are made in the blib/script directory and will be copied into the final script directory (/usr/local/bin) during the installation phase.

Packing for CPAN

When packing up your module and makefile for CPAN, all you need to do is clean the extension or module directory for your application and then use **tar** and **gzip** to package the entire directory. You'll need to delete any unnecessary files and also clean the directory of any of the build files specific to your development platform. For the former, it's a case of manually deleting those files; for the latter, the easiest way to do this is to change to your directory and then type

```
$ make distclean
```

To actually package the module up, use something like this

```
$ tar cf - ./MyModule|gzip -c - >MyModule.tar.gz
```

where **MyModule** is the name of your module. When supplying to CPAN, you should include the version number and then separate the module name from the version by a single hyphen; for example, MyModule-1.13.tar.gz.

Alternatively, make sure your MANIFEST file is up to date and then use

```
$ make dist
```

This will package up all the files listed in MANIFEST into a tar file and then zip them using **gzip**. The name of the resultant file will be based on the **NAME** and **VERSION** options in the Perl makefile.

Packing for PPM/VPM

The Perl Package Manager is actually very similar to the **CPAN** module, and it provides a way for users of the ActivePerl distribution to download and install modules precompiled for a number of platforms, but primarily the Windows series. This is the only major difference between a traditional **MakeMaker** package and PPM—with PPM you package up a precompiled version of the module, rather than its raw source.

You need to develop the Perl makefile and the options and other tricks you use with **MakeMaker** as normal, build it on your target platform, and then produce a separate file, the PPD, which contains all of the information about the module required by the PPM system. There is, of course, a simple way of doing this.

For example, consider this makefile template:

```
use ExtUtils::MakeMaker;

WriteMakefile(
    'NAME' => 'MyModule',
    'VERSION_FROM' => 'MyModule.pm',
    ($] ge '5.005') ? (
        'AUTHOR' => 'Me (me@me.org)',
        'ABSTRACT' => 'Does my stuff',
    ) : (),
);
```

Normally at this point, with all the modules and the Perl makefile ready-written, we'd package everything up into a distributable package ready for posting on CPAN. However, we need to perform the build process on behalf of the end-user, since we cannot guarantee they will have the utilities required to extract the file themselves. To do this, type:

```
C:\> perl Makefile.PL
C:\> nmake
```

If you don't have a copy of **nmake** (which comes with Visual Studio) you can download a copy from **ftp://ftp.microsoft.com/Softlib/MSLFILES/nmake15.exe**.

This will go through the build process creating the standard directory structure used by **MakeMaker**. PPM uses this base structure when installing the module into its final location—normally this would be handled by **make** or a similar utility. You might see output like the following, although it will depend on the **make** utility you are using.

```
mkdir blib
mkdir blib/lib
mkdir blib/arch
mkdir blib/arch/auto
mkdir blib/lib/auto
mkdir blib/man3
copy MyModule.pm blib/lib/MyModule.pm
```

You now need to package the **blib** directory up using **tar** and **gzip**. You can get these utilities from a variety of places—ActiveState recommends **http://www.itribe.net/virtunix/**. For example:

```
C:\> tar cvf MyModule.tar blib
C:\> gzip MyModule.tar
```

This will create a file called **MyModule.tar.gz**.

The final step is to create the PPD (Perl Package Definition) file that specifies the package information required by PPM. This is, in essence, a condensed version of the information that is normally extracted from a number of files by the **CPAN** module. The PPD is read by PPM/VPM when you are searching for a given package. To make the process easier, the **MakeMaker** utility places the necessary steps into the makefile, based on the definitions you've already provided, so we can type

```
C:\> nmake ppd
```

The resulting file that is produced should be called MyModule.PPD, and it'll look something like this:

```
<SOFTPKG NAME="MyModule" VERSION="1,0,0,0">
    <TITLE>MyModule</TITLE>
    <ABSTRACT>Does my stuff</ABSTRACT>
    <AUTHOR>Me (me@me.org)</AUTHOR>
    <IMPLEMENTATION>
        <OS NAME="MSWin32" />
        <ARCHITECTURE NAME="MSWin32-x86-object" />
        <CODEBASE HREF="" />
    </IMPLEMENTATION>
</SOFTPKG>
```

The file is actually in XML format and defines all of the information required by PPM when you search a repository. You will need to change the value of the **CODEBASE** property to point to the location of the source package file.

If you want to actually supply your final package to a public repository, like the one at ActiveState, you need to put the MyModule.tar.gz file in an x86 directory, and then Zip the x86 directory and send it to the repository concerned. (See Chapter 2 for more information on PPM/VPM repositories.)

FINE-TUNING
APPLICATIONS

The
Complete
Reference

Part V

Appendixes

The Complete Reference

Perl

Appendix A

Function Reference

This appendix is a quick guide to the functions and major operators (including regular expression and quoting mechanisms) support by Perl v5.7 (the latest developmental release at the time of writing).

Because of the way in which most of the Perl functions operate, it's difficult to give a strict or coherent meaning to all of the functions. Most of the functions and operators have their own special meaning and treatment, depending on the context in which they are used. It's also impossible to qualify functions according to what they return, since different functions return different information according to their context. For example, the **localtime** function returns a date/time string in scalar context, but the individual time and date components when used in a list context.

Each function description includes details of the function's operation and the effects of the function (using the short codes listed in Table A-1). References to other functions, chapters, or modules that may extend or provide a better interface to the facilities offered by the function are also mentioned.

For a quick reference to some of the more popular problems and effects of the Perl built-in functions, see Table A-2. This lists functions and the variables they use or modify, or the types of exceptions they raise. The same codes are used within the function definitions. The column descriptions for Table A-2 are given in Table A-1.

Effect	Description
$_	Uses **$_**, **@_**, or similar as a default value if no arguments have been supplied
$!	Sets **$!** on an error
$@	Raises an exception that can be trapped by embedding the call within **eval**, setting the value of **$@** with the error string
$?	Sets **$?** when a child process exits
T	Taints the data returned by this function
XA	Raises an exception when supplied an invalid argument
XR	Raises an exception if you modify a read-only argument
XT	Raises an exception if fed tainted data
U	(Support is only guaranteed on Unix) Raises an exception if unsupported on the current platform; you should be able to trap the function call and error using **eval**

Table A-1. *Effect Codes Used on Functions*

Function	$_	$!	$@	$?	T	XA	XR	XT	U
abs	X								
accept	X					X			X
alarm	X								X
atan2									
bind		X				X		X	X
binmode						X			
bless						X			
caller									
chdir		X						X	
chmod		X						X	
chomp	X						X		
chop	X						X		
chown		X						X	X
chr	X								
chroot	X	X						X	X
close		X		X		X			
closedir		X				X			X
connect		X				X		X	X
cos	X								
crypt									X
dbmclose		X							X
dbmopen		X							X
defined	X								
delete									
die			X						
do (block)									

Table A-2.   *Attributes for Built-In Perl Functions*

Function	$_	$!	$@	$?	T	XA	XR	XT	U
do (file)	x				X			X	
do (subroutine)			X						
dump									
each									
endgrent									X
endhostent									X
endnetent									X
endprotoent									X
endpwent									X
endservent									X
eof						X			
eval	X							X	
exec		X						X	
exists									
exit									
exp	X								
fcntl		X				X	X	X	X
fileno						X			
flock		X				X			X
fork		X							X
format									
formline									
getc					X	X			
getgrent									x
getgrgid									x
getgrnam									x

Table A-2. *Attributes for Built-In Perl Functions* (continued)

Function	$_	$!	$@	$?	T	XA	XR	XT	U
gethostbyaddr									x
gethostbyname									x
gethostent									x
getlogin									x
getnetbyaddr									x
getnetbyname									x
getnetent									x
getpeername		X				X			x
getpgrp		X							X
getppid									X
getpriority		X							X
getprotobyname									X
getprotobynumber									X
getprotoent									X
getpwent					X				X
getpwnam					X				X
getpwuid					X				X
getservbyname									X
getservbyport									X
getservent									X
getsockname		X				X			X
getsockopt		X				X			X
glob	X		X		X			X	
gmtime									
goto			X						
grep									

Table A-2.   *Attributes for Built-In Perl Functions* (continued)

Function	$_	$!	$@	$?	T	XA	XR	XT	U
hex	X								
import									
index									
int	X								
ioctl		X				X	X	X	X
join									
keys									
kill		X				X		X	X
last			X						
lc	X				X				
lcfirst	X				X				
length	X								
link		X						X	X
listen		X				X			X
local									
localtime									
log	X		X						
lstat	X	X							X
m//					X			X	
map									
mkdir		X						X	
msgctl		X							X
msgget		X							X
msgrcv		X							X
msgsnd		X							X
my									

Table A-2. *Attributes for Built-In Perl Functions* (continued)

Function	$_	$!	$@	$?	T	XA	XR	XT	U
next			X						
no			X						
oct	X								
open		X				X		X	X
opendir		X				X		X	X
ord	X								
pack			X						
package									
pipe		X				X			X
pop									
pos	X								
print	X	X				X			
printf	X	X				X			
prototype						X			
push									
quotemeta	X								
rand									
read		X			X	X	X		
readdir		X			X	X			X
readline		X			X	X			
readlink	X	X			X				X
readpipe		X		X	X			X	X
recv		X			X	X	X		X
redo			X						
ref	X								
rename		X						X	

Table A-2. *Attributes for Built-In Perl Functions* (continued)

Function	$_	$!	$@	$?	T	XA	XR	XT	U
require	X	X	X					X	
reset									
return			X						
reverse									
rewinddir		X				X			X
rindex	X	X						X	
rmdir									
s///					X		X	X	
scalar									
seek		X				X			
seekdir		X				X			X
select (filehandle)						X			
select (files)		X							X
semctl		X							X
semget		X							X
semop		X							X
send		X				X			X
setgrent									X
sethostent									X
setnetent									X
setpgrp		X						X	X
setpriority		X						X	X
setprotoent									X
setpwent									X
setservent									X
setsockopt		X				X			X

Table A-2.   *Attributes for Built-In Perl Functions* (continued)

Function	$_	$!	$@	$?	T	XA	XR	XT	U
shift									
shmctl		X							X
shmget		X							X
shmread		X							X
shmwrite		X							X
shutdown		X				X			X
sin	X								
sleep									
socket		X				X		X	X
socketpair		X				X		X	X
sort			X						
splice			X						
split	X				X				
sprintf									
sqrt	X		X						
srand									
stat	X	X				X			
study	X								
sub									
substr			X			X	X		
symlink		X						X	X
syscall		X					X	X	X
sysopen		X				X			
sysread		X	X		X	X	X		
sysseek		X				X			
system		X		X				X	

Table A-2. *Attributes for Built-In Perl Functions* (continued)

APPENDIXES

Function	$_	$!	$@	$?	T	XA	XR	XT	U
syswrite		X	X			X			
tell						X			
telldir						X			X
tie			X						
tied									
time									
times									
tr///						X			
truncate		X				X		X	X
uc	X				X				
ucfirst	X				X				
umask								X	X
undef						X			
unlink	X	X						X	
unpack			X						
unshift									
untie									
use		X	X						
utime		X						X	X
values									
vec						X			
wait		X		X					X
waitpid		X		X					X
wantarray									
warn		X							
write		X	X			X			
y///						X			

Table A-2. *Attributes for Built-In Perl Functions* (continued)

-X

```
-X FILEHANDLE
-X EXPR
```

This performs a file test, where **X** is one or more of the letters listed in Table A-3. The function takes one operator, either a file name (contained in **EXPR**) or a **FILEHANDLE**. The function tests the file and then returns true if the test was true and false otherwise. Some tests may also return a value, which will be zero (false) under some circumstances. If **EXPR** and **FILEHANDLE** are omitted, the function tests **$_**, except for **-t**, which tests **STDIN**.

Test	Result
-r	File is readable by effective uid/gid.
-w	File is writable by effective uid/gid.
-x	File is executable by effective uid/gid.
-o	File is owned by effective uid.
-R	File is readable by real uid/gid.
-W	File is writable by real uid/gid.
-X	File is executable by real uid/gid.
-O	File is owned by real uid.
-e	File exists.
-z	File has zero size.
-s	File has non-zero size (returns the file size in bytes).
-f	File is a plain file.
-d	File is a directory.
-l	File is a symbolic link.
-p	File is a named pipe (**FIFO**), or **FILEHANDLE** is a pipe.
-S	File is a network socket.
-b	File is a block special file.

Table A-3.   *File Tests*

APPENDIXES

Test	Result
-c	File is a character special file.
-t	File is opened to a tty (terminal).
-u	File has setuid bit set.
-g	File has setgid bit set.
-k	File has sticky bit set.
-T	File is a text file.
-B	File is a binary file (opposite of **-T**).
-M	Age of file in days when script started
-A	Time of last access in days when script started
-C	Time of last inode change when script started

Table A-3.   *File Tests* (continued)

Effects	*$_*
Returns in Scalar Context	*Returns in List Context*
0 if false	
1 if true	
Special conditions exist for some	
operators; see Table A-3	

See also Chapter(s)	*Function(s)*	*Module(s)*
Chapter 7	**stat**	

abs

```
abs EXPR
```

Returns the absolute value of **EXPR** or **$_**.

Effects	**$_**
Returns in Scalar Context	*Returns in List Context*

Absolute value

See also Chapter(s)	*Function(s)*	*Module(s)*
Chapter 8		

 ## accept

```
accept NEWSOCKET, GENERICSOCKET
```

Accepts an incoming connection on the existing **GENERICSOCKET**, which should
have been created with **socket** and bound to a local address using **bind**. The new
socket, which will be used for communication with the client will be **NEWSOCKET**.
GENERICSOCKET will remain unchanged.

Effects	**$_, XA, U**
Returns in Scalar Context	*Returns in List Context*

0 on failure
Packed address of remote host on success

See also Chapter(s)	*Function(s)*	*Module(s)*
Chapter 12	**connect, listen**	**IO::Socket**

 ## alarm

```
alarm EXPR
alarm
```

Sets the "alarm," causing the current process to receive a **SIGALRM** signal in **EXPR**
seconds. If **EXPR** is omitted, the value of **$_** is used instead. The actual time delay is not
precise, since different systems implement the **alarm** functionality differently. The
actual time may be up to a second more or less than the requested value. You can only
set one alarm timer at any one time. If a timer is already running and you make a new

call to the alarm function, the alarm timer is reset to the new value. A running timer can be reset without setting a new timer by specifying a value of 0.

Effects	$_, U
Returns in Scalar Context	*Returns in List Context*
Integer, number of seconds remaining for previous timer	

See also Chapter(s)	*Function(s)*	*Module(s)*
Chapter 14		

---

atan2

    atan2 Y,X

Returns the arctangent of Y/X in the range . to - .

Effects	None
Returns in Scalar Context	*Returns in List Context*
Floating point number	

See also Chapter(s)	*Function(s)*	*Module(s)*
Chapter 8		

---

bind

    bind SOCKET, ADDRESS

Binds the network **ADDRESS** to the filehandle identified by **SOCKET**. The **ADDRESS** should be a packed address of the appropriate type for the socket being opened.

Effects	$!, XA, XT, U
Returns in Scalar Context	*Returns in List Context*
0 on failure 1 on success	

See also Chapter(s)	*Function(s)*	*Module(s)*
Chapter 12	connect, accept, socket	IO::Socket

binmode

binmode FILEHANDLE

Sets the format for **FILEHANDLE** to be read from and written to as binary on the operating systems that differentiate between the two. Files that are not in binary have **CR LF** sequences converted to **LF** on input, and **LF** to **CR LF** on output. This is vital for operating systems that use two characters to separate lines within text files (MS-DOS), but has no effect on operating systems that use single characters (Unix, Mac OS, QNX).

Effects	**XA**
Returns in Scalar Context	*Returns in List Context*

undef on failure or invalid **FILEHANDLE**
1 on success

See also Chapter(s)	*Function(s)*	*Module(s)*
Chapter 7		

bless

bless REF, CLASSNAME
bless REF

Tells the entity referenced by **REF** that it is now an object in the **CLASSNAME** package, or the current package if **CLASSNAME** is omitted. Use of the two-argument form of **bless** is recommended.

Effects	**XA**
Returns in Scalar Context	*Returns in List Context*

The reference to an object blessed into
CLASSNAME

See also Chapter(s)	*Function(s)*	*Module(s)*
Chapter 10	**ref**	

APPENDIXES

caller

```
caller EXPR
caller
```

Returns information about the current subroutines caller. In a scalar context, returns the caller's package name or the package name of the caller **EXPR** steps up.

In a list context, with no arguments specified, **caller** returns the package name, file name and line within the file for the caller of the current subroutine:

```
($package, $filename, $line) = caller;
```

If **EXPR** is specified, **caller** returns extended information for the caller **EXPR** steps up. That is, when called with an argument of 1, it returns the information for the caller (parent) of the current subroutine, with 2 the caller of the caller (grandparent) of the current subroutine, and so on. The information returned is

```
($package, $filename, $line, $subroutine,
  $hasargs, $wantarray, $evaltext, $is_require) = caller($i);
```

The **$evaltext** and **$is_require** values are only returned when the subroutine being examined is actually the result of an **eval( )** statement.

Effects	None
Returns in Scalar Context	*Returns in List Context*
undef on failure	Basic information when called with no *arguments*
	Extended information when called with an argument
See also Chapter(s)	*Function(s)*	*Module(s)*
Chapter 21		

chdir

```
chdir EXPR
chdir
```

Changes the current working directory to **EXPR**, or to the user's home directory if none is specified.

Effects	$!, XT
Returns in Scalar Context	*Returns in List Context*
0 on failure	
1 on success	

See also Chapter(s)	*Function(s)*	*Module(s)*
Chapter 7		**Cwd**

chmod

```
chmod MODE, LIST
```

Changes the mode of the files specified in **LIST** to the **MODE** specified. The value of **MODE** should be in octal. You must check the return value against the number of files that you attempted to change to determine whether the operation failed.

Effects	$!, XT
Returns in Scalar Context	*Returns in List Context*
Integer, number of files successfully changed	

See also Chapter(s)	*Function(s)*	*Module(s)*
Chapter 7	−X, stat	

chomp

```
chomp EXPR
chomp LIST
chomp
```

Removes the last character if it matches the value of **$/** from **EXPR**, each element of **LIST,** or **$_** if no value is specified. Note that this is a safer version of the **chop** function because it only removes the last character if it matches **$/**. Removes all trailing newlines from the string or strings if in paragraph mode (when **$/ = ''**).

Effects	$_, XR
Returns in Scalar Context	Returns in List Context
Integer, number of bytes removed for all strings	

See also Chapter(s)	Function(s)	Module(s)
Chapter 8	chop	

chop

```
chop EXPR
chop LIST
chop
```

Removes the last character from **EXPR**, each element of **LIST**, or **$_** if no value is specified.

Effects	$_, XR
Returns in Scalar Context	Returns in List Context
The character removed from EXPR	The character removed from the last element of LIST

See also Chapter(s)	Function(s)	Module(s)
Chapter 8	chomp	

chown

```
chown USERID, GROUPID, LIST
```

Changes the user and group to the IDs specified by **USERID** and **GROUPID** on the files specified in **LIST**. Note that **USERID** and **GROUPID** must be the numeric IDs, not the names. If you specify a value of -1 to either argument, then the user or group ID are not updated. Note that you must compare the number of files that were actually changed against the number of files you wanted to change to determine if the operation was successful.

Effects	$!, XT, U
Returns in Scalar Context	*Returns in List Context*

Number of files successfully changed

See also Chapter(s)	*Function(s)*	*Module(s)*
Chapter 7	**chmod**	

---

chr

```
chr EXPR
chr
```

Returns the character represented by the numeric value of **EXPR**, or **$_** if omitted, according to the current character set. Note that the character number will use the Unicode character numbers for numerical values above 127.

Effects	$_
Returns in Scalar Context	*Returns in List Context*

Character

See also Chapter(s)	*Function(s)*	*Module(s)*
Chapter 8	**ord**	

---

chroot

```
chroot EXPR
chroot
```

Changes the root directory for all pathnames beginning with "/" to the directory specified by **EXPR**, or **$_** if none is specified. For security reasons, this function, which is identical to the system **chroot( )** function, is restricted to the superuser and cannot be undone.

Effects		$\$\_$, $\$!$, **XT**, **U**	
Returns in Scalar Context		*Returns in List Context*	
0 on failure			
1 on success			
See also Chapter(s)	*Function(s)*		*Module(s)*
Chapter 7	**chdir**		

close

```
close FILEHANDLE
close
```

Closes **FILEHANDLE**, flushing the buffers, if appropriate, and disassociating the **FILEHANDLE** with the original file, pipe, or socket. Closes the currently selected filehandle if none is specified.

Effects		$\$!$, $\$?$, **XA**	
Returns in Scalar Context		*Returns in List Context*	
0 on failure			
1 if buffers were flushed and			
the file was successfully closed			
See also Chapter(s)	*Function(s)*		*Module(s)*
Chapters 7, 12	**open, socket**		**IO::File,\IO::Socket**

closedir

```
closedir DIRHANDLE
```

Closes the directory handle **DIRHANDLE**.

Effects	**$!, XA, U**
Returns in Scalar Context	*Returns in List Context*
0 on failure	
1 on success	

See also Chapter(s)	*Function(s)*	*Module(s)*
Chapter 7	**opendir**	

connect

```
connect SOCKET, EXPR
```

Connects to the remote socket using the filehandle **SOCKET** and the address specified by **EXPR**. The **EXPR** should be a packed address of the appropriate type for the socket.

Effects	**$!, XA, XT, U**
Returns in Scalar Context	*Returns in List Context*
0 on failure	
1 on success	

See also Chapter(s)	*Function(s)*	*Module(s)*
Chapter 12	**accept, socket**	**IO::Socket**

continue

```
continue BLOCK
```

Not a function. This is a flow control statement that executes **BLOCK** just before the conditional for the loop is evaluated.

Effects	None
Returns in Scalar Context	*Returns in List Context*
Nothing	

See also Chapter(s)	*Function(s)*	*Module(s)*
Chapter 5		

cos

```
cos EXPR
cos
```

Returns the cosine of **EXPR**, or **$_** if **EXPR** is omitted. The value should be expressed in radians.

Effects		**$_**	
Returns in Scalar Context		*Returns in List Context*	
Floating point number			
See also Chapter(s)	*Function(s)*		*Module(s)*
Chapter 8	**atan2, sin**		**Math::Trig**

crypt

```
crypt EXPR,SALT
```

Encrypts the string **EXPR** using the system **crypt( )** function. The value of **SALT** is used to select an encrypted version from one of a number of variations. Note that there is no equivalent decryption function. You cannot (easily) decrypt a string that has been encrypted in this way. It's normally used one way, first to encrypt a string, and then to encrypt a password to compare against the encrypted string. If you're using it in this form, then consider supplying the encrypted password as the **SALT**.

Effects		**U**	
Returns in Scalar Context		*Returns in List Context*	
Encrypted string			
See also Chapter(s)	*Function(s)*		*Module(s)*
Chapter 11	**getpw***		

dbmclose

```
dbmclose HASH
```

Caution   *Use of this function is heavily deprecated.*

Closes the binding between a hash and a DBM file. Use the **tie** function with a
suitable module.

Effects		**$!, U**	
Returns in Scalar Context		*Returns in List Context*	
0 on failure			
1 on success			
See also Chapter(s)	*Function(s)*		*Module(s)*
Chapter 13	**dbmopen, tie**		**DBM_File, GDBM_File, SDBM_File**

█ dbmopen

   dbmopen HASH, EXPR, MODE

█ **Caution**   *Use of this function is heavily deprecated.*

Binds the database file specified by **EXPR** to the hash **HASH**. If the database does not
exist, then it is created using the mode specified by **MODE**. The file **EXPR** should be
specified without the .dir and .pag extensions. Use is now deprecated in favor of **tie**
and one of the tied DBM hash modules, such as **SDBM_File**.

Effects		**$!, U**	
Returns in Scalar Context		*Returns in List Context*	
0 on failure			
1 on success			
See also Chapter(s)	*Function(s)*		*Module(s)*
Chapter 13	**dbmclose, tie**		**DBM_File, GDBM_File, SDBM_File**

defined

```
defined EXPR
defined
```

Returns true if **EXPR** has a value other than the **undef** value, or checks the value of **$_** if **EXPR** is not specified. This can be used with many functions to detect a failure in operation, since they return **undef** if there was a problem. A simple Boolean test does not differentiate between false, zero, an empty string, or the string "0", which are all equally false.

If **EXPR** is a function or function reference, then it returns true if the function has been defined. When used with entire arrays and hashes, it will not always produce intuitive results. If a hash element is specified, it returns true if the corresponding value has been defined, but does not determine whether the specified key exists in the hash.

Effects		**$_**	
Returns in Scalar Context		*Returns in List Context*	
0 if EXPR contains **undef**		0 if EXPR has not been defined	
1 if EXPR contains a valid value or reference		1 if EXPR has been defined	
See also Chapter(s)	*Function(s)*		*Module(s)*
Chapters 4, 8			

delete

```
delete LIST
```

Deletes the specified keys and associated values from a hash, or the specified elements from an array. The operation works on individual elements or slices. For example:

```
delete $array[0];
delete $hash{$key};
```

Note that deleting from the **$ENV** hash modifies the current environment, and deleting from a hash tied to a DBM database deletes the entry from the database file. Also note that when deleting an array item, only the item's value is emptied; it doesn't remove the item from the list or close the gap between the preceding and subsequent item(s).

Effects   None

Returns in Scalar Context   *Returns in List Context*

undef if the key does not exist   **undef** if the key does not exist
Value associated with the deleted hash Value associated with the deleted hash
key or array index.   key or array index.

See also Chapter(s)   *Function(s)*   *Module(s)*

Chapters 4, 8

---

die

| die LIST

Prints the value of **LIST** to **STDERR** and calls **exit** with the error value contained in $!.
If **$!** is 0, then it prints the value of (**$? >> 8**) (for use with **backtick** commands). If (**$? >> 8**) is 0, then the exit status value returned is 255.

Inside an **eval**, the value of **LIST** is inserted in the $@ variable, and the **eval** block exits with an undefined value. You should therefore use **die** to raise an exception within a script.

If the value of **LIST** does not end in a newline, then Perl adds the current script and input line number to the message that is printed. If **LIST** is empty and $@ already contains a value, then the string "\t...propagated" is appended, and if **LIST** is empty, the string "Died" is printed instead.

If you want to insert the filename and line into the output yourself, make sure to add a newline to the end of the list, and then use __FILE__ and __LINE__ accordingly.

Effects $@

Returns in Scalar Context   *Returns in List Context*

Nothing

See also Chapter(s)   *Function(s)*   *Module(s)*

Chapters 7, 9, 15, 16, 21   **exit, eval, warn**

---

do

| do BLOCK
| do EXPR
| do SUB(LIST)

When supplied a block, **do** executes as if **BLOCK** were a function, returning the value of the last statement evaluated in the block. When supplied with **EXPR**, **do** executes the file specified by **EXPR** as if it were another Perl script. This is usually used to import the contents of a script for loading subroutines or values, and is essentially equivalent to

```
scalar eval `ls`;
```

If supplied a subroutine, **SUB**, **do** executes the subroutine using **LIST** as the arguments, raising an exception if **SUB** hasn't been defined.

Effects	None for **do {}**
	$_, T, XT for **do file**
	$@ for **do subroutine**

Returns in Scalar Context	*Returns in List Context*
undef if file is not accessible	
(for **do EXPR**)	
0 on failure (not a Perl script, for **do EXPR**)	
1 on success	

| *See also Chapter(s)* | *Function(s)* | *Module(s)* |
| Chapter 15 | **eval** | |

dump

```
dump LABEL
```

Dumps the currently executing Perl interpreter and script into a core dump. Using the **undump** program, you can then reconstitute the dumped core into an executable program. If so, execution in the dumped program starts at **LABEL**. The process is usually unsuccessful, since core dumps do not necessarily make good fodder for a new program. If you want to produce an executable version of a Perl script, use the Perl-to-C compiler.

Effects	None
Returns in Scalar Context	*Returns in List Context*
Nothing	
See also Chapter(s)	*Function(s)*	*Module(s)*
Chapter 22		

each

```
each HASH
```

In a list context, returns a two-element list referring to the key and value for the next element of a hash, allowing you to iterate over it. In a scalar context, returns only the key for the next element in the hash. Information is returned in a random order, and a single iterator is shared among each—keys and values. The iterator can be reset by evaluating the entire hash or by calling the **keys** function in a scalar context.

Effects	None
Returns in Scalar Context	*Returns in List Context*
In a scalar context, undef at end of hash	In a list context, null array at end of hash
In a scalar context, key only for the next element of a hash	In a list context, key *and* value for the next element of a hash

See also Chapter(s)	*Function(s)*	*Module(s)*
Chapters 4, 8	**keys, values**	

endgrent

```
endgrent
```

Tells the system you no longer expect to read entries from the groups file using **getgrent**. Under Windows, use the **Win32API::Net** function to get the information from a domain server.

Effects	U
Returns in Scalar Context	*Returns in List Context*
Nothing	

See also Chapter(s)	*Function(s)*	*Module(s)*
Chapter 11	**getgrent, setgrent**	**Win32API::Net**

endhostent

```
endhostent
```

APPENDIXES

Tells the system you no longer expect to read entries from the hosts file using **gethostent**.

Effects	**U**	
Returns in Scalar Context	*Returns in List Context*	
Nothing		
See also Chapter(s)	*Function(s)*	*Module(s)*
Chapter 12	**gethostent, sethostent**	

endnetent

     endnetent

Tells the system you no longer expect to read entries from the networks list using **getnetent**.

Effects	**U**	
Returns in Scalar Context	*Returns in List Context*	
Nothing		
See also Chapter(s)	*Function(s)*	*Module(s)*
Chapter 12	**getnetent, setnetent**	

endprotoent

endprotoent

Tells the system you no longer expect to read entries from the protocols list using **getprotoent**.

Effects	**U**	
Returns in Scalar Context	*Returns in List Context*	
Nothing		
See also Chapter(s)	*Function(s)*	*Module(s)*
Chapter 12	**getprotoent, setprotoent**	

endpwent

```
endpwent
```

Tells the system you no longer expect to read entries from the password file using
getpwent. Under Windows, use the **Win32API::Net** function to get the information
from a domain server.

Effects	**U**	
Returns in Scalar Context	*Returns in List Context*	
Nothing		
See also Chapter(s)	*Function(s)*	*Module(s)*
Chapter 11	**getpwent, setpwent**	**Win32API::Net**

endservent

```
endservent
```

Tells the system you no longer expect to read entries from the services file
using **getservent**.

Effects	**U**	
Returns in Scalar Context	*Returns in List Context*	
Nothing		
See also Chapter(s)	*Function(s)*	*Module(s)*
Chapter 12	**getservent, setservent**	

eof

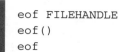

```
eof FILEHANDLE
eof()
eof
```

Returns true if the next read on the specified **FILEHANDLE** will return an end-of-file condition, or if **FILEHANDLE** is not currently associated with an open file. If **FILEHANDLE** is not specified, it returns the condition for the last accessed file.

If the **eof( )** format is used, it checks the input status of the list of files supplied on the command line and hence allows you to detect the end of the file list, instead of the end of the current file.

Normally, you should never need to use **eof**, because all filehandle-compatible functions return false values when no data remains, or if there was an error.

Effects	**XA**
Returns in Scalar Context	*Returns in List Context*

undef if **FILEHANDLE** is not
at end of file
1 if **FILEHANDLE** will report end
of file on next read

See also Chapter(s)	*Function(s)*	*Module(s)*
Chapters 7, 12		while, open, close

---

eval

```
eval EXPR
eval BLOCK
```

Evaluates **EXPR** at execution time as if **EXPR** were a separate Perl script. This allows you to use a separate, perhaps user-supplied, piece of Perl script within your program. An **eval EXPR** statement is evaluated separately each time the function is called. The second form evaluates **BLOCK** when the rest of the script is parsed (before execution).

In both cases, the evaluated **EXPR** or **BLOCK** has access to the variables, objects, and functions available within the host script. Any exceptions raised by the interpreter, **die**, or **warn** are contained in **$@**.

Effects	**$_, XT**
Returns in Scalar Context	*Returns in List Context*

Value of last evaluated statement in **EXPR**
or **BLOCK**

See also Chapter(s)	*Function(s)*	*Module(s)*
Chapter 15		

exec

```
exec EXPR LIST
exec LIST
```

Executes a system command (directly, not within a shell) and never returns to the calling script, except if the command specified does not exist and has been called directly, instead of indirectly through a shell. The operation works as follows:

- If there is only one scalar argument that contains no shell metacharacters, then the argument is converted into a list and the command is executed directly, without a shell.

- If there is only one scalar argument that contains shell metacharacters, then the argument is executed through the standard shell, usually **/bin/sh** on Unix.

- If **LIST** is more than one argument, or an array with more than one value, then the command is executed directly without the use of a shell.

If called with **EXPR** and **LIST**, then **EXPR** is used in the same way as the indirect object in **print** or **printf**. Here, **EXPR** is used as the real path to the command to be executed, and the first argument of **LIST** is used as the name that the program was executed as. This is useful for calling programs like **gzip** or **gunzip**, which are usually the same program, but operate differently based on the name used to execute them.

The **EXPR** and **LIST** format can also be used to execute a program defined in a single element list.

You should use **system** if you want to run a subcommand as part of a Perl script.

Effects	**$!, XT**
Returns in Scalar Context	*Returns in List Context*
0 only if the command specified cannot be executed	

See also Chapter(s)	*Function(s)*	*Module(s)*
Chapter 15	**system**	

exists

```
exists EXPR
```

Returns true if the specified hash key exists, regardless of the corresponding value, even if it's **undef**. If **EXPR** is a subroutine, then **exists** will return 1 if the subroutine has been declared (but not necessarily defined), 0 if not.

Effects	None
Returns in Scalar Context	*Returns in List Context*
0 if hash element or array index does not exist, or if the subroutine has not been declared	
1 if hash element or array index does exist, or if the subroutine has not been declared	

See also Chapter(s)	*Function(s)*	*Module(s)*
Chapters 4, 8	**undef, delete**	

exit

```
exit EXPR
exit
```

Evaluates **EXPR**, exits the Perl interpreter, and returns the value as the exit value. Always runs all **END{}** blocks defined in the script (and imported packages) before exiting. If **EXPR** is omitted, then the interpreter exits with a value of 0. Should not be used to exit from a subroutine; either use **eval** and **die** or use **return**.

Effects	None
Returns in Scalar Context	*Returns in List Context*
Nothing	

See also Chapter(s)	*Function(s)*	*Module(s)*
Chapters 11, 14, 15		

exp

```
exp EXPR
exp
```

Returns *e* (the natural logarithm base) raised to the power of **EXPR**, or **$_** if omitted.

Effects	**$_**	
Returns in Scalar Context	*Returns in List Context*	
e raised to the power		
See also Chapter(s)	*Function(s)*	*Module(s)*
Chapter 8		

---

fcntl

```
fcntl FILEHANDLE, FUNCTION, SCALAR
```

The Perl version of the system **fcntl( )** function. Performs the function specified by **FUNCTION**, using **SCALAR** on **FILEHANDLE**. **SCALAR** either contains a value to be used by the function or is the location of any returned information. The functions supported by **fcntl( )** are entirely dependent on your system's implementation. If your system does not support **fcntl( )**, then a fatal error will occur.

Effects	**$!, XA, XR, XT, U**	
Returns in Scalar Context	*Returns in List Context*	
undef on failure		
0 but true if the return value from the		
fcntl( ) is 0		
Value returned by system		
See also Chapter(s)	*Function(s)*	*Module(s)*
Chapter 7	**ioctl**	Fcntl

---

fileno

```
fileno FILEHANDLE
```

Returns the file descriptor number (as used by C and POSIX functions) of the specified **FILEHANDLE**. This is generally useful only for using the **select** function and any low-level tty functions.

Effects	**XA**
Returns in Scalar Context	*Returns in List Context*
undef if **FILEHANDLE** is not open	
File descriptor (numeric) of	
FILEHANDLE	

See also Chapter(s)	*Function(s)*	*Module(s)*
Chapter 7	**select**	**IO::File, IO::Handle**

 # flock

> flock FILEHANDLE, OPERATION

Supports file locking on the specified **FILEHANDLE** using the system **flock( )**, **fcntl( )** locking, or **lockf( )**. The exact implementation used is dependent on what your system supports. **OPERATION** is one of the static values defined in Table A-4.

In nearly all cases, file locking is generally advisory, especially if the underlying implementation is through the **flock( )** function.

Effects	**$!, XA, U**
Returns in Scalar Context	*Returns in List Context*
0 on failure to set/unset lock	
1 on success to set/unset lock	

See also Chapter(s)	*Function(s)*	*Module(s)*
Chapter 7	**fcntl**	

Operation	**Result**
LOCK_SH	Set shared lock.
LOCK_EX	Set exclusive lock.
LOCK_UN	Unlock specified file.
LONG_NB	Set lock without blocking.

Table A-4. *Locking Operations*

fork

```
fork
```

Forks a new process using the **fork( )** system call. Any shared sockets or filehandles are duplicated across processes. You must ensure that you **wait** on your children to prevent "zombie" processes from forming.

When you call **fork** and then use **exec** to execute a program, only the filehandles up to the value of **$^F ($SYSTEM_FD_MAX)** are inherited by the new program. The default value is 2, allowing only **STDIN**, **STDOUT**, and **STDERR** to be inherited. You can correct this behavior by increasing the value of **$^F** *before* opening the filehandles that you want to have inherited.

 Note   *The **fork( )** system call is emulated within Perl under Windows by using threads and multiple Perl interpreters. You might be better off using threads or the **Win32::Process** module.*

Effects	**$!, U**
Returns in Scalar Context	*Returns in List Context*

undef on failure to fork
Child process ID to parent on success
0 to child on success

See also Chapter(s)	*Function(s)*	*Module(s)*
Chapter 15	**wait**	**Win32::Process**

format

```
format NAME =
picture line
LIST
. . .
```

Declares a picture format for use by the **write** function.

Effects	None
Returns in Scalar Context	*Returns in List Context*

Nothing

See also Chapter(s)	*Function(s)*	*Module(s)*
Chapter 16	**write**	

formline

formline PICTURE, LIST

An internal function used by the **format** function and related operators. It formats **LIST** according to the contents of **PICTURE** into the output accumulator variable **$^A**. The value is written out to a filehandle when a write is done.

Effects	None
Returns in Scalar Context	*Returns in List Context*
1 (always)	

See also Chapter(s)	*Function(s)*	*Module(s)*
Chapter 16	**format, write**	

getc

getc FILEHANDLE
getc

Reads the next character from **FILEHANDLE** (or **STDIN** if none specified), returning the value.

Effects	T, XA
Returns in Scalar Context	*Returns in List Context*
undef on error or end of file Value of character read from **FILEHANDLE**	

See also Chapter(s)	*Function(s)*	*Module(s)*
Chapter 7	**read**	**IO::File, IO::Handle**

getgrent

getgrent

Iterates over the entries in the /etc/group file. Returns the following in a list context:

```
($name, $passwd, $gid, $members)
```

The **$members** scalar contains a space-separated list of the login names that are members of the group. Returns the group name only when used in a scalar context. Under Windows, consider using the **Win32API::Net** module.

Effects	**U**
Returns in Scalar Context	*Returns in List Context*
Group name	Group record (name, password, group ID, and member list)

See also Chapter(s)	*Function(s)*	*Module(s)*
Chapter 11	**getgrgid, getgrnam**	**Win32API::Net**

---

getgrgid

```
getgrgid EXPR
```

Looks up the group file entry by group ID. Returns the following in a list context:

```
($name, $passwd, $gid, $members)
```

The **$members** scalar contains a space-separated list of the login names that are members of the group. Returns the group name in a scalar context. For a more efficient method of retrieving the entire groups file, see **getgrent**. Under Windows, consider using the **Win32API::Net** module.

Effects	**U**
Returns in Scalar Context	*Returns in List Context*
Group name	Group record (name, password, group ID, and member list)

See also Chapter(s)	*Function(s)*	*Module(s)*
Chapter 11	**getgrnam, getgrent**	**Win32API::Net**

getgrnam

 getgrnam EXPR

Looks up the group file entry by group name. Returns the following in a list context:

(\$name, \$passwd, \$gid, \$members)

The **\$members** scalar contains a space-separated list of the login names that are members of the group. Returns the group ID in a scalar context. For a more efficient method of retrieving the entire groups file, see **getgrent**. Under Windows, consider using the **Win32API::Net** module.

Effects	**U**
Returns in Scalar Context	*Returns in List Context*
Group ID in a scalar context	Group record (name, password, group ID, and member list)

See also Chapter(s)	*Function(s)*	*Module(s)*
Chapter 11	**getgrent, getgrgid**	**Win32API::Net**

 gethostbyaddr

 gethostbyaddr ADDR, ADDRTYPE

Contacts the system's name-resolving service, returning a list of information for the host **ADDR** of type **ADDRTYPE**, as follows:

(\$name, \$aliases, \$addrtype, \$length, @addrs)

The **@addrs** array contains a list of packed binary addresses. In a scalar context, returns the host address.

Effects	U
Returns in Scalar Context	*Returns in List Context*
undef on error	Empty list on error
Host name	Host record (name, aliases, address type, length, list of addresses)

See also Chapter(s)	*Function(s)*	*Module(s)*
Chapter 12	**gethostbyname**	

gethostbyname

```
gethostbyname NAME
```

Contacts the system's name-resolving service, returning a list of information for **NAME**, as follows:

```
($name, $aliases, $addrtype, $length, @addrs)
```

The **@addrs** array contains a list of packed binary addresses. In a scalar context, returns the host address.

Effects	U
Returns in Scalar Context	*Returns in List Context*
undef on error	Empty list on error
Host address	Host record (name, aliases, address type, length, list of addresses)

See also Chapter(s)	*Function(s)*	*Module(s)*
Chapter 12	**gethostbyaddr**	

gethostent

```
gethostent
```

Returns the next entry from the hosts file as a list:

    ($name, $aliases, $addrtype, $length, @addrs)

Effects	U
Returns in Scalar Context	*Returns in List Context*
undef on error	Empty list on error
Host name	Host record (name, aliases, address type, length, list of addresses)

See also Chapter(s)	*Function(s)*	*Module(s)*
Chapter 12	**sethostent, endhostent**	**Net::hostent**

getlogin

    getlogin

Returns the user's name, as discovered by the system function **getlogin( )**. Under Windows, use the **Win32::LoginName( )** function instead.

Effects	U
Returns in Scalar Context	*Returns in List Context*
undef on failure	Empty list on error
User's login name	Host record (name, aliases, address type, length, list of addresses)

See also Chapter(s)	*Function(s)*	*Module(s)*
Chapter 11	**getpwuid**	**Win32::LoginName( )**

getnetbyaddr

    getnetbyaddr ADDR, ADDRTYPE

In a list context, returns the information for the network specified by **ADDR** and type **ADDRTYPE**:

    ($name, $aliases, $addrtype, $net)

In a scalar context, returns only the network address.

Effects	**U**
Returns in Scalar Context	*Returns in List Context*
undef on error	Empty list on error
Network address	Network record (name, aliases, address type, network address)

See also Chapter(s)	*Function(s)*	*Module(s)*
Chapter 12	**getnetbyname**	**Net::netent**

getnetbyname

```
getnetbyname NAME
```

In a list context, returns the information for the network specified by **NAME**:

```
($name, $aliases, $addrtype, $net)
```

In a scalar context, returns only the network address.

Effects	**U**
Returns in Scalar Context	*Returns in List Context*
undef on error	Empty list on error
Network address	Network record (name, aliases, address type, network address)

See also Chapter(s)	*Function(s)*	*Module(s)*
Chapter 12	**getnetbyaddr**	**Net::netent**

getnetent

```
getnetent
```

Gets the next entry from the /etc/networks file, returning:

```
($name, $aliases, $addrtype, $net)
```

Effects	U
Returns in Scalar Context	*Returns in List Context*
undef on error	Empty list on error
Network name	Network record (name, aliases, address type, network address)

See also Chapter(s)	*Function(s)*	*Module(s)*
Chapter 12	**setnetent, endnetent**	**Net::netent**

getpeername

```
getpeername SOCKET
```

Returns the packed socket address of the remote host attached to **SOCKET**.

Effects	$!, XA, U
Returns in Scalar Context	*Returns in List Context*
undef on error	Empty list on error
Packed socket address	Network record (name, aliases, address type, network address)

See also Chapter(s)	*Function(s)*	*Module(s)*
Chapter 12	**accept, bind, socket**	**IO::Socket**

getpgrp

```
getpgrp EXPR
getpgrp
```

Returns the process group for the process ID specified by **EXPR**, or the current process group if none is specified.

Effects	$!, U
Returns in Scalar Context	*Returns in List Context*
Process group ID	

See also Chapter(s)	*Function(s)*	*Module(s)*
Chapter 14	**setpgrp**	**Win32::Process**

getppid

    getppid

Returns the process ID of the parent process.

| *Effects* | **U** |
| *Returns in Scalar Context* | *Returns in List Context* |

Process ID of the parent process

| *See also Chapter(s)* | *Function(s)* | *Module(s)* |
| Chapter 14 | | |

getpriority

    getpriority WHICH, WHO

Returns the current priority for a process (**PRIO_PROCESS**), process group
(**PRIO_PGRP**) or user (**PRIO_USER**). Use the constants defined in the **BSD::Resource**
module. The argument **WHICH** specifies what entity to set the priority for, and **WHO**
is the process ID or user ID to set. A value of 0 for **WHO** defines the current process,
process group, or user. This produces a fatal error on systems that don't support the
system **getpriority( )** function.

| *Effects* | **$!, U** |
| *Returns in Scalar Context* | *Returns in List Context* |

undef on error
Current priority

See also Chapter(s)	*Function(s)*	*Module(s)*
Chapter 14	**setpriority**	**BSD::Resource,**
		Win32::Process

getprotobyname

    getprotobyname NAME

Translates the protocol **NAME** into its corresponding number in a scalar context, and its number and associated information in a list context:

```
($name, $aliases, $protocol_number)
```

Effects   U

Returns in Scalar Context   *Returns in List Context*

undef on error   Empty list on error
Empty list in a list context   Protocol record (name, aliases,
                                                 protocol number)

See also Chapter(s)	*Function(s)*	*Module(s)*
Chapter 12	**getprotobynumber**	

getprotobynumber

```
getprotobynumber NUMBER
```

Translates the protocol **NUMBER** into its corresponding name in a scalar context, and its name and associated information in a list context:

```
($name, $aliases, $protocol_number)
```

Effects   U

Returns in Scalar Context   *Returns in List Context*

undef on error   Empty list on error
Protocol name   Protocol record (name, aliases,
                                                 protocol number)

See also Chapter(s)	*Function(s)*	*Module(s)*
Chapter 12	**getprotobyname**	

getprotoent

```
getprotoent
```

Returns the next entry from the list of valid protocols:

```
($name, $aliases, $protocol_number)
```

Effects	**U**
Returns in Scalar Context	*Returns in List Context*
undef on error	Empty list on error
Protocol name	Protocol record (name, aliases, protocol number)

See also Chapter(s)	*Function(s)*	*Module(s)*
Chapter 12	**setprotoent, endprotoent**	

---

getpwent

```
getpwent
```

Returns the next password entry from the /etc/passwd file. This is used in combination with the **setpwent** and **endpwent** functions to iterate over the password file. In a list context, returns

```
($name, $passwd, $uid, $gid, $quota,
 $comment, $gcos, $dir, $shell) = getpwent;
```

In a scalar context, just returns the user name.

Effects	**T, U**
Returns in Scalar Context	*Returns in List Context*
User name	User record (name, password, user ID, group ID, quote, comment, real name, home directory, shell)

See also Chapter(s)	*Function(s)*	*Module(s)*
Chapter 11	**getpwnam, getpwent**	**Win32API::Net**

 # getpwnam

```
getpwnam EXPR
```

In a list context, returns a list of fields, as extracted from the /etc/passwd file, based on the user name specified by **EXPR**. It's generally used like this:

```
($name, $passwd, $uid, $gid, $quota,
 $comment, $gcos, $dir, $shell) = getpwnam($user);
```

In a scalar context, returns the numeric user ID. If you are trying to access the whole /etc/passwd file, you should use the **getpwent** function. If you want to access the details by user ID, use **getpwuid**.

Effects	**T, U**
Returns in Scalar Context	*Returns in List Context*
User ID	User record (name, password, user ID, group ID, quote, comment, real name, home directory, shell)

See also Chapter(s)	*Function(s)*	*Module(s)*
Chapter 11	**getpwent, getpwuid**	**Win32API::Net**

---

getpwuid

```
getpwuid EXPR
```

In a list context, returns a list of fields, as extracted from the /etc/passwd file, based on the user name specified by **EXPR**. It's generally used like this:

```
($name, $passwd, $uid, $gid, $quota,
 $comment, $gcos, $dir, $shell) = getpwuid($uid);
```

In a scalar context, returns the user name. If you are trying to access the whole /etc/passwd file, you should use the **getpwent** function. If you want to access the details by user name, use **getpwnam**.

Effects	**T, U**
Returns in Scalar Context	*Returns in List Context*
User name	User record (name, password, user ID, group ID, quote, comment, real name, home directory, shell)

See also Chapter(s)	*Function(s)*	*Module(s)*
Chapter 11	**getpwent, getpwnam**	**Win32API::Net**

getservbyname

```
getservbyname NAME, PROTO
```

Translates the service **NAME** for the protocol **PROTO**, returning the service number in a scalar context and the number and associated information in a list context:

```
($name, $aliases, $port_number, $protocol_name)
```

Effects	**U**
Returns in Scalar Context	*Returns in List Context*
undef on error	Empty list
Service number	Service record (name, aliases, port number, protocol name)

See also Chapter(s)	*Function(s)*	*Module(s)*
Chapter 12	**getservbyport**	

getservbyport

```
getservbyport PORT, PROTO
```

Translates the service number **PORT** for the protocol **PROTO**, returning the service name in a scalar context and the name and associated information in a list context:

```
($name, $aliases, $port_number, $protocol_name)
```

APPENDIXES

Effects	**U**
Returns in Scalar Context	*Returns in List Context*
undef on error	Empty list on error
Service name	Service record (name, aliases, port number, protocol name)

See also Chapter(s)	*Function(s)*	*Module(s)*
Chapter 12	**getservbyname**	

---

getservent

```
getservent
```

Gets the next entry from the list of service entries, returning:

```
($name, $aliases, $port_number, $protocol_name)
```

Effects	**U**
Returns in Scalar Context	*Returns in List Context*
undef on error in scalar context	Empty list on error
Protocol name	Service record (name, aliases, port number, protocol name)

See also Chapter(s)	*Function(s)*	*Module(s)*
Chapter 12	**setservent, endservent**	

---

getsockname

```
getsockname SOCKET
```

Returns a packed address of the local end of the network socket **SOCKET**.

Effects	**$!, XA, U**
Returns in Scalar Context	*Returns in List Context*
undef on error	Empty list on error
Packed address of local socket	Service record (name, aliases, port number, protocol name)

See also Chapter(s)	*Function(s)*	*Module(s)*
Chapter 12	**getpeername, socket**	**IO::Socket**

getsockopt

getsockopt SOCKET, LEVEL, OPTNAME

Gets the socket options set on **SOCKET** at the socket implementation level **LEVEL** for the option **OPTNAME**. Some sample values for **OPTNAME** at a socket level are given in Table A-5. The values are defined in the **Socket** package.

Effects	**$!, XA, U**
Returns in Scalar Context	*Returns in List Context*
undef on error	Empty list on error
Option value	Service record (name, aliases, port number, protocol name)

See also Chapter(s)	*Function(s)*	*Module(s)*
Chapter 12	**setsockopt**	**IO::Socket**

OPTNAME	Result
SO_DEBUG	Get status of recording of debugging information
SO_REUSEADDR	Get status of local address reuse
SO_KEEPALIVE	Get status of keep connections alive
SO_DONTROUTE	Get status of routing bypass for outgoing messages
SO_LINGER	Get status of linger on close if data is present
SO_BROADCAST	Get status of permission to transmit broadcast messages
SO_OOBINLINE	Get status of out-of-band data in band
SO_SNDBUF	Get buffer size for output
SO_RCVBUF	Get buffer size for input
SO_TYPE	Get the type of the socket
SO_ERROR	Get and clear error on the socket

Table A-5. *Options for **getsockopt***

glob

```
glob EXPR
glob
```

Returns a list of files matching **EXPR** as they would be expanded by the standard Bourne shell. If the **EXPR** does not specify a path, uses the current directory. If **EXPR** is omitted, the value of **$_** is used.

From Perl 5.6 on, expansion is done internally, rather than using an external script. Expansion follows the **csh** (and any derivatives, including **tcsh** and **bash**) style of expansion, which translates as the following:

- Files beginning with a single period are ignored unless **EXPR** explicitly matches.

- The * character matches zero or more characters of any type.

- The ? character matches one character of any type.

- The [..] construct matches the characters listed, including ranges, as per regular expressions.

- The ~ characters matches the home directory; **~name** matches the home directory for the user **name**.

- The {..} construct matches against any of the comma-separated words enclosed in the braces.

Use **File::Glob** if you want to expand more complex files, including those with spaces.

Effects	$_, $@, T, XT
Returns in Scalar Context	*Returns in List Context*
undef on error	Empty list on error
First file in the list of expanded names	List of expanded file names

See also Chapter(s)	Function(s)	Module(s)
Chapter 7	**chdir**	**File::Glob**

gmtime

```
gmtime EXPR
gmtime
```

Returns a list of values corresponding to the date and time as specified by **EXPR**, or date and time returned by the **time** function if **EXPR** is omitted, localized for the standard Greenwich mean time. The values returned are as follows:

```
# 0     1     2     3     4     5     6     7     8
($sec,$min,$hour,$mday,$mon,$year,$wday,$yday,$isdst) = gmtime(time);
```

The array elements are numeric, taken from the system **struct tm**. The value of **$mon** has a range of **0..11**, **$wday** has a range of **0..6** (Sunday–Saturday), and **$year** is returned as the number of years from 1900; so 2010 is 110, not 10.

If you want to convert a list of individual time values, use the **Time::Local** module.

Effects	None
Returns in Scalar Context	*Returns in List Context*
Returns a string of the form: Thu Sep 21 14:52:52 2000	Returns the individual time component values (seconds, minutes, hours, day of month, month, year, day of week, day of year, daylight savings time)

See also Chapter(s)	*Function(s)*	*Module(s)*
Chapter 11	**localtime, time**	**Time::gmtime, Time::Local**

goto

```
goto LABEL
goto EXPR
goto &NAME
```

The first form causes the current execution point to jump to the point referred to as **LABEL**. A **goto** in this form cannot be used to jump into a loop or external function—you can only jump to a point within the same scope. The second form expects **EXPR** to evaluate to a recognizable **LABEL**. In general, you should be able to use a normal conditional statement or function to control the execution of a program, so its use is deprecated.

The third form substitutes a call to the named subroutine for the currently running subroutine. The new subroutine inherits the argument stack and other features of the original subroutine; it becomes impossible for the new subroutine even to know that it was called by another name.

Effects		$@
Returns in Scalar Context		*Returns in List Context*
Nothing		
See also Chapter(s)	*Function(s)*	*Module(s)*
Chapters 5, 6		

grep

```
grep BLOCK LIST
grep EXPR, LIST
```

Similar to the standard Unix **grep** command. However, the selection process is more widespread and limited to regular expressions. Evaluates the **BLOCK** or **EXPR** for each element of **LIST**, returning the list of elements that the block or statement returns true.

Effects		None
Returns in Scalar Context		*Returns in List Context*
Number of times the expression returned **true**		List of elements that matched the expression
See also Chapter(s)	*Function(s)*	*Module(s)*
Chapter 8	**map**	

hex

```
hex EXPR
hex
```

Interprets **EXPR** as a hexadecimal string and returns the value, or converts **$_** if **EXPR** is omitted.

Effects	$_
Returns in Scalar Context	*Returns in List Context*

Numeric value

See also Chapter(s)	*Function(s)*	*Module(s)*
Chapters 8	**oct**	

import

```
import CLASSNAME LIST
import
```

Not a built-in function, but supported by the **Exporter** (and other) modules as a method for importing functions, variables, and objects from another package into the current namespace.

Effects	None
Returns in Scalar Context	*Returns in List Context*

See also Chapter(s)	*Function(s)*	*Module(s)*
Chapter 6	**use, require**	Exporter

index

```
index STR, SUBSTR, POSITION
index STR, SUBSTR
```

Returns the position of the first occurrence of **SUBSTR** in **STR**, starting at the beginning (starting at zero), or from **POSITION** if specified.

Effects	None
Returns in Scalar Context	*Returns in List Context*

-1 on failure
Position of matching string (starting at zero for the first character).

See also Chapter(s)	*Function(s)*	*Module(s)*
Chapter 8	**Substr**	

int

```
int EXPR
int
```

Returns the integer element of **EXPR**, or **$_** if omitted. The **int** function does not do rounding. If you need to round a value up to an integer, you should use **sprintf**.

Effects	**$_**	
Returns in Scalar Context	*Returns in List Context*	
Integer		
See also Chapter(s)	*Function(s)*	*Module(s)*
Chapter 8	**abs, sprintf**	

ioctl

```
ioctl FILEHANDLE, FUNCTION, SCALAR
```

Performs the function **FUNCTION** using the system function **ioctl( )**, using **SCALAR** to set or receive information when appropriate. The available values for **FUNCTION** are completely system independent. You should refer to your ioctl.h C header file, if you have one available, for suitable values.

Effects	**$!, XA, XR, XT, U**	
Returns in Scalar Context	*Returns in List Context*	
undef on failure		
0 but true if the return value		
from the **ioctl( )** is 0		
Value returned by system		
See also Chapter(s)	*Function(s)*	*Module(s)*
Chapter 7	**abs, sprintf**	

join

```
join EXPR, LIST
```

Combines the elements of **LIST** into a single string using the value of **EXPR** to separate each element. It is effectively the opposite of **split**. Note that **EXPR** is only interpolated between pairs of elements in **LIST**; it will not be placed either before the first or after the last element in the string. To join together strings without a separator, supply an empty string rather than **undef**.

Effects	None	
Returns in Scalar Context	*Returns in List Context*	
Joined string		
See also Chapter(s)	*Function(s)*	*Module(s)*
Chapter 8	**Split**	

keys

```
keys HASH
```

Returns all the keys of the **HASH** as a list. The keys are returned in random order but, in fact, share the same order as that used by **values** and **each**. Using **keys** to reevaluate the hash, in either scalar, list, or void context will reset the iterator for all three functions. If used as an lvalue, then it presets the number of buckets used to store the hash data.

Effects	None	
Returns in Scalar Context	*Returns in List Context*	
Number of keys in the hash	List of keys	
See also Chapter(s)	*Function(s)*	*Module(s)*
Chapters 4, 8	**each, values**	

kill

```
kill EXPR, LIST
```

Sends a signal of the value **EXPR** to the process IDs specified in **LIST**. If the value of **EXPR** is negative, it kills all processes that are members of the process groups specified. If **EXPR** is 0, then it sends the signal to all the members of the same group as the current process—you can use this to send signals to your children without having to explicitly track their process IDs. The **EXPR** can be specified with the signal number (non-portable) or a suitable string. Using an unrecognized signal name raises an exception that is trappable with **eval**.

The precise list of signals supported is entirely dependent on the system implementation, but Table A-6 shows the main signals that should be supported by all POSIX-compatible operating systems.

Effects	**$!, XA, XT, U**
Returns in Scalar Context	*Returns in List Context*
Nothing	

See also Chapter(s)	*Function(s)*	*Module(s)*
Chapter 14		

Name	Effect
SIGABRT	Aborts the process
SIGARLM	Alarm signal
SIGFPE	Arithmetic exception
SIGHUP	Hang up.
SIGILL	Illegal instruction
SIGINT	Interrupt
SIGKILL	Termination signal
SIGPIPE	Write to a pipe with no readers.
SIGQUIT	Quit signal.
SIGSEGV	Segmentation fault
SIGTERM	Termination signal
SIGUSER1	Application-defined signal 1
SIGUSER2	Application-defined signal 2

Table A-6.   *POSIX-Compatible Signals*

last

```
last LABEL
last
```

Not a function. The **last** keyword is a loop-control statement that immediately causes the current iteration of a loop to become the last. No further statements are executed, and the loop ends. If **LABEL** is specified, then it drops out of the loop identified by **LABEL** instead of the currently enclosing loop.

Effects	$@	
Returns in Scalar Context	*Returns in List Context*	
Nothing		
See also Chapter(s)	*Function(s)*	*Module(s)*
Chapter 5	**next, redo**	

lc

```
lc EXPR
lc
```

Returns a lowercased version of **EXPR**, or **$_** if **EXPR** is omitted.

Effects	$_, T	
Returns in Scalar Context	*Returns in List Context*	
String		
See also Chapter(s)	*Function(s)*	*Module(s)*
Chapter 8	**lcfirst**	

lcfirst

```
lcfirst EXPR
lcfirst
```

Returns the string **EXPR** or **$_** with the first character lowercased.

Effects	$_, T	
Returns in Scalar Context	**Returns in List Context**	
String		
See also Chapter(s)	**Function(s)**	**Module(s)**
Chapter 8	**lc**	

length

```
length EXPR
length
```

Returns the length, in characters, of the value of **EXPR**, or **$_** if not specified. Use scalar context on an array or hash if you want to determine the corresponding size. You'll need to use the **bytes** pragma to get the size of a string in bytes.

Effects	$_	
Returns in Scalar Context	**Returns in List Context**	
Integer		
See also Chapter(s)	**Function(s)**	**Module(s)**
Chapter 8	**scalar**	**bytes**

link

```
link OLDFILE,NEWFILE
```

Creates a new file name, **NEWFILE**, linked to the file **OLDFILE**. The function creates a hard link; if you want a symbolic link, use the **symlink** function.

Effects	$!, XT, U	
Returns in Scalar Context	**Returns in List Context**	
0 on failure		
1 on success		
See also Chapter(s)	**Function(s)**	**Module(s)**
Chapter 7	**symlink**	

listen

```
listen SOCKET, EXPR
```

Configures the network socket **SOCKET** for listening to incoming network connections. Sets the incoming connection queue length to **EXPR**. You might want to consider using the **IO::Socket** module, which provides a much easier way of creating and listening to network sockets.

Effects	**$!, XA, U**
Returns in Scalar Context	*Returns in List Context*
0 on failure	
1 on success	

See also Chapter(s)	*Function(s)*	*Module(s)*
Chapter 12	**accept, connect**	**IO::Socket**

 # local

```
local LIST
```

Sets the variables in **LIST** to be local to the current execution block. If more than one value is specified, you *must* use parentheses to define the list. Note that **local** creates a local *copy* of a variable, which then goes out of scope when the enclosing block terminates. The localized value is then used whenever it is accessed, including any subroutines and formats used during that block.

Unless otherwise stated, the new variable has an initial value of **undef** (for scalars) or an empty list (for arrays or hashes). If you are trying to create a lexically scoped variable then use **my**.

Effects	None
Returns in Scalar Context	*Returns in List Context*
Nothing	

See also Chapter(s)	*Function(s)*	*Module(s)*
Chapter 6	**my**	

localtime

```
localtime EXPR
```

In a list context, converts the time specified by **EXPR**, returning a nine-element array with the time analyzed for the current local time zone. The elements of the array are

```
#  0     1     2     3     4     5     6     7     8
($sec,$min,$hour,$mday,$mon,$year,$wday,$yday,$isdst) = localtime(time);
```

If **EXPR** is omitted, uses the value returned by **time**.

In a scalar context, returns a string representation of the time specified by **EXPR**, roughly equivalent to the value returned by **ctime( )**. Use the **Time::Local** module if you want to convert a set of time values into an epoch value.

Note that you should be using **gmtime** if you want to compare times reliably—using **localtime** will give skewed results when used across time-zone boundaries.

Effects	None
Returns in Scalar Context	*Returns in List Context*
Returns a string of the form: Thu Sep 21 14:52:52 2000	Returns the individual time component values (seconds, minutes, hours, day of month, month, year, day of week, day of year, daylight savings time)

See also Chapter(s)	*Function(s)*	*Module(s)*
Chapter 11	**gmtime, time**	**Time::Local**

log

```
log EXPR
log
```

Returns the natural logarithm of **EXPR**, or **$_** if omitted.

Effects	**$_, $@**
Returns in Scalar Context	*Returns in List Context*
Floating point number	

See also Chapter(s)	*Function(s)*	*Module(s)*
Chapter 8		

lstat

```
lstat FILEHANDLE
lstat EXPR
lstat
```

Performs the same tests as the **stat** function on **FILEHANDLE** or the file referred to by **EXPR** or **$_**. If the file is a symbolic link, it returns the information for the link, rather than the file it points to. Otherwise, it returns the information for the file.

Effects	**$_, $!, U**	
Returns in Scalar Context	*Returns in List Context*	
0 on failure		
1 on success		
See also Chapter(s)	*Function(s)*	*Module(s)*
Chapter 7	**stat**	

m//

```
m//
```

Match operator. Parentheses after initial **m** can be any character and will be used to delimit the regular expression statement.

Effects	**T, XT**	
Returns in Scalar Context	*Returns in List Context*	
0 on failure to match	List of values in a grouped regular	
1 on success	expression *match*	
See also Chapter(s)	*Function(s)*	*Module(s)*
Chapter 8	**s///, tr///, quotemeta, study**	**re**

map

```
map EXPR, LIST
map BLOCK LIST
```

Evaluates **EXPR** or **BLOCK** for each element of **LIST**. For each iteration, **$_** holds the value of the current element, which can also be assigned to allow the value of the element to be updated.

Effects	None	
Returns in Scalar Context	*Returns in List Context*	
List of values		
See also Chapter(s)	*Function(s)*	*Module(s)*
Chapter 8	**grep**	

mkdir

```
mkdir EXPR,MODE
```

Makes a directory with the name and path **EXPR** using the mode specified by **MODE**, which should be supplied as an octal value for clarity.

Effects	$!, XT	
Returns in Scalar Context	*Returns in List Context*	
0 on failure		
1 on success		
See also Chapter(s)	*Function(s)*	*Module(s)*
Chapter 7	**chdir**	**Cwd**

msgctl

```
msgctl ID, CMD, ARG
```

Calls the system function **msgctrl( )** with the arguments **ID, CMD**, and **ARG**. You may need to include the **IPC::SysV** package to obtain the correct constants.

Effects $!, U

Returns in Scalar Context   *Returns in List Context*

undef on failure
0 but true if the system function returns 0
1 on success

See also Chapter(s)	*Function(s)*	*Module(s)*
Chapter 14	**msgget, msgsnd, msgrcv**	**IPC::SysV**

msgget

```
msgget KEY, FLAGS
```

Returns the message queue ID, or **undef** on error.

Effects $!, U

Returns in Scalar Context   *Returns in List Context*

undef on error
Message queue ID

See also Chapter(s)	*Function(s)*	*Module(s)*
Chapter 14	**msgctl, msgsnd, msgrcv**	**IPC::SysV**

msgrcv

```
msgrcv ID, VAR, SIZE, TYPE, FLAGS
```

Receives a message from the queue **ID**, placing the message into the variable **VAR**, up to a maximum size of **SIZE**.

Effects $!, U

Returns in Scalar Context   *Returns in List Context*

0 on error
1 on success

See also Chapter(s)	*Function(s)*	*Module(s)*
Chapter 14	**msgctl, msgsnd, msgrcv**	**IPC::SysV**

msgsnd

```
msgsnd ID, MSG, FLAGS
```

Sends the message **MSG** to the message queue **ID**, using the optional **FLAGS**.

Effects		**$!, U**
Returns in Scalar Context		*Returns in List Context*
0 on error		
1 on success		
See also Chapter(s)	*Function(s)*	*Module(s)*
Chapter 14	**msgctl, msgget, msgrcv**	**IPC::SysV**

my

```
my TYPE LIST : ATTRIBUTES
my LIST : ATTRIBUTES
my TYPE LIST
my LIST
```

Declares the variables in **LIST** to be lexically scoped within the enclosing block. If more than one variable is specified, all variables must be enclosed in parentheses.

If **TYPE** is used, then it should specify the type of the scalar or scalars listed in **LIST**. Note that currently **TYPE** should be the class of object that you want the scalar or scalars to be blessed into. The **ATTRIBUTES** should list the initial values of the object's fields.

Effects		None
Returns in Scalar Context		*Returns in List Context*
Nothing		
See also Chapter(s)	*Function(s)*	*Module(s)*
Chapter 6	**local, our**	**strict, warnings**

next

```
next LABEL
next
```

Not a function. Causes the current loop iteration to skip to the next value or next evaluation of the control statement. No further statements in the current loop are executed. If **LABEL** is specified, then execution skips to the next iteration of the loop identified by **LABEL**.

Effects		*$@*	
Returns in Scalar Context		*Returns in List Context*	
Nothing			
See also Chapter(s)	*Function(s)*		*Module(s)*
Chapter 5	**last, redo**		

no

```
no MODULE LIST
no MODULE
```

If **MODULE** supports it, then **no** calls the **unimport** function defined in **MODULE** to unimport all symbols from the current package, or only the symbols referred to by **LIST**. Has some special meanings when used with pragmas; see Chapter 19 for more information.

Effects		*$@*	
Returns in Scalar Context		*Returns in List Context*	
Nothing			
See also Chapter(s)	*Function(s)*		*Module(s)*
Chapters 6, 19	**use, do, eval**		

APPENDIXES

oct

```
oct EXPR
oct
```

Returns **EXPR**, or **$_** if omitted, as a decimal by interpreting **EXPR** as an octal value.

Effects	**$_**
Returns in Scalar Context	*Returns in List Context*
Decimal value	

See also Chapter(s)	*Function(s)*	*Module(s)*
Chapter 8	**hex**	

open

```
open FILEHANDLE, EXPR, LIST
open FILEHANDLE, EXPR
open FILEHANDLE
```

Opens the file specified by **EXPR**, associating it with **FILEHANDLE**. If supplied with three or more arguments, then **LIST** is taken as the filename or arguments to pass to **exec** if using a pipe, and **EXPR** becomes the mode to be used when opening the file. If you are using the multiargument form, the normal rules for **exec** program execution apply, except that a **fork** is implied before **exec** is called.

If **EXPR** is not specified, then the file name specified by the scalar variable of the same name as **FILEHANDLE** is used instead. The format of **EXPR** defines the mode in which the file is opened, as shown in Table A-7.

You should not ignore failures to the **open** command, so it is usually used in combination with **warn**, **die**, or a control statement.

Note that you may need to use **binmode** on the filehandle on operating systems other than Unix and Mac OS that use multicharacter line termination—most notably Windows. Alternatively, Perl v5.6 or above allows you to specify the encoding format to be used when reading and writing to and from a filehandle by supplying the format as part of the **EXPR** argument, and supplying the name of the file to be opened in **LIST**. To specify the encoding formation, you must supply the modes shown in Table A-8. For example:

```
open(FILE, "<:para:crlf", 'myfile');
```

Expression	Result
"filename"	Opens the file for reading only; does not create the file if it does not already exist
"<filename"	Opens the file for reading only; does not create the file if it does not already exist
">filename"	Truncates and opens the file for writing
">>filename"	Opens the file for appending (places pointer at end of file), but existing data cannot be either read or overwritten—appending is enforced.
"+<filename"	Opens the file for reading and writing; does not create the file if it does not already exist
"+>filename"	Truncates and opens the file for reading and writing
"+>>filename"	Opens the file for appending (places pointer at end of file); existing data can be read but not overwritten—appending is enforced.
"| command"	Runs the command and pipes the output to the filehandle
"command |"	Pipes the output from filehandle to the input of command
"-"	Opens **STDIN**
">-"	Opens **STDOUT**
"<&FILEHANDLE"	Duplicates specified **FILEHANDLE** or file descriptor if numeric for reading
">&FILEHANDLE"	Duplicates specified **FILEHANDLE** or file descriptor if numeric for writing
"<&=N"	Opens the file descriptor matching **N**, essentially identical to C's **fdopen( )**
"|-" and "-|"	Opens a pipe to a forked command

Table A-7. *Options for Opening Files*

Discipline	Meaning
:raw	Binary mode—no line input processing; equivalent to calling **binmode**
:text	Text processing—the basic mode supported by versions prior to v5.6
:def	Default—as declared by the **use open** pragma
:latin1	Use the ISO-8859-1 format.
:lctype	Use the **LC_CTYPE** format.
:utf8	Use the **UTF-8** (Unicode) format.
:utf16	Use the **UTF-16** (Unicode) format.
:utf32	Use the **UTF-32** (Unicode) format.
:uni	Intuit Unicode (**UTF-***) format.
:any	Intuit **Unicode/Latin1/LC_CTYPE**
:xml	Use the file-specified encoding format.
:crlf	Intuit newlines.
:para	Paragraph mode
:slurp	Slurp mode

Table A-8.   *File Format Encoding Disciplines*

If you are looking for the equivalent of the system function **open( )**, see **sysopen**.

Effects	**$!, XT, XR, U**	
Returns in Scalar Context	*Returns in List Context*	
0 on failure 1 on success		
See also Chapter(s)	*Function(s)*	*Module(s)*
Chapter 7	**print, sysopen, close**	**IO::Handle, IO::File**

opendir

```
opendir DIRHANDLE, EXPR
```

Opens the directory **EXPR**, associating it with **DIRHANDLE** for processing, using the **readdir** function.

Effects	**$!, XT, XR, U**	
Returns in Scalar Context	*Returns in List Context*	
0 on failure 1 on success		
See also Chapter(s)	*Function(s)*	*Module(s)*
Chapter 7	**readdir, rewinddir**	**IO::Dir**

ord

```
ord EXPR
ord
```

Returns the ASCII numeric value of the character specified by **EXPR**, or $_ if omitted.

Effects	**$_**	
Returns in Scalar Context	*Returns in List Context*	
Integer		
See also Chapter(s)	*Function(s)*	*Module(s)*
Chapter 8	**chr**	

our

```
our TYPE LIST : ATTRIBUTES
our LIST : ATTRIBUTES
our TYPE LIST
our LIST
```

Defines the variables specified in **LIST** as being global within the enclosing block, file, or **eval** statement. It is effectively the opposite of **my**—it declares a variable to be global within the entire scope, rather than creating a new private variable of the same name. All other options are identical to **my**; see the **my** entry for more information.

Effects	None
Returns in Scalar Context	*Returns in List Context*
Integer	

See also Chapter(s)	*Function(s)*	*Module(s)*
Chapter 6	**local, my**	

pack

```
pack EXPR, LIST
```

Evaluates the expressions in **LIST** and packs them into a binary structure specified by **EXPR**. The format is specified using the characters shown in Table A-9.

Character	Description
@	Null fill to absolute position
a	An ASCII string, will be null padded
A	An ASCII string, will be space padded
b	A bitstring (ascending bit order)
B	A bitstring (descending bit order)
c	A signed char (8-bit) value
C	An unsigned char (8-bit) value
d	A double-precision float in the native format
f	A single-precision float in the native format
H	A hex string (high nibble first)

Table A-9. *pack Format Characters*

Character	Description
h	A hex string (low nibble first)
i	A signed integer value
I	An unsigned integer value
l	A signed long value (32 bits)
L	An unsigned long value (32 bits).
N	A long (32 bits) in "network" (big-endian) order
n	A short (16 bits) in "network" (big-endian) order
p	A pointer to a null-terminated string
P	A pointer to a fixed-length string
q	A signed quad (64-bit) value
Q	An unsigned quad (64-bit) value
s	A signed short value (16 bits)
S	An unsigned short value (16 bits)
u	A uuencoded string
U	A Unicode character number.
V	A long (32 bits) in "VAX" (little-endian) order
v	A short (16 bits) in "VAX" (little-endian) order
w	A BER compressed integer
x	A null byte (effectively skips forward one byte)
X	Backs up a byte
Z	A null-terminated (and null-padded) string of bytes

Table A-9. *pack* Format Characters (continued)

APPENDIXES

Each character may be optionally followed by a number, which specifies a repeat count for the type of value being packed—that is nibbles, chars, or even bits, according to the format. A value of * repeats for as many values remain in **LIST**. Values can be unpacked with the **unpack** function.

Using the / character allows you to specify within **FORMAT** the size of the following value according to **length/string**. For example:

```
pack 'C/a','\04Martin';
```

returns "Mart". Note that **string** must be one of **A**, **a**, or **Z**; if you supply * (as in **a***) the * will be ignored.

Appending the ! character to **s**, **S**, **l**, or **L** forces **pack** to use native short and long values, rather than the strict 16-bit and 32-bit formats used by default.

Effects		*$@*	
Returns in Scalar Context		*Returns in List Context*	
Formatted string			
See also Chapter(s)	*Function(s)*		*Module(s)*
Chapters 8, 13	**unpack**		

package

```
package NAME
package
```

Changes the name of the current symbol table to **NAME**. The scope of the package name is until the end of the enclosing block. If **NAME** is omitted, there is no current package, and all function and variables names must be declared with their fully qualified names.

Effects		None	
Returns in Scalar Context		*Returns in List Context*	
Nothing			
See also Chapter(s)	*Function(s)*		*Module(s)*
Chapter 6	**use, do, eval, no**		

pipe

```
pipe READHANDLE, WRITEHANDLE
```

Opens a pair of connected communications pipes: **READHANDLE** for reading and **WRITEHANDLE** for writing.

Effects	**$!, XA, U**
Returns in Scalar Context	*Returns in List Context*
0 on failure	
1 on success	

See also Chapter(s)	*Function(s)*	*Module(s)*
Chapters 7, 12, 14	**open**	**IO::Open2, IO::Open3, IO::Pipe**

pop

```
pop ARRAY
pop
```

Returns the last element of **ARRAY**, removing the value from the array. Note that **ARRAY** must explicitly be an array, not a list. If **ARRAY** is omitted, it pops the last value from **@ARGV** in the main program, or when called within **eval STRING**, or the **BEGIN, CHECK, INIT,** or **END** blocks. Otherwise, it attempts to pop information from the @_ array within a subroutine. It is the opposite of **push**, which when used in combination, allows you to implement "stacks."

Effects	None
Returns in Scalar Context	*Returns in List Context*
undef if list is empty	
Last element from the array	

See also Chapter(s)	*Function(s)*	*Module(s)*
Chapter 8	**push, shift, unshift**	

pos

```
pos EXPR
pos
```

Returns the position(s) within **EXPR**, or **$_**, where the last **m//g** search left off.

Effects	**$_**
Returns in Scalar Context	*Returns in List Context*
Integer	The positions of all the matches within the regular expression

See also Chapter(s)	*Function(s)*	*Module(s)*
Chapter 8	**m//**	

print

```
print FILEHANDLE LIST
print LIST
print
```

Prints the values of the expressions in **LIST** to the current default output filehandle, or to the one specified by **FILEHANDLE**. If set, the **$** variable will be added to the end of the **LIST**. If **LIST** is empty, the value in **$_** is printed instead. Because **print** accepts a list of values, every element of the list will be interpreted as an expression. You should therefore ensure that if you are using **print** within a larger **LIST** context, you enclose the arguments to **print** in parentheses.

Effects	**$_, $!, XA**
Returns in Scalar Context	*Returns in List Context*
0 on failure	
1 on success	

See also Chapter(s)	*Function(s)*	*Module(s)*
Chapters 7, 8	**printf, sprintf**	

printf

```
printf FILEHANDLE FORMAT, LIST
printf FORMAT, LIST
```

Prints the value of **LIST** interpreted via the format specified by **FORMAT** to the current output filehandle, or to the one specified by **FILEHANDLE**. Effectively equivalent to

```
print FILEHANDLE sprintf(FORMAT, LIST)
```

Remember to use **print** in place of **printf** if you do not require a specific output format. The **print** function is more efficient. Table A-10 shows the list of accepted formatting conversions.

Format	Result
%%	A percent sign
%c	A character with the given ASCII code
%s	A string
%d	A signed integer (decimal)
%u	An unsigned integer (decimal)
%o	An unsigned integer (octal)
%x	An unsigned integer (hexadecimal)
%X	An unsigned integer (hexadecimal using uppercase characters)
%e	A floating point number (scientific notation)
%E	A floating point number (scientific notation using "E" in place of "e")
%f	A floating point number (fixed decimal notation)
%g	A floating point number (**%e** or **%f** notation according to value size)
%G	A floating point number (as **%g**, but using "E" in place of "e" when appropriate)
%p	A pointer (prints the memory address of the value in hexadecimal)
%n	Stores the number of characters output so far into the next variable in the parameter list

Table A-10. *Conversion Formats for **printf***

Format	Result
%I	A synonym for **%d**
%D	A synonym for C **%ld**
%U	A synonym for C **%lu**
%O	A synonym for C **%lo**
%F	A synonym for C **%f**

Table A-10.   *Conversion Formats for **printf*** (continued)

Perl also supports flags that optionally adjust the output format. These are specified between the % and conversion letter, as shown in Table A-11.

Flag	Result
space	Prefix positive number with a space
+	Prefix positive number with a plus sign
-	Left-justify within field
0	Use zeros, not spaces, to right-justify
#	Prefix non-zero octal with "0" and hexadecimal with "0x"
number	Minimum field width
.number	Specify precision (number of digits after decimal point) for floating point numbers
l	Interpret integer as C-type "long" or "unsigned long"
h	Interpret integer as C-type "short" or "unsigned short"
V	Interpret integer as Perl's standard integer type
v	Interpret the string as a series of integers and output as numbers separated by periods or by an arbitrary string extracted from the argument when the flag is preceded by *.

Table A-11.   *Formatting Flags for **printf** Conversion Formats*

Effects	$_, $!, XA
Returns in Scalar Context	*Returns in List Context*

0 on failure
1 on success

See also Chapter(s)	*Function(s)*	*Module(s)*
Chapters 7, 8	**print, sprintf**	

---

prototype

```
prototype EXPR
```

Returns a string containing the prototype of the function or reference specified by
EXPR, or **undef** if the function has no prototype. You can also use this to check the
availability of built-in functions. If **EXPR** starts with **CORE::**, then the rest is taken as
the name of a built-in function, and the call raises an exception. If the function does
exist, but does not behave like a function, then it returns **undef**.

Effects	XA
Returns in Scalar Context	*Returns in List Context*

undef if no function prototype

See also Chapter(s)	*Function(s)*	*Module(s)*
Chapter 6		

---

push

```
push ARRAY, LIST
```

Pushes the values in **LIST** onto the end of the list **ARRAY**. Used with **pop** to
implement stacks.

Effects	None
Returns in Scalar Context	*Returns in List Context*

Number of elements in new array

See also Chapter(s)	*Function(s)*	*Module(s)*
Chapter 8	**pop, shift, unshift**	

quotemeta

```
quotemeta EXPR
quotemeta
```

Returns the value of **EXPR** or **$_** with all nonalphanumeric characters backslashed.

Effects	**$_**	
Returns in Scalar Context	*Returns in List Context*	
String		
See also Chapter(s)	*Function(s)*	*Module(s)*
Chapter 8	**study, m//, s///**	

rand

```
rand EXPR
rand
```

Returns a random fractional number between 0 and the positive number **EXPR**, or 1 if not specified. Automatically calls **srand** to seed the random number generator unless it has already been called.

Effects	None	
Returns in Scalar Context	*Returns in List Context*	
Floating point number		
See also Chapter(s)	*Function(s)*	*Module(s)*
Chapter 8	**srand**	

read

```
read FILEHANDLE, SCALAR, LENGTH, OFFSET
read FILEHANDLE, SCALAR, LENGTH
```

Tries to read **LENGTH** bytes from **FILEHANDLE** into **SCALAR**. If **OFFSET** is specified, then reading starts from that point within the input string, up to **LENGTH** bytes. Uses the equivalent of the C **fread( )** function. For the equivalent of the C **read( )** function, see **sysread**.

Effects	**$!, T, XA, XR**
Returns in Scalar Context	*Returns in List Context*
undef on error	
0 at end of file	
Number of bytes read	

See also Chapter(s)	*Function(s)*	*Module(s)*
Chapter 7	**sysread**	

---

readdir

> readdir DIRHANDLE

In a scalar context, returns the next directory entry from the directory associated with **DIRHANDLE**. In a list context, returns all of the remaining directory entries in **DIRHANDLE**.

Effects	**$!, T, XA, U**
Returns in Scalar Context	*Returns in List Context*
undef on failure (end of entries)	Empty list on failure
File path	List of file *paths*

See also Chapter(s)	*Function(s)*	*Module(s)*
Chapter 7	**opendir, rewinddir**	

---

readline

> readline EXPR

Reads a line from the filehandle referred to by **EXPR**, returning the result. If you want to use a **FILEHANDLE** directly, it must be passed as a typeglob. In a scalar context, only one line is returned; in a list context, a list of lines up to end-of-file is returned.

Ignores the setting of the **$/** or **$INPUT_RECORD_SEPARATOR** variable. You should use the <> operator in preference.

Effects	**$!, T, XA**
Returns in Scalar Context	*Returns in List Context*
undef on error	Empty list on error
One record (line)	List of records (lines)

See also Chapter(s)	*Function(s)*	*Module(s)*
Chapter 7		

---

readlink

```
readlink EXPR
readlink
```

Returns the pathname of the file pointed to by the link **EXPR**, or **$_** if **EXPR** is not specified.

Effects	**$_, $!, T, U**
Returns in Scalar Context	*Returns in List Context*
undef on error	
String	

See also Chapter(s)	*Function(s)*	*Module(s)*
Chapter 7	**link, symlink**	

---

readpipe

```
readpipe EXPR
```

Executes **EXPR** as a command. The output is then returned as a multiline string in scalar text, or with the line returned as individual elements in a list context.

Effects		**$!, $?, T, XT, U**	
Returns in Scalar Context		*Returns in List Context*	
String		List	
See also Chapter(s)	*Function(s)*		*Module(s)*
Chapter 7	**system, open**		**IO::Pipe, IO::Handle**

recv

```
recv SOCKET, SCALAR, LEN, FLAGS
```

Receives a message on **SOCKET** attempting to read **LENGTH** bytes, placing the data read into variable **SCALAR**. The **FLAGS** argument takes the same values as the **recvfrom( )** system function, on which the function is based. When communicating with sockets, this provides a more reliable method of reading fixed-length data than the **sysread** function or the line-based operator **<FH>**.

Effects		**$!, T, XA, XR, U**	
Returns in Scalar Context		*Returns in List Context*	
undef on error			
Number of bytes read			
See also Chapter(s)	*Function(s)*		*Module(s)*
Chapter 12	**send, socket, accept**		**IO::Socket**

redo

```
redo LABEL
redo
```

Restarts the current loop without forcing the control statement to be evaluated. No further statements in the block are executed (execution restarts at the start of the block).

A **continue** block, if present, will not be executed. If **LABEL** is specified, execution restarts at the start of the loop identified by **LABEL**.

Effects	$@	
Returns in Scalar Context	*Returns in List Context*	
Nothing		
See also Chapter(s)	*Function(s)*	*Module(s)*
Chapters 5, 6	**next, last, continue**	

ref

```
ref EXPR
ref
```

Returns a true value if **EXPR**, or **$_** if **EXPR** is not supplied, is a reference. The actual value returned also defines the type of entity the reference refers to. The built-in types are

```
REF
SCALAR
ARRAY
HASH
CODE
GLOB
LVALUE
IO::Handle
```

If the reference has been blessed into a package, the package name is returned instead.

Effects	$_	
Returns in Scalar Context	*Returns in List Context*	
Empty string if not a reference		
String if a reference		
See also Chapter(s)	*Function(s)*	*Module(s)*
Chapter 10		

rename

```
rename OLDNAME, NEWNAME
```

Renames the file with **OLDNAME** to **NEWNAME**. Uses the system function **rename( )**, and so it will not rename files across file systems or volumes. If you want to copy or move a file, use the **copy** or **move** command supplied in the **File::Copy** module.

Effects	**$!, XT**
Returns in Scalar Context	*Returns in List Context*
0 on failure	
1 on success	

See also Chapter(s)	*Function(s)*	*Module(s)*
Chapter 7		**File::Copy**

require

```
require EXPR
require
```

If **EXPR** (or **$_** if **EXPR** is omitted) is numeric, then it demands that the script requires the specified version of Perl in order to continue. If **EXPR** or **$_** are not numeric, it assumes that the name is the name of a library file to be included. You cannot include the same file with this function twice. The included file must return a true value as the last statement.

    This differs from **use** in that included files effectively become additional text for the current script. Functions, variables, and other objects are not imported into the current name space, so if the specified file includes a package definition, then objects will require fully qualified names.

Effects	**$_, $!, $@, XT**
Returns in Scalar Context	*Returns in List Context*
Nothing	

See also Chapter(s)	*Function(s)*	*Module(s)*
Chapter 6	**use**	

APPENDIXES

reset

```
reset EXPR
reset
```

Resets (clears) all package variables starting with the letter range specified by **EXPR**. Generally only used within a **continue** block or at the end of a loop. If omitted, resets **?PATTERN?** matches.

Effects	None
Returns in Scalar Context	*Returns in List Context*
1 (always)	

See also Chapter(s)	*Function(s)*	*Module(s)*
Chapter 8		

return

```
return EXPR
return
```

Returns **EXPR** at the end of a subroutine, block, or **do** function. **EXPR** may be a scalar, array, or hash value; context will be selected at execution time. If no **EXPR** is given, returns an empty list in list context, **undef** in scalar context, or nothing in a void context.

Effects	$@
Returns in Scalar Context	*Returns in List Context*
List, which may be interpreted as scalar, list, or void context	

See also Chapter(s)	*Function(s)*	*Module(s)*
Chapter 6		

reverse

```
reverse LIST
```

In a list context, returns the elements of **LIST** in reverse order. In a scalar context, returns a concatenated string of the values of **LIST**, with all bytes in opposite order.

Effects	None
Returns in Scalar Context	*Returns in List Context*
String	List

See also Chapter(s)	*Function(s)*	*Module(s)*
Chapter 8	**sort, keys, values**	

rewinddir

```
rewinddir DIRHANDLE
```

Resets the current position within the directory specified by **DIRHANDLE** to the beginning of the directory.

Effects	$!, XA, U
Returns in Scalar Context	*Returns in List Context*
0 on failure	
1 on success	

See also Chapter(s)	*Function(s)*	*Module(s)*
Chapter 7		

rindex

```
rindex STR, SUBSTR, POSITION
rindex STR, SUBSTR
```

Operates similar to **index**, except it returns the position of the last occurrence of **SUBSTR** in **STR**. If **POSITION** is specified, returns the last occurrence at or before that position.

Effects	$_, $!, XT
Returns in Scalar Context	*Returns in List Context*
undef on failure	
Integer	

See also Chapter(s)	*Function(s)*	*Module(s)*
Chapter 8	**index, substr**	

---

rmdir

```
rmdir EXPR
rmdir
```

Deletes the directory specified by **EXPR**, or $_ if omitted. Only deletes the directory if the directory is empty.

Effects	None
Returns in Scalar Context	*Returns in List Context*
0 on failure	
1 on success	

See also Chapter(s)	*Function(s)*	*Module(s)*
Chapter 7	**mkdir, chdir**	**Cwd**

---

s///

```
s/PATTERN/REPLACE/
```

Not a function. This is the regular expression-substitution operator. Based on the regular expression specified in **PATTERN**, data is replaced by **REPLACE**. Like **m//**, the delimiters are defined by the first character following **s**.

Effects		
	T, XR, XT	
Returns in Scalar Context	*Returns in List Context*	
0 on failure		
Number of substitutions made		
See also Chapter(s)	*Function(s)*	*Module(s)*
Chapter 8	**m//, tr///, quotemeta, study**	

scalar

```
scalar EXPR
```

Forces the evaluation of **EXPR** to be in scalar context, even if it would normally work in list context.

Effects		
Returns in Scalar Context	*Returns in List Context*	
Scalar		
See also Chapter(s)	*Function(s)*	*Module(s)*
Chapters 4, 6, 7, 8		

seek

```
seek FILEHANDLE, POSITION, WHENCE
```

Positions the file pointer for the specified **FILEHANDLE**. **seek** is basically the same as the **fseek( )** C function. The position within the file is specified by **POSITION**, using the value of **WHENCE** as a reference point, as shown in Table A-12. The constants are defined within the **IO::Seekable** and **POSIX** modules.

If you are accessing a file using **syswrite** and **sysread**, you should use **sysseek** due to the effects of buffering.

Value	Constant	Description
0	**SEEK_SET**	Sets the new position absolutely to **POSITION** bytes within the file
1	**SEEK_CUR**	Sets the new position to the current position plus **POSITION** bytes within the file
2	**SEEK_END**	Sets the new position to **POSITION** bytes, relative to the end of the file

Table A-12.   *Offset Values and Constants for **seek***

The **seek** function also clears the **EOF** condition on a file when called, even if you are still potentially at the end of a file.

Effects	**$!, XA**
Returns in Scalar Context	*Returns in List Context*
0 on failure	
1 on success	

See also Chapter(s)	*Function(s)*	*Module(s)*
Chapter 7	**tell, sysseek**	**IO::File, IO::Handle**

seekdir

 `seekdir DIRHANDLE, POS`

Sets the current position within **DIRHANDLE** to **POS**. The value of **POS** must be a value previously returned by **telldir**.

Effects	**$!, XA, U**
Returns in Scalar Context	*Returns in List Context*
0 on failure	
1 on success	

See also Chapter(s)	*Function(s)*	*Module(s)*
Chapter 7	**rewinddir, telldir**	**IO::Dir**

select (filehandle)

```
select FILEHANDLE
select
```

Sets the default filehandle for output to **FILEHANDLE**, setting the filehandle used by functions such as **print** and **write** if no filehandle is specified. If **FILEHANDLE** is not specified, then it returns the name of the current default filehandle.

Effects	**XA**
Returns in Scalar Context	*Returns in List Context*
Previous default filehandle if **FILEHANDLE** specified Current default filehandle if **FILEHANDLE** is not specified	

See also Chapter(s)	*Function(s)*	*Module(s)*
Chapters 7, 12	**print, autoflush, write**	**IO::Handle, IO::File, IO::Select**

select (files)

```
select RBITS, WBITS, EBITS, TIMEOUT
```

Calls the system function **select( )** using the bits specified. The **select** function sets the controls for handling non-blocking I/O requests. Returns the number of filehandles awaiting I/O in scalar context, or the number of waiting filehandles and the time remaining in a list context.

TIMEOUT is specified in seconds, but accepts a floating point instead of an integer value. You can use this ability to pause execution for milliseconds instead of the normal seconds available with **sleep** and **alarm** by specifying **undef** for the first three arguments.

Effects	**$!, U**
Returns in Scalar Context	*Returns in List Context*
The number of filehandles awaiting I/O	The number of filehandles and time remaining

See also Chapter(s)	*Function(s)*	*Module(s)*
Chapter 7	**open**	**IO::Handle, IO::File, IO::Select**

semctl

> semctl ID, SEMNUM, CMD, ARG

Controls a System V semaphore. You will need to import the **IPC:SysV** module to get the correct definitions for **CMD**. The function calls the system **semctl( )** function.

Effects		**$!, U**
Returns in Scalar Context		*Returns in List Context*
undef on failure		
0 but true if the return value from		
the **semctl( )** is 0		
Value returned by system		

See also Chapter(s)	*Function(s)*	*Module(s)*
Chapter 14	**semget, semop**	**IPC::SysV,**
		Win32::Semaphore

 ## semget

> semget KEY, NSEMS, FLAGS

Returns the semaphore ID associated with **KEY**, using the system function **semget( )**.

Effects		**$!, U**
Returns in Scalar Context		*Returns in List Context*
undef on error		
Semaphore ID		

See also Chapter(s)	*Function(s)*	*Module(s)*
Chapter 14	**semctl, semop**	**IPC::SysV,**
		Win32::Semaphore

 ## semop

> semop KEY, OPSTRING

Performs the semaphore operations defined by **OPSTRING** on the semaphore ID associated with **KEY**. **OPSTRING** should be a packed array of **semop** structures, and each structure can be generated with

```
$semop = pack("sss", $semnum, $semop, $semflag);
```

Effects   **$!, U**

Returns in Scalar Context   *Returns in List Context*

0 on failure
1 on success

See also Chapter(s)	*Function(s)*	*Module(s)*
Chapter 14	**semctl, semget**	**IPC::SysV,** **Win32::Semaphore**

send

```
send SOCKET, MSG, FLAGS, TO
send SOCKET, MSG, FLAGS
```

Sends a message on **SOCKET** (the opposite of **recv**). If the socket is unconnected, you must supply a destination to communicate to with the **TO** parameter. In this case, the **sendto** system function is used in place of the system **send** function.

The **FLAGS** parameter is formed from the bitwise **or** of 0 and one or more of the **MSG_OOB** and **MSG_DONTROUTE** options. **MSG_OOB** allows you to send out-of-band data on sockets that support this notion. The underlying protocol must also support out-of-band data. Only **SOCK_STREAM** sockets created in the **AF_INET** address family support out-of-band data. The **MSG_DONTROUTE** option is turned on for the duration of the operation. Only diagnostic or routing programs use it.

Effects   **$!, XA, U**

Returns in Scalar Context   *Returns in List Context*

undef on error
Integer, number of bytes sent

See also Chapter(s)	*Function(s)*	*Module(s)*
Chapter 12	**recv, socket**	**IO::Socket**

setgrent

```
setgrent
```

Sets (or resets) the enumeration to the beginning of the set of group entries. This function should be called before the first call to **getgrent**.

Effects	U	
Returns in Scalar Context	*Returns in List Context*	
Nothing		
See also Chapter(s)	*Function(s)*	*Module(s)*
Chapter 11	**getgrent, endgrent**	**Win32API::Net**

sethostent

```
sethostent STAYOPEN
```

Sets (or resets) the enumeration to the beginning of the set of host entries. This function should be called before the first call to **gethostent**. The **STAYOPEN** argument is optional and unused on most systems.

Effects	U	
Returns in Scalar Context	*Returns in List Context*	
Nothing		
See also Chapter(s)	*Function(s)*	*Module(s)*
Chapter 11	**gethostent, endhostent**	

setnetent

```
setnetent STAYOPEN
```

Sets (or resets) the enumeration to the beginning of the set of network entries. This function should be called before the first call to **getnetent**. The **STAYOPEN** argument is optional and unused on most systems.

Effects	U
Returns in Scalar Context	*Returns in List Context*
Nothing	

See also Chapter(s)	*Function(s)*	*Module(s)*
Chapter 12	**getnetent, endnetent**	

setpgrp

```
setpgrp PID, PGRP
```

Sets the current process group for the process **PID**. You can use a value of 0 for **PID** to change the process group of the current process. If both arguments are omitted, defaults to values of 0. Causes a fatal error if the system does not support the function.

Effects	$!, XT, U
Returns in Scalar Context	*Returns in List Context*
undef on failure	
New parent process ID	

See also Chapter(s)	*Function(s)*	*Module(s)*
Chapter 15	**getpgrp**	

setpriority

```
setpriority WHICH, WHO, PRIORITY
```

Sets the priority for a process (**PRIO_PROCESS**), process group (**PRIO_PGRP**), or user (**PRIO_USER**). The argument **WHICH** specifies what entity to set the priority for, and **WHO** is the process ID or user ID to set. A value of 0 for **WHO** defines the current process, process group, or user. Produces a fatal error on systems that don't support the system **setpriority( )** function.

Effects	$!, XT, U
Returns in Scalar Context	*Returns in List Context*
0 on error	
1 on success	

See also Chapter(s)	*Function(s)*	*Module(s)*
Chapter 14	**getpriority**	**Win32::Process**

setprotoent

setprotoent STAYOPEN

Sets (or resets) the enumeration to the beginning of the set of protocol entries. This function should be called before the first call to **getprotoent**. The **STAYOPEN** argument is optional and unused on most systems.

Effects	U	
Returns in Scalar Context	*Returns in List Context*	
Nothing		
See also Chapter(s)	*Function(s)*	*Module(s)*
Chapter 12	**getprotoent, endprotoent**	

setpwent

setpwent

Sets (or resets) the enumeration to the beginning of the set of password entries. This function should be called before the first call to **getpwent**.

Effects	U	
Returns in Scalar Context	*Returns in List Context*	
Nothing		
See also Chapter(s)	*Function(s)*	*Module(s)*
Chapter 11	**getpwent, endpwent**	**Win32API::Net**

setservent

setservent STAYOPEN

Sets (or resets) the enumeration to the beginning of the set of service entries. This function should be called before the first call to **getservent**. The **STAYOPEN** argument is optional and unused on most systems.

Effects	**U**
Returns in Scalar Context	*Returns in List Context*

Nothing

See also Chapter(s)	*Function(s)*	*Module(s)*
Chapter 12	**getservent, endservent**	

setsockopt

```
setsockopt SOCKET, LEVEL, OPTNAME, OPTVAL
```

Sets the socket option **OPTNAME** with a value of **OPTVAL** on **SOCKET** at the specified **LEVEL**. You will need to import the **Socket** module for the valid values for **OPTNAME** shown in Table A-13.

OPTNAME	Description
SO_DEBUG	Enable/disable recording of debugging information.
SO_REUSEADDR	Enable/disable local address reuse.
SO_KEEPALIVE	Enable/disable keep connections alive.
SO_DONTROUTE	Enable/disable routing bypass for outgoing messages.
SO_LINGER	Linger on close if data is present.
SO_BROADCAST	Enable/disable permission to transmit broadcast messages.
SO_OOBINLINE	Enable/disable reception of out-of-band data in band.
SO_SNDBUF	Set buffer size for output.
SO_RCVBUF	Set buffer size for input.
SO_TYPE	Get the type of the socket (get only).
SO_ERROR	Get and clear error on the socket (get only).

Table A-13.   *Socket Options*

APPENDIXES

Effects	**$!, XA, U**	
Returns in Scalar Context	*Returns in List Context*	
undef on failure		
1 on success		
See also Chapter(s)	*Function(s)*	*Module(s)*
Chapter 12	**getsockopt, socket**	**IO::Socket**

shift

```
shift ARRAY
shift
```

Returns the first value in an array, deleting it and shifting the elements of the array list to the left by one. If **ARRAY** is not specified, shifts the @_ array within a subroutine, or **@ARGV** otherwise. **shift** is essentially identical to **pop**, except values are taken from the start of the array instead of the end.

Effects	None	
Returns in Scalar Context	*Returns in List Context*	
undef if the array is empty		
First element in the array		
See also Chapter(s)	*Function(s)*	*Module(s)*
Chapter 8	**pop, push, unshift**	**IO::Socket**

shmctl

```
shmctl ID, CMD, ARG
```

Controls the shared memory segment referred to by **ID**, using **CMD** with **ARG**. You will need to import the **IPC::SysV** module to get the command tokens defined in Table A-14.

Command	Description
IPC_STAT	Places the current value of each member of the data structure associated with **ID** into the scalar **ARG**
IPC_SET	Sets the value of the following members of the data structure associated with **ID** to the corresponding values found in the packed scalar **ARG**
IPC_RMID	Removes the shared memory identifier specified by **ID** from the system and destroys the shared memory segment and data structure associated with it
SHM_LOCK	Locks the shared memory segment specified by **ID** in memory
SHM_UNLOCK	Unlocks the shared memory segment specified by **ID**

Table A-14. *Commands for Controlling Shared Memory Segments*

Effects	**$!, U**
Returns in Scalar Context	*Returns in List Context*

undef on failure
0 but true if the return value from the
shmctl( ) is 0
Value returned by system

See also Chapter(s)	*Function(s)*	*Module(s)*
Chapter 14	**shmget, shmread**	IPC::SysV

shmget

```
shmget KEY, SIZE, FLAGS
shmget KEY
```

Returns the shared memory segment ID for the segment matching **KEY**. A new shared memory segment is created of at least **SIZE** bytes, providing that either **KEY** does not already have a segment associated with it or that **KEY** is equal to the constant **IPC_PRIVATE**.

Effects	$!, U
Returns in Scalar Context	Returns in List Context
Shared memory ID	

See also Chapter(s)	Function(s)	Module(s)
Chapter 14	shmctl, shmread, shmwrite	IPC::SysV

shmread

```
shmread ID, VAR, POS, SIZE
```

Reads the shared memory segment **ID** into the scalar **VAR** at position **POS** for up to **SIZE** bytes.

Effects	$!, U
Returns in Scalar Context	Returns in List Context
0 on failure	
1 on success	

See also Chapter(s)	Function(s)	Module(s)
Chapter 14	shmctl, shmget, shmwrite	IPC::SysV

shmwrite

```
shmwrite ID, STRING, POS, SIZE
```

Writes **STRING** from the position **POS** for **SIZE** bytes into the shared memory segment specified by **ID**. The **SIZE** is greater than the length of **STRING**. **shmwrite** appends null bytes to fill out to **SIZE** bytes.

Effects	**$!, U**
Returns in Scalar Context	*Returns in List Context*
0 on false	
1 on success	

See also Chapter(s)	*Function(s)*	*Module(s)*
Chapter 14	**shmctl, shmget, shmread**	**IPC::SysV**

shutdown

```
shutdown SOCKET, HOW
```

Disables a socket connection according to the value of **HOW**. The valid values for **HOW** are identical to the system call of the same name. A value of 0 indicates that you have stopped reading information from the socket. A value of 1 indicates that you've stopped writing to the socket. A value of 2 indicates that you have stopped using the socket altogether.

Effects	**$!, XA, U**
Returns in Scalar Context	*Returns in List Context*
0 on failure	
1 on success	

See also Chapter(s)	*Function(s)*	*Module(s)*
Chapter 12	**accept**	**IO::Socket**

sin

```
sin EXPR
sin
```

Returns the sine of **EXPR**, or **$_** if not specified.

Effects		**$_**
Returns in Scalar Context		*Returns in List Context*
Floating point		
See also Chapter(s)	*Function(s)*	*Module(s)*
Chapter 8	**atan2, cos**	**Math::Trig**

sleep

```
sleep EXPR
sleep
```

Pauses the script for **EXPR** seconds, or forever if **EXPR** is not specified. Returns the number of seconds actually slept. Can be interrupted by a signal handler, but you should avoid using **sleep** with **alarm**, since many systems use **alarm** for the **sleep** implementation.

Effects		None
Returns in Scalar Context		*Returns in List Context*
Integer, number of seconds actually slept		
See also Chapter(s)	*Function(s)*	*Module(s)*
Chapter 14	**alarm, select**	**IO::Select**

socket

```
socket SOCKET, DOMAIN, TYPE, PROTOCOL
```

Opens a socket in **DOMAIN**, of **TYPE**, using **PROTOCOL**, and attaches it to the filehandle **SOCKET**. You will need to import the **Socket** module to get the correct definitions. For most systems, **DOMAIN** will be **PF_INET** for a TCP/IP-based socket. **TYPE** will generally be one of **SOCK_STREAM** for streams-based connections (TCP/IP) or **SOCK_DGRAM** for a datagram connection (UDP/IP). Values for **PROTOCOL** are system defined, but valid values include **TCP** for TCP/IP, **UDP** for UDP, and **RDP** for the "reliable" datagram protocol.

Consider using the **IO::Socket** module instead to create both client and server sockets, since it handles all of this detail for you.

Effects	**$!, XA, XT, U**
Returns in Scalar Context	*Returns in List Context*
0 on failure	
1 on success	

See also Chapter(s)	*Function(s)*	*Module(s)*
Chapter 12	**accept, bind**	**IO::Socket**

socketpair

```
socketpair SOCKET1, SOCKET2, DOMAIN, TYPE, PROTOCOL
```

Creates an unnamed pair of connected sockets in the specified **DOMAIN**, of the specified **TYPE**, using **PROTOCOL**. If the system **socketpair( )** function is not implemented, then it causes a fatal error.

Effects	**$!, XA, XT, U**
Returns in Scalar Context	*Returns in List Context*
0 on failure	
1 on success	

See also Chapter(s)	*Function(s)*	*Module(s)*
Chapter 12	**pipe, socket**	**IPC::Open2, IPC::Open3, IO::Socket**

sort

```
sort SUBNAME LIST
sort BLOCK LIST
sort LIST
```

Sorts **LIST** according to the subroutine **SUBNAME** or the anonymous subroutine specified by **BLOCK**. If no **SUBNAME** or **BLOCK** is specified, then it sorts according to normal alphabetical sequence. If **BLOCK** or **SUBNAME** is specified, then the subroutine should return an integer less than, greater than, or equal to zero, according to how the elements of the array are to be sorted.

Effects	$@
Returns in Scalar Context	*Returns in List Context*
	List

See also Chapter(s)	*Function(s)*	*Module(s)*
Chapter 8	**reverse**	

splice

```
splice ARRAY, OFFSET, LENGTH, LIST
splice ARRAY, OFFSET, LENGTH
splice ARRAY, OFFSET
```

Removes the elements of **ARRAY** from the element **OFFSET** for **LENGTH** elements, replacing the elements removed with **LIST**, if specified. If **LENGTH** is omitted, removes everything from **OFFSET** onwards.

Effects	$@
Returns in Scalar Context	*Returns in List Context*
undef if no elements removed	Empty list on failure
Last element removed	List of elements removed

See also Chapter(s)	*Function(s)*	*Module(s)*
Chapter 8	**substr, map, grep**	

split

```
split /PATTERN/, EXPR, LIMIT
split /PATTERN/, EXPR
split /PATTERN/
split
```

Splits a string into an array of strings, returning the resultant list. By default, empty leading fields are preserved and empty trailing fields are deleted.

In a scalar context, returns the number of fields found and splits the values into the @_ array using **??** as the pattern delimiter. If **EXPR** is omitted, splits the value of $_. If **PATTERN** is also omitted, it splits on white space (multiple spaces, tabs). Anything matching **PATTERN** is taken to be a delimiter separating fields and can be a regular expression of one or more characters.

If **LIMIT** has been specified and is positive, splits into a maximum of that many fields (or fewer). If **LIMIT** is unspecified or zero, splitting continues until there are no more delimited fields. If negative, then **split** acts as if an arbitrarily large value has been specified, preserving trailing null fields.

A **PATTERN** of a null string splits **EXPR** into individual characters.

Effects	**$_, T**
Returns in Scalar Context	*Returns in List Context*
Integer, number of elements	List of split elements

See also Chapter(s)	*Function(s)*	*Module(s)*
Chapter 8	**join**	

---

sprintf

```
sprintf FORMAT, LIST
```

The **sprintf** function uses **FORMAT** to return a formatted string based on the values in **LIST**. Essentially identical to **printf**, but the formatted string is returned instead of being printed. The **sprintf** function is basically synonymous with the C **sprintf** function, but Perl does its own formatting; the C **sprintf** function is not used (except for basic floating-point formatting).

The **sprintf** function accepts the same format conversions as **printf** (see Table A-10). Perl also supports flags that optionally adjust the output format. These are specified between the % and conversion letter and are the same as those for **printf** (see Table A-11).

Effects	None
Returns in Scalar Context	*Returns in List Context*
undef on error	
Preformatted string according to **FORMAT** and **LIST**	

See also Chapter(s)	*Function(s)*	*Module(s)*
Chapters 7, 8	**print, printf**	

APPENDIXES

sqrt

```
sqrt EXPR
sqrt
```

Returns the square root of **EXPR**, or **$_** if omitted.

Effects	**$_, $@**
Returns in Scalar Context	*Returns in List Context*
Floating point number	

See also Chapter(s)	*Function(s)*	*Module(s)*
Chapter 8		

srand

```
srand EXPR
srand
```

Sets the seed value for the random number generator to **EXPR** or to a random value based on the time, process ID, and other values if **EXPR** is omitted.

Effects	None
Returns in Scalar Context	*Returns in List Context*
Nothing	

See also Chapter(s)	*Function(s)*	*Module(s)*
Chapter 8	**rand**	

stat

```
stat FILEHANDLE
stat EXPR
stat
```

Returns a 13-element array giving the status info for a file, specified by either
FILEHANDLE, EXPR, or **$_**. The list of values returned is shown in Table A-15. If used
in a scalar context, returns 0 on failure, 1 on success. Note that support for some of
these elements is system dependent—check the documentation for a complete list.

Effects	**$_, $!, XA**
Returns in Scalar Context	*Returns in List Context*
0 on failure in scalar context	Empty list on failure
1 on success in scalar context	List of file statistics (*see* table)

See also Chapter(s)	*Function(s)*	*Module(s)*
Chapter 7	**-X, lstat**	

Element	Description
0	Device number of file system
1	Inode number
2	File mode (type and permissions)
3	Number of (hard) links to the file
4	Numeric user ID of file's owner
5	Numeric group ID of file's owner
6	The device identifier (special files only)
7	File size, in bytes
8	Last access time since the epoch
9	Last modify time since the epoch
10	Inode change time (*not* creation time!) since the epoch
11	Preferred block size for file system I/O
12	Actual number of blocks allocated

Table A-15.   *Values Returned by* **stat**

study

```
study EXPR
study
```

Takes extra time to study **EXPR** in order to improve the performance on regular expressions conducted on **EXPR**. If **EXPR** is omitted, uses **$_**. The actual speed gains may be very small, depending on the number of times you expect to search the string. You can only study one expression or scalar at any one time.

Effects	**$_**	
Returns in Scalar Context	*Returns in List Context*	
Nothing		
See also Chapter(s)	*Function(s)*	*Module(s)*
Chapter 8	**m//, s///**	**re**

sub

```
sub NAME PROTO ATTRS BLOCK# Named, prototype, attributes, definition
sub NAME ATTRS BLOCK       # Named, attributes, definition
sub NAME PROTO BLOCK       # Named, prototype, definition
sub NAME BLOCK             # Named, definition
sub NAME PROTO ATTRS       # Named, prototype, attributes
sub NAME ATTRS             # Named, attributes
sub NAME PROTO             # Named, prototype
sub NAME                   # Named
sub PROTO ATTRS BLOCK      # Anonymous, prototype, attributes, definition
sub ATTRS BLOCK            # Anonymous, attributes, definition
sub PROTO BLOCK            # Anonymous, prototype, definition
sub BLOCK                  # Anonymous, definition
```

The **sub** keyword defines a new subroutine. The arguments shown above follow these rules:

- **NAME** is the name of the subroutine. Named subroutines can be predeclared (without an associated code block) with, or without, prototype specifications.

- Anonymous subroutines *must* have a definition.

- **PROTO** defines the prototype for a function, which will be used when the function is called to validate the supplied arguments.

- **ATTRS** define additional information for the parser about the subroutine being declared.

Effects	None
Returns in Scalar Context	*Returns in List Context*
Nothing	

See also Chapter(s)	*Function(s)*	*Module(s)*
Chapter 7	**prototype**	

substr

```
substr EXPR, OFFSET, LEN, REPLACEMENT
substr EXPR, OFFSET, LEN
substr EXPR, OFFSET
```

Returns a substring of **EXPR**, starting at **OFFSET** within the string. If **OFFSET** is negative, starts that many characters from the end of the string. If **LEN** is specified, returns that number of bytes, or all bytes up until end-of-string if not specified. If **LEN** is negative, leaves that many characters off the end of the string. If **REPLACEMENT** is specified, replaces the substring with the **REPLACEMENT** string.

If you specify a substring that passes beyond the end of the string, it returns only the valid element of the original string.

Effects	$@, **XA**, **XR**
Returns in Scalar Context	*Returns in List Context*
String	

See also Chapter(s)	*Function(s)*	*Module(s)*
Chapter 8	**splice, m//**	

symlink

```
symlink OLDFILE, NEWFILE
```

Creates a symbolic link between **OLDFILE** and **NEWFILE**. On systems that don't support symbolic links, causes a fatal error.

Effects		**$!, XT, U**	
Returns in Scalar Context		*Returns in List Context*	
0 on failure			
1 on success			
See also Chapter(s)	*Function(s)*		*Module(s)*
Chapter 7	**link, lstat**		

syscall

    syscall EXPR, LIST

Calls the system function **EXPR** with the arguments **LIST**. Produces a fatal error if the specified function does not exist.

Effects		**$!, XR, XT, U**	
Returns in Scalar Context		*Returns in List Context*	
-1 on failure of system call			
Value returned by system function			
See also Chapter(s)	*Function(s)*		*Module(s)*
Chapter 14			

sysopen

    sysopen FILEHANDLE, FILENAME, MODE, PERMS
    sysopen FILEHANDLE, FILENAME, MODE

Equivalent to the underlying C and operating system call **open( )**. Opens the file specified by **FILENAME**, associating it with **FILEHANDLE**. The **MODE** argument specifies how the file should be opened. The values of **MODE** are system dependent, but some values are historically set. Values of 0, 1, and 2 mean read-only, write-only, and read/write, respectively. The supported values are available in the **Fcntl** module, and are summarized in Table A-16. Note that **FILENAME** is strictly a file name; no interpretation of the contents takes place (unlike **open**), and the mode of opening is defined by the **MODE** argument.

If the file has to be created, and the **O_CREAT** flag has been specified in **MODE**, then the file is created with the permissions of **PERMS**. The value of **PERMS** must be specified in traditional Unix-style hexadecimal. If **PERMS** is not specified, then Perl uses a default mode of 0666 (read/write on user/group/other).

Effects	$!, XA
Returns in Scalar Context	*Returns in List Context*
0 on failure	
1 on success	

See also Chapter(s)	*Function(s)*	*Module(s)*
Chapter 7	**sysread, syswrite, sysseek**	Fcntl, IO::File, IO::Handle

Flag	Description
O_RDONLY	Read only.
O_WRONLY	Write only.
O_RDWR	Read and write.
O_CREAT	Create the file if it doesn't already exist.
O_EXCL	Fail if the file already exists.
O_APPEND	Append to an existing file.
O_TRUNC	Truncate the file before opening.
O_NONBLOCK	Non-blocking mode.
O_NDELAY	Equivalent of **O_NONBLOCK**.
O_SYNC	Write data physically to the disk, instead of write buffer.
O_EXLOCK	Lock using **flock** and **LOCK_EX**.
O_SHLOCK	Lock using **flock** and **LOCK_SH**.
O_DIRECTOPRY	Fail if the file is not a directory.
O_NOFOLLOW	Fail if the last path component is a symbolic link.
O_BINARY	Open in binary mode (implies a call to **binmode**).
O_LARGEFILE	Open with large (>2GB) file support.
O_NOCTTY	Don't make the terminal file being opened the processes-controlling terminal, even if you don't have one yet.

Table A-16. *Modes for Opening Files with* **sysopen**

APPENDIXES

sysread

```
sysread FILEHANDLE, SCALAR, LENGTH, OFFSET
sysread FILEHANDLE, SCALAR, LENGTH
```

Tries to read **LENGTH** bytes from **FILEHANDLE**, placing the result in **SCALAR**. If **OFFSET** is specified, then data is written to **SCALAR** from **OFFSET** bytes, effectively appending the information from a specific point. If **OFFSET** is negative, it starts from the number of bytes specified counted backward from the end of the string. This is the equivalent of the C/operating system function **read( )**. Because it bypasses the buffering system employed by functions like **print**, **read**, and **seek**, it should only be used with the corresponding **syswrite** and **sysseek** functions.

Effects	**$!, $@, T, XA, XR**
Returns in Scalar Context	*Returns in List Context*

undef on error
0 at end of file
Integer, number of bytes read

See also Chapter(s)	*Function(s)*	*Module(s)*
Chapter 7	**syswrite, sysseek**	**IO::File, IO::Handle**

sysseek

```
sysseek FILEHANDLE, POSITION, WHENCE
```

Sets the position within **FILEHANDLE** according to the values of **POSITION** and **WHENCE**. This function is the equivalent of the C function **lseek( )**, so you should avoid using it with buffered forms of **FILEHANDLE**. This includes the <FILEHANDLE> notation and **print**, **write**, **seek**, and **tell**. Using it with **sysread** or **syswrite** is OK, since they too ignore buffering.

The position within the file is specified by **POSITION**, using the value of **WHENCE** as a reference point, as shown in Table A-17.

Value	Constant	Description
0	**SEEK_SET**	Sets the new position absolutely to **POSITION** bytes within the file
1	**SEEK_CUR**	Sets the new position to the current position plus **POSITION** bytes within the file
2	**SEEK_END**	Sets the new position to **POSITION** bytes, relative to the end of the file

Table A-17.   *Offset Values and Constants for* **seek**

Effects		**$!, XA**	
Returns in Scalar Context		*Returns in List Context*	

undef on failure
A position of 0 is returned as
the string 0 but true
Integer, new position (in bytes) on success

See also Chapter(s)	*Function(s)*	*Module(s)*
Chapter 7	**tell, seek**	**IO::File, IO::Handle**

system

```
system PROGRAM, LIST
system PROGRAM
```

Executes the command specified by **PROGRAM**, passing **LIST** as arguments to the command. The script waits for execution of the child command to complete before continuing. If **PROGRAM** is the only argument specified, then Perl checks for any shell metacharacters and, if found, passes **PROGRAM** unchanged to the user's default command shell. If there are no metacharacters, then the value is split into words and passed as an entire command with arguments to the system **execvp** function.

APPENDIXES

The return value is the exit status of the program as returned by the **wait** function. To obtain the actual exit value, divide by 256. If you want to capture the output from a command, use the backticks operator.

Effects	**$!, $?, XT**	
Returns in Scalar Context	*Returns in List Context*	
Exit status of program as returned by **wait**		
See also Chapter(s)	*Function(s)*	*Module(s)*
Chapter 14	**exec**	

syswrite

```
syswrite FILEHANDLE, SCALAR, LENGTH, OFFSET
syswrite FILEHANDLE, SCALAR, LENGTH
```

Attempts to write **LENGTH** bytes from **SCALAR** to the file associated with **FILEHANDLE**. If **OFFSET** is specified, then information is read from **OFFSET** bytes in the supplied **SCALAR**. This function uses the C/operating system **write( )** function, which bypasses the normal buffering. You should therefore avoid using functions such as **print** and **read** in conjunction with this function.

Effects	**$!, $@, XA**	
Returns in Scalar Context	*Returns in List Context*	
undef on error		
Integer, number of bytes written		
See also Chapter(s)	*Function(s)*	*Module(s)*
Chapter 7	**sysread, sysseek**	**IO::File, IO::Handle**

tell

```
tell FILEHANDLE
tell
```

Returns the current position (in bytes) within the specified **FILEHANDLE**. If **FILEHANDLE** is omitted, then it returns the position within the last file accessed.

Effects   **XA**

Returns in Scalar Context   *Returns in List Context*

Integer, current file position (in bytes)

See also Chapter(s)	*Function(s)*	*Module(s)*
Chapter 7	**seek, sysseek**	**IO::File, IO::Handle**

---

telldir

```
telldir DIRHANDLE
```

Returns the current position within the directory listing referred to by **DIRHANDLE**.

Effects   **XA, U**

Returns in Scalar Context   *Returns in List Context*

Integer

See also Chapter(s)	*Function(s)*	*Module(s)*
Chapter 7	**opendir, readdir, closedir**	**IO::Dir**

---

tie

```
tie VARIABLE, CLASSNAME, LIST
```

Ties the **VARIABLE** to the package class **CLASSNAME** that provides implementation for the variable type. Any additional arguments in **LIST** are passed to the constructor for the entire class. Typically used to bind hash variables to DBM databases.

Effects   **$@**

Returns in Scalar Context   *Returns in List Context*

Reference to tied object

See also Chapter(s)	*Function(s)*	*Module(s)*
Chapter 10	**tied, untie**	**Tie::Array, Tie::Handle, Tie::Hash, Tie::RefHash, Tie::Scalar, Tie::SubstrHash**

tied

tied VARIABLE

Returns a reference to the object underlying the tied entity **VARIABLE**.

Effects	None
Returns in Scalar Context	*Returns in List Context*
undef if **VARIABLE** is not tied to a package	

See also Chapter(s)	*Function(s)*	*Module(s)*
Chapter 10	**tie, untie**	**Tie::Array, Tie::Handle, Tie::Hash, Tie::RefHash, Tie::Scalar, Tie::SubstrHash**

time

time

Returns the number of seconds since the epoch (00:00:00 UTC, January 1, 1970, for most systems; 00:00:00, January 1, 1904, for Mac OS). Suitable for feeding to **gmtime** and **localtime**.

Effects	None
Returns in Scalar Context	*Returns in List Context*
Integer, seconds since epoch	

See also Chapter(s)	*Function(s)*	*Module(s)*
Chapter 11	**gmtime, localtime**	

times

times

Returns a four-element list giving the user, system, child, and child system times for the current process and its children.

Effects	None
Returns in Scalar Context	*Returns in List Context*
User, system, child, child system times as integer	

See also Chapter(s)	*Function(s)*	*Module(s)*
Chapter 11		

tr///

```
tr/SEARCHLIST/REPLACEMENTLIST/
```

Not a function. This is the transliteration operator; it replaces all occurrences of the characters in **SEARCHLIST** with the characters in **REPLACEMENTLIST**.

Effects	XR
Returns in Scalar Context	*Returns in List Context*
Number of characters replaced or deleted	

See also Chapter(s)	*Function(s)*	*Module(s)*
Chapter 8	**m//, s///**	

truncate

```
truncate FILEHANDLE, LENGTH
```

Truncates (reduces) the size of the file specified by **FILEHANDLE** to the specified **LENGTH** (in bytes). Produces a fatal error if the function is not implemented on your system.

Effects	$!, XA, XT, U
Returns in Scalar Context	*Returns in List Context*
undef if the operation failed 1 on success	

See also Chapter(s)	*Function(s)*	*Module(s)*
Chapter 7	**open, sysopen**	**IO::File, IO::Handle**

uc

```
uc EXPR
uc
```

Returns an uppercased version of **EXPR**, or **$_** if not specified.

Effects	**$_, T**
Returns in Scalar Context	*Returns in List Context*
String	

See also Chapter(s)	*Function(s)*	*Module(s)*
Chapter 8	**lc, lcfirst, ucfirst**	

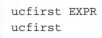
ucfirst

```
ucfirst EXPR
ucfirst
```

Returns the value of **EXPR** with only the first character uppercased. If **EXPR** is omitted, then uses **$_**.

Effects	**$_, T**
Returns in Scalar Context	*Returns in List Context*
String	

See also Chapter(s)	*Function(s)*	*Module(s)*
Chapter 8	**lc, lcfirst, uc**	

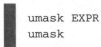
umask

```
umask EXPR
umask
```

Sets the umask (default mask applied when creating files and directories) for the current process. Value of **EXPR** must be an octal number. If **EXPR** is omitted, simply returns the previous value.

Effects	**XT, U**
Returns in Scalar Context	*Returns in List Context*
Previous **umask** value	
See also Chapter(s)	*Function(s)*	*Module(s)*
Chapter 7	**open, sysopen, mkdir**

 ## undef

```
undef EXPR
undef
```

Undefines the value of **EXPR**. Use on a scalar, list, hash, function, or typeglob. Use on a hash with a statement such as **undef $hash{$key}**; actually sets the value of the specified key to an undefined value. If you want to delete the element from the hash, use the **delete** function.

Effects	**XR**
Returns in Scalar Context	*Returns in List Context*
undef	
See also Chapter(s)	*Function(s)*	*Module(s)*
Chapters 4, 6	**delete**

 ## unlink

```
unlink LIST
unlink
```

Deletes the files specified by **LIST**, or the file specified by **$_** otherwise.

Effects	**$_, $!, XT**
Returns in Scalar Context	*Returns in List Context*
Number of files deleted	
See also Chapter(s)	*Function(s)*	*Module(s)*
Chapter 7		

unpack

```
unpack FORMAT, EXPR
```

Unpacks the binary string **EXPR** using the format specified in **FORMAT**. Basically reverses the operation of **pack**, returning the list of packed values according to the supplied format.

You can also prefix any format field with a **%<number>** to indicate that you want a 16-bit checksum of the value of **EXPR**, instead of the value.

Effects		*$@*
Returns in Scalar Context		*Returns in List Context*
List of unpacked values		
See also Chapter(s)	*Function(s)*	*Module(s)*
Chapters 8, 10, 13	**pack**	

 # unshift

```
unshift ARRAY, LIST
```

Places the elements from **LIST**, in order, at the beginning of **ARRAY**.

Effects		None
Returns in Scalar Context		*Returns in List Context*
Number of new elements in **ARRAY**		
See also Chapter(s)	*Function(s)*	*Module(s)*
Chapter 8	**shift, pop, push**	

 # untie

```
untie VARIABLE
```

Breaks the binding between a variable and a package, undoing the association created by the **tie** function.

Effects		None	
Returns in Scalar Context		*Returns in List Context*	
0 on failure			
1 on success			
See also Chapter(s)	*Function(s)*		*Module(s)*
Chapters 10, 13	**tie**		**Tie::Array, Tie::Handle, Tie::Hash, Tie::RefHash, Tie::Scalar, Tie::SubstrHash**

use

```
use MODULE LIST
use MODULE
```

Imports all the functions exported by **MODULE**, or only those referred to by **LIST**, into the name space of the current package. Effectively equivalent to

```
BEGIN
{
    require "Module.pm";
    Module->import();
}
```

Also used to impose compiler directives (pragmas) on the current script, although essentially these are just modules anyway.

Note that a **use** statement is evaluated at compile time. A **require** statement is evaluated at execution time.

Effects		$!, $@	
Returns in Scalar Context		*Returns in List Context*	
Nothing			
See also Chapter(s)	*Function(s)*		*Module(s)*
Chapter 6	**require, no, package**		

APPENDIXES

utime

```
utime ATIME, MTIME, LIST
```

Sets the access and modification times specified by **ATIME** and **MTIME** for the list of files in **LIST**. The values of **ATIME** and **MTIME** must be numerical. The inode modification time is set to the current time.

Effects	$!, XT, U
Returns in Scalar Context	*Returns in List Context*
Number of files updated	

See also Chapter(s)	*Function(s)*	*Module(s)*
Chapter 11	-X, stat	

 values

```
values HASH
```

Returns the list of all the values contained in **HASH**. In a scalar context, returns the number of values that would be returned. Uses the same iterator, and therefore order, used by the **each** and **keys** functions.

Effects	None
Returns in Scalar Context	*Returns in List Context*
Number of values	List of values

See also Chapter(s)	*Function(s)*	*Module(s)*
Chapters 4, 8, 10, 13	each, keys	

 vec

```
vec EXPR, OFFSET, BITS
```

Treats the string in **EXPR** as a vector of unsigned integers and returns the value of the bit field specified by **OFFSET**. **BITS** specifies the number of bits reserved for each entry in the bit vector. This must be a power of two from 1 to 32.

Effects	**XR**
Returns in Scalar Context	*Returns in List Context*
Integer	

See also Chapter(s)	*Function(s)*	*Module(s)*
Chapters 8, 13		

---

wait

```
wait
```

Waits for a child process to terminate, returning the process ID of the deceased process. The exit status of the process is contained in **$?**.

Effects	**$!, $?, U**
Returns in Scalar Context	*Returns in List Context*
-1 if there are no child processes	
Process ID of deceased process	

See also Chapter(s)	*Function(s)*	*Module(s)*
Chapter 14	**waitpid**	

---

waitpid

```
waitpid PID, FLAGS
```

Waits for the child process with ID **PID** to terminate, returning the process ID of the deceased process. If **PID** does not exist, then it returns -1. The exit status of the process is contained in **$?**.

If you import the **POSIX** module, you can specify flags by name, although all Perl implementations support a value of 0. Table A-18 lists the flags supported under

Solaris. You will need to check your implementation for the flags your operating system supports.

Effects		**$!, $?, U**	
Returns in Scalar Context		*Returns in List Context*	
-1 if process does not exist			
Process ID of deceased process			
See also Chapter(s)	*Function(s)*		*Module(s)*
Chapter 14	**wait**		

wantarray

    wantarray

Returns true if the context of the currently executing function is looking for a list value. Returns false in a scalar context.

Effects		None	
Returns in Scalar Context		*Returns in List Context*	
undef if no context		1 if lvalue expects a list	
0 if lvalue expects a scalar			
See also Chapter(s)	*Function(s)*		*Module(s)*
Chapter 6			

Flag	Description
WIFEXITED	Wait for processes that have exited
WIFSIGNALED	Wait for processes that received a signal
WNOHANG	Nonblocking wait
WSTOPSIG	Wait for processes that received STOP signal
WTERMSIG	Wait for processes that received TERM signal
WUNTRACED	Wait for processes stopped by signals

Table A-18. *Flags for* **waitpid**

warn

```
warn LIST
```

Prints the value of **LIST** to **STDERR**. Basically the same as the **die** function except that no call is made to the exit and no exception is raised within an **eval** statement. This can be useful to raise an error without causing the script to terminate prematurely.

If the variable **$@** contains a value (from a previous **eval** call) and **LIST** is empty, then the value of **$@** is printed with "\t...caught" appended to the end. If both **$@** and **LIST** are empty, then "Warning: Something's wrong" is printed.

Effects	**$!**	
Returns in Scalar Context	*Returns in List Context*	
Nothing		
See also Chapter(s)	*Function(s)*	*Module(s)*
Chapters 9, 21	**die**	

write

```
write FILEHANDLE
write
```

Writes a formatted record, as specified by **format** to **FILEHANDLE**. If **FILEHANDLE** is omitted, then writes the output to the currently selected default output channel. Form processing is handled automatically, adding new pages, headers, footers, and so on, as specified by the format for the filehandle.

Effects	**$!, $@, XA**	
Returns in Scalar Context	*Returns in List Context*	
0 on failure		
1 on success		
See also Chapter(s)	*Function(s)*	*Module(s)*
Chapter 16	**format**	

y///

y/SEARCHLIST/REPLACEMENTLIST/

Identical to the **tr///** operator; translates all characters in **SEARCHLIST** into the corresponding characters in **REPLACEMENTLIST**.

Effects   XR

Returns in Scalar Context   *Returns in List Context*

Number of characters modified

See also Chapter(s)   *Function(s)*   *Module(s)*

Chapter 8   **tr///**

The
Complete
Reference

Perl

Appendix B

Standard Perl Library

993

The standard Perl library comes with a range of modules that have been deemed useful, if not essential, to developing Perl applications. Some of these modules, such as **AutoLoader, AutoSplit,** and much of the **ExtUtils** hierarchy, are an essential part of the development process. Others are utility modules, such as the **Text::Tabs** module that supports the expanding and compressing of tabs to and from spaces.

Although what's included here is not an exhaustive list of all the modules in the Standard Perl Library, it is an attempt to concentrate on the modules you are most likely to need or use. With that in mind, please note the following:

- References to the **CORE** module refer to the core functions and operators supported natively by the Perl interpreter.
- The actual location of the files will vary according to platform and version. You may need to search the entire Perl 5 library directory to find a specific module. The titles given here will work inside any standard Perl script.
- The list of modules available on your system may be different from that listed here because of differences between the supported features of different operating systems.
- Only genuine modules have been included here. Older Perl libraries (with a .pl suffix) are not included.
- Pragmas—which control the execution of a Perl program—are described in detail in Chapter 19.

AnyDBM_File

```
use AnyDBM_File;
```

This module imports a suitable DBM module to enable you to use a DBM database. Care should be taken, since you cannot normally mix DBM formats. By default, any program wanting to use a DBM file can use this module, which will try to inherit a DBM-handling class first from **NDBM_File** (which is also compatible with **ODBM_File**). Then the module tries to inherit its classes in turn from **DB_File**, **GDBM_File**, **SDBM_File** (which is part of the Perl distribution), and finally, **ODBM_File**.

To use, specify the DBM type as **AnyDBM_File** within the **tie** statement:

```
use Fcntl;
use AnyDBM_File;

tie %myhash, "AnyDBM_File", "mydbm", O_RDWR, 0644;
```

You can override the default list and sequence by redefining the contents of the **@ISA** array within the **AnyDBM_File** module:

```
@AnyDBM_File::ISA = qw(GDBM_File ODBM_File);
```

You can also specify your own preference by importing your DBM module directly. This is less portable, but if you are relying on the feature set of a DBM implementation, especially with the special capabilities of **DB_File** and **GDBM_File** in mind, then you may want to use the module directly.

References   Chapter 13; *see also* **DB_File, GDBM_File, NDBM_File, ODBM_File, SDBM_File**

AutoLoader

This module provides a method for automatically loading Perl subroutines from external files that have been split by the **AutoSplit** module. Each subroutine is stored in an individual file within the ./auto directory with the rest of the Perl library modules. For example, the function **Auto::foo** would be in a file ./auto/Auto/foo.al.

```
package Auto;
use Exporter;
use AutoLoader;
@ISA = qw/Exporter AutoLoader/;
```

Any module using the **AutoLoader** should have the special marker _ _**END**_ _ prior to any subroutine declarations. These will be used as the declarations for subroutines to be autoloaded from the corresponding .al files. Any code before the marker will be parsed and imported when the module is first used. Any subroutine declared that is not already in memory will then be loaded from the corresponding file by looking into the ./auto directory tree.

Since the _ _**END**_ _ ends the current scope, you will need to use package globals rather than lexical variables declared with **my**. Either use **our** or use the **vars** pragma to declare them if you are also using the **strict** pragma.

The easiest way to create a module supporting **AutoLoader** is to use the **AutoSplit** module. You may also want to see the **SelfLoader** module, which provides a similar mechanism for loading subroutines.

Also note that this is related to but does not provide the support for the **AUTOLOAD** special subroutine. See Chapter 5 for more information.

References   Chapters 6, 20; *see also* **AutoSplit, SelfLoader, strict, vars**

AutoSplit

This module provides a method for splitting modules into the individual files required by the **AutoLoader** module. This is generally used by the standard Perl library modules, and by the XS and **MakeMaker** systems to split C extensions into individual loadable subroutines. The main function is **autosplit**, and it supports the splitting process in a single hit. The typical use is

```
perl -MAutoSplit -e 'autosplit(FILE, DIR, KEEP, CHECK, MODTIME)'
```

where **FILE** is the module to split, and **DIR** is the base directory into which the file should be split. The **KEEP** argument defines whether existing .al files should be deleted as the module is split. This is the operation when false; if true, files are kept even if the functions do not appear in the new module.

The **CHECK** argument tells **AutoSplit** to check whether the specified module actually includes the **AutoLoader** module. If false, no checks are made. The **MODTIME** argument, if true, only splits the module if its modification time is later than that of the autosplit.ix index file.

Only those functions specified after the _ _**END**_ _ marker are split; other functions are forced to load when the module is imported.

You will be warned if the functions to be split exceed the permitted length for file names on the desired file system. Because of the use of function names as file names, it presents possible naming conflicts that should be resolved. You will also be warned if the directory that you want to split the module into does not exist.

This module is normally only used as part of the **MakeMaker** process.

References   Chapters 20, 25; *see also* **AutoLoader, ExtUtils::MakeMaker**

B

This module is part of the Perl compiler. The compiler uses many of the objects and methods defined within the **B** module and its hierarchy in order to provide the script with the necessary hooks into its own internals. The module does this by providing its own suite of classes, which allow a Perl script to examine its own objects and classes in detail.

```
use B;
```

Although this module provides the information required during the compilation process of a Perl script into a stand-alone executable, use of this module is not required to make a stand-alone program.

The bulk of the **B** module is the methods for accessing the fields of the objects that describe the internal structures. Note that all access is read-only: you cannot modify the internals by using this module.

The **B** module exports a variety of functions: some are simple utility functions; others provide a Perl program with a way to get an initial "handle" on an internal object. These are listed in Table B-1.

Function	Description
main_cv	Returns the (faked) **CV** corresponding to the main part of the Perl program.
main_root	Returns the root opcode of the main part of the Perl program.
main_start	Returns the starting op of the main part of the Perl program.
Comppadlist	Returns the **AV** object of the global comppadlist.
sv_undef	Returns the **SV** object corresponding to the C variable **sv_undef** (the undefined value).
sv_yes	Returns the **SV** object corresponding to the C variable **sv_yes** ("true").
sv_no	Returns the **SV** object corresponding to the C variable **sv_no** ("false").
walkoptree(OP, METHOD)	Does a tree-walk of the syntax tree starting at the opcode referenced by **OP**, calling **METHOD** on each opcode in the tree it visits. Each parent node is visited before its children.
walkoptree_debug(DEBUG)	Returns the current debugging flag for **walkoptree**. If the optional **DEBUG** argument is non-zero, it sets the debugging flag to that value.
walksymtable(SYMREF, METHOD, RECURSE)	Walks the symbol table starting at **SYMREF** and calls **METHOD** on each symbol visited. When the walk reaches package symbols **Foo::**, it invokes **RECURSE** and only recurses into the package if that sub returns true.

Table B-1.   *Functions in the **B** Module*

Function	Description
svref_2object(SV)	Takes any Perl variable and turns it into an object in the appropriate **B::OP**-derived or **B::SV**-derived class.
ppname(OPNUM)	Returns the **PP** function name (for example, **pp_add**) of opcode number **OPNUM**.
hash(STRING)	Returns a string in the form "$0x$...", representing the hexadecimal value of the internal hash function used by Perl on string **STR**.
cast_I32(I)	Casts **I** to the internal **I32** type used by the current Perl interpreter.
minus_c	Does the equivalent of the **–c** command line option.
cstring(STR)	Returns a double-quote–surrounded escaped version of **STR**, which can be used as a string in C source code.
class(OBJECT)	Returns the class of an object without the part of the class name preceding the first **::**.
threadsv_names	In a Perl interpreter compiled for threads, this returns a list of the special per-thread **threadsv** variables.
byteload_fh(FILEHANDLE)	Loads the contents of **FILEHANDLE** as bytecode.

Table B-1.   *Functions in the B Module* (continued)

A more in-depth discussion on the use of the Perl compiler, of which the **B** module is a critical part, can be found in Chapter 19.

References   *See* **O**; Chapter 22

B::Asmdata

This module is used internally by **B::Bytecode** and other modules to generate data about Perl opcodes.

References   *See* **B::Bytecode**, **O**; Chapter 22

B::Assembler

The module used by the **O** Perl compiler interface to assemble Perl bytecode into executable opcodes.

References   *See* **B::Bytecode, O**; Chapter 22

B::Bblock

The module used by the **O** Perl compiler interface to produce a report of the basic blocks that make up a Perl program.

References   *See* **O**; Chapter 22

B::Bytecode

This module provides the necessary code for translating Perl scripts into Perl bytecode as used by the **O** module and the Perl compiler. For example, you can convert any Perl script into bytecode using

```
$ perl -MO=Bytecode foobar.pl
```

References   *See* **O**; Chapter 22

B::C

The basic underlying module used by the Perl compiler that produces raw C code in a nonoptimized format, suitable for compiling into a stand-alone program. For an optimized version, you should use the **B:CC** module. The default operation creates a C file that can be separately compiled:

```
$ perl -MO=C foobar.pl
```

If you want to compile a Perl script directly, then use the **perlcc** command:

```
$ perlcc foobar.pl
```

This will generate a stand-alone application called **foobar**.

References   *See* **O**; Chapter 22

B::CC

This is the optimized interface for creating C code from Perl scripts for compilation into stand-alone applications. For example:

```
$ perl -MO=CC foobar.pl
```

Relatively simple optimizations are supported for the purposes of improving the performance of Perl code into C code.

References *See* **O**; Chapter 22

B::Debug

This module produces a Perl syntax tree, providing debug-level information about the opcodes being used. For example:

```
$ perl -M=Debug
```

For a simpler version, you should try the **B::Terse** compiler interface module.

References *See* **O**; Chapter 22

B::Deparse

An interface used by the Perl compiler and the **O** module that regurgitates a Perl script based on the internal structure used by the Perl interpreter. The source output matches the format of the script after being parsed by the interpreter and may not match the original source script. It is normally used with the **O** module.

```
$ perl -MO=Deparse foobar.pl
```

References *See* **O**; Chapter 22

B::Disassembler

The backend used by the Perl compiler to translate compiled bytecode into raw source code.

References *See* **B::Bytecode**, **O**; Chapter 22

B::Lint

This module expands on the warnings provided by the **–w** switch with additional warnings for some specific statements and constructs in the Perl code. It is used as a backend to the Perl compiler.

```
$ perl -MO=Lint foobar.pl
```

References   *See* **O**; Chapter 22

B::Showlex

A Perl compiler backend, used with the **O** module. The module produces a list of lexical values used within functions and files.

References   *See* **O**; Chapter 22

B::Stackobj

A helper module for the Perl compiler.

References   *See* **O**; Chapter 22

B::Terse

Used with the Perl compiler to provide the syntax tree for a Perl script. Unlike in the **Debug** backend, information about individual opcodes within the tree is kept to a minimum.

```
$ perl -MO=Terse foobar.pl
```

References   *See* **O**; Chapter 22

 # B::Xref

A Perl compiler backend that produces a report detailing and cross-referencing the variables, subroutines, and formats used in a Perl script on a line-by-line and file-by-file basis.

References   *See* **O**; Chapter 22

Benchmark

```
use Benchmark;
```

This module provides a constant and consistent interface to aid in the production of
benchmarking figures. You can use the **Benchmark** module to time the execution of
any Perl statement or function, or even the entire script.

There are three main functions: **timeit**, **timethis**, and **timethese**:

```
timeit(COUNT, 'CODE');
```

times the execution of a single piece of **CODE**, for **COUNT** iterations. Note that **CODE**
is a string containing the code to benchmark. Use the object method shown next to
benchmark an arbitrary piece of code.

For example, the code

```
$t = timeit(1000000,'cos(3.141)');
```

will place the timing information for a million iterations of the calculation into **$t**,
which will be a reference to a **Benchmark** object. See below for more information on
the object interface.

```
timethis(COUNT, 'CODE')
```

uses **timeit** to run a piece of code, also printing a header to state that it is timing a piece
of code and the resulting timing information.

```
timethese(COUNT, CODEHASH)
```

runs **timethis** on multiple pieces of code. Each piece of code should be placed into the
value of a hash element, and the corresponding key will be used as a label for the
reported figures.

Note that in all the preceding cases, the code is embedded into a **for** loop and then
eval'd in its entirety. As such, lexical values declared outside the **eval** block will not be
available within it.

If you want to time arbitrary requests, you need to use the object interface to the module:

```
$ta = new Benchmark;
&render_object();
$tb = new Benchmark;
print "Calculation time: ", timestr(timediff($ta,$tb)), "\n";
```

The **timediff** function returns a new object detailing the time difference between two **Benchmark** objects, and you can then print a string of the time difference information with **timestr**.

In all cases, the times reported use the **times** function, so both CPU and user times are reported. The CPU time is the most important, since it should not be affected by other processes. Because it uses the **times** function, measurements are in milliseconds. You should aim to support enough iterations for a reasonable timing figure. Times of at least five seconds are advised; ten seconds or more may give a more precise figure.

References   Chapters 11, 21

Carp

This module provides a simplified method for reporting errors within modules. A **die** call from a package will report an error with reference to the package file in which it was called. This can cause problems if you are trying to trace errors in a calling script. The **Carp** module provides three functions: **carp**, **croak**, and **confess**. With each function, the location of the error is specified relative to the package that called the function.

```
carp "Didn't work";
```

Equivalent of **warn**, reports an error to **stderr**.

```
croak "Definitely didn't work";
```

Equivalent of **die**.

```
confess "Failed around about there";
```

This is equivalent to **croak** except that a stack trace is printed.

For example, imagine that you have a package called **T**, used in a script called **tm.pl**. The package defines a single function, **only**, which calls **warn** and **carp**; the result is

```
Warning! at T.pm line 11.
Carp warning! at tm.pl line 3
```

You can see from this that the first message, using **warn**, reports the error with reference to the module. The second, using **carp**, reports an error with reference to the original script in which it was called.

The reference is obtained using **caller** and goes up exactly one level; so if another package calls a **carp**-using function, the error will be reported with reference to the calling package.

Reference Appendix A

CGI

This module provides a set of functions for drawing HTML pages, and for both creating HTML forms and post-processing them using the CGI interface.

```
use CGI;
```

The module's primary use is for producing web forms, and parsing their contents once the information has been filled in and returned by a client. The module defines a simple CGI class that can be used to build the pages, although use of the class methods is not exclusive; they can be used as normal functions as well.

For example, to create a "Hello World!" page using the object method:

```
use CGI;
$page = new CGI;
print $page->header,
    $page->start_html('Hello World!'),
    $page->h1('Hello World!'),
    $page->end_html;
```

You can achieve the same result with the functional interface as follows:

```
use CGI qw/:standard/;

print header,
    start_html('Hello World!'),
    h1('Hello World!'),
    end_html;
```

The module provides three main elements: the HTTP header, HTML-formatted text, and a parsing engine for accepting input from browsers and forms using the various request methods available. In addition, it supports frames, cascading style sheets, cookies, and server-push technologies. Refer to Chapter 15 for more information on the use of the **CGI** module when writing HTML/CGI scripts.

Import Sets

The module supports the import sets shown in Table B-2.

Reference   Chapter 18

Import Set	Exported Symbols/Symbol Sets
html2	h1 h2 h3 h4 h5 h6 p br hr ol ul li dl dt dd menu code var strong em tt u i b blockquote pre img a address cite samp dfn html head base body Link nextid title meta kbd start_html end_html input Select option comment
html3	div table caption th td TR Tr sup sub strike applet Param embed basefont style span layer ilayer font frameset frame script small big
netscape	blink fontsize center
form	textfield textarea filefield password_field hidden checkbox checkbox_group submit reset defaults radio_group popup_menu button autoEscape scrolling_list image_button start_form end_form startform endform start_multipart_form isindex tmpFileName uploadInfo URL_ENCODED MULTIPART
cgi	param path_info path_translated url self_url script_name cookie dump raw_cookie request_method query_string accept user_agent remote_host remote_addr referer server_name server_software server_port server_protocol virtual_host remote_ident auth_type http use_named_parameters save_parameters restore_parameters param_fetch remote_user user_name header redirect import_names put Delete Delete_all url_param

Table B-2.   *Import Sets for the **CGI** Module*

Import Set	Exported Symbols/Symbol Sets
ssl	https
cgi-lib	ReadParse PrintHeader HtmlTop HtmlBot SplitParam
html	html2 html3 netscape
standard	html2 html3 form cgi
push	multipart_init multipart_start multipart_end
all	html2 html3 netscape form cgi internal

Table B-2. *Import Sets for the **CGI** Module* (continued)

CGI::Apache

This module supports the use of the **CGI** module when used within the confines of the Perl-Apache API, as supported by the **mod_perl** CPAN module.

```
require CGI::Apache;

my $query = new Apache::CGI;
$query->print($query->header);
```

The module provides a slightly modified interface in order to allow the **CGI** module to work when executing scripts with the Perl-Apache API environment. This imports, and also overrides, some of the methods defined by the **CGI** module.

References *See* **CGI, CGI::Switch**

CGI::Switch

This module attempts to load **CGI** constructors from different modules until it successfully loads one.

```
use CGI::Switch;
```

The default packages it attempts to load, in order, are **Apache::CGI**, **CGI::XA**, and **CGI**. You can define a different order or a different selection of modules by specifying them explicitly:

```
use CGI::Switch qw/CGI CGI::Apache/;
```

A call to the **new** method in **CGI::Switch** will return an object of the first found type:

```
$query = new CGI::Switch;
```

Reference   *See* **CGI**

Class::Struct

This module supports the construction of **struct**-like data types as Perl classes.

```
use Class::Struct;
```

It supports only one function, **struct**, which builds a new class based on the information you supply. The new class can be made up of multiple elements composed of scalars, arrays, hashes, and further class definitions. This is primarily used for designing or emulating C **struct** structures within Perl. The function has three forms:

```
struct(CLASS_NAME => [ ELEMENT_LIST ]);
struct(CLASS_NAME => { ELEMENT_LIST });
struct(ELEMENT_LIST);
```

The first two forms explicitly define the new class to be created, and the third form assumes the current package name as the new class. The first form creates an array-based class, which is fast; the second and third create a hash-based class, which is slower but more flexible and practical.

The newly created class must not be a subclass of anything other than **UNIVERSAL**. This is because it will inherit methods, including **new**, from its base class, which will override the methods generated by **struct**.

The **ELEMENT _LIST** argument has the format of a typical hash assignation:

```
NAME => TYPE
```

The **NAME** is the name of each element in the new class, and **TYPE** is one of '**$**', '**@**', or '**%**', to create a new scalar, array, or hash entry; or it can be the name of another class.

For example, to create a Perl version of the **hostent** structure:

```
struct('hostent' => {
                    'h_name' => '$',
                    'h_aliases' => '@',
                    'h_addrtype' => '$',
                    'h_length' => '$',
                    'h_addr_list' => '@',
                });
```

The name of the new class is **hostent**, but you need to create a new object in order to make use of it; **struct** merely constructs the class definition. Thus,

```
$host = new hostent;
```

will create a new **hostent** structure.

Using Scalar Elements

The scalar is initialized with **undef**. To access the scalar:

```
$obj->scalar
```

To set the value of the scalar:

```
$obj->scalar(value)
```

When defined, if the element type is stated as '**$**', then the element value is returned. If it is defined as '***$**', then a reference to the scalar element is returned.

Using Array Elements

The array is initialized as an empty list. To access the entire array:

```
$obj->array
```

Note that because there is no leading @ sign, you will need to use block notation to use the array in its entirety with many functions, for example,

```
sort @{$obj->array};
```

To access an element from the array,

```
$obj->array(index)
```

where **index** is the numerical index within the array.

To set a value in the array,

```
$obj->scalar(index, value)
```

where **index** is the numerical index within the array, and **value** is the value to be assigned.

When defined, if the element type is stated as '@', then the element value is returned. If it is defined as '*@', then a reference to the element is returned.

Using Hash Elements

The hash is initialized as an empty list. To access the entire hash:

```
$obj->array
```

Note that because there is no leading @ sign, you will need to use block notation to use the array in its entirety with many functions, for example,

```
sort @{$obj->array};
```

To access an element from the hash,

```
$obj->array(key)
```

where **key** is the string value.

To set a value in the hash,

```
$obj->scalar(key, value)
```

where **key** is the string index within the array, and **value** is the value to be assigned. When defined, if the element type is stated as '%', then the element value is returned. If it is defined as '*%', then a reference to the element is returned.

Using Class Elements

The element's value must be a reference blessed to the named class or to one of its subclasses. The assigned class can have methods and structures and can be used like any other method, albeit within the confines of the class created by **struct**. The main use for this element is to support nested data structures within a **Class::Struct** created class.

Example

The code that follows builds on the **hostent** structure and populates it with the correct information for the host given.

```
use Class::Struct;
use Socket;

struct('hostent' => {
    'h_name' => '$',
    'h_aliases' => '@',
    'h_addrtype' => '$',
    'h_length' => '$',
    'h_addr_list' => '@',
});

($name, $aliases, $addrtype, $length, @addresses) = gethostbyname($hostname);

my $host = new hostent;

$host->h_name($name);

@aliases = split / /, $aliases;
foreach($i=0;$i<@aliases;$i++)
{
    $host->h_aliases($i, $aliases[$i]);
}
$host->h_addrtype($addrtype);
$host->h_length($length);

for($i=0;$i<@addresses;$i++)
{
    $host->h_addr_list($i,inet_ntoa($addresses[$i]));
}
```

References   Chapters 7, 10

Config

This module provides an interface to the configuration information determined during the build process.

```
use Config;
```

The module exports a single hash, **%Config**, which can be used to access individual configuration parameters by name, for example,

```
print "Built with: $Config{'cc'} $Config{'ccflags'}\n";
```

You can also optionally import the **myconfig**, **config_sh**, and **config_vars** functions:

```
myconfig
```

This returns a text summary of the main Perl configuration values. This is the method used by the **-V** command line option.

```
config_sh
```

This returns the entire set of Perl configuration information in the form of the config.sh file used during the building process.

```
config_vars(LIST)
```

sends the configuration values for the names specified in **LIST** to **STDOUT**. The information is printed as you would output the values in a simple loop. Thus, the code

```
use Config qw/config_vars/;

config_vars(qw/cc ccflags ldflags/);
```

outputs

```
cc='gcc -B/usr/ccs/bin/';
ccflags='-I/usr/local/include';
ldflags=' -L/usr/local/lib';
```

The information contained in the **Config** module is determined during the build process. Since this module could be modified and/or overwritten or copied, the actual configuration information may not match the binary you are currently using.

References   Chapters 20, 24, 25; *see also* **ExtUtils::MakeMaker**

CPAN

This module provides a simple, and programmable, interface for downloading and installing modules from the CPAN archives. The module takes into account the requirements of the module you are downloading, automatically including the required modules during the installation process. The module makes use of the **Net::FTP** or **LWP** modules if they are available, or it uses the **lynx** web browser and even an external **ftp** client to download the information and modules it needs.

The **CPAN** module, therefore, takes out a lot of the manual work required when downloading and installing a **CPAN** module. It is, in fact, the best way to download **CPAN** modules, as it guarantees that you will get the latest version while also ensuring that any required modules will be downloaded and installed.

It works in one of two ways: either within an interactive shell, which is invoked like this:

```
$ perl -MCPAN -e shell;
```

or via a Perl script:

```
use CPAN;
```

Interactive Shell Interface

The shell interface, also known as interactive mode, puts Perl into a simple shell-style interface using the readline line input system. The first time the shell interface is run, you will go through a configuration process that sets up your environment for using the **CPAN** module. This includes configuration of the internal system used to access raw data from the Internet, your preferred download location, and proxy information.

The shell interface supports the commands listed in Table B-3. You can use the shell to query the CPAN archives and also to download and install modules.

To install a module with the interactive shell, the easiest method is to use the **install** command:

```
$ perl -MCPAN -e shell
cpan> install Nice
```

Command	Argument	Description
a	EXPR	Searches authors. **EXPR** should be a simple string, in which case a search will be made for an exact match with the author's ID. Alternatively, you can supply a regular expression that will search for matching author IDs and name details.
b		Displays a list of bundles.
d	EXPR	Performs a regular expression search for a package/module.
m	EXPR	Displays information about the expression matching **EXPR**.
i	EXPR	Displays information about a module, bundle, or user specified in **EXPR**.
r	EXPR	Displays a list of reinstallation recommendations, comparing the existing module list against installed modules and versions. If **EXPR** is not specified, lists all recommendations.
u	EXPR	Lists all modules not currently installed, but available on CPAN.
make	EXPR	Downloads the module specified in **EXPR**, builds it, and installs it. No check is performed to ensure that you need to install the module; it just does it. Use **install** if you want to update a module according to its version number.
test	EXPR	Runs **make test** on the module specified in **EXPR**.
install	EXPR	Downloads and installs the module specified in **EXPR**. Runs **make install**. If **EXPR** is a module, it checks to see if the currently installed version of the module specified in **EXPR** is lower than that available on CPAN. If it is, it downloads, builds, and installs it. If **EXPR** is a distribution file, then the file is processed without any version checking.
clean	EXPR	Runs a **make clean** on the specified module.

Table B-3. *Commands for the Interactive Shell*

Command	Argument	Description
force	**make** | **test** | **install EXPR**	Forces a **make**, **test**, or **install** on a command within the current session. Normally, modules are not rebuilt or installed within the current session.
readme		Displays the README file.
reload	**index** | **cpan**	Loads the most recent CPAN index files, or the latest version of the **CPAN** module.
h | **?**		Displays the help menu.
o		Gets and sets the various configuration options for the **CPAN** module.
!	**EXPR**	Evaluates the Perl expression **EXPR**.
q		Quits the interactive shell.

Table B-3. *Commands for the Interactive Shell* (continued)

To install a CPAN bundle:

```
cpan> install Bundle::LWP
Fetching with Net::FTP:
  ftp://ftp.demon.co.uk/pub/mirrors/perl/CPAN/authors/id/GAAS/
  libwww-perl-5.42.tar.gz

  CPAN: MD5 security checks disabled because MD5 not installed.
  Please consider installing the MD5 module.

x libwww-perl-5.42/, 0 bytes, 0 tape blocks
x libwww-perl-5.42/t/, 0 bytes, 0 tape blocks
x libwww-perl-5.42/t/net/, 0 bytes, 0 tape blocks
x libwww-perl-5.42/t/net/cgi-bin/, 0 bytes, 0 tape blocks
x libwww-perl-5.42/t/net/cgi-bin/test, 526 bytes, 2 tape blocks
...
```

In addition to the commands in Table B-3, the interactive shell supports two commands that should only be used by experienced users: **autobundle** and **recompile**.

The **autobundle** function writes a bundle file into the **$CPAN::Config->{cpan_ home}/Bundle** directory. The new bundle contains all of the modules currently installed in the current Perl environment that are also available from CPAN. You can then use this file as the source for installing the same bundle of modules on a number of machines.

The **recompile** function forces the reinstallation of all the installed modules that make use of the XS extension system. This solves problems when an update to the operating system breaks binary compatibility. The function will re-download the necessary modules and rebuild them under the updated environment.

Programmable Interface

Depending on what you are trying to achieve, you might find the programmable interface to be more useful. All of the commands available in the interactive shell are also available as **CPAN::Shell** methods within any Perl script. The methods take the same arguments as their shell interface equivalents.

The **CPAN** module works with a series of subclasses for handling information about authors, bundles, modules, and distributions. The classes are **CPAN::Author**, **CPAN::Bundle**, **CPAN::Module**, and **CPAN::Distribution**. Individual methods are identical to those outlined in the shell in Table B-3.

The core of the system is still the **CPAN::Shell** module. Individual methods are identical to their command equivalents; but instead of outputting a list to **STDOUT**, the methods return a list of suitable IDs for the corresponding entity type. This allows you to combine individual methods into entire statements—something not available in the shell. For example,

```
$ perl -MCPAN -e 'CPAN::Shell->install(CPAN::Shell->r)'
```

will reinstall all of the outdated modules currently installed.

The **CPAN::Shell** module also supports a further function, **expand**:

```
expand(TYPE, LIST)
```

This returns an array of **CPAN::Module** objects expanded according to their correct type. The **LIST** is the list of entries to expand. For example, you can expand and install a number of modules at once, using

```
for $module (qw/Bundle::libnet Bundle::LWP/)
{
    my $object = CPAN::Shell->expand('Module',$module);
    $object->install;
}
```

References   Chapter 2, Web Appendix B (**www.osborne.com**)

CPAN::FirstTime

This is a utility for configuring the **CPAN** module:

```
CPAN::FirstTime::init();
```

The **init** function asks some simple questions about the current environment and updates the **CPAN::Config** file that will be used by the **CPAN** module when downloading and building extensions.

Reference   *See* **CPAN**

CPAN::Nox

This module supports the normal **CPAN** functionality but avoids the use of XS extensions during execution.

```
$ perl -MCPAN::Nox -e shell
```

This is intended for use when the binary compatibility has been broken between the Perl binary and the extensions. The preceding command puts you into the familiar **CPAN** interactive state.

Reference   *See* **CPAN**

Cwd

This module provides a platform-independent interface for discovering the current working directory. The module provides three functions:

```
use Cwd;
$dir = cwd();
$dir = getcwd();
$dir = fastcwd();
```

The **cwd** function provides the safest method for discovering the current working directory. The **getcwd** function uses the **getcwd()** or **getwd()** C functions, if they are available on your platform.

The **fastcwd** function is a much faster version and can be used in situations in which speed may be of great importance. However, it is not a reliable method and may mistakenly indicate that you can **chdir** out of a directory that you cannot change back into. As such, it shouldn't be relied on.

The **Cwd** module also optionally provides a replacement for the CORE **chdir** function that updates the value of the **PWD** environment variable:

```
use Cwd qw/chdir/;
chdir('/usr/local');
print $ENV{PWD};
```

References   Chapter 8; *see also* **File::Spec**

Data::Dumper

This module provides methods for resolving a data structure (including objects) into a string format that can be used both to "dump" the data for printing and to make an evaluation so that a dumped structure can be reconstituted with **eval** into a valid internal structure.

```
use Data::Dumper;
```

The primary function is **Dumper**:

```
Dumper(LIST)
```

This function accepts a list of scalar references to data structures or objects. The return value is a string representation of the structure, produced in normal string syntax format. For example:

```
use Data::Dumper;

my $ref = { "Name" => "Martin",
            "Size" => "Medium",
            "Dates" => { "Monday" => "170599",
                         "Tuesday" => "180599"
                       }
          };

print Dumper($ref);
```

generates the following:

```
$VAR1 = {
          'Dates' => {
                        'Monday' => 170599,
                        'Tuesday' => 180599
                     },
          'Name' => 'Martin',
          'Size' => 'Medium'
        };
```

Note that references to anonymous variables are labeled with **$VARn**, where **n** is a sequential number relating to the references as they were supplied.

References   See Chapters 10, 13

DB_File

This module provides access to the Berkeley DB system—probably the most flexible implementation of the DBM database system. Beyond the basic capabilities of supporting a hash-style database, **DB_File** also provides the necessary functions and methods for accessing the database structures, and for creating and managing B-Tree structures. The Berkeley DB system also supports a system based on fixed- and variable-length record numbers, which is supported within Perl as a hash using numerical rather than string references.

```
use DB_File ;

[$X =] tie %hash,  'DB_File', [FILENAME, FLAGS, MODE, $DB_HASH] ;
[$X =] tie %hash,  'DB_File', FILENAME, FLAGS, MODE, $DB_BTREE ;
[$X =] tie @array, 'DB_File', FILENAME, FLAGS, MODE, $DB_RECNO ;

# Methods for Hash databases
$status = $X->del(KEY [, FLAGS]);
$status = $X->put(KEY, VALUE [, FLAGS]);
$status = $X->get(KEY, VALUE [, FLAGS]);
$status = $X->seq(KEY, VALUE, FLAGS) ;
$status = $X->sync([FLAGS]);
$status = $X->fd;
```

```
# Methods for BTree databases
$count = $X->get_dup(KEY);
@list  = $X->get_dup(KEY);
%list  = $X->get_dup(KEY, 1);

# Methods for Record Number databases
$a = $X->length;
$a = $X->pop;
$X->push(LIST);
$a = $X->shift;
$X->unshift(LIST);


untie %hash;
untie @array;
```

The different database types are defined in the last argument to the **tie** function, using **DB_HASH** for hashes, **DB_BTREE** for binary trees, and **DB_RECNO** for the record number database.

A **DB_HASH** is identical in most respects to Perl's internal hash structure, except that the key/data pairs are stored in data files, not memory. The functionality provided is basically identical to that provided by the other DBM-style database engines. **DB_File** uses its own hashing algorithm for storing and retrieving the key/data pairs, but you can supply your own system if you prefer.

The **DB_BTREE** format follows the same key/data pair structure, but the pairs are stored in a sorted, balanced binary tree. By default, the keys are sorted in lexical order, although you can supply your own comparison routine for use by the binary sorting subsystem.

DB_RECNO supports the storage of fixed- and variable-length records in a flat text using the same key/value hash interface. This may be more suitable to your requirements than using the DBI toolkit, covered later in this appendix. In order to make the record numbers more compatible with the array system employed by Perl, the offset starts at zero rather than one (as in the Berkeley DB).

You can also create an in-memory database (which is held entirely within memory, just like a standard hash) by specifying a NULL file name (use **undef**). You can use any of the database types for the in-memory database.

References Chapter 13; *see also* **AnyDBM_File, GDBM_File, NDBM_File, ODBM_File, SDBM_File**

APPENDIXES

Devel::SelfStubber

This module generates subroutine stubs for use with modules that employ the **SelfLoader** module.

```
use Devel::SelfStubber;

Devel::SelfStubber->stub(MODULE, LIBDIR);
```

It analyzes the module specified in **MODULE** (which should be specified as if it were being imported). The **LIBDIR** argument specifies the directory to search for the module; if it is left as a blank string, the current directory is used.

The generated output displays the list of subroutine stubs you need to put before the __DATA__ token in order to support autoloading via the **SelfLoader** module. The stub also ensures that if a method is called, it will get loaded according to the classes and normal inheritance rules, taking into account the effects of autoloading in the inherited modules and classes.

The basic method only produces a list of the correct stubs. To output a complete version of the whole module with the stubs inserted correctly, you need to set the value of the **$Devel::SelfStubber::JUST_STUBS** to zero. For example:

```
use Devel::SelfStubber;

$Devel::SelfStubber::JUST_STUBS = 0;
Devel::SelfStubber->stub(MODULE, LIBDIR);
```

The module uses the **SelfLoader** module to generate its list of stub subroutines, and so can be useful if you want to verify what the **SelfLoader** thinks the list of stubs should be.

References   *See* **SelfLoader**

DirHandle

This module supplies an object/method-based interface for directory handles.

```
use DirHandle;
```

It provides an object interface to the directory handle functions **opendir**, **readdir**, **closedir**, and **rewinddir**:

```
$dir = new DirHandle '.';
```

The only argument to the **new** method is the directory to be read, as specified in the **opendir** function. The supported methods then work in a manner identical to their functional equivalents, except that they are known as **open**, **read**, **close**, and **rewind**.

References   Chapter 8, Appendix A

DynaLoader

This module supports the dynamic loading of C libraries into Perl code.

```
package MyPackage;
require DynaLoader;
@ISA = qw/DynaLoader/;

bootstrap MyPackage;
```

It provides a generic interface to the various dynamic linking mechanisms available on the different platforms. This is primarily used with the XS extension system to load external C libraries and functions into the consciousness of the Perl interpreter. The **DynaLoader** module is designed to be easy to use from the user's point of view, in that using a module should be easy, even though the module itself may involve more complex processes to load the module.

In order to make use of the system within your own module, you only need to supply the information just described, which will work whether your module is statically or dynamically linked. The Perl and C functions that need to be called in order to load the dynamic modules are automatically produced for you during the compilation of an XS interface.

The internal interface for communicating with the lower-level dynamic loading systems supported under SunOS/Solaris, HP-UX, Linux, VMS, Windows, and others is high level and generic enough to cover the requirements of nearly all platforms. However, the **DynaLoader** does not produce its own glue code between Perl and C—you must use the XS, SWIG, or other systems for that purpose.

Please refer to the **DynaLoader** man page for details on how to use the internal interface.

References   Chapter 6; *see* also **AutoLoader, SelfLoader**

English

This module produces a set of aliases that provide full text versions of the standard variables. These match those available in **awk**, and may also make more sense to most users. See Table B-4.

Reference   Chapter 4

Perl	English
$_	$ARG
$&	$MATCH
$`	$PREMATCH
$'	$POSTMATCH
$+	$LAST_PARENT_MATCH
@+	@LAST_MATCHED
@–	@LAST_MATCH_START
$.	$NR $INPUT_LINE_NUMBER
$/	$RS $INPUT_RECORD_SEPARATOR
$|	$AUTOFLUSH $OUTPUT_AUTOFLUSH
$,	$OFS $OUTPUT_FIELD_SEPARATOR
$\	$ORS $OUTPUT_RECORD_SEPARATOR
$"	$LIST_SEPARATOR
$;	$SUBSEP $SUBSCRIPT_SEPARATOR
$%	$FORMAT_PAGE_NUMBER
$=	$FORMAT_LINES_PER_PAGE
$–	$FORMAT_LINES_LEFT
$~	$FORMAT_NAME
$^	$FORMAT_TOP_NAME
$:	$FORMAT_LINE_BREAK_CHARACTERS

Table B-4. *Perl and English Variable Names*

Perl	English
$^L	$FORMAT_FORMFEED
@_	@ARG
$^A	$ACCUMULATOR
$?	$CHILD_ERROR
$^C	$COMPILING
$^D	$DEBUGGING
$!	$ERRNO $OS_ERROR
%!	%ERRNO %OS_ERROR
$^E	$EXTENDED_OS_ERROR
$@	$EVAL_ERROR
$$	$PID $PROCESS_ID
$<	$UID $REAL_USER_ID
$>	$EUID $EFFECTIVE_USER_ID
$(	$GID $REAL_GROUP_ID
$)	$EGID $EFFECTIVE_GROUP_ID
$0	$PROGRAM_NAME
$]	$OLD_PERL_VERSION
$^F	$SYSTEM_FD_MAX
$^O	$OSNAME
$^P	$PERLDB

Table B-4. *Perl and English Variable Names* (continued)

Perl	English
$^R	$LAST_REGEXP_CODE_RESULT
$^S	$EXCEPTIONS_BEING_CAUGHT
$^T	$BASETIME
$^V	$PERL_VERSION
$^W	$WARNING
$^X	$EXECUTABLE_NAME

Table B-4. *Perl and English Variable Names* (continued)

Env

This module imports environment variables into the current package as real scalars, rather than forcing you to use the **%ENV** hash. To import all the variables defined within the **%ENV** hash, just import the whole module:

```
use Env;
```

To import specific environment variables, specify them during the import:

```
use Env qw/PATH/;
```

You can now use and update **$PATH** as if it were **$ENV{PATH}**.

The internal method for supporting this is actually to tie scalar values to the **%ENV** hash. The tie remains in place until the script exits, or until you remove a tied variable with **undef**:

```
undef $PATH;
```

References   Chapters 7, 11, 14, 15

Errno

This module defines and exports the constants defined in errno.h for error numbers on your system.

```
use Errno;
```

Importing this module has the added effect of exporting %!. This allows you to access $!{} as a hash element, retaining the look and feel of the special $! variable. Each key of the hash is one of the exported error numbers. When an error occurs, the corresponding error(s) that occurred have a non-zero value. Thus, you can do more complex error trapping and management by identifying and handling individual error types.

Exporter

This module implements the default import method for modules.

```
package MyModule;
use Exporter;
@ISA = qw/Exporter/;
```

It implements a default **import** method that is called during the **use** statement. Although it is possible for any module to define its own **import** method, this module supplies a sample **import** method that can be inherited by your module to enable you to export symbols to the calling script.

The **Exporter** module and the supplied **import** method use the **@EXPORT**, **@EXPORT_OK**, and **%EXPORT_TAGS** variables to select which symbols to import. The symbols in **@EXPORT** are exported by default, and the symbols in **@EXPORT_OK** only when specifically requested. The **%EXPORT_TAGS** hash defines a number of import sets that can be used to import a named set of symbols at one time.

For example, if the module defines the following variables,

```
@EXPORT       = qw/A B C D E F/;
@EXPORT_OK    = qw/G H I J K L/;
%EXPORT_TAGS = (FIRST => [qw/D E F/],
                SECOND => [qw/J K L/]
                );
```

then you can use the following constructs in a calling script:

```
use MyModule;                      # Imports all of @EXPORT
use MyModule qw/G H/               # Only symbols G and H
use MyModule qw/:DEFAULT/;         # All the symbols in @EXPORT
use MyModule qw/:FIRST A B C/;     # The symbols in group FIRST and A B C
use MyModule qw(/^[ACGH]/);        # Only the symbols matching the regex
use MyModule qw/!:FIRST/;          # Only A B C
```

A leading colon indicates that you want to load the symbols defined in the specified group, as defined by **%EXPORT_TAGS**. Note that the symbols exported here must appear either in **@EXPORT** or **@EXPORT_OK**.

A leading exclamation mark indicates that you want to delete the specified symbols from the import list. If such a definition is the first in the import list, then it assumes you want to import the **:DEFAULT** set.

A // regular expression imports the symbols defined in **@EXPORT** and **@EXPORT_OK** according to the regular expression.

You can display the list of symbols to be imported as they are determined by setting the value of **$Exporter::Verbose** to true. You'll need to do this in a **BEGIN** block:

```
BEGIN { $Exporter::Verbose = 1 }
```

Unknown Symbols

You can prevent certain symbols from being exported. You should place the names of symbols that should not be listed into the **@EXPORT_FAIL** array. Any attempt to import any of these symbols will call the **export_fail** method (in the host module) with a list of failed symbols.

If **export_fail** returns an empty list, no error is recorded and the requested symbols are exported. If the list is not empty, an error is generated for each return symbol and the export fails. The default **export_fail** method supported by **Exporter** just returns the list of symbols supplied to it.

Tag-Handling Functions

You can modify the contents of the **@EXPORT_OK** and **@EXPORT** arrays using the tag sets defined by the **%EXPORT_TAGS** hash, and the **Exporter::export_tags** and **Exporter::export_ok_tags** methods.

For example, consider our original example, in which you could have built the contents of **@EXPORT** and **@EXPORT_OK** using

```
@EXPORT      = qw/A B C/;
@EXPORT_OK   = qw/G H I/;
%EXPORT_TAGS = (FIRST  => [qw/D E F/],
                SECOND => [qw/J K L/]
                );
Exporter::export_tags('FIRST');
Exporter::export_ok_tags('SECOND');
```

This would populate the arrays with your original values, without requiring you to specify the symbols explicitly. Any names not matching a tag defined in **%EXPORT_TAGS** will raise a warning when the **–w** command line switch is enabled.

Version Checking

The **require_version** method validates that the module being loaded is of a value equal to or greater than the supplied value. The **Exporter** module supplies this method for you, or you can define your own. In the case of the **Exporter** version, it uses the value of the **$VERSION** variable in the exporting module.

Note that the comparison made is numeric, so version 1.10 will be treated as a lower version than 1.9. You should, therefore, use an explicit two-digit (or more) format for the version number, for example, 1.09.

Reference   Chapter 7

ExtUtils::Command

This function is used under Win32 implementations to provide suitable replacements for core Unix commands used by the extension development process. You should not need to use this module directly, but it defines the following functions/commands:

```
cat
eqtime src dst
rm_f files....
touch files ...
mv source... destination
cp source... destination
chmod mode files...
mkpath directory...
test_f file
```

APPENDIXES

ExtUtils::Embed

This module provides the necessary command line options and other information for use when you are embedding a Perl interpreter into an application. It supports the following functions.

    xsinit

generates code for the XS initializer function.

    ldopts

generates command line options for linking Perl to an application.

    ccopts

generates command line options for compiling embedded Perl programs.

    perl_inc

generates the command line options for including Perl headers.

    ccflags

outputs the contents of the **$Config{ccflags}** hash element.

    ccdlflags

outputs the contents of the **$Config{ccdlflags}** hash element

    xsi_header

outputs the string defining the **EXTERN_C** macro used by perlmain.c and includes statements to include perl.h and EXTERN.h.

    xsi_protos(LIST)

outputs the corresponding **boot_MODULE** prototypes for the modules specified in **LIST**.

```
xsi_body(LIST)
```

returns a list of the calls to **newXS** that glue each module **bootstrap** function to the **boot_MODULE** function for each module specified in **LIST**.

References   Chapter 25; *see also* **Config, ExtUtils::MakeMaker**

ExtUtils::Install

This module defines two functions: **install** and **uninstall**. These are used during the installation process by the **MakeMaker** system to install files into the destination directory.

ExtUtils::Installed

This module defines a suite of functions that can be used to query the contents of the .packlist files generated during module installation. If you call the **new** function, it constructs the internal lists by examining the .packlist files. The **modules** function returns a list of all the modules currently installed. The **files** and **directories** both accept a single argument—the name of a module. The result is a list of all the files installed by the package. The **directory_tree** function reports information for all the related directories. In all cases, you can specify **Perl** to get information pertaining to the core Perl installation.

The **validate** function checks that the files listed in .packlist actually exist. The **packlist** function returns an object as defined by **ExtUtils::Packlist** for the specified module. Finally, **version** returns the version number of the specified module.

ExtUtils::Liblist

This module defines the libraries to be used when building extension libraries and other Perl-based binaries. The information provided here broaches much of the complexity involved in getting an extension to work across many platforms; the bulk of the code relates to the information required for individual platforms.

ExtUtils::MakeMaker

The **MakeMaker** package provides a Perl-based system for producing standard **make** files suitable for installing Perl applications and, more specifically, Perl extensions.

Reference   Chapter 25

ExtUtils::Manifest

This module provides the functions that produce, test, and update the MANIFEST file. Five of the functions are the most useful, beginning with **mkmanifest**, which creates a file based on the current directory contents. The **maincheck** function verifies the current directory contents against the MANIFEST file, while **filecheck** looks for files in the current directory that are not specified in the MANIFEST. Both **maincheck** and **filecheck** are executed by the **fullcheck** function, and **skipcheck** lists the files in the MAINFEST.SKIP file.

ExtUtils::Miniperl

This module provides the list of base libraries and extensions that should be included when building the **miniperl** binary.

ExtUtils::Mkbootstrap

This module makes a bootstrap file suitable for the **DynaLoader** module.

ExtUtils::Mksymlists

This module produces the list of options for creating a dynamic link library.

ExtUtils::MM_OS2

MakeMaker specifics for the OS/2 operating system are produced by this module.

ExtUtils::MM_Unix

MakeMaker specifics for the Unix platform are produced by this module. It also includes many of the core functions used by the main **MakeMaker** module irrespective of the host platform.

ExtUtils::MM_VMS

This module produces **MakeMaker** specifics for VMS.

ExtUtils::MM_Win32

This module produces **MakeMaker** specifics for Windows 95/98/NT.

ExtUtils::Packlist

This module supplies the **Packlist** object used by the **ExtUtils::Installed** module.

Reference   *See* **ExtUtils::Installed**

Fatal

This module provides a system for overriding functions that normally provide a true or false return value so that they instead fail (using **die**) when they would normally return false. For example,

```
use Fatal qw/open/;
```

overrides **open** so that a failure will call **die** automatically and raise an exception that can be caught with a suitable **$SIG{__DIE__}** handler. This allows you to bypass the normal checking that you would conduct on each call to **open**, and instead install a global handler for all **open** calls.

To trap your own calls:

```
sub mightfail {};
import Fatal 'mightfail';
```

Note that you cannot override the **exec** and **system** calls.

Reference   Chapter 9

Fcntl

This module supplies the constants that are available as standard within the fcntl.h file in C. This supplies all the constants directly as functions—the same as other modules. This information is gleaned during the installation and build process of Perl and should be correct for your operating system, supporting a compatible set of constants.

The module exports the following constants by default. The exact list will vary from system to system; this list comes from MacPerl 5.2.0r4:

```
F_DUPFD F_GETFD F_GETLK F_SETFD F_GETFL F_SETFL F_SETLK F_SETLKW
FD_CLOEXEC F_RDLCK F_UNLCK F_WRLCK
O_CREAT O_EXCL O_NOCTTY O_TRUNC
O_APPEND O_NONBLOCK
O_NDELAY O_DEFER
O_RDONLY O_RDWR O_WRONLY
O_EXLOCK O_SHLOCK O_ASYNC O_DSYNC O_RSYNC O_SYNC
F_SETOWN F_GETOWN
O_ALIAS O_RSRC
```

The following symbols are available, either individually or via the **flock** group:

```
LOCK_SH LOCK_EX LOCK_NB LOCK_UN
```

To import this group:

```
use Fcntl qw/:flock/;
```

Reference   Chapter 8

FileCache

This module enables you to keep more files open than the system permits.

```
use FileCache;
```

It remembers a list of valid pathnames that you know you will want to write to, and opens and closes the files as necessary to stay within the maximum number of open files supported on your machine. To add a path to the list, you call the **cacheout** function:

```
cacheout $path;
```

FileHandle

This module supports an object-based interface for using filehandles.

```
use FileHandle;
```

The **new** method creates a new **FileHandle** object, returning it to the caller. Any supplied arguments are passed on directly to the **open** method. If the **open** fails, the object is destroyed and **undef** is returned. The newly created object is a reference to a newly created symbol as supported by the **Symbol** module.

```
$fh = new FileHandle;
```

Alternatively, you can use the **new_from_fd** method to create a new **FileHandle** object. It requires two parameters that are passed to **FileHandle::fdopen**.

The **open** method attaches a file to the new filehandle:

```
$fh->method(FILE [, MODE [, PERMS]])
```

The **open** method supports the options as the built-in **open** function. The first parameter is the file name. If supplied on its own, you can use the normal **open** formats such as > or >>, and then it uses the normal **open** function.

If you supply a **MODE** in the format of the **POSIX fopen()** function—for example, "w" or "w+"—then the built-in **open** function is also used. If given a numeric **MODE**, then the built-in **sysopen** function is used instead. The module automatically imports the **O_*** constants from **Fcntl** if they are available.

The **fdopen** method is like **open** except that its first argument should be a filehandle name, **FileHandle** object, or a file descriptor number.

If supported on your system, the **fgetpos()** and **fsetpos()** functions are available as the **getpos** and **setpos** methods, respectively. The **getpos** works like **tell** and returns the current location. You can then revisit the location within the file using **setpos**.

The **setvbuf** method is available to you if your system supports the **setvbuf()** function, and it sets the buffering policy for the filehandle:

```
$fh->setvbuf(VAR, TYPE, SIZE)
```

The **VAR** parameter should be a suitable scalar variable to hold the buffer data, and **SIZE** defines the maximum size of the buffer. The **TYPE** is specified using a constant, and these are exported by default by the module. The constants are described in Table B-5.

Constant	Description
_IOFBF	Causes the input and output to be fully buffered.
_IOLBF	Causes the output to be line buffered. The buffer will be flushed when a newline character is written to the filehandle, when the buffer is full, or when input is requested on the handle.
_IONBF	Causes the input and output to be completely unbuffered.

Table B-5. *Options for the **FileHandle->setvbuf** Method*

Caution *You should not modify the contents of the scalar variable you use for the buffer while it is in use.*

The **FileHandle** module also supports the following methods, which are simply aliases for the corresponding functions. See Chapter 3, Chapter 6, and/or Appendix A for more information on the following functions:

clearerr	close	eof	fileno	getc
gets	print	printf	seek	tell

The module also supports methods for setting the individual variables that affect the use of the filehandle directly:

autoflush	format_formfeed
format_line_break_characters	format_lines_left
format_lines_per_page	format_name
format_page_number	format_top_name
input_line_number	input_record_separator
output_field_separator	output_record_separator

Finally, the module also supports two further methods for reading lines from the file:

```
$fh->getline
$fh->getlines
```

The **getline** method returns a single line from the filehandle, just like the **<$fh>** operator when used in a scalar context. The **getlines** method returns a list of lines in a manner identical to the **<$fh>** operator in a list context. The **getlines** method will **croak** if called in a scalar context.

References   Chapter 8; *see also* **Symbol, POSIX**

File::Basename

This module supports the **basename** and **dirname** functions for extracting file and directory names for complete paths. It also supports more complex file path parsing functions.

```
use File::Basename;
```

The **File::Basename** module supplies functions for parsing pathnames and extracting the directory; the file name; and, optionally, the extension. The extraction can be made to account for different operating systems and can, therefore, be used as a cross-platform tool for parsing paths.

   The main function is **fileparse**:

```
fileparse PATH, EXTENSION
```

The **fileparse** function separates **PATH** into its components: a directory name, a file name, and a suffix. The directory name should contain everything up to and including the last directory separator in **PATH**. The remainder is then separated into the file name and suffix based on the **EXTENSION** definitions you supply.

   This argument should be a reference to an array, in which each element is a regular expression used to match against the end of the file name. If the match succeeds, the file is split into its file name and extension. If it does not match, the whole file name is returned and the suffix remains empty.

   For example:

```
($name, $path, $suffix) = fileparse('/usr/local/bin/script.pl', '\.pl');
```

This will return "script," "/usr/local/bin/," and ".pl," in that order. Note that this is not the same as the order you might expect. The function guarantees that if you combine the three elements returned, you will end up with the original file path.

The syntax used to separate the path depends on the setting of the module. You can change the specification syntax using the **fileparse_set_fstype** function:

```
fileparse_set_fstype EXPR
```

The supplied expression defines the operating system syntax to be used. If **EXPR** contains one of the substrings "VMS," "MSDOS," or "MacOS," then the corresponding syntax is used in all future calls to the **fileparse** function. If **EXPR** does not contain one of these strings, the Unix syntax is used instead. Note that the default operation depends on the value of **$Config{osname}** as determined during the build process.

Two functions, **basename** and **dirname**, are supplied for Unix compatibility:

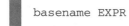

```
basename EXPR
```

The **basename** function returns the file name of a path. The function uses **fileparse** for its result.

```
dirname EXPR
```

The **dirname** function returns the directory portion of a file path. The result depends on the current syntax being used to extract the information. When using VMS or MacOS, the result is the same as the second argument returned by **fileparse**. If Unix or MSDOS syntax is used, the value matches what would be returned by the **dirname** Unix command. The function uses **fileparse** for its result.

Reference   Chapter 8

File::CheckTree

This module provides a mechanism for validating a series of files using the standard built-in tests for files. The method is to call the **validate** function with a textual list of files and tests, for example,

```
use File::CheckTree;
$errors += validate(q{
/test/test.c              -e  || die "Can't find test.c"
/test/test.o              -e  || warn "Object file not found"
/test/test               -ex || warn
});
```

The preceding tests that the **test.c** file exists; a failure will cause a call to **die**. Warnings are produced if the object and executable do not exist, and also if the executable is not actually executable. The default method is to produce a warning (effectively, | | **warn**) if a file is not specified. Note that the files must be specified exactly. See the **File::Find** module for another alternative.

You can also use a method of **cd**, which indicates the following entries are within the specified directory. Thus, the preceding example could be rewritten:

```
use File::CheckTree;
$errors += validate(q{
/test
   test.c                    -e  || die "Can't find test.c"
   test.o                    -e  || warn "Object file not found"
   test                      -ex || warn
});
```

In all cases, providing a fatal error has not occurred, the return value is the number of files that failed the test.

Reference   *See* **File::Find**

File::Compare

This module compares files or filehandles.

```
use File::Compare;
```

To compare files, you use the **compare** function:

```
print "Equal\n" if (compare('f1','f2') == 0);
```

Either argument to the function can be a file name or filehandle. The function returns zero if the files are equal, 1 otherwise, or –1 if an error was encountered.

File::Copy

This module copies or moves files or filehandles.

```
use File::Copy;
```

It supports two functions: **copy** and **move**. The **copy** function accepts two arguments and copies from the first to the second file. Either argument can be a file name or filehandle. The following examples are valid:

```
copy('f1', 'f2');
copy(\*STDIN, 'console');
copy('f1', \*STDOUT);
```

The **move** function will move a file from one location to another:

```
move('f1', 'f2');
```

If possible, it will rename the file; but if this does not work, the contents will be copied to the new file, and the old file will be deleted when the copy is complete.

Both functions are platform independent and return 1 on success, 0 on failure.

Reference   *See* **Shell**

File::DosGlob

This module provides a DOS-like globbing functionality, with the addition that wildcards are supported in directory and file names.

```
require 5.004;
use File::DosGlob qw/glob/;
```

Note that this function overrides the **CORE** function within the scope of the current package. To override the function in all packages:

```
use File::DosGlob qw/GLOBAL_glob/;
```

You can use spaces to separate individual patterns within the file specification given, for example,

```
$executables = glob('*.exe *.com');
```

Note that in all cases you may have to double the backslashes in file specifications to override the normal parsing that Perl does on quoted strings. Alternatively, use the **q//** operator.

Reference   Chapter 8

File::Find

This module supports the traversal of a directory tree.

```
use File::Find;
```

It supports two functions: **find** and **finddepth**. The **find** function accepts at least two arguments:

```
find(\&wanted, '/foo', '/bar');
```

The first argument is a reference to a subroutine called each time a file is found. This is called the "wanted" function and is used to process each file as it is found. Further arguments specify the individual directories to traverse.

Because the wanted function is called each time a file is found, the function can perform whatever functions or verifications on each file it needs to. The **$File::Find::dir** variable contains the name of the current directory. Note that the function calls **chdir** to change into each found directory. The special **$_** variable contains the current file name. You can also access **$File::Find::name** to get the full pathname of the current file. Setting the value of **$File::Find::prune** prunes the directory tree.

For example, the script that follows would print files and directories in the /usr/local tree that are executable by the real and effective uid/gid:

```
use File::Find;

find(\&wanted, '/usr/local');

sub wanted
{
    next unless (-x $_ and -X _);
    print "$File::Find::name\n";
}
```

If you are creating complex wanted functions and know how to use the Unix **find** command, you can use the **find2perl** script, which generates the necessary stand-alone code for you. For example,

```
$ find2perl /usr/local -name "*.html" -mtime -7
```

produces the following stand-alone script:

```
#!/usr/local/bin/perl
    eval 'exec /usr/local/bin/perl -S $0 ${1+"$@"}'
        if $running_under_some_shell;

require "find.pl";

# Traverse desired filesystems


&find('/usr/local');

exit;
sub wanted {
    /^.*\.html$/ &&
    (($dev,$ino,$mode,$nlink,$uid,$gid) = lstat($_)) &&
    (int(-M _) < 7);
}
```

The **finddepth** function is identical to **find** except that it does a depth first search, rather than working from the lowest depth to the highest.

References   Chapters 8, 20

File::Path

This module creates or removes a directory tree.

```
use File::Path;
```

It supplies two functions, **mkpath** and **rmtree**, which make and remove directory trees.

```
mkpath(ARRAYREF, PRINT, MODE)
```

The **ARRAYREF** should be either the name of the directory to create, or a reference to a list of directories to be created. All intermediate directories in the specification will also be created as required. If **PRINT** is true (default is false), the name of each directory created will be printed to **STDOUT**. The **MODE** is the octal mode to be used for the newly created directories. The function returns a list of all the directories created. For example, to create a typical /usr/local structure:

```
mkpath(['/usr/local/bin',
        '/usr/local/etc',
        '/usr/local/lib'], 0, 0777);
```

The **rmtree** function deletes a directory subtree. All of the directories specified will be deleted, in addition to the subdirectories and files contained within them.

```
rmtime(ARRAYREF, PRINT, SKIP)
```

The **ARRAYREF** should either be the name of a directory to delete or a reference to an array of directories to be deleted. The directory specified and all its subdirectories and files will be deleted.

The **PRINT** argument, if set to true, prints each file or directory, and the method used to remove the file or directory. The default value is false. The **SKIP** argument, if set to true, causes the function to skip files and directories that it is unable to remove due to access privileges. The default value for **SKIP** is false.

The function returns the number of files successfully deleted.

Note that you will need to use a **$SIG{__WARN__}** handler to identify files or directories that could not be deleted.

References   Chapters 8, 24

File::Spec

This module is a cross-platform–compatible library for performing operations on file names and paths.

```
use File::Spec;
```

The module is supported by a number of platform-specific modules that are imported as required, depending on the platform on which the script is running. You shouldn't need to import the support modules individually; use the **File::Spec** module and let it decide which module is required. See the **File::Spec::Unix** module for a list of the supported methods. Other modules override the necessary methods that are specific to that platform.

Since the interface is object oriented, you must call the functions as class methods:

```
$path = File::Spec->('usr','local');
```

References   Chapter 24; *see also* **File::Spec::Mac, File::Spec::OS2, File::Spec::Unix, File::Spec::VMS, File::Spec::Win32**

File::Spec::Mac

This module supports the MacOS-specific methods for manipulating file specifications.

```
use File::Spec::Mac;
```

It overrides the default methods supported by **File::Spec**. Note that you should not normally need to use this module directory. The methods overridden by this module are given here.

```
canonpath
```

returns the path it's given; no process is required under MacOS.

```
catdir
```

concatenates directory names to form a complete path ending with a directory. Under MacOS, these rules are followed:

- Each argument has any trailing : removed.
- Each argument except the first has any leading : character removed.
- All arguments are then joined by a single : character.

To create a relative rather than absolute path, precede the first argument with a : character, or use a blank argument.

```
catfile
```

concatenates directory names and a file into a path that defines an individual file. Uses **catdir** for the directory names. Any leading or trailing colons are removed from the file name.

```
curdir
```

returns a string defining the current directory.

> ```
> rootdir
> ```

returns a string defining the root directory. Under MacPerl, this returns the name of this startup volume; under any other Perl, it returns an empty string.

> ```
> updir
> ```

returns the string representing the parent directory.

> ```
> file_name_is_absolute
> ```

returns true if the supplied path is absolute.

> ```
> path
> ```

returns the null list under MacPerl, since there is no execution path under MacOS. When used within the MPW environment, returns the contents of **$ENV{Commands}** as a list.

Reference   *See* **File::Spec**

File::Spec::OS2

This module supports methods for manipulating file specifications under the OS/2 platform.

> ```
> use File::Spec::OS2;
> ```

It overrides the default methods supported by **File::Spec**. Note that you should not normally need to use this module directory. The supported methods are detailed in the **File::Spec:Unix** module.

Reference   *See* **File::Spec**

File::Spec::Unix

This module supports Unix-specific methods for file specifications.

> ```
> use File::Spec::Unix;
> ```

APPENDIXES

It imports and overrides the methods supported by **File::Spec**. It is normally imported by **File::Spec** as needed, although you can import it directly if required. The following methods are supplied.

canonpath

cleans up a given path, removing successive slashes and /.. Note that the physical existence of the file or directory is not verified.

catdir

concatenates one or more directories into a valid path. This strips the trailing slash off the path for all but the root directory.

catfile

concatenates one or more directories and a file name into a valid path to a file.

curdir

returns a string representing the current directory (.).

rootdir

returns a string representing the root directory (/).

updir

returns a string representing the parent directory (. .).

no_upwards

removes references to parent directories from a given list of file paths.

file_name_if_absolute

returns true if the given path is absolute.

path

returns the **$ENV{PATH}** variable as a list.

 join

is identical to **catfile**.

References   *See* **File::Spec**

File::Spec::VMS

This module supports VMS-specific methods for file specifications.

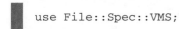
```
use File::Spec::VMS;
```

It is imported and overrides the methods supplied by **File::Spec** under the VMS platform. The following methods are supported.

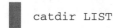 catdir LIST

concatenates a list of specifications and returns a VMS syntax directory specification.

 catfile LIST

concatenates a list of specifications and returns a VMS syntax file specification.

 curdir

returns the current directory as a string.

 rootdir

returns the root directory as a string.

 updir

returns the parent directory as a string.

path

translates the logical VMS path defined in **DCL$PATH** rather than splitting the value
of **$ENV{PATH}**.

    file_name_is_absolute

checks that a VMS directory specification is valid. Note that this does not check the
physical existence of a file or directory, only that the specification is correct.

Reference   *See* **File::Spec**

File::Spec::Win32

This module provides Win32-specific methods for file specifications.

    use File::Spec::Win32;

This is the module imported internally by **File::Spec** under Win32 platforms. The
package overrides the following methods supported by the **File::Spec** module.

    Catfile LIST

concatenates one or more directory names and a file name to form a complete path to a
file.

    canonpath EXPR

cleans up a supplied pathname for use on Win32 platforms.

Reference   *See* **File::Spec**

FindBin

This module exports variables that define the directory of the original Perl script.

    use FindBin;

It locates the full path to the script's parent directory, as well as the name of the script. This can be useful if you want to install a script in its own directory hierarchy but do not want to hard code the directory location into the script.

The variables available are shown in Table B-6. The variables are not exported by default; you must explicitly request them or use the fully qualified values.

Note that if the script was invoked from **STDIN** or via the **-e** command line option, the value of **$Bin** is set to the current directory.

GDBM_File

This module provides an interface to the GDBM database system. The main benefit of GDBM over other systems (except Berkeley DB) is that it provides rudimentary database locking and does not have a restricted bucket size, allowing you to store any size object within a GDBM database.

```
use GDBM_File;
tie %db, 'GDBM_File', 'db', &GDBM_WRCREAT, 0640;
untie %db;
```

Instead of using the modes for opening the database that are ordinarily supplied by the **Fcntl** module, the **GDBM_File** module provides its own constants, listed in Table C-7.

References   Chapter 13; *see also* **AnyDBM_File, DB_File, NDBM_File, ODBM_File, SDBM_File**

Variable	Description
$Bin	Path to the directory where the script was located
$Script	The name of the script that was invoked
$RealBin	The value of **$Bin** with all the links resolved
$RealScript	The value of **$Script** with all the links resolved

Table B-6.   *Variables Available via* ***FindBin***

Constant	Description
GDBM_READER	Open for read only.
GDBM_WRITER	Open for read/write.
GDBM_WRCREAT	Open for read/write, creating a new database if it does not already exist, using the mode specified.
GDBM_NEWDB	Open for read/write, creating a new database even if one already exists, using the mode specified.

Table B-7. *Modes for Opening GDBM Tied Databases*

Getopt::Long

This module is suitable for simple scripts and argument passing. However, it falls over if you try to do more complex processing or want to place the extracted information into specific variables and structures. The **Getopt::Long** module implements a more advanced system. It is **POSIX** compliant and, therefore, suitable for use in scripts that require **POSIX** compliance.

POSIX compliance allows not only the standard single-character matching supported by the **Getopt::Std** module, but also string arguments. For example:

```
$ script.pl --inputfile=source.txt
```

The command line option in this case is **– – inputfile**. Note that long names as arguments are supported by both the single and double hyphen, although the double hyphen is the **POSIX** default.

Note   *The + sign is also supported, but the use of this is deprecated and not part of the **POSIX** specification.*

The selection of additional arguments to command line options is supported by appending a specific character sequence to the end of the option name. The list of available modifiers is defined in Table B-8.

Any elements in the argument list not identified as options remain in the **@ARGV** array.

Option Specified	Description
!	The option does not accept an optional piece of information and may be negated by prefixing **no**. For example, **opt!**, will set the value of an option **--opt** to one, and **--noopt** to zero.
+	The option does not accept an additional piece of information. Each appearance in the command line options will increment the corresponding value by one, such that **--opt --opt --opt** will set a value of three, providing it doesn't already have a value.
=s	The option requires an additional string argument. The value of the string will be placed into the corresponding variable.
:s	The option accepts an optional string argument. The value of the string will be placed into the corresponding variable.
=i	The option requires an integer argument. The value will be placed into the corresponding variable.
:i	The option accepts an optional integer argument. The value will be placed into the corresponding variable.
=f	The option requires a real number argument. The value will be placed into the corresponding variable.
:f	The option accepts an optional real number argument. The value will be placed into the corresponding variable.

Table B-8.   *Options for the **Getopt::Long** Module*

Linkage

When using a hash reference as the first argument to the **GetOptions** function, additional facilities are available to you for processing more complex command lines. By default, the operation is identical to the **getopts** function. You can also use a trailing @ or % sign to signify that an array or hash reference should be returned. In the case of an array reference, this allows you to supply multiple values for a single named option.

For a hash, it supports "–option name=value" command line constructs, where **name** and **value** are the key and value of the returned hash.

If you do not specify a hash reference as the first argument, the function will instead create a new variable of the corresponding type, using the argument name prefixed by **opt_**. So a function call

```
GetOptions("file=s","files=s@","users=s%");
```

may result in a similar assignment to the following:

```
$opt_file = "source.txt";
@opt_files = ('source.txt', 'sauce.txt');
%opt_users = ( 'Bob'  => 'Manager',
               'Fred' => 'Salesman' );
```

You can also use the hash argument feature to update your own variables directly:

```
GetOptions("file=s"   => \$file,
           "files=s@" => \@files,
           "users=s%" => \%users);
```

This last specification method also supports a function that will handle the specified option. The function will receive two arguments—the true option name (see the next section) and the value supplied.

Aliases

You can support alternative argument names by using | characters to separate individual names. For example:

```
GetOptions("file|input|source=s");
```

The "true" name would be "file" in this instance, placing the value into **$opt_file**. This true name is also passed to a function if specified (see previous section).

Callback Function

If **GetOptions** cannot identify an individual element of the **@ARGV** array as a true argument, you can specify a function that will handle the option. You do this by using a value of <> as the argument name, as in

```
GetOptions("<>" => \&nonoption);
```

Remember that the **GetOptions** function removes identifiable arguments from @**ARGV** and leaves the remainder of the elements intact if you don't use this facility. You can then process the arguments as you wish after **GetOptions** has completed successfully.

Return Values

The **GetOptions** function returns true (1) if the command line arguments could be identified correctly. If an error occurs (because the user has supplied a command line argument the function wasn't expecting), the function returns false and uses **warn** to report the bad options. If the definitions supplied to the function are invalid, the function calls **die**, reporting the error.

Customizing GetOptions

You can control the operation of the **GetOptions** function by passing arguments to **Getopt::Long::Configure**. The list of options is shown in Table B-9. The values shown in the table *set* the option; to unset, prefix the option with **no_**.

For example, to set auto-abbreviation and allow differentiation between upper- and lowercase arguments:

```
Getopt::Long::Configure('auto_abbrev','no_ignore_case');
```

Option	Description
Default	Sets all configuration options to their default values.
auto_abbrev	Supports abbreviated option names, providing the arguments supplied can be identified uniquely. This is the default operation, unless the **POSIXLY_CORRECT** environment variable is set.
getopt_compat	Supports the use of **+** as the prefix to arguments. This is the default operation, unless the **POSIXLY_CORRECT** environment variable is set.

Table B-9. *Configuration Options for **GetOpt::Long***

APPENDIXES

Option	Description
require_order	This specifies that your options must be supplied first on the command line. This is the default operation, unless the **POSIXLY_CORRECT** environment variable is set. This is the opposite of **permute**. If **require_order** is set, processing terminates on the first nonorder item found in the argument list.
permute	Specifies that nonoptions are allowed to be mixed with real options. This is the default operation, unless the **POSIXLY_CORRECT** environment variable is set. This is the opposite of **require_order**.
bundling	Setting this allows single-character options to be bundled into single strings. For example, if this is set, the string "-vax" will be equivalent to "-v -a -x." This option also allows for integer values to be inserted into the bundled options, such that "-d256aq" is equivalent to "-d 256 -a -q."
bundling_override	If set, the **bundling** option is implied. However, if an option has been defined with the same full name as a bundle, it will be interpreted as the name, not the individual options. For example, if "vax" was specified, then "-vax" would be interpreted as "-vax," but "-avx" would be interpreted as "-a -v -x."
ignore_case	Default; string command line options are interpreted ignoring case.
ignore_case_always	When **bundling** is set, case is also ignored on single-character options.
pass_through	Unrecognized options remain in the **@ARGV** array, instead of producing and being flagged as errors.
prefix	Takes the next argument to the function as a string defining the list of strings that identify an option. The default value is (−−|-|\+), or (−−|-) if the **POSIXLY_CORRECT** environment variable is set.
debug	Enables debugging output.

Table B-9.   *Configuration Options for **GetOpt::Long*** (continued)

Variables

You can monitor the version number of the **Getopt::Long** module with the **$Getopt::Long::VERSION** variable. You can also identify the major and minor versions using the **$Getopt::Long::major_version** and **$Getopt::Long::minor_version** variables. If you want to identify the version number during import, use the usual

```
use Getopt::Long 3.00;
```

When using the callback function (with <>) you may want to report an error back to the main **GetOptions** function. You can do this by incrementing the **$Getopt::Long::error** variable.

Reference   Chapter 16

Getopt::Std

This module provides two functions: **getopt** and **getopts**.

```
use Getopt::Std;

getopt('ol');
getopts('ol:');
```

Both functions require a single argument that specifies the list of single-letter arguments you would like to identify on the command line.

In the case of the **getopt** function, it assumes that all arguments expect an additional piece of information. With the **getopts** function, each character is taken to be a Boolean value. If you want to accept arguments with additional information, append a colon.

Variables are created by the function with a prefix of **$opt_**. The value of each variable is one in the case of a Boolean value, or the supplied additional argument. If the command argument is not found, the variable is still created, but the value is **undef**.

In addition, for either function, you can supply a second argument that should be a reference to a hash:

```
getopts('i:',\%opts);
```

APPENDIXES

Each supplied argument will be used as the key of the hash, and any additional information supplied will be placed into the corresponding values. Thus, a script using the preceding line when called,

```
$ getopts -i Hello
```

will place the string "Hello" into the **$opts{'i'}** hash element.

If you have the **use strict 'vars'** pragma in effect (see Chapter 16), you will need to predefine the **$opt_** and hash variables before they are called. Either use a **my** definition before calling the function, or, better still, predeclare them with **use vars**.

Reference   Chapter 16

I18N::Collate

The functionality of the **I18N::Collate** module (which allows strings to be sorted according to their current locale, rather than by the ordinal values in the ASCII table) has been integrated into Perl from version 5.003_06. See the **perllocale** man page for details.

IO

This module automatically imports a number of base IO modules.

```
use IO;
```

It doesn't provide any modules or functionality on its own, but does attempt to import the following modules for you:

```
IO::File
IO::Handle
IO::Pipe
IO::Seekable
IO::Socket
```

References   Chapter 8; *see also* **IO::File, IO::Handle, IO::Pipe, IO::Seekable, IO::Socket**

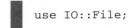

IO::File

This module supports the methods for accessing and using filehandles.

```
use IO::File;
```

The **new** method creates a new filehandle, and any arguments are passed to the **open** method. If **open** fails, the object is destroyed; otherwise, it is returned to the caller.

```
new_tmpfile
```

Creates a new filehandle opened for read/write on the newly created temporary file. Once created, the object supports the following methods:

```
open(FILENAME [, MODE [, PERMS]])
```

The **open** method supports the options as the built-in **open** function. The first parameter is the file name. If supplied on its own, you can use the normal **open** formats, such as > or >>, and then it uses the normal **open** function.

If you supply a **MODE** in the format of the **POSIX fopen()** function—for example, "w" or "w+"—the built-in **open** function is also used. If given a numeric **MODE**, the built-in **sysopen** function is used instead. The module automatically imports the **O_*** constants from **Fcntl** if they are available.

The **fdopen** method is like **open** except that its first argument should be a filehandle name, **FileHandle** object, or a file descriptor number.

Additional methods are inherited from **IO::Handle** and **IO::Seekable**.

References   *See* **IO, IO::Handle, IO::Seekable**

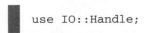

IO::Handle

This module supports the object methods available for use with other IO handles.

```
use IO::Handle;
```

It provides the base class from which all other IO handle classes inherit.

new

The **new** method creates a new **IO::Handle** object.

new_from_fd(FD, MODE)

Creates a new **IO::Handle** object. The **FD** and **MODE** are passed on to the **fdopen** method.

Additional methods match the functionality supported by the following functions. See Chapters 4, 8, and Appendix A for more details.

close	**fileno**	**getc**	**eof**	**read**
truncate	**stat**	**print**	**printf**	**sysread**
syswrite				

The following methods are handle-specific versions of the corresponding Perl variables. See Chapter 4 for more information.

autoflush	**format_formfeed**
format_line_break_characters	**format_lines_left**
format_lines_per_page	**format_name**
format_page_number	**format_top_name**
format_write	**input_line_number**
input_record_separator	**output_field_separator**
output_record_separator	

Additional module-specific methods are described here.

$fh->fdopen(FD, MODE)

This opens the file like the built-in **open**. The **FD** parameter takes a filehandle name, **IO::Handle** object, or a file descriptor number. The **MODE** is a valid **Fcntl** mode, and the module attempts to import the **O_*** series of constants from **Fcntl**, but doesn't **croak** if the modules cannot be imported.

$fh->opened

returns true if the object is currently a valid file descriptor.

```
$fh->getline
$fh->getlines
```

The **getline** method returns a single line from the filehandle, just like the **<$fh>** operator when used in a scalar context. The **getlines** method returns a list of lines in a manner identical to the **<$fh>** operator in a list context. The **getlines** method will **croak** if called in a scalar context.

```
$fh->ungetc(ORD)
```

pushes the character that is the ordinal value **ORD** onto the input stream.

```
$fh->write(BUF, LEN [, OFFSET ] )
```

writes **BUF** of size **LEN** to the filehandle. This is the implementation of the **write()** C function. If given, then **OFFSET** specifies the location within the file to write the data, without requiring you to move to that spot, and without modifying the current file pointer. Note that this is identical to the **pwrite()** C function.

```
$fh->flush
```

flushes the filehandle's buffer.

```
$fh->error
```

returns true if the filehandle has experienced any errors.

```
$fh->clearerr
```

clears the error indicator.

```
$fh->untaint
```

marks the data received on the handle as taint safe.

The **setvbuf** method is available if your system supports the **setvbuf()** function, and it sets the buffering policy for the filehandle:

```
$fh->setvbuf(VAR, TYPE, SIZE)
```

The **VAR** parameter should be a suitable scalar variable to hold the buffer data, and **SIZE** defines the maximum size of the buffer. The **TYPE** is specified using a constant, and these are exported by default by the module. The constants are described in Table B-10.

 You should not modify the contents of the scalar variable you use for the buffer while it is in use.

References *See* IO, IO::File, Symbol

IO::Pipe

This module supports methods for pipes.

```
use IO::Pipe;
```

It provides an object interface for creating pipes between processes.

```
new([READER, WRITER])
```

This creates a new object (as supplied by the **Symbol** package). It takes two optional arguments, which should be **IO::Handle** objects, or an object that is a subclass of **IO::Handle**. These arguments will be used during the **pipe()** system call. If no arguments are supplied, the **handles** method is called.

Supported methods are described here.

```
reader([ARGS])
```

Constant	Description
_IOFBF	Causes the input and output to be fully buffered.
_IOLBF	Causes the output to be line buffered. The buffer will be flushed when a newline character is written to the filehandle, when the buffer is full, or when input is requested on the handle.
_IONBF	Causes the input and output to be completely unbuffered.

Table B-10.   *Options for the **FileHandle->setvbuf** Method*

The object is reblessed into a subclass of **IO::Handle** and is the handle at the reading end of the pipe. Any supplied **ARGS** are used when calling **exec** after a **fork**.

```
writer([ARGS])
```

The object is reblessed into a subclass of **IO::Handle** and is the handle at the writing end of the pipe. Any supplied **ARGS** are used when calling **exec** after a **fork**.

```
handles
```

This method returns two objects blessed into **IO::Pipe::End** or a subclass thereof.

References   *See* **IO, IO::Handle, Symbol**

IO::Seekable

This module supplies base seek methods for IO objects.

```
use IO::Seekable;
package IO::Package;
@ISA = qw/IO::Seekable/;
```

It provides base methods for other **IO::*** modules to implement the positional functionality normally handled by the **seek** and **tell** built-in functions. Note that the module does not support any constructor methods of its own. The methods support the seek and location within file descriptors, using the **fgetpos()** and **fsetpos()** C functions. The methods are supported within **IO::File** as **IO::File::getpos** and **IO::File::setpos** methods, respectively. See the **seek** and **tell** functions in Appendix A for more information.

References   Chapters 4, 8, Appendix A; *see also* **IO, IO::File**

IO::Select

This module supports an object-oriented interface to the **select()** system call.

```
use IO::Select;
```

The module allows you to monitor which **IO::Handle** objects are ready for reading or writing, or have an error pending, just like the **select** built-in function.

You can create a new **IO::Select** object with the **new** method:

```
new([HANDLES])
```

The optional **HANDLES** argument is a list of **IO::Handle** objects to initialize into the **IO::Select** object.

Once created, the new object supports the following, more pragmatic, interface to the **select** function.

```
add(HANDLES)
```

adds the list of **IO::Handle** objects, integer file descriptor, or array reference, where the first element is an **IO::Handle** object or integer. It is these objects that will be returned when an event occurs. This works by the file descriptor number (as returned by **fileno**), so duplicated handles are not added.

```
remove(HANDLES)
```

removes the given handles from the object.

```
exists(HANDLE)
```

returns true if **HANDLE** is a part of the set.

```
handles
```

returns an array of all the handles within the set.

```
can_read([TIMEOUT])
```

returns an array of handles that are ready for reading. The method blocks for a maximum of **TIMEOUT** seconds. If **TIMEOUT** is not specified, the call blocks indefinitely.

```
can_write([TIMEOUT])
```

returns an array of handles that are ready for writing. The method blocks for a maximum of **TIMEOUT** seconds. If **TIMEOUT** is not specified, the call blocks indefinitely.

```
has_error([TIMEOUT])
```

returns an array of handles that have a pending error condition. The method blocks for a maximum of **TIMEOUT** seconds. If **TIMEOUT** is not specified, the call blocks indefinitely.

```
count
```

returns the number of handles that will be returned when a **can_*** method is called.

```
bits
```

returns a bitstring suitable for passing to the built-in **select** function.

```
IO::Select::select(READ, WRITE, ERROR, [, TIMEOUT])
```

The **select** method is a static method that must be called with the package name, as just shown. The function returns an array of three elements. Each is a reference to an array holding the reference to the handles that are ready for reading, are ready for writing, and have error conditions waiting, respectively.

The **READ, WRITE,** and **ERROR** arguments are **IO::Select** objects, or **undef**. The optional **TIMEOUT** value is the number of seconds to wait for a handle to become ready.

References   Chapter 8, 12; *see* **IO, IO::File, IO::Handle**

IO::Socket

This module supports an object interface for socket communications.

```
use IO::Socket;
```

This class supports socket-based communication. It exports the functions and constants supported by **Socket** and also inherits methods from **IO::Handle**, in addition to defining a number of common methods suitable for all sockets. The **IO::Socket::INET** and **IO::Socket::UNIX** classes define additional methods for specific socket types.

The **new** method creates a new **IO::Socket** object using a symbol generated by the **Symbol** package.

```
$socket = IO::Socket->new(Domain => 'UNIX');
```

The constructor only identifies one option, **Domain**, which specifies the domain in which to create the socket. Any other options are supplied to the **IO::Socket::INET** or **IO::Socket::UNIX** constructor accordingly.

The newly created handle will be in autoflush mode. This is the default operation from versions above 1.1603 (Perl 5.004_04). You will need to specify this explicitly if you want to remain compatible with earlier versions.

The class supports the following methods:

```
accept([PKG])
```

This accepts a new socket connection like the built-in **accept** function, returning a new **IO::Socket** handle of the appropriate type. If you specify **PKG**, the new object will be of the specified class, rather than that of the parent handle. In a scalar context, only the new object is returned; in a list context, both the object and the peer address are returned. The method will return **undef** or an empty list on failure.

```
timeout([VALUE])
```

If supplied without any arguments, the current time-out setting is returned. If called with an argument, it sets the time-out value. The time-out value is used by various other methods.

```
sockopt(OPT [, VALUE])
```

gets/sets the socket option **OPT**. If the method is only supplied **OPT**, it gets the current value of the option. To set a value, use the two-argument form.

```
sockdomain
```

returns the numerical value of the socket domain type.

```
socktype
```

returns the numerical value of the socket type.

```
protocol
```

returns the numerical value of the protocol being used on the socket. If the protocol is unknown, zero is returned.

> peername

This is identical to the built-in **getpeername** function.

> sockname

This is identical to the built-in **getsockname** function.

The class also supplies frontend methods for the following built-in functions:

> socket
> socketpair
> bind
> listen
> send
> recv

Please refer to Chapter 9 and Appendix A for more information on these functions/methods.

IO::Socket::INET

The **IO::Socket::INET** class provides a constructor to create a socket within the **AF_INET** family/domain. The constructor accepts a hash that takes the options shown in Table B-11.

If passed a single argument, the constructor assumes that it's a **PeerAddr** specification. For example, to create a connection to a web server on port 80,

```
$socket = IO::Socket::INET->new(PeerAddr => 'www.mcwords.com:http(80)');
```

Or to create a local socket for listening:

```
$socket = IO::Socket::INET->new(LocalAddr => 'localhost',
                                LocalPort => '7000',
                                Listen    => '5',
                                Proto     => 'tcp');
```

Note that by specifying **LocalAddr** and **Listen**, the constructor builds a local socket suitable for acting as a server-side socket. You can use the **accept** method (inherited from **IO::Socket**), which works just like the built-in function.

Beyond the methods that are inherited from **IO::Socket** and **IO::Handle**, the **IO::Socket::INET** class also supports the following methods:

> sockaddr

Option	Format	Description
PeerAddr	hostname[:port]	Remote host address (and port). The **address** can be specified as a name (which will be resolved) or as an IP address. The **port** (if specified) should be a valid service name and/or port number as defined in **PeerPort**.
PeerPort	service(port) | port	The service port name and number, or number only.
LocalAddr	hostname[:port]	Local host address to bind to.
LocalPort	service(no) | no	The local service port name and number, or number only.
Proto	"tcp" | "udp" | . . .	The protocol name or number. If this is not specified and you give a service name in the **PeerPort** option, then the constructor will attempt to derive **Proto** from the given service name. If it cannot be resolved, then "tcp" is used.
Type	SOCK_STREAM | SOCK_DGRAM | . . .	The socket type, specified using a constant as exported by **Socket**. This will be deduced from **Proto** if not otherwise specified.
Listen		The queue size for listening to requests.
Reuse		If true, then it sets the **SO_REUSEADDR** option before binding to the local socket.

Table B-11.   *Options for Creating an **IO::Socket::INET** Object*

returns the 4-byte packed address of the local socket.

```
sockport
```

returns the port number used for the local socket.

```
sockhost
```

returns the IP address in the form *xxx.xxx.xxx.xxx* for the local socket.

peeraddr

returns the 4-byte packed address of the remote socket.

peerport

returns the port number used for the remote socket.

peerhost

returns the IP address in the form *xxx.xxx.xxx.xxx* for the remote socket.

IO::Socket::UNIX

The **IO::Socket::UNIX** class provides a constructor to create a socket within the **AF_UNIX** family/domain. The constructor accepts a hash that takes the options shown in Table B-12.

Like the **IO::Socket::INET** class, this class supports the methods inherited from **IO::Socket** and **IO::Handle**, in addition to the following methods:

hostpath

returns the pathname to the FIFO file at the local end.

Option	Description
Type	The socket type, **SOCK_STREAM**, **SOCK_DGRAM**, or one of the other constants supported in **Socket**.
Local	Path to the local FIFO file.
Peer	Path to the peer FIFO file.
Listen	If set to true, it creates a socket that can be used to accept new client connections.

Table B-12.   *Options for Creating a New IO::Socket::Unix Object*

```
peerpath
```

returns the pathname to the FIFO file at the peer end.

References   Chapter 13; *see also* **IO::Handle, IO::Socket, Socket**

IPC::Msg

This module is an object-oriented interface to the System V message system.

```
use IPC::Msg;
```

It provides an alternative interface to the **msg*** range of IPC message queue functions. The **new** method creates a new message queue.

```
new KEY, FLAGS
```

creates a new message queue associated with **KEY** using **FLAGS** as the permissions for accessing the queue. You will need to import suitable constants from **IPC::SysV**. A new object is created only under the following conditions:

- **KEY** is equal to **IPC_PRIVATE**.
- **KEY** does not already have a message queue associated with it.
- **FLAGS** contains the **IPC_CREAT** constant.

Once created, the following methods are supported:

```
id
```

returns the system message queue identifier.

```
rcv BUF, LEN [, TYPE [, FLAGS]])
```

receives a message from the queue into the variable **BUF**, up to a maximum length **LEN**.

```
remove
```

removes (destroys) the message queue from the system.

```
set STAT
set(NAME => VALUE [, NAME => VALUE...])
```

sets the values using either an **IPC::Msg::stat** object or the specified hash. Supported elements are **uid**, **gid**, **mode**, and **qbytes**.

```
snd
```

sends a message to the queue of **TYPE**.

```
stat
```

returns an **IPC::Msg::stat** object that is a subclass of the **Class::Struct** class. The object consists of the following fields:

uid	gid	cuid	cgid	mode	qnum	qbytes
lspid	lrpid	stime	rtime	ctime		

References   Chapter 14; *see also* **Class::Struct**, **IPC::SysV**

IPC::Open2

This module allows you to open a piped process for both reading and writing.

```
use IPC::Open2;

$pid = open2(READER, WRITER, LIST);
```

The **open2** function supports the functionality not provided in the built-in **open** function to allow you to open a command for both reading and writing. The **READER** and **WRITER** arguments should be references to existing filehandles to be used for reading from and writing to the piped command. The function does not create the filehandles for you. The **LIST** is one or more arguments defining the command to be run. For example:

```
$pid = open2(\*READ, \*WRITE, '|bc|');
```

The returned value is the process ID of the child process executed. Errors are raised by an exception matching **/^open2:/**. You should probably use this within an **eval** block.

If **READER** is a string and it begins with ">&", then the child will send output directly to that filehandle. If **WRITER** is a string that begins with "<&", then **WRITER** will be closed in the parent, and the child process will read from the filehandle directly. In both cases, the filehandle is duplicated with **dup()** instead of **pipe()**.

Note *The function assumes you know how to read from and write to the child process while preventing deadlocking. Commands that use a fixed input or output length (specified in a number of characters or lines) should prevent the problem.*

References   Chapters 8, 14, 15; *see also* **IPC::Open3**

IPC::Open3

This module is similar to **IPC::Open2**, but it opens a command for reading, writing, and error handling.

```
use IPC::Open3;

$pid = open3(WRITER, READER, ERROR, LIST);
```

The **WRITER, READER,** and **ERROR** should be references to existing filehandles to be used for standard input, standard output, and standard error from the command and arguments supplied in **LIST**. Note that the order of the **READER** and **WRITER** arguments is different from that in **open2**. If **"** is given as the argument for **ERROR**, then **ERROR** and **READER** use the same filehandle.

All other details are identical to the **open2** call, including the warning on deadlocking.

References   Chapters 8, 14 ,15; *see also* **IPC::Open2**

IPC::Semaphore

This module is an object class definition for System V semaphore–based IPC.

```
use IPC::Semaphore;
```

It provides an object interface to the System V semaphore system used for interprocess communication. The **new** method creates a new **IPC::Semaphore** object:

```
$sem = new IPC::Semaphore(KEY, NSEMS, FLAGS);
```

Creates a new semaphore set associated with **KEY**, with **NSEMS** semaphores in the set. The value of **FLAGS** is a list of permissions for the new semaphore set. You will need to import suitable constants from the **IPC::SysV** module.

A new semaphore is created only under the following conditions:

- **KEY** is equal to **IPC_PRIVATE**.
- **KEY** does not already have a semaphore identifier associated with it.
- **FLAGS** contains the **IPC_CREAT** constant.

Once created, the new object supports the following methods:

```
getall
```

returns the values contained in the semaphore set as a list.

```
getnccnt SEM
```

returns the number of processes waiting for **SEM** to become greater than the current value.

```
getpid SEM
```

returns the process ID of the last process that used **SEM**.

```
getval SEM
```

returns the current value of **SEM**.

```
getzcnt SEM
```

returns the number of processes waiting for **SEM** to become zero.

```
id
```

returns the system identifier for the semaphore set.

```
op OPLIST
```

performs a specific operation on the semaphore set. **OPLIST** is a multiple of a three-value list that defines the operation to perform. The first argument is the semaphore number, the second is the operator, and the last is the **FLAGS** value.

```
remove
```

removes (destroys) the semaphore set.

```
set STAT
set(NAME => VALUE [, NAME => VALUE...])
```

sets the **uid**, **gid**, and **mode** of the semaphore set. Accepts either an **IPC::Semaphore::stat** object, as returned by the **stat** method (see the example that follows), or a hash.

```
setall LIST
```

sets all the values in the set to those given in **LIST**. The **LIST** must be of the correct length.

```
setval N, VALUE
```

sets the value of the semaphore at index **N** to **VALUE**.

```
stat
```

returns an **IP::Semaphore::stat** object that is a subclass of the **Class::Struct** class. The object consists of the following fields:

uid	**gid**	**cuid**	**cgid**	**mode**	**ctime**	**otime**	**nsems**

References   Chapter 14; *see also* **Class::Struct**, **IPC::SysV**

IPC::SysV

This module supplies the System V IPC constants used by the built-in IPC calls.

```
use SysV::IPC;
```

Note that the module does not import any symbols implicitly. You need to specify the symbols you want to use. The list of available symbols is shown here:

GETALL	GETNCNT	GETPID	GETVAL
GETZCNT			
IPC_ALLOC	IPC_CREAT	IPC_EXCL	IPC_GETACL
IPC_LOCKED	IPC_M	IPC_NOERROR	IPC_NOWAIT
IPC_PRIVATE	IPC_R	IPC_RMID	IPC_SET
IPC_SETACL	IPC_SETLABEL	IPC_STAT	IPC_W
IPC_WANTED			
MSG_FWAIT	MSG_LOCKED	MSG_MWAIT	MSG_NOERROR
MSG_QWAIT			
MSG_R	MSG_RWAIT	MSG_STAT	MSG_W
MSG_WWAIT			
SEM_A	SEM_ALLOC	SEM_DEST	SEM_ERR
SEM_ORDER	SEM_R	SEM_UNDO	
SETALL	SETVAL		
SHMLBA			
SHM_A	SHM_CLEAR	SHM_COPY	SHM_DCACHE
SHM_DEST	SHM_ECACHE	SHM_FMAP	SHM_ICACHE
SHM_INIT	SHM_LOCK	SHM_LOCKED	SHM_MAP
SHM_NOSWAP	SHM_R	SHM_RDONLY	SHM_REMOVED
SHM_RND	SHM_SHARE_MMU	SHM_SHATTR	SHM_SIZE
SHM_UNLOCK	SHM_W		
S_IRUSR	S_IWUSR	S_IRWXU	
S_IRGRP	S_IWGRP	S_IRWXG	
S_IROTH	S_IWOTH	S_IRWXO	

You can also optionally import the **ftok** function:

```
ftok(PATH, ID)
```

This creates a unique key suitable for use with the **msgget**, **semget**, and **shmget** functions.

References   *See* **IPC::Msg, IPC::Semaphore**

Math::BigFloat

This module supports the use of floating point numbers of arbitrary length.

```
use Math::BigFloat;
$bigfloat = Math::BigFloat->new($string);
```

The **new** method creates a new floating point object based on the supplied string.

Most operators are overloaded to support the new floating point objects, providing you create the number with

```
$bigfloat = new Math::BigFloat '1.23456789012345678901234567890';
```

In addition, you can use the following methods.

```
fadd(STRING)
```

adds the number **STRING** to the object, returning a number string.

```
fsub(STRING)
```

subtracts the number **STRING** from the object, returning a number string.

```
fmul(STRING)
```

multiplies the object by the number **STRING**, returning a number string.

```
fdiv(STRING [,SCALE])
```

divides the object by the number **STRING**, to the specified **SCALE** places.

```
fneg()
```

negates the number.

```
fabs()
```

returns the absolute number.

fcmp(STRING)

compares the object to the number **STRING**, returning a value less than, equal to, or greater than zero, according to whether the number is less than, equal to, or greater than the given number.

fround(SCALE)

rounds the number object to **SCALE** digits, returning the number strings.

ffround(SCALE)

rounds the number at the **SCALE**th place within the number.

fnorm()

normalizes the floating point, returning a number string.

fsqrt([SCALE])

returns the square root of the number object, rounded to the specified **SCALE** if supplied.

Reference   *See also* **Math::BigInt**

Math::BigInt

Supports math with integer values of arbitrary sizes.

```
use Math::BigInt;
$int = Math::BigInt->new($string);
```

Basic operators are overloaded, providing you create the new integer with

```
$int = new Math::BigInt '123456789012345678901234567890123456789012345678890';
```

The following methods are supported by the new object.

```
bneg return BINT                      negation
```

negates the integer, and returns an integer string.

| babs

returns the absolute value as an integer string.

| bcmp(STRING)

compares the object with the supplied integer **STRING**, returning a value smaller, equal to, or greater than zero, depending on the relationship between the object and the supplied **STRING**.

| badd(STRING)

adds **STRING** to the object.

| bsub(STRING)

subtracts **STRING** from the object.

| bmul(STRING)

multiplies the object by **STRING**.

| bdiv(STRING)

divides the object by **STRING**, returning the quotient and remainder as strings.

| bmod(STRING)

returns the modulus of the object and **STRING**.

| bgcd(STRING)

returns the largest common divisor.

| bnorm

normalizes the object.

Reference   *See also* **Math::BigFloat**

Math::Complex

This module supports the use of complex numbers in mathematical computations.

```
use Math::Complex;
```

You create a new complex number with the **make** method,

```
$z = Math::Complex->make(1,2);
```

the **cplx** function,

```
$z = cplx(1, 2);
```

or directly, using complex notation:

```
$z = 3 + 4*i;
```

In addition, you can specify them in the polar form:

```
$z = Math::Complex->emake(5, pi/3);
$x = cplxe(5, pi/3);
```

The first argument is the modulus, and the second is the angle in radians.

The module also overloads the following operations to allow complex math directly within Perl, where **z** is an imaginary variable.

```
z1 + z2 = (a + c) + i(b + d)
z1 - z2 = (a - c) + i(b - d)
z1 * z2 = (r1 * r2) * exp(i * (t1 + t2))
z1 / z2 = (r1 / r2) * exp(i * (t1 - t2))
z1 ** z2 = exp(z2 * log z1)
~z = a - bi
abs(z) = r1 = sqrt(a*a + b*b)
sqrt(z) = sqrt(r1) * exp(i * t/2)
exp(z) = exp(a) * exp(i * b)
log(z) = log(r1) + i*t
sin(z) = 1/2i (exp(i * z1) - exp(-i * z))
cos(z) = 1/2 (exp(i * z1) + exp(-i * z))
atan2(z1, z2) = atan(z1/z2)
```

You can also use the following methods:

Im(z)	**Re(z)**	**abs(z)**	**acos(z)**
acosh(z)	**acot(z)**	**acoth(z)**	**acsc(z)**
acsch(z)	**arg(z)**	**asec(z)**	**asech(z)**
asin(z)	**asinh(z)**	**atan(z)**	**atanh(z)**
cbrt(z)	**cosh(z)**	**cot(z)**	**coth(z)**
csc(z)	**csch(z)**	**log10(z)**	**logn(z,n)**
sec(z)	**sech(z)**	**sinh(z)**	**tan(z)**
tanh(z)			

Math::Trig

This module defines the full set of trigonometric functions.

```
use Math::Trig;
```

The supplied functions are as follows.

```
tan
```

returns the tangent.

```
csc, cosec, sec, cot, cotan
```

The cofunctions of sine, cosine, and tangent. The **csc** and **cosec** are aliases for each other, as are **cot** and **cotan**.

```
asin, acos, atan
```

The arcus (inverse) of sin, cos, and tan.

```
atan2(y, x)
```

The principle value of the arctangent of **y/x**.

```
acsc, acosec, asec, acot, acotan
```

The arcus cofunctions.

```
sinh, cosh, tanh
```

The hyperbolic functions.

```
csch, cosech, sech, coth, cotanh
```

The cofunctions of the hyperbolics.

```
asinh, acosh, atanh
```

The arcus of the hyperbolics.

```
acsch, acosech, asech, acoth, acotanh
```

The arcus cofunctions of the hyperbolics.
The module also defines the constant **pi**.

Net::Ping

This module supports a simplified interface, to the process of determining a remote host's accessibility.

```
use Net::Ping;
```

The module uses an object-oriented interface and makes use of the **alarm** function and associated signal to test for a suitable time-out value. To create a new **Ping** object:

```
Net::Ping->new([PROTO [, TIMEOUT [, BYTES]]]);
```

The **PROTO**, if specified, should be one of "tcp," "udp," or "icmp." You should use "udp" or "icmp" in preference to "tcp" due to network bandwidth. The default is "udp."

The default **TIMEOUT** should be specified in seconds and be greater than zero. The default value is five seconds. The **BYTES** parameter specifies the number of bytes to be sent to the remote host. The minimum value should be 1 if the protocol is "udp," 0 otherwise. The maximum size is 1024 bytes.

The following methods are supported by the new object.

```
ping(HOST [, TIMEOUT]);
```

Pings the remote **HOST** and waits for a response. The method waits the number of seconds defined when the object was created, or **TIMEOUT** seconds if specified. The method returns 1 if the lookup was successful, 0 otherwise. The **undef** value is returned if the host cannot be resolved.

```
close();
```

Closes the network connection. The connection is automatically closed if the object goes out of scope.

The module also supports a single function, **pingecho**, for backward compatibility:

```
pingecho(HOST [, TIMEOUT])
```

This pings **HOST** using the **tcp** protocol, returning 1 if the host can be reached, 0 otherwise. If the **HOST** cannot be resolved, the function returns **undef**.

Reference   Chapter 12

NDBM_File

```
use NDBM_File;
use Fcntl;

tie(%db, 'NDBM_File', 'db', O_RDWR|O_CREAT, 0640);
untie %db;
```

This module is an interface supporting, via **tie**, the new (standard) DBM data storage format.

References   Chapter 13; *see also* **AnyDBM_File, DB_File, GDBM_File, ODBM_File, SDBM_File**

O

This module supports the generic interface to the Perl compiler backends.

```
perl -MO=Backend[OPTIONS] foo.pl
```

Most backends support the following **OPTIONS**. These should be supplied a comma-separated list of words without white space.

-V   Puts the backend into verbose mode

-oFILE   Specifies the name of the output **FILE**

-D   Switches on backend debugging flags

References   Chapter 22; *see also* **B, B::Asmdata, B::Bblock, B::Bytecode, B::C, B::CC, B::Debug, B::Deparse, B::Disassembler, B::Lint, B::Showlex, B::Stackobj, B::Terse, B::Xref**

ODBM_File

```
use ODBM_File;
use Fcntl;
tie(%db, 'ODBM_File', 'db', O_RDWR|O_CREAT, 0640);
untie %db;
```

This is an interface supporting, via **tie**, the old DBM data storage format.

References   Chapter 13; *see also* **AnyDBM_File, DB_File, GDBM_File, NDBM_File, SDBM_File**

Opcode

This module is
used by the **Safe** module and **ops** pragma to disable named opcodes when compiling Perl scripts.

```
use Opcode;
```

An opcode is the smallest executable element of a Perl program, and it is the internal format of a Perl script once it has been compiled. You shouldn't normally need to use this module; the **Safe** and **ops** interfaces are more practical. However, the information provided here is useful background and reference for both modules.

The module works by creating an opcode mask using the supported functions and defined opcode names and sets. Once the opcode mask has been created, you can execute your program. The execution will croak if an attempt is made to use an opcode defined in the current mask. Note that the created opcode mask only affects the *next* compilation, that is, one executed by **eval**. It does not affect the current script.

Functions

Most functions accept a number of arguments, and these are defined as **OPNAME**, which is the individual name of an opcode; **OPTAG**, for a group of opcodes; or an **OPSET**, which is a binary string that holds a set of zero or more operators. Functions are provided for building **OPSET** strings. Both **OPNAME** and **OPTAG** can be negated by prefixing the name or set with an exclamation mark. **OPTAG** names start with a colon.

```
opcodes
```

In a scalar context, returns the number of opcodes in the current Perl binary. In a list context, returns a list of all the opcodes. This is not yet implemented, so use

```
@names = opset_to_opts(full_opset);
```

to get the full list.

```
opset(OPNAME, ...)
```

returns an **OPSET** containing the listed operators.

```
opset_to_ops(OPSET)
```

returns a list of operator names corresponding to those operators in the **OPSET**.

```
opset_to_hex(OPSET)
```

returns a string representation of an **OPSET**.

`full_opset`

returns an **OPSET** that includes all operators.

`empty_opset`

returns an **OPSET** that contains no operators.

`invert_opset(OPSET)`

returns an **OPSET** that is the inverse set of the one supplied.

`verify_opset(OPSET, ...)`

returns true if **OPSET** is valid; returns false otherwise. If you supply a second argument and it is true, the function calls **croak** if the **OPSET** is invalid.

`define_optag(OPTAG, OPSET)`

creates **OPTAG** as a symbolic name for **OPSET**.

`opmask_add(OPSET)`

adds **OPSET** to the current opcode mask. You cannot unmask opcodes once added.

`opmask`

returns the **OPSET** corresponding to the current opcode mask.

`opdesc(OPNAME, ...)`

returns a list of descriptions for the supplied **OPNAME**s.

`opdump(PAT)`

prints to **STDOUT** a list of opcode names and corresponding descriptions. If **PAT** is supplied, only lines that match the pattern will be listed.

Opcode Sets

A number of predefined **OPSET** values are supplied as standard. They are logically divided into both function and security-conscious sets.

:base_core

aassign	abs	add	aelem
aelemfast	and	andassign	anoncode
aslice	av2arylen	bit_and	bit_or
bit_xor	chomp	chop	chr
complement	cond_expr	const	defined
delete	die	divide	each
enter	entersub	eq	exists
flip	flop	ge	gt
helem	hex	hslice	i_add
i_divide	i_eq	i_ge	i_gt
i_le	i_lt	i_modulo	i_multiply
i_ncmp	i_ne	i_negate	i_postdec
i_postinc	i_predec	i_preinc	i_subtract
index	int	keys	lc
lcfirst	le	leave	leaveeval
leavesub	leavesublv	left_shift	length
lineseq	list	lslice	lt
match	method	method_named	modulo
multiply	ncmp	ne	negate
nextstate	not	null	oct
or	orassign	ord	pop
pos	postdec	postinc	pow
predec	preinc	prototype	push

pushmark	qr	quotemeta	return
reverse	right_shift	rindex	rv2av
rv2cv	rv2hv	rv2sv	sassign
scalar	schomp	schop	scmp
scope	seq	setstate	sge
sgt	shift	sle	slt
sne	splice	split	stringify
stub	study	substr	subtract
trans	uc	ucfirst	undef
unshift	values	vec	wantarray
warn	xor		

:base_mem

concat	repeat	join	range
anonlist	anonhash		

:base_loop

enteriter	enterloop	goto	grepstart
grepwhile	iter	last	leaveloop
mapstart	mapwhile	next	Redo
unstack			

:base_io

enterwrite	eof	formline	getc
leavewrite	print	rcatline	read
readdir	readline	recv	rewinddir
seek	seekdir	send	sysread
sysseek	syswrite	tell	telldir

:base_orig

bless	crypt	dbmclose	dbmopen
entertry	gelem	getpgrp	getppid
getpriority	gmtime	gv	gvsv
leavetry	localtime	padany	padav
padhv	padsv	pipe_op	prtf
pushre	ref	refgen	regcmaybe
regcomp	regcreset	rv2gv	select
setpgrp	setpriority	sockpair	sprintf
srefgen	sselect	subst	substcont
tie	untie		

:base_math

atan2	cos	exp	log
rand	sin	sqrt	srand

:base_thread

lock	threadsv

:default

This set is made up of the following other sets.

:base_core	:base_mem	:base_loop	:base_io
:base_orig	:base_thread		

:filesys_read

fileno	ftatime	ftbinary	ftblk
ftchr	ftctime	ftdir	fteexec
fteowned	fteread	ftewrite	ftfile

ftis	ftlink	ftmtime	ftpipe
ftrexec	ftrowned	ftrread	ftrwrite
ftsgid	ftsize	ftsock	ftsuid
ftsvtx	fttext	fttty	ftzero
lstat	readlink	stat	

:sys_db

egrent	ehostent	enetent	eprotoent
epwent	eservent	getlogin	ggrent
ggrgid	ggrnam	ghbyaddr	ghbyname
ghostent	gnbyaddr	gnbyname	gnetent
gpbyname	gpbynumber	gprotoent	gpwent
gpwnam	gpwuid	gsbyname	gsbyport
gservent	sgrent	shostent	snetent
sprotoent	spwent	sservent	

:browser

This collection of opcodes is more practical than the **:default** set.

:default	:filesys_read	:sys_db

:filesys_open

binmode	close	closedir	open
open_dir	sysopen	umask	

:filesys_write

chmod	chown	fcntl	link
mkdir	rename	rmdir	symlink
truncate	unlink	utime	

:subprocess

backtick	fork	glob	system
wait	waitpid		

:ownprocess

exec	exit	kill	time	tms

:others

This set holds a list of other opcodes that are not otherwise handled and don't deserve their own tags.

msgctl	msgget	msgrcv	msgsnd
semctl	semget	semop	shmctl
shmget	shmread	shmwrite	

:still_to_be_decided

accept	alarm	bind	caller
chdir	connect	dbstate	dofile
entereval	flock	getpeername	getsockname
gsockopt	ioctl	listen	pack
require	reset	shutdown	sleep
socket	sort	ssockopt	tied
unpack			

:dangerous

These are possibly dangerous tags not mentioned elsewhere.

syscall	dump	chroot

Pod::Functions

Used by the internal **Pod** libraries. You shouldn't need to use this function on its own, unless you are developing your own Pod interface.

References   Chapter 23; *see also* **Pod::Html**, **Pod::Text**

Pod::Html

Supports a single function, **pod2html**, for translating POD formatted documents into HTML documents.

```
use Pod::Html;
pod2html("pod2html",
            "--podpath=lib",
            "--podroot=/usr/local/lib/perl5/5.00502/",
            "--htmlroot=/usr/local/http/docs",
            "--recurse",
            "--infile=foo.pod",
            "--outfile=/perl/foo.html");
```

For a full list of supported options, see Table C-13.

References   Chapter 23; *see also* **Pod::Text**

Pod::Text

Supports the **pod2text** script for translating documents from POD format to normal text.

```
use Pod::Text;
pod2text(LIST);
```

If **LIST** is only one argument, it is taken as the name of a file to translate. The translated output is automatically sent to **STDOUT**. If a second argument is specified, it is taken as a reference to a filehandle to which the output should be sent.

APPENDIXES

Option	Description
--flush	Flushes the contents of the item and directory caches created during the parsing of a POD document.
--help	Prints a help message.
--htmlroot	The base directory from which you reference documents relatively. This is required if you expect to install the generated HTML files onto a web server. The default is /.
--index	Generates an index of **=head1** elements at the top of the HTML file that is generated (default).
--infile	The file name to convert. You don't have to use this element; the first nonhyphenated argument is taken as a file name. If you don't specify a file by either method, it will accept input from standard input.
--libpods	A colon-separated list of pages searched when referencing **=item** entries. These are not the file names, just the page names, as they would appear in **L<>** link elements.
--netscape	Uses Netscape-specific browser directives when necessary.
--nonetscape	Prevents the use of Netscape-specific browser directives (default).
--outfile	The destination file name for the generated HTML. Uses standard output if none is specified.
--podpath	A colon-separated list of directories containing pod files and libraries.
--podroot	The base directory prepended to each entry in the **podpath** command line argument. The default is "."—the current directory.
--noindex	Don't generate an index at the top of the HTML file that is generated.
--norecurse	Don't recurse into the subdirectories specified in the **podpath** option.
--recurse	Recurse into the **subdirectories** specified in the **podpath** option (this is the default behavior).
--title	The contents of the <TITLE> tag in the created HTML document.
--verbose	Produces status and progress messages during production.

Table B-13. *Options for Translating POD to HTML*

You can optionally insert two arguments before the input file. The **-a** option instructs the function to use an alternative format that does not make assumptions about the capabilities of the destination output stream. Without this option, termcap may be used to format the document (you can force this by setting **$Pod::Text::termcap** to a value of one); or if termcap is not available, backspaces will be used to simulate boldfaced and underlined text.

The **-width** argument should be the width of the output device, where **width** is the number of characters to use (the default value is 72 characters), or the value of your terminal if this can be determined with termcap.

References   Chapter 23; *see also* **Pod::Html**

POSIX

 use POSIX;

The **POSIX** module provides an interface to the POSIX standard—a set of standards designed to provide a common set of features across operating systems, primarily Unix. The **POSIX** module also supports many of the constants and static definitions required when using **fcntl**, **ioctl**, and other I/O-related functions.

The full range of the POSIX functions has been the subject of many books. The best of these is *The POSIX Programmers Guide* by Donald Lewine (O'Reilly & Associates, Sebastopol, CA, 1991).

When possible, the interface to the underlying POSIX library is made as Perl compatible as possible. This means that some of the interface is handled by functions and some is handled by objects and classes. As a general rule, when a structure would normally be returned by a function, the Perl equivalent returns a list.

The list of functions supported by the module is shown in Table B-14. Note that some functions are C specific and, therefore, are not supported within the interface.

Supported Classes

The **POSIX** module provides three new classes: **POSIX::SigSet**, **POSIX::SigAction**, and **POSIX::Termios**.

Constant	Description
_exit	Exits the current process.
abort	Aborts the current script, sending the **ABRT** signal to the Perl interpreter.
abs	Identical to the Perl function; returns the absolute value.
access	Returns true if the file can be accessed to the specified level.
acos	Returns the arc cosine of a number.
alarm	Identical to the Perl **alarm** function.
asctime	Converts a time structure to its string equivalent.
asin	Returns the arcsine of a number.
assert	Currently unimplemented. Aborts the current program if the assertion fails.
atan	Returns the arctan of a number.
atan2	Identical to the Perl function.
atexit	Not supported. Use an **END{}** block instead.
atof	C specific.
atoi	C specific.
atol	C specific.
bsearch	Not supported. The functionality can normally be supported by using a hash.
calloc	C specific.
ceil	Identical to the C function; returns the smallest integer value greater than or equal to the supplied value.
cfgetispeed	Method for obtaining the input baud rate. See the section on the **POSIX::Termios** import set.
cfgetospeed	Method for obtaining the output baud rate. See the section on the **POSIX::Termios** import set.
cfsetispeed	Method for setting the input baud rate. See the section on the **POSIX::Termios** import set.

Table B-14.   *Functions in the POSIX Module*

Constant	Description
cfsetospeed	Method for setting the output baud rate. See the section on the **POSIX::Termios** import set.
chdir	Identical to the Perl function.
chmod	Identical to the Perl function.
chown	Identical to the Perl function.
clearerr	Not supported. Use the **FileHandle::clearerr** function.
clock	Returns an approximation of the amount of CPU time used by the program.
close	Closes the file descriptor created by the **POSIX::open** function.
closedir	Identical to the Perl function.
cos	Returns the cosine of a value.
cosh	Returns the hyperbolic cosine of a value.
creat	Creates a new file, returning the file descriptor.
ctermid	Returns the pathname to the device for controlling terminal for the current program.
ctime	Returns a formatted string for the supplied time. Similar to the scalar value returned by **localtime**.
cuserid	Returns the current user name.
difftime	Returns the difference between two times.
div	C specific.
dup	Duplicates an open file descriptor.
dup2	Duplicates an open file descriptor.
errno	Returns the value of **errno**.
execl	C specific. Use the built-in **exec** function instead.
execle	C specific. Use the built-in **exec** function instead.
execlp	C specific. Use the built-in **exec** function instead.
execv	C specific. Use the built-in **exec** function instead.

Table B-14.   *Functions in the POSIX Module* (continued)

Constant	Description
execve	C specific. Use the built-in **exec** function instead.
execvp	C specific. Use the built-in **exec** function instead.
exit	Identical to the Perl function.
exp	Identical to the Perl function.
fabs	Identical to the built-in **abs** function.
fclose	Use the **FileHandle::close** method instead.
fcntl	Identical to the Perl function.
fdopen	Use the **FileHandle::new_from_fd** method instead.
feof	Use the **FileHandle::eof** method instead.
ferror	Use the **FileHandle::error** method instead.
fflush	Use the **FileHandle::flush** method instead.
fgetc	Use the **FileHandle::getc** method instead.
fgetpos	Use the **FileHandle::getpos** method instead.
fgets	Use the **FileHandle::gets** method instead.
fileno	Use the **FileHandle::fileno** method instead.
floor	Returns the largest integer not greater than the number supplied.
fmod	Returns the floating point remainder after dividing two numbers using integer math.
fopen	Use the **FileHandle::open** method instead.
fork	Identical to the Perl function.
fpathconf	Returns the configural limit for a file or directory using the specified file descriptor.
fprintf	C specific. Use the built-in **printf** function instead.
fputc	C specific. Use the built-in **print** function instead.
fputs	C specific. Use the built-in **print** function instead.
fread	C specific. Use the built-in **read** function instead.

Table B-14. *Functions in the POSIX Module* (continued)

Constant	Description
free	C specific.
freopen	C specific. Use the built-in **open** function instead.
frexp	Returns the mantissa and exponent of a floating point number.
fscanf	C specific. Use <> and regular expression instead.
fseek	Use the **FileHandle::seek** method instead.
fsetpos	Use the **FileHandle::setpos** method instead.
fstat	Gets the file status information for a given file descriptor.
ftell	Use the **FileHandle::tell** method instead.
fwrite	C specific. Use the built-in **print** function instead.
getc	Identical to the Perl function.
getchar	Returns one character read from **STDIN**.
getcwd	Returns the path to the current working directory.
getegid	Returns the effect group ID for the current process. Use **$)**.
getenv	Returns the value of the specified environment variable. Use **%ENV**.
geteuid	Identical to the Perl function.
getgid	Returns the current process's real group ID. Use **$(**.
getgrgid	Identical to the Perl function.
getgrnam	Identical to the Perl function.
getgroups	Identical to the Perl function.
getlogin	Identical to the Perl function.
getpgrp	Identical to the Perl function.
getpid	Gets the current process ID. Use the **$$** value.
getppid	Identical to the Perl function.
getpwnam	Identical to the Perl function.
getpwuid	Identical to the Perl function.

Table B-14.   *Functions in the POSIX Module* (continued)

Constant	Description
gets	Returns a line from **STDIN**.
getuid	Gets the current user ID. Use the value of $<.
gmtime	Identical to the Perl function.
isalnum	Returns true if the string is composed only of letters (irrespective of case) or numbers.
isalpha	Returns true if the string is composed only of letters (irrespective of case).
isatty	Returns true if the specified filehandle is connected to a TTY device.
iscntrl	Returns true if the string is composed only of control characters.
isdigit	Returns true if the string is composed only of digits.
isgraph	Returns true if the string is composed only of printable characters, except space.
islower	Returns true if the string is composed only of lowercase characters.
isprint	Returns true if the string is composed only of printable characters, including space.
ispunct	Returns true if the string is composed only of punctuation characters.
isspace	Returns true if the string is composed only of white-space characters. Within the default C and POSIX locales are space, form feed, newline, carriage return, horizontal tab, and vertical tab.
isupper	Returns true if the string is composed only of uppercase characters.
isxdigit	Returns true if the string is composed only of hexadecimal characters, "a–z", "A–Z", "0–9".
kill	Identical to the Perl function.
labs	C specific. Use the built-in **abs** function.
ldexp	Multiplies a floating point number by a power of 2 (**ldexp(num,pow)**).

Table B-14. *Functions in the POSIX Module* (continued)

Constant	Description
ldiv	C specific. Use **int($a/$b)** instead.
localeconv	Gets numeric formatting information. See the **locale_h** import set entry later in this appendix.
localtime	Identical to the Perl function.
log	Identical to the Perl function.
log10	Computes the logarithmic value in base 10.
longjmp	C specific. Use **die** instead.
lseek	Moves the read/write pointer within an open file descriptor.
malloc	C specific.
mblen	Returns the length of a multibyte string.
mbstowcs	Converts a multibyte string to a wide character string.
mbtowc	Converts a multibyte character to a wide character.
memchr	C specific. Use the built-in **index** function.
memcmp	C specific. Use **eq** instead.
memcpy	C specific. Use = instead.
memmove	C specific. Use = instead.
memset	C specific. Use **x** instead.
mkdir	Identical to the Perl function.
mkfifo	Creates a fifo (named pipe).
mktime	Converts date and time information to a calendar time.
modf	Returns the integral and fractional parts of a floating point number.
nice	Changes the execution priority of a process.
offsetof	C specific.
open	Opens a file, returning a file descriptor. Accepts three arguments: the file name, mode, and permissions (in octal).
opendir	Identical to the Perl function.

Table B-14. *Functions in the POSIX Module* (continued)

Constant	Description
pathconf	Gets configuration values for a specified file or directory.
pause	Suspends the execution of a process until it receives a signal with an associated handler.
perror	Prints the error message associated with the error in **errno**.
pipe	Creates an interprocess communication channel returning file descriptors for use with **open** and related functions.
pow	Raises a number to the specified power (**pow(num,power)**).
printf	Identical to the Perl function.
putc	C specific. Use the built-in **print** instead.
putchar	C specific. Use the built-in **print** instead.
puts	C specific. Use the built-in **print** instead.
qsort	C specific. Use the built-in **sort** instead.
raise	Sends the specified signal to the current process.
rand	Not supported. Use the built-in **rand** function.
readdir	Identical to the Perl version.
realloc	C specific.
remove	Identical to the Perl **unlink** function.
rewind	Seeks to the beginning of the specified filehandle.
rewinddir	Identical to the Perl version.
scanf	C specific. Use the <> operator and regular expressions.
setbuf	Sets how a filehandle will be buffered.
setgid	Sets the group ID for the process. Equivalent to setting the value of **$(**.
setjmp	C specific. Use **eval** instead.
setlocale	Sets the current locale. See the **local_h** import set section, later in this appendix.
setpgid	Sets the process group ID.

Table B-14. *Functions in the POSIX Module* (continued)

Constant	Description
setsid	Creates a new session and sets the process group ID of the current process.
setuid	Sets the user ID. Equivalent to setting the value of $<.
setvbuf	Sets and defines how the buffer for a filehandle works.
sigaction	Defines a signal handler. See the upcoming **POSIX::SigAction** section.
siglongjmp	C specific. Use the **die** function instead.
signal	C specific. Use the **%SIG** hash instead.
sigpending	Returns information about signals that are blocked and pending. See the upcoming **POSIX::SigSet** section.
sigprocmask	Changes or examines the current process's signal mask. See the upcoming **POSIX::SigSet** section.
sigsetjmp	C specific. Use **eval** instead.
sigsuspend	Installs a signal mask and suspends the process until a signal arrives. See the upcoming **POSIX::SigSet** import set section.
sin	Returns the sine for a given value.
sinh	Returns the hyperbolic sine for a given value.
sleep	Identical to the Perl function.
sprintf	Identical to the Perl function.
sqrt	Identical to the Perl function.
srand	Identical to the Perl function.
sscanf	C specific. Use regular expressions.
stat	Identical to the Perl function.
strcat	C specific. Use .= instead.
strchr	C specific. Use the built-in **index** function instead.
strcmp	C specific. Use **eq** instead.
strcoll	Compares two strings using the current locale.
strcpy	C specific. Use = instead.

Table B-14. *Functions in the POSIX Module* (continued)

Constant	Description
strcspn	C specific. Use regular expressions instead.
strerror	Returns the error string for a specific error number.
strftime	Returns a formatted string based on the supplied date and time information.
strlen	C specific. Use the built-in **length** function instead.
strncat	C specific. Use **.=** or **substr** instead.
strncmp	C specific. Use **eq** or **substr** instead.
strncpy	C specific. Use **eq** or **substr** instead.
strpbrk	C specific.
strrchr	C specific. Use **eq** or **substr** instead.
strspn	C specific.
strstr	Identical to the Perl **index** function.
strtod	C specific.
strtok	C specific.
strtol	C specific.
strtoul	C specific.
strxfrm	Transforms the supplied string.
sysconf	Retrieves values from the system configuration tables.
tan	Returns the tangent of a value.
tanh	Returns the hyperbolic tangent of a value.
tcdrain	See the section on **POSIX::Termios**.
tcflow	See the section on **POSIX::Termios**.
tcflush	See the section on **POSIX::Termios**.
tcgetattr	See the section on **POSIX::Termios**.
tcgetpgrp	See the section on **POSIX::Termios**.
tcsendbreak	See the section on **POSIX::Termios**.
tcsetattr	See the section on **POSIX::Termios**.

Table B-14. *Functions in the POSIX Module* (continued)

Constant	Description
tcsetpgrp	See the section on **POSIX::Termios**.
time	Identical to the Perl function.
times	Similar to the Perl function, but returns five values (realtime, user, system, childuser, and childsystem) counted in clock ticks rather than seconds.
tmpfile	Use the **FileHandle::new_tmpfile** method instead.
tmpnam	Returns the name for a temporary file.
tolower	Identical to the Perl **lc** function.
toupper	Identical to the Perl **uc** function.
ttyname	Returns the path to the terminal associated with the supplied filehandle.
tzname	Returns the offset and daylight saving time settings for the current time zone.
tzset	Sets the current time zone using the **$ENV{TZ}** variable.
umask	Identical to the Perl function.
uname	Returns the system name, node name, release, version, and machine for the current operating system.
ungetc	Use the **FileHandle::ungetc** method instead.
unlink	Identical to the Perl function.
utime	Identical to the Perl function.
vfprintf	C specific.
vprintf	C specific.
vsprintf	C specific.
wait	Identical to the Perl function.
waitpid	Identical to the Perl function.
wcstombs	Converts a wide character string to a multibyte character string.
wctomb	Converts a wide character to a multibyte character.
write	Writes to a file descriptor opened with **POSIX::open**.

Table B-14.   *Functions in the POSIX Module* (continued)

POSIX::SigSet

This provides an interface to the **sigset** function for creating signal sets. For installing handlers for these sets, use the **SigAction** class. See the **signal_h** import set for information about the available signal constants to use with the methods.

```
$sigset = POSIX::SigSet->new;
```

creates a new **SigSet** object. Additional methods are described here.

```
addset SIGNAL
```

adds a **SIGNAL** to an existing set.

```
delset SIGNAL
```

deletes a **SIGNAL** from a set.

```
emptyset
```

empties a signal set.

```
fillset
```

populates a signal set with all the available signals.

```
ismember SIGNAL
```

returns true if the signal set contains the specified signal.

POSIX::SigAction

This installs a signal handler against a specific **SigSet** object.

```
$sigaction = POSIX::SigAction->new('main::handler', $sigset, $flags);
```

The first parameter must be the fully qualified name of the signal handler routine. The second argument is the previously created **SigSet** object. The value of flags is a list of signal actions.

POSIX::Termios

This supports an interface to the termios interface driving system.

```
$termios = POSIX::Termios->new;
```

creates a new **Termios** object. The following additional methods are supported.

```
getattr FD
```

gets the attributes for the file descriptor specified. Uses zero (**STDIN**) by default.

```
getcc EXPR
```

gets the value from the **c_cc** field. The information is an array, so you must use an index value.

```
getcflag
```

returns the value of the **c_cflag**.

```
getiflag
```

returns the value of the **c_iflag**.

```
getispeed
```

returns the input baud rate.

```
getlflag
```

returns the value of the **c_lflag**.

```
getoflag
```

returns the value of the **c_oflag**.

```
getospeed
```

returns the output baud rate.

```
setattr FD, EXPR
```

sets the attributes for the file descriptor **FD**.

```
setcc EXPR, INDEX
```

sets the value of the **c_cc** field. The information is an array, so you must specify an index value.

```
getcflag EXPR
```

sets the value of the **c_cflag**.

```
getiflag EXPR
```

sets the value of the **c_iflag**.

```
getispeed EXPR
```

sets the input baud rate.

```
getlflag EXPR
```

sets the value of the **c_lflag**.

```
getoflag EXPR
```

sets the value of the **c_oflag**.

```
getospeed EXPR
```

sets the output baud rate.

See the **termios_h** import set for the lists of supported constants.

Symbol Sets

For convenience and compatibility, the functions and constants defined within the **POSIX** module are also grouped into symbol sets to import the required elements. The sets are grouped by the name of the header file that would be required if you were programming directly in C. To use, specify the header name, substituting underscores for periods, and prefixing the name with a colon. For example, to include the elements of the fcntl.h file:

```
use POSIX qw/:fcntl_h/;
```

For reference, the sets and functions they import, along with the constant they define, are listed under the headings that follow.

assert_h

This symbol set imports the following function: **assert**.
    The following constant function is also imported: **NDEBUG**.

ctype_h

This symbol set imports the following functions:

isalnum	Isalpha	iscntrl	isdigit
isgraph	Islower	isprint	ispunct
isspace	Isupper	isxdigit	tolower
toupper			

dirent_h

There are no imported elements for this symbol set, since the functions of dirent.h are supported as built-in functions within Perl.

errno_h

The constants defined within errno.h are those that specify the numerical error number normally contained within $!. The list of imported constants is as follows:

E2BIG	EACCES	EADDRINUSE
EADDRNOTAVAIL	EAFNOSUPPORT	EAGAIN
EALREADY	EBADF	EBUSY
ECHILD	ECONNABORTED	ECONNREFUSED
ECONNRESET	EDEADLK	EDESTADDRREQ
EDOM	EDQUOT	EEXIST
EFAULT	EFBIG	EHOSTDOWN
EHOSTUNREACH	EINPROGRESS	EINTR
EINVAL	EIO	EISCONN

EISDIR	ELOOP	EMFILE
EMLINK	EMSGSIZE	ENAMETOOLONG
ENETDOWN	ENETRESET	ENETUNREACH
ENFILE	ENOBUFS	ENODEV
ENOENT	ENOEXEC	ENOLCK
ENOMEM	ENOPROTOOPT	ENOSPC
ENOSYS	ENOTBLK	ENOTCONN
ENOTDIR	ENOTEMPTY	ENOTSOCK
ENOTTY	ENXIO	EOPNOTSUPP
EPERM	EPFNOSUPPORT	EPIPE
EPROCLIM	EPROTONOSUPPORT	EPROTOTYPE
ERANGE	EREMOTE	ERESTART
EROFS	ESHUTDOWN	ESOCKTNOSUPPORT
ESPIPE	ESRCH	ESTALE
ETIMEDOUT	ETOOMANYREFS	ETXTBSY
EUSERS	EWOULDBLOCK	EXDEV

fcntl_h

This symbol set imports the following function: **creat**.
This symbol set imports the following constants:

FD_CLOEXEC	F_DUPFD	F_GETFD	F_GETFL
F_GETLK	F_RDLCK	F_SETFD	F_SETFL
F_SETLK	F_SETLKW	F_UNLCK	F_WRLCK
O_ACCMODE	O_APPEND	O_CREAT	O_EXCL
O_NOCTTY	O_NONBLOCK	O_RDONLY	O_RDWR
O_TRUNC	O_WRONLY	SEEK_CUR	SEEK_END
SEEK_SET	S_IRGRP	S_IROTH	S_IRUSR
S_IRWXG	S_IRWXO	S_IRWXU	S_ISBLK
S_ISCHR	S_ISDIR	S_ISFIFO	S_ISGID
S_ISREG	S_ISUID	S_IWGRP	S_IWOTH
S_IWUSR			

float_h

This symbol set imports the following constants:

DBL_DIG	DBL_EPSILON	DBL_MANT_DIG
DBL_MAX	DBL_MAX_10_EXP	DBL_MAX_EXP
DBL_MIN	DBL_MIN_10_EXP	DBL_MIN_EXP
FLT_DIG	FLT_EPSILON	FLT_MANT_DIG
FLT_MAX	FLT_MAX_10_EXP	FLT_MAX_EXP
FLT_MIN	FLT_MIN_10_EXP	FLT_MIN_EXP
FLT_RADIX	FLT_ROUNDS	LDBL_DIG
LDBL_EPSILON	LDBL_MANT_DIG	LDBL_MAX
LDBL_MAX_10_EXP	LDBL_MAX_EXP	LDBL_MIN
LDBL_MIN_10_EXP	LDBL_MIN_EXP	

limits_h

This symbol set imports the following constants:

ARG_MAX	CHAR_BIT	CHAR_MAX
CHAR_MIN	CHILD_MAX	INT_MAX
INT_MIN	LINK_MAX	LONG_MAX
LONG_MIN	MAX_CANON	MAX_INPUT
MB_LEN_MAX	NAME_MAX	NGROUPS_MAX
OPEN_MAX	PATH_MAX	PIPE_BUF
SCHAR_MAX	SCHAR_MIN	SHRT_MAX
SHRT_MIN	SSIZE_MAX	STREAM_MAX
TZNAME_MAX	UCHAR_MAX	UINT_MAX
ULONG_MAX	USHRT_MAX	_POSIX_ARG_MAX
_POSIX_CHILD_MAX	_POSIX_LINK_MAX	_POSIX_MAX_CANON
_POSIX_MAX_INPUT	_POSIX_NAME_MAX	_POSIX_NGROUPS_MAX
_POSIX_OPEN_MAX	_POSIX_PATH_MAX	_POSIX_PIPE_BUF
_POSIX_SSIZE_MAX	_POSIX_STREAM_MAX	_POSIX_TZNAME_MAX

locale_h

This symbol set imports the following functions:

locateconv   setlocale

The **localeconv** function returns a reference to a hash with the following self-explanatory elements:

currency_symbol	decimal_point	frac_digits
grouping	int_curr_symbol	int_frac_digits
mon_decimal_point	mon_grouping	mon_thousands_sep
n_cs_precedes	n_sep_by_space	n_sign_posn
negative_sign	p_cs_precedes	p_sep_by_space
p_sign_posn	positive_sign	thousands_sep

This symbol set imports the following constants:

LC_ALL	LC_COLLATE	LC_CTYPE
LC_MONETARY	LC_NUMERIC	LC_TIME
NULL		

math_h

This symbol set imports the following functions:

acos	asin	atan	ceil
cosh	fabs	floor	fmod
frexp	ldexp	log10	modf
pow	sinh	tan	tanh

This symbol set imports the following constant: **HUGE_VAL**.

setjmp_h

This symbol set imports the following functions:

longjmp	setjmp	siglongjmp	sigsetjmp

signal_h

This symbol set imports the following functions:

raise	sigaction	signal	sigpending
sigprocmask	sigsuspend		

This symbol set imports the following constants:

SA_NOCLDSTOP	SA_NOCLDWAIT	SA_NODEFER
SA_ONSTACK	SA_RESETHAND	SA_RESTART
SA_SIGINFO	SIGABRT	SIGALRM
SIGCHLD	SIGCONT	SIGFPE
SIGHUP	SIGILL	SIGINT
SIGKILL	SIGPIPE	SIGQUIT
SIGSEGV	SIGSTOP	SIGTERM
SIGTSTP	SIGTTIN	SIGTTOU
SIGUSR1	SIGUSR2	SIG_BLOCK
SIG_DFL	SIG_ERR	SIG_IGN
SIG_SETMASK	SIG_UNBLOCK	

stddef_h

This symbol set imports the following function: **offsetof**.
This symbol set imports the following constant: **NULL**.

stdio_h

This symbol set imports the following functions:

clearerr	fclose	fdopen	feof	ferror
fflush	fgetc	fgetpos	fgets	fopen
fprintf	fputc	fputs	fread	freopen
fscanf	fseek	fsetpos	ftell	fwrite
getchar	gets	perror	putc	putchar
puts	remove	rewind	scanf	setbuf

setvbuf	sscanf	stderr	stdin	stdout
tmpfile	tmpnam	ungetc	vfprintf	vprintf
vsprintf				

This symbol set imports the following constants:

BUFSIZ	EOF	FILENAME_MAX	L_ctermid
L_cuserid	L_tmpname	NULL	SEEK_CUR
SEEK_END	SEEK_SET	STREAM_MAX	TMP_MAX

stdlib_h

This symbol set imports the following functions:

abort	atexit	atof	atoi	atol
bsearch	calloc	div	free	getenv
labs	ldiv	malloc	mblen	mbstowcs
mbtowc	qsort	realloc	strtod	strtol
strtoul	wcstombs	wctomb		

This symbol set imports the following constants:

EXIT_FAILURE	EXIT_SUCCESS	MB_CUR_MAX	NULL
RAND_MAX			

string_h

This symbol set imports the following functions:

memchr	memcmp	memcpy	memmove	memset
strcat	strchr	strcmp	strcoll	strcpy
strcspn	strerror	strlen	strncat	strncmp
strncpy	strpbrk	strrchr	strspn	strstr
strtok	strxfrm			

This symbol set imports the following constant: **NULL**.

sys_stat_h

This symbol set imports the following functions:

fstat   mkfifo

This symbol set imports the following constants:

S_IRGRP	S_IROTH	S_IRUSR	S_IRWXG	S_IRWXO
S_IRWXU	S_ISBLK	S_ISCHR	S_ISDIR	S_ISFIFO
S_ISGID	S_ISREG	S_ISUID	S_IWGRP	S_IWOTH
S_IWUSR	S_IXGRP	S_IXOTH	S_IXUSR	

sys_utsname_h

This symbol set imports the following function: **uname**.

sys_wait_h

This symbol set imports the following constants:

WEXITSTATUS	WIFEXITED	WIFSIGNALED	WIFSTOPPED
WNOHANG	WSTOPSIG	WTERMSIG	WUNTRACED

termios_h

This symbol set imports the following functions:

cfgetispeed	cfgetospeed	cfsetispeed	cfsetospeed
tcdrain	tcflow	tcflush	tcgetattr
tcsendbreak	tcsetattr		

This symbol set imports the following constants:

B0	B110	B1200	B134
B150	B1800	B19200	B200
B2400	B300	B38400	B4800
B50	B600	B75	B9600
BRKINT	CLOCAL	CREAD	CS5
CS6	CS7	CS8	CSIZE

CSTOPB	ECHO	ECHOE	ECHOK
ECHONL	HUPCL	ICANON	ICRNL
IEXTEN	IGNBRK	IGNCR	IGNPAR
INLCR	INPCK	ISIG	ISTRIP
IXOFF	IXON	NCCS	NOFLSH
OPOST	PARENB	PARMRK	PARODD
TCIFLUSH	TCIOFF	TCIOFLUSH	TCION
TCOFLUSH	TCOOFF	TCOON	TCSADRAIN
TCSAFLUSH	TCSANOW	TOSTOP	VEOF
VEOL	VERASE	VINTR	VKILL
VMIN	VQUIT	VSTART	VSTOP
VSUSP	VTIME		

time_h

This symbol set imports the following functions:

asctime	clock	ctime	difftime
mktime	strftime	tzset	tzname

This symbol set imports the following constants:

CLK_TCK	CLOCKS_PER_SEC	NULL

unistd_h

This symbol set imports the following functions:

_exit	access	ctermid	cuserid
dup	dup2	execl	execle
execlp	execv	execve	execvp
fpathconf	getcwd	getegid	geteuid
getgid	getgroups	getpid	getuid
isatty	lseek	pathconf	pause
setgid	setpgid	setsid	setuid
sysconf	tcgetpgrp	tcsetpgrp	ttyname

This symbol set imports the following constants:

F_OK	NULL
R_OK	SEEK_CUR
SEEK_END	SEEK_SET
STDIN_FILENO	STDOUT_FILENO
STRERR_FILENO	W_OK
X_OK	_PC_CHOWN_RESTRICTED
_PC_LINK_MAX	_PC_MAX_CANON
_PC_MAX_INPUT	_PC_NAME_MAX
_PC_NO_TRUNC	_PC_PATH_MAX
_PC_PIPE_BUF	_PC_VDISABLE
_POSIX_CHOWN_RESTRICTED	_POSIX_JOB_CONTROL
_POSIX_NO_TRUNC	_POSIX_SAVED_IDS
_POSIX_VDISABLE	_POSIX_VERSION
_SC_ARG_MAX	_SC_CHILD_MAX
_SC_CLK_TCK	_SC_JOB_CONTROL
_SC_NGROUPS_MAX	_SC_OPEN_MAX
_SC_SAVED_IDS	_SC_STREAM_MAX
_SC_TZNAME_MAX	_SC_VERSION

References   Chapters 6, 10, 11, 12, 13, 14, 15, 21, 22, Appendix A

Safe

This module creates a safe compartment for executing a Perl script.

```
use Safe;

$compartment = new Safe;
```

The created compartment has the following attributes:

■ A new name space. The new package has a new root name space, and code within the compartment cannot access the variables outside of this root name space. The parent script can optionally insert new variables into the name space, but the reverse is not true. Only the "underscore" variables ($_, @_, and %_) are shared between the parent and safe compartment.

■ An operator mask. This is generated using the opcode names and tags as defined in the **Opcode** module. Executing code within the new compartment that contains a masked operator will cause the compilation of the code to fail. By default, the operator mask uses the **:default** opcode set.

To create a new compartment:

```
$compartment = new Safe;
```

An optional argument specifies the name of the new root name space. The module then supports the following methods.

```
permit(OP, ...)
```

adds the specified opcodes or sets to the mask when compiling code in the compartment.

```
permit_only(OP, ...)
```

exclusively sets the specified opcodes or sets in the mask when compiling code in the compartment.

```
deny(OP, ...)
```

deletes the specified opcodes or sets from the current mask.

```
deny_only(OP, ...)
```

denies only the listed opcodes or sets.

```
trap(OP, ...)
```

is synonymous with **deny**.

```
untrap(OP, ...)
```

is synonymous with **permit**.

```
share(NAME, ...)
```

shares the specified variables with the compartment.

```
share_from(PACKAGE, ARRAY)
```

shares the list of symbols defined in the array of references **ARRAY** from the specified **PACKAGE** with the compartment.

```
varglob(VARNAME)
```

returns a glob reference for the symbol table entry of **VARNAME** with the package of the compartment.

```
reval(STRING)
```

evaluates **STRING** within the compartment.

```
rdo(FILENAME)
```

executes the script **FILENAME** in the compartment.

```
root(NAMESPACE)
```

returns the name of the package that is the root of the compartment's name space.

```
mask(MASK)
```

When **MASK** is not specified, returns the entire operator mask for the compartment. If **MASK** is specified, then it sets the compartment's operator mask.

References   Chapter 15; *see also* **Opcode, ops**

SDBM_File

```
use SDBM_File;
use Fcntl;

tie(%db, 'SDBM_File', 'db', O_RDWR|O_CREAT, 0640);
untie %db;
```

This is an interface supporting access to the Perl-supplied **SDBM** database using tie.

References   Chapter 13; *see also* **AnyDBM_File, DB_File, GDBM_File, NDBM_File, ODBM_File**

Search::Dict

```
use Search::Dict;
look *FILEHANDLE, $key, $dict, $fold;
```

The **look** function sets the current location within the **FILEHANDLE** to the first occurrence of **$key**, or the closest match that is greater than or equal to it. This can be used, as the name suggests, to locate a word within a dictionary that lists words, one per line. If **$dict** is true, the search is conducted in strict dictionary (alphabetical) order, ignoring everything that is not a word character. The dictionary file should have been sorted with the Unix **sort** command and the **-d** option. If **$fold** is true, the case is ignored.

References   Chapter 13; *see also* **Text::Abbrev, Text::Soundex**

SelectSaver

This module provides an alternative to the **select** function for selecting the default output filehandle.

```
use SelectSaver;
```

You use it within a block:

```
use SelectSaver;

#STDOUT is selected
{
    my $saver = new SelectSaver(MYOUT);
    #MYOUT is selected
}
#STDOUT is selected again
```

Once the block exits, the selected filehandle returns to the value selected before the block.

References Chapters 4, 7

SelfLoader

This module provides a system similar to **AutoLoader** except that functions are self-loaded from the script rather than from separate files.

```
package MyPackage;
use SelfLoader;
```

Like **AutoLoader**, the module delays the loading of functions until they are called. Unlike **AutoLoader**, the functions themselves are defined after the _ _DATA_ _ token. This token signifies to Perl that the code to be compiled has ended, and the functions defined in _ _DATA_ _ are available via the **MyPackage::DATA** filehandle.

The _ _DATA_ _ definitions for a single package can span multiple files, but the last _ _DATA_ _ token in a given package is the one accessible via the **MyPackage::DATA** filehandle. Reading from the **DATA** filehandle ends when it sees the _ _END_ _ token. But it will restart if the _ _END_ _ token is immediately followed by a **DATA** token (not to be confused with the _ _DATA_ _ token).

The method used by the **SelfLoader** package is to read in the contents of the filehandle to identify the defined functions. When the function is first called, it uses **eval** to parse the requested subroutine. The **SelfLoader** exports an **AUTOLOAD** subroutine to be used for loading the packages from the **DATA** filehandle.

Unlike **AutoLoader**, there is a small overhead for having the definitions parsed once at compile time. Other than that, execution will seem faster because functions are only compiled when used, thus negating the need to compile unused functions. There is no advantage to defining often-used functions with **SelfLoader**.

Note that lexically defined values (via **my**) are visible to functions only up to the _ _DATA_ _ token. Functions that rely on lexicals cannot be autoloaded, either by

AutoLoader or SelfLoader. Remember to use the **vars** pragma if you are also using the **strict** pragma.

References   Chapters 6, 20, 25; *see also* **AutoLoader, Devel::SelfStubber**

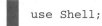
Shell

This module allows you to use shell commands directly without the need to use backticks or the **system** function.

```
use Shell;
```

If you do not explicitly specify any commands, then all are assumed.
    Once loaded, you can use the shell commands just like a normal Perl function:

```
use Shell;

print ps('-ef');
```

If you want to use them without parentheses, either import explicitly or declare the shell command as a function before you use it:

```
use Shell;
sub ps;
print ps -ef;
```

The actual method of supporting this operation is to use the **AUTOLOAD** system to call the supported command.

References   Chapters 14, 15

Socket

This module defines the core functions and utility routines for supporting socket-based communication.

```
use Socket;
```

The module defines a core set of functions, as shown in Table B-15.

References   Chapter 12; *see also* **IO::Socket**

Function	Description
inet_aton HOSTNAME	Returns a 4-byte packed IP address for **HOSTNAME**, or **undef** if it cannot be resolved.
	Returns a string in the form *x.x.x.x* based on the supplied 4-byte packed IP address.
inet_ntoa IP_ADDRESS	Returns a 4-byte packed string defining the wildcard address for accepting connections.
INADDR_BROADCAST	Returns a 4-byte packed string defining the broadcast address.
INADDR_LOOPBACK	Returns a 4-byte packed string defining the loopback address for the current host.
INADDR_NONE	Returns a 4-byte packed string defining the invalid IP address.
sockaddr_in PORT, ADDRESS	Packs **PORT** and **ADDRESS** into a **sockaddr_in** structure.
sockaddr_in SOCKADDR_IN	Unpacks and returns the **SOCKADDR_IN** structure into port and IP address.
pack_sockaddr_in PORT, ADDRESS	Packs **PORT** and **ADDRESS** into a **sockaddr_in** structure.
unpack_sockaddr_in SOCKADDR_IN	Unpacks and returns the **SOCKADDR_IN** structure into port and IP address.
sockaddr_un PATHNAME	Packs **PATHNAME** into a **sockaddr_un** structure.
sockaddr_un SOCKADDR_UN	Unpacks **SOCKADDR_UN** structure into a pathname.
pack_sockaddr_un PATHNAME	Packs **PATHNAME** into a **sockaddr_un** structure.
unpack_sockaddr_un SOCKADDR_UN	Unpacks **SOCKADDR_UN** structure into a pathname.

Table B-15. *Functions Defined in the **Socket** Module*

Symbol

This module provides a set of functions for manipulating Perl symbols and their names.

```
use Symbol;

$glob = gensym;
print qualify($symbol, $pkg);
print qualify_to_ref($symbol, $pkg);
```

The **gensym** function returns a reference to an anonymous glob. The resulting reference is suitable for use as a file or directory handle. This is useful when you want to use a filehandle but do not want to name it directly.

The **qualify** function returns a string containing the qualified variable name for the supplied **$symbol** (which should be a string). If you supply **$pkg**, it will be used as the default package for variables not defined within a separate package in place of the normal **main::**. In all cases, the returned string contains the true qualification, such that function **foo** in package **Bar** will always resolve to **Bar::foo**. These two lines would print the same value:

```
print qualify('foo','Bar'),"\n";
print qualify('foo','foo'),"\n";
```

References are assumed to be glob references and, therefore, return their true, qualified name by their very nature.

The **qualify_to_ref** function is identical to **qualify** except that it returns a glob reference rather than a string.

The optional **delete_package** function deletes all of the symbol table entries and, therefore, the related variables, functions, and other structures:

```
use Symbol qw/delete_package/;

delete_package('Foo');
```

Reference   Chapter 6

Sys::Hostname

This module provides a semi-reliable method of determining a host's name by trying every conceivable method until the hostname is found.

```
use Sys::Hostname;
print "Hostname is ", hostname, "\n";
```

It tries **syscall(SYS_gethostname), 'hostname', 'uname -n'**, and the file /com/host, stripping any white space, line termination, or null characters as necessary. If it is still unable to find the hostname, it calls **croak**.

Note that this method may fail on non-Unix operating systems.

References   Chapter 9; *see also* **Carp**

Sys::Syslog

This module supports an interface to the Unix **syslog** logging system.

```
use Sys::Syslog;
```

There are four main functions imported by default: **openlog**, **syslog**, **setlogmask**, and **closelog**:

```
openlog IDENT, LOGOPT, FACILITY
```

Opens the system log. The string **IDENT** will prepend every message. The **LOGOPT** is a comma-separated list of options that equate to the standard **openlog** constants. See Table B-16 for a list.

The **FACILITY** argument is a string that defines the part of the system for which to record the log entries. Valid values are **user** for user-level entries, **kern** for kernel problems, and **daemon** for system daemons. These equate to the **LOG_USER**, **LOG_KERN**, and **LOG_DAEMON** constants used in the C interface. The exact list of supported values is system dependent.

```
syslog PRIORITY, FORMAT, LIST
```

APPENDIXES

String	C Constant	Description
pid	LOG_PID	Logs the process ID with each message.
ndelay	LOG_NDELAY	Opens the connection to the **syslogd** daemon immediately. Normally, the interface waits until the first message is posted to open the log.
cons	LOG_CONS	Writes messages to the system console if the **syslogd** daemon cannot be contacted.
nowait	LOG_NOWAIT	Don't wait for child processes (from **fork**) to log messages to the console.

Table B-16.   *Syslog* Options in Perl

This records an entry in the system log, of the level specified by **PRIORITY**. Note that the priority definition is the same as for the **LOGOPT** parameter to the **openlog** function and should be expressed as a string. See Table B-17. Individual priorities can be combined using the | symbol. The **FORMAT** and **LIST** are passed to **sprintf** to format and output the supplied arguments in a formatted format. The resulting string is then used as the log entry.

The **FORMAT** string supports one additional option not supported by **printf**. The **%m** format inserts the value of the latest error message found in **$!**.

```
setlogmask MASK
```

sets the mask priority for further **syslog** calls. Returns the old mask value.

```
closelog
```

closes the connection to the **syslogd** daemon.

You can optionally import the **setlogsock** function, which allows you to change the type of socket used to communicate with the **syslogd** daemon.

```
setlogsock SOCKTYPE
```

Valid values for **SOCKTYPE** are "unix," for Unix domain sockets, and "inet" for INET domain sockets. The function returns true on success and **undef** on failure.

References   Chapters 11, 14, 15, Appendix A

String	C Constant	Description
emerg	LOG_EMERG	A panic condition, normally broadcast to all users.
alert	LOG_ALERT	An urgent problem that needs immediate attention.
crit	LOG_CRIT	Critical error such as a hardware error/failure.
err	LOG_ERR	Simple errors.
warning	LOG_WARNING	Warning messages.
notice	LOG_NOTICE	Notification of particular events. Not considered critical, but may still require immediate attention.
info	LOG_INFO	Informational messages.
debug	LOG_DEBUG	Debugging information, normally of no use outside a debugging procedure.

Table B-17. *Syslog* Priorities

Term::Cap

This module provides a simplified interface to the termcap terminal driver system.

```
use Term::Cap;
```

The module supports an object interface to **Tgetent**:

```
Tgetent(TERM)
```

The **Tgetent** function extracts the entry of the specified terminal type **TERM**, returning a reference to a **Term::Cap** object. For example:

```
$terminal = Tgetent Term::Cap { TERM => 'vt220', OSPEED => $ospeed };
```

The **OSPEED** is the output bitrate for the terminal, specified either in POSIX format (absolute bitrates such as 9600), or as BSD-style relative values, where 13 equals 9600.

```
$terminal->Trequire(LIST)
```

The **Trequire** method enables you to specify the list of required capabilities for the terminal driver.

```
$terminal->Tgoto(EXPR, COL, ROW, HANDLE)
```

This decodes a cursor addressing string **EXPR,** passing it **COL** and **ROW.** The value of the string is returned, or printed directly to the **HANDLE** if specified.

```
$terminal->Tputs(EXPR, COUNT, HANDLE)
```

caches the control string **EXPR** for **COUNT** times, returning the string. Alternatively, you can have it sent directly to **HANDLE** if specified.

You can access the extracted termcap entry by accessing the **TERMCAP** hash key element.

Reference   Chapter 17

Term::Complete

This module provides an interface for completing words on a command line interface, similar to that provided by the Bourne Again SHell (**bash**).

```
use Term::Complete;
```

It supports a single function, **Complete**:

```
Complete(PROMPT, LIST)
```

This provides **PROMPT** to the screen and supports completion on the words in **LIST.** The return value is the completed word:

```
$input = Complete('$ ', qw/echo ls/);
```

You can type any character into the prompt. Pressing TAB completes the word (if possible). The default ^D prints a list of completion words. The ^U combination deletes the current line, and the DEL and BACKSPACE keys work as you would expect. You can modify the keys used for the last four options using the **$Term::Complete::complete, $Term::Complete::kill, $Term::Complete::erase1,** and **$Term::Complete::erase2** variables.

Specification should be done using the normal **stty** values, and the **stty** command is required for the module to function correctly. Note that you can continue to edit the line using the preceding keyboard sequences. The completion value is not returned until ENTER is pressed.

References   Chapter 17; *see also* **Text::Abbrev**

Term::ReadLine

This module supports an interface to the available readline packages.

```
use Term::ReadLine;
```

Readline is a function library that supports the input of text in a line-by-line editable format. The interface is object based:

```
use Term::ReadLine;

$line = new Term::ReadLine 'Line Interface';
$input = $line->readline('Name? ');

print "Got $input\n";
```

The supported methods are described here.

```
readline(EXPR)
```

returns the string entered, using the value of **EXPR** as a prompt. The trailing newline character is removed from the returned value.

```
ReadLine
```

returns the name of the actual package being used to support the readline operation.

```
new
```

creates a new **Term::ReadLine** object. You can optionally supply two arguments that specify the input and output filehandles to use for the readline operation.

```
addhistory(EXPR)
```

adds **EXPR** to the history of input lines.

```
IN
OUT
```

returns the filehandles for input or output.

```
MinLine(EXPR)
```

if specified, defines the minimal size of a line to be included in the history list.

```
findConsole
```

returns an array of two strings containing the names for files for input and output, specified in the normal **shell** style of **<file** and **>file**.

```
Attribs
```

returns a hash reference describing the internal configuration parameters of the package.

```
Features
```

returns a hash reference describing the features of the current readline package being used.

References   Chapter 17

Test

This module provides a simple framework for writing Perl test scripts, using a format similar to Perl's own testing systems.

```
use Test;
```

You use the framework by importing the module and then using a **BEGIN** block to specify the parameters for the tests you are about to conduct. For example,

```
use Test;
BEGIN { plan tests => 2}

ok(1);
ok(0);
```

Each call to **ok** should indicate a successful test or failure. The resulting report and output matches the format used by Perl's own testing system available when Perl has been built from a raw distribution. For example, the preceding script would output

```
1..2
ok 1
not ok 2
# Failed test 2 in test.pl at line 5
```

Note that each call to **ok** iterates through the available test numbers, and failures are recorded and reported.

You can embed expressions into the **ok** call:

```
ok(mytest());
```

The return value or resolved expression must be expected to return true or false according to the success or otherwise of the test. You can also use a two-argument version that compares the values of the two arguments:

```
ok(mytest(),mytest());
```

If you want to trap additional information with the error, you can append additional arguments to the **ok** function:

```
ok(0,1,'Math Error');
```

The resulting error and mismatch information is reported when the script exits:

```
1..2
ok 1
not ok 2
# Test 2 got: '0' (test.pl at line 5)
#    Expected: '1' (Didnt work)
```

You can mark tests as "to do" tests by specifying which test numbers are to be fixed directly within the test suite. These tests are expected to fail. You specify the information to the **plan** function during the **BEGIN** block:

```
use Test;
BEGIN { plan tests => 2, todo = [2]}

ok(1);
ok(0);
```

The resulting failure message notes the existence of an expected failure,

```
1..2 todo 2;
ok 1
not ok 2 # (failure expected in test.pl at line 5)
```

and also warns you when it sees a success in a test it was expecting to fail:

```
1..2 todo 2;
ok 1
ok 2 # Wow! (test.pl at line 5)
```

You can skip tests based on the availability of platform-specific facilities, using the **skip** function:

```
skip(TEST, LIST)
```

TEST is a test that evaluates to true only if the required feature is *not* available. Subsequent values in **LIST** work identically to the **ok** function.

You can supply a subroutine to handle additional diagnostics after the tests have completed. The function is passed an array reference of hash references that describe each test failure. The keys of each hash are **package**, **repetition**, and **result**. To configure the function, specify its reference in the call to **plan** in the **BEGIN** block:

```
BEGIN { plan tests => 2, onfail => \&errdiags }
```

The resulting function is executed within an **END** block and is, therefore, subject to the normal limitations of such a block.

References   Chapters 9, 11, 21

Test::Harness

This module processes the output of multiple Perl test scripts and reports the success or failure of the scripts accordingly.

```
use Test::Harness;
runtests(LIST)
```

LIST should be a list of valid test scripts to be executed. It parses the output produced by a typical Perl test script and analyzes the output. The output produced by the **Test** module is suitable for correct parsing.

For example, a nine-test script with three failures would output the following:

```
t.p................# Failed test 2 in t.pl at line 5
# Failed test 5 in t.pl at line 8
# Failed test 9 in t.pl at line 12
FAILED tests 2, 5, 9
        Failed 3/9 tests, 66.67% okay
Failed Test  Status Wstat Total Fail  Failed  List of failed
-------------------------------------------------------------------
t.pl                     9    3  33.33%  2, 5, 9
Failed 1/1 test scripts, 0.00% okay. 3/9 subtests failed, 66.67% okay.
```

References   Chapter 9, 11, 21; *see also* **Test**

Text::Abbrev

Given a list of words, this module generates an abbreviation table in a hash. The generated list accounts for possible duplications of abbreviations within the supplied list.

```
use Text::Abbrev;
%abbrev = ();
abbrev(\%abbrev, LIST);
```

For example, the call

```
abbrev(\%abbrev, 'better');
```

will produce a hash like this:

```
b       => better,
be      => better,
bet     => better,
bett    => better,
bette   => better,
better  => better,
```

while the call

```
abbrev(\%abbrev, qw/be bet better/);
```

will populate the **%abbrev** hash with

```
b       => be,
be      => be,
bet     => bet,
bett    => better,
bette   => better,
better  => better,
```

Reference   *See also* **Term::Complete**

Text::ParseWords

This module parses an array of lines into a list of words using a specified delimiter. Any words or strings contained within quotes are treated as single words, effectively ignoring the supplied delimiter.

```
use Text::ParseWords;
@words = quotewords($delim, $keep, LIST);
```

The **$delim** element is the delimiter to use. This can be a raw string or a regular expression. The **$keep** element affects the way text within the lines is treated. If set to true, quotes are retained in the list of words returned; otherwise, they are removed. Also, if **$keep** is true, then t`he backslashes are preserved in the returned list. If false, then a double backslash is converted to a single backslash, and a single backslash disappears entirely.

References   Chapter 8, Appendix A

Text::Soundex

The **Text::Soundex** module generates a four-character soundex string using the algorithm designed by Donald Knuth. The algorithm translates individual words into the string, which can then be used for comparison and hashing of the supplied words as they sound when they are spoken, rather than how they are spelled.

```
use Text::Soundex;

soundex LIST
```

The **soundex** function hashes the words supplied in **LIST**, returning a list of soundex codes. Each code is made up of a single character, matching the first character of the supplied word, and three digits. For example,

```
print join(' ',soundex('Martin', 'Brown'),"\n");
```

prints

```
M635 B650
```

On the other hand,

```
print join(' ',soundex('Martin', 'Martian'),"\n");
```

produces

```
M635 M635
```

Note that the soundex string produced cannot be mapped back to the original string. The preceding example should demonstrate the fact, since M635 refers both to "Martin" and "Martian." Note however that the algorithm is not completely fail-safe:

```
print join(' ',soundex('Wood', 'Would'),"\n");
```

This produces the following, perhaps incorrect, sequence:

```
W300 W430
```

If a suitable soundex string cannot be produced, then the function returns **$soundex_nocode**, which is initially set to the undefined value. You can, however, set the value of this variable for your own purposes.

Text::Tabs

This module expands tabs into spaces and "unexpands" spaces into tabs.

```
use Text::Tabs;

$tabstop = 8;
expand LIST
unexpand LIST
```

The **$tabstops** scalar specifies the number of spaces to replace a single tab with **expand**, or the number of spaces to convert into a single tab with **unexpand**. Both functions accept a list of scalars, and each scalar should contain a string to be expanded or unexpanded as appropriate. Each element of **LIST** should not contain any newlines; they should be **split** first into a suitable list. The return value is a list of converted elements.

For example, here is a script for expanding the tabs of files supplied on the command line into four spaces:

```
#!/usr/local/bin/perl -pi.bak

BEGIN
{
        use Text::Tabs;
        $tabstop = 4;
}

$_ = expand $_;
```

You can now do

```
$ expand file.txt
```

To convert it back, create a new script with **unexpand** instead of **expand**:

```
#!/usr/local/bin/perl -pi.bak

BEGIN
{
        use Text::Tabs;
        $tabstop = 4;
}

$_ = unexpand $_;
```

Text::Wrap

This module intelligently wraps text into paragraphs.

```
use Text::Wrap;

$Text::Wrap::columns = 70;
wrap PREFIRST, PREOTHER, EXPR
```

The width of the resulting paragraph is specified directly in the **$Text::Wrap::columns** scalar. The **wrap** function then wraps **EXPR**, indenting the first line of the paragraph with **PREFIRST** and subsequent lines in the paragraph with **PREOTHER**.

Tie::Array

This module provides some simple base class definitions for tying arrays. You normally use this module to inherit base methods from, for example:

```
package MyArray;
use Tie::Array;
@ISA = qw/Tie::Array/;
```

It provides stub **DELETE** and **EXTEND** methods, and also **PUSH**, **POP**, **SHIFT**, **UNSHIFT**, **SPLICE**, and **CLEAR** in terms of basic **FETCH**, **STORE**, **FETCHSIZE**, and **STORESIZE**, in addition to the mandatory **new** method for creating the new object.

When developing your own tied-array classes, you will need to define the following methods:

```
TIEARRAY classname, LIST
STORE this, index, value
FETCH this, index
```

```
FETCHSIZE this
STORESIZE this, count
EXTEND this, count
CLEAR this
DESTROY this
PUSH this, LIST
POP this
SHIFT this
UNSHIFT this, LIST
SPLICE this, offset, length, LIST
```

Reference   Chapter 10

Tie::Handle

This module provides core methods for tying handles.

```
package MyHandle;
use Tie::Handle;
@ISA = qw/Tie::Handle/;
```

It supports the basic **new** method in addition to **TIESCALAR**, **FETCH**, and **STORE**.
    For developing your own tied-handle classes, you will need to define the following methods:

```
TIEHANDLE classname, LIST
WRITE this, scalar, length, offset
PRINT this, LIST
PRINTF this, format, LIST
READ this, scalar, length, offset
READLINE this
GETC this
DESTROY this
```

Reference   Chapter 10

Tie::Hash

This module provides base class definitions for tied hashes. It provides the **new**, **TIEHASH**, **EXISTS**, and **CLEAR** methods.

```
package MyHash;
use Tie::Hash;
@ISA = qw/Tie::Hash/;
```

When developing your own class for tying hashes, you will need to implement the following methods:

```
TIEHASH classname, LIST
STORE this, key, value
FETCH this, key
FIRSTKEY this
NEXTKEY this, lastkey
EXISTS this, key
DELETE this, key
CLEAR this
```

Reference   Chapter 10

Tie::RefHash

This module supports the facility to use references as hash keys through a tied hash. This is normally not allowed; and if **strict refs** is switched on, Perl will fail on compilation.

```
use Tie::RefHash;
tie %hash, 'Tie::RefHash', LIST;
```

Reference   Chapter 10

Tie::Scalar

This module provides base class definitions for tying scalars. The basic **Tie::Scalar** package provides the **new, TIESCALAR, FETCH,** and **STORE** methods.

```
package myScalar;
use Tie::Scalar;
@ISA = qw/Tie::Scalar/;
```

If you are developing your own tied scalars, you will need to define the following methods:

```
TIESCALAR classname, LIST
FETCH this
STORE this, value
DESTROY this
```

Reference   Chapter 10

Tie::SubstrHash

This module provides a class for supporting a hash with fixed key and value sizes. The resulting hash algorithm is a factor of the key and value sizes specified, and the hash is optimized for the specified size. This improves performance, but also limits the size of the hash you create. Any attempt to add keys into the hash beyond the specified size results in a fatal error.

```
require Tie::SubstrHash;
tie %hash, 'Tie::SubstrHash', KEYLEN, VALUELEN,  TABLE_SIZE;
```

These lines create a hash in **%hash**. Each key within the hash will be **KEYLEN** long (in bytes), and values will be **VALUELEN** long. Note that **KEYLEN** and **VALUELEN** are not maximum sizes; they are fixed. Attempts to insert data with a key size greater or less than **KEYLEN** will cause a fatal error, as will storing values that are greater or less than **VALUELEN**. The maximum size for the hash is specified as the number of key/value pairs, as specified in **TABLE_SIZE**.

There are two main benefits to this system: speed and memory. With a fixed-size hash, the memory footprint is much smaller; and the resulting internal tables used to look up individual key/value pairs are, therefore, much smaller, resulting in faster and more efficient searches for information.

Reference   Chapter 10

Time::Local

This module provides the reverse functionality of the **localtime** and **gmtime** functions—that is, it converts a date and time specified in individual variables into the number of seconds that have elapsed since the epoch:

```
use Time::Local;

$time = timelocal(SEC, MIN, HOURS, MDAY, MON, YEAR);
$time = timegm(SEC, MIN, HOURS, MDAY, MON, YEAR);
```

The functions accept the arguments in the same range as the corresponding **localtime** and **gmtime** functions, such that the code

```
use Time::Local;

$time = time;

print "Time!" if ($time = (timelocal((localtime)[0..5])));
```

should always print "Time!"

Both **timelocal** and **timegm** return –1 if the upper limit is reached for the integer that stores the time value. On most systems this will be Jan 1 2038.

Reference Chapter 11

Time::gmtime

Overrides the built-in **gmtime** function with one that returns an object based on the **Time::tm** module. The individual methods within the returned object are the individual fields of the new time structure. For example:

```
use Time::gmtime;

$time = gmtime;

print "Date is: ",
      join('/',$time->mday,($time->mon+1),($time->year+1900)), "\n";
```

The individual methods (fields) match the names of the **struct tm** structure, that is, **sec**, **min**, **hour**, **mday**, **mon**, **year**, **wday**, **yday**, and **isdst**.

It's also possible to obtain the time from the last **gmtime** call via predefined variables. These variables have the same name as the structure fields and object methods with a **tm_** prefix. For example:

```
use Time::gmtime qw/:FIELDS/;
```

```
gmtime;

print "Date is:
        ",join('/',$tm_mday,($tm_mon+1),($tm_year+1900)),"\n";
```

The time variables will not be updated until **gmtime** is called again.

You can access the original **CORE::gmtime** function in a scalar context using the new **gmctime** function:

```
print gmctime(time);
```

To use the object-oriented interface without overriding the **CORE::localtime** function, import the module with an empty import list, and then call the functions explicitly:

```
use Time::gmtime qw//;

$time = Time::gmtime::gmtime;

print "Date is: ",
        join('/',$time->mday,($time->mon+1),($time->year+1900)), "\n";
```

References   Chapter 11; *see also* **Time::tm**

Time::localtime

This module overrides the built-in **localtime** function with one that returns an object based on the **Time::tm** module. The individual methods within the returned object are the individual fields of the new time structure. For example:

```
use Time::localtime;

$time = localtime;

print "Time is: ",join(':',$time->hour,$time->min,$time->sec),"\n";
```

The individual methods (fields) match the names of the **struct tm** structure, that is, **sec, min, hour, mday, mon, year, wday, yday,** and **isdst**.

It's also possible to obtain the time from the last **localtime** call via predefined variables. These variables have the same name as the structure fields and object methods with a **tm_** prefix. For example:

```
use Time::localtime qw(:FIELDS);

localtime;

print "Time is: ",join(':',$tm_hour,$tm_min,$tm_sec),"\n";
```

The time variables will not be updated until **localtime** is called again.

You can access the original **CORE::localtime** function in a scalar context using the new **ctime** function:

```
print ctime(time);
```

To use the object-oriented interface without overriding the **CORE::localtime** function, import the module with an empty import list, and then call the functions explicitly:

```
use Time::localtime qw//;

$time = Time::localtime::localtime;

print "Time is: ",join(':',$time->hour,$time->min,$time->sec),"\n";
```

References   Chapter 11; *see also* **Time::tm;**

Time::tm

This module supports the internal functionality of the **Time::localtime** and **Time::gmtime** modules.

References   *See* **Time::localtime, Time::gmtime**

UNIVERSAL

The **UNIVERSAL** module provides the base class from which all other classes are based. This module provides the essential grounding for all blessed references within.

APPENDIXES

Because all new objects inherit from the base class, the **UNIVERSAL** module also provides some base methods that are automatically inherited by all classes and objects. Two of the methods, **can** and **isa**, are supported both as methods and functions:

```
isa(TYPE)
UNIVERSAL::isa(REF, TYPE)
```

returns true if the object or **REF** is blessed into the package **TYPE** or has inherited from the package **TYPE**.

```
can(METHOD)
UNIVERSAL::can(REF, METHOD)
```

returns a reference to the subroutine supporting **METHOD** if **METHOD** is supported within the class of the object or **REF**. If the specified method does not exist, then it returns **undef**.

```
VERSION ([REQUIRE])
```

returns the contents of the **$VERSION** variable within the object's class. If the **REQUIRE** value is specified, the script will die if **REQUIRE** is less than or equal to the **$VERSION** variable.

Reference   Chapter 10

User::grent

This module supports an object-oriented interface to the built-in **getgr*** functions:

```
use User::grent;
$grent = getgrnam('staff');
```

Individual fields are then available as methods to the **$grent** object. The supported methods are **name**, **passwd**, **gid**, and **members**. This last item returns a reference to a list; the first three simply return scalars.

Reference   Chapter 11; *see also* **User::pwent**

User::pwent

This module provides an object-based interface to the built-in **getpw*** functions.

```
use User::pwent;
$pwent = getpwnam('root');
```

Once retrieved, individual fields of the password entry are available as methods to the newly created object. For example,

```
print "User ID: ",$pwent->uid,"\n";
```

prints the uid of the **root** user. The list of methods supported is **name**, **passwd**, **uid**, **gid**, **quota**, **comment**, **gecos**, **dir**, and **shell**.

References   Chapter 11; *see also* **User::grent**

utf8

The **utf8** pragma tells Perl to use the UTF-8 (Unicode) character set for internal string representation. The pragma is block scoped. For most installations, there are no differences between Unicode and normal ASCII representation, since the first 128 characters of the ASCII code are stored within a single byte. For patterns that are greater than this value, or for multibyte characters, the differences are significant.

```
use utf8;
```

Once switched on, you can switch off Unicode operation with **no**:

```
no utf8;
```

The main effects of the module are as follows:

- Strings and patterns may contain characters that have an ordinal value greater than 255. You can explicitly specify a Unicode character by specifying the hexadecimal prefix with braces and the Unicode character in a 2-byte hexadecimal string, for example \x{263A}.
- Symbol table entries within Perl may be specified in Unicode format.

APPENDIXES

- Regular expressions match characters (including multibyte characters) instead of individual bytes.

- Character classes in regexps match characters instead of bytes.

- You can match Unicode properties using **\p{}** (which matches a property) and **\P{}** (which does not match a property).

- The **\X** pattern match matches any extended Unicode string.

- The **tr///** operator translates characters instead of bytes.

- Case translation with the **uc**, **lc**, **ucfirst**, and **lcfirst** functions uses internal Unicode tables for conversion.

- Functions that use or return character positions, return positions correctly in characters, not bytes.

- The **pack** and **unpack** functions are unaffected (the "c" and "C" letters still pack single-byte characters). The "U" specifier can instead be used to pack Unicode characters.

- The **chr** and **ord** functions work on Unicode characters.

- Use of **reverse** in a scalar context works correctly on characters, not bytes.

References   Chapter 8; *see also* **File::Find, File::CheckTree**

Appendix C

Resources

erl has been around for many years, and as one of the primary languages for Internet development, it's sparked up numerous web sites, as well as a huge book and article industry. It's not very difficult to find information about Perl, but it is difficult to find the right sort of information from all of the sources available.

Although this book is a complete reference guide to Perl, there will be times when you want some more specific examples, ready-to-run information, or more in-depth background information on a particular topic. So, for this last appendix, I've tried to produce a condensed directory of the most popular sites, journals, and books that will help guide you through programming with Perl.

Supplied Documentation

Your first port of call after this guide should be the documentation supplied with Perl. There's a more detailed guide to the contents of the Perl documentation in Chapter 24, but I've included a quick guide here.

Unix Documentation

If you are using Unix, then the documentation will have been installed in the form of manual pages, which can be viewed using the **man** utility. The primary page is **perl**, and that gives you a further list of the other man pages within the Perl systems. For example, the **perlop** page gives you information about Perl operators and **perlfunc** about the functions.

In addition, most modules also have their own manual pages, which you can access directly; for example, the **Net::SMTP** module can be read using

```
$ man Net::SMTP
```

If you use the **emacs** editor, you can use the **man** command (**M-x man**) and supply the name of the manual page you want to view. Once you're viewing the page, typing **M-x man** again will populate the default selection with the current word—useful if you want to cross reference and view a number of pages easily.

As a final solution, I've written a script (**perlman.cgi**, available from my web site, **www.mcwords.com**) that enables you to convert POD-formatted manual pages into HTML on the fly, so you can view an HTML-formatted version of the pages in your favorite web browser. It retains the linking abilities, so you can click directly through to related pages, and because it uses the POD and module files directly, you can be sure that the information is up to date. Better still, if you install an updated version of a module, you'll be viewing the updated version without having to do a manual conversion.

Windows Documentation

Under Windows, the manuals are installed as HTML. The ActiveState installers all include a full set of online documentation that includes all of the core documents, the supplied modules and extensions, and the **Win32** module set, all converted and linked, ready for viewing. You'll need something that is able to display frames to see the documentation properly—Netscape Communicator/Navigator 4.*x*, or Internet Explorer 4.*x*, or above.

The documentation installed includes

- Complete guide to the ActivePerl applications, release notes, an installation guide, and information on using the Perl Package Manager (PPM) to install additional third-party modules

- ActivePerl component guide to the different ActivePerl application packages

- A Frequently Asked Questions (FAQ) section that covers both Win32-specific queries and compatibility queries when you are moving from the Unix platform

- HTML versions of all the core Perl documentation normally supplied with the Unix version of the Perl interpreter, including the FAQ sections

- HTML versions of all the POD documentation included within the Perl standard library

- Documentation for all the Win32 modules supplied as standard with the ActivePerl distribution

You can access the main documentation page through the Start menu.

As a background to the Windows libraries, you'll need to be familiar with the Windows environment before you are able to make the best use of the extensions. In particular, the documentation supplied with Win32 modules takes a number of liberties and assumes an awful lot about the reader's knowledge of the Windows platform.

The best source for more detailed information about what some of the features, functions, and constants really mean is the Microsoft Developer Network (MSDN) documentation that comes with any of the Visual Studio development products. If you don't have access to a Visual Studio product, you can try the online Developer Network site on the Web. See below for details on how to access the site.

Mac OS Documentation

The MacPerl installer provides an additional application, called **shuck**, which takes raw POD documents and formats them on screen in a normal Macintosh window. The **shuck** application includes a built-in menu that will take you to all of the Perl documentation and the Mac OS–specific elements. It also retains and honors the linking system so you can click through to other documentation pages.

If you've downloaded a module or POD document that you want to view, just drag and drop it on the **shuck** application to view it. Make sure, however, that the document has been recognized as a Perl file—it'll need a type and creator code of "TEXT" and "McPL", respectively. Use **FileTyper** to change the code, or simply open the text file in MacPerl itself, and resave it.

Other Platforms

Because Perl documentation is written using the POD standard, it can be easily converted to other formats. Unless you have a particular preference, the best solution is to convert the documentation into HTML format and use a web browser to view it. See Chapter 23 for more information.

Books

While it's impossible to list all the books, journals, and other publications that promote Perl as a programming language, there are some standard books that all Perl programmers should probably keep on their bookshelf.

ActivePerl Developers Guide. **Brown, M. C. 2000. New York, NY: McGraw-Hill**

A guide to programming Perl, using the ActiveState Perl distribution for Windows. As well as a guide to the ActivePerl modules and tools, it also provides a cross-reference for programmers migrating from both Unix and Visual Basic environments to the Perl language.

DeBugging Perl. **Brown, M. C. 2000. Berkeley, CA: Osborne/McGraw-Hill**

Much more than just debugging, the *DeBugging Perl* title also looks at how to write better, cleaner Perl code, how to avoid adding potential problems, and how to trap and resolve errors within the code so that your users don't bear the brunt of the problems. The book also covers information on how to optimize and deliberately break your code when it's running within the production environment, from stressing disk and CPU time, to environment variables, web servers, and other external factors.

Perl Annotated Archives. **Brown, M. C. 1999. Berkeley, CA: Osborne/ McGraw-Hill**

The Annotated Archives series takes real-world scripts and then annotates them on a line-by-line basis to demonstrate the semantics of the Perl language and the algorithms and tricks required to complete the program. The title includes scripts for processing text files and logs, using Perl for networking. There is even a special section on developing and managing websites using Perl. The book should help both beginners and advanced users, and it is an excellent companion to *Perl: The Complete Reference*.

Perl Programmers Reference. **Brown, M. C. 1999. Berkeley, CA: Osborne/ McGraw-Hill**

A condensed version of *Perl: The Complete Reference*, this book contains a quick reference guide to the features you will probably use most often within Perl. This includes the semantics, built-in functions, the standard Perl library, and the Perl debugger.

Object Oriented Perl. **Conway, D. 2000. Greenwich, CT: Manning Publications**

The most comprehensive reference to using Perl in an object-oriented fashion that you'll ever find. Covers everything from building objects in the first place through to inheritance-tied variables and persistence, with everything in between.

Perl Black Book. **Holzner, S. 1999. Scottsdale, AZ: CoriolisOpen Press**

A practical guide to Perl programming covering the basics and more advanced topics using a number of different examples. Contains an excellent and practical web guide at the end of the book that looks at a variety of problems and solutions.

Cross-Platform Perl. **Johnson, E. F. 1996. Foster City, CA: IDG Press**

This book concentrates on creating code that can be easily transported between Unix and Windows NT hosts. Special attention is given to scripts that deal with systems administration and websites, although the book covers a wide range of other topics.

Perl 5 Interactive Course: Certified Edition. **Orwant, J. 1997. Corte Madera, CA: Waite Group**

This book is a thorough guide to Perl 5 programming, taking the reader through a series of different tasks and topics that range from building basic scripts to the proper use of variables, functions, and Perl-style regular expressions.

Learning Perl on Win32 Systems. **Schwartz, R. L., E. Olson, and T. Christiansen. 1997. Sebastopol, CA: O'Reilly**

This is a modified version of the *Learning Perl* title, customized to include information about using Perl on Windows systems. Unfortunately, it is now quite out of date and fails to mention many of the features now present in ActivePerl and other Windows-specific builds.

Advanced Perl Programming. **Srinivasan, S. 1997. Sebastopol, CA: O'Reilly**

This book is an excellent guide to data modeling, networking, and the Tk widget interface. It also covers the internal workings of Perl, which will help the advanced programmer write more efficient and smaller code, while providing all the information necessary for extending Perl with external C code.

Programming Perl. **3rd ed. Wall, L., T. Christiansen, and J. Orwant. 2000. Sebastopol, CA: O'Reilly**

Written by the three modern Perl architects, this is the definitive guide to Perl programming. Heavily updated, and now in its third edition, the new version is almost twice the size and covers everything from the basics to the advanced topics of compilers, threads, and non-Unix platform support. *Programming Perl* is affectionately known as the "Camel," since that's the motif used on the cover.

Perl Cookbook. **Wall, L., T. Christiansen, and N. Torkington. 1998. Sebastopol, CA: O'Reilly**

This cookbook of recipes for programming in the Perl language is written by the same team as the classic Camel book and is based on two chapters from the original first edition. It covers all sorts of algorithms and problems in Perl using a series of annotated examples, and it deftly shows Perl's flexibility.

 Journals/Websites

There are a variety of printed and online journals that now cover Perl, including the updated O'Reilly Net/Perl site. Most of these provide up-to-date guides and examples covering both the topical and traditional topics. Most of the old traditional websites have turned into regularly updated magazine-style sites, and most of the older journals are now available entirely online.

The Perl Journal (www.tpj.com)

A periodical devoted entirely to Perl, *The Perl Journal* covers a wide range of topics from basic principles for beginners to the advanced topics of Perl internals. The Journal also includes book and product reviews and guides to writing better Perl. Although it's available as a paper manual, you can also read the journal online at **www.tpj.com**.

Internet.com (www.internet.com)

The Internet.com website is actually a collection of other sites that concentrate on different topics. As well as some of the more basic channels, there are specific sites for handling web programming, e-commerce, Linux programming, and others that cover many of the most-used aspects of the Perl language. Although not strictly a journal site, the articles are updated daily so that there is a regular influx of new material and topics to choose from.

Server/Workstation Expert Magazine (sun.expert.com)

Although this magazine is aimed at Unix (specifically Solaris and AIX), this magazine often includes examples of text processing and includes a regular column written by Aeleen Frisch on integrating Windows and Windows NT into a Unix environment called NTegration. This often includes script examples that help to bridge the gap between the two platforms. A sister publication, *WebServer Online Magazine*, concentrates on the web production process.

TechWeb (www.techweb.com)

Another of the portal sites offering information and guides on many different topics that has particular channels covering network, web, and Unix/Linux programming and that includes a number of Perl articles each month.

Web Resources

In addition to the journal-style sites, there are also a number of sites that simply provide updates and information on the Perl community, and that offer extensions, modules, and FAQ style guides for some of your problems. You can see a list of some of the choice sites in Table C-1. If you can't find what you are looking for here, try visiting Yahoo (**www.yahoo.com**) or AltaVista (**www.altavista.com**).

Site	Description
www.perl.com	Now the home of Perl, and sponsored by O'Reilly, this should be your first port of call for Perl information and resources. The site is managed by the main Perl development team, which includes Larry Wall, Tom Christiansen, and Randal L. Schwartz, among others. As well as providing the usual links and other information about Perl, the site also supports a magazine format, with guest editorial and regular articles covering different aspects of Perl programming.
www.cpan.org	The Comprehensive Perl Archive Network (CPAN) is an online library of scripts, modules, and extensions to Perl. The organization can sometimes leave something to be desired, and it can take you some time to find what you want, but it's undoubtedly the best all-round resource for Perl modules and scripts.
www.ActiveState.com	ActiveState is the home of Perl under Win32, and you can download installers for all the different distributions available from ActiveState. You can also download 30-day trial licenses of the commercial Perl development tools.
www.roth.net/perl	This site is maintained by Dave Roth, the author of the **Win32::AdminMisc** and **Win32::ODBC** modules. The site also includes some general information and tips about programming Perl under Win32.

Table C-1.   *Perl Websites*

APPENDIXES

Site	Description
dada.perl.it	Aldo Calpini develops the **Win32::GUI** and is also a general Perl consultant. This site is a mixture of information about his own modules and other Win32-related modules and extensions.
www.scriptics.com	The home of the Tk interface builder and Tcl programming language. You can download the necessary installers and libraries from this site to enable Tk on your machine. You'll need to use the PPM utility to install the Tk module.
msdn.microsoft.com	The main developer pages for Microsoft products. This contains an updated version of the MSDN documentation, which is required reading if you want to make the best of the ActivePerl distribution of Perl.
www.perl.com/CPAN-local/ ports/win32/Standard/x86/	This is Gurusamy Sarathy's archive of the standard ActivePerl Win32 extensions, modified so that they work with the core distribution.
www.geocities.com/Silicon Valley/Way/6278/perl-win32-d atabase.html	Matt Sergeant's Database FAQ—an excellent resource for database programming within Perl when using the **Win32::ODBC** driver.

Table C-1.   *Perl Websites* (continued)

Mailing Lists

Mailing lists fall into two distinct categories: announcements and discussions. If the list is for announcements, you are not allowed to post to the group. These tend to be low volume and are useful for keeping in touch with the direction of Perl. If it's a discussion list, you can post and reply to messages just as you would in a Usenet newsgroup (for historical messages, try **www.dejanews.com**). These are higher volume lists, and the number of messages can become unmanageable very quickly.

That said, a discussion list is likely to have the experts and users in it that are able to answer your questions and queries with authority.

General Mailing Lists

Perl Institute Announce

This list carries announcements from the Perl Institute on general Perl issues. To subscribe, send an email to **majordomo@perl.org** with "subscribe tpi-announce" in the body of the message.

Perl-Unicode (from the Perl Institute)

This list is concerned with issues surrounding Unicode and Perl at both porting and using levels. To subscribe, send an email to **majordomo@perl.org** with "subscribe perl-unicode" in the body of the message.

Perl5-Porters

If you are porting Perl or Perl modules or want to help in the development of the Perl language in general, you should be a member of this discussion list. Don't join if you are just interested. This is a high-volume, highly technical mailing list. To subscribe, send an email to **majordomo@perl.org** with "subscribe perl5-porters" in the body of the message.

Windows-Specific Mailing Lists

Windows Users

The Perl-Win32-Users mailing list is targeted for Perl installation and programming questions. There are two versions: standard and digest. To subscribe to the standard version, send an email to **ListManager@ActiveState.com** with "SUBSCRIBE Perl-Win32-Users" in the body of the message. To subscribe to the digest version, send an email to **ListManager@ActiveState.com** with "DIGEST Perl-Win32-Users" in the body of the message.

Windows Announce

This mailing list is for announcements of new builds, bugs, security problems, and other information. To subscribe to the standard version, send an email to **ListManager@ActiveState.com** with "SUBSCRIBE Perl-Win32-Announce" in the body of the message. To subscribe to the digest version, send an email to **ListManager@ActiveState.com** with "DIGEST Perl-Win32-Announce" in the body of the message.

Windows Web Programming

This focuses on using Perl as a CGI programming alternative on Windows NT servers. To subscribe to the standard version, send an email to **ListManager@ActiveState.com** with "SUBSCRIBE Perl-Win32-Web" in the body of the message. To subscribe to the

APPENDIXES

digest version, send an email to **ListManager@ActiveState.com** with "DIGEST Perl-Win32-Web" in the body of the message.

Windows Admin

Here you will find information and discussion on using Perl for administering and managing Windows 95 and NT machines. To subscribe to the standard version, send an email to **ListManager@ActiveState.com** with "SUBSCRIBE Perl-Win32-Admin" in the body of the message. To subscribe to the digest version, send an email to **ListManager@ActiveState.com** with "DIGEST Perl-Win32-Admin" in the body of the message.

Newsgroups

To reach a more general Perl audience, you might want to post a question or announcement to one of the many Perl newsgroups. These are available on many ISP's Usenet news servers, and many will be happy to add them to their list if you ask nicely. The list is summarized in Table C-2. If you want to browse existing and "expired" messages, check out the **www.dejanews.com** website, which archives these and many other groups for you.

Newsgroup	Description
comp.infosystems.www.authoring.cgi	Deals with using Perl as a tool for writing CGI programs. This is a general CGI discussion group; it is not specifically targeted at Perl users. However, it does provide a lot of useful information on extracting, receiving, and returning information from web servers and clients.
comp.lang.perl.announce	Used to announce news from the Perl world. This includes new book releases, new version releases, and occasionally major Perl module releases.

Table C-2. *Perl-Friendly Newsgroups*

Newsgroup	Description
comp.lang.perl.misc	A general discussion forum for Perl. Everything from queries about how best to tackle a problem to the inside machinations of Perl is discussed here. Some of the discussions can get quite technical and be more biased to someone interested in the internal Perl workings, but it still represents the best port of call if you are having trouble with a problem or Perl script.
comp.lang.perl.modules	This was set up to specifically discuss the use and creation of Perl modules. Unlike **comp.lang.perl.misc**, you should only find problems related to modules in this group. If you are having trouble with something downloaded from CPAN, this is the best place to start asking questions.
comp.lang.perl.tk	Tk is a toolkit that provides a set of functions to support a graphical user interface (GUI) within Perl. Tk was originally developed in combination with Tcl (Tool Command Language) but has been massaged to work with other scripting systems, including Perl.

Table C-2.   *Perl-Friendly Newsgroups* (continued)

You may also want to refer to "Joseph's Top Ten Tips for Answering Questions Posted to comp.lang.perl.misc," available at **www.5sigma.com/perl/topten.html**. This will provide you with some hints and tips on how best to make use of the question-and-answer nature of many of these groups. The site is a little tongue-in-cheek, but still a good resource.

Index

NOTE: Page numbers in *italics* refer to illustrations or tables.

A

P

X

Y

Z